THE UNCONQUERABLE KEANE

JOHN KEANE
AND
THE RISE
OF
WATERFORD HURLING

David Smith

ORIGINAL WRITING

© 2010 David Smith

All rights reserved. No part of this publication may be reproduced in any form or by any means—graphic, electronic or mechanical, including photocopying, recording, taping or information storage and retrieval systems—without the prior written permission of the author.

978-1-907179-59-4

A CIP catalogue for this book is available from the National Library.

Published by Original Writing Ltd., Dublin, 2010.

Printed by Cahill Printers Limited, Dublin.

For my wife Anne and daughters Jean, Susan, Gillian and Mary.

I also remember, with great affection, aunties May, Molly, Babby, Kitty and Queenie, uncles Thomas and Josie and especially my mother Peggy. All of them *imithe, anois, ar Shlí na Fírinne*, but I felt them looking over my shoulder as I wrote this biography of a beloved husband and brother.

ACKNOWLEDGEMENTS

The writing of this book is all mine but many people contributed to the final result. From the beginning I have had the unstinting support of John's sons and daughters. Tom, John and Gerard assisted me in many ways to bring the book to fruition and I hereby acknowledge their support and their many insightful suggestions which helped immeasurably. They were very generous in sharing their recollections as well as family artefacts such as books, magazines, match programmes, photographs and memorabilia. To Gerard and Tom I owe a special word of thanks. Gerard wrote the computer program for the Index and Tom spent weeks checking it manually. I also acknowledge the support I received from my cousins Tomás O Cinnéide and Nicholas Hartery. Tomás read every word I wrote and added many personal touches to the book but just as importantly he reassured me and restored my confidence whenever I had those dark nights of the soul and felt inadequate to the task.

This book would have been all the poorer without the special contributions of Pat and Larry Fanning – both of whom could not have loved John more if he had been their brother. I thank Pat's grandson, Eoin Fanning, who lent me the two invaluable scrapbooks compiled by the Goode family of Dungarvan and my sincerest thanks go to the Mount Sion H&F club for the use of the club's minutes from 1936 to date. I could not have written this book without such an incredible resource. I have had formal and informal interviews with former hurlers and others who knew John personally. My sincere thanks are due to my interviewees Andy Fleming, Jim O'Meara, Tom 'Gum' Kennedy, Austin Flynn, Jack O'Neill, James Grant and John Barron who gave willingly of their valuable time. Over the years I have had extended conversations with Peggy Keane, Tommy Keane, Mary Doyle, Pat Kelly and Paddy Greene – all of whom shared the special relationship they had with John. My thanks also go to the always courteous and helpful staff at Waterford Municipal Library, Waterford County Library and Kilkenny County Library.

My son-in-law Gabriel Doherty had an immense influence on the book. Without his expert advice I doubt that it would ever have been finished. My wife Anne and my daughters Jean, Susan, Gillian and Mary were very tolerant of a somewhat absent and distant father during the almost three years it took to research and write the book. My deepest gratitude goes to them for their patience and understanding especially when I rambled on and on about a match or an incident that happened sixty or seventy years ago. To them I dedicate this book with love and affection.

The author has made every effort to trace the copyright owners of all the photographs used in this book. If any infringement of copyright has occurred it is inadvertent and the photographs will be removed from all subsequent editions.

A special word of thanks is due to my publishers, who responded to my every request with patience and understanding.

Preface

Eddie Keher called him a legend of hurling; Jack O'Neill, a Waterford local historian, called him a great man. Those comments are two sides of the same coin. The great Kilkenny hurler's comment alluded to John Keane's position amongst the heroes of the game, and while it was, indeed, the hurling that defined John he would have been remarkable even if he had never played the game. O'Neill referred to his character as a man. When I interviewed Jack for this book his first words were: 'That's a book that's long overdue. He was a remarkable man.' Jack had first met John when both were members of the Local Defence Force (LDF) during the Emergency and further contact in subsequent years had only reinforced his opinion that here was a man to be admired for his qualities as a human being – he was intelligent, moral, trustworthy, disciplined, friendly and modest, despite his great fame.

Keher's comment had come during a chance meeting that I had in Tramore with the great Kilkenny hurler shortly after the Millennium hurling team had been announced. John's name came up in the ensuing conversation and prompted the above mentioned comment from Keher, who also asked if I had ever seen John play? That question made me realise that time passes by, inexorably, and that even legendary figures can be forgotten. It also impressed on me how important it was to get the record of John's life and career down on paper so that he would be properly celebrated for the contribution he made to Irish life and culture – and to hurling, the greatest game of all.

Here, then, is the story of John Keane, Waterford's greatest hurler, and the era in which he played. Having already made his mark at minor level he played on the Waterford senior hurling team for seventeen years and was, in addition, the trainer/manager of the county's greatest team – that which took the field between 1957 and 1963. His story, therefore, is also the story of Waterford hurling, from the 1930s to the early 1960s. While this book is by no means a definitive history of Waterford hurling during this period, that history unfolded in parallel with the story of John Keane, and forms the first part of this work.

Before and after making his mark at inter-county, and inter-provincial, level, however, John Keane was the quintessential clubman and his name and that of the Mount Sion club were, for many years, virtually synonymous. He was present at its creation and was a central figure in its activities for the rest of his life, right up to his premature death in 1975. His story is the story of Mount Sion's rise to greatness and the second part of the book is dedicated to this aspect of his life. You will read about the foundation of the club; its symbiotic relationship with Mount Sion school; how it nearly broke up over the 'Paddy O'Connor' case and how it became a parallel family with all the highs and lows associated with families – squabbles, rows and achievements; its great struggle for supremacy in the county with the clubs of Portlaw, Dungarvan, Tallow and especially Erin's Own; and about its games with the champion clubs of Cork, Tipperary and Kilkenny.

I will describe John's great clashes and friendships with the stars of his era: men such as Mick Mackey, Jackie Power, Timmy Ryan and the others on the Limerick team he regarded as being the greatest ever; Jack Lynch and Christy Ring of Cork; and Jimmy Langton and Jimmy Walsh of Kilkenny. In keeping with many of these figures John has been regularly selected as a member of all the 'greatest-ever' hurling teams and, while the selection of such teams is essentially a diverting parlour-game, the consistency in the vote for John over a period of forty-one years indicates his position in the first-rank of hurlers and marks him as a legend of the game.

Legends, by their very nature, have many stories told about them – some true, but most invented. There are quite a number of anecdotes in this book but all those who related them are given due acknowledgement and where I have found mention of John in books and articles I have endeavoured to check such references against the historical record, discarding those found to be deficient in this regard. I have also endeavoured to avoid any vague and uncorroborated quotes in an effort to keep the work accurate; each source is fully documented in either the general text or in footnotes. This book, therefore, will not be of the type epitomised by the Irish saying, *Dúirt fear liom go ndúirt fear leis* (A man told me that a man told him).

My primary sources were my own memories of John and the reminiscences of the wider Keane family. These consisted mainly of extended conversations with John's wife and children, his sisters, brothers, nephews and nieces; minutes of the Mount Sion Hurling and Football club; national and local newspapers; discussions with former players and officials; and manuscript letters. My secondary sources were books, magazines, scrapbooks and match programmes. Two points should be noted, one relating to such sources, the other purely terminological. Firstly, the style of newspaper reporting for most of John's early career meant that only rarely would one see comments about a hurler's individual contribution to a match and this leaves gaps in my re-creation of his playing record. Secondly, the county ground in Waterford city, now known as Walsh Park, is referred to consistently in this book as the Gaelic Field because that was how it was known during John's playing career.

This is the story of a great player's love for hurling and for those who played it; of his loyalty to club and county; of heartbreaking defeat, frustration and, at one time, even disenchantment – and of his ultimate triumph. The story of an ordinary man who was at one with the people of his neighbourhood but who achieved greatness by extraordinary and heroic deeds on the hurling fields of Ireland and thereby made us all feel better about ourselves. He was a true hero, for despite all his fame John Keane remained to the end a friendly, quiet, humorous and utterly modest man.

Contents

Acknowledgements   v
Preface   ix
Introduction   1

PART ONE

Chapter One – The Beginning   11

Chapter Two – Schooldays 1923-34   17

Chapter Three – County Senior Debut   32

Chapter Four – Keane versus Mackey   39

Chapter Five – A County Comes Of Age   48

Chapter Six – The Emergency   66

Chapter Seven – The Unconquerable Keane   72

Chapter Eight – The Greatest Man In Ireland   86

Chapter Nine – Building a Team   98

Chapter Ten – Senior All-Ireland   107

Chapter Eleven – Post-1948   128

PART TWO

CHAPTER TWELVE – MOUNT SION	137
CHAPTER THIRTEEN – THREE IN A ROW	150
CHAPTER FOURTEEN – JOHN RESIGNS	162
CHAPTER FIFTEEN – CHAMPIONS AGAIN	171
CHAPTER SIXTEEN – MOUNT SION DOUBLE UP	179
CHAPTER SEVENTEEN – JOHN GOES FORWARD	186
CHAPTER EIGHTEEN – JOHN KEANE'S SCORING MACHINE	197
CHAPTER NINETEEN – RETIREMENT FROM HURLING	205
CHAPTER TWENTY – TRAINER, COACH, PSYCHOLOGIST	217
CHAPTER TWENTY ONE – ENDGAME	224
CHAPTER TWENTY TWO – EPILOGUE	229
Appendix 1 – Statistical record of John's career	234
Appendix 2 – Graveside Oration	242
Appendix 3 – Tributes	246
Appendix 4 – Greatest-ever hurling teams	250
Bibliography	256
Index	263

INTRODUCTION

There had always been a strong tradition of hurling in Waterford, especially in its Irish-speaking areas. The local poet Donncha Ruadh macConmara was reputed to be a fine hurler and in his epic poem *Eachtra Ghiolla an Amaráin*, written c1750, he wrote of a hurling match between the scholars of his school in Waterford and the youths of the district. A hundred years later, however, at the time when Thomas Francis Meagher had grown to manhood, hurling had almost died in the city.[1] When Meagher was a young man, hurling had been very popular in such districts of the city as Ballybricken, Ballytruckle, Gallows Hill (Upper Gracedieu) and the Yellow Road, while tradition has it that Butlerstown and Ballyduff, just outside the city, had produced hurlers capable of holding their own against the best that Kilkenny and Tipperary could throw at them. In earlier decades, the seafarers of Waterford had played hurling in their leisure moments ashore in Newfoundland and the Americas.[2]

The reasons for the decline of hurling were many and complex, but it was a problem that was not exclusive to Waterford for it pervaded almost the whole country. As a result of the Great Famine much of the culture, folklore, historical memory, genealogy, religious practices and social structures of the people had been swept away, amidst a tide of modernisation and Anglicisation. Of course the Famine was not the sole cause – it had been preceded by centuries of anti-Irish propaganda, institutional, legislative and literary. There had been a concerted attack upon the Irish people's religion, language and culture and, over time, all classes of the Irish poor, both urban and rural, were exposed to

---

1   Meagher attended Mount Sion schools for a short time before being sent to Clongowes Wood College
2   McCarthy, Kevin, *Gold, Silver and Green: The Irish Olympic Journey 1896-1924*, (Cork University Press, Cork, 2010), p. 78

colonial theories about the inferiority of Irish culture.³ Even the leaders of the people, the native clergy, joined with the authorities in this approach, actively discouraging patterns and sports gatherings, claiming that they gave rise to riots and disorder. As early as April 1828 the diarist Amhlaoibh Ó Súilleabháin wrote, 'Easter Sunday. Boys were playing hurley [sic] near Droichead na nGabhar [near Callan county Kilkenny] in the evening. The sticks and hips were busy, when Fr Croíoch came and chased away the hurlers. They ran before him like a flock of sheep before a lion.'⁴

The Fenian Charles J. Kickham saw such behaviour by the authorities and clergy as an attack on the things he held most dear. In a leading article in the *Irish People* entitled 'National Sports' he wrote

> Now, why all this anxiety to put down our old sports and pastimes? ... We hear it said that young men would murder one another if hurling were permitted. This is a calumny invented by our enemies. It is simply telling us that we are savages. More blows have been struck at fairs and markets, and even at Sundays and holidays after Mass, than ever were struck at hurlings ... Our fathers and grandfathers hurled and leaped and danced, and we cannot see why we should not do the same. ... The people know it cannot be for love for them that makes their tyrants so anxious to discourage athletic exercises among them. Our masters see that manly sports have a tendency to foster manliness. And manliness they will not have in Ireland, if they can help it.⁵

R. V. Comerford in his biography maintains that Kickham anticipated the development of the Gaelic Athletic Association

---

3   Doherty, Gillian, *The Irish Ordnance Survey: history, culture and memory*, (Four Courts, Dublin, 2004), p. 149
4   de Bhaldraithe, Tomás (trans. & ed.), *Diary of an Irish countryman*, (Mercier, Cork, 1979), p. 51
5   *Irish People*, 15 October 1864

(GAA) in that 'he had an awareness of the political significance of organised sport, and especially its affinity to the processes that go to make a nationalist movement.'[6] But in so doing Kickham had, in his thoughts and sentiments, merely echoed Thomas Francis Meagher. Sixteen years earlier, in 1848, Meagher had formulated, quite clearly, the value of native, gaelic, games in fostering an Irish spirit amongst the people. After a political rally conducted on Ballybricken Green for the 1848 Waterford by-election, he recited the following quatrain which showed his true feelings for the game and his distress at its demise in the city and county:

You have the Irish dances yet,
Where is the hurling gone?
Of two such pastimes why forget
The nobler and the manlier one![7]

Meagher and Michael Doheny (two of the prime movers in the 1840s Confederacy in Ireland) then co-led two teams of twenty one men each onto the green to play a game of hurling. This was an attempt to revive interest in the game locally because Meagher realised that those games and pastimes were the best mediums for inculcating in the people a love of their native land. Furthermore, he believed fervently that the practice of athletics was the best means of training them for active service in their country's interest.

When the Famine finally ended with over two million having either died or emigrated, the remaining people lay shocked and hopeless. Charles Gavan Duffy, the Young Irelander, was quoted as saying, on his departure from Ireland to Australia, 'that there was no more hope [for Ireland] than for the corpse on the dissecting table.'[8] The countryside lay ravaged and the populace dispirited. The native games were in a parlous state and near

---

6 Comerford, R. V., *Charles J. Kickham* (Wolfhound, Dublin, 1979), p. 185
7 1948 All-Ireland hurling final programme
8 *The Nation*, 25 August 1855

to extinction, but efforts still continued in an attempt to revive hurling locally. In 1858 Denis Cashman, the noted Waterford Fenian, attempted the task and he organised one of the very last games in the old tradition, a hurling match in Knockhouse, just outside the city, when twenty one men from the city opposed a like number from Kilmacthomas.[9] A further ten years passed before a similar occasion occurred in the city. A writer in the *Waterford News* of 11 February 1938 recalled that his friend, Thomas Sexton (one of Parnell's chief lieutenants), who had always been interested in old Irish games and customs, told him of a hurling match he had once witnessed, in 1868, at An Slí Caol (Slievekeale Road) between twenty one hurlers from that locality and a team from Gracedieu. It lasted for an hour and a half and ended in a drawn game. That seems to have been the dying kick of the hurling tradition in the city because in 1884, when the GAA was founded by Michael Cusack, football was the dominant sport.

However Waterford city was not alone in this regard. Hurling was almost unknown in many of the major towns and in the year 1886, for instance, Kilkenny saw its first hurling game for twenty years.[10] Waterford had responded enthusiastically to Michael Cusack's call when he founded the GAA and in 1887, when the first statistics of the Association's membership were compiled, the county had thirty affiliated clubs. This number had fallen drastically, however, to only six just three years later.[11] This was due to the split in the Association as a result of its 'take-over' by the Irish Republican Brotherhood (IRB) and the subsequent onslaught on it by the Catholic hierarchy. Throughout all this turmoil and disruption the county had, however, played its part in the Association and its football clubs were very active, but it was

---

9   Cronin, Jim, *Munster GAA story* (Clare Champion, Ennis, 1986), p. 9
10 de Búrca, Marcus, *The GAA: a history* (Second edition, Gill & Macmillan, Dublin, 1999), p. 22
11 de Búrca, *The GAA: a history*, p.22

not until 1902 that a hurling championship game was played in county Waterford.

From the earliest days of the GAA the hurlers of Mooncoin had crossed to the south bank of the Suir on a Sunday evening in summer and played hurling against the young boys in county Waterford. Their motives were not wholly altruistic however because when they rowed back across the river they took with them ash-boughs that were cut in the woods of Mount Congreve and subsequently fashioned into hurleys.[12] The young Waterford boys showed great interest in hurling and this prompted a city man named Ned 'Gaelic' Phelan to make another attempt to revive hurling in the city and county. Phelan was known as the pioneer of hurling in Waterford and in the spring of 1902, when he retired from active participation in the sport, he set himself the task of getting the game going on competitive lines in the city and county. He searched around for some one to aid him in his objective and, realising that a figure of great authority in Waterford GAA was needed, the man he chose was the well-known official Willie Walsh, after whom Walsh Park is named.

A better choice could not have been made. Walsh, a small-boned wiry man, who lived in the city's Griffith Place, was a noted administrator in Waterford GAA circles. He was also a famous referee and he later took charge of six All-Ireland senior hurling finals (1915-19 and 1921) and the football All-Ireland finals in 1920 and 1921. Later still he was prevailed upon to come out of retirement to referee the second replay of the 1931 hurling final between Cork and Kilkenny. After his attendance at the 1916 Easter GAA Congress in Dublin, he was arrested by British forces at Waterford Railway station and interned. In 1902 Phelan and Walsh visited Knockboy where they met Charlie Walsh, an old hurler, and discussed the possibility of forming a team in the area. Willie Walsh agreed to interview some friends in different parts of the county and this resulted in the formation of clubs in Clonea and Durrow. Three hurling teams affiliated to contest the first county championship, Clonea (the

---

12   *Irish Independent*, 3 September 1938

eventual champions), Durrow and Knockboy. Two more teams affiliated the following year, Gracedieu and De la Salle, both from the city. The first tentative steps had been made behind the scenes to set hurling on a proper foundation in the city and county.

Waterford had won its first senior Munster championship match in 1903 when Kerry were the opponents but what followed was a twenty-two year long catalogue of defeat after defeat. That generation of hurlers, however, had established a tradition of picking themselves up and resuming the struggle – a tradition of never giving up. It would take another generation for a leader to appear and bring Waterford into a new era where they would challenge for the highest honours in the game. The scene had been set for the emergence of John Keane, the subject of this story and the county's greatest-ever player.

Part One

John Keane

Chapter One

The beginning

There are three Keane septs in Ireland: Ó Caháin of Ulster, Mac Catháin of West Clare and Ó Céin of Munster. McLysaght writes of the name (O) Keane that when it is not used as a variant of the Ulster Ó Cahan (Ó Catháin), it is generally understood to refer to Ó Céin of Munster and that, inevitably, Keane has been substituted for Kane.[13] In Griffith's Property Survey of 1848-64 the most numerous Keane households were found in Galway (240), Clare (182) and Waterford (182). Seán de Bhulbh states that while the name Ó Catháin is quite general in Munster, the Ó Céin name relates specifically to Waterford.[14] It is quite clear, therefore, that John's branch (sometimes rendered without the final e) is that of a quite distinct county Waterford sept. The surname was Ó Céin although John was given the name Seán Ó Catháin when he started school and was so named all through his life.

This Ó Céin sept had settled in county Waterford, specifically in the triangle of land between Kilmacthomas, Bunmahon and Tramore, and it was from the latter area that John could trace his ancestry, the family originating in the area between the Tramore townlands of Islandikeane (Oileán Uí Chéin) and Moonvoy (Móin Bhuídh). In Canon Power's *The place names of Decies* he concludes that Islandikeane derived its name from the ancient occupation of a Celtic warrior chief, but recent DNA studies indicate that some of the Keane families in Ireland descended from a Viking line that adopted the disguise of a Gaelic

---

13 MacLysaght, Edward, *The surnames of Ireland* (Irish Academic Press, Dublin, 1985), p. 171
14 de Bhulbh, Seán, *Sloinnte uile Éireann* (Comhar-chumann Íde naofa teo, Luimneach, 2002) p. 287

clan.[15] It would be interesting to discover if John, with his tall stature, blond hair and ruddy complexion, owed more to a Viking lineage than to a Celtic one.

John's paternal grandfather, Thomas Keane, had come into Waterford city from the Tramore area to find work. Having settled down there he married Mary Walsh, a cloak-maker from Mayor's Walk, in Ballybricken church on 30 January 1864. Their first child, Thomas (John's father), was born on Thursday 12 April 1866. The family lived at Bachelor's Walk at this time and John's father obtained a position as a horse-groom with Widger's, the famous horse dealers, who were one of the largest suppliers of cavalry horses in Europe.

Tom Keane, John's father.
(Photo courtesy of Tosh Widger, Waterford)

In 1895 the Widger family won the Aintree Grand National with a horse named 'The wild man from Borneo.' Thomas Keane was the groom who looked after the horse.

John's maternal great-grandfather, John Darmody, was born c1815 in Crowbally, Mullinavat, county Kilkenny. In the middle 1830s he had journeyed the fifteen miles into Waterford city to look for work. With his farming background he was soon employed and in *Shearman's Commercial Guide to Waterford and Tramore* in 1839 he is described as a 'Butcher attending The Shambles,' the public slaughtering house. He mar-

---

15 http://www.familytreedna.com/public/keaneYDNAwebsite/default.aspx

ried Catherine Kennedy from Gracedieu on 9 September 1843, after which they lived in Morrison's Road and had nine children, five sons and four daughters. All were educated in Mount Sion and the Presentation Convent schools, thus beginning a long family association with both schools. Their second son, Tom Darmody, was the father of Katie Darmody, John's mother.

John's parents, Tom Keane and Katie Darmody, were married on 7 July 1898, when Tom was thirty two years old and she was only nineteen. They had nine children, with John being the youngest boy and the second youngest child, born on 18 February 1917. John's father was known affectionately to the whole family as 'Da' and while he was the head of the household and had the final word in family matters it was his wife Katie who effectively ran the family. Da was quite content to let Katie make the decisions and he trusted her judgment in all things.

John's family surname was anglicized to sound as Kane and John's father signed his name as Thomas Kane at the registration of the birth of John's second-eldest sister Mary (Molly). By the time John was born, however, the name was being written as Keane, but whilst John spelt his name thus, the old pronunciation lingered and everyone in Waterford pronounced his name as John Kane. Many years later (in 1948) this led to an amusing comment in the *Dungarvan Leader* when the Gaelic games writer, reporting on the Waterford v Cork Munster final, wrote that someone had suggested to him that he should caption his report with the title 'Waterford gives Cork a Keaning [caning]' punning on the local pronunciation of the name but also implying that John's performance in the match had been such that he had been the chief architect of Waterford's win.[16]

John's family on both sides was steeped in the traditions of Gaelic Ireland. His childhood years were spent among likeminded neighbours for the people in the area around John's home in Barrack Street were very nationalistic despite the two British military barracks in the street – or maybe because of them. Another reason was the strong influence of the Christian

---

16 *Dungarvan Leader*, 7 August 1948

Brothers in Mount Sion. The Brothers were ultra nationalistic; all of them were Irish speakers and the language was in wide use throughout the schools. The language was very important to the Brothers and they imbued the boys in their charge with the same zeal. In 1927, when John was a pupil, the school was adjudged the best school in Munster for proficiency in Irish and was presented with the Dáil cup.

The schools were situated at the eastern end of Barrack Street and directly across the road stood the Infantry barracks, a constant reminder to the Brothers of the military occupation of the country. Just as Mount Sion was confronted by a British military barracks so too was the Keane house at the western end of the street – by the Artillery/Cavalry barracks. The people of the area got on reasonably well, for the most part, with the soldiers: the men drank side by side with them in the public houses in the area but there were many arguments amongst them, especially when the pubs had closed and the alcohol had taken its effect. These arguments sometimes exploded into fights and, on occasion, serious injuries and deaths. One such incident deeply affected John's family and only reinforced their advanced nationalism. John's father and mother had married in 1898, living in Newgate Street at first but moving to Barrack Street when the houses were built there in 1900. The incident with the soldiers happened on 10 September 1904 when the Keane household consisted of John's maternal grandmother, his father and mother and three children, Biddy and the two boys Thomas and Josie.

A group of local men had been drinking with two soldiers and at closing time the two soldiers left the pub and walked to the Cavalry barracks with two of the civilians. As they approached the barracks they were surrounded by a group of civilians numbering about twenty or thirty. Heated words were exchanged and after about five minutes of insults and jostling the soldiers had to fight their way through the hostile crowd into the barracks. At this time there was about one hundred and fifty young men and women gathered outside the barracks gate, having been attracted by the shouting and arguing. One of the soldiers went to his room to get his gun, after which he placed a ladder against the inside wall of the barracks, climbed it and fired into the crowd gathered outside, shooting a young boy of fifteen years named Matthew Hayes of Slievekeale Road. The boy had been at Confession in Ballybricken church earlier and was walking home with his sister past the Keane house directly opposite the barracks when he was hit. On hearing the shot John's grandmother rushed out and dragged the boy into her kitchen where he died on the floor. The police were called to the scene where they tried to gain admittance to the barracks to question the soldiers but were not allowed entrance for quite some time. When they were eventually admitted they could find no rifle that bore traces of having recently been discharged but some civilians said that they had seen soldiers climbing out over the wall of the barracks and running down the hill at Prior's Knock.[17]

John's grandmother fed her grandchildren with a diet of such stories. John's eldest brother, Thomas, who was four years old when young Hayes died in the house, subsequently joined the Irish Republican Army (IRA) as a young man and took the Republican side in the Civil War. He was captured by Free State forces on 9 February 1923 and was interned in Waterford, Kilkenny and the Curragh. He took part in the nationwide IRA hunger strike and was released under the general amnesty with all the other IRA prisoners on 21 December 1923. His eldest son, Tommy, subsequently played with John on the Mount Sion and Waterford senior hurling teams.

John was born in the area and it had been men from Barrack Street who first brought the game of hurling to the American continent in the years when Waterford city had very close links with Newfoundland. Many of the old songs of Waterford had verses about Waterford men's adventures in Newfoundland and one of these old songs, which contained many phrases in the Irish language, was entitled *The Hurlers from Faha Stoogeen.*

---

17   From Keane family lore. See also *Munster Express* 17 September 1904, 24 September 1904 and 30 June 1905

It was a lament about their departure from Barrack Street and failure to return. John's home was part of an area known locally as 'Up the roads' a term given to all of the western suburbs. Most of this area was laid out in a grid formation and John was particularly lucky in that his terrace was the southern edge of a square, with Morrison's Road at the west, St Ignatius Street at the north and Mount Sion Avenue at the east. The houses faced outwards to the streets and the backs of the houses enclosed a common green where the children of the area played together, safe and sound under the watchful eyes of the women and out of sight of members of the newly-formed Gárda Síochána, who were zealous in their pursuit of children found ball-playing on the streets. It was in this small field that the very young John, together with the other little boys, and some girls, learned the art and craft of hurling. The field measured approximately fifty yards by fifty; large enough for young boys to play on, but it was uneven and bumpy and skill was at a premium. Of course the little hurlers didn't have the field to themselves but had to share it with a veritable host of others: the women of the area who sat knitting and talking, girls playing with dolls and prams, others minding babies and yet more girls playing with their goats – a favourite pet in those times.

John and his friends were within five minutes walk of the Gaelic Field, where all of Waterford's, and even some of Kilkenny's, championship games were held. The boys made this area their second home, especially in the summer evenings when there was constant activity in the field. The boys always carried makeshift cut-down hurleys that were cobbled together out of broken hurleys procured from the field of play. One evening the boys were playing in Slievekeale Road, between the Gaelic Field and the Presentation Convent and were being observed by a man named Maurice Lucas, who was employed by the nuns to look after the convent grounds. John was playing with a bent stick and Lucas, who obviously saw something different about John that made him stand out from the others, gave John his first, proper, boy's hurley, thus setting the young boy on the road to glory.

CHAPTER TWO

SCHOOLDAYS 1923-34

John's great uncle, Michael Darmody, had been born in 1860 and had attended Mount Sion primary and secondary schools, graduating in 1878. Michael had left for the United States to join his brother James (b.1847) and family in Chicago, where he found work as a labourer. He felt he had a vocation to be a Christian Brother and eventually joined the Order of the Christian Brothers at Glencoe, Missouri, only to find that he had, in fact, joined the De la Salle Brothers.[18] Notwithstanding the error, however, Michael was very happy in the De la Salle Order, and though he left after a few years to become a priest he never forgot the welcome he had received from the Brothers in Glencoe. He always retained a great affection for them and he requested that after his death he wanted to be buried in the De la Salle Brothers' cemetery there.

When school beckoned for John, the Keane family found itself in a quandary. Mount Sion was the preferred school for John (as it had been for two generations of the family before him) but a complication had arisen.

---

18 Murray, Robert J., *A church grows on a tree claim: a history of Sacred Heart parish, Aberdeen, SD., USA*, (North Plains press, Aberdeen SD, 1981), p. 18. The error was in the naming and was easy to understand. When Br Rice had founded his Order there was another Order already in existence known throughout the world as the Order of the Christian Brothers (more commonly known in Ireland as the De la Salle Brothers) so Br Rice, to avoid confusion, named his Order the Irish Christian Brothers.

John's mother, Katie in 1937. (Photo courtesy of the Smith family)

Fr Darmody sent money home on a regular basis to his relations, including his niece Katie Keane (John's mother), and he stipulated that some of the money was to have John educated in the De la Salle schools in Waterford. When John reached school age, therefore, he was enrolled in the De la Salle's Stephen's Street school, although, as already stated, all of his male forebears had been educated in Mount Sion. It is not known how the family got round this rather delicate situation, but they did, and after only one year he transferred to Mount Sion on 25 April 1924, when he was seven years old.

John thrived in Mount Sion and was a very good student. In his fifth standard examinations in 1929 he achieved 100% in six subjects: comprehension and reading, Irish, history, geography, drawing and grammar; 90% in writing skills and 80% in arithmetic.[19] The future course of his life had been firmly set and to the day he died he remained very closely tied to the Brothers in Mount Sion schools.

Mount Sion had been founded by Brother Edmund Rice in 1802 and was the mother-house of the Irish Christian Brothers. The ethos of the school was Catholic, Gaelic and nationalist. Irish was the language of the school and Irish culture played a large part in its life – its language, history and music. The boys were immersed in what is known in Irish as *Tír grádh agus teanga grádh* – that love of country and love of the language summed up in the term 'Faith and Fatherland,' so indelibly as-

---

19 Waterford city archives, EDU1/1/1

sociated with the Brothers. A Christian Brother from Limerick city, Br A. S. Malone had arrived in the school in 1925 and he subscribed fully to those ideals.

The importance of Br Malone and his fellow Brothers in their role of moulding their young pupils cannot be overestimated. Br Malone quickly set about establishing Gaelic games throughout the city and environs. He organised a competition amongst the four Christian Brothers schools in the city but only three of them participated: Mount Sion, St John's and St Patrick's. This school league ran for several years in one form or another and Andy Fleming, later a star with Mount Sion, Waterford and Munster, told me about the time when he and John played in it. During the time in question St Patrick's school couldn't field a team so the inter-school league had five teams from Mount Sion and one from St John's (the Manor) school.

Br Malone, who is regarded as the first founder of the Mount Sion H&F club

> John and I captained the two best teams. John's team played on Saturdays and mine on Tuesdays. I lived near Stradbally, in the county, and as I went home on the train every night I couldn't play on Saturdays because I was needed at home. As luck would have it, both our teams reached the final of the league which had been fixed for a Saturday. I told the Brother that I couldn't play but he, after thinking about it, suggested that I ask my father if he would allow me to stay over for the final. He told me to tell my father that, if he agreed, my accommodation would be arranged for Friday night and that

the Brother would put me on the train after the final. My father agreed that I could stay and play but the Brother told me not to tell any of the players. In the week before the game the talk was about how much I would be missed and that John's team would thrash us in the final so you can imagine the consternation when I turned out for the final and helped in beating John's team. I never let John forget that.[20]

The dominant hurling force in the county at that time was the great city club, Erin's Own. Br Malone had been urging the club for some considerable time to form a minor team but he was becoming increasingly frustrated with that club's negative response to what he could see was the right way forward. He was great friends with Charlie Ware, Erin's Own's great player, and kept stressing to him that he had a conveyor belt of very good hurlers in the school. Erin's Own were not interested in minor hurlers, however, as they assumed that they would continue to get all the best players from the school, which they regarded as a nursery for their club. But Br Malone had registered the Mount Sion school team as a minor club under the name Éire Óg and this team competed in the county minor championship in 1930. It was at this time that John made his championship debut at left half-back – he was only thirteen years of age.[21] Mount Sion beat Portlaw in the Eastern final and the star of the game was the seventeen years old Locky Byrne at midfield for Mount Sion, who won the game on the score 9-4 to 1-1. Mount Sion/Éire Óg went on to win the 1930 county minor title by beating Dungarvan on a score of 8-2 to 0-0, and John had won his first county medal.[22]

Br Malone was transferred from Mount Sion schools in August 1930. His loss to the school and to Gaelic games in the city was immeasurable, for it was to him more than to anyone else that credit was due for the formation of the minor clubs in the

---

20   Interview with Andy Fleming
21   *Waterford News*, 30 January 1931
22   *Waterford News*, 2 April 1931

district and it was through his efforts that juvenile hurling and football became a virile force in the development of the Association in the city. In his years at the school, his love of hurling, his enthusiasm for the language, and his total commitment to all things Gaelic and national had influenced all with whom he came in contact. He was a man of magnetic personality, a man who inspired by example, a man born to lead. Under his direction hurling in Mount Sion achieved a new dimension. He had a philosophy of teaching that carried over to his hurling coaching and it was embodied in his mantra, *Múin beagáin, ach múin go maith* (Teach little, but teach well) – in other words, teach the basics. It was through him that the national game became a very significant part of the school tradition and his hope was that the spirit of the school would continue and endure through a GAA club that would carry the name and reflect the character of the monastery.

John was now playing minor hurling and football for his school and was beginning to be noticed by the public at large. Billy Howlett, a good friend and work colleague of mine, played minor hurling for Portlaw at that time and in later years we often spoke about John as a minor hurler. He said that John was a very powerful athlete with enormous skill and was almost a one-man team when Mount Sion appeared to be in trouble. It was his opinion that John was worth about four points to Mount Sion before the game even started, despite the fact that John was usually at full back in those days. Billy added, 'He *was* Mount Sion.'

He said that everyone could see that John was an extraordinary hurler, even at that early stage in his development. John had a decided advantage over most other players in that he was big for his age. Billy Howlett (who was a big man) told me that he could match John for strength but that John had the added attribute of being incredibly skilful and this, together with his speed of thought and action, made him an exceptional player. He also told me that John was a natural leader and that even as a very young man he earned the respect of men who were much older than he and who were more experienced and mature. Billy said that John had that indefinable quality that all leaders possess. He could be in any company and people would defer to him because he exuded what nowadays is called charisma.

John's school team played a series of challenge games with schools in Waterford and Kilkenny and were very successful, winning most of them. The Harty cup team defeated Kilkenny CBS in Kilkenny and then beat Callan CBS (a team augmented by several ex-pupils) in Waterford. The style of newspaper reporting in the 1930s meant that only rarely would one see comments about a hurler's individual attributes, and almost never about juveniles, so it is a measure of John's impact on the local scene that we read, in a preview of the Callan game, that 'we will be all watching out for the wizardry of Mount Sion's star full-back – John Keane – a boy scarcely sixteen years of age.'[23] The minor team, which was in effect the school team, was expected to win the 1932 county final against Lismore but injuries to Paddy Greene and John meant that two of Mount Sion's stars could not play and Lismore swept to victory on the back of a marvellous exhibition by a future Waterford senior player, Mick Regan.

Pat Fanning, future president of the GAA, remembered the time when he first became aware of John as a hurler.

> I was eighteen months younger than John and in a class below him in school, but I knew of him. Everyone did. John was already a legend in the school. Everybody knew of his prowess. He was big for his age with the perfect build for an athlete. He had a massive presence about him on the field of play. I remember a school match down in [New] Ross. I was rather small as a boy and I was put on goal for my first appearance with the school team. John was at full-back but he got a belt and had to go off and suddenly I realised the vastness of the field. There was total protection for me in goal when John

---

23   *Waterford News*, 11 November 1932

stood at full-back but when John was off the field I felt horribly exposed.[24]

In 1932 John was selected, at fifteen years of age, for the Waterford minor hurlers to play against Cork in the Munster championship; he played at centre-field and was one of six Mount Sion players on the team. A wonderful display by the Waterford boys resulted in the beating of Cork (who had the fifteen year old Jack Lynch, the future Taoiseach, playing at right half back) on a score of 4-1 to 3-2. This win set up a Munster semi-final clash in Thurles with Tipperary, the 'kings' of minor hurling in the 1930s, who dominated this grade for many years winning six consecutive titles from 1930 to 1935. Jack Lynch recalled, years later, that every sub that Tipperary brought on during a game at that time seemed to be bigger and better than the player who was taken off.[25] Tipperary duly beat Waterford by 4-7 to 3-1 with John playing at left half forward. The minor game had been the preliminary to the senior match between the All-Ireland champions Cork and Limerick, the team that was to dominate the 1930s. The fifteen year old John sat on the sidelines and saw in action, for the first time, the new sensation of hurling, Mick Mackey of Limerick, with whom he would become indelibly linked in the folklore of the game just five years hence.

---

24 Interview with Pat Fanning. Pat was John's great friend, and closest colleague and confidant. He was president of the GAA 1970-73, chairman of the Munster council 1962-5, and chairman of the Waterford county board on three occasions (1955-62, 1969-70 and 1975-87). At club level he is life president of Mount Sion, was secretary 1940-55 and chairman 1955-70 and 1977-85. As a player with Mount Sion he won seven senior hurling championship medals, one minor hurling medal and one for junior football. He also played senior hurling for Waterford.
25 Ó Tuama, Liam, *Where he sported and played: Jack Lynch, a sporting celebration*, (Blackwater, Dublin, 2000), p. 15

In the 1933 Munster championship John was selected at right full-back on the Waterford minor team that drew with Tipperary. The two teams put on an exhibition of top class hurling with Tipperary scoring the equalising point from a seventy yard free only just before the end. In the replay Waterford lost by two goals but the game never reached the heights of the drawn match.

John's eldest brother, Thomas (Photo courtesy of the Keane family)

John was a very intelligent boy with a keen brain and he excelled in mathematics[26] and business studies. Notwithstanding his obvious scholastic ability, however, he was taken out of full-time schooling and sent to work at Messrs Graves & Co., timber merchants, who had their premises at Park Road. The reason why this action was taken was all too common in Ireland in the hungry thirties; families were large, work was scarce and every penny was needed.

Two brothers (Thomas and Josie) and two sisters (Molly and Babby) were married at this time but six people were still living at home (John, Kitty, Peggy, Queenie and parents) and John's father was still working although he was now sixty seven years of age. He was taking home about £2 10s per week from his job on the outdoor staff of Waterford Corporation but as there was no pension the family would be without his income if he retired. John continued attending Mount Sion on a part-time basis, studying business and commerce. An added benefit for so doing was that

---

26   He obviously passed on this facility to his three sons, Tom, John and Gerard because all three graduated from university with honours degrees in the subject.

he thereby qualified to play for his school in colleges competitions such as the Dr Harty cup.

In April 1933 three Mount Sion school players, Michael Doyle, Paddy O'Donovan and John, were chosen on the Munster colleges' team for the annual inter-provincial final series with Leinster. John was selected at full back and all three played in Munster's thrilling win by six points over Leinster in Nowlan Park. St Kieran's college had supplied nine players to the Leinster team and their forward division was incorporated *en bloc*. The *Irish Independent* reported that 'the Munster back division was almost impregnable and defied the best efforts of the St Kieran's forwards.'[27]

John's brother Josie (Photo courtesy of David Smith)

John's sisters Babby, Kitty, Queenie, Peggy and Molly (Photo courtesy of David Smith)

---

27   *Irish Independent*, 1 May 1933

The inter-provincial college series was held every year between Munster and Leinster and the venue for the games alternated between Cork and Kilkenny. The teams travelled the day before the game and stayed for two nights. On the night of the game there was a dinner for both teams, the winners got their medals and afterwards the boys mingled and fraternised. John played for three years in the series and it was at these gatherings that John forged lasting friendships with Jack Lynch of Cork, Tony Brennan of Tipperary and hurlers from other counties – friendships that lasted all their lives.

Jack Lynch with John at a Munster final in the 1960s

The following story which showed the depth of these friendships was told to me by Pat Kelly, an old work-mate of mine. Pat's father, Tommy, worked as a ticket checker on the Waterford/Dublin trains and when John was in the Mater hospital in early 1975 it was Tommy's practice to visit him whenever he had time off in Dublin. On one such day there was a sudden flurry of activity in the ward and the matron rushed in to see if everything was in order because a distinguished visitor had arrived to see John. The visitor came down the ward hot on her heels – it was none other than the former Taoiseach and leader of Fianna Fáil, Jack Lynch. Tommy was a bit embarrassed, being in his work uniform, and he rose to leave but was stopped by John who put his arm on Tommy's and said, quite firmly, 'Stay where you are Tommy. Jack is here, not as the former Taoiseach or leader of Fianna Fáil, but as a friend – just as you are.'

As well as playing schools and colleges hurling for Mount Sion and Munster, John was also playing minor hurling and football and senior hurling for his club, and minor and junior hurling and football for Waterford (no talk of burn-out, then). He was usually at full back in hurling but played as a forward for the county in football. The newspapers of the time devoted very little space to sport so it is impossible to re-create all his sporting activity at that time but I have, however, recorded all that has been documented about John and his participation in hurling and football during his career and this information is included as an appendix to this book.

He was also involved in many other sporting and recreational activities and like all great athletes he would have excelled at a myriad of sports. He played quite a lot of Handball; he played Badminton in the school and was the school's star gymnast. At the time Mount Sion school was a centre of excellence in schools' gymnastics and John always took centre-stage during gymnastic exhibitions. This latter ability was manifested in a rather unusual way whilst John was still a young boy. At times he would travel to school by walking the length of Barrack Street on his hands. In later years when he was training the great Waterford team of 1957-63 he showed that he had lost little of his gymnastic prowess. On the way to a game when the team cars stopped to allow the players stretch their legs John would walk on his hands along the side of the road.

During my youth it was often said that John's first medal was won at soccer but the truth was that he never played the game competitively. This canard arose from a half-truth. He was keen on a girl from Poleberry in the lower part of the city and joined with the boys of the area in street soccer matches. Soccer was quite strong in that area (the headquarters of Waterford junior soccer, then as now, being located in Ozier Park in Poleberry) and he evidently impressed the Poleberry lads because they tried to get him to play the game competitively. Paddy Hodgers, a former Mount Sion pupil and hurler (who was also going-out with a girl from the area) noticed this and was concerned that John might be seduced away from hurling. He approached John and had a long talk with him but John assured him that there was no danger of anything like that happening – he was a hurler and he intended to stay a hurler.

John was also a very strong swimmer and did most of his swimming in Tramore. As a youth, he swam regularly from the pier to the strand, a formidable feat even for an adult. I had the personal experience of seeing John and his brother-in-law, Johnny Hartery (the international soccer player) swimming the length of Tramore strand. John is reputed to have once saved a man from drowning in the river Suir. When the rescue was accomplished, however, the man pointed out that his hat was still in the river whereupon John dived in and retrieved the hat.[28]

In politics John's family supported the new government of Mr deValera's Fianna Fáil party (as did John) but in the 1930s Waterford city was a hotbed of left-wing political action and the local Irish Republican Army (IRA) under the leadership of Peter O'Connor and Frank Edwards was very active in social issues such as slum housing and workers' rights. John had a leaning towards the IRA's social policies; his strong sense of justice would have dictated that course of action but he became alienated from the local IRA leadership when they became even more radicalised. Some of the leaders joined the Communist party of Ireland and started indulging in actions that were likely to lead to criminal prosecutions. That course was a step too far for John and he reverted to more mainstream politics. He was never doctrinaire in his politics though and he was not above supporting independent candidates, especially in local politics. In the 1954 General Election he had signed the papers (as one of the assentors) of Billy Kenneally, the Fianna Fáil candidate but in the 1955 Municipal elections he nominated Dick Jones as an Independent candidate.

Back with hurling John played for Munster in the 1934 colleges' inter-provincial at Nowlan Park as Leinster won for the very first time in the series with Jack Lynch making his debut for Munster at left half back. A hectic year continued with the

---

28   Keane family lore

junior hurling win over Kerry in the Munster championships and a minor championship win over the same opposition with John at full back. Just a week after the minor hurling game he lined out for the Waterford minor footballers who outclassed Limerick in the championship by 3-4 to 0-1, and a month later he was at full back as the All-Ireland champions Tipperary beat Waterford in the Munster minor hurling final at Cork. There were nine Mount Sion boys on the team, including Andy Fleming and Paddy Greene.

Waterford had also reached the Munster finals in minor football against Tipperary and junior hurling against Cork and both finals were fixed for Waterford on the same day, 12 August 1934. The selectors had a dilemma. It was obvious that John could not play in both games and the selectors decided, inexplicably, that he would sit out the junior hurling game and play for the minor footballers. Sense eventually prevailed and he played for the hurlers who took the Munster title after a thrilling tussle with Cork. The *Munster Express* reported, prophetically, on the junior hurling match:

> It was a great game, punctuated with thrills and resulting in as fine an exhibition of the code as has ever been seen in Waterford. ... To say that the result came as a surprise is but to state what is true. Only to the most intimate supporters could it be known that there was such fine hurling material in our county – material, it can be safely stated, which has in it the moulding of a senior combination of which much may be heard in the not too distant future.[29]

Out of four Munster finals that Waterford contested that year (senior, junior and minor hurling and minor football) the county had won just one. Later in the same month Waterford beat Galway in the All-Ireland home junior hurling semi-final with John one of the stars of a dull game. The county had reached its second junior final in four years and looked for a repeat of the victory last achieved in 1931.

---

29   *Munster Express*, 17 August 1934

Waterford, All-Ireland junior champions 1934. John is the young seventeen year old in dead centre of photo (extreme left of the three players in the middle row).
(Photo courtesy of Tom 'Gum' Kennedy)

The All-Ireland junior hurling home final between Waterford and Kildare was fixed for Wexford Park on 14 October 1934. Kildare had a team drawn mainly from the Army's Curragh camp and all the leading hurling counties were represented on its team whilst Waterford's team was based almost exclusively on the previous year's minor team, although a few of the 1934 minor team also figured.[30] The game itself was a rather disappointing one with Waterford gaining an easy victory thus qualifying them to meet London in the final proper. London had stylish hurlers in keeping with the eleven Cork men on the team, their star player being Morgan Madden who had played for Cork in the three memorable games against Kilkenny in the 1931 senior All-Ireland final. In the match the exiles went within an ace of causing a sensation for they were on a level basis with the home champions right up to the end of the game. Although they were

---

30   *Munster Express*, 12 October 1934

being led by five points near the end they made a great fighting rally and decreased the margin by a goal, but poor finishing by their forwards lost the opportunities that offered them the winning scores. Waterford had scraped through and John, at seventeen years of age and playing at full back, had won his first All-Ireland medal. Mount Sion's win in the county junior final of 1934 meant that John would be playing senior hurling for his club when the 1935 season started.

Chapter three
County senior debut

The seventeen year old John, still a schoolboy, made his debut for the county seniors at right half forward in the National League game against Cork at the Mardyke on 10 February 1935. He was joined by his Mount Sion clubmate John 'Hopper' Walsh together with six players from Erin's Own, three each from Tallow and Dungarvan and one from Lismore. He got honourable mention as the best of the forwards but Cork were comfortable winners on a score of 5-4 to 2-1. Another league match followed quickly, this time against Kilkenny, but now he was at left half-back marking the famous 'Lovely' Johnny Dunne who had been the hero of Kilkenny's All-Ireland win in 1933 when he scored the winning goal that gave him his nickname. John was again in good form and kept Dunne scoreless but Kilkenny won on a score line of 4-6 to 3-3 with Locky Byrne scoring two goals for the winners. A week later, John was in action at right full back for Munster colleges as they beat Leinster in the inter-provincial at Cork.

Waterford had won the 1934 junior hurling All-Ireland final and some half a dozen players had staked a claim for inclusion on the senior team. John was establishing himself as a regular on the county senior team but a surprise was caused when the team to play in the Munster championship against Tipperary was announced. Many of the western players from the successful 1934 junior team were missing and not one of the promising youngsters (including Christy Moylan and John) was selected. The public were clearly unhappy but it didn't prevent them from travelling to the game in their thousands. Two special trains left Waterford on a boiling hot day in July and twelve thousand people were packed into Davin Park before the game began. The selectors had delayed announcing the team until a week before the game but as the team paraded behind the Carrick brass band it was evident that unauthorised changes had been made to the expected line out.

After about twelve minutes the Waterford crowd might as well have gone home because Tipperary had already scored three goals. Tipperary scored eight goals in total as they humiliated Waterford by 8-4 to 1-2 and the eagerly awaited clash between the two veterans Charlie Ware and Martin Kennedy (the man many people regarded as the greatest ever full forward) had resulted in the latter scoring four goals. Public reaction was swift and the Erin's Own club (which had the responsibility for the county selection) was blamed for the debacle and the changes in the team. Whatever the reason, another Munster championship had come and gone and a season that had promised so much for Waterford was in tatters.

After Erin's Own had won the 1935 county final the club committee met in a public house in Grattan square, Dungarvan and selected a team to represent Waterford in the upcoming National League match with Limerick. They instructed their representatives to present the list of the selected team to the county board, as a *fait accompli*, at the next meeting of that body. The board was outraged with the action of Erin's Own and selected its own team. Erin's Own then withdrew all its players from the county team and at a special meeting of the county board the Erin's Own club was suspended for six months.

When the team was selected for the National League match versus Tipperary on 17 November the Erin's Own players were ignored and most of the young players who had been dropped so sensationally for the Munster championship game with Tipperary were brought back. The newcomers included John, who was never dropped again and right up to his retirement was an automatic choice for the county. He had been selected at full back to mark no less a man than the famous Martin Kennedy, who had 'roasted' the great Charlie Ware to the tune of four goals in the championship match. This was his biggest challenge to date and many must have wondered how the eighteen year old would acquit himself against the greatest full-forward the game had seen up to then. To the shock of the hurling world Waterford confounded all predictions by defeating Tipperary, 4-4 to 3-3. P. D. Mehigan (Pat'O in the *Irish Times*) wrote 'Surprises continue through the National Leagues ... last Sunday's results ... found the lowly county of Waterford astonishing all and sundry by defeating a strong Tipperary side.'[31] The *Irish Independent* heaped praise on the young Waterford team that turned over at half time with a three goal lead as Tipperary scored only a solitary point, per Kennedy. The paper continued: 'Showing considerable improvement in the second half they [Tipperary] attacked repeatedly and were it not for the fine defensive tactics of Keane, who frustrated Kennedy in many attempts, the scoreboard at the close might have read differently.'[32] Kennedy, who was near the end of his great career, as John was starting his, used all his guile, craft and vast experience to the full but to no avail as John, with his physical strength and tactical nous, limited Kennedy to three points and made the hurling world sit up and take notice. The *Munster Express*, quoting the *Evening Mail* wrote: 'Introducing Keane (late of the minor team) and Doyle of Tallow, these two youngsters were two valuable finds for Waterford ... by securing victory Waterford have re-established themselves ... the success of the younger players will have a splendid effect.'[33]

After the appeal by Erin's Own to the Munster council had been rejected, the club surrendered the selection of the county team to the county board and were re-instated. Waterford completed their National League fixtures with their first ever visit to Connacht in December where they were narrowly defeated by Galway. John was at full back in this game and was one of Waterford's best players. He had established himself as a regular on the team and looked set for a long career on the team, even with the imminent recall of the Erin's Own players. But Erin's Own resentment at the county board's action in suspending the

---

31   *Irish Times*, 19 November 1935
32   *Irish Independent*, 18 November 1935
33   *Munster Express*, 22 December 1935

club still rankled and it was to manifest itself once more in an extraordinary and unprecedented manner in the coming year.

John's first Munster championship

At the Easter Congress of the GAA in 1936 a motion was moved by Willie Walsh of Waterford, that 'the county borough of Waterford should be returned to the jurisdiction of the Waterford county board.' The city suburbs of Ferrybank and Sallypark had been transferred to Kilkenny in 1932 and several high-profile players had been lost to the Waterford county team, the most famous being Locky Byrne. Mr Gibbons TD opposed the motion on behalf of Kilkenny but after Mr Clifford (Limerick) spoke in favour, saying that Waterford was contending with foreign influences, it was carried on a show of hands and Ferrybank was back in Waterford for GAA purposes.[34]

The Waterford senior hurling selection committee announced an eighteen man panel for the league and championship: six players from Mount Sion, five from Erin's Own, three from Dungarvan and two each from Tallow and Dunhill. It was a powerful panel and one that the public could certainly support with a good expectation of success.[35] The importance of Ferrybank's return was seen in the selection of Locky Byrne and Bill Lynch (two ex-Mount Sion schoolboys) for Waterford's Munster championship first round match – both players had transferred from Mooncoin to Ferrybank and had declared for Waterford.

John had retained his place for what would be his first-ever appearance in the Munster senior championship. Prospects for the county were looking decidedly good and as the thousands

---

34   *Munster Express*, 17 April 1936
35   The panel consisted of Bon Ryan, George Keogh, Paddy Duggan, Dottie Hogan, John Keane, Brian Doyle (Mount Sion); Charlie Ware, Johnny Fanning, Lukie Ryan, Fad Browne, Sonny Wyse (Erin's Own); Christy Moylan, Tom Greaney, Declan Goode (Dungarvan); Pa Sheehan, D. Doyle (Tallow), Mick Skehan, Jack McGrath (Dunhill).

journeyed to Fermoy for the double-header against Clare the Waterford supporters looked forward in high anticipation to seeing their new team advance to the semi-finals. The weather was favourable, the arrangements were good – but the day was disastrous. Clare won both games and the Waterford players and supporters were in total disarray and confusion. It was not just the results alone, however, that were responsible but the startling and unprecedented situation that unfolded before the start of the senior game. When the team assembled it was discovered that six players had not turned up viz., Sonny Wyse, Fad Browne (both Erin's Own); the two Ferrybank players, Locky Byrne and Bill Lynch; and two substitutes Mick Wyse and Charlie Ware (also Erin's Own). The team had to be hurriedly re-arranged and it was no surprise that Waterford were beaten. Equally unsurprising was the reaction of the county board – all hell broke loose.

A meeting of the board was called to inquire into the non-attendance of the six players. During the course of the discussion the chairman, Vincent O'Donoghue, said that ever since the match he had been listening to whispers, statements and rumours about what was going on in Waterford city. He said that 'he had heard that attempts were made and deliberately made, whether through motives of jealousy or not I cannot say, to sabotage this team, and I have no doubt that the majority of these men who absented themselves were deliberately got at.' The board then heard the reasons, or excuses, for the players' actions. Sonny Wyse was suspended for six months; Charlie Ware's letter of explanation was accepted, although the chairman expressed his dissatisfaction with the decision; Fad Browne and Mick Wyse produced doctors' certificates stating that they were unfit to play and these were accepted, but the cases of Lynch and Byrne were more serious as neither gave any reason for their non-appearance in Fermoy. Lynch was given a six month suspension, but the board's fury was primarily directed at Byrne who received a nine month suspension.

The chairman said that Byrne had not only let down his county but had treated the board with silent contempt and that he had given Waterford a dirty break. Willie Walsh said that in his opinion the suspension would not affect Byrne in the slightest because he believed that Byrne was not a registered member of the GAA in Waterford at all. 'He can smack his fingers at us,' said Walsh 'because he is not a member of any club in Waterford to my knowledge.' Walsh was correct. Byrne's transfer from Mooncoin to Ferrybank was not completed until the Tuesday after Waterford's game with Clare. The chairman then ruled that as Byrne was not eligible to play for Waterford at the time, the decision of the Waterford county board suspending him had no effect. Locky later played for Mooncoin in the Kilkenny senior championship and with Kilkenny in their defeat by Limerick in the All-Ireland final. Despite the excuses offered by the players most people believed that the 'no-show' was a protest by the Erin's Own club against its previous suspension by the county board.

John was now the county captain after Mount Sion's victory in the 1936 county championship (subsequently lost on an objection) and was selected at centre-field in the team to play Dublin in the National League at Croke Park. Many changes had been made to the team and it was obvious that the selectors were hoping to start the league in the hope that the new team would re-establish lost prestige. The team responded magnificently when after being despairingly in arrears they fought back to win a thrilling game by 4-5 to 4-4. Dublin led by five points at half-time and had increased that lead to eleven when John began the Waterford comeback. The team responded to his inspired leadership at centre-field and he started the revival by scoring a goal and a point and the team began to gain the upper hand. Further goals by Con Ryan and Paddy Greene sealed the victory. The game against Dublin showed a facet of John's play that was to become a trademark of his – the surge into the forward line in an attempt to revive his team whenever it was in trouble. Dónal Foley has remarked on this feature of John's play.

Keane's leadership was such that he could start a resurgence on his own. Indeed, many a time I watched him snatch victories for his beloved Mount Sion against great clubs like Mooncoin, Tullaroan or Thurles Blues. John had the ability to take the ball right up the field on his own hurley while men tackled him from all sides.[36]

It was just the tonic that the county needed and two weeks later Waterford stood at the head of the league when Cork were soundly beaten by nine points in Lismore.

---

36   *Irish Times*, 4 October 1975

Chapter Four
Keane versus Mackey

1936 had ended on a high note for John. His club had won the county title on the field and he had captained the county team to two great wins in the league – the coming year promised much for Waterford and Mount Sion. John's performances in 1936 had caused many people to take notice of him and to feel that here was the genuine article. Confirmation of this came early in 1937 with his selection on Munster's Railway cup team and he made his cup debut at right half back against Connacht in the semi-final. He was nineteen years old and was the first Mount Sion club man to be so honoured. All the team had previous Railway cup experience except John and fellow Waterford player Christy Moylan. The *Weekly Irish Times* previewing the match commented that 'John Keane, of Waterford, is a recent league product. His display against E. Wade in the Waterford-Dublin game was very impressive – he has power and resource, whilst his tackling is of typical Munster keenness. He is a powerful back who tackles well.'[37]

After Connacht had been defeated, both Moylan and John retained their places on the team to play Leinster in the final on St Patrick's Day in Croke Park. This game was scheduled for a live radio broadcast and John's parents had arranged to hear the broadcast in the home of Mikie Norris, the Keane's local grocer, publican and good friend of family – and the only person in the street to possess a radio (or wireless set as it was called back then). They were to be disappointed however when Radio Éireann cancelled the proposed broadcast because the GAA objected to one of the two commentators and wanted one of their own. John lined out at right-full-back and had a good game,

---

37 *Weekly Irish Times*, 9 January 1937

holding his immediate opponent scoreless and in the process winning his first Railway cup medal.

If the Waterford selectors were still undecided as to John's best position on the team no such doubts were entertained by his club. Paddy Greene, a Mount Sion and Waterford colleague, remembered John at that time.

> During a match he directed the Mount Sion team's operations from centre half-back. He had a commanding presence about him and he seemed to defy the opposing forwards. He was only nineteen years of age and already one of the best hurlers in the country. He had become our natural leader, on and off the field, even though he was younger than all of us. We would have followed him to hell and back. But that wasn't just because of his hurling ability – after the match everybody wanted to be in his company because he was fun to be with. He was the centre of attraction wherever he went. He was the greatest I have ever seen and he bested every hurler he ever met. Mackey, Ring, Langton, Kennedy – all had to give way to Keane. He had everything; he was out on his own.[38]

His first outing for the county team that year was in the National League when Waterford played Tipperary in Clonmel. This game was special in John's career because it marked the first time that he played at centre-half-back for the county. Although Waterford were well beaten in a match played in dreadful conditions John again started the revival when he ran the length of the field in the second half to score a vital goal thus igniting Waterford into scoring three goals in the last ten minutes. The Mount Sion club was concerned over the selection of the Waterford team and suspected that its players were being deliberately excluded. It was believed widely that secret deals were being done between some clubs regarding the selection of the county team. It was decided that the club committee 'should send a letter to the county secretary protesting that the team

---

38 Conversation with Paddy Greene

for the upcoming game with Galway was selected by an illegal committee that had been disbanded at the [county] Convention' and it was also decided to nominate John for a place on the senior hurling selection committee.[39] This indicates the stature he had obtained in the local game at only twenty years of age.

The league game with Galway was won at Dungarvan but Kilkenny had an easy victory over Waterford at Nowlan Park. John reverted to full-back for this match but with Kilkenny leading by four goals at half-time Waterford made several changes in position, the most notable being to place John at centre-forward. The changes worked immediately and Waterford became a much improved team in the second half. The selectors were still unsure how to best utilise John. He had shown leadership of a high order against Tipperary and had also shown his versatility in three league games when he played in three different positions. The selectors, therefore, had a huge decision to make: could this vital position be entrusted to a twenty year old in the Munster championship – and against Mick Mackey?

John Keane in July 1937 two weeks after he had first played against Mick Mackey. (Photo courtesy of the Smith family)

John had become a fixture at centre back for Mount Sion and the county selectors had also finally agreed that this was his best position for Waterford. The team was settling in nicely and was the best county combination since Waterford had joined the elite hurling counties in 1931. Waterford and Limerick had both won their opening championship matches and the eagerly

---

39 Mount Sion club minutes, 28 February 1937

awaited clash between the two victors was set for Clonmel on the 4 July. Waterford had a good team and had defeated Dublin, Cork, Galway and Clare in the league – but Limerick were the overwhelming favourites. They were the All-Ireland champions, having appeared in three successive finals, and they had also won in 1934. They had won both the Munster championship and the National League for the fourth year in a row – and they had Mick Mackey! John is defined by many people in the light of how he performed against Mackey in their first great tussle in 1937, but while Mackey was the standard by which all players were judged at that time, John was much more than 'the man who stopped Mackey' – although it was that first clash that had all Ireland talking. The eminent GAA writer Séamus Ó Braonáin included John, more than once, in his top three of the greatest ever hurlers, the other two being Ring and Mackey. This is what he wrote about them in a fascinating article in the *Munster GAA story* entitled 'Ring or Mackey?'

> In my youth, Mick Mackey was the talk of the land, the fear of his opponents, and the pride of Limerick. John Keane, of Waterford, was his implacable opponent, a wonderful centre-half back, who later won an All-Ireland at centre-forward, and who had many a great tussle with Mackey. And just beginning to appear over the horizon was Ring, who was to go on to be every Corkman's choice as the greatest of all time. It was a formidable age to be young in, and those were formidable stars who set our standards for us … It makes it hard for the players we see to-day to achieve any sort of eminence in our eyes: they must inevitably stand the test against a boyhood view of Mackey and Ring and Keane. In Waterford they will tell you that the only reason why Keane and Christy Moylan are not universally accepted as the game's greatest ever is that Waterford as a team lost three or four matches in the thirties by a point or two points, while Limerick won them, and that in the forties they lost another three or four while Cork won

them. It is truly the dilemma which faces one in any assessment of the greatest hurlers.[40]

John, like Christy Ring, seemed to have sprung into hurling eminence fully grown as it were and without any hurling pedigree, but Mackey was bred in the purple – he was born to be a hurler. The Mackey family had been connected with the GAA from its foundation: a forebear, Anthony Mackey, was treasurer of the central council in the late 1880s; John Mackey, Mick's grandfather, was a noted player with Castleconnell and Mick's father, John 'Tyler' Mackey, was one of the greatest figures in Munster hurling and was a famous captain of the Limerick team. In 1913 Limerick GAA supporters (aided by Cork GAA men) presented 'Tyler' with a purse of a hundred sovereigns to show their appreciation of him and in recognition of his services to native games, a gesture unheard of in the GAA before or since.

It can be said with truth that it was Mick Mackey who *made* the GAA. Thousands flocked to see him when he reigned supreme, and it was his clashes with John Keane that fired the imagination of all Ireland and had everyone talking. Mackey was an elemental force of nature, a human whirlwind of a player who single-handedly electrified the adoring thousands who came to pay homage to his genius. He was the original playboy of hurling: he always came to defeat you, but he did it with a wink and a smile. There are many stories to illustrate this facet of Mackey's game. John told me of a Waterford match with Limerick when Mackey's direct opponent was Christy Moylan of Dungarvan. During a torrid first half both players took lumps out of each other. At half-time Mackey sauntered over to the sideline, asked if anyone had an orange, and when several oranges were thrown onto the field Mackey took one, broke it in two, ate one half and tossed the other half to Moylan as he passed him. The crowd broke into a spontaneous ovation on

---

40   Cronin, *Munster GAA story*, pp. 358-9

seeing the gesture. It was human touches such as this that endeared him to the spectators wherever he played.

It was said that if it was Mackey's father who had invented the solo run it was his son who perfected the art. The crowds stood enthralled as Mick came thundering down the field seemingly indifferent to all attempts to stop him. A story that gained currency was that in some of his solo runs he pretended to hop the ball on his hurley with the right hand whilst the ball was gripped tightly in the other. When asked once if that were true he just smiled and winked. He was as solid as a tank and with his low centre of gravity he was almost impossible to knock over. John told the *Irish Independent* writer John D. Hickey that 'when Mackey hit you with a hip you thought a big wall had fallen on you.'[41]

In 1935 hurling judges regarded Mackey's display in the Munster semi-final against Cork as one of the most brilliant and spectacular individual displays of hurling ever seen. In 1936 he captained Limerick for the first time and in the Munster final versus Tipperary he gave another brilliant individual performance, rampaging all over the field and scoring 5-3 out of Limerick's total of 8-5 to Tipperary's 4-6. In the All-Ireland final they easily beat Kilkenny 5-6 to 1-5. Such was Limerick's consistency in the 1930s that they contested four All-Ireland and six league finals in a row, winning five of them. Two All-Irelands titles in 1934 and 1936 was scant reward for their efforts. Over a four and a half year period from October 1933 to April 1938 they played sixty-five games of which they won fifty-eight while four of the remaining games were drawn – and Mackey was at the heart of every game. An example of how he was regarded is seen in the remark of Garrett Howard, the famous old Limerick hurler who said that 'the likes of Mackey should have five wives, for his breed should never be let die out.'[42] And this was

---

41 *Irish Independent*, 8 February 1956
42 Houlihan, Elaine Burke (comp), *Tipperary: A Treasure Chest* (Relay Books, Nenagh, 1995), p. 72

the hurling giant that the young Waterford man stopped dead in his tracks.

Pat Fanning still has a vivid memory of John at that time when he was just twenty years of age and about to face the twenty five year old Mackey, who was then a colossus of the hurling world. '[John] was magnificent in his youth, a magnificent figure of a man, strong, well-built, a head with fair hair set on his shoulders, a massive body and with plenty of speed. He outmatched Mackey that day. It was that that bred the belief that they could come [good].'[43]

When John was selected for Munster for the first time in early 1937 he was given an excellent chance to study Mackey at close quarters for he knew that he would have to clash with him in the near future. He was once asked if he had detected any weakness in Mackey's game and he replied that Mackey was slow to double on a ball. He quickly added that it was not a weakness of course but that Mackey was not as great in that respect as he was in all others. He said that Mackey was a great man entirely and that it was ridiculous to talk of Mick and a hurling flaw, for he had none.[44] Séamus Ó Braonáin once questioned John about Mackey, and how it was that he managed to subdue him.

> Well, he said, I was a terribly long time thinking about it. God forgive me, even at Mass it used to come into my head. But, in the end I decided that there was only one possible way to beat Mackey – get out in front of him for every ball and never let it reach him at all. But, John, we said, weren't you taking a terrible risk. Supposing you missed the ball, Mackey would be through – on his own. Ah, but that's the thing, you see, said John as though speaking to a rather dense child, I wouldn't miss.[45]

---

43   Keane, Colm, *Hurling's top 20* (Mainstream, Edinburgh, 2003), p. 23
44   *Irish Independent*, 8 February 1956
45   *Gaelic Sport*, November 1975

The veteran Gaelic games writer for the *Limerick Leader*, Seamus Ó Ceallaigh (a Kilkenny man long domiciled in Limerick), wrote:

> The Shannonsiders then encountered Waterford in Clonmel. The game was played on July 4th, 1937, a date that will not be forgotten by Suirside, as it marked the commencement of a new era for Waterford hurling, when the county, after years of earnest endeavour, at last joined the ranks of the top-class hurling counties. Best man of the thirty that day was John Keane, then a mere youth, who figured in many rare duels with Mick Mackey. To add that he more than held his own with the famous Limerickman is sufficient tribute to his great ability. The newspapers greeted his display thus: The fair-haired Mount Sion youth, who shone a few years ago as a minor, was the spanner in the Shannonside scoring machine. Nimble and fast, he was like a man on springs.[46]

On previous form it appeared that Waterford did not have a chance of extending the champions but sport is maintained by the fact that the unexpected can happen at any time. Certainly that game provided the unexpected in such a way that those who witnessed it remembered it for the rest of their lives.

> To say that Waterford extended the champions is to put it mildly ... Mackey and Keane were soon having duels and there was considerable 'barracking' by the crowds and eventually the referee intervened. Keane is undoubtedly one of the best players in the game, and is not easily subdued, but Mackey undoubtedly played into the hands of this wily Waterford player.[47]

---

46 Seamus Ó Ceallaigh's GAA collection (from the *Limerick Leader*) in Limerick city library.
47 *Munster Express*, 9 July 1937

Waterford led with only seconds remaining in lost time when Dave Clohessy flashed in the winning goal for Limerick. Amidst the tumult and the cheering Limerick had qualified for their fifth Munster final in a row and Waterford were left, once again, to wait for another year and after a supreme effort. The writer 'Green Flag,' in the *Irish Press* the following day, said that 'the hero of the day was John Keane, the Waterford centre half-back who was the inspiration of his side and the master of the redoubtable Mick Mackey right through the hour. Waterford's hurling name holds a higher niche; the champions were almost dethroned.'[48]

So why had Waterford lost? Willie Walsh, the former all-Ireland referee, had no doubts as to the cause – slow motion watches! Referring to the 1937 Waterford v Limerick match he said that the duration of *actual playing* in the second half (excluding stoppages) was some seconds in excess of thirty five minutes and it was in the last minute of this extra time that Limerick snatched victory.[49] The game had been stolen from Waterford and, as a result, the county's breakthrough had been delayed once again. It was common practice at the time for referees to favour the champions. The spectators wanted to see the great teams and, by extension, great players in finals, and referees allowed them great latitude in that regard. Lax time-keeping was prevalent and the two minute rule allowed for injuries was rarely observed. John recalled on more than one occasion that in the 1937 match Waterford's speedy momentum was broken many times by the Limerick players' apparent injuries and that they all seemed to get 'injured' at very inopportune times for Waterford.

---

48   *Irish Times*, 10 July 1937
49   *Munster Express*, 2 September 1938

Chapter Five
A county comes of age

After his displays in 1937 John was selected by the *Weekly Irish Times* as one of the outstanding hurlers of that year. The list also included Timmy Ryan of Limerick, Jimmy Cooney of Tipperary, and Paddy Phelan of Kilkenny. John was described thus:

> John Keane of Waterford who hurls at home for [the] Mount Sion Club ... came into prominence for the first time in the 1936 league. At half-back or midfield, Keane is equally at home. He is strong and bony; he fears nothing, and loves to match his young prowess against some famous hurling star. Against Dublin, Cork, Limerick, Tipperary, Kilkenny and Clare, the Waterford City man has played powerful hurling. Ground work is his strongest suite (sic), yet he can lift and drive long balls to the area. He is the most promising of our young hurlers.[50]

He was selected to play for Munster in the 1938 Railway cup competition for the second year in succession. Tipperary, the All-Ireland champions, had five players on the team as did Limerick; Cork and Waterford had two (Christy Moylan and John); and Clare had one, as Munster beat Leinster in the final to give John his second medal. The game marked Jack Lynch's first game with Munster when he came on as a substitute in the second half.

At the beginning of the year long-running divisions between the eastern and western factions in Waterford re-emerged, and for a time it seemed likely that the county would split in two.

---

50   *Irish Weekly Times*, 8 Jan 1938

A 'peace convention' was proposed by the Munster council and with the Munster championship first round match with Cork getting ever closer it was vital that the 'convention' should have a positive outcome. The *Irish Independent* reported on the Wednesday before the match that:

> A breach of long standing in GAA administration within the county has been healed and that all hands are now as one, united in a wholehearted effort to ensure that the best available fifteen are fielded against Cork and that in the matter of training and preparation by the players nothing will be left undone ... Everything in the nature of disunity and discussion has disappeared. There is now perfect harmony and friendship. East has joined West. Old grievances are forgotten in one big effort to bring All-Ireland honours to Waterford for the first time.[51]

Time would tell if that goodwill would last. Meanwhile, Dungarvan town geared up for its biggest match in a generation – Waterford versus Cork in the Munster championship. For the occasion the Waterford team had changed from wearing its traditional royal blue jersey to all-white jerseys with blue collars and cuffs. As they came out on the field to a huge welcome from the crowd of fifteen thousand a deluge of rain started and continued unceasingly all through the game, drenching the crowd which had taken up every vantage point on the green banks, with many more crowding the sidelines and even encroaching on the playing area. The pitch was like a skating rink in the second half with many players finding it difficult to keep their feet. The Waterford defence stood up to everything that Cork threw at them and the match was halted twice due to fisticuffs. In the second bout of fighting, and with just one minute to go, one player from each side was dismissed with Waterford losing its captain, Mick Hickey. The conditions should have favoured Cork who were the heavier team by far but it was Waterford's

---

51   *Irish Independent*, 6 July 1938

speed and combination that won the day as they demolished Cork by 5-2 to 1-3, having led by three clear goals at half time. The team was now in the Munster final where their opponents would be Clare.

1938 Munster championship. Waterford players L-R: Declan Goode (Dungarvan), Charlie Ware (Erin's Own), Locky Byrne (Mount Sion), Pa Sheehan (Tallow), Tom Greaney (Mitchelstown), Jackie Butler (Faughs), John Keane (Mount Sion). (Photo courtesy of the Smith family

Tipperary, the All Ireland champions, had defeated Clare in the semi-final and had included the wonder-boy, Jimmy Cooney, in their side. Cooney, who had been selected as one of the outstanding hurlers of 1937, had admitted attending a rugby international the previous February, thus automatically suspending himself from the Association. Perversely, however, Tipperary stated that they were going to play Cooney in the semi-final even though Clare had intimated before the game that if he played they would object. Tipperary won, the Clare officials objected, with the result that Clare were awarded the match and Tipperary were expelled from the championship. Waterford were expected to roll-over Clare, especially after the heroics displayed against Cork, but Clare refused to lie down, could have won the match in the last minute, and were defeated by a solitary goal 3-5 to 2-5.

Waterford had just had a narrow escape but there was no time to dwell on such matters because the semi-final with Galway was taking place on the following Sunday in Ennis, county Clare. It would be not only a test of hurling ability but one of every facet of the team's game, and it called for an almighty effort combining character and self discipline. Waterford were set for a bruising encounter because Galway had the reputation of being a very physical team, and the team knew that it was in for a very tough hour. In those times of religious certainty it was common practice for every house to have a holy-water font at the front door and whenever John was leaving for a match his mother would sprinkle him with the holy water and say 'Look after your self, John. Please God you won't get hurt today.' To her dying day she was fearful of Galway and their reputation for taking no prisoners. Mick Hickey, the Waterford captain, spoke for all when he said that 'We cannot take any chances against those Galway men. They are a sturdy and resourceful team, but on the whole I think that the superior speed and craft of Waterford will carry them through.'[52] True to expectations the game was a tough encounter with the *Irish Independent* describing it thus:

> [It was] a tough, hard-fought battle, featured by keen tackling, which in the first half-hour provoked a few bitter exchanges. Under a broiling sun, and on a sod still heavy from recent rains, it was a trying test for the players, but Waterford, although closely pressed until near the end, put in a strong finish, and were, in all respects, deserving winners.[53]

The *Connacht Tribune* noted that 'John Keane in the centre half-line, was a tower of strength to the Waterford defence, and

---

52   *Irish Independent*, 6 August 1938
53   *Irish Independent*, 8 August 1938

when the ball did get past him there was Charlie Ware to clear ... they emerged with flying colours.'[54] The *Waterford News* reported that 'John Keane stood out on his own. He gave as brilliant an exhibition of defence work as I have ever seen and his eighty yard solo-run, in which he beat some five opponents, was the grandest effort I have seen since the eclipse of Mick Mackey.'[55] Waterford had won by double scores, 4-8 to 3-1, but that score line was less than the Galway men deserved for they had matched Waterford for fifty minutes of the sixty.

The county had made the big break-through at last and for the players it was a time of mixed emotions: joy, satisfaction and pride – but mostly relief. The promise shown in their hurling over the previous few years had finally borne fruit and they looked forward with some optimism to the final. However, the very first action of the county board unwittingly sowed the seeds of defeat. Acting in what they perceived to be in the best interests of the county team the board appointed Paul Russell, the famous Kerry footballer, as trainer of the team for the final. Russell was a garda sergeant stationed in Dungarvan and had been elected as the chairman of the west Waterford GAA board in January of 1938. He was a distinguished Gaelic footballer with Dublin and his native Kerry, and was regarded as being one of football's greatest players. Hindsight is a wonderful thing, and foresight better still – but whatever about the former attribute the board was certainly not overly-endowed with the latter and Russell's training routine almost completely destroyed what Mick Hickey had rightly identified as Waterford's greatest weapon – their superior speed. Waterford had the fastest team that hurling had seen for years; their game consisted of first-time striking from the ground allied to a dazzling interchanging of positions among the forwards with the speedy corner forwards playing wide on the wings. Russell, however, initiated a training regime that was more suited to marathon running. He believed in long slow runs of eight to ten miles a

---

54 *Connacht Tribune*, 13 August 1938
55 *Waterford News*, 12 August 1938

session designed to build up endurance (which it undoubtedly did) but at a cost of blunting the speed that was essential to Waterford's success.

John disagreed fundamentally with this training but, unfortunately perhaps, he made no formal protest. Being the youngest player on the team he felt that it wasn't his place to do so. The Waterford forwards were small and light and John felt it would have been unwise for them to come to close quarters with their opponents. They should, rather, have put their faith in speed and on the golden maxim – make the ball do the work. Many years later when he was training the 1957-9 team he elaborated on this philosophy of training. 'The first man to the ball nearly always wins possession, so I was a great believer in short sprints as a means of developing the quick burst.' When asked if he ever feared that the players might burn themselves out in the first three quarters of the match and have nothing left for the vital last fifteen minutes he replied 'No. I advised them to go steadily into it, raising the tempo of their play as the game progressed so that they would reach their peak in the last quarter.'[56]

As the day of the final approached the public had become increasingly uneasy at the reports coming from the training camps in Dungarvan and Waterford. Willie Walsh was alert to those fears and he felt it necessary to issue a statement to the press in an effort to try and allay the belief that training was not going well.

> The fear has been expressed in some quarters that our hurlers have become over-trained, and I wish to avail myself of this opportunity to dispel all such fear. The Munster champions are in the capable hands of Paul Russell, and what Russell does not know about the art of training is not worth knowing. He possesses six senior All-Ireland medals, won with his native Kerry.

In the light of modern knowledge, however, his training methods can now be seen as disastrous. But Russell's training

---

56 *Sunday Independent*, 18 April 1965

John Keane, 1938 All Ireland final. (Photo courtesy of Independent Newspapers Ltd)

was not the sole cause of Waterford's failure in the final. The weight of history was also against them for few teams had won the title at the first attempt. Their opponents, Dublin, had some very experienced players and the team was contesting its third final in five years (including one draw). In all, Dublin had won five titles from nine appearances while Waterford was contesting its first senior final. Withal, Waterford was highly regarded and had some excellent hurlers including several junior All-Ireland medallists and two with senior final experience, Locky Byrne with Kilkenny in 1935 and 1936 and Seán Feeney with Dublin in 1934. The Waterford team was very small in stature and weight, the average height being just five feet eight inches, the average weight eleven stones seven pounds, and the average age twenty six years. John was exceptionable amongst them for he was the youngest at twenty one years, the heaviest (along with Johnny Fanning) at thirteen stones, and the tallest at six feet. We are recalling a different Ireland of seventy years ago when people were much smaller than today – and Waterford men, especially those from the city, were particularly small. In 1957, after the All-Ireland final between Kilkenny and Waterford, the social diarist of the *Evening Press*, Terry O'Sullivan, described a visit he made to the respective hotels of both teams. He remarked that 'The Kilkenny men and their supporters are the largest number of tall men we have ever seen. By contrast, the Waterford men remind us of the Welsh men who turn up here for the occasional rugby internationals ... small, lean, wiry.'[57]

---

57   *Evening Press*, 7 September 1957

In the 1930s health-care was poor and the average life expectancy of a man who was twenty years old in 1937 (like John) was only 66.8 years.[58] Almost all men partook of alcoholic drink in some form and most were also heavy smokers, and John was no exception. He smoked cigarettes all his life and took a drink until 1943 (the reasons for his subsequent teetotalism will be given later), but he gloried in his strength and athleticism and, like most youths, never gave a thought to the future. People from Cork, Kilkenny and Tipperary cannot understand the fever that grips the followers of an

Programme for 1938 All-Ireland finals

unsuccessful county when that county reaches a final. That hysteria was bound to affect the team and the way it played – and that's just what happened. John always regarded the 1938 team as the best Waterford team of his era, yet they lost the final. The difference was that Dublin played as a team for most of the match while Waterford played as a collection of individuals, only coming together in the last ten minutes when the match finally sparked into life. An anonymous columnist got it right when he wrote about the match under the headline 'Hotfoot John sizzled.'

---

58 Central Statistics Office, *Irish life tables no. 14 2001-2003, table 3*, (CSO, Dublin, 2004).

The pace was sizzling from the start, and after only ten minutes John Keane's feet began to smoke. The correct procedure for dealing with that situation was already well established by Limerick's Mick Mackey – the ceremonial unlacing of the boots, the wriggling of the toes, the flourish as the offending footwear sailed in the direction of the nearest touch-judge. So hotfoot with John to the sideline to put his boots out of play and back again to play the game of his life for the next fifty minutes.

Waterford were firm believers in the efficacy of private enterprise, as represented by brilliant individualism. It had got them that far, with no set plan of campaign, such as would be favoured by neighbouring Cork and Kilkenny. Centre half-back John Keane, most brilliant individual of the lot, might have had different ideas; so, too, might … Locky Byrne, full forward, and full-back Charlie Ware. But even three swallows don't make a summer.[59]

Waterford trailed by 2-3 to 1-3 at half-time with Dec Goode scoring the goal and John (0-2) and Locky Byrne (0-1) the points. With ten minutes to go Dublin were five points ahead but tiring and Mick Daniels, the Dublin captain, who had played himself to a standstill, collapsed from exhaustion. John pointed; Locky added another; and with three minutes to go John had another point from a seventy yard free. Waterford were all over Dublin at this stage but it was too late and the metropolitans held out for the win.

Waterford had ended as gallant losers but they had spoiled their chance by over-eagerness; they had played the type of game that suited Dublin, and there's no profit in playing a man at his own game unless you can play it better than he can. Although John had played a magnificent game and finished as Waterford's top scorer it was to no avail. That elusive title was still to be won; a win that would have fed the appetite for more. The sup-

---

59 Undated clipping in the Goode family scrapbooks, courtesy of Eoin Fanning.

porters returned home like an army that had lost a battle but with flags still flying. The only immediate benefit from Waterford's success in winning the Munster championship and reaching the All-Ireland final was that the number of affiliated clubs in the county rose from forty in 1937 to sixty five in 1939.[60]

Waterford team, All Ireland finalists 1938. Back Row (L to R): J Keane, C Moylan, C Ware, T Halpin, W Walsh, M Hickey (Capt), M Curley, L Byrne; Front Row (L to R): T Greaney, J Fanning, J Mountain, W Barron, S Feeney, P Sheehan. Dec Goode is missing from photograph. When he arrived in Croke Park he found that he had left behind a holy medal that he always wore. He raced back to his hotel to retrieve the medal and missed the team photograph.
(Photo courtesy of Independent Newspapers Ltd)

Limerick were due in town for the opening match of the National League against Waterford, and there was, therefore, the likelihood of another tussle between Mick Mackey and John. This was something to savour because in the 1930s and 1940s there was no greater clash. It must be understood that in that era

---

60   de Búrca, *The GAA*, p. 161

the meeting of great players in direct opposition to each other had a fascination all its own. While the match result was always of prime concern there was also a secondary issue that was only slightly less important and that was the outcome of any personal clash between each team's champion players, and many people travelled to see which man came out on top. Furthermore, if one of the two champions was switched during play the move was regarded as a victory for the other and for that reason some players were extremely reluctant to move to another position when so instructed by selectors. This is perfectly illustrated in a comment made by Willie John Daly, one of Cork's great players, when he was interviewed by Brendan Fullam for the latter's book *Giants of the Ash*. In the Cork versus Tipperary Munster championship match of 1949 Tommy Doyle had held Christy Ring to only one point in a game where the two players were hip to hip. In the replay all eyes were on the clash to see who would come out on top but Daly knew that a different strategy was needed and on a number of occasions he said to Ring to keep away from Doyle. Ring refused to move, however, his response being, 'The crowd, what about the crowd, what will the crowd think?'[61]

In the National League game, however, the expected duel between Mick Mackey and John did not happen because Mackey played at centre-field while his brother John (almost as great a player) went centre-forward. The *Irish Independent* described the game.

> ... ten minutes from the end it appeared as if Limerick ... would emulate Dublin's All-Ireland victory over the Suirsiders. Then Waterford's positional changes had an electrifying effect, the team putting in rare dash and determination which thrilled the spectators to the core. A deficiency of three points was converted into a gain of five points with two majors and a minor which followed each other with lightning-like rapidity.[62]

---

61   Fullam, Brendan, *Giants of the ash* (Wolfhound, Dublin, 1991), p. 52
62   *Irish Independent*, 9 October 1938

Limerick had led by 1-3 to 0-1 at half time and was still leading with ten minutes left when Waterford sent John to centre-forward and Charlie Ware to full-forward. This galvanised the attack which had spluttered into life only intermittently and with John scoring two goals defeat was turned into victory. The *Independent* reported that 'Keane once more covered himself with glory.' The following week saw John in league football action at centre-forward and scoring a goal as a second string Waterford side were defeated by Wicklow. The following month saw the age-old rivalry between Waterford and Kilkenny sparkle in a tremendous tussle before a record crowd in Dungarvan for a league game. The home team deservedly won by four points but not before spectators spilled onto the pitch and fighting ensued between them for several minutes before order could be restored. At the end of the year the Waterford team sat proudly on top of the National League.

Captain of Munster

This last year of peace before the outbreak of the Second World War was one of John's busiest. He played in twenty eight games and was also included on the panel of referees of the county's eastern board. He refereed several games in both Waterford and Kilkenny, including the Waterford senior hurling semi-final between Erin's Own and St Stephen's, the winner of which was scheduled to meet John's Mount Sion in the final – something one could not imagine happening nowadays. He played in nine football games that year and represented the county in football at both junior and senior grades. John loved playing Gaelic football. The reasons were twofold – it was a much tougher game, physically, than hurling, and John loved a physical challenge; and in football he usually played in the forward line thus giving him a chance to score. He was noted for his fisted goals which usually came when he leaped highest in a goalmouth to punch the ball into the net. An amusing incident happened in a national football league game in March against

Wexford when 'in the first half Hayes (Wexford) knocked himself badly out with a "hay-maker" of an uppercut intended for the ball.'[63]

John would now be captain of Waterford and Munster. It was an exciting time for him – Waterford had just won its first Munster title and had played in the All-Ireland final; the team stood at the top of the National League and it seemed to be only a matter of time before major honours would come, at last, to the county. Waterford had four players on the Munster team to play Connacht in the Railway cup semi-final. John captained the team at right half-back with Mick Curley in goal, Christy Moylan at left half-forward and Locky Byrne at full forward.

John Keane, captain of Munster team 1939, 3rd from left front row. Other Waterford players are Christy Moylan (3rd left, back row), Mick Curley (5th left, back row) and Locky Byrne, extreme left, front row). Mick Mackey is 2nd from left, back row. (Photo courtesy of the Keane family and with the permission of Independent Newspapers Ltd)

---

63 *Munster Express*, 17 March 1939

It was the county's largest representation ever and the Irish Times commented;

> Though Waterford are Provincial champions, they are more of a uniform side than brilliant individualists, so it was no surprise to find five Limerick men selected, as against four from Waterford. ... Munster's hurling selectors had a long and arduous duty with five strong counties holding claims. I think they have done very well. ... Munster's half-line is the best I have seen, and a good half-line is the backbone of any fifteen. Here we have Keane (Waterford) and Barrett (Cork) flanking Clohessey – a powerful line.[64]

Having beaten Connacht easily by 8-5 to 0-2 Munster then beat Leinster by seven points on St Patrick's Day and the Railway cup came to Waterford for the very first time. This was the first national senior trophy won by a team captained by a Waterford man, and over the next few weeks hundreds of people came to John's home in Barrack Street to see the cup. What springs to mind is the Irish sean-fhocal *An rud is annamh is iontach* (what's seldom is wonderful) and such scenes would not have happened in the more successful counties.

John Keane 1939, with Railway Cup. Photo by Phillips of Waterford. (Photo courtesy of the Smith family)

---

64   *Irish Times*, 11 January 1939

At the beginning of February Waterford beat Clare in the National League and then drew with Cork to set up a semi-final match with Wexford. This game in New Ross saw the speedy Waterford men up against a big and strong Wexford team. It was in this game that the future great player, Vin Baston, played his first senior game for Waterford. The eighteen year old Baston had been the star player with the Mount Sion school team and with Munster colleges and he was selected at midfield. This game also saw the twenty year old Andy Fleming play at right half-back for the first time and, in years to come both Andy and John would form the celebrated half-back line with Paddy Dowling for both Mount Sion and Waterford. It was a game that Waterford won relatively easily despite shooting eleven wides in the first ten minutes and then having to withstand a storming finish by Wexford. This result meant that Waterford would contest its first national hurling league final where the opponents would be Dublin.

With three weeks to prepare for the final the county board decided, unwisely, that the county hurling team should go into special training – the eastern representatives to train in the evenings in the city and the westerners to do likewise in Dungarvan. Then on certain specified days both camps were to undergo collective training at both venues. Like the preparations for the All-Ireland hurling final in 1938, it was another recipe for disaster. During the league campaign the team had beaten Limerick, Kilkenny, Clare and Wexford and had drawn with

No. 12—JOHN KEANE (Waterford & Munster)
Big, blonde and brawny. Quick on the caman, 'and can "box" a ball with the best. Captained Munster in their win over Leinster in the Railway Cup, and an All-Ireland Finalist with Waterford. Mount Sion's magnificent mainstay in many matches

Cartoon sketch from Munster Express 1939 (With the permission of the Munster Express)

Cork – all on the back of regular training – and, in hindsight, to have changed the training for the final was perverse. In the midst of this period John was selected for three games on the one day. Mount Sion had a senior hurling tournament engagement with Mooncoin at Fiddown (which they won easily) but the county board had also arranged two games, in hurling and football, between the east and west divisions for Dungarvan. The latter matches were trials for the hurling and football county teams and, as John was a certainty for the hurling team, he opted to play in the senior football trial.

Waterford were regarded as the favourite to take the hurling league title because of having to surmount far stiffer opposition than Dublin on the way to the final. Dublin had beaten Westmeath, Tipperary, Galway and Laois but the weak showing of the Dublin players with Leinster in the Railway cup final had introduced a note of uncertainty to their prospects against Waterford. The final in Thurles on the last day of April was very disappointing. The match was similar to the All-Ireland final of the previous September between the two teams in that Waterford failed to launch any coherent challenge in the first half and the resurgence came only when John was moved to centre-field after half-time, with Christy Moylan taking over at centre half-back. This changed the game dramatically and Waterford starting forcing the play with Greaney and John driving the team on from centre-field. Dublin finished the stronger, however, and a late goal and a point clinched the title.

Shortly before the Munster championship hurling match against Cork the great full-back Charlie Ware announced his retirement from inter-county hurling. He had been playing for a total of seventeen years and he was almost irreplaceable. Known as the prince of full-backs he had had a glorious career. Though born in Cork he had declared for Waterford shortly after his arrival in the city and had given exceptional service to the county and was the first Waterford player to win a Railway cup medal. His retirement was a huge headache for the selectors and a frantic search started for someone to replace him. Two tournament games were scheduled before the Munster championship game and the selectors decided to try John in the full-back position. Of course this left a gaping hole in the centre-back position and for the first of those games (versus Wexford in Enniscorthy) the big Portlaw man Mick O'Regan was drafted in to replace John in a team that was selected mainly from the eastern division. Although Waterford defeated Wexford the experiment was not a success and the back-line only played as a cohesive unit when John was restored to centre-back and Johnnie Fanning moved from the corner to full-back. The problem remained unsolved and as the Cork game drew nearer a successful appeal was made to Charlie Ware to return, if only for one game.

Twenty two thousand people crammed into Fermoy's Gaelic pitch to see the game. Six trains from Cork and three from Waterford brought full contingents of fans on a baking hot day to see Cork attempt to reverse the 1938 result. It was a thrilling battle until just near the end and Waterford went down with flying colours. Although Cork led by ten points at one stage in the first half Waterford had reduced this lead to only two points at the interval. When Cork scored a goal just after the re-start John was switched to centre-forward in an effort to get the forward line moving but this weakened the backs and Cork scored three quick goals to go into a thirteen point lead. John did succeed in scoring a goal near the end but Cork finished as well-deserved winners. The problem with Waterford was that the forwards were very inconsistent. They could be brilliant one day and very poor the next and the county had only one 'go-to' man, someone who could change a game by his own efforts and who could lead by example. The stronger counties like Cork, Tipperary and Kilkenny had several such men on their teams to whom they could turn in an emergency without weakening the overall team but Waterford's crisis solution of pushing John into the forward line only weakened the defence and left a gap of 'barn-door' dimensions.

It was Charlie Ware's last game for Waterford and the selectors still had the problem of finding his replacement. For the remaining games in that year John was again selected as full-back. Waterford fielded an experimental side against Limerick in the National League at Limerick and though they lost the game by six points John, who played at full-back, was once again the best man of the thirty. A writer in the *Cork Examiner* gave a splendid tribute to him when, speaking of the general run of the play, he wrote:

> Amongst the exceptions was John Keane, who gave a magnificent display at full back for Waterford. In fact the Waterford captain gave one of his best displays of the year, and it was due to his craft, soundness and sure striking that there was not a bigger score against the Decies county. ... Keane was proving a tower of strength in the Waterford defence.[65]

Despite John's heroics, however, Waterford lost all those games because, splendidly though he played, his commanding presence was badly missed at centre-back.

---

65   *Cork Examiner*, 9 October 1939

Chapter Six
The Emergency

The outbreak of the Second World War (or the 'Emergency' as it was officially called by the government) in September 1939 meant that the country faced into a period of great uncertainty and anxiety. The government created a local security force (LSF) in May 1940 as an auxiliary police service. This force incorporated both defence and police elements and was created from a network of volunteers in every locality who carried out local security duties. In June 1940 it was decided to divide the force into two groups; the 'A' group to be an auxiliary to the army and the 'B' group to continue as an auxiliary to the police. By the end of 1940 the army had more or less completed its expansion to a war-time footing and was then in a position to take over the control of the 'A' group from the Gárdaí. On the first day of January 1941, therefore, this force was handed over to the command and control of the Army and was given the new title of the local defence force (LDF) more commonly known in later years as *An Fórsa Cosanta Áitiúil* (FCA, or 'Free Clothing Association' as some wag christened it). From the military point of view the LDF was the equivalent of many additional battalions to the defence forces. John joined up as a member of the LDF and, after his initial recruitment period was complete, he was assigned to the company of engineers where he served for the duration of the war.

Eamonn de Valera had declared Ireland's neutrality and, as a result, the country became isolated from the rest of the world. Rationing of everyday household items caused serious hardship; its effect was severe everywhere but more so in the cities and towns, where it was just not possible to augment the food and clothing rations as easily as could be done in rural areas. The people desperately needed something to relieve their increasingly desperate situation as the effects of war began to bear down, especially from 1942 onwards. This was ultimately to the benefit of the GAA and interest in the games soared to unprecedented levels despite the hardships entailed for players and spectators. The local county championship matches were the chief beneficiaries as huge crowds attended because of the short journeys involved but the number of spectators at inter-county games fell dramatically for a time because of the difficulty in traveling.

Petrol rationing had already begun and private motoring had almost completely ceased by 1943. Bus and train services were reduced so much as to be completely inadequate and unreliable where they did operate. This caused extreme hardship to players and clubs as they had to find new and novel ways to travel to matches and players were forced to cycle or walk to local venues. However the attraction of the games forced spectators to use innovative ways to overcome these difficulties and the bicycle was brought increasingly into use. On Sunday after Sunday the roads became thronged with many groups of fifty or more cyclists, young boys and girls, as they travelled to the major games, especially in Munster. Those who lived a distance from the match venue would often set out on the evening before or very early on Sunday morning. The roads were of poor quality and punctures were so common that everyone carried a repair kit, but a new problem arose when bicycle tyres became scarce due to the lack of rubber. The pony and trap were brought out of storage and some people even walked to the games; the newspapers of the time were full of such stories.

Most GAA players were manual workers, whether on the farm or in factories, and the working day was very long. All food was organic and though life was hard and health care was poor the general populace was much fitter than today. People generally walked or cycled to work and there were fewer injuries. Pulled muscles were rare and it was postulated that walking and cycling stretched the hamstrings, the bane of the modern athlete. As a consequence an athlete at his peak did not require as much physical training as would be needed nowadays and training concentrated largely on perfecting hurling skills interspersed with short, explosive sprints.

The game was played in a different fashion from that which we see today. The most common feature of the game was the overhead striking of the ball and the first-time pulling on the ground, with the ball being made to do the work. With a heavier and bigger sliotar every delivery from goal landed around the halfway line and it was a foolhardy player who attempted to catch the ball in his hand due to the skilful overhead doubling when the ball travelled the length of the field without touching the ground. The 'shemozzle' (as Mícheál O'Hehir called it) was rarely seen in outfield play and only rarely would one see a group of players scrabbling round the sliotar with all of them trying to lift it into their hands. Different counties had perfected their own styles and Munster's was generally more robust than Leinster's. Ground striking was a familiar feature of Munster hurling and Tipperary was famous for its hip-to-hip style of play. Waterford played an expansive type of first-time ground hurling although they were also heavily influenced by the Kilkenny style. The hurlers of Kilkenny and Wexford favoured the lifting and handling game although there were differences even there for it was subsequently maintained that Kilkenny's was 'sharper, more fluent and economical, scientific almost to the point of mathematical calculation and technical precision.'[66]

The playing gear of the 1940s was light years away from the ergonomically designed shoes and clothing of today. Jerseys were made of wool; they itched on very warm days and became very uncomfortable and heavy in rain. Some jerseys shrank in the wash and one would sometimes see teams appearing with sleeves shrunk to the elbow and so tight fitting that they were almost impossible to wear. The wool jerseys were also usually full of moth-holes and had to be darned frequently. The club provided the jersey but the player was responsible for everything else. In those times of austerity, when cloth was hard to

---

66   *Irish Times*, 7 October 1975

procure, a player's shorts (togs or knicks) were usually homemade by a sister or mother using any material that came readily to hand and from which the finished article would resemble an approximation of a proper shorts. If one looks at any team photograph from that era one would usually see a variety of shorts and it was the rare team that did not contain a variety of different colours. Flour bags were most commonly used as shorts material and usually with great success but Jim Cronin in his excellent book *Making connections: a Cork GAA miscellany* tells an amusing tale of one such effort that had a surprising outcome. He wrote that 'a Dursey Island woman made a pair of togs out of a flour bag for her son who was playing with Garnish. In the next game as the Dursey man was soloing up the wing ... printed across his backside was "Sunburst Flour, 140lb net weight."' Cronin also tells of an enterprising player who 'came along with light blue shorts which he had made himself by the simple process of cutting away some (as he said unnecessary) elastic from a sister's [under]garment.'[67] Players wore heavy leather boots, some with strengthened toe-caps, and they became almost rigid over time unless they were regularly treated with a cream such as 'Dubbin,' which was almost impossible to get in wartime Ireland. These boots usually had nailed-in cogs and sometimes an inexpertly nailed cog caused the nail (or cog) to come up through the sole of the boot. Sometimes the heavy boots were very uncomfortable on hard, sun-baked, ground and this was the reason why some players (like John in the All-Ireland final of 1938) discarded the boots during a game.

The game could, of course, proceed without boots, jersey and shorts but a hurley and sliotar were the two absolute essentials and both bore little resemblance to those used today. In contrast to the small, white, impermeable and almost golf ball-like sliotar in use today the 1930s-40s sliotar was much bigger and was almost brown in colour. It sometimes became irregular in shape through excessive wear and was then very difficult to control.

---

67   Cronin, Jim, *Making connections: a Cork GAA miscellany* (Coiste chontae Chorcaí CLG, Corcaigh, 2005), pp. 346-7

When saturated with rain it tended to swell and developed the consistency of a Christmas pudding. This restricted the number of scores in a game and a feature of games was the low number of points. As already explained most games were played using ground-hurling and the design of the hurley (particularly the *bos,* which had a pronounced hook) also militated against the lifting game. Despite all these deficiencies in equipment the players were adept at using them to their advantage and the scoring of points from placed balls hit from the ground (such as side-line cuts) was a feature. The Waterford player Declan Goode usually took his seventy-yard frees from the ground and I remember Mount Sion's Martin Óg Morrissey scoring points from ground strokes, in the 1950s and 1960s. But the absolute master in Waterford was Matty Creed of Erin's Own. He made his own hurleys and for ground strokes he fashioned them with a particularly thick bottom to the heavy *bos*. After every training session he could be seen practicing the striking of side-line cuts from various distances.

During the war years the supply of hurleys became a problem and a carpenter was a prized member of a club because he could repair them, and, if necessary, even make some. All hurlers had to supply their own hurleys and at a cost of seven shillings and sixpence this was a great drain on people who could ill afford it. This caused Mount Sion to introduce a concession that if one was broken in a match the affected player was thrown a replacement that he could later purchase at half price. Whilst this was a welcome move Larry Fanning told me that he broke eight hurleys in one year and, as he earned only eight shillings a week as an apprentice printer, the cost of replacing his broken hurleys was crippling. When John was interviewed about the problem he gave it as his opinion that

> The hurley problem is, I consider, the root cause of many of hurling's ills and it is time something really big was done. I know that in Munster and I expect it is the same elsewhere,

the Provincial Council gives generous grants to juvenile leagues for the purpose of buying hurleys for the youngsters. This is grand as far as it goes, but the problem is far from being solved. The need for a good quality stick at a reasonable price for every grade is of vital importance. For years I have had my own pet solution. I think that the Association should set up its own plant for the manufacture of suitable hurleys for minors, juniors and seniors. An indication that such a move was under consideration might overnight give us cheaper and better camans.[68]

---

68 Undated interview in the *Sunday Press*

Chapter seven
The unconquerable Keane

For all of the latter part of 1939 John had played as full back for Waterford and this was a probable cause for his relegation to the substitute's bench in the 1940 Railway cup competition along with Jack Lynch and Timmy Ryan. The chosen fifteen came in for a great deal of criticism and the comments of the *Irish Times* Gaelic games writer, P. D. Mehigan were representative of the general feeling amongst his colleagues.

> Munster's hurling selection was eagerly awaited on all sides. ... I had personally picked a side ... and it differs in just four places from the final selection. I could not leave John Keane (Waterford), Tim Ryan (Limerick) or J. Lynch (Cork) out of the side. The fact is that Munster has a surplus of high-grade hurlers to defend last year's cup.[69]

John came on as a substitute in the final, however, unlike Jack Lynch who was left, inexplicably, on the sideline. In those years selection for the Munster Railway cup team was comparable to selection on the current All-Star teams and was a great affirmation of one's ability – every hurler in the province dreamed of wearing the famous light-blue jersey of Munster and competition for places was fierce amongst Munster's enormously strong pool of players. In the thirteen years that spanned John's participation in the competition (1937 to 1949) Munster won the cup on eleven occasions, with Leinster and Connacht winning once each. To further show Munster's dominance of hurling during John's years of senior inter-county hurling (between 1936 to 1951) the All-Ireland senior hurling title was won by Munster

---

69   *Irish Times*, 22 February 1940

counties on thirteen occasions out of sixteen with Tipperary and Cork winning five titles each, Limerick two and Waterford one. Reputations counted for little in the Munster selection process and one had to earn one's place by current performance. Timmy Ryan, the great Limerick centre-field player, was a perfect example; one of the hurlers of the year in 1937 he had found himself on the bench in 1938 along with Jack Lynch.

Waterford had been drawn to meet Limerick in the Munster championship but the Munster council certainly did not have the Waterford followers in mind

The Unconquerable Keane. (Photo from the Fanning family collection & courtesy of Tom Partridge)

when it selected Killarney as the venue. Those Waterford fans who did eventually make the long journey saw a magnificent game and were treated to a ferocious clash between the two captains, Mick Mackey and John – the latter showing, once again, that he had no peer at centre-half back by holding Mackey to just one point in the match. With his club-mates Fleming on his right and Paddy Dowling on his left John was the linchpin of a half-back line that proved beyond yea or nay that it was the best line of defence in the game. In typical war-time parlance it was described by a local Waterford paper as the 'Hindenberg Line.' John and Andy also comprised two thirds of Munster's half-back line and there are many people in Waterford who maintain that a great injustice was done to Paddy Dowling over the fact that he was never chosen for his province – there were suspicions that Cork and Tipperary selectors had colluded to prevent Waterford (and Mount Sion) providing all three half-back positions on the Railway cup team. Andy expressed to Larry Fanning on one occasion that he thought John preferred Paddy Dowling as his wing-man. Larry could understand how Andy might have formed this opinion because John was constantly talking to Dowling during play but left Andy to get along with what Andy could do to perfection – take complete control of his zone of operations.

The Waterford selection had been severely criticised in the week before the game so it created a first class surprise by holding to level scores a strong and widely fancied Limerick side. The Waterford goal-keeper George O'Grady, deputising for the injured Jim Ware, had a magnificent game and he was the main reason why Limerick's lead at half-time was limited to five points. The game was brimful of incidents, especially in the second period when the Waterford hurlers were at their best and were threatening to sweep the Limerick defence off its feet. In the words of the *Waterford News*, 'These full-blooded thrusts, originating from the Fleming, Keane and Dowling section, were carried right through up to the Limerick goal-posts, but usually the brilliant goal-keeping of Scanlon stood between the fiery attackers and their sorely coveted objective.'[70] Towards the end of the third quarter Waterford pressed so strongly that Mick Mackey was forced to move to the defence in a desperate attempt to keep the Waterford attacks at bay and this undoubtedly saved Limerick from defeat. Christy Moylan equalised for Waterford and then the same player put Waterford ahead from a free amidst a welter of excitement. After a seventy yard free by Mackey was only partially cleared a tussle in the Waterford goalmouth led to a goal by Limerick and when Dave Clohessy scored a point they led by a clear goal with only a few minutes left in the match. Desperate measures require desperate actions and it was then that John decided to take matters into his own hands. He won the ball in midfield and struck out in a solo run

---

70 *Waterford News*, 21 June 1940

for the opponent's goal, brushing through the uncompromising tackles of the Limerick defenders. When he got within sight of the goal area he unleashed a tremendous shot that Scanlon only parried but John, following through, lashed the rebound to the net to secure a well merited draw for Waterford.

Twenty seven years later there was an interesting sequel to the above match. John's nephew, Tomás Ó Cinnéide, was employed in Tralee where at weekends he indulged in mountain-walking and climbing. On one occasion Tomás and a group of colleagues were on the mountains overlooking Killarney on a day when Kerry were playing Cork in a Munster championship final in Fitzgerald Stadium. During their walk they encountered an elderly Kerryman who stopped to talk and, in the course of the conversation and having ascertained the county affiliations of everyone, enquired as to why they weren't at the football game. When the group asked why he, a Kerryman, wasn't at the match he replied that he had given up on football and said that hurling was his game. Knowing that Tomás came from Waterford but not knowing that he was John's nephew, he said:

> It was a county man of yours that turned me on to hurling. There was a hurling game down there (pointing towards the town) in 1940 – it was a novelty to us so we went to the match and there I saw a man called John Keane who gave an exhibition of hurling. He hurled the Limerick team off the field. I never saw anything like it. I was a hurling follower after that, or maybe I should say I was a follower of John Keane after that. I went all over the country to see him play. He was the best I ever saw. Tell me, do you know him at all?[71]

The replay was scheduled for Clonmel exactly one month after the drawn game and a packed ground was treated to a superb game in which Waterford led for most of the game but just lost out in a hectic finish. Waterford had gone down fighting gloriously after leading most of the game – but Limerick had won

---

71 Interview with Tomás Ó Cinnéide

once again. Hope springs eternal, however, and the *Waterford News* echoed the thoughts of many Waterford followers when writing 'Never before have I remembered a defeat being so well taken as by Waterford's supporters in Clonmel. ... One thing certain – we have now lost, at last, our inferiority complex.' Writing of John it continued 'The critics unanimously proclaim John Keane the best man of the thirty players and mark him out as the outstanding figure in hurling in Ireland today.'[72]

The match was remembered for the number of duels between noted rivals, chief of these being the mighty clashes between John and Mackey. *The Irish Independent* reported thus: 'In a game featured by dash and determination, John Keane, the Waterford half back, was the outstanding player of the day, and it was certainly no fault of his that Waterford had to accept defeat.'[73] *The Waterford News* commented that 'Mackey could not master the Waterford skipper and we found him changing to right-wing forward and centre-half back at different stages of the game.'[74] There was no denying, however, that it was the steadying influence of Mackey in the Limerick back line in the closing five minutes that held the game for Limerick. After the game a *Munster Express* reporter went to Hearn's hotel to have his tea, and having replenished the inner man was introduced by his companion, a Limerick man, to Timmy Ryan, the Limerick centre-field player who had played a great game. Ryan said that it had been the toughest match he had played since 1936 and he then paid an unsolicited tribute to John saying that 'he was a very fine player indeed and that it was hard to get his equal.'[75]

Seamus Ó Braonáin told a lovely story about an incident that happened after the game.

> John Keane loved hurling so much and [he] knew and understood, deep in his heart, the way the people felt about hurling and how they wanted to touch the edge of the garment of the

---

72   *Waterford News*, 19 July 1940
73   *Irish Independent*, 15 July 1940
74   *Waterford News*, 19 July 1940
75   *Munster Express*, 19 July 1940

man who made them feel so proud. There are many stories that illustrate this. One of the best is probably that of the man who had cycled the thirty or so miles to ... Clonmel. Steering along the street after the game, he suddenly spotted Keane in his ordinary clothes walking to the team's hotel. In his excitement at recognizing him and never having seen him except in hurling togs, he lost all his bearings and shouting out 'Poor John Keane, it wasn't your fault, anyway' he cycled straight up on the pavement and crashed into a shop-front, his eyes still on his hero. Keane went to his rescue with the others nearby. He was patched up and brought home. But John went to the trouble of finding out who the man was, where he lived, and from that day until he died used to drop in to the home of that man to say a few words when he was in the area.[76]

John's character

John was only twenty three years of age but he had already achieved an iconic status among hurling followers in Waterford; amongst them he had reached a level of hero-worship and popularity never seen before. Growing up in the Waterford of seventy years ago John Keane was our own original hero – and he was ours to see almost whenever we desired. One could just saunter into the Gaelic Field to see him training with his club, Mount Sion. Afterwards, when training was over, one could join the crowds of boys (and men) who would gather near the dressing rooms to catch a glimpse of him and listen as he spoke to some acquaintance. Or he could be seen on occasions as he walked through the city, followed usually by a posse of boys too respectful to bother the great man. They were just happy to follow him as he went about his business and to be in reasonably close proximity to their hero – for hero he undoubtedly was. The word hero denotes a man who shows courage out of the ordinary when faced with great odds and who is admired

---

[76] Ó Braonáin, Séamus, *Gaelic Sport*, November 1975

for his achievements and noble qualities. John had those qualities in abundance for it was usually he, more than anyone, who stood between his team and defeat on the hurling field. He was playing, remember, for a county team that, for most of its existence, had achieved very little.

There is, however, an inherent danger in making the acquaintance of one's boyhood heroes for they tend, on closer contact, to have feet of clay. 'Idolatry does not suit human beings for they are by nature unable to sustain the ideals which little boys build about them. But no man lived up to what one's boyhood ideal made him as did John.'[77] It is difficult to imagine, in these very cynical times, just how much John was hero-worshipped – and not just by small boys. Those boys would not have dared to speak to him for to them he was a god. If only they had known, for John was the most approachable of men and he loved to talk about hurling and hurling men. Whenever John's name appeared in print his name was always prefixed by the words 'The great' or followed by the words 'the idol of Waterford people everywhere.' John was the most famous person of his time in Waterford and people lost all their critical faculties when they were in his company. A good example of this was given by a contributor to the Gaelic games website, *An Fear Rua*, who wrote:

> As for John Keane, all I can say is that he was my father's especial hero and I grew up listening to the stories. I think the thing about Keane that stood out, apart from being our greatest ever, was the fact that he was a gentleman to boot. Anyway, a treasured memory I have, which I mentioned here before, is of me about eight years of age and my father bringing me over to meet John Keane and Frankie Walsh at a match in Cappoquin and how they gave me a hurley and sliotar, and how I never got my hands on them because my Da was so star

---

77   Ó Braonáin, Séamus, *Gaelic Sport*, November 1975

struck he never let them out of his possession. They definitely don't make [th]em like that anymore.[78]

The traits that people found appealing in John's character were threefold. He had never strayed from his Barrack Street roots; he was a gentleman; and he carried his fame lightly on his shoulders. People felt at ease with him for he was at ease with himself. He was always the same John Keane as far as the people were concerned and all of them felt that they knew him personally. They liked who he was, and what he was. He could walk with princes and not lose the common touch. He was a social animal and was very gregarious. He liked nothing better than to be in the company of hurling people and would speak all day about hurling with anyone, be he the greatest bore or the most knowledgeable individual – the only qualification needed was that one was a hurling man. On the field he was tough and uncompromising when necessary, but he was never denigrating of his opponents. He had shown character and courage on the field of play for many years but always in a sporting manner and, of course, he was a gifted hurler who had earned the unanimous respect of his peers in a golden era of hurling prowess from the mid 1930s to the late1940s. His popularity in Waterford knew no bounds and lasted a lifetime, but this popularity also transcended county boundaries. Pat Fanning told me that during his presidency of the GAA he invited John to sit with him on several occasions in the presidential box and that he was constantly reminded of John's stature in the game by the excitement engendered when nearby spectators realised that John was present. It was as if no one else in the stadium mattered; people clambered over seats to shake his hand and wish him well – and this was twenty years after he had retired from the game.

John believed that hurling was so important to the Irish people that no one should be excluded from playing or watching the game. This raised the thorny question of charging people for admittance. The money so obtained was for many clubs their

---

78 http://www.anfearrua.com

chief source of funds, gained from the many challenge matches with other clubs. Many people could not afford to pay the admission price because of lack of work and there was always a small group of people (usually pensioners, old hurling followers who had, as was said, 'paid their dues') hanging round outside the gates hoping for a nod or a wink from an understanding gateman. John squared that particular circle by saying that children, pensioners and the unemployed should be admitted without charge. He acted on this conviction with such regularity that he became the bane of all the gatekeepers in the Gaelic Field. He always stopped to talk with the old men outside the ground, irrespective of their club affiliations, and the result was always the same: the deserving few usually walked in scot-free in John's wake.

This came to a head one day when Waterford had a national hurling league match in the Gaelic Field. John attempted to shepherd several old timers through the gate but was stopped by the gateman who enquired as to who was going to pay for John's entourage. John was rather taken aback and, though he was a modest man, he said to the gateman 'Do you know who I am?' John's attempted use of his fame on behalf of the old men was out of character but showed how deeply he felt about them. The ploy didn't work, however, because the gateman replied that he still required payment for the 'hangers-on' as he called them. John replied that if his 'friends' were refused admittance then he too would stay outside and wouldn't bother with the match. Meanwhile, as the throw-in approached, the county secretary, Declan Goode, was frantically searching all over the place for his captain and greatest player. Someone mentioned that he had seen John, earlier, outside the ground so Goode ran to the entrance in a state of great agitation, and a lather of sweat, to find the impasse at the gate. Goode told the gateman to admit John and the 'hangers-on' but the gateman refused adamantly to which Goode retorted 'Do you know who I am?' All were then admitted very quickly but the poor gateman (who was, after all, only doing his job) got a tongue-lashing that day from Goode that he didn't forget for a long while.

Waterford's third clash with Limerick in as many months came in the National League at Waterford. It was at this time that John was given the title of the 'Unconquerable Keane' by a local scribe. It was a memorable appellation and it described exactly how Waterford people felt about him.[79] His standard of performance had reached such a high level of excellence and consistency that no player could defeat him. He had played against the game's greatest players – Mackey, Lynch, Ring, Kennedy and Walsh – and none of them had bested him. For the next three years he was undoubtedly one of the top two hurlers in the country and only Jack Lynch could claim to be on a par with him. Five thousand people turned up to see the latest instalment in the contest between Keane and Mackey, and they got full value for money as the sparks flew between the pair in innumerable clashes. *The Munster Express* reported that 'John Keane, the Waterford captain, was in tip-top form ... [and] the two captains gave no quarter to each other, and it was a great thrill to see such a well-matched pair oppose each other at centre-field and other quarters.' The game was played in a downpour but both teams provided a classic match despite the conditions. Mackey started at centre-forward but was soon roving all over the field. After John had driven a forty yard free all the way to the net midway through the first half, Waterford led by a point at half-time. Mackey started at mid-field in the second half but was often seen in defence especially towards the end of the game when Limerick were desperately defending a one point lead. With full-time fast approaching and Waterford in arrears by just one point, John took a free puck from thirty yards out and it was none other than Mick Mackey who plucked the piledriver from just under the bar to save the day for his team.

---

79   *Waterford News*, 4 October 1940

Wartime restrictions

As the year 1941 began the war-time restrictions started to take effect and there was a huge question mark over the continuance of sport - but an effort had to be made. The Munster Railway cup selectors selected their team but must have wondered if it would ever take the field. John was selected for the fifth year in succession; indeed, the *Waterford News* reported in its issue of the 10 January that there had been only two automatic choices on the team – Paddy Scanlon in goal and John at centre-back. His automatic selection was a well merited reward for his magnificent play all through the previous year when he had dominated every game he played. Jack Lynch was again named as a substitute and he was joined there by Christy Ring whose name appeared for the first time on a Munster panel. Munster played without Mick and John Mackey due to a family bereavement but Leinster's one point win, their first win since 1936, was still a surprise.

Further petrol rationing was announced in May 1941 but the big story that month was the reporting of five cases of foot and mouth disease, the worst affected areas being in Kilkenny, Tipperary and Carlow. Waterford were due to play Tipperary in the Munster championship at the end of May but the game was postponed because of the travel restrictions that were put in place. All games in Tipperary were called off; no games at all were played until the end of July and the GAA found that it was becoming increasingly difficult to continue with anything resembling a normal schedule. The Second World War was raging in Europe and rationing was in place in Ireland but even without the problems posed by war and the shortage of fuel there was little traffic and movement of people and animals compared with the present. There were very few matches played in Ireland that year. The Cork senior hurling team played its first game in September – and that was in the Munster final (an arranged match as the whole championship had been curtailed). The National Leagues were suspended due to the national crisis and clubs were left to their own devices, by and large. The Munster championship match with Tipperary which had been postponed due to the foot and mouth epidemic was re-scheduled for the 27 July. However John did not play in this game as a mark of sympathy for his brother-in-law, Patrick Kennedy, who had died on the Tuesday before the game. Patrick had been a member of the Mount Sion club since 1937, before which he had been captain of the O'Rourke's club for a number of years. The *Waterford News* reported on the match:

> The defeat of our senior hurlers by Tipperary came as a big surprise and disappointment to all Gaelic fans in Waterford. It would appear that the absence of John Keane through a family bereavement completely upset the team and with the exception of A. Fleming and Paddy Dowling none of the players showed their usual form.[80]

Another year had passed and the promise of the previous year still remained unfulfilled.

In 1942 there was even more doubt that the championship could be completed at all due to the war restrictions that were becoming worse each day. On Wednesday 13 May the Minister for Supplies, Seán Lemass, ordered all cars and vehicles (except for public purposes) off the roads.[81] On the following Wednesday the garage proprietors in the city reported that they had run out of petrol and that there was no prospect of having any of the precious fuel before Tuesday, at least, of the following week. Petrol coupons were, therefore, entirely useless and only those people who had petrol in stock and who had received a license from the Ministry of Supplies could use their cars.[82] The situation got worse. With a view to preventing the excessive wear and tear of tyres caused by high speeds the Government made an order restricting the speed of all motor vehicles. Motor

---

80 *Waterford News*, 1 August 1941
81 *Munster Express*, 15 May 1942
82 *Munster Express*, 22 May 1942

vehicles of less than two tons in un-laden weight were restricted to a maximum speed of thirty miles per hour while single-deck buses and vehicles of over two tons were restricted to thirty five miles per hour.[83] Sport in provincial Ireland was going to be badly affected.

It was time to get out the bicycles, but this raised another problem for the harassed public – bicycle rustling. The theft of bicycles reached epidemic proportions and the courts were dealing severely with the culprits. In Waterford District Court the judge sentenced such a thief to two months imprisonment with hard labour and he remarked that he would not be surprised if bicycle thieves were beaten and even lynched and that the time for bicycle stealing was long past.[84] A new phenomenon then appeared – the theft of bicycles just to get the precious rubber tyres. You could ask your own price for a set of tyres (even old ones) and a bicycle repair kit was an absolute necessity when contemplating any journey – long or short. Even teams were forced to cycle to matches

The petrol shortage also put inter-county matches in jeopardy although the railway company stepped into the breach and put on special trains to cater for the crowds. Train travel was not without its difficulties, however, and in one week in May trains from Tralee, Cork and Galway to Dublin broke down so many times that passengers were obliged to spend all day and all night on them. Two clergymen informed the *Munster Express* that they spent twenty one hours in the Tralee to Dublin train without any food or heat.[85]

The few Waterford people who managed to travel to see Waterford play Limerick in the Munster championship at Cork at the end of May saw a great game in which John had another wonderful game against Mick Mackey, the *Irish Independent* describing John as 'the outstanding player on view.'[86] However

---

83   *Irish Times*, 6 June 1942
84   *Munster Express*, 22 May 1942
85   *Munster Express*, 15 May 1942
86   *Irish Independent*, 1 June 1942

the end result was as usual – Waterford lost by five points despite having enough chances to win the game. The team could win an occasional match but did not have a scoring forward line that was consistently deadly in front of goal and all the defending in the world by a set of heroic backs just could not win a series of matches without sufficient scores being put on the board. The usual tactic in this situation was for John to be sent up to the forward line but this inevitably left a weakened defence and the usual result was that Waterford still lost. What the county needed was another very good player, preferably in a forward position or, failing that, a defender that could to step in at centre half-back so that John could take up a permanent position in the attack. But where was such a man to be found? John had a man in mind to take on that role but the war was frustrating his plan and it would be another seven months before he could act.

Chapter eight
The greatest man in Ireland

In John's long career as an inter-county senior hurler there were six outstanding years: 1937 to 1940, 1943 and 1948. The latter year would be the obvious choice for a lot of people; it was, after all, the year when Waterford won its first All-Ireland senior title in which John played more than one man's part. Others might choose 1937 when he exploded on the hurling scene and subdued the mighty Mick Mackey. Yet again some might favour 1940 when John earned the epithet 'The unconquerable Keane' by virtue of his magnificent displays throughout the year especially in the games against Limerick (and Mackey). But many close followers of the game regard 1943 as being his greatest year. Certainly, his courage, hurling ability, loyalty and leadership were put to the severest test, out of which he came with his reputation greatly enhanced. Yet that year ended with him in the centre of a controversy that was not of his own making.

After the disastrous years of 1941 and 1942 John had begun 1943 with two objectives foremost in his mind: the first was to secure Waterford's future as a contending county by unearthing a few new, good players; the second was to revive Mount Sion's fortunes and regain the county title. As already mentioned there was a potentially great player that he had in mind for the county and he set out to procure him almost immediately the season began. John knew the man for the job and was actively pursuing his objective but the war was thwarting him in his efforts. The man in mind was Vincent 'Vin' Baston, an ex-Mount Sion schoolboy from Passage East, who had already played for Waterford. He was training to be an officer in the Army Cadet School at Renmore barracks in Galway where he had been attached, since 1940, to the army's Irish-speaking battalion. His army duties made it very difficult for him, however, to make a permanent commitment to play for Waterford and a further problem was the distance involved in making the journeys, especially in war-time. He had decided, therefore, to play for Galway.

John's first opportunity to speak with Baston came when Munster played Connacht in the Railway cup semi-final at Nenagh on 14 February. John was at centre-back for Munster with Andy Fleming on his right, the latter directly opposing Baston who was making his first appearance for Connacht. After the game John had a long discussion with Baston and told him that there was a chance of an All-Ireland title for him with Waterford. His plan was to move to centre-forward thus enabling Baston to take over at centre-back. Baston was receptive to the idea (assuming that his Army commitments and the travel problem could be solved) and after thinking about it for a while he declared for Waterford in April 1943. He also mentioned that he would like to join the Mount Sion club but the problem of residency interfered with that idea as he would have had to travel to Waterford every week to meet the residency requirement. Baston's decision to play for Waterford had inserted a major cog into the wheel that would propel Waterford to its first All-Ireland senior title but not even John, the architect of the plan, could foresee that it would take another six years for the plan to come to fruition.

Connacht ran Munster close but it was a timely warning for Munster and the selectors made several positional changes for the final. John retained the centre-back position with Andy Fleming on his right and both played splendidly in a magnificent match that Munster won by just one point, scored by Christy Ring with almost the last stroke of the game. This was John's sixth Railway cup medal in seven years and Andy Fleming's first at his inaugural attempt.

The transport situation became worse as the war entered its fourth year. Walking and cycling now became the norm and the roads were full of cyclists. People became used to the idea

In Dublin for the 1943 Railway Cup. M Hayes, John Keane and Martin Cullen (Photo courtesy of the Keane family)

of cycling everywhere and distance became no object. Players and spectators cycled to local matches and even officials took to the road. The east Waterford board meetings rotated between the city and Portlaw and at the January meeting all the officials present expressed their willingness to cycle to the meetings as the cost of hiring two cars would be considerable.[87] More games were arranged locally and John was reported to have played nineteen matches in the year as well as refereeing some others.

Waterford had drawn Tipperary in the Munster championship but a potential disaster happened only two weeks before the match. John was crossing the timber-yard at work when he attempted to leap over a pile of timber, but landed awkwardly and damaged his ankle. He knew immediately that the injury was serious; the pain was intense, the ankle swelled up like a balloon and he was unable to put weight on the injured leg. The doctor diagnosed a fracture of the ankle with associated tendon rupture and he told John that he was definitely out of action for several months. It seemed that John's championship date with Tipperary was out of the question and, remembering what had happened two years previously when he didn't play because of a family bereavement, it boded ill for

---

87   *Munster Express*, 15 January 1943

the county team. John had been selected at centre-back and the team was expected to win, although the selection of four veteran players was heavily criticised by the general public. The correspondent for the *Waterford News* commented:

> Judging the team all round, it is a strong combination which will, I believe, lower the Tipperary colours. ... The half-line of backs would be an Atlantic rampart – strong in depth and range – but for the doubt about John Keane's fitness. At the moment it is not quite certain if his damaged ankle can stand up to the strain of the pivotal half-back position but, unless ill-luck dogs him, Keane will be in the thick of the fray on Sunday.[88]

The salient question was not whether John's fractured ankle could stand the strain but, rather, whether he could even stand on the ankle. There was a quiet confidence amongst the general public that 1943 was going to be Waterford's year and that confidence weighed heavily on John's mind when the time arrived to make a decision as to whether he should play or not. The doctor was adamant in his refusal to allow his patient to play because of the damage that might ensue but John was determined to play – and so he did. The outcome was astonishing because John gave one of the greatest displays of courage and determination ever seen. It was, perhaps, his greatest personal triumph as he stood at centre-back and almost alone defied the whole Tipperary forward line. The *Waterford News* reported that despite 'the handicap of his injured ankle, the Mount Sion skipper played one of the best games of his career. With wonderful anticipation he was always under the fall of the ball and his lengthy clearances were responsible for many scores.'[89] Pat Fanning recalled the occasion for me.

---

88 *Waterford News*, 11 June 1943
89 *Waterford News*, 18 June 1943

John was simply magnificent. I have never seen such raw courage. I remember at the final whistle when John hobbled over to the sideline to lie down on the grass because he couldn't make it the dressing rooms. We tried to remove his boots but couldn't do so because the ankle had swollen so much. I had to borrow a knife and cut the laces but the boot still wouldn't come away. Eventually I had to cut the boot from the swollen foot and when I removed his sock the extent of the injury became evident because the ankle was unrecognisable as such. A crowd had gathered round John as he lay on the ground and I well remember the old Tipperary man (he was in his seventies but was wizened in appearance) who pushed his way through that throng of admirers to where John lay and, bending down and thrusting out his hand, he said that he wanted to shake the hand of John Keane, the greatest man in Ireland.[90]

Limerick were Waterford's opponents in the Munster semi-final at Cork just two weeks after the game with Tipperary. The Limerick team were in transition and were comprised of a majority of veterans who had vast experience in how to win, in contrast to Waterford who had youth and speed on their side. Speed won the day – but only just. It was not a good game from a hurling standpoint. The *Munster Express* reported that 'Limerick had the craft and the experience but from start to finish they were beaten for speed. ... Waterford thoroughly deserved their fine victory. Two men were outstanding ... Jim Ware in goal and John Keane at centre-half.'[91] Limerick were always one of the hardest teams to beat and though Waterford deserved to win it was a close run thing. Ware was unbeatable in goal and he frequently put his body where others would not put a hurley. John was simply irrepressible. When goals were needed he was not found wanting and scored two magnificent goals from frees to rejuvenate his team when it looked as if Limerick would prevail, the *Irish Press* headline being 'John Keane spe-

---

90   Interview with Pat Fanning
91   *Munster Express*, 9 July 1943

cials wreck Limerick hopes.[92] John's protégé, Vin Baston, was a great midfield partner for Mick Hickey and with Willie Barron (of Dungarvan) flying at wing-forward the team were gaining confidence with every game. There was a belief in Waterford that the All-Ireland that year would be between Waterford and Kilkenny, with Waterford coming out the victor; it was a view that was also shared by a lot of hurling people from other counties. It was, therefore, with great confidence, that the thousands prepared to invade the southern capital for the final because Waterford had lost the toss for venue and the match was to be played in Cork.

LDF duties had still to be attended to and at midnight on Saturday 17 July John and his colleagues in the 46th Battalion received a surprising mobilization order. Within a few minutes of its issue the city streets rang with the sound of hurrying feet as members of the battalion from all over the city hurried to their unit's assembly point. The full exercise followed, despite the terrible weather, and concluded about four o'clock in the morning. Units of the battalion in Dunmore East, Passage East, Tramore, Butlerstown, Slieverue, Kilmacow as well as the Waterford Company Maritime Inscription also took part. This had been a general mobilisation but smaller exercises were a constant feature of LDF life and were a grim and constant reminder to all that there were other important issues to be faced.[93]

The Great Southern Railway refused to provide any match-trains so the supporters got out their bicycles in readiness for the long journey. At a time when the train journey from Waterford city through Kilmacthomas, Dungarvan, Lismore, Fermoy, Mallow and Glanmire to Cork city took six hours one can only imagine the hardship involved on such a journey by bicycle. But still, the hurling had to be played and although John's ankle was still not right he had been magnificent through two Munster championship matches and with a Munster final next on the agenda against the All-Ireland champions he was not going

---

92   *Irish Press*, 5 July 1943
93   *Munster Express*, 23 July 1943

to let his damaged ankle prevent him from playing. Another injury, however, played havoc with Waterford's chances. Vin Baston received a serious injury when playing in an army game just a few days before the Munster final and was unable to play thus breaking up the midfield partnership with Mick Hickey. Notwithstanding the injuries Waterford were confident and P. D. Mehigan described why.

> Waterford were a tried and true team, having raced Tipperary off their feet in Dungarvan and put out a fancied Limerick side on these Cork grounds a month ago. No wonder Waterford were confident and for myself I thought local betting all wrong – 6 to 1 on Cork, fours against Waterford. Events proved that Waterford's moderate display against Limerick had led the Leeside critics to underestimate the Déiseacht strength. As a matter of fact they shook the Cork champions to the foundations – the red jerseys were in arrears five times in the hour – and stood hip-high with Cork in every corner of the field. Many times the title-holders were beaten in every race to a ball and until … [the] final whistle Waterford looked dangerous for scores that would dethrone the champions, and add one more shock to the many surprises of a surprising year.[94]

It rained the proverbial 'cats and dogs' all through that Sunday morning and the hundreds of cyclists who had ventured on the long road to Cork were drenched to the skin long before they reached their destination. The sky cleared about mid-day but the afternoon was spoiled by frequent showers making things miserable for the spectators, although they were treated to a memorable Munster final. John played at centre-back and in the first half of an epic game he gave one of the great attacking displays of the Munster championship. Despite Christy Ring's presence at centre-forward John was outstanding and it was he that drove-on the Waterford forwards who were inspired and enthused by his performance. Cork rang all the changes in an

---

94   *Carbery's Annual* (1943-4), p. 87

effort to grab control of the game but John stood like a rock and defied every move made by the Cork selectors. When half-time arrived Waterford went to the dressing rooms with a two point advantage and as the second half began it was noticed that Ring had been switched off John with Bernie Murphy being tried in his place. But it was when Cork, in desperation, placed Jack Lynch at centre-forward that the Cork men started to come into the game. Lynch had been playing brilliantly at centre-field but something had to be done to curb John's attacking play and Lynch, with his power and height, was just the man for the job. He was told to lie-in on John and prevent the latter's famous surges into the forward line. Gradually Cork started to score and went into a two point lead as the Waterford men tired but a further surge by Waterford yielded a great goal by Hickey and Waterford led once more. Cork levelled as the match entered its last quarter but Cork were staying the pace better and with John's ankle now 'crocked' the home team pulled away to win by two points. Cork had won its three-in-a-row of titles.

Jim Ware, the Waterford captain, spoke for all Waterford men when he said in an interview after the game 'Naturally we are disappointed, but not disheartened. ... I thought that we deserved at least a draw. Our ill-luck to be short Vincent Baston, and the disadvantage of having to play Cork at home made all the difference.'[95] Andy Croke, in the *Sunday Independent*, wrote that were it not for the superb hurling of Jack Lynch and the many positional changes ordered by the astute Cork mentors the Munster crown might have left the Leeside. He continued by saying that 'It is not taking from any of the Decies fifteen to mention two players as [being] outstanding, John Keane and Jim Ware. Seldom have I seen a more brilliant half-back than Keane.'[96] John D. Hickey, writing about that game some thirteen years later and in wonder at John's performance, recalled 'that epic struggle of 1943 when John, single-handed, almost

---

95 *Munster Express*, 6 August 1943
96 *Sunday Independent*, 8 August 1943

carried his county to a sensational victory over mighty Cork.'[97] In a retrospective look at John's career in 1973 a writer for the GAA magazine *An Cúl* wrote that 'No one can fully understand what Keane meant to Waterford: even when the county was weak. John was still freely acknowledged through the length and breadth of the country as the greatest hurler in the game – the man who could play Mackey and Ring and subdue them.'[98]

Imagine the feelings of the Waterford team and supporters when they learned shortly afterwards that Antrim had sensationally beaten Kilkenny in the All-Ireland semi-final and that if Waterford had beaten Cork the All-Ireland final would have been between Waterford and Antrim. There seemed to be a curse on the Waterford team. Kilkenny's defeat led to an amusing story about a Waterford-based old Kilkenny man who frequented 'The Well' public house in the city's Yellow Road. At a time when few people had wireless (radio) sets at home some pubs had one installed for their patrons, just as most pubs now have TV's. When the sports results were read out the old man listened in disbelief to the announcement that Kilkenny had been beaten and he jumped up and roared at the wireless, 'You liar! You liar!' Without showing any disrespect to Antrim, who had also beaten Galway, this would have been a game in which Waterford would have been outstanding favourites as shown by Cork's demolition job of Antrim in the final which they won by 5-16 to 0-4. Another chance of that elusive break-through had vanished.

Dropped by Munster

After John's magnificent year in 1943 he was surely a certainty for the 1944 Railway cup team but, to general amazement, he was dropped and was not even included among the reserves. The *Munster Express* reporter spoke for the majority

---

97 *Irish Independent*, 8 February 1956
98 *An Cúl* (vol. 4, no. 2, Aibreán 1973), p. 13

when he wrote 'When we opened our morning paper and had a look at the names we got a bit of a shock at not seeing the name of John Keane. He was not even picked as a sub. It makes one wonder.'[99]

He would have wondered all the more if he had known of the circumstances behind John's non-selection because it became clear, some time afterwards, that other forces were at play and that the Munster selectors had been misled and misinformed. The revelation happened to come out by chance. Later in the year a fellow Mount Sion committee man, Aidan MacNamara, fell into company with several newspaper reporters from the national press and during the conversation the selection of the Munster hurling team was raised. A discussion ensued and MacNamara realised that the journalists were privy to inside information regarding the selection process. He raised the fact that John had been dropped and asked if any one knew why this had happened. Seán Coghlan, who wrote under the pen-name of 'Green Flag' for the *Irish Press*, replied that the question would be more properly addressed to Waterford's selectors for the Munster team. On further probing it was revealed that it had been intimated at the selection committee meeting that John should not be considered as he was suffering from ill-health (tuberculosis was implied) and that he might not be playing hurling for very long more. There was, of course, no truth whatsoever in that story. The comment of the *Waterford News* reporter that 'it makes one wonder' recalled the same reporter's comment about the selectors when Seán Veale of Stradbally was dropped from the 1941 Munster Railway cup football team. On that occasion the reporter wrote 'perhaps the fault lies with our own representatives at the Munster council.'[100] It was a sad episode and it took another two years for John to regain his place on the Munster team.

John suffered a very serious head injury in a county championship match early in 1944 and, as a consequence, was out of

---

99 *Munster Express*, 3 December 1943
100 *Waterford News*, 10 January 1941

hurling for six months. In his absence his club were eliminated from the county championship and Waterford were beaten by Tipperary in the Munster championship. He was sorely missed because both teams appeared leaderless. As the months of inaction passed it was a worrying time because it looked as if he might never again return to top-flight hurling action. This was a very frustrating time and he only made his re-appearance on 29 October for Waterford's match against Cork in the Br Rice Memorial Tournament final. To commemorate the centenary of Br Rice's death the GAA had organised a great tournament of hurling and football involving the top counties, the hurling final to be held in Waterford – but neither Waterford nor Tipperary were invited to take part, the standard of hurling in both counties not being considered to be good enough. This was an incongruous decision but the tournament proceeded despite vehement objections from the Waterford county board. Cork and Dublin qualified for the final but Dublin couldn't travel and nominated Waterford as their replacement. And so it came about that Waterford, the team that were considered not good enough at the start of the tournament, would now face Cork, the all-conquering, four-in-a-row, All-Ireland champions.

Apart from the association of the city with the founder of the Christian Brothers the game had an exceptional appeal. When Waterford had been beaten by Cork in the Munster final of 1943 the Waterford players were adamant that with home advantage and a full team they would have prevailed. The subsequent defeat in a re-match had not altered that opinion and the exclusion of the team from the initial rounds of the Br Rice tournament had rankled. It would be a game to savour. John was very eager to make his come-back in this game and with his doctor's blessing he declared himself open to selection. The team selected was a strong one and John resumed his place at centre-back. Cork had strengthened their team since the All-Ireland final and had six players from the Glen Rovers club that had won the Cork senior hurling final on the previous Sunday.

It was a magnificent game that had the crowd enthralled. The result was a huge shock because in the early stages it looked as if it would be a one-sided affair in favour of the champions. As the game advanced, however, and particularly in the second half, Waterford dominated the exchanges and proved their superiority in almost every department. The result evoked some caustic comments from the Waterford supporters in view of the fact that the standard of hurling in the county had been so lowly regarded by the organisers. It was a great source of pride to the Mount Sion community that Waterford had four past pupils on the team: John, Andy Fleming and Paddy Dowling had formed the mighty half-back line and Vin Baston had starred in the forward line. There was a reception after the game after which John quietly presented Br O'Connor with the gold medal that had been specially struck for the winners. It was a gesture typical of John – he wanted to recognise in a tangible way the role of Br O'Connor all those years ago when he was one of that small group that had founded the Mount Sion club. The gesture was much appreciated by Br O'Connor who wore the medal on his watch-chain until the day he died.

Chapter Nine
Building A Team

Waterford's inter-county team had little to boast about in its 1945 engagements. In the league they lost every game and in the Munster championship Tipperary inflicted a crushing defeat to the tune of 3-6 to 0-3. John had been omitted again from the Munster selection for the Railway cup but this time there was such a public outcry over the team that the Munster selectors were forced to assuage the discontent of the general public by picking a second team labelled the 'Rest of Munster' to play a challenge against the 'official' Munster team. Two Waterford players, Andy Fleming (Mount Sion) and Jim Ware (Erin's Own), were picked for Munster and four of their Waterford colleagues lined out with 'The Rest' team, viz., John Keane and Paddy Dowling (Mount Sion), Christy Moylan (now playing with Portlaw) and Willie Barron (Dungarvan). The game took place in the University College Cork grounds at the Mardyke before a huge attendance and the Munster selectors would have taken comfort from the resounding win of the 'official' team, although the *Irish Independent* reported that the difference in scores was not a true reflection of the run of play and that the Rest of Munster forwards missed innumerable chances.[101] The real difference between the teams was Jim Ware in the Munster goal whose saves were incredible. P. D. Mehigan described his performance in that year's *Carbery's Annual* thus: 'Jim Ware in the Munster goal was a treat to watch. He could stop "turnip-seed" if it were thrown at him.'[102] The three members of the great Mount Sion half back-line, Fleming, Keane and

---

101   *Irish Independent*, 26 February 1945
102   *Carbery's Annual* (1945-6), p. 60

Dowling played in this game but what a pity it was that all three were not playing together as a unit for Munster.

The Waterford selectors embarked on a policy of trying out new players in the weeks leading up to the Munster championship meeting with Tipperary but suffered a series of defeats without unearthing any new talent. The team had been well beaten by Wexford, Kilkenny and Cork in league and tournament games and this led to the disaffection of Vin Baston who had become discouraged at Waterford's lack of success. He had not appeared for the game with Cork and was thinking of declaring once more for Galway, and it took all John's persuasive skills to keep him at Waterford's service. The breakthrough promised by John had not happened and it was as frustrating for John as well as for Baston. No one expected any great showing against Tipperary and so it proved on the day although for half the game the Waterford goalkeeper, Jim Ware, gave Waterford great hope with an incredible series of saves. Ware was injured early in the game but continued to play so brilliantly that up to half-time Tipperary had failed to score against him. Then, during the interval, he collapsed and was unable to resume. This seriously affected the morale of the team and Tipperary went on to win easily.

Mount Sion had regained the county title in 1945 and, as county champions, were automatically given two of the five positions on the county senior hurling selection committee. Mick Gallagher and John were the club's nominees and they were joined by F. Roche (Portlaw), the county chairman Vincent O'Donoghue (Lismore) and Tom Kyne from Dungarvan. The new county selection committee set out to try as many newcomers as possible and the team responded with two splendid wins, the first over Wexford in the league and then over Tipperary, the All-Ireland champions, in which John had a magnificent game in his usual centre-back role. A disturbing aspect of these early season matches, however, was the absence of Vin Baston who was becoming restless again. He had not been selected for Munster in the Railway cup competition and was thinking again about leaving Waterford and declaring for Galway.

John renewed his efforts to keep Baston and had promised him that he would be selected for the county team at either centre-back or centre-field in the coming Munster championship. This meant that that John would move permanently to the centre-forward position. The first opportunity to do so came with a challenge match with Cork when he played in that position, scoring a goal, but from Waterford's display it was obvious that the county was going to need Baston for the championship match against Cork.

This match took place at Clonmel in front of a packed attendance. Both teams fielded as selected but Waterford made one positional change; Baston had been chosen at centre-back, as promised, with John at centre-field. However, when the teams lined up for the throw-in it was seen that the two players had switched positions with each other. John had a magnificent match, rampaging all over the field and playing in three different positions during the game. Waterford were on top of Cork in the first half but were one point in arrears when the latter scored a simple goal, the ball dribbling between the Waterford goalkeeper's legs. The *Irish Independent* reported that the switch between Baston and John certainly justified itself as both played outstanding games, with John having a grip on Christy Ring, 'the Cork flier.' The paper continued that positional changes in the second-half, which brought John to centre-field in place of Hayes, gave Waterford a pull at this sector. John then went to centre-forward and 'though the Cork defence was very solid up to a point they were not so impressive when Keane got in amongst them.'[103]

The reporter's comment that Keane had a grip on Ring brings up the matter regarding the performances of both hurlers when pitted in direct opposition to each other. This point was raised in Val Dorgan's wonderfully entertaining biography of Ring in the following terms:

---

103 *Irish Independent*, 1 July 1946

Before one game against the formidable Waterford centre back John Keane, Ring walked ten miles every day for about two months. He told a friend of mine after he had outplayed Keane—'my legs were like rocks, I knew I could run forever.' This was in the early forties when hurlers generally did nothing like the same physical preparation as today.[104]

Keane versus Ring

Dorgan's quote intrigued me for three reasons. Firstly, Ring and John (who were friends and had great respect for each other) had rarely opposed one another directly on the field of play; secondly, the source is not named; and thirdly, the statement 'after he had outplayed Keane' does not concur with the available evidence. I examined the newspaper archives for the period 1940 to 1946 and found that the two great hurlers met only four times in direct opposition to each other with the following results. In April 1940 Ring, at nineteen years of age, was not mentioned in any match report. In August 1943, as we have seen, John was superb at centre-back and was winning the championship game for Waterford when Cork, in desperation, switched Ring (and others) and put Jack Lynch at centre forward in an effort to try and curb John's attacking display. In November 1944 Ring scored a goal from a seventy yard free. Then, in 1946 (regarded by many people as Ring's greatest year), John was reported to have got the better of Ring. In the 1940s, of course, John was usually at centre-back and Ring's best position was at wing forward and both would have been switched to suit the needs of each team. It is fair to say that while John was never bested when faced by Ring the latter was often doing severe damage to Waterford elsewhere on the field.

With regard to John's opinion of Ring and the other hurlers of his time I often heard him say that, in his opinion, the greatest hurlers he had seen were, in no particular order, Mick

---

104 Dorgan, Val, *Christy Ring* (Ward River, Dublin, 1980), p. 187

Mackey, Paddy Scanlon and Jackie Power of Limerick; Christy Ring and Jack Lynch of Cork; Jimmy Langton and Paddy Phelan of Kilkenny; and Andy Fleming and Christy Moylan of Waterford. Whilst all of the above-named were his contemporaries, John was forward-looking and was not one of those ex-hurlers whose head was stuck permanently in the sands of time – he believed that the general standard of the game was improving constantly with each succeeding generation. He gave second place to no one in his admiration for the wonderful hurlers on the Waterford team of 1957-63 and he regarded the centre-field partnership of Philly Grimes and Séamus Power as being the greatest ever, in any county. He also mentioned, in a letter to Seamus O'Brien, the long-time Waterford central council representative, that he believed Pat McGrath to be one of Mount Sion's, and Waterford's, greatest-ever players.[105] One can only wonder what he would think of the present day Mount Sion and Waterford hurlers Tony Browne (grandson of his friend 'Fad' Browne of Erin's Own) and Ken McGrath (son of the aforementioned Pat McGrath). He was adamant, however, that the great players of his era (Mackey, Ring, Lynch, Langton, Phelan et al) were super-stars of the game and that we would be lucky if even one hurler in each generation came near their standards.

Erin's Own had effectively ended Mount Sion's hopes of a repeat county title when they won their championship clash and they duly became county champions for 1946. The club held a special meeting where the non-selection (especially for the Munster championship match with Cork) of any of its players for Waterford in that year was discussed. The club sent a letter to the county secretary, also published in the local newspapers, calling for the resignations of the county board chairman and the members of the senior hurling selection committee. The letter was published in the newspapers on Friday the 1 November and in the league game on the following Sunday none of the six players Erin's Own players selected to play turned up for the match. This was a serious challenge to the county board and

---

105 Conversation with Seamus O'Brien

that body called a special meeting to deal with the situation. After a long debate the club was suspended for twelve months. The club appealed the suspension to the Munster council, which upheld the county board decision, thereby placing the very future of the club in doubt.

The last action of the year saw Waterford defeat Cork, thus shattering Cork's hopes of National League honours. The match was played in appalling weather conditions and the referee wanted to abandon the game after ten minutes of the second half but the teams insisted on playing to a finish. Cork fielded only five players from their All-Ireland winning team while Waterford, who made all the running, had only four of the team that had played in the Munster championship. John had another outstanding game and must have had hopes of returning to the Munster team for the 1947 Railway cup competition. Sure enough when the team was announced he was named at full-back and Waterford had been given its second highest representation ever with four players selected. Joining John and Andy Fleming on the team were Vin Baston and the Butlerstown player, Mick Hayes who were both making their first appearance for Munster. Baston had been a tremendous addition to the Waterford team and another find was Hayes, who was a very talented player as well as being big and strong.

Back with Munster

If ever a team had an easy passage into a Railway cup final it was Munster, who scored at will against Ulster at Croke Park on 16 March. It had been intended to play the semi-finals and final over the two days but due to the appalling weather conditions the hurling final was postponed to another day. At the half-way stage Ulster were nineteen points behind and though the Munster forwards treated themselves to a liberal supply of goals and points it was Vin Baston at centre-field who was the best player on view. The *Irish Independent* reported that Baston stood head and shoulders over all and his masterly control of the ball under such frightful conditions was truly marvellous. 'Needless to remark, the Munster defence was never really tested. In fact, for most of the second half at full back, J. Keane was busily engaged swinging his hands to keep them from becoming numb with the cold and rain.'[106] Munster had won by 9-7 to 0-0 but it was a pity that the team hadn't reserved a few of the scores for the final because when it was finally played the Connacht men totally outclassed the holders, who were held to a score of only 1-1, Connacht thus registering its first win in the competition. Although John had held his man scoreless no one on the Munster team enhanced his reputation.

Back home Waterford had an easy victory over Wexford at Enniscorthy and were in sight of a play-off place in the National League. The most encouraging aspect of the win was the performance of Johnny O'Connor, the youngest player on the team, who had assisted the Munster Colleges' team on the previous Sunday. He gave an outstanding display at right half-back after being catapulted into the side when Andy Fleming cried off at the last minute. He was still a schoolboy and was understandably nervous but, years later, in an interview with the *Irish Independent*, he gave great credit to John who had given constant verbal encouragement to him all through the match. In O'Connor's words, 'That encouragement coming from such a man as John Keane would make a dead man hurl.'[107] Waterford had discovered another outstanding player and the selectors' practice of trying out talented youngsters was paying off. There was now a strong nucleus of very good players, John, Andy Fleming, Vin Baston, Mick Hayes, Jackie Goode and Johnny O'Connor, and with moves afoot to re-instate the Erin's Own club the future prospects for the county were positive.

Vigorous efforts were being made to try and rescind the suspension on the Erin's Own club but the Munster council had refused to countenance their appeal against suspension. It appeared that unless the latter club backed down the status quo

---

106 *Irish Independent*, 17 March 1947
107 *Irish Independent*, 22 February 1966

would remain. Then, at the end of March, Erin's Own gave up the fight and apologised. The club was reinstated but it had been an embarrassing episode and a humbling experience in power politics for the club. But they were back, and with a vengeance, as would be seen later in 1948, to John's detriment. Three Erin's Own players were selected to play against Cork in the Munster championship and the return of Jim Ware to the goal was universally welcomed. Waterford lost, as expected, but the issue was in doubt for long periods and a surprise seemed imminent. Indeed, only one minute of normal time remained when Ring and Kelly scored goals and Ring pointed to give Cork an eleven point victory. The *Irish Independent* was surprised at Waterford's display and reported:

> Waterford made a much better showing than the score suggests and they had a real star in V. Baston at centre-field. He was superior to either Lynch or Condon ... The effectiveness of Cork's attack was blunted to some extent by the fact that J. Keane, the Waterford full-back, held D. O'Riordan, well throughout.[108]

That match convinced John that he was needed more amongst Waterford's forwards than he was amongst the backs. John D. Hickey wrote in 1956 that some people in the county held that Waterford might have earned more rewards at a time when they had great teams if John had been turned into a forward earlier in his career. Recalling the Munster final against Cork in 1948 and his subsequent brilliance in the All-Ireland when John was again at centre-forward he agreed that there was much to be said for the contention. Hickey maintained, however, that no blame should attach to the Waterford selectors for not switching John earlier than they did. 'They brought a boy to Clonmel and he stopped Mick Mackey. In those days it would have looked like hurling suicide to switch him.'[109]

---

108 *Irish Independent*, 30 June 1947
109 *Irish Independent*, 8 February 1956

The year closed with four National League matches in which John alternated between full-back and centre-back playing brilliantly in both positions, but that was business as normal. The most heartening and pleasing aspect of those games, however, was that the other 'big' men on the team, Fleming, Baston, Ware, Hayes and Goode were all playing at a very high level of consistency and the newcomers, Johnny O'Connor, Eddie Carew, Willie Galvin, Ned Daly and John Cusack looked ready to join them. The days when Waterford had a team of four brilliant individuals, plus eleven others, appeared to be over. The 'hard core' of the team was getting bigger and it looked as if the team would be a serious contender for the title in the coming year.

Chapter Ten

Senior All-Ireland

Did anyone really expect that 1948 would be Waterford's year? Not many, to be honest! Cork and Kilkenny had played one of the greatest-ever All-Ireland finals in 1947 and looked set to dominate the scene for several years to come, yet there were some who felt that this Waterford team was building nicely. The county had produced some great teams since it had gained admission into the top tier of hurling counties in 1931 but those teams had failed mainly because of a lack of penetration amongst the forwards. John had told Vin Baston back in 1943 that he would be moving to the forward division to make way for Baston at centre-back but circumstances had not allowed him to do so until now. He judged that the time had finally arrived and he announced, publicly, that he was leaving the defence for good and henceforth was going to play exclusively in the forwards. Perhaps this was the key to the success he had promised Baston!

If Erin's Own had been rather paranoid about Mount Sion's role in the senior hurling selection process in 1946 then Mount Sion certainly had similar feelings about Erin's Own in 1948 – and with good reason. The county board elected a senior hurling selection committee comprising Martin Cullen and Charlie Ware (Erin's Own), John Keane (Mount Sion), Dave Shanahan (Clonea) and Tom Lannen (Dungarvan). Mount Sion were unhappy with the composition of this selection committee and at a meeting of the club it was decided that 'owing to the peculiar composition of this committee [that] John Keane should continue as a member and attend all meetings regardless of possible developments and tactics likely to be adopted by the selectors.'[110] At the AGM of

---

110 Mount Sion club minutes, 11 March 1948

the Mount Sion club the chairman, Mick Gallagher, stepped down from his position and John was elected as chairman for the coming year and was also elected as trainer of the senior hurling team.[111] He was now chairman of the club, captain and trainer of the club's senior hurling team, a member of the panel of county referees and a member of the county selection committees for senior hurling and minor football. He was also playing football with the Mount Sion and Waterford junior teams and, because Mount Sion did not have a senior football team, he played senior football with St Otteran's, a divisional team.

John's first game for Waterford under the new regime resulted in a loss to Dublin in the National League where John had been chosen at full-back by the county selection committee despite his objections. Furthermore, three members of the Mount Sion team had been dropped for the game – a fact that John reported to his club as per instructions stating that the three players 'had been dropped apparently for no other reason but their membership of this club.' The club meeting discussed the position fully and agreed that John should continue to act on the county selection committee and await further developments.[112]

As the first round of the Munster Senior Hurling championship match drew near there was tension within the county selection committee. John had quickly realised that the other four selectors had obviously entered into a voting pact that excluded him and it appeared that team selection was being made, unofficially and illegally, outside the committee room. James Grant, the subsequent county secretary, told me of the first time this became a matter of public notice.

> I remember the day well. I was about seventeen years of age and I was standing with my father outside the dressing rooms in Dungarvan where the selectors were having a meeting. I remember hearing the door of the dressing rooms slamming shut and looked up to see John walking out and he was quite vis-

---

111 Mount Sion club minutes, 14 March 1948
112 Mount Sion club minutes, 15 March 1948

ibly upset. My father Ritchie, who was an official of the Erin's Own club and a friend and neighbour of John in the city, saw that John was upset and he called out to John asking him if he was all right. John stopped and replied 'I am, Ritchie, but I'm just wasting my time in there' waving his hand in the direction of the dressing rooms. Then, with a shake of his head he was gone on his way.[113]

John was unhappy and frustrated at what he believed to be an act of betrayal by the other four committee members and felt that he should resign. However, as he had been instructed by his club to continue as a member of the committee he decided that he would report back as arranged and await the decision of the club. The first game for Waterford in the Munster championship was against Clare, the winners to go straight to the Munster final. Waterford qualified, but only just. The team were slow to settle down but struck a wonderful spell midway through the first half that brought three goals and two points, for an interval lead of nine points. In addition to that advantage Waterford entered the second half aided by a strong breeze and everything in its favour. The nine points lead was maintained until ten minutes from the end when, inexplicably, the centre of Waterford's defence collapsed and Clare quickly scored two goals and two points to bring them perilously close to earning at least a draw. It was then that John acted, on his own and without any reference to his fellow selectors on the sideline. Noticing the danger he raced back to the defence and took over at centre-back, placing Mick Hayes in his rightful position at left half-back and sending Phil Grimes to centre-forward. With John standing like a rock at centre-back the collapse was immediately stopped and Waterford survived the last ten minutes. Mick Healy always maintained that John's intervention that day had certainly saved, if not won, an All-Ireland for Waterford.

The Waterford minors had also qualified for the Munster final when, with a magnificent display, they beat Clare on a score

---

113 Interview with James Grant

of 9-5 to 0-4 with Maurice 'Budgie' McHugh scoring 6-1. The *Dungarvan Leader* lauded the minors but was very pessimistic about the senior team's chances in the Munster final.

> Were it not for John Keane who came from centre forward to centre back and Vince Baston who was an inspiration at centre field, Waterford would certainly have suffered defeat as these two broke up raid after raid by the Banner county men. Vin Baston was outstanding – there is nothing more I can say about him. ... There were only two forwards worth mentioning, John Keane and Ned Daly. Keane was his old self. I don't believe that he failed once to beat his man in the whole hour. His distribution of the ball to his wing men was something which I have never seen before in a Waterford team.[114]

The Munster final was still more than two months away but the problem within the senior hurling selection committee was becoming apparent to the public at large. Waterford had played Wexford in a challenge match in preparation for the final and had been beaten by one point but there was great public disquiet about the selection. The *Munster Express* reported soberly that the attendance, which numbered two thousand, 'were very disappointed at the scrappy selection that Waterford sent out to do duty. They considered that the home team should have been more representative in view of their entry into the Munster final.'[115] The public and press were becoming agitated and, after another game, the *Dungarvan Leader* was not so understanding of the selectors and commented 'The majority [of the players] were like dead men who forgot to lie down ... In passing I would like to comment on the selectors ... Selectors should not treat county teams as a joke.'[116]

When the team to play Cork was selected a storm arose about the way the selection had been made. Declan Goode, the

---

114 *Dungarvan Leader*, 29 May 1948
115 *Munster Express*, 18 June 1948
116 *Dungarvan Leader*, 17 July 1948

county secretary, had been appointed by the county board at the beginning of the year to act as recording secretary to the senior hurling selection committee. Although he attended the meetings he had no function other than to record the process by which the team was selected and report back to the county board. He was unable to be present at the team selection meeting for the Munster final and he asked Pat Fanning, the Mount Sion secretary, to deputise for him. Pat agreed and was outraged at what he heard and witnessed; it was obvious that the team had been selected beforehand by four of the selectors at an unofficial meeting and that the 'official' meeting was only a sham.[117] He reported his concerns to the county board and the latter body discussed the matter but decided to take no action. John, as chairman of Mount Sion, convened a meeting of the club committee so that he might get its views on the matter. At the meeting he explained the circumstances in which the team to play Cork had been selected. He reported to the meeting on the recent county board meeting at which the actions of the senior hurling committee was discussed and he protested that the only people who had spoken against the actions of the committee were Vincent O'Donoghue, the county board chairman, and Pat Fanning. The club decided to endeavour to have a special meeting of the county board called to discuss the irregular manner in which team was selected.[118] Pat was very concerned that John's hurling would be affected by the matter and prevailed upon him to resign from the selection committee, a view shared by the Mount Sion club committee. Pat then drafted a letter to the county board from John in which was explained the reason for his resignation.

A special meeting of the county board was called to discuss the selection of the team in view of a telegram received, a letter from the acting secretary of the selection committee (Pat Fanning) and two letters of resignation from that committee. When the special meeting met to consider the matter the chairman of

---

117 Interview with Pat Fanning
118 Mount Sion club minutes, 23 July 1948

the county board decided not to read the contents of the telegram because it was unsigned. The two letters of resignation were then read. The first one was from Martin Cullen, one of the Erin's Own representatives. This letter, which had been the cause of debate at a previous board meeting but had not been read in its entirety, was now read in full. The second letter of resignation, in which John gave his reasons for resigning, sparked off a heated discussion amongst the board members regarding the method of selection adopted by the selection committee. At the end of the debate a vote was taken and the board refused to accept John's resignation. Despite this vote John insisted that he was going to resign and another proposal was put to the board to accept the resignation. This time it was accepted. The board then considered a proposal to nominate a substitute to fill the vacant position on the selection committee but this was rejected and it was decided to proceed with just four selectors. Before the meeting concluded *the county board, on a vote, expressed its disapproval of the team selected to do duty in the Munster final, thus censuring its own committee.*[119]

The letter that Pat Fanning had drafted on behalf of John and the Mount Sion club and Mount Sion's call to the county board for action against the selection committee were to have serious repercussions for the two Fanning brothers. Larry had been dropped from the Munster final team as the scapegoat for the collapse against Clare but, as he pointed out, the collapse had occurred at centre half-back and not in his position at full-back. He added further, that his opponent had scored only one goal in the entire match. Pat had been a member of the senior panel for the two Munster championship games but he was now dropped from the panel without any explanation and was never re-instated. Some time later, Paddy Greene, a member of the Mount Sion club and a former Waterford county player, met the chairman of the selectors on the street and asked him why Pat had been dropped from the panel, especially as he had not even played a game. He was answered rather sarcastically 'If he was

---

119 *Waterford Star*, 30 July 1948

as good a player as he is a letter-writer he might still be on the panel' to which Paddy replied to the chairman's back as the latter walked on, 'So it's personal then!'[120] Such were the politics in Waterford hurling in the momentous year of 1948.

The Munster final was scheduled for Thurles and so confident were the Cork supporters of victory that they stayed at home in great numbers and opted to go to the seaside instead. The railway company had four trains ready at Glanmire station but only two were needed for Thurles and the other two went to Youghal, packed to capacity with erstwhile Cork hurling supporters. It was not so in Waterford and five special trains left the Waterford North station as the city and county moved en-bloc to Thurles. Every available means of transport was used as the county responded to a first-ever Waterford appearance in a Munster final in Thurles. It was a memorable and unforgettable occasion for the supporters. Most city people travelled to the match by train and from the moment they stepped on to the platform of Thurles railway station they were caught up in a maelstrom of excitement and passion that didn't subside for one minute during their stay in the town. It was extraordinary to see a match take over a town so completely and in a manner that would have been impossible in a city.

When the supporters arrived in Cathedral square the sight of about thirty thousand people crammed into that small area, all consumed by the match, was breath-taking. Bishops and parish priests jostled side-by-side with factory workers, farmers and farm labourers as they all sought to get a drink or a meal in the various bars, cafés, and unofficial eating establishments where the ubiquitous 'meat-teas' signs proliferated in the windows of private houses. As they left the Square to take the long road to the ground some joined the large crowd of people who were peering in through the large windows of the Glenmorgan House to catch a glimpse of the team having its pre-match meal. What a thrill that was, because normally you would never see those players except when they were fully rigged-out for the

---

120 Conversation with Paddy Greene

game. Fiddlers, banjo players and singers were everywhere and on the way to the ground the mass of humanity was regaled by a variety of entertainers: dancers, fiddlers, box players, three-card-trick men, and ballad makers who sang their own compositions (usually about some previous match) and tried their best to sell their ballad-sheets for sixpence or whatever they could charm out of the passers-by. The future Tipperary goalkeeper and Gaelic games writer, John O'Grady, who hailed from just outside Thurles town and who wrote so beautifully about hurling under the pen-name 'Cúlbáire,' vividly remembered the 1948 final.

> There's no trouble pin-pointing '48 out of the mass of memories – Waterford's first All-Ireland gave it strong identity. Thurles again – one is tempted to say 'of course'; John Keane, centre-forward on Paddy O'Donovan; perennial Jim Ware in 'numero uno'; Vin Baston, smoothest left-hander, I think, till Jimmy Doyle, at wing-back; a big, capable Decies team, absolutely entitled in every respect to pull off the most appreciated of wins over Cork, and later over Dublin. It was one of the tensest of Thurles finals, with everybody bar Cork wishing Waterford well. The day was improved further for them by the minor victory in which several great future seniors were concerned – I've always said those minors were about the best I've ever seen for evenness and ball-control.[121]

Ah yes, that Waterford minor team! Tipperary had been the dominant force in Munster minor hurling since the competition started in 1928 and had won six titles in succession in the 1930s. The minor championship had been suspended for three years during war-time but Tipperary continued to dominate the series after it was resumed in 1945 and had won the title three times in a row when they lined out against Waterford in

---

121 O'Grady, John (Cúlbáire), 'Tipperary viewpoint' in Cronin, *Munster GAA story*, p. 349

1948.¹²² The home supporters were in for an almighty shock, however, as the Waterford minors ran riot and won by 3-6 to 0-3. The lighter Waterford boys simply outclassed Tipperary in every way – in team-work, in speed and in the finer points of the game. They hit first, hit faster and placed the ball with such precision that the scoring was almost all one way. Despite some rallies by the Tipperary team in the second half the Déise boys played with a coolness and self-possession that never left the issue in doubt. Tom Keith quoted the comment of an elderly Franciscan priest who was in Thurles that day and who had followed the game of hurling all his life. The Friar turned to his companion as the final whistle blew and said, 'You can take me home now, I have seen hurling played like I never thought I would in my lifetime.'¹²³

The win by the minor team was undoubtedly very encouraging to the senior team as it took the field. The senior match was an epic encounter with all the passion of the greatest of Munster finals. Most people regarded the outcome as a foregone conclusion for the Cork men. After all, in 1947 hadn't Cork played the greatest-ever All-Ireland against Kilkenny, only losing in the last minute to what Jack Lynch described as 'the usual point' and hadn't they won five of the previous six All-Ireland finals? But Waterford hurled as if they were the champions and had Cork on the back foot from the start. The *Dungarvan Leader* began its report:

> Someone suggested to me that I should caption [this] story with the title 'Waterford gives Cork a Keaning' and I was tickled by it. ... John Keane at centre forward was the old maestro of the game and whenever he got the ball and it was very, very, often, he proved a headache for the Cork defence. He engineered many grand openings to leave his wing men

---

122 In the eighteen years between 1945 and 1962 Tipperary won fifteen Munster minor hurling titles

123 Keith, Tom, *The colours blue & white* (Coiste chontae Phort Láirge CLG, Port Láirge, 1998), p.124

through and scored some decisive points himself at crucial moments.[124]

The centre-field pair of Eddie Carew and Johnny O'Connor subdued the Cork midfield pair, Christy Ring and Bernie Murphy, and laid the foundation for Waterford's stunning victory. O'Connor played so well on Ring that he made it necessary for the Cork mentors to switch Ring to the forwards late in the game. The *Irish Independent* claimed that the midfielders' efforts might well have been in vain without the splendid support of Jim Ware, Vin Baston and John Keane. Writing of John the reporter commented, 'Invariably the mainspring of the attack J. Keane was once again the main danger to the Cork defence, and it seemed a strange coincidence that each time the holders seemed likely to go in front Keane added the point which pinned them back again.'[125]

The end of the game proved heart-stopping for the Waterford supporters. Waterford led by five points going into lost time but a defensive blunder let Cork through for a goal. Only two points then separated them and that lead was reduced to the minimum when Willie John Daly scored a point. Then an error by Vin Baston almost cost Waterford the victory. Waterford were awarded a line ball and Baston moved out from centre-back to take it. Jim Barry, the Cork trainer, was immediately on his feet motioning several Cork players to attempt a block. Ring had moved to the position vacated by Baston and he gathered the ball when the sideline cut was deflected. Visions of a replay loomed when Ring started a solo run of about thirty yards until he reached to within forty yards of the Waterford goal and with time to take aim he struck the ball cleanly and high. Time stood still as, spinning through the air, Ring's shot looked good. For a brief moment in time, everything appeared to happen in slow motion and the world seemed to stop spinning on its axis. Waterford players and supporters watched helplessly and in horror

---

124 *Dungarvan Leader*, 7 August 1948
125 *Irish Independent*, 2 August 1948

as the ball rose in what seemed its unerring flight towards the posts, but it drifted to the right and missed by a whisker. Waterford had gained an historic and astonishing victory. Tomás Ó Cinnéide, John's nephew, remembers the long walk back into the square after the game.

> After my father died in 1941 we went to live in the house at Barrack Street. John was still living there and he took a particular interest in me as I was the only boy in my family. John married Auntie May in 1945 but he continued to care for me and he brought me to matches everywhere he could. I have a vivid memory of that 1948 game and of walking back to Thurles from the field with John, who was still in his togs, and the multitudes of people cheering him and clapping him on the back. But the memory that made the greatest impression on me was the sight of his two hands covered in dried blood and his knuckles torn to shreds. It made me realise that hurling was a man's game and that there was a price to be paid for all the cheering and back-slapping.[126]

On the Tuesday following the Munster final, the county board met in Dungarvan and there were calls for specialised training to be initiated in preparation for the All-Ireland semi-final. A motion to that effect was proposed but, thankfully, wiser heads prevailed and it was decided that no specialised training would be sanctioned for the county team and the motion was defeated – surely someone had remembered the disastrous, and failed, experiment in 1938.

The important games came tumbling one on top of the other. One week after that historic hurling double the county faced into its third Munster final of the year, this time in junior football. John and his team-mates travelled to Dromcollogher in county Limerick to take on the home team. With victories over Clare and Cork they had no fear of Limerick who had disposed of a fancied Tipperary team in the semi-final. Their optimism

---

126 Interview with Tomás Ó Cinnéide

was justified when they defeated Limerick and gave Waterford a third Munster title for that year. Two members of the hurling team played in the football game, Tom Curran joining John in the forward line, and both came through the match without any injury. It was an anxious time because the All-Ireland semi-final against Galway was scheduled for the following Sunday. Vin Baston was the only injury worry but it was expected that his injured fingers would have recovered to enable him to take his place at centre-back. Baston had finally been placed there for the Munster final and he had played a great game as had Eddie Carew and Johnny O'Connor at centre field and John at centre-forward. It was in this triangle that Waterford's hopes were centred and in an effort to curb John's attacking play Galway introduced a new centre-half. The *Connacht Tribune* was concerned about the new man and reported:

> Nestor is still somewhat of an unknown quantity in the centre half berth. He is a good sticky player but may need to call on more speed than he has shown in the trials. A defect in this sector could open the way to many Waterford scores. He will be matched against John Keane, a strong skilled player.[127]

The call for Nestor to show more speed when facing John calls up an interesting fact about John. He was now thirty one years old and in his thirteenth year of inter-county competition but he still retained that speed to the ball that was one of his strengths. John believed that possession invariably went to the first man to the ball and he constantly and assiduously practiced his short explosive sprints. The *Tribune* reporter was perceptive in his comments because it was in this vital area that Waterford broke the deadlock that occurred in the first half. It had been a poor game and the issue was in doubt for the first twenty five minutes when Waterford failed to capitalise on their overwhelming outfield superiority and Seanie Duggan in the Galway goal had saved everything thrown at him by the

---

127 *Connacht Tribune*, 14 August 1948

Waterford forwards. The *Cork Examiner* commented that 'It would be difficult to over-emphasise the part which Waterford's veterans, Keane and Moylan, played in their victory. They were at the peak of their form, Keane being too good for Nestor, the Sarsfields hurler.'[128]

Waterford led by only 1-4 to 0-3 with four minutes left in the first half, although aided by the sun and a strong breeze, and were in urgent need of a breakthrough. It was then that John struck, scoring two brilliant goals in the space of two minutes. The first came after a scramble between backs and forwards had culminated in John stealing the ball and calmly flicking the ball past Duggan. The second goal was completely different. Some good combined play between Galvin and Carew gave John a second opening and from twenty-five yards he blasted the ball low and into the corner of the net past a diving goalkeeper. The match was effectively over and despite a short rally by Galway the Waterford men strolled to the final by a margin of seven points. It was an incredible day for Waterford because the minors had demolished Galway in the first game by 8-12 to 3-2. That minor team is still considered to be one of the greatest teams in the history of hurling (if not the all-time greatest) and had now scored twenty goals and twenty three points in three championship games while conceding only three goals and nine points. However, their sternest test, in the shape of Kilkenny, still awaited them.

John had played championship matches for three successive Sundays but his playing commitments were not yet at an end. On the Sunday following the Galway match he was in action again as he lined out for Waterford in the All-Ireland junior football semi final against Dublin. Waterford had the advantage of strong wind and sun in the first half and led by 1-2 to 0-2 at half time, the only goal being scored by John. In the second period, however, Dublin had the conditions in their favour and simply toyed with the opposition before winning on a score of 5-11 to 1-3. The *Irish Independent* remarked that 'Waterford's

---

128 *Cork Examiner*, 16 August 1948

only players of merit were their three All-Ireland Senior Hurling finalists, Keane, Curran and Moylan.'[129]

All-Ireland final

Then it was on to the All-Ireland finals, with the minors playing Kilkenny, and the seniors taking on Dublin. A sensation was caused in the week preceding the game when Mick Hickey was chosen at right half-back. Hickey, the captain of Waterford in 1938, had been suspended for six months in June 1946 for an incident in a club game and had not played for Waterford since then. Indeed it was to be his only game for Waterford that year and his selection threw into focus the irregular way in which the senior hurling team had been selected, for there were strong rumours that the selectors had made some kind of deal with him. But whatever the reason it cannot be denied that Hickey deserved his chance at winning an All-Ireland medal. His pedigree in the GAA was of the best. His father, Martin Hickey, was a member of the American 'Invasion' team of 1888 and Mick maintained that his father was the first man to take a hurley into Carrick-on-Suir. He told Brendan Fullam that his father 'had walked from Carrick to Mooncoin to get a pattern and, having returned, set about making a hurley.'[130] Brendan Fullam also relates an amusing story about Mick and his mother in relation to Mick's penchant for road running as part of his training. Andy Fleming had shown Fullam a scrapbook in which a reporter had recounted the story that Mick had run past his own house during his training and his mother saw him. 'Is that Mickey?' she enquired from a neighbour. The reply was in the affirmative. 'I declare,' replied the good woman. 'Will he ever grow up?'[131] Mick Hickey was known throughout the province as 'the hard man of Munster,' a label that belied his slender physique – he was close to six feet in height but was only ten stones nine pounds in weight. He was a

---

129 *Irish Independent*, 23 August 1948
130 Fullam, *Giants of the ash*, p. 100
131 Fullam, *Giants of the ash*, p. 100

fearsome competitor and his reputation went before him, causing him to be a target for referees. Larry Fanning testified to his toughness and said that while he was a very fair competitor, woe-betide any man who pulled a dirty stroke on him because, as Larry said, 'Hickey would kill you.'[132]

For the first-ever time, plane-loads of supporters arrived in Collinstown airport, Dublin for the big game and no less than six aircraft brought Waterford exiles from the USA in a mass invasion. The city and county were deserted of all but old people and children on All-Ireland Sunday as Waterford came to Dublin. Pat Fanning recalled the occasion.

> All through that morning, all the buses and lorries and everything that was capable of moving were on the road. I don't think there was ever an exodus like it from any county, even though other counties have the population and we're a small county, relatively speaking. You often talk about pulling down the shutters after the last man has left. Certainly, in 1948 the number of people left in Waterford must have been very few. Our minors, incidentally, were based in Naas. The sight of so many Waterford people going through Naas and into Dublin was most extraordinary.[133]

The supporters and the press were confident that Waterford could take both crowns and the two teams were also in a positive frame of mind. The minor game was a classic and at half-time, Waterford, who had played some scintillating hurling, led by 2-7 to 0-1. But in the second half Kilkenny scored four goals and caused many of the Waterford followers to look anxiously at their watches as the game neared its conclusion. The game finished with Waterford still three points ahead, and the minor title had returned to Waterford for the first time since 1929 - before any of the team was even born.

---

132 Interview with Larry Fanning
133 Keane, *Hurling's top 20*, p. 25

*Waterford All Ireland senior hurling champions 1948
(Courtesy of the Keane Family and with the permission of
Independent Newspapers Ltd)*

When the senior team took the field it had the distinction of being the heaviest Waterford team up to that point, averaging twelve stones ten pounds compared to 1938's eleven stones seven pounds. The average height was five feet ten inches opposed to five feet eight inches, and the average age was twenty eight years compared to twenty six years. The age profile suggested that the team would not suffer from any nerves and so it proved because they settled down very quickly and were never headed in the match. Pat'O in the *Irish Times* summed up the reasons why Waterford had won when he wrote, 'Waterford, minors and seniors, rarely dallied with the ball. They hit it as it sped ... it was Waterford's first-time hitting that confounded Dublin's plans ... they usually outpaced a far younger side, and were so accurate in their approach shots that flag-umpires were kept busy.'[134] It had been a comprehensive victory; youth versus experience was the keynote of the clash and experience won the day. In a series of articles on famous All-Ireland finals the *Irish Independent* remarked about the 1948 final:

---

134 *Irish Times*, 7 September 1948

This was a talented Waterford team and while one and all played their part in securing victory none was more brilliant than John Keane, whose artistry on the 40 yard mark left Dublin centre half-back, J. Butler, in a state of bewilderment. Well as Butler played ... he more often than not found Keane that vital split second ahead of him.[135]

Andy Fleming remembered John's display that day when he was asked to recall the 1948 final for Colm Keane of RTÉ:

> John Keane was fantastic. He was put into centre-forward to strengthen the half-forward line. ... He dominated the whole half-forward line against Dublin. He organised all the moves. If he got the ball and couldn't hit it he'd distribute it. He'd pass it out for someone to run onto it. He was able to find loopholes in the Dublin back line.[136]

It is a mark of the really great players that they perform best on the big occasion and John, on that day, epitomised all that was great in hurling for he gave an exhibition of centre forward play. On the Sunday following the match the Gaelic games writer for the *Sunday Dispatch* eulogised John's performance.

> He has got a senior medal: but, what is more, he has been told – by officials, team-mates, supporters, opponents, commentators – that without him there might have been no taking home of the McCarthy championship Cup for the first time. ... John Keane has been chief builder of Waterford's all-conquering fifteen. He has encouraged young players to persevere and practice in the search for his own perfection of ground-hitting, lofting, passing and shooting. He has inspired colleagues to give of their very best all the time. He has brought peak form out of attacking colleagues who benefitted from Keane's craft and experience. ... He is a

---

135 *Irish Independent*, 28 March 1950
136 Keane, *Hurling's top 20*, p. 26

net-conscious centre half-forward – a 31 year-old-wizard whose opportunism, tricks, marksmanship and co-operation with his wingers all combine to bewilder the defence.

In generations to come when there is reference to Waterford's breaking-of-the-ice by taking the GAA's 61st senior hurling championship, praise in plenty will be given to Keane's big part in the 1948 decider. Not alone was he top scorer for the winners on September 5 – he raised five of Waterford's thirteen flags, getting three goals and two points out of the total of 6-7 – but he was the man of the match in other ways also. Sequel was that, when the excitement really blazed up, with the referee blowing for full time and a glorious Waterford win, it was to John Keane that most of the other players and thousands of supporters rushed first – to congratulate him, hug him, kiss him, cry over him, carry him in wild tribute all around Croke Park. ... It was a fitting climax to a decade and a half of sporting endeavour.[137]

John felt a sense of relief when it was all over. His wife, May, had sat in the Hogan Stand wearing on a necklace the All-Ireland junior hurling medal that John had won fourteen years previously. He had told her – without boasting but with every reason for optimism – that he would present her with an All-Ireland senior medal before he retired from inter-county hurling and now that promise would be fulfilled.

John could be forgiven if had relaxed for the rest of the season for surely there must have been a sense of anti-climax after all the heroics he had already performed in that year. But the county championship still had to be completed (Mount Sion wanted back that county title) and there was a match to be played that, given the geographical and other contexts, was almost as important as the All-Ireland final – the Oireachtas tournament semi-final where Kilkenny would be the opponents. Kilkenny people would never accept that any county were the true cham-

---

137 *Sunday Dispatch*, 12 September 1948

pions until that county had defeated their own team.

The match was set for the Gaelic Field almost exactly one month after the All-Ireland final. Never before had a match in Waterford assumed such an importance in the minds of the two rival camps. No match between Waterford and Kilkenny is insignificant, due to the two counties' geographical proximity and to the supporters' ties of work, kinship and marriage. But there was another element added to the age-old rivalry, for the hitherto lowly county of Waterford were now claiming to be Ireland's champions! It is true to say that never before, or since, has such a huge gathering been seen in the Gaelic Field. Seven trains were run to Waterford by the Railway Company and every mode of conveyance, bus, car, traps, bicycle and shanks' mare, was used to swell the crowd. From noon the crowds began their trek to the grounds as the Kilkenny supporters poured across the Suir in their many thousands to add to the huge Waterford throng already ensconced. So large was the attendance that the gates were closed half an hour before the game began and the overflow had to be seated on the grass margin of the field.

Programme for the 1948 All Ireland finals

The teams paraded around the pitch to a mighty roar from the expectant crowd and headed by three bands. Waterford fielded without four of their All-Ireland final team; John Cusack, Mick Hickey, Christy Moylan and Tom Curran while Kilkenny were at full strength. The All-Ireland champions of 1947 had a star-studded team. In defence were Ramie Dowling, Paddy Grace, Diamond Hayden, Mark Marnell, Jimmy Walsh, Jack Mulcahy and Willie Walsh; at centre field were Dowling and Kennedy while the half forward line of Shem Downey, Terry Leahy and Jimmy Langton would have graced any team in Ireland and Kilkenny men were at a loss to explain their defeat by Laois in the championship. It was an enthralling game featuring many thrilling passages of hurling and despite the exceptionally keen rivalry between the two counties the players entered into the spirit of the game with exemplary sportsmanship without one incident to blemish a great occasion. The opening half was very keenly contested and Waterford led by a solitary point at half time 1-4 to 0-6. At the start of the second half Waterford began to get the upper hand and with the teams level at half way, Ned Daly scored a goal that sent the crowds into ecstasy. That score was quickly followed by two points and Waterford led by five with only ten minutes left. Kilkenny tried valiantly but Waterford were now in control all over the field and won eventually by three points on a score of 2-6 to 0-9. Dublin won the final, however, reversing the result of the All-Ireland final.

The following letter appeared in the Waterford News of 10 September 1948
By kind permission of the Waterford News & Star

To the Editor,
"Waterford News."
8th Sept., 1948.

Dear Sir,—John Keane! What glorious memories are conjured up by the mention of that famous name. From minor days, through inter-provincial college finals, junior inter-county, and then in 1935 while still in his 'teens he came to grace our senior inter-county teams. His wonderful record in inter-county and Railway Cup games speaks for itself; and now, 1948, he has crowned all with achievements which will be spoken of in Waterford whenever and wherever hurlers and hurling followers meet.

How often has the question been asked:—"Who was the greatest hurler of all time," and how varied the answers given? We have listened to the glories of Eudie Coughlan, Christy Ring, Mick Mackey, Lory Meagher, "Builder" Walsh, Bob Mockler, Paddy Phelan, Mick D'Arcy, Matt Gargan, and other giants of the past, but can we in Waterford not be proud of our own John Keane and put him on that pedestal? Has he not proved himself the most versatile of them all—the greatest all-round player the game has known. Full-back, wing back, centre and wing-half back, centre-field and centre-forward, they come all the same to John—a master in his craft.

Let us hope that his inspiration and leadership will remain with our teams for many years to come for John has remained unspoiled in all his triumphs—surely a king among hurling kings!

"OLD HURLER".

Chapter eleven
Post-1948

Retirement from inter-county competition was now clearly on John's mind. He had achieved a lifetime ambition in winning that senior All-Ireland medal; he had married in late 1945 (see Part 2) and he now had a young and growing family to occupy his mind. He already was the proud father of two children, Tom (born in 1946) and Margaret (1947), and a third (John) arrived in1949. The family was completed with the births of Gerard in 1953 and Catherine in 1957.

John's family in 1960 - John & May with (L-R) John, Margaret, Tom, Catherine, Gerard (Photo courtesy of the Keane family)

He judged that it was time to move on with his GAA life and to take a more active role in the administrative side of the Association. At the 1949 annual convention of the Waterford county board GAA he contested the position of treasurer. There were seven nominations but five withdrew leaving the issue between John from Mount Sion and Alderman Kenneally from Ballytruckle. The result was an overwhelming victory for John on a vote of one hundred and five to fifty seven for his opponent. John, returning thanks for his election, was accorded prolonged applause by the delegates.[138] His course seemed set for a continuing career in the administrative affairs of both club and county.

He had still not made up his mind about retiring from inter-county hurling but the announcement of the Munster hurling team for the Railway cup semi-final against Leinster decided him to continue for at least another year. John was selected at centre-forward and had also been appointed as captain.[139] Five of his Waterford colleagues had also been selected; Andy Fleming and Jackie Goode at right and left full-back respectively, Vin Baston and Eddie Carew at midfield and Ned Daly at full-forward. In addition Mick Hayes was selected as a substitute. It was a great honour for the county and just reward for their successes in the past year. In a preview of the semi-final the *Irish Independent* recalled Munster's great winning sequences in the competition and remarked 'Another peak period in Munster's successes was from 1937 to 1940, and the only remaining link with that winning run is Waterford's centre-half forward, J. Keane, who played as far back as twelve years ago. The passing of time has meant little to this great player.'[140]

The chosen goalkeeper, Cork's Tom Mulcahy, could not travel due to business reasons and Jim Ware was called to action although he had not been named on the original team. It was just as well for Munster because Ware and some sterling

---

138 *Munster Express*, 4 February 1949
139 *Dungarvan Leader*, 8 January 1949
140 *Irish Independent*, 11 February 1949

defensive work by the full back line kept Munster in the game and it was only when Christy Ring was switched to corner forward that Munster got the two late goals that decided the issue in their favour. John had shown flashes of his best but otherwise had a quiet match. Langton and Ring had been the stars of the match and Munster were decidedly fortunate. Ware kept his place for the final against Connacht and again Munster had to come from behind to win. With only ten minutes to go and Connacht leading by two goals 'Carbery' reported that 'when Jim Barry [the Munster trainer] switched out John Keane of Waterford to the left corner, he won the game for the holders.'[141] The *Connacht Tribune* reported that 'the weakness on the Munster full-forward line was to a great extent eliminated when John Keane was moved to … the left corner. Within a few minutes the positions of the teams as shown on the scoring board underwent a big change,'[142] and the *Irish Independent* wrote that 'the switching of J. Keane to fill the vacant forward position, marked the first signs of a Munster recovery.'[143] The full forward line came into its own having failed dismally until then and a blizzard of goals resulted in just a few minutes. Waterford's Ned Daly scored the first goal which was quickly followed by another goal from John, which levelled the match and another by Daly of Clare. Munster had stolen a match they had deserved to lose.

It was to be John's last appearance in the Railway cup and it was fitting that, after being so long at the heart of Munster's defence, it was he who won the game for Munster in his only appearance in the forward line. He had made nine appearances over twelve years (seven in succession), successfully captaining the team on two of those occasions, and winning seven medals.

John had decided to limit his playing activities during that year and he subsequently made only five appearances for the county compared to twelve in 1948. He was preparing for his

---

141 *Carbery's Annual* (1949-50), p. 38
142 *Connacht Tribune*, 26 March 1949
143 *Irish Independent*, 18 March 1949

retirement and he opted out of a number of inter-county matches so that younger players could be given a chance. He had played in the defeat to Dublin in the opening round of the National League and then Waterford played two games in quick succession as preparation for its first defence of its Munster title. On a brilliantly sunny day two special trains from Waterford and Cork brought the rival supporters to Dungarvan to see the home team comprehensively beat Cork in a challenge. Waterford fielded thirteen of the 1948 championship winning fifteen and played excellently all through the field. The team then journeyed to Belfast where it crushed Antrim with John scoring two goals in a fine performance. This all came to nought however when Limerick surprised the hurling world with a five points defeat of the champions in the Munster championship. It was the Limerick youngsters who fashioned the victory and showed Waterford that hurling is, essentially, a young man's game. John felt that it was time to retire although he hesitated making such an announcement.

In 1950, with Mount Sion beating everyone in sight and John playing so consistently well, he came under tremendous pressure to join the Waterford squad for the 1950 Munster semi-final. He eventually agreed to come back, a fact that was greeted with enthusiasm amongst the Waterford supporters, but the match against Cork was a dreadful affair and even stars like Christy Ring and John failed to shine. The *Irish Independent* summed up the scene: 'Like the weather, the Munster Senior Hurling championship semi-final between Cork and Waterford at Thurles, yesterday, was exceedingly dull and the crowd ... were as apathetic as the players.'[144] Cork won by two points but only due to an incredible save in the last minute by the Cork full-back who seemed to come from nowhere to pluck the ball almost out of the net. That score would have given Waterford a most improbable one point victory.

Early in 1951 John told the Waterford selectors that he had retired from inter-county hurling but he was implored to play

---

144 *Irish Independent*, 26 June 1950

one last Munster championship match and, when he agreed, he was selected at corner-forward for the first round clash with Tipperary. A huge crowd turned up on what was to be his last appearance with the Waterford hurlers and they saw Waterford outplay the All-Ireland champions right through the hour. The Munster crown sat precariously on Tipperary's head for most of the game and Waterford supporters believed that only the absence of Vin Baston prevented Waterford from dethroning the champions. When the Waterford selectors needed a man to get the forwards going they turned to John, who went centre-forward. He scored one point and made several others and it was only the greatness of Tipperary's Jimmy Finn at left half-back that saved Tipperary, who eventually won on a score of 2-10 to 1-10.

John had brought down the curtain on a glorious inter-county career after seventeen successive years as the county's leader. Many years later Pat Fanning reminisced about John and his impact on Waterford teams.

> I'm not exaggerating the situation when I say that in all the critical games in which Waterford was engaged during his period and during my time, he was the man who made the difference. Even in defeat, he was a man who stood out, just as in 1937 the magnificence of him standing there at centre-back and throwing back the hordes of Limerick forwards that bore down on him. These are the pictures and images I have of John Keane. So it was in 1948, also, when he was gone past his zenith, I would say. He was on a down curve but he was still the great man. Of course, his hurling brain stood to him, he was the master of tactics and he was the natural leader of men who responded to his urgings.[145]

---

145 Keane, *Hurling's top 20*, p. 26

Part two

Chapter twelve
Mount Sion

Billy Howlett once said that John Keane *was* Mount Sion, and while there was far more to the club than this one man, the statement rang true for most people. During his schooldays he had been the team's best player and had been a member of the Mount Sion/Éire Óg team that won the county minor title in 1930 when he was only thirteen years old. He was present at that first meeting when the decision was made to start a new club that would bear the school name and he was elected, at age fourteen, to its first committee. On his retirement in 1951, after Mount Sion had won its eighth county senior title he remained the only man who had shared in all those triumphs.

The great Erin's Own team of the late 1920s regarded the Mount Sion school as a nursery for their club and most of their players had attended the school. The school team's guiding genius, Br Malone, was great friends with the Erin's Own captain, Charlie Ware, and constantly exhorted him to start a minor team in the club – but without any success. After the Mount Sion school team's success in winning the 1930 minor hurling championship it was obvious that some people in Erin's Own felt uneasy about the future. Br Malone, their great friend and supporter, had been transferred from Mount Sion and they could not be sure that his successor would feel the same way about the Erin's Own club and might not urge the pupils to continue their association with the club. As a consequence, the Erin's Own club decided at their Annual General Meeting (AGM) in January 1931 to inaugurate a minor team and to devote more than ordinary attention to it.[146]

---

146 *Waterford News*, 31 January 1931

As the 1931 year progressed, it became quite apparent that the Erin's Own club's decision to form a minor club was not being implemented in any shape or form. Consequently a small group of current and former Mount Sion schoolboys gathered in the front parlour of the Mount Sion monastery to discuss whether a new club bearing the name of Mount Sion should be formed to which the present and future minors could progress. The reaction was positive and it was decided to call a public meeting. The *Munster Express* of 18 September 1931 reported:

> A meeting was held at Mount Sion last week for the purpose of forming a junior hurling club and electing a committee. There was a large and enthusiastic attendance, consisting mainly of present and past pupils of Mount Sion Schools, and the following officers were elected: Hon. President, Rev. Bro. Walker; Hon. Vice-Presidents, Rev. Brothers Malone and O'Toole; chairman, Mr. Jos. Duggan; vice-chairman, Mr. J. Kelly [sic; this was Pat Kelly, John's brother-in-law]; treasurer, Mr. Seán Hogan; hon. sec. Mr. S. Hayes. Committee: Messrs. Keane, Walsh and Byrne, with the captain and vice-captain (to be elected).

John had been elected to the committee together with his friends Locky Byrne and John 'Hopper' Walsh. All three were under eighteen years old and John was only fourteen.

The full complement of all those who were present that evening is unknown but we are certain that Br O'Connor, Michael Doyle and Michael Dowling were also present.[147]

Circumstantial evidence would suggest that Jack Flavin was also present – he was an officer (along with Doyle and Dowling) of Éire Óg, the minor/school club, and it seems doubtful that two officers would have attended the meeting but not the third. Little did the members of that group envisage that their club would go on to dominate the Waterford GAA for the next seventy odd years and become one of the most famous clubs in the Associa-

---

147 Interview with Pat Fanning

Very early Mount Sion junior team in 1932. John, age 15 is 2nd from right second row. Also in photo are Pat Kelly, Denis Harte, Martin Bolger, Michael Doyle, Brian Doyle, Paddy Duggan, Paddy Fanning, Bon Ryan and Sonny Wyse who is at extreme right in front row. (Photo courtesy of the Cooney family)

tion. The boys who had gathered together that night had a strong allegiance to the school and to the Brothers who lived there – and they were all dedicated to the game of hurling.

John's Mount Sion minor team lost the 1932 minor championship but won the county championship in 1933 against Dungarvan on a score of 9-3 to 1-0 – giving him, at age sixteen, his second county minor medal. The *Munster Express* reported that the Mount Sion team left no doubt as to their supremacy in minor hurling ranks: 'From the start they monopolised the play and had matters much their own throughout. They led by a substantial margin at half-time and could have made it larger if they had put their best into it.'[148] The Mount Sion junior team had also won the county final against the same opposition on a score of 6-3 to 2-5. Dungarvan would have been closer to the

---

148 *Munster Express*, 26 January 1934

winners but for an imperious display by John at centre-field, the *Munster Express* observing that he 'was instrumental in saving his side on many occasions.'[149] This junior success meant that Mount Sion would play in the senior championship in 1934. John would, therefore, play minor and senior for the club in the coming year.

John was not the only member of the Keane family to achieve success in hurling that year however because his sister Peggy was at midfield as her team St Colmcille's won the Waterford senior camogie title. Later that year, she starred in a great game against Kilkenny in the All-Ireland series, won by a point by Kilkenny who, typically, scored a goal in the last minute. John often remarked to me in later life, 'You know, Peggy was a great hurler. She would have got her place on any Mount Sion team.' High praise indeed! Peggy told me how John got his first full-size hurley. She was almost three years older than John and had started working while John was still at school. A man named Mickey Grant from Sexton Street was selling a full-size hurley but as John couldn't afford to buy it Peggy suggested that she and John should buy it between them which they did. They shared the hurley for a while, she playing camogie and he playing hurling.

The very first senior match that Mount Sion played was in the Gaelic Field on 4 February 1934 against a strong De La Salle side that included many players from other counties who were attending the teachers training college. The result was a win for Mount Sion by 3-6 to 2-3 and a new era in Waterford club hurling had begun.[150] With the club now in senior ranks it sought to test itself against senior opposition, mostly from within the

---

149 *Munster Express*, 27 October 1933
150 *Munster Express*, 9 February 1934. For the record, the following is the list of players that lined out for Mount Sion's first senior hurling match: Mick Parle (Goal); Paddy Fanning; John Keane; 'Dottie' Hogan; J. Buggy (1-0); Paddy Duggan; Johnny O'Hanlon; George Kehoe (Capt.) (0-1); Brian Doyle; Michael Doyle; Connors; Eddie Dowling (1-2); John 'Hopper' Walsh (1-0); Martin Bolger; Paddy Greene (0-3).

county but also from other counties. The city club was ideally placed geographically for such a programme. Mooncoin, Carrickshock and Mullinavat (all regular county final aspirants in Kilkenny) were just across the river in south Kilkenny; Carrick Swan and Carrick Davins were just a little farther away in south Tipperary but still within easy reach. The ultimate objective was, of course, the county senior hurling title which Erin's Own had just won for the seventh successive year. In March Mount Sion played Mooncoin twice in challenge games, losing at home (4-2 to 3-1) and in Mooncoin (5-4 to 3-1). John played in both games and was opposed directly by his good friend Locky Byrne.

Then came John's first senior championship match – he was seventeen years old. As only four teams had affiliated for the Eastern Division senior championship it was decided to run the championship on a league system. Mount Sion had an easy victory over De La Salle, and Erin's Own beat Dunhill; the scene was thus set for the first ever meeting of the two clubs in a senior hurling game. That historic game took place on 23 September 1934 and interest in the game was sky high. Mount Sion, the younger and lighter side, were out to dethrone the champions of the previous seven years. Mount Sion started at a furious pace and led at half time on a score of 1-3 to 0-3 but when the second half started Erin's Own, with the breeze and sun at their backs, mounted some fierce pressure. The Mount Sion defence was magnificent with Hogan, Keane and O'Connor outstanding. Points were exchanged and Mount Sion were still in the lead with just ten minutes to go. The excitement became intense as Erin's Own mounted wave after wave of attacks on the Mount Sion goal. Bon Ryan, the Mount Sion goalkeeper, was injured as Erin's Own scored a goal and thus gained the lead for the first time in the game. With an injured goalkeeper the Mount Sion resistance collapsed and in the last five minutes, Erin's Own found the net three times to leave them winners by 4-8 to 1-6.

In 1935, because of the small number of teams, it was decided to organise two divisional teams, one from the junior clubs in the city and one from the country clubs. Mount Sion beat the city divisional team and Dunhill beat the country team. Mount

Sion then beat Dunhill by 4-0 to 3-2 in a magnificent game. Mount Sion led by 4-0 to 0-0 at half time due mainly to a very strong breeze and the brilliance of 'Dottie' Hogan and John who marshalled a defence that was described as unbeatable. Notwithstanding the twelve point deficit Dunhill resumed their onslaught on the Mount Sion goal during a stirring second half and with just a few minutes to go had reduced the margin to just two points. Mount Sion prevailed by one point and thus set up a clash with Erin's Own in the eastern final.[151] It was early September before the teams met and when they took the field both team were wearing the same blue jerseys, the only difference being that Erin's Own had numbers on the back. After a hurried conference no team would agree to change so the referee decided to carry on. Very little interest was aroused by the clash, many believing the result a foregone conclusion. Heavy rain on the Saturday and a downpour just a before the game made the pitch very heavy, a decided advantage for the stronger Erin's Own team who won by 3-5 to 1-3, but they had to withstand a serious challenge from Mount Sion, a young, speedy and determined fifteen. It was their superior field craft and experience that eventually won through for Erin's Own who later won the county title for the ninth successive year.

First county senior final

Mount Sion had been drawn against Erin's Own in the 1936 senior championship first round match and in a sensational game the champions were beaten for the first time in the championship in ten years. Under the fusillade of attacks that Mount Sion launched against them they were beaten, 4-3 to 2-5, by a combination of skill and determination. John at centre-half back was the star of the Mount Sion team and Frank Penkert played a stylish game for Erin's Own but lacked support. Mount Sion then played and beat Dunhill in the Eastern final

---

151 *Munster Express*, 20 September 1935

but Dunhill objected to the result claiming that Mount Sion had played an illegal player, the man in question being Paddy O'Connor. He was a carpenter who couldn't find work in Waterford and had travelled to Enniscorthy in county Wexford where he gained employment on a building site. Charlie Ware had heard from his trades union contacts that O'Connor had played hurling whilst domiciled there and, judging that it was too late to object to Mount Sion's win over Erin's Own, urged the Dunhill officials to object to the result of their match before it was too late.[152] Dunhill couldn't produce enough proof to be awarded the match but they established a doubt in the minds of the county board and the latter offered Dunhill a replay. Dunhill gambled that they could beat Mount Sion and accepted the replay but lost by a point.

Mount Sion, county champions 1936. The match was subsequently lost on an objection. The nineteen year old John is on the extreme left, back row. (Photo from the Fanning family collection & courtesy of Tom Partridge)

---

152 Interview with Tom 'Gum' Kennedy

Mount Sion had thus qualified for their first county senior hurling final where their opponents would be Tallow, the match being played in Lismore on 27 September 1936. Tallow had been the defeated finalists in four of the previous five years and had a very good team but Mount Sion went into the game as firm favourites, if only by virtue of their victory over Erin's Own. Mount Sion won the final on a score of 2-6 to 1-5 and although the game resulted in one of the fastest and most brilliant exhibitions of high-class hurling seen in Lismore for years, the final score was hardly a true reflection of the nature of the play. Tallow proved to be stubborn opponents but the best team won owing to their greater combination and speed and Mount Sion had achieved its goal, a first county title, in only its third year of senior competition. It was a great achievement and there was great satisfaction at a job well done. The main celebration would come later and preparations for a gala night were put in motion.

At a county board meeting that met in Lismore after the Cork match an objection by Tallow to Mount Sion's win in the county final was heard. The objection covered ten points but the main point concerned the playing of Paddy O'Connor. Mount Sion felt that they were entitled to play O'Connor because the county board's decision on the Dunhill objection clearly implied that O'Connor was a legal player. The chairman appealed to the representatives of Mount Sion and Tallow to retire from the room to consider some means whereby an amicable agreement might be reached between the two clubs and stated that a replay was out of the question. The two clubs returned to say that no agreement had been reached and the chairman then deferred the matter to the next board meeting and requested the named player to appear and give his evidence.

At the end of November the chairman of the county board over-ruled the Tallow objection saying that there was a doubt on the point raised and Mount Sion were confirmed as county champions. Tallow responded by informing the meeting that they were going to appeal to the Munster council. Mount Sion, now officially the county champions, held a victory céilidh in city hall with dancing from 9.00pm until 3.00am. Those celebrations were a little premature, however. Tallow's appeal to the Munster council resulted in that body ruling that the Waterford county board should hear the matter again. At a general meeting of the Mount Sion club it was agreed that the Tallow objection should be left with the county board to decide and that Paddy O'Connor should be asked to attend the relevant county board meeting.[153]

The meeting of the county board was held on Friday evening of the 12 March 1937 at the Gaelic League rooms in Waterford. Those present included Paddy O'Connor, the man at the centre of the storm and Mr. Keogh, secretary of Wexford county board. The latter, who spoke in Irish, said he recognised Paddy O'Connor as a man who had played with Wexford in an inter-county game and with the Rapparees club of Enniscorthy. Paddy Duggan, one of the Mount Sion club representatives then spoke and said that the club would accept whatever suspension was imposed on it. The chairman asked if the case was admitted as far as O'Connor was concerned and Duggan replied in the affirmative. O'Connor then left the room with the permission of the chairman but as he was leaving he made a personal remark about Mr Keogh. Keogh reacted by claiming that the remark was a gross insult which brought the Association into disrepute. The chairman said that he had heard only part of O'Connor's statement but that what he heard was a very improper remark and he asked one of the Mount Sion delegates to go after O'Connor and to bring him back to the meeting. Paddy Duggan obeyed the chairman's orders and when he returned after about five minutes absence he stated that he conveyed the chairman's request to O'Connor whose reply was that he had no time to return. It was proposed that O'Connor be suspended until he apologised in writing to the board and Mr. Keogh. The

---

153 Mount Sion club minutes, 23 January 1937

end result was that Tallow's objection was upheld and they were declared county champions for 1936.

Br O'Connor

A very tense and acrimonious meeting of the Mount Sion club was held in the week following the County Board decision and a long and bitter discussion ensued about what action the club should take following on the suspension of Paddy O'Connor and the loss of the county title. There were many voices advocating that the club the club should disband in protest at the decision; more argued that the club should continue the fight in the press and elsewhere but Br O'Connor brought an incipient rebellion within the club to an abrupt end when he spoke tersely on the matter and with barely controlled emotion added that no useful purpose would be served by Press reports or letters.[154]

The contentious bubble was burst and a meeting that had at one time threatened to split the club ended with the decision that no further action be taken. The irony of the whole situation was that Paddy O'Connor, the man whose actions could have destroyed the club, was the club's most popular member.

The 1937 county championships had begun with Portlaw defeating Erin's Own and Mount Sion annihilating Dunhill. The latter match was described as one of the worst for violence that had been seen for years. The referee told a subsequent Eastern board meeting that he had seen a deliberate attack being made with hurleys by two Dunhill players on Paddy Greene, the Mount Sion forward. A delegate said that it was one of the most disgraceful thing he had seen for a long time and the Mount

---

154   Mount Sion club minutes, 18 March 1937

Sion delegate told the meeting that Greene had lost two weeks work with the consequent loss of wages and doctor's bills. The Mount Sion club asked the board to compensate Greene for his loss but, unbelievably, no action was taken. The way was clear for the Eastern final where Portlaw shocked Mount Sion in a magnificent match that reached inter-county standard at times and Portlaw eventually won the county title.

The last games of the local season saw two very competitive games in a tournament at Portlaw involving the Waterford teams Portlaw, Mount Sion and Erin's Own and Mooncoin from Kilkenny. Tournaments are unknown in the modern game but in their hey-day they were second only to the local and provincial championships. They were usually organised to benefit some local cause and had lucrative prizes. Some tournaments offered gold watches (always welcome) but the most favoured of all were those that offered suit-lengths for the winners. Very few men had a really good suit and if they had, it was usually reserved for Mass on Sunday morning and was then put away until the following week. Another favoured tournament was one that offered hurleys to the winner because not many clubs could afford to have an adequate supply and the chance of getting some free hurleys was always an incentive to take part. Furthermore, tournament organisers always invited the home team and three other teams that were usually the champion teams of their respective counties and this encouraged the supporters of those teams to travel, thus swelling the gate money and benefitting the cause for which the tournaments were organised. Thousands attended and one could always rely on at least one band (but usually two or three) to add colour and excitement to the occasion.

Portlaw drew with Mooncoin and Mount Sion beat Erin's Own by one point, 3-2 to 2-4. The latter game was notable for the first appearance of Locky Byrne in the Mount Sion senior team and his selection was the cause of an objection to the referee before the game even started. Charlie Ware (Erin's Own) objected to Byrne and Paddy Greene and claimed that both players were illegal. The ploy (for ploy it was) was rejected by the referee and his decision was later upheld by the county board. The supporters were keyed-up to fever pitch in this contest as there was more at stake than just the trophies. The fact that Mount Sion had broken Erin's Own's long run of successes in the championship and that Erin's Own had turned the tables on Mount Sion in a tournament lent added interest to the third in the series. Mount Sion won the rubber but it was a near thing. Excitement ran high and at one period an encroachment took place. Some scuffles happened between rival supporters at the end of the game and this was to be an unwelcome feature of games between the two clubs for the next decade.

Pat Fanning had this to say about the bitterness that became prevalent between Mount Sion and Erin's Own:

> All that stuff was mainly between the supporters of both clubs. For instance, my first cousin Johnny Fanning was one of Erin's Own's great players. His mother, my aunt Lizzy [Barnes], was an out and out Erin's Own supporter and I'll never forget one day after a Mount Sion/Erin's Own county final when she said to me in exasperation: 'How could anyone expect Erin's Own to win when ye had all the Brothers in Mount Sion down on their knees every night saying rosary's and novenas for ye?'[155]

John blamed all the trouble on the provision of sideline seats that enabled spectators to have easy access to the pitch both during and after a match.[156] He believed that if players were left alone there would be very little trouble because players respected each other and very few went out to deliberately injure their opponents. Most of the players from both clubs were from 'Up the roads' and there were great friendships between some of the players. They drank together in the local pubs, some were work friends, and almost all were past pupils of Mount Sion school

---

155 Interview with Pat Fanning
156 Undated *Sunday Press* clipping from the Goode family scrapbooks, courtesy of Eoin Fanning

where they would have sat side by side. However, for about a week before a match the call of 'no fraternisation' would go out from both clubs. It was time for the serious business.

But whilst the bitterness was mainly between rival supporters there was also an edginess between officials of both clubs and at the AGM of the Mount Sion club a motion was passed that the secretary should write to the eastern and county boards protesting against the action of some members of the Erin's Own club who were approaching playing members of Mount Sion asking them to join their rivals. The real prize being sought, of course, was John.

Another year had passed and that elusive title for Mount Sion was no nearer.

Chapter thirteen
Three in a row

The Mount Sion AGM at the end of 1937 had elected John as vice-captain of the senior hurling team and made the winning of the 1938 senior hurling title its absolute priority. All players were exhorted to turn up for training in the Gaelic Field at 6.45pm on Monday, Wednesday and Friday of each week. Furthermore, Pat Kelly (John's brother-in-law) was appointed as team manager with the responsibility of liaising with the club's senior hurlers to ensure that all reported regularly for training. To have the team ready for the championship clash with Tallow the club had set out on a series of challenge and tournament matches against all-comers and over the previous five months had remained undefeated against Mooncoin, Carrigtohill, Erin's Own and Carrick Swan.

Although Mount Sion were regarded as hot favourites against Tallow they had to scramble for their lives in a tense struggle in atrocious conditions in Dungarvan. They led at half time on a score of 3-2 to 2-2 but facing a gale and driving rain in the second half they were quickly in arrears and with five minutes to go were five points in arrears. A point for Mount Sion was followed by a brilliant goal from Locky Byrne and then in the dying moments Paddy O'Connor sailed right round the Tallow defence and sent the leather into the right-hand corner of the net for a sensational victory. After the incident in 1936 that had given Tallow the county title it was poetic justice that it was O'Connor who scored the winner. But the game was a 'wake-up call' for Mount Sion and though their county title aspirations were still alive they knew that sterner tasks lay ahead. Pat Fanning recalled an amusing story about that match.

The game in Dungarvan was one of the toughest we ever played. Tallow had a great team that challenged every year for the county title. We led at half-time but the weather was terrible – a gale force wind and lashing rain – and we had to face both in the second half. We went behind fairly quickly and with the weather the way it was, our prospects didn't look good. We were all very young and few of us had money to spare. Whatever we had was being minded by Jim Meara who looked after the clothes, hurleys and, on match days, the money. Jim was running up and down the sideline urging on Mount Sion and, with that great confidence he had in the Mount Sion team, was fairly vocal about what he regarded as our inevitable victory. This was too much for the Tallow supporters so they challenged Jim to put his money where his mouth was. 'Right' says Jim, 'I'll take all your bets.' And he did – with everyone else's money.[157]

In the semi-finals Erin's Own had defeated Dungarvan after three memorable games and Mount Sion had easily beaten P. H. Pearse, so the final between the 'big two' was eagerly awaited. Mount Sion had been undefeated in all competitions and against all comers during 1938 but Erin's Own were still a very good team and were determined to retain the title that it had owned between 1927 and 1935. It was a unique occasion – the first county final between the two great clubs – and the supporters were in a frenzy of excitement all over the Christmas and New Year periods. Interest in the final spread far beyond the county and a bumper crowd was expected. The game was to take place in the Gaelic Field, a home venue for both clubs for they both trained at the ground and sometimes shared the pitch. Larry Fanning told me about that time and how the tension between both clubs manifested itself in training.

> Both teams used the pitch lengthways, Mount Sion using the Presentation Convent side while Erin's Own trained on the

---

157 Interview with Pat Fanning

Griffith Place side. Hurling balls were very scarce and both clubs would have had only three or four at any given time. If any player hit a ball astray into the other team's territory he would have to wait until someone hit it back to him. He would never cross over to retrieve the sliotar. That would only be asking for trouble. Only John could do that, unchallenged.[158]

At the club's AGM the chairman, Jack Flavin, had appealed to all the senior hurlers 'to prepare assiduously for the county final on 8 January, stressing the fact that they were up against a well trained team in Erin's Own and one which would prove worthy opposition to the best.'[159] When Mount Sion announced its team it was noticed that Pat Fanning was placed at right corner forward in direct opposition to his first cousin, Johnny Fanning. Two sections of Erin's Own supporters taunted Pat in the days before the game. One lot said that the only reason he was pitted against his cousin was because he knew that Johnny wouldn't hit him while the other group said that Johnny would take the head off him. As it turned out Pat was indeed hit, but not by his cousin. On match-day and before a very big crowd the backs went to their positions and the centre-fielders and forwards lined up in the middle of the field for the throw-in. Then there occurred an incident that was recalled many years later by Tom Humphries of the *Irish Times* who wrote, 'The 1938 county final is remembered for an early intervention on Locky Byrne's part. His county team-mate Charlie Ware, playing full back for the legendary Erin's Own team of the time, announced his presence in time-honoured, physical fashion. Locky Byrne stepped in and issued an injunction.'[160]

The incident happened right at the start of the match when the ball was whipped down towards the Erin's Own goal and the Mount Sion forwards ran to take up their positions. Charlie Ware pulled across Pat Fanning's shins by way of an introduction. Locky

---

158 Interview with Larry Fanning
159 Mount Sion club minutes, 24 November 1938
160 *Irish Times*, 10 August 2002

Byrne, running behind Pat to take up his left half forward position, saw the incident and, continuing his run, did exactly to Ware what Ware had just done to Fanning. Then pointing his hurley at Ware, his former club team-mate, he said 'Now, Charlie, leave the young fellow alone. If you want to play the game that way, just try it on me.'[161] It was a tempestuous start and it set the tone for the rest of the game. The marking was very tight and it took a firm referee to control the players. Just before the interval when tempers threatened to spill over into dangerous play the referee, Declan Goode, sent Mick Gallagher (Mount Sion) and Nicky Fardy (Erin's Own) to the sideline. At half-time Mount Sion led by two points but Erin's Own would have the advantage of a strong breeze after the interval and within twelve minutes they had levelled the scores. Then, in a dramatic surge, Mount Sion, out-hurling their opponents, scored three goals in quick succession per Paddy Duggan, Locky Byrne and Pat Fanning. It looked as they would go on to win easily but the Erin's Own veterans rallied and in a magnificent final ten minutes they scored two goals and a point as they laid siege to the Mount Sion goal. It was an heroic effort but when time ran out Mount Sion had won its first county senior title by two points. This time, however, it would not be taken away from them in the committee room.[162]

The club was dealt a bad blow early in 1939 with the news that Paddy Duggan, the secretary, full-back and captain, was being transferred by his employers, the Prudential Assurance Company, to its Swords branch in Dublin. As he could not travel up and down from Dublin to Waterford on a regular basis he received a transfer to the Faughs hurling club in Dublin. He was a big loss to Mount Sion both on and off the field. As John had been vice-captain of the senior hurling team he now

---

161 Interview with Pat Fanning
162 The Mount Sion team on the day was: Paddy Dowling (Goal), Dick Breen, Paddy Duggan (Capt), Paddy O'Connor, Mick Gallagher, John Keane, John 'Hopper' Walsh, Brian Doyle, Wattie Morrissey, Bill Lynch, Frank Minogue, Locky Byrne, Pat Fanning, Larry Duggan, Paddy Greene.

Mount Sion, County champions 1938-40.
Back Row: J.Flynn, S.Murphy, M.Simpson, J.Donnelly, D. Breen, B.Lynch, P.Greene, N.Cooke, J.Hanlon, M.Doyle, J.Meara.
Second Row: S.McGabhann, J.Flavin, M.Gallagher, L.Duggan, B.Doyle, Br Kenneally, P.O'Connor, A.McNamara, L.Byrne, M.Dowling, D.Harte.
Front Row: P.Dowling, J.Walsh, J.Keane, P.Duggan, F.Minogue, W.Morrissey, P.Fanning. The young boy is Tommy Morrissey.

stepped in as captain, a position he retained for the next twelve years. In that era most team captains of GAA clubs were mere ciphers and had no authority or special functions on the field and the captaincy was regarded as a reward for his club winning his county's championship and had no other significance. Most captains were also men of mature years so Mount Sion was breaking the mould with the selection of John as captain. His youth could have been a handicap amongst the older players but that was overcome by the magnificence of his hurling for he was quite clearly Mount Sion's greatest player and, indeed, one of the best hurlers in the country. It had been recognised almost from the start of his career that he was a born leader, a man who could get others to willingly follow him. He had a presence about him that made others look up to him and he had all the attributes that made others defer to his will. He inspired by example, he was honest in everything he did, and he gave credit where credit was due. He also had great integrity and he could be trusted implicitly because he never deviated from his strong inner values and, to cap it all, he had a warm and winning personality.

His first game as captain was in a convincing win over P. H. Pearse in the senior hurling championship and this was quickly followed by the county semi-final against Dungarvan where he played at full-back in the absence of Paddy Duggan. The Mount Sion team pulverised its opponent 9-3 to 1-2 in a game that was played in terrible conditions. There were many injuries: Hopper Walsh had his collar-bone broken and Locky Byrne had several stitches inserted in his lip. This game became notable for what happened to Locky subsequently. After about ten minutes of the second half he suffered the injuries to his lip when he was struck in the face and had to retire. His father 'Dashy' had a fixation about players not keeping their clothes dry on wet days and he was forever gathering up clothes that had been thrown on the ground. He was also noted for admonishing players who ignored his pleas to keep themselves dry. It was unfortunate for Locky that the aforesaid 'Dashy' was, unusually, not present that day in Portlaw for when Locky came off the field he sat down in his wet clothes and that was the beginning of the end for him. It was as a result of his actions that day that he contracted the tuberculosis that eventually killed him at the age of only twenty seven years.

As Erin's Own had beaten St Stephen's in the second semifinal of the county championship the way was now cleared for a game that everyone wanted to see – a repeat of the 1938 county final. A huge and very vociferous crowd were present to see the match on a perfect day for hurling and the game did not disappoint, for it had everything that such a passionate crowd expected – brilliant hurling, great scores, tight marking, two men sent off, crowd trouble, great champions and gallant losers. Mount Sion were dominant in the first half when they were aided by a strong wind but they had to withstand sustained pressure from Erin's Own in the second period and but for the marvellous displays by Paddy O'Connor and John they might have relinquished their title. The star of the Erin's Own team was Jim Ware in goal who made saves in the first half that bounded on the miraculous when he almost single-handedly defied the speedy Mount Sion forwards of whom Paddy Greene (1-2), Larry Duggan (1-0), Brian Doyle (0-1) and Locky Byrne (0-1) were the best. Mount Sion had won its second senior title on a score of 2-4 to 2-2.

Exactly one week later the team lost its two year unbeaten record when going down to the Kilkenny finalists Carrickshock who thus gained revenge for Mount Sion's win just over a year previously. The south Kilkenny team were exceptional and in the nine year period between 1938 and 1946 they contested all nine Kilkenny county finals winning five, including four in a row – a feat unequalled in Kilkenny hurling until 2009. In that period both teams played each other five times with Mount Sion winning three, Carrickshock one, with one drawn. Mount Sion had a great relationship, and rivalry, with its great Kilkenny rivals not least because of John's lifetime friendship with Carrickshock's captain, Jimmy Walsh. Walsh was one of John's best friends and the depth of friendship between the two is illustrated in a gesture by Walsh when Waterford reached the All-Ireland final in 1948. He travelled to Waterford and, as a token of the esteem in which he held John, presented him with the hurley that he had used in the 1939 All-Ireland final.[163]

At the Mount Sion AGM on 22 November 1939 John was re-elected as the senior hurling team captain with Locky Byrne as vice-captain. Locky had been unwell but no one suspected that his condition would deteriorate so quickly and that he would never again be seen on the hurling field. He had played his last-ever game in a senior hurling tournament final on 12 November 1939, in which Mount Sion had a facile win over Erin's Own during which he scored two goals in the 3-2 to 0-3 win. Over the next year, however, his health grew steadily worse. Pat Fanning told me of meeting Locky, sometime in late 1940, on Waterford's Parnell Street when Locky was leaving a doctor's

---

163 *Munster Express*, 10 September 1948

office. Locky had stopped to talk with Pat and Pat recalled over sixty years later the shock he experienced at seeing his friend's appearance. Locky's condition had deteriorated so quickly that Pat remarked that he had seen 'death on his face.'

Locky left an abiding influence on the Mount Sion club He had always been keen to establish a youth policy for Mount Sion and he wanted young fellows to make their way on to the senior teams as quickly as possible. He had no time at all for established stars who stayed beyond their time, and who thus, however inadvertently, blocked the way for aspiring youngsters. Once upon a time he was discussing the problem with Mick Gallagher and said, 'Mick, we won't overstay our welcome; we'll know when to pull out and leave the field to the young lads.' Locky's thinking became Mount Sion policy and on to each county championship fifteen came one, two, or three minors of that particular year to proclaim the fact that youth would not be denied. That was his legacy to Mount Sion.

The big news of the year had nothing to do with the GAA although it was to have enormous repercussions for the Association. On the day of the All-Ireland hurling final the British Prime Minister announced that his country was now at war with Germany. The Second World War had started and normal life changed forever. Ten days after the war began the Government announced on Radio Éireann that petrol would be rationed from the following Saturday.[164] This measure was but the start of the privations that the general public would have to endure and it would also have a massive effect on how the GAA conducted its affairs for the next six years.

With Mount Sion striving in 1940 to take its third title in succession the rivalry with Erin's Own became very intense. Every match between the two city clubs was ratcheting-up the tension another notch but John's popularity transcended club loyalties and even club tribalism. There was no greater rivalry than that which existed between Erin's Own, the old champions, and Mount Sion, the newcomers who threatened to take over where

---

164 *Munster Express*, 15 September 1939

the former had left off. Here was tribalism at its worst: both sets of followers were cut from the same cloth; both came from the same area, even from the same families. It was like a miniature civil war, yet John had many admirers and friends among what were apparent enemies. His best friends amongst the Erin's Own players were Sonny Wyse and Fad Browne (grandfather of the current Waterford and Mount Sion player Tony Browne), a man admired greatly by John as a hurler and as a man. John described him as an honest, decent, gentleman and a wonderful hurler. Sonny Wyse had captained the Mount Sion school team and was one of John's original heroes. He was the supreme stylist, of whom Martin Kennedy of Tipperary once said: 'The finest corner forward who ever played beside me.'[165]

However, whilst players respected each other it was a different matter altogether with supporters – yet John won them over too. James Grant, subsequently the long-time secretary of the Waterford county board, illustrates the latter very well.

> Even at a tender age affiliations ran high, and I must proclaim that although a Mount Sion CBS pupil, my loyalty at that time rested with Erin's Own, chiefly because my father was for many years chairman of that great club. But as far as the playing field was concerned, none could supplant the adolescent worship yours truly held for John Keane. He was to me the absolute perfection when it came to hurling; a master tactician, a skilful ball player, a leader of men, and above everything else a sportsman to his very fingertips. Little did I imagine, during my school-going days, that I would have the privilege of playing along side the great John Keane in a championship match for Mount Sion, and I can vividly recall one particular occasion in an important senior football match versus Kill at Walsh Park, when my task was to take on the illustrious Tom McGrath (RIP) in the middle of the field. Everyone [who] was entitled to [do so], had his say in the dressing room beforehand, but John Keane in his own inimi-

---

165 *An Cúl* (vol. 4, no. 2, Aibreán 1973), p. 13

table style took this then teen-ager aside, and told him how to go about his business, emphasising ... the exemplary qualities of his opponent, and how imperative it was to be first to the ball at all times. Whether I succeeded in putting such words of wisdom into effect remains a matter of conjecture, at any event Mount Sion duly won the game and went on to reach yet another county final.[166]

Mount Sion had qualified for the county championship senior hurling semi-final where the opponents would again be Erin's Own. As had become usual by now when those rivals were pitted against each other the city was ablaze with wild rumours and speculation in the week leading up to the match. Jim O'Meara, newly recruited to the Mount Sion club, recalled that time. He had played Dr Harty cup hurling with the school and when he graduated from there he joined Ferrybank, his local club, and played with them for a number of years. However, the siren call of his *alma mater* was still ringing in his ears and he joined the Mount Sion club at the end of 1939. It was to be the first time that Jim would play for Mount Sion against Erin's Own and the tension was palpable. He knew, of course, about the great rivalry that had built up between the two clubs over the previous few years, but because he lived and worked across the river in Ferrybank he really had no idea of the extent of the passions that were aroused between the rival supporters. Andy Fleming and Jim got an instruction from the club that they were not to go directly to the hurling field on the Sunday of the match but were to assemble at the Mount Sion schools instead.

> I remember thinking at the time that this was rather strange. On arrival at the school we heard a story that was extraordinary, to me at least. Relations between supporters had reached such a pitch that some people had threatened, apparently, to assault individual Mount Sion players as they made their way to the ground so, as a precaution, it had been decided that we would march as a

---

166 *Portláirge '84*, (Waterford, 1984), p.7

team to the Gaelic Field. So there we were, on the day of a county semi-final, marching up Barrack Street and Slievekeale with hurleys at the ready in case we were attacked. Everything worked out all right in the end, but it was an extraordinary thing.[167]

It was only hurling that could arouse such controversy and passion. The famous Dónal Foley, the *Irish Times* columnist, was a native of Ferrybank. A reporter for the *Irish Examiner* subsequently wrote about how important the game had been to Foley and his friends.

> Sporting options were limited ... [at] the time, he [Foley] remembered. They were aware of the professional soccer team in Waterford while rugby they regarded as a 'game for snobs played by bank clerks,' and Gaelic football 'a bastard version of mixed up soccer and rugby.' One game stood out. Other sports were merely games or pastimes. Hurling was different, and a way of life.[168]

The semi-final passed off without incident and Mount Sion won handily enough by five points, although, as usual, Erin's Own put in a strong finish. Mount Sion had qualified for another county final where the opponents would be Dungarvan, who had a very good, young team. Mount Sion, having defeated the old enemy, were complacent and the match was a draw. With Mount Sion three points down it was John who came to his team's rescue when he went to centre-forward and changed the whole direction of the game. After he had scored a great goal the game underwent a transformation and it was the champions who took control, swarming around the Dungarvan goal in the fruitless search for a winning score. They would have to fight all over again.

At the Mount Sion AGM that followed it was stressed that the team would have to ready for the Dungarvan challenge and the

---

167 Interview with Jim O'Meara
168 *Irish Examiner*, 5 September 2008

team was encouraged to train assiduously for the replay. To that end a new and more vigorous training schedule was announced for weekdays and Sunday mornings in the Gaelic Field. John was confirmed as the senior hurling captain with Paddy Duggan (who had returned to Waterford) replacing Locky Byrne as vice-captain. A tribute was paid to Locky for the help given by him to the club in the past and the meeting also expressed the hope that he would soon recover from his illness.[169] It was clear that Locky's illness was serious and that he was not expected to return to the team for a long time.

In the county final replay the Mount Sion juggernaut duly flattened the challengers by more than double scores. Leading at half-time by three goals and two points they emerged well-deserved victors by three goals and three points. The *Waterford News* reported that 'John Keane was the best man of the thirty, playing a wonderful game and well supported by Dowling and Fleming he made the task of the full-back line an easy one and plied the forward line incessantly during the hour.'[170] Mount Sion had completed its first three-in-a-row of county titles and it seemed that the club would continue to dominate for a long time to come. This was not to be, however, for both the war and pressures within the club would seriously threaten its future. John would play a central role in this dark period as will be seen in the next chapter.

---

169 Mount Sion club minutes, 30 October 1940
170 *Waterford News*, 1 November 1940

CHAPTER FOURTEEN
JOHN RESIGNS

Locky Byrne died in a Dublin nursing home on Saturday, 18 January 1941 at the age of twenty seven years. The suddenness of his death caught everyone by surprise, although he had been seriously ill for several months. His body was removed to Waterford on the Saturday night and despite the drenching downpour many hundreds of people had assembled at the Waterford North railway station to meet the remains. Locky's Mount Sion team-mates John Keane (club captain), Paddy Duggan, Bunny Doyle, Michael Dowling, Paddy O'Connor and Mick Gallagher carried the coffin to the waiting hearse and then formed a guard of honour as the hearse made its way to the Chapel-of-Ease in Ferrybank through the many hundreds more who stood bareheaded in the torrential rain as they lined the route. On Monday a huge crowd, representative of Waterford city and county and the neighbouring counties of Kilkenny, Wexford and Tipperary, attended the burial as a pitiless rain, following a storm of snow and sleet, swept the graveyard. Once again the members of the Mount Sion club acted as guard of honour but this time they were joined by a like number from the Mooncoin club. The enormous crowd waited until the last shovelful of earth had been placed on the grave and then knelt and prayed in tribute to a man who had been one of the most popular players in the history of the game. Locky's Mount Sion colleague, Jim O'Meara, told me that as the cortege made its way to the grave he overheard Locky's father, 'Dashy' Byrne, say to a friend 'I thought he was made of steel.' For the Mount Sion club Locky's death was a hammer-blow and it presaged a year that saw the club go steadily downhill until it was rocked by a sensation involving John at the club's AGM in November 1941.

A major tournament had been organized for the Gaelic Field on 23 March; Mount Sion were set to play against Mullinavat (defeated Kilkenny finalists in 1940) and Eire Óg were pitted against their great Kilkenny rivals, Carrickshock. Mount Sion were defeated by one point, only its second defeat against all-comers since July 1937 but the main talking point was that three players, Mick Gallagher, Paddy Greene and Paddy Dowling had refused to play in the match. This was a serious breach of club discipline and the dispute dragged on without any resolution for a full two months. Eventually all three players gave an undertaking to abide by majority rule, thus defusing the situation, but severe damage had been done to the unity of the club and it would subsequently pay a heavy price for the episode.

Amidst all this trouble hurling continued as best it could, given the restrictions of war-time. John was reported to have played only ten games in 1941 compared with twenty-two in 1940 and twenty-eight in 1939. The few local games that were played saw attendances swell enormously, however, and the championships benefited financially. After Erin's Own had defeated St Stephen's they faced Mount Sion in the Eastern Final. As was usual by now the city was ablaze with speculation about the upcoming match and passions ran high. It was felt that the old champions had the capability to beat Mount Sion but the match turned out to be a damp squib. In front of a huge crowd Mount Sion swamped their great rivals and were it not for the large tally of wides in the first half they would have had the game finished at half-time, the *Waterford News* reporting that 'The mainstay of Mount Sion's defence rests in the half line, when Keane, Fleming and Dowling broke up everything that came their way and, at centre-field, Mount Sion, in O'Meara and Morrissey, were on top all through.' At full-time the champions had won by twelve points and it looked as if there was no one to stop them from taking their fourth title in a row. But there was disunity in the ranks.

A drinking culture had developed amongst some of the younger players and this problem was very much exercising the minds of the club officials. John was a member of that drinking group although he was never a heavy drinker. He was a very gregarious and sociable man and there was nothing he liked better than to sit down in a pub after a match with his colleagues (and some opponents if they were so inclined) and have a drink and a smoke. He gave up drink in 1943 and became a 'Pioneer,' a member of the Pioneer Total Abstinence Association (PTAA), but he remained a heavy smoker of cigarettes all his life and that habit undoubtedly contributed to his early death from athero-sclerosis. In that period it was extremely rare to find a man who didn't drink and smoke and the culture of the time made it almost *de rigueur* to do so – it was almost expected that one began smoking and drinking simultaneously with the wearing of long-pants.

Club officials were becoming alarmed because the drinking was bringing problems of indiscipline. Their worst fears were confirmed after a game in Portlaw when the drinking faction became unruly on the bus and, after some heated words were exchanged, a row broke out in which one of the officials was assaulted by a player. The offending player was expelled by the club and, although the vote for his expulsion was unanimous, it left a residue of resentment that took a long time to dissipate. John was clearly upset because, although he was a member of the committee that had expelled the player, he was also a great friend, drinking pal and work-mate of the offender. The club became divided and indiscipline crept in as the results in 1941 and 1942 would subsequently confirm.

Mount Sion had played just one championship game but in this truncated year it was sufficient to put the club into another county final where the opponents would be Dungarvan, the defeated finalists of 1940. Mount Sion were a surprisingly ill-prepared team for the county final. The attendance of the senior hurling panel at training sessions had been poor; there was an apathy amongst the members that was hard to explain and cliques were starting to develop amongst the club officers. It should have been no surprise, therefore, when Mount Sion lost their crown to Dungarvan, although the three-time champions were warm favourites after their easy victory over Erin's Own.

The result was unexpected, nevertheless, although Dungarvan had an excellent young team and had beaten Portlaw in the semi-final after a good game. The final never reached a high standard of hurling due to the close marking and rough play which were the order of the day. Stoppages due to injuries were frequent and the game lasted nearly two hours. The year had been one that left the club dispirited and in disarray but the events of the AGM provided a sensation that rocked it to its very foundation.

There had been only three general meetings of the club in that year and attendance of members had been only fair, but a large crowd of junior and minor players attended the AGM on 2 November. The attendance of the senior players, however, left a lot to be desired. The meeting began in the usual way when the secretary rose to give his review of the past year. Referring to the problems within the club he issued a dire warning to the club members that if the 'dry-rot' was allowed to continue unchecked it would, in a short time, seriously threaten the club's existence. Unknown to the members present, there was a piece of paper lying on the table in front of him that contained a shock of seismic proportions for the club and which had the potential to tear its heart out. After the treasurer's report had been debated and adopted a discussion ensued that only emphasised the problems with the senior team. It was unanimously decided that the chairman and the secretary should call on all members of the senior team that were absent from the meeting and ask if they would be agreeable to play in all the club's future engagements. If anyone replied in the negative then he would be regarded as not being on the club's playing strength. It was clear that the problems in the club ran deep.

When the secretary rose again he announced that he had received from the club captain, John Keane, a letter which he proposed to read in full. In this letter John informed the club that he would not be taking part in any games for a long time and that he would be thankful if the club would accept this decision as his final word on the matter. In other words he was resigning from Mount Sion and, consequently, retiring from hurling because he could not contemplate playing with any other team. In a brief coda to the letter he admitted that he was wrong about the 'Portlaw affair' (a reference to the fracas that had broken out on the team bus mentioned above) and he wished the club well in its forthcoming matches. This was a bombshell to all present and while the members were trying to digest the import of what they had just heard it was proposed and seconded that the meeting adjourn to another date because the junior players had to leave to play a league match.[171]

When the meeting resumed three weeks later it was noticed that the attendance was much larger than at the previous meeting with almost all the senior hurlers in attendance. Sensation piled upon sensation when chairman, Jack Flavin, read out a letter of resignation from the secretary, Paddy Duggan. The split within the club was out in the open. There had been two high profile resignations from the club; firstly the club captain and now the secretary. Both were men of principle and honour; both had resigned over the same issue with each man at the opposite ends of the argument. A general discussion then took place on the situation created by the secretary's resignation and on the proposal of Paddy O'Connor, seconded by Pat Kelly, it was decided that two members of the club should call on Paddy Duggan and ask him to return to the club as a playing member. Paddy O'Connor and Frank Minogue were appointed to the task and were asked to report back to the committee. It was at this stage that committee member Mick Gallagher rose and also tendered his resignation.[172] The club members, many of whom had not attended a meeting all year, were left reeling in disbelief. The club had a serious problem that had to be addressed promptly or the club would not see another year.

John had put himself out on a limb with his plea for the club 'to accept this decision as his final word on the matter.' No one approached him to re-join the club because he had asked to be left alone. He was twenty four years of age, mature in hurling

---

171 Mount Sion club minutes, 2 November 1941
172 Mount Sion club minutes, 23 November 1941

skills but less so in the machinations of the committee room, and after he was elected to the committee he had been dragged into a dispute between two older committee members. He was also unhappy over certain decisions made by the club in which he had played a part and he had become disenchanted and disillusioned with the lack of commitment shown by a large section of the senior team. The drinking culture within the club had the potential to cause serious divisions and John was a confused and disheartened man when he made his decision to resign. A bad year had ended disastrously.

The new year of 1942 opened with no ease to John's torment in sight. Weeks had past and he was very unhappy with his lot. He had made his decision and he could see no way back without losing face. He had been lucky in one aspect, however, because there was very little hurling during the time of his resignation and retirement. Although he had never intended his resignation to be permanent he found that as the weeks passed with no sign of resolution he had become depressed; redemption of a sort was at hand, however. As if he were compensating for the lack of hurling in his life, he immersed himself in his LDF activities where he found a new life with his comrades in uniform. After enrolling with his workmates from Messrs Graves he spent some months with the Recruit Training Department and then, when his training was completed, he was assigned to the Company of Engineers which was the most active one within the LDF. It was composed of men with special skills that would be invaluable in time of war: comrades of John who had specific building-skills and others like those from the Railway Company who had engineering skills; also men with explosives expertise, builders, machinists, carpenters etc. The volunteers were young and patriotic and most were highly motivated. Some were married but most were young single men who willingly gave up their spare time to the LDF activities which increased greatly as the war progressed. The Engineering Company took part in rifle and foot drilling, route marches, weekend camps and lectures and demonstrations on the uses of explosives and allied matters. There were concerts and dances and, of course, sports.

An athletic club was established and the Engineering Company also organised a hurling team.

Although John loved the life in the LDF he missed the hurling and the day to day activities of his club. It was a terrible time for him and his family and it was just when he was at his lowest that an extraordinary event happened. He was drinking in the local public house when several men came knocking on the door of his Barrack Street home enquiring if they could see him about a business proposition. John's mother invited them in for a cup of tea and sent for John. When he arrived the men asked if they could speak to him in private and a discussion ensued for a long while. The visitors were business-men from Cork and they promised John a supervisory job in that city and told him he could take his pick of either Ford or Dunlop, the most sought after jobs in Cork. There was a catch, though – the job was conditional on John playing hurling for Cork. The visitors stressed that they were acting entirely alone and on behalf of no one else and were doing so purely for the benefit of Cork hurling; in other words, the Cork county board had, ostensibly, nothing to do with the approach. John promised to think about it and the visitors said they would be back in a few weeks to hear his answer. John's sister Peggy recalled the family's reaction:

> We were all in a state of shock and the prospect of John leaving Waterford and Mount Sion was unthinkable. Some weeks later my mother decided to confront John and being a mother who knew her son inside-out she found the right words to say. Reaching up she put her two hands on John's shoulders and said 'John, would you do that to the Brothers?' to which John immediately answered 'No, mother. I would not!'[173]

His mother's words had gone straight to the core of his being – loyalty, duty and honour. He was a Waterford man, a Mount Sion man, and so he was going to remain. John's torment was over and he reconciled with his Mount Sion colleagues. It is

---

173 Interview with Peggy Keane

tantalizing to speculate, however, about which club he would have joined if he had gone to Cork. Given his friendship at that time with Jack Lynch and Paddy O'Donovan he would, almost certainly, have played with Glen Rovers, and one can only surmise, if such an outcome had come to pass, how many more Cork titles the 'Glen' would have won. There is a very interesting sequel to that incident and it happened thirteen years later. The old Waterford hurler, Larry Fanning, told me that he and a small group of Mount Sion hurlers went to see the 1954 All-Ireland hurling final in which Christy Ring won his eighth senior medal. John had been an umpire at that All-Ireland final and after the match he re-joined his Mount Sion colleagues and went for a meal and a drink. Later that evening the group was standing outside the Cork team's hotel when Ring and a few Cork players came down the steps. John and Christy both saw each other at the same time and came together to shake hands. John congratulated Ring saying 'Well done, Christy! What a marvellous achievement – winning eight All-Ireland medals.' Ring looked up at John and replied 'Yerra, John, what are you talking about! If you had come to play for us you'd have won a bucketful of those medals!' It was quite obvious from Ring's reply that he knew of the proposal made to John all those years before.[174]

Back in the game

When John returned to hurling he picked up where he had left off – still captain of his club. The county championship had been arranged on a geographic basis to facilitate the clubs by minimizing travel and Mount Sion were drawn against Portlaw in the first round of a league system, the game to take place in Portlaw at the beginning of May. The home club had been strengthened by the addition of the new Cork star Willy Campbell, and in front of a record crowd they beat Mount Sion de-

---

174 Interview with Larry Fanning

cisively, by a margin of eleven points. John played at full back and although Andy Fleming had a great game at centre-back the team lacked cohesion. It was quite obvious that there were still divisions in the club, with the morale of the senior team in particular being very low. Mount Sion had been drawn against Erin's Own in the second round but got a lifeline when the latter were sensationally beaten by St Stephen's in its first round match. The second round championship match with Erin's Own was won easily by the latter and that effectively ended Mount Sion's championship campaign for 1942.

It had been a bad year for Mount Sion. Not one of its five teams across hurling and football had won even an eastern title and now the club was losing players to emigration. It was time for some straight talking and that was provided at the AGM when a full and frank discussion took place. Hope lay with the juniors and minors who had played well all year without achieving the ultimate success and it was with cautious confidence that all looked forward to the coming year; but only time would tell if that confidence was founded on a firm foundation. It was true to say that 1943 was going to be a defining one for Mount Sion. There were recriminations in the club over the team's tame exit from the championship and at a general meeting Brian Doyle called for a change in club policy and advocated that the policy of non-interference with the junior hurling team should be abandoned especially as the senior team was losing players to emigration. The treasurer then revealed that the club was financially insolvent and that there was nothing in the 'kitty.'[175]

---

175 Mount Sion club minutes, 11 October 1942

Chapter Fifteen
Champions Again

The transport situation became worse as the war entered its fourth year. Walking and cycling now became the norm and the roads were full of cyclists. People became used to the idea of cycling everywhere and distance became no object. More games were arranged locally and John was reported to have played nineteen matches in the year as well as refereeing some others.

John had fractured his ankle in an accident at work but had played for Waterford in the championship match against Tipperary where he had given a sensational display. There appeared to be no chance, however, of him being fit enough to play for Mount Sion in the county championship first round match against Erin's Own which was scheduled for the following weekend. But John was really determined to play against the old enemy, no matter what the consequences might be. Not only did he play in this match, however, but he was quite outstanding, with the *Munster Express* reporting that 'John Keane [was] here, there and everywhere, his weight, skill and driving power being marvellous.'[176] Erin's Own led at half time but Mount Sion started the second half well with John scoring a goal direct from a seventy yard free. Jim O'Meara was having a great tussle at centre-field with Fad Browne of Erin's Own but the scores were not coming for Mount Sion. After ten minutes John switched to the half-forward line and shortly afterwards Mount Sion scored another goal to leave them only a point behind. The excitement was now intense and after Jim Ware had saved a point-blank shot John doubled on a high ball and sent to the net to give Mount Sion the lead. Just before the end Jim

---

176 *Munster Express*, 25 June 1943

O'Meara sent over the bar to give Mount Sion victory by a three point margin. The quest to regain the county title was still alive but John's fractured ankle was not healing and the two games he had played did not help in his recovery.

Mount Sion had qualified to meet Portlaw in the eastern senior hurling final at Ballyduff and as the club was extremely anxious about the state of the field the chairman of the club, Jack Flavin was requested to accompany John to the field and endeavour to have it put in order for the game. They were also instructed to hire a room at deLacy's, Ballyduff, in which the team might strip. Such were the conditions prevailing for GAA teams at that time.[177] The team duly cycled from the city to Ballyduff where they pulverised Portlaw. Although John played in this game his ankle was still troubling him and was not showing any signs of healing. He was at centre-back when the county final was played out at Dungarvan despite the motion to have it played in Waterford which was carried at the county convention in 1941. This was a bruising game and John was carried off after only ten minutes play with a severe injury to his head. The standard of hurling quickly deteriorated and the match became one that tested the nerves and courage of all – it was more like a war than a county hurling final. Andy Fleming had been switched to centre-back to take up John's position and was faced by a huge six foot-plus Gárda from Galway. Andy remembered the day well.

> When John was injured after about ten minutes things were looking bad for us because Tallow were in control. I went to mark the big fellow and he was way bigger than I was. I remember in the second half when a high ball came into us and we both pulled on it in the air. There was great aerial play in those days. No one would put up his hand to catch the ball because his arm would be taken off at the elbow. Anyway, he creased me (over my right eye) and I creased him but it was I who connected and sent the ball down the field. As we both

---

177 Mount Sion club minutes, 4 August 1943

lay on the ground, with blood pouring out of us, the ball came back and I got up and sent it straight back over the bar. But we won! That was a great day for us.[178]

It was a day of injuries and Mount Sion had more injuries to deal with apart from those to John and Andy. Pat Fanning also had stitches inserted in a head wound and Jim O'Meara dislocated a sinew in his neck. Pat Fanning described what subsequently happened:

> John received a terrible head wound and there was blood everywhere. He was taken to the local hospital while we remained to fight like savages to win the county title. After the match we hurried to the hospital where the nurse assured us that every effort was being made to contact the doctor but that there was nothing to do but wait. Shortly after she had left, a man opened the door of the room and stepped inside. He was dressed from top to toe in hunting clothes and he carried a hunting rifle on his arm. He was an extraordinary sight but not as extraordinary as we were – Andy and I had bandaged and bloodied heads and John was still in his togs which were covered in blood. The place looked like a crime scene. The man studied us for a moment before deciding that John was the most badly injured and walking over to him he said 'That's a nasty wound.' Before he could say another word I jumped up in my rather impetuous way, came between them, and said rather peremptorily 'No one is to touch that man until he sees a doctor' to which he replied with the immortal phrase 'I am the doctor.'[179]

Mount Sion had completed its rehabilitation and had won its fourth senior title. After the match the winners retired for a victory meal at Miss Phelan's café in the Main Street where thirty meat teas had been ordered. Later they visited a public house

---

178 Interview with Andy Fleming
179 Interview with Pat Fanning

in Grattan Square where they celebrated well into the night. Long after closing time the hard drinking set amongst them was still celebrating when the Gárdaí raided the pub and the county champions had to make an ignominious exit by scrambling over the back wall and out to safety.

Larry Fanning related the story to me and said that John got such a shock at the thought of the story being splashed all

Mount Sion, 1943 County champions
Back Row (L-R): Jack Gallagher, Mick O'Brien, Richard Cooper, Paddy Dowling
Second Row (L-R): Jim O'Meara, Mick Gallagher, Joe O'Shea, Paddy O'Connor, 'Doyle' Walsh, Brian Doyle, Jimmy Walsh, Paddy Greene
Front Row (L-R): Andy Fleming, Larry Fanning, Jack Flavin, John Keane (Capt.), Frank Minogue, John Baston, Pat Fanning. Boy in front is Billy Connors (Ard na Gréine). (Photo by Phillips of Waterford, courtesy of Eoin Fanning)

over the newspapers that he never took a drink after that night. While it is true that John foreswore alcoholic drink from that day, the reason for so doing was very different, and romantic. The true reason was that John had met his beloved May – the lady who was to become his wife. I use the word lady quite deliberately. At the present time when the word is used indiscriminately and is interchangeable with the word 'woman' it is salutary to recall that at the time of which I write the title had to be earned. There was never any doubt that May Dunne was a lady, for she embodied all that such an appellation implied. Her quiet dignity, graciousness, demeanour, behaviour, deportment and gentleness all bespoke a person of refinement. May was also a committed Pioneer, a member of the PTAA, and John's life changed from that moment. He not only gave up the alcohol but, under May's influence, he also became a Pioneer and wore the Pioneer pin for the rest of his days. It was only during his last illness that on his doctor's advice he took a shot of whiskey with an aspirin.

The old year was near an end but there was one very interesting and important game to be played before closing time was called on 1943. The National Army's 7th Brigade, flushed with victory over all other Army teams, laid down a challenge to Waterford's unbeaten 46th Battalion of the LDF and agreed to play the game in Waterford. This was a game to savour because both teams had a host of inter-county stars, the greatest of them being John for the LDF and Mick Mackey for the Army. In a magnificent game it looked like a rout for the Army who scored five goals and four points in the first twenty minutes in reply to Paddy Greene's solitary goal for the LDF. However, shrewd positional switches by the LDF put a halt to the Army's gallop and gradually the game changed and when the 46th went into the lead the game reached inter-county standard. The match finished with the 46th the victors on a score-line of 6-8 to 5-5 leaving the combination of Waterford and Kilkenny hurlers still undefeated against all-comers.

John's fractured ankle had finally healed after a year when his hurling had reached such a degree of brilliance that only Jack Lynch stood on the same level. He was then twenty six years of age and at the peak of his career and his personal life had entered a new and happier phase now that he had met the woman who was to be his wife. He still smoked heavily but he had given up alcohol and his general health was good, although he had received some serious injuries. His club, Mount Sion, had regained the county senior hurling title and he was confident that the Waterford team were on the brink of making that longed-for breakthrough.

The economic conditions imposed by the war were worsening and clubs were losing players all the time due to emigration. The haemorrhaging of players from Mount Sion continued and shortly after the game against Cork in Waterford, Paddy Dowling, the great wing half-back, had announced that he was leaving Waterford to take up employment in England. Another Mount Sion man who left, this time to Tralee, was Brian Doyle and these departures, allied to the previous emigration of Bill Lynch, were severe body-blows to the newly crowned champions. The following year was going to test Mount Sion's resources to the limit. A further war-time restriction that would severely impact on clubs and counties was announced in December. The Government decreed that hackney vehicles would no longer be allowed to travel to any sports meeting unless with the prior sanction of the Minister of Supplies and that a permit from the Department would be required for each journey. Furthermore, hackney cars would only be allowed where no public transport was available and even then the playing members of a team would be allowed to travel by hackney only if at least three were travelling together. One must have wondered if sport could continue at all.

Serious injury

At the club's AGM in March 1944, John was confirmed as club captain with Andy Fleming as vice-captain. The senior team suffered another body-blow when Frank Minogue announced that he was leaving to seek work in England and Mick Gallagher retired from hurling due to injury and ill-health. Mount Sion would, therefore, start the defence of the county title without five of its senior team. The club's bid to retain the county senior hurling title was seriously threatened before a ball had been struck. A further threat to Mount Sion's title was the arrival on the county championship scene of a team from the 3rd Battalion of the Army that was now quartered in the Waterford Military Barracks. It was going to be an interesting year. The Army team showed its strength early in the year when it played a draw with Mount Sion in a tournament game but it was in the replay when all the drama occurred. In this game on 27 April John suffered a severe blow to the head when he was accidentally struck by Private Mick Barry of the Army team. All present that day will never forget the sickening sound of the hurley striking John's head for it seemed to reverberate around the ground. He was taken from the field and rushed to the county and city infirmary where for three days he passed into unconsciousness on several occasions. It was an awful time and the prognosis was not good. Eventually his great physical fitness, allied to his enormous strength, helped him greatly to recover but the doctors were concerned about his heart and after some weeks in the Infirmary he was eventually transferred to a Dublin hospital where he spent a week undergoing tests before he was released home on 27 May. He had been in hospital for a month but he was still under the doctor's care and was forbidden to play hurling. One interesting fact revealed by the tests was that John had an abnormally slow heart-rate, a condition shared by many great athletes.

During his absence the Mount Sion team were beaten by both Erin's Own and the Army team and Waterford were eliminated from the Munster championship by Tipperary. He was sorely missed because both teams appeared leaderless. As the months of inaction passed it was a worrying time for John because it looked as if he might never again return to top-flight hurling action. In total, his absence from the playing field lasted a full six months from his injury on the 27 April to his re-appearance on 29 October for Waterford against Cork in the Br Rice Memorial Tournament final.

The year ended on a very sad note for John with the sudden death of his beloved father on Christmas Day, shortly after he had attended early mass in Ballybricken church. He had been employed on the outdoor staff of Waterford Corporation for over twenty years but towards the end of his life he had been placed on light duties because of his advanced age. He was seventy eight years old at his death and had worked two days in the previous week, his last working day being Christmas Eve.

Chapter sixteen
Mount Sion double up

John could have been forgiven if during 1945 his mind had been elsewhere than on hurling for he was preparing for his marriage, which took place in St John's church in Waterford on the first of August, his best man being his Mount Sion and Waterford hurling colleague, Paddy Dowling.

Mount Sion had won its first round match in the county championship rather easily against P. H. Pearse but John missed the second round clash with De La Salle which took place while he was on his honeymoon. De La Salle had lost two games already and many thought this game would be a one-sided affair but De La Salle had the ex-champions fully extended and were unlucky to lose. With full-time approaching and Mount Sion just three points ahead, their opponents hit the crossbar and eventually lost by only two points. John couldn't come back fast enough as far as Mount Sion was concerned because the next opponents would be the old enemy, Erin's Own. Mount Sion made wholesale positional changes and the famous half-back line was broken up. John went centre-forward, Jim O'Meara went to centre-back, Andy Fleming was at full-back and Paddy Dowling went to centre-field to partner Mick Healy who was making his championship debut. Healy was an extraordinarily good club player and John always said that when selecting a Mount Sion team for any game he would put Mick Healy's name at centre-field and then start from there. No man could ask for a finer tribute and no man deserved it more. Healy is not remembered as an inter-county hurler, though he played many a fine game for Waterford, but as a club hurler he became one of Mount Sion's greatest players.

The match itself had everything in abundance; great scores, goalmouth incidents, brilliant hurling, a disputed goal, crowd

Wedding photo 1945. John sitting at left with his wife May. The best man was John's team-mate Paddy Dowling and the bridesmaid was May's sister Delia.
(Photographer Annie Brophy, Waterford City Archives and by courtesy of the Keane family)

trouble and, unfortunately, two shocking incidents in which John was unwittingly involved – one during the match and the other after it was all over. Erin's Own led by two points at half-time but the stormy action was reserved for the second half which was close and exciting. The play was being stubbornly contested and the marking became close and sometimes over aggressive culminating in a physical attack on John that had the crowd in an uproar. John had been struck on the head from behind and with no chance to defend himself. The offending player was sent off the field and, subsequently, both John and he were called to a county board meeting to give their accounts of what happened. The offending player, who had not turned up as requested, received a suspension of twelve months.

The attack made on John emphasised that hurling was a man's game and was no place for 'shrinking violets.' John abhorred 'dirty' play which he called 'cowardly' but he had been brought up in what was called 'the school of hard knocks' and had learned, from the beginning, to take care of himself. He played in an era where courage was a prerequisite for playing the game. There was an accepted, though unwritten, code in hurling which demanded that if one were deliberately hit by another player one immediately struck back, because failure to do so was almost a licence to the other player to strike at will. Also, if any team-mates were deliberately hit it was regarded as an assault on the whole team. John was a powerful man and his size and strength ensured that he was not intimidated by anyone but he was very protective of smaller, lighter comrades and he often switched positions with such players during a game so as to take on the 'mullickers', as he called them. He hated to see anyone hurt during a game and one of his favourite sayings after a game was 'A grand day and no one hurt, thank God.'

Many people at the match, remembering the blows that John had received in 1943 at the county final and the serious injury he suffered less than twelve months later, were incensed at what they saw as a deliberate attempt to seriously injure, if not maim, a great player. When the offender was sent off the field a section of the crowd had tried to attack him and he was hurried away to the dressing rooms which were then locked. The match was held up for attention to John whose wound was bleeding profusely and was still bleeding as the match ended in a storm of protest at the disallowing of a goal that would have secured a draw for Mount Sion. The goal umpire was then threatened and was escorted, with difficulty, to the dressing rooms where he remained barricaded as the mob tried to gain entrance. The Gárdaí were called and fully three-quarters of an hour passed before order was restored and the ground was cleared. Amidst all this riotous behaviour the Mount Sion team and officials could not gain entrance to the dressing rooms and decided to remain on the field for their own safety as small pockets of fans had started fighting each other. John was lying on the sideline being attended by first-aid people when a most shocking and unforgiveable incident happened.

A neighbour of the Keane family, who was the mother of an Erin's Own player, approached John who rose and held out his hand to greet her on the assumption that she was going to enquire about his injury. Instead, she reached up and spat in his face. The incident was over before anyone could react but it left an indelible impression on the few who witnessed it. The whole episode was an example of tribalism gone mad and was a most reprehensible and disgusting insult, especially since John had done nothing untoward and was the injured party in every respect. It was the nadir of relations between the two sets of supporters, a relationship that had always been difficult but had never before descended to such a level.

Although the Mount Sion team had been beaten in that game against Erin's Own they were still in the championship, and a very difficult assignment lay in wait – a crunch match with the Army's 3rd battalion, the reigning county champions. If Mount Sion beat the Army and Erin's Own dealt similarly with P. H. Pearse a play-off would be required between the two city clubs. John had had been playing well in all his matches since his six month lay-off in 1944 but had not yet displayed the brilliance that he had consistently shown ever since his entry to senior ranks. However he showed signs in the game against the army that he was coming back to his best. Although Mount Sion were led by five points at the interval a storming second half left them comfortable winners by 10-2 to 5-6, the high number of goals being attributed to the substitute goalkeepers on both sides. A showdown with Erin's Own was on the cards but a series of revelations about the illegal constitution of the Erin's Own team that had beaten Mount Sion in a previous round led to an objection being lodged by the latter. The objection was lodged on four points; the county board chairman accepted three, and upheld the complaint. Erin's Own appealed to the Munster council but the next meeting of that body also upheld the objection and the match was awarded to Mount Sion, thus paving the way for a county final meeting with Dungarvan. The Mount Sion minor team had also reached the final and for the first ever time the club had a chance of doing the hurling double.

It was a great occasion for both school and club. Br O'Connor had succeeded in bringing his minor team to the county final in the first year since his return to the school but he recognised that he had a group of gifted young hurlers, two of whom, Tommy Keane and Philly Grimes, had already played with the senior team. Tommy Keane was John's nephew, but was more like a brother, being only ten years younger. He was a great goal-scorer (he had already scored seven goals in one game with the minor team) and he would go on to have a long and distinguished career with the senior team. Like Mick Healy he would prove to be a great club player although he could never nail-down a regular place on the Waterford team.

Qualifying two teams for the county finals brought its own problems, however, not least being the financial one. The problems were discussed at a committee meeting of the club when the secretary submitted a list of forty seven members entitled to travel to the finals comprising nineteen senior players, twenty one minors and seven committee members and selectors. Finance was then discussed and it was reckoned that cars would cost twenty eight pounds while catering would cost eight pounds. The problem for the club was that there was only £25-17-0 in the coffers. Hurleys would also have to be purchased as the club had only seven spare hurleys on hand. Money was the least of the problems, however, because there remained the vexed issue of getting permits from the Department of Supplies. The war had ended but the Government restrictions continued. The secretary stated that he had made application for permits for five cars to transport the seniors and had received the permits – but his application for permits for the minors had been refused. The situation was serious. Various schemes to obtain the permits were proposed (such as asking four of the car drivers to make double journeys) but eventually it was decided that Br O'Connor should be asked to ring the Department and stress that the minor team was essentially a school team. This suggestion worked and the required permits were granted. When the finals were won, and the year had ended, the club found itself eleven pounds in debt.[180]

A record county final attendance at Dungarvan saw the Mount Sion minor team beat Cappoquin in the first game. The minor team had to line out without Seamus Power and Philly Grimes (who were injured) but great play by Tommy Keane,

---

180 Mount Sion club minutes, 13 October 1945

Mount Sion 1945 County Champions
(Photo courtesy of Jim O'Meara)

Billy Mulcahy and Mick Flannelly saw off a game opposition. The senior game, in which Mount Sion defeated Dungarvan by 3-8 to 2-5, was memorable for John's magnificent performance; fittingly, he had chosen the county final to return to his usual brilliance. The *Dungarvan Leader* reported that the senior clash provided thrilling hurling which delighted the large crowd and it was one of the best county hurling finals played at the venue for many years. The paper continued:

> From the throw-in a lightning pace was set and a very high standard of play was witnessed. The initial placings of the Mount Sion men saw John Keane figure at centre forward, but a short time had only elapsed when a switch was noticed, Keane going to centre field and O'Meara going to the pivotal position. This change made a remarkable difference and ultimately was the deciding factor in the city team's great victory. The hurling of the Mount Sion captain was reminiscent of

the great John Keane of a few years back and showed that this magnificent player has lost none of the prowess which has earned for him the honour of being styled one of the best hurlers in Ireland. His stick work and anticipation Sunday last earned rounds of applause, even from staunch supporters of the Old Boro' team and he was indeed the inspiration of his team.[181]

The *Munster Express* was similarly enraptured with the standard of hurling and reported that

Seldom, if ever, has such a standard of hurling been witnessed in Waterford City or county. ... The hero of the hour, however, was John Keane, the idol of Waterford hurling fans. His perfect control, uncanny precision and typical solo runs showed that he has lost none of his speed or craft. His last point, from a '70,' was a fitting conclusion to a great display.[182]

John had ended the season on a high note with his performances returning to the consistent brilliance of his displays before his serious injury of 1944. He had started the year in his usual position of centre half-back but had moved to midfield and centre-forward towards the end of the season. This experiment would continue during the next two years before he moved permanently to the centre-forward position in 1948.

---

181 *Dungarvan Leader*, 27 Oct 1945
182 *Munster Express*, 26 October 1945

Chapter seventeen
John goes forward

John had been successful in his efforts to coax Vin Baston to declare for Waterford and Baston had also indicated his desire to play for Mount Sion. The latter ambition was being stymied, however, by his inability to satisfy the residency qualification but he was eligible to play for the club in challenge and tournament games. To accommodate Baston John had played in a variety of positions for Waterford and was thinking of moving permanently to the forward line. He had played a few games at centre half-forward in 1945 but it was in 1946 that he played the majority of matches in that position although he also played at centre-back, full-back and centre-field.

In preparation for the county championship Mount Sion arranged a series of challenge games with Éire Óg, the Kilkenny champions and Mullinavat – and lost both. The team was in transition, having lost players to emigration and retirement and was trying out new players including some of the successful minor team of 1945. John's friendship with Jack Lynch was the catalyst for the very first meeting between Mount Sion and Glen Rovers of Cork, the latter agreeing to come to Waterford. The Glen had a star-studded team but Mount Sion emerged victorious by 3-5 to 2-3. It was a great win for Mount Sion, the one disappointing feature being the absence of Christy Ring from the Glen Rovers team. With John playing at centre-forward and Andy Fleming at centre-back, Baston was placed at wing-back for Mount Sion and all three starred in a memorable match.

In the vital championship match against Erin's Own which was played in wretched conditions in Dungarvan, Erin's Own effectively ended Mount Sion's hopes of a repeat county title when they won 3-3 to Mount Sion's 1-2. Although John had performed heroics at centre-back and centre-field, scoring

Mount Sion's only goal, Erin's Own became county champions for 1946.

In 1947 Mount Sion were determined to win back the county title and embarked on a series of challenge games with clubs from outside the county. First up was the Cork club, Blackrock, which Mount Sion defeated by two points at Lismore followed two weeks later by a demolition of Carrick Swan. John had finally relinquished the centre back role with Mount Sion and had taken over at centre-forward on a permanent basis and in the first round county championship game against Butlerstown he gave a master-class of centre-forward play when he outclassed no less a man than Munster's Mick Hayes. His performance that day is still talked about amongst all who were privileged to see it. Then there followed two games against the great Kilkenny team, Carrickshock, who had contested the previous nine Kilkenny senior finals, winning five. They, too, fell to Mount Sion, who appeared at this stage to be unstoppable.

The county championship draw had ensured that Mount Sion and Erin's Own would play each other provided they won their preliminary games but both teams had shocks when barely scraping wins against opposition that were not highly regarded. The two city clubs had qualified to play each other in the semi-final and in a magnificent match the champions, Erin's Own, belied the veteran tag and came out on top by two points. Injuries were frequent as a result of the full-blooded encounters and the First-Aid men were the kept busy all afternoon. John always referred to this match as the match of 'O'Meara's thumb.' Jim O'Meara was having a wonderful game at centre-field for Mount Sion who went into a lead of five points midway through the second half and were bombarding the Erin's Own goal when O'Meara received a very severe injury to his thumb and had to retire. The broken thumb never healed properly and is quite visibly distorted to this day, over sixty years later. The retirement of O'Meara halted Mount Sion's momentum and Erin's Own scored a dramatic and unexpected win. In subsequent years John mused, wistfully, that it was O'Meara's thumb that caused him to miss out on captaining the Waterford team in 1948.

Champions again

In 1948 Mount Sion signified their intention to regain the county title in a magnificent first-round game which saw them decisively defeat old rivals Erin's Own by 7-7 to 1-2.

Mount Sion had given three of the All-Ireland winning minors, Máirtín Morrissey, Mick Flannelly and Tom Gallagher, a place on the club senior team and with the latter two youngsters as his speedy wing-men John found that he was enjoying club hurling more than ever. He seemed rejuvenated. The club had cruised to the county final where the opponents were Avonmore, the Western champions, a team composed of the best junior hurlers in that Division. It turned out to be a facile victory for Mount Sion, a feature of the game being the inter-play between John and his wing-men with the artistry of John allied to the speed and skill of Gallagher and Flannelly keeping the Avonmore defence under severe pressure. John scored 1-3, Flannelly 1-0 and Gallagher 1-3 in a total of nine goals and eight points to Avonmore's five points.

Three stalwarts of Mount Sion's win over Erin's Own – Andy Fleming, Mick Heffernan and Jim O'Meara – still going strong in 2010

This was the beginning of a golden period in the club's history and it won eight championships in the 1948 season — five in the eastern division (senior, junior and minor hurling and junior and minor football), and three county championships (senior and minor hurling and junior football). The minor hurling team celebrated its fourth successive county championship (a winning streak that would eventually stretch to a record six) and in a period of three years from the end of August 1947 to the end of July 1950, the club's senior hurling team lost only one match during which it played against all-comers from Waterford and the surrounding counties.

Another Cup for Mount Sion. Andy Fleming, John Keane, Mick Gallagher

The club was advancing the policy enunciated by Locky Byrne when he advocated that the older players should know when to bow out and 'leave the field to the young lads.' John was excited by the club's successes and by the young players that were now making their way onto the senior team. Tommy Keane and Philly Grimes, both protégés of John, had been among the first to be promoted and while both had established themselves as regular senior players Philly had decided to go to the USA to find work. He was an exceptional player, even at that early stage, and had quickly made his mark on the Waterford senior team, playing in the first round tie against Clare and thus qualifying for an All-Ireland senior medal. Philly lived in Mount Sion Avenue, just round the corner from John's house in Barrack Street, and John had been a father-figure to him. Philly recalled two stories about this facet of their relationship for Brendan Fullam's book *Giants of the Ash*. In Philly's young days, when he had no jersey, he told Fullam of receiving from John a present of one of John's Railway cup jerseys and feeling ten feet tall when he wore it.

> Another kindly act that Phil recalled about John went back to 1945, when the minor championships were revived [having been suspended due to the War]. Phil was picked to play with Waterford; but two weeks before the match he broke his collar-bone. On the day of the match he was standing at the Tower Clock [sic], feeling very dejected as he watched his colleagues take off for the game. John Keane saw him, opened the door of his car, put Phil sitting on his knee and took him to the match.[183]

Those acts of John's kindness to a young, eager and aspiring player were typical of the man and made such an impression on the young Grimes that they were remembered and recounted almost forty years later. Such acts of friendship and encouragement to a young player from his idol have started many a hurler on the road to All-Ireland glory and the whole world changes and takes on a new meaning when he is treated with such kindness. One can only imagine with what eagerness the young Grimes hurried to his next training session and the pride he felt when he pulled on that Munster jersey – remember it was not just any Munster jersey but one given him by John Keane. Any young player with even an atom of ambition would have been strengthened in his desire to prove himself worthy of the deed. Philly returned from the USA after a few years in New York and became the bright shining star of the greatest Mount Sion and Waterford teams.

---

183 Fullam, *Giants of the ash*, p. 90

John leading out Mount Sion in the 1948 county championship. (Photo from the Fanning family collection & courtesy of Tom Partridge)

Ireland's greatest team

The success of the Mount Sion senior hurling team in 1948 and the continued success of a succession of great minor teams had made John realise that he still had something to give his club on the playing field. He had been enthused and invigorated by the quality of the minor hurlers who had been introduced to the senior team and with the prospect of giving those players the benefit of his experience he decided, therefore, to defer any thought of retirement until he saw how things developed during the year. When the 1949 season began he had attained a position in the club that was unchallenged by any other member. He was the club's leader on the field and also in the committee room for he was at once the club's chairman, captain and greatest player and also the trainer and selector of the club's senior hurling team. He was also a county referee, a county selector in senior hurling and minor football and the newly elected county treasurer. Something had to give and John intimated to the club committee that he did not intend to contest the position of club chairman for the year 1949, saying that he found he would not have sufficient time to devote to the job. The members expressed regret at his decision and Mick Gallagher paid tribute to his wonderful work for the club during the past year and that John 'by his own conduct was an inspiration to the whole club', a sentiment echoed by each committee member.[184]

John played in a flurry of matches with his club, Mount Sion. The first was in the Gaelic Field tournament semi-final against the old enemy Erin's Own. There was disarray in the Erin's Own camp due to internal rows and there were rumours that they might not be able to field a team. Despite this lack of interest the club decided to enter teams in all grades of hurling in 1949. The result of the match against Mount Sion was a disaster for Erin's Own who suffered the club's heaviest defeat in the history of its clashes against Mount Sion up to that point,

---

184 Mount Sion club minutes, 25 February 1949

losing by 6-11 to 1-0. This defeat caused more unrest within the Erin's Own club because the team had been composed mostly of juniors who felt that they had been the sacrificial lambs offered up to slaughter.[185] Mount Sion then defeated Carrickshock (Kilkenny) in the Tournament final but suffered its first defeat in two years when being defeated by the Tipperary title holders, Holycross, in a close game.

Over the next year, more young players were brought into the Mount Sion senior team. The senior hurling championship began at Carrick-on-Suir in front of a large crowd that was augmented by over four hundred people who had travelled from Waterford in a special train. They saw Mount Sion crush St Molleran's but not before enduring a bruising encounter where tempers became frayed and players resorted to frequent bouts of fisticuffs. This brought about a second round match against the divisional team, Thomas Francis Meagher's, who were similarly brushed aside to leave Mount Sion to play against Erin's Own in the county semi-final.

When the two teams had met at the beginning of the year the Erin's Own club had been in a bad way both on and off the pitch. The champion club of 1946 and 1947 had withered away; some said that the problem was due to internal rows while others blamed the policy of introducing players from other counties instead of promoting from within the club. Despite all its woes, however, the club had, somehow, found its way into the semi-final where a formidable foe now stood in its path. The Mount Sion team, John Keane's scoring machine, had justified its nickname by going on scoring sprees throughout that year. The score in the match against the Meagher's is unknown but Mount Sion had won easily. However, in its five previous games the team had scored twenty-two goals and thirty-five points but no one in his wildest dreams could have imagined what was about to happen on 21 August 1949. As the championship clash approached the Erin's Own club was almost non-existent and

---

185 Kennedy, Tom, Erin's Own hurling club story (CD ROM, 2007)

there was serious doubt about its ability to field a team against Mount Sion. At a meeting of the Mount Sion club the club delegates to the county board were instructed to appeal to the Erin's Own delegates attending the next county board meeting to continue in the senior championship.[186]

On the day of the game Ritchie Grant, the chief mentor of the Erin's Own minor team, had arranged a challenge game for his minor team, against Dicksboro of Kilkenny, as a curtain raiser to the senior game. When the minor match ended and the time came for the senior teams to take the field it became apparent that Erin's Own had not a team or even another club officer present. Grant was in a terrible dilemma. He had no official function with the senior team but in the absence of any senior team officials he had to decide what to do. The obvious course was to concede a walk-over but because of his life long pride in the club he felt that this action would be ignominious for Erin's Own and inconsistent with the club's great record. He decided, therefore, to cobble together a scratch team of minors, juniors and anyone else from the club who happened to be present and who was willing to play. The result was a foregone conclusion and the *Munster Express* described, in a few words, what happened.

> Mount Sion hurlers (Waterford) ran up what is believed to be a record score in the long history of the GAA when, at Waterford Gaelic Field on Sunday last, they defeated Erin's Own in the county senior championship semi-final by 22 goals and 12 points to nil. Erin's Own were depleted when they took the field, and were demoralised at the close of the 60 minutes, in which Mount Sion had scored at the rate of more than a point a minute.[187]

Every time that Mount Sion team attacked (which was nearly all match long) the players found themselves almost alone in

---

186 Mount Sion club minutes, 30 July 1949
187 *Munster Express*, 26 August 1949

front of goal. When I asked Larry Fanning why so many goals were scored he answered by posing me the question, 'What were we supposed to do? Hit it wide?' He said that they realised the low standard of the Erin's Own team that had appeared but that Mount Sion had taken every chance of scoring a goal because that was what you were supposed to do. After a short while, however, it became quite evident that there was no danger of an upset and that the Erin's Own opposition had collapsed. The match then became embarrassing but Larry's question then comes into play. The situation was reminiscent of the Munster final of 1982 when Ray Cummins of Cork palmed the ball over the bar for a point to Cork when he found himself in front of an empty goal and Waterford about thirty points in arrears. Every Waterford supporter who remembers that incident has always regarded Cummins's action as a humiliation and all agree he should have taken the goal. The huge score achieved by Mount Sion became a nine day wonder and there was, surprisingly, very little comment about the result of the match. People just accepted that Erin's Own had many problems and that the club might not survive.

Mount Sion had qualified for the county final against Clonea but had first to fulfil a long standing Dr Kinane Cup semi-final engagement against Tullaroan, the Kilkenny champions of 1948. Vin Baston's transfer to Mount Sion had come through at last and he was immediately selected on the team to face Tullaroan.[188] There was a strange anomaly at work here. He was now officially a member of the Mount Sion club but was not eligible to play in the championship until the residency qualification was satisfied, although he was entitled to play for the club in challenge and tournament games. There was a large crowd present to see the teams march behind the band and, as both teams had qualified for their respective county finals, a great game was anticipated. The crowd was not disappointed. It was a cracking match although the Mount Sion lads pulled away from the opposition in the second half and won comprehensively by

---

188 Mount Sion club minutes, 12 September 1949

nine points. John had opted out of the National League clash with Dublin, thus signalling the end of his inter-county career, but continued playing for his club as Mount Sion cruised to another county title when Clonea were crushed by twelve points. It was time for John to consider his options; he had indicated towards the end of 1949 that his inter-county career was finished but he had a major decision to make regarding his further involvement as a player with Mount Sion. His natural inclination was to make a full retirement but he hesitated because of two factors: firstly, he loved the game so much that he knew it would be a terrible wrench to give it up completely; secondly, he was excited at the thought of the potentially great players that were coming through the Mount Sion minor teams and he wanted to play side-by-side with them to give them the benefit of his great experience. He would think about the problem over the winter months.

Chapter eighteen
John Keane's scoring machine

At the beginning of 1950 John had indicated that he did not wish to be considered for the upcoming national hurling league fixtures. It appeared that his career with the county team was over although he had not made up his mind about continuing to play with Mount Sion. However, a motion at the county convention sponsored by the Clonea club 'that no Waterford city club should be allowed to select players residing outside the city boundary' became a major factor in his decision to continue playing with his club. As justification for the motion the proposer said that one city club had won senior, minor and junior championships in one year and that it had the help of country players. Mount Sion had not been mentioned by name but the implication was sufficiently strong. The motion was passed overwhelmingly by eighty seven votes to forty after only a short but lively debate where the Mount Sion delegates argued that this move would seriously restrict the city clubs while putting no barrier to country clubs going all over the county in their search for players. John and the other Mount Sion delegates were incensed at the vote against their club at the convention, and although he had wavered about continuing to play club matches for another year he needed little persuasion to continue after the motion was passed. There was certainly an anti-Mount Sion majority at the convention but that did not apply to John, personally, because he was re-elected as county treasurer when all the other candidates withdrew their nominations in his favour.

Mount Sion 4-11 v Tullaroan 2-8 in the Dr Kinane Cup semi-final, 1949. John (wearing his Munster jersey) is leading out the Mount Sion team followed by Larry Fanning and Vin Baston. Andy Fleming (also in a Munster jersey) is third from the back. (Photo courtesy of Eoin Fanning)

Mount Sion had defeated Tullaroan, the 1948 Kilkenny champions, when both clubs had been preparing for their respective 1949 county finals but, whilst Mount Sion had won its final, Tullaroan had been beaten by Graigue, the Kilkenny champions for 1949. Graigue then challenged Mount Sion almost immediately but the club could not accept the challenge at that time for a variety of reasons. The first opportunity to play Graigue arose in a tournament game in Davin Park, Carrick-on-Suir at the end of March when the champions of the four neighbouring counties, Waterford, Tipperary, Cork and Kilkenny were invited. Glen Rovers were drawn against Borrisoleigh and Mount Sion were set to meet Graigue. It was a massive occasion. The railway company ran special trains from Thurles and Waterford and four bands took part in a massed-band parade before the two semi-finals, in the first of which the Glen defeated their rivals in a game devoid of any spectacular hurling. The second game was closely contested and both teams played some excellent hurling, but Mount Sion proved to be too strong for the Kilkenny champions, winning by five points. John had a great game and alternated throughout the game between centre-forward and centre-field, scoring 1-1. It is interesting to note, in view of the anti-Mount Sion motion at the convention, that all the Mount Sion players who played in Carrick were not only all Waterford city men but all had been past pupils of the school.

That match against Graigue was the first in an astonishing series of games that Mount Sion played against the cream of all the top hurling counties. In an eight week period the 'scoring machine' met and defeated Holycross and Borrisoleigh of Tipperary, Dungarvan United, Glen Rovers of Cork, Avonmore of Waterford in the county championship and the two Kilkenny clubs Graigue and Éire Óg, thus earning for itself the title of 'Ireland's greatest team.' The team was scoring goals for fun and the nickname 'John Keane's scoring machine' was never more apt. In the Dr Kinane Cup final Tipperary's Holycross were comprehensively defeated and two weeks later the Tipperary champions Borrisoleigh came to town and Mount Sion ran riot to the tune of ten goals in a match that left the Tipperary men bewildered. The greatest test that the Mount Sion team was given thus far happened in the next game when a Dungarvan United team, comprised of the best hurlers within that area, scored seven goals but the 'scoring machine' answered with nine of their own. The combination play of the Mount Sion half-forward line was breath-taking. John said on more than one occasion that it was his happiest time in hurling. He had nothing but the highest praise for his two wing men, Mick Flannelly and Tom Gallagher. Both had graduated from the All-Ireland winning Waterford minor team of 1948 where 'Flan' had been the general of the team. Now it was John who was directing the forward line, spraying passes into the path of his two flying wingers. Both were speed merchants but they also showed brilliant stick-work that was executed at top speed.

The sternest test appeared to be in the Carrick-on-Suir tournament final when John's Mount Sion would face Christy Ring's

Glen Rovers. In the event the Waterford team maintained its winning record in a match that provided some brilliant hurling but Mount Sion were superior all round and won convincingly, scoring six goals. When Mount Sion defeated Avonmore, the western divisional team, the newspapers remarked that Mount Sion were regarded as being nearly invincible but also lamented, however, that Mount Sion scored only four goals and twelve points in the match – it was obviously becoming difficult to please everybody. Kilkenny's champions, Graigue, fell to the Waterford juggernaut for the second time in eight weeks and then, only four days later, came the clash that everyone expected would be the game of the season: the senior hurling challenge for the benefit of the Mount Sion club funds between Mount Sion and Éire Óg of Kilkenny. The Kilkenny team had not been county champions since 1947 but were destined to reach the subsequent Kilkenny county final as were Mount Sion in Waterford. It was a powerful team, nonetheless, and full of stars such as Ramie Dowling, 'Diamond' Hayden, Jack Mulcahy, Nick O'Donnell (later of Wexford fame), Eddie Carew, Liam Reidy, Joe Gargan and the irrepressible Jimmy Langton. But Mount Sion had its stars too.

As usual the crowds flocked from all parts of south Kilkenny and Waterford and there was a festive atmosphere when the game began. Both teams produced a real classic of hurling in a challenge that held a championship tempo. There were some rare tussles between John at centre-forward and Nick O'Donnell, who lined out at centre-back for the visitors. For at least three-quarters of an hour it seemed anybody's game and it was only then that Mount Sion raised its game and held on to its record of being unbeaten for over a year. Over the three years since its defeat by Erin's Own in the county senior championship on 24 August 1947 the team had played twenty nine matches losing only once (to Holycross of Tipperary) and during that period played against all the major hurling clubs. The *Waterford News* claimed that 'last night's game has stamped Mount Sion as the country's leading hurling club.'[189] It was a statement that no one could dispute.

---

189 *Waterford News*, 26 May 1950

Cartoon by Gay from Munster Express, 2 June 1950

Cartoon by Gay from Munster Express, 9 June 1950

Mount Sion breezed through its remaining game in the county championship and were set for a date with the western hopefuls Tourin in the final. No one gave that young team a chance against the all-conquering city-men. Tourin, the junior champions of 1949, faced a seemingly impossible task; it was the first year for the team in the senior grade and only one player, Davy Walsh, had experienced inter-county hurling at senior level. It had, however, a strong backbone of very big men who were also skilled, if inexperienced, hurlers. Tourin contacted Mount Sion in the weeks before the match to know of its attitude towards Jim Fives, a cadet in the military college at the Curragh, who was prevented by the residency rule from playing with his club. The club committee decided after a full debate that they could not enter into any agreement with Tourin on this matter because under the same rule (and with the exact same circumstances) Vin Baston was denied the right to play for Mount Sion in the match.[190]

A huge crowd attended the game to see the biggest shock for years as the challengers ousted the red-hot favourites in a pulsating match. John was once again at the centre of the action, but not only for his hurling. After ten minutes of the match had been played, and with Mount Sion leading into a stiff breeze by 1-2 to 0-2, an incident happened that had a major bearing on the ultimate result. The *Munster Express* described what happened. 'Following a bout of hard pulling between two rival players, the referee was about to send the Tourin man to the line when John Keane sportingly interceded and he was allowed to remain on.'[191] Pat Fanning, who was also playing that day, had joined with John in his appeal to the referee and I subsequently asked him why they both had so done. 'Well,' said Pat, 'it was the county final, there was a huge crowd present and we were overwhelming favourites. I suppose we didn't want the occasion spoiled.' Larry Fanning had a different take on the occasion when he remarked ruefully, 'We were over-confident. We didn't

---

190 Mount Sion club minutes, 13 August 1950
191 *Munster Express*, 15 September 1950

want to beat them out the gate and especially if they were going to have only fourteen men on the field. We thought we would win easily. John and Pat lost us a county title.'

Mount Sion's greatest, John Keane and Andy Fleming

The referee had erred, of course, and there was intense speculation in the following week as to the attitude of the county board to the referee's report, and the matter was addressed at the next committee meeting of the Mount Sion club. The chairman, Michael Doyle, after congratulating the minor hurling team on its wonderful victory in the county final, expressed regret that the senior team had failed to retain the senior crown. He acknowledged, however, that they had been beaten by a better team on the day and that it might do some good for the game in the county. He added that the club secretary had already sent a congratulatory letter to the victors. The committee then unanimously adopted a motion that Mount Sion would not accept a re-match should the county board, acting on the referee's report, decide on this line of action. They stated, furthermore, that should the board insist on awarding the game to Mount Sion the club would offer Tourin a replay rather than accept victory in the board room.[192]

Both clubs were anxious to cash-in on the excitement engendered by Tourin's victory and quickly arranged a return match in Cappoquin, with both sides to share the gate money. Tourin showed that the county final result was no fluke when they again beat Mount Sion in front of the biggest crowd ever seen at the venue up to that time. Dick Doocey, a Tourin player, told me an interesting and extraordinary fact about that game. Because the match was for the benefit of both clubs, all the Mount Sion officials and players paid their own admittance money to the ground.

Philly Grimes had returned home after two years in New York where he had played with the Tipperary team. He wished to rejoin Mount Sion and there was jubilation when his transfer from New York to Mount Sion was confirmed to the club members at a committee meeting on the 6 December 1950. At the last committee meeting of the club on 18 December a motion for the county convention was proposed by Pat Fanning 'that the by-law enacted at the last county convention confining membership of Waterford city teams to players resident in the urban area of Waterford be rescinded.'

The coming year would be an interesting one for John and Mount Sion – but just how dramatic could not even be imagined.

---

192 Mount Sion club minutes, 18 September 1950

Chapter nineteen
Retirement from hurling

A sequel to the incident at the 1950 county final between Mount Sion and Tourin was provided at a meeting of the county board early in 1951 when the player for whom Pat Fanning and John had interceded was suspended for two years. The county chairman in moving the suspension motion said that the man's conduct had been most aggressive and that this was the only appropriate method of dealing with the problem. Looking at the incident in retrospect one can only wonder at why John and Pat had wanted the player to remain on the pitch.

Mount Sion's defeat in the 1950 county championship had not affected the club's status amongst the top teams in the country and the club was inundated with requests for participation in tournaments and challenge matches from Tullaroan, Dicksboro, Éire Óg, Graigue, Carrick Swan, Rathnure and Cork Sarsfields. The Mount Sion club had itself initiated a challenge to Carrickshock and the problem now was to find dates on which all clubs could agree. Furthermore the club had finally leased a plot of ground from Waterford Corporation on which to construct a playing field and club premises and the committee was heavily involved in that activity. John had given strong hints that this year would be his last as a player but he was a very active member of the club committee and he threw himself whole-heartedly into the construction of the new club headquarters. The club was fortunate in that it had a variety of trades represented amongst its membership and men like John (with his building expertise), Tommy and Séamus Keane, Paddy O'Connor, Philly Grimes, Dick Culleton and Wal Casey did trojan work in ensuring that Mount Sion would have a centre befitting the premier club in the county. It was the first tentative steps towards what would in time be the first club centre built in the county through the GAA's club development scheme.

Mount Sion, County finalists 1950

Back Row (L-R): Jack Flavin, Brian Doyle, Johnny O'Regan, Aidan McNamara, Pat Fanning, Davy Walsh, Paddy O'Connor, Mick Healy, Mick Gallagher, Tommy Keane, Willie Gallagher, John Keane (Capt.), Paddy Curran, Jack Gallagher, Tom Gallagher, Watty Morrissey.

Front Row (L-R): Davy Power, Billy Gaffney, Mick Heffernan, Mick Flannelly, Máirtín Morrissey, Andy Fleming, Seán Hayden, Tom Kennedy, Mick Doyle.

After Mount Sion's two defeats to Tourin in 1950, many people waited with interest to see the team's form in the early season matches in 1951. It turned out to be business as usual as Mount Sion swept to victory in the Carrick Swan tournament, which included a win over the Kilkenny champions Dicksboro. The scoring machine then moved into top gear as the team went on the rampage against three Kilkenny teams, Tullaroan, Mooncoin and Carrickshock, scoring a total of eighteen goals in the three games. It was understood generally that this year was to be John's last as a player and big crowds were present at each Mount Sion match in case it proved to be his final game. The huge crowd that had gathered to see the match with Tullaroan was thrilled at the home team's great performance although disappointed that John did not play. He was limiting his playing activity and was saving himself for the more important championship games ahead. The great Andy Fleming, however, judged that it was now time for him to retire. It was not generally known that a serious eye injury sustained in a football game in 1948 had never really been cured and for several weeks had begun to affect his play so that, time and again, he had to depend on his great experience and hurling 'sense' to see him through difficult situations. His loss to club and county was inestimable but it was typical of the man that he left the game only when he was convinced the future of the team was assured

    The Kilkenny clubs were coming at Mount Sion in waves. The next challenge came from Jimmy Langton's club, Éire Óg. The teams had met three times over the last few years with the series result standing at two to one in favour of Éire Óg. Another huge crowd had paid to see the game which was regarded as one of the greatest matches ever at Waterford's Gaelic Field, the hurling being brilliant and the crowd fanatical in its support. Both teams fielded at full strength, Philly Grimes coming on to the Mount Sion team as a direct replacement for Andy Fleming. This showed the depth of talent available to Mount Sion – one of the club's greatest-ever players retired and was replaced by another. The clashes between the star players on both sides were fierce, but fair, and one incident in particular showed up the difference between Munster and Leinster hurling. In a tussle for a high ball at centre-field the Mount Sion centre-back, Larry Fanning, received a blow on the head from behind. As he cleared the ball he turned and saw that only Jimmy Langton of the opposition was near him. Just then a high ball came back towards Larry and as he positioned to hit it he heard John roaring 'My ball.' Larry and all the Mount Sion players in the vicinity ducked (out of self-preservation) because John had a tremendous stroke on a ball and was brilliant at overhead play but, as Larry said 'poor Langton put up his hand to catch the ball and John nearly cut it off at the wrist.' Langton exclaimed, in his pain, 'John, John, that's not hurling' to which John answered, 'That's Munster hurling, Jimmy.' Nowadays, an incident like that would have meant instant dismissal but at that time overhead striking of the ball was a major feature of the game and any ball in the air was regarded as fair game.

The match was also notable for an incident when an elderly woman ran on to the field and began hitting Jimmy Langton with her handbag. The mistaken impression amongst the crowd was that Langton had hit the woman with his hurley and uproar ensued. A large section of the crowd invaded the pitch and many blows were exchanged between rival supporters. From then until the referee blew the final whistle there was trouble in the ground and when the match finally ended with Éire Óg winning by 0-13 to 0-8 there were pockets of spectators still on the pitch. John immediately went to his old friend, Langton, and escorted him off the field in case anyone tried to assault him. John told me subsequently that he had been prepared to hit anyone who dared to attempt such an action.

The trouble was not yet over however. The belief persisted that Langton had assaulted the woman and as the Éire Óg bus left to go to Mackey's café on the Quay (where Mount Sion had arranged a meal for the visiting team) a crowd followed and a rock was thrown through a window at the back of the bus, smashing the glass. Fortunately, no-one was injured.[193] The club was naturally concerned that the trouble that day would reflect badly on its reputation, but such worries were allayed by a swift invitation from Éire Óg for a return match in Kilkenny.

The county championship clash that everyone wanted to see was the first round meeting of the county champions, Tourin, and the team they had deposed, Mount Sion. Over five thousand spectators witnessed a game that proved the greatest disappointment seen for many years. It was a match marred by violent scenes that occurred during play and the referee brought the game to an end before full-time. The Mount Sion players were the complete masters and never relented in their determined attack on the Tourin goal. With ten minutes remaining in the first half a Tourin player was ordered off the field and, amidst fighting, the referee was attacked. Mount Sion led at

---

193 *Munster Express*, 8 June 1951

half time by 3-7 to Tourin's 1-4. Tourin did make a spirited attempt to catch-up after the start of the second half but Mount Sion were completely focused on their objective and drove on without cease until near the end when scenes of rowdyism broke out for the second time. When all efforts failed to restore order the referee brought the game to a premature end with the score at 4-12 to 1-6 in Mount Sion's favour. At a subsequent county board meeting the Tourin player who had allegedly struck a Mount Sion player with a hurley was suspended from the Association for three years while another Tourin player was ordered to appear before the board. Two Mount Sion players were given a 'slap on the wrist' with a minimum suspension of two months. The Mount Sion players had made no secret of their desire to win the county championship in John's final year and they were now into the semi-final.

Another huge crowd was present in Dungarvan when Cappoquin squared up to Mount Sion. Towards the end of the game the crowd on the sidelines was so great that they gradually encroached on to the playing area and it became almost impossible to follow the play. It was apparent that every hurling follower wanted to be present whenever John played just in case it turned out to be his last-ever game. He didn't disappoint them. The *Waterford Star* reported that, 'In attack, John Keane once more was the man of the match and in what may have been the second last match of his career gave the spectators an object lesson in hurling.'[194] John was the prototype of the unselfish centre-forward and he was usually content to manufacture scoring opportunities for his wing-men and full-forward line – but not on this day. He was in devastating form and by half-time had already scored three goals and a point. Mount Sion were in complete control in the second half and John added two more goals – the first of which broke the net, such was the ferocity of the shot – and he also hit the post. Another pile-driver was only parried by the goalkeeper who was knocked into the back of the net by the force of the shot. The ball looped into the air and

---

194 *Waterford Star*, 12 October 1951

John's nephew, Tommy Keane, scored a goal from the rebound. The Cappoquin side had been stunned by John's goal-feast and thoroughly demoralised by a six goal defeat. John was going to leave the playing arena with a bang, not a whimper, but no one could foresee the sensation that was to occur in his very last game.

The county final was set for Dungarvan and it was a match to savour because Mount Sion were opposed by the home club. It was a gala occasion with an enormous crowd present to see the final game of John's hurling career. For the first fifteen minutes it was a closely contested affair with Mount Sion leading by 0-5 to 0-3. Then the incident occurred that completely changed the course of the game and turned what might have been a narrow victory into a riot of scoring for Mount Sion.

> Mount Sion's captain, John Keane, was involved with an opposing player in a trivial incident which seemed to have ended when, to the consternation of his team-mates, and – if the stony silence which greeted the decision be any indication – to the amazement of the entire crowd, the Mount Sion star was ordered to the sidelines by the referee. Always the perfect sportsman, Keane obeyed this harsh instruction without demur and the game continued – but with a difference. The extraordinary and inexplicable decision of the referee galvanised the remaining Mount Sion men into furious action and they settled down to give the most determined and sustained exhibition of hurling since their epic clashes with Erin's Own a decade or so ago. Another result of the referee's action was to swing the entire neutral section of the crowd in Mount Sion's favour which was rather hard on a gallant Dungarvan team which was in no way responsible for the unfortunate development.[195]

---

195 Unidentified newspaper clipping from the Goode family scrapbooks, courtesy of Eoin Fanning

Thus the 1951 championship ended with the return of the championship to Mount Sion for the eighth time. Following the final whistle the Mount Sion team (aided by several Dungarvan players) chaired their captain in triumph from the field in a spontaneous tribute to the only man in their club who had participated in all of its championship wins.

Mount Sion, County champions 1951

Back Row (L-R): John Keane (Capt.), Johnny O'Regan, Tom Gallagher, Wal Casey, Sean Hayden, Mick Healy, Billy Gaffney, Tommy Keane, Larry Fanning, Máirtín Morrissey, Noel Jackman, Davy Power

Front Row (L-R): Billy Mulcahy, Mick Heffernan, Mick Flannelly, Philly Grimes, Tom Kennedy, Jim Hurley, Tom Vereker, Paddy Curran, Tom Connolly

The club committee subsequently debated the matter of the sending-off (the first in John's career and in his last match) and decided that the club delegates would not make an issue of it as it would not be desirable to drag John's name into an unseemly controversy. The committee was informed that John's attitude towards the issue was that the club were now the county champions and could afford to ignore the whole matter.[196] A long and colourful hurling career had been brought to its close in a rather unexpected fashion.

A last hurrah

Although John had retired from top-class hurling he was a committed GAA man and he embraced the new challenges his free-time now allowed. He had resigned from the club committee but continued as a selector for the club's senior hurling team and was also, along with Pat Fanning, the club's nominee as selector for the county team. He also began to referee more matches. A new initiative was introduced to the GAA locally in 1952 – the business houses league. With the growth of industrial Waterford a regular competition had been organised and thirteen teams were entered in what was known locally as the 'Factory league' and John was asked to play for the Graves & Co. team. He played in the first game against Goodbody's Jute Factory and scored three goals in double quick time before retiring. The aim of the competition was to unearth new talent for the local game and to provide recreation for the workers and John felt that he was taking up a place on the team that could be given more beneficially to a younger player. He was chosen by the GAA to adjudicate in some high-profile games either as referee or umpire, the most notable being as referee in the Junior All-Ireland final in London (1952), the minor All-Ireland hurling final (1953), and several National League hurling matches. He was also one of the umpires at the All-Ireland senior hurling finals of 1954 and 1956.

His most challenging role, however, came with his selection as trainer of the Mount Sion senior hurling team. His great hurling brain and astute tactical sense made him an obvious candidate but his first year in the position came to a grinding halt when Mount Sion, the county champions, were beaten by Clonea who went on to take the title in 1952. This led to calls

---

196 Mount Sion club minutes, 17 October 1951

from several members of the club for John to make a come-back to the senior hurling team for 1953. When the matter of his possible return was raised at a meeting on 8 July 1953 the committee decided that this was an issue that should be left entirely up to himself; when approached he expressed his belief that the team was quite capable of winning county championships without his presence on the field. No more was heard of the matter and that team went on to win the next nine Waterford senior hurling titles. Mount Sion's record at the end of that period was astonishing – in the eighteen years between 1948 and 1965 the club won fifteen county senior hurling titles – and John was associated as player and coach with every success.

His presence on the playing field was not over, however. In a surprise move the club senior football selectors made a special request to him to make a return to the team for the 1953 championships. John had always loved playing football and he agreed to return to the panel. To the surprise of everyone Mount Sion went on to win the senior football title (the club's first) and although John did not play he was listed as first substitute and won his first senior football medal.

He continued playing football and although Mount Sion were defeated in the divisional final in the following year hopes were high for 1955. John was then thirty eight years old but was still one of the club's best footballers and the *Munster Express* reported on their first round championship victory thus:

> A feature ... was the return to active service of the fabulous John Keane and present indications are that he will be again included in the "Monastery" attack on Sunday. John Keane introduced that effective leadership into the Mount Sion forward division when the side triumphed over St Otteran's [1-7 to 1-4], and his inclusion against Kill looks a certainty.[197]

The game against Kill in the divisional senior football semi-final was the third match that the club played in four days. On

---

197 *Munster Express*, 5 August 1955

Thursday evening 4 August the hurlers had defeated Mooncoin at Waterford. On the following day they then travelled to Cork where they defeated the local team, Sarsfields, in a thrilling match before returning to Waterford where two days later twelve of the hurling team played against, and defeated, Kill in the county football championship. In that hard-fought game at Portlaw Mount Sion triumphed by a point on a score of 1–6 to 1–5 with John contributing 1–2 to his team's total. He was the star of the game, a newspaper claiming that 'Hero of the hour, as far as the winners were concerned, was the outstanding display given by former hurling star, John Keane. Besides scoring the all-important goal, Keane also helped his side with two well-taken points.'[198]

The team drew with Dunhill in the county football semi-final thereby causing a huge problem for the club for with the continued success of both hurling and football teams a clash of fixtures happened. The day came to pass on Sunday 28 August when the replay of the senior football semi-final coincided with the senior hurling semi-final. At 3.00pm the hurlers defeated De La Salle in the city, and the club then travelled to Portlaw where, at 7.30pm, most of the hurlers played for John's football team that defeated Dunhill by 0–6 to 0–3. It was a remarkable performance of skill and physical fitness demonstrated by this exceptional group of players.

The football and hurling teams had now qualified for their respective county finals and it was strange for John to be playing for the footballers and not for the hurlers. After the senior and minor hurlers had won their respective county titles it was time for the footballers to attempt to bring the third title to the club for 1955. It was a tough match against Brickey Rangers and one that was destined to end in a storm of controversy. Scores were level twice in a game that was attended by a then record crowd for a football final. The score that brought Mount Sion back into the game was a goal that was punched to the net by John when he doubled on a fifty yard free kick as players and

---

198 *Munster Express*, 12 August 1955

spectators engaged in fisticuffs on the end line. This goal, which brought Mount Sion to within one point of their opponents, was the signal for an invasion of the pitch by hundreds of spectators as Brickey Rangers officials called for the abandonment of the game. Order was restored after some time but just as the players were prepared to resume 'hostilities' a bizarre scene unfolded as two horses galloped on to the field scattering the players who tried to avoid being knocked down. The two horses had been grazing on the green area behind the city goal and in the turmoil of the pitch invasion someone had opened the gate to the sideline and hunted the two horses on to the pitch. When the horses were eventually driven off, the game (immortalised thereafter as the 'giddy-up' final) resumed for the final five minutes and Frankie Walsh scored the equalising point for Mount Sion from a close-in free. The game finished 1-2 to 0-5 with John scoring the goal and Walsh the two points.

The replay was eagerly anticipated and all records for a football final were broken as the teams squared off for the second time in a game that was abandoned before the final whistle. It was a rip-roaring match that saw the Brickey's lead for only a short period in the game. Just before half time and with Mount Sion leading by 1-3 to 0-4 John gathered the ball from a close-in free and headed straight for the goal but was dragged down in the square. Frankie Walsh blazed hard for a goal but the goalie deflected the ball over the bar for a point. The Brickey's scored their last point after ten minutes of the second half had passed and from then to the finish the Mount Sion midfielders Séamus Power and Philly Grimes dominated the match and the Mount Sion defence held firm. It was a shame that with only about five minutes left in the match and Mount Sion leading by 1-6 to 0-6 a section of the crowd invaded the pitch. The referee, aided by board officials and stewards, tried vainly to clear the grounds but without success.

It was an unsatisfactory end to the championship and the issue was never resolved. A proposal to the county board that the final be declared abandoned was carried and no champions were recorded for that year. It had been John's last appearance on the field of play and although the Mount Sion players were the moral victors no county championship medals were ever given to the team. In compensation, Fr John Grace, a committee member of the Mount Sion club, had special medals struck and he presented them to the football team at a function for the Mount Sion county winning teams of 1955.

Chapter Twenty
Trainer, coach, psychologist

John had now most definitely retired from playing and was concentrating solely on training the players that he considered to be the golden generation of Mount Sion hurlers.

The Mount Sion club was at the zenith of its power and when the 1956 season ended it had won an unprecedented four county titles – senior hurling and football and minor hurling and football – and one player, Freddie O'Brien, was a playing member of all four teams. It is a record that has stood the test of time. The first signs that Waterford had the basis of a great team were evident in the Munster championship match lost to Cork in Fermoy in June 1956. Waterford were the masters for three-quarters of the game with Philly Grimes and Johnny Kiely dominating the centre of the field and would have won but for the disastrous switching of Grimes to the forward line in the second half when victory was in sight. Six of John's Mount Sion team played in that match and John was ready and willing to have a say in the county's future in whatever capacity the county board deemed fit. That offer came in early 1957 when he was appointed trainer and one of a selection panel of five, the other Mount Sion representative being Pat Fanning.

The first training session for the 1957 Waterford panel is burnt forever in Austin Flynn's memory. The great full-back had come on to the Waterford panel in 1952 for a short while but then was dropped and drifted away, being quite content playing for his club, Abbeyside, doing a bit of fishing from a boat he had just made with his brother, and going off on trips with the local scout troop He spoke to me at length in 2008 about John and the Waterford team of 1957-63.[199]

---

199 Interview with Austin Flynn

> When I first got the invitation to join the county team I remember feeling a bit ambivalent about it. I remember going down the village and meeting some of the club officials and they were so excited about my call-up that I was taken a bit aback. I told them that I wasn't sure if I would go to training and they nearly exploded and insisted that I had to do it for the village. To tell you nothing but the truth I never thought I was that good. But that first night! I'll never forget it! There were a few officials around but I remember only two—Pat Fanning and John Keane.

Austin recalled that he knew John only from reputation and that John had been his idol as a player but he had met Pat many years before when Austin was a schools player. Austin continued with his reminiscence of that first night's training in 1957.

> Both Pat and John were charismatic but each of them had the same effect on you. They made you believe in yourself as a hurler and that belief grew the more you were in their company. Each had a totally different approach. Pat was the orator – and what an orator! He was the most inspirational speaker I have ever heard. I still remember his words to us that night. He told us that we were starting a journey that would take us to an All-Ireland title. 'As God is my judge,' he said 'I believe there's the winning of an All Ireland in this team. It will take a great effort. You will all have to give yourselves totally to the cause, give until it hurts and then give even more. You will have to have pride in the Waterford jersey. Cork and Tipperary and Kilkenny have their tradition. But we also have our tradition. Being beaten and picking yourself up and coming back for more – that's our tradition. We will never give up.

Austin then spoke about John.

> Talk about being overawed! Here was this legendary figure treating me as an equal and without any condescension. He

was a great man. He had a knack of putting you at your ease. You know, he never raised his voice. He didn't need to. He had done it all and when he spoke about hurling he did so with authority. We often hear of managers who break down doors and who never stop roaring and shouting at players. That was not John's way. His approach was the quiet word in your ear. He was a sport psychologist long before that type of person was even thought of in Ireland. He never criticised a player in front of others. He never even took us aside from the others to speak to us. When he had to impart advice or otherwise you would suddenly realise that you and he had somehow drifted apart from the others without anyone noticing and then, after your talk, you would rejoin the group, again without anyone noticing. We all appreciated that.

Another player from that team who reminisced with me on many occasions was John Barron. He told of an occasion in a match when a decision by the referee went against him and he reacted badly, throwing his hurley to the ground in disgust. Afterwards, amidst the noise and clamour of the dressing room, he realised that John was sitting beside him talking quietly about the match. The trainer referred to the incident on the pitch and told him that a player should never let his opponent see that he was rattled and that he should never broadcast his mistakes. It was advice that Barron never forgot. He told me that it was all the more effective in the way it was transmitted to him. John Barron also discussed John's method of training.

> It consisted mainly of hurling skills allied to explosive sprints. The training was enjoyable but intense. We didn't know how much work we were doing because of the way John operated. He had enormous hands, you know, and he had wrists like steel cords. He would stand in the midst of a group of players with the hurley in his right hand and flick the ball one-handed for a player to chase and hit, right or left. What we didn't re-

alise was that he kept hitting the ball just that little bit farther each time so that we were doing these really intense sprints that were getting progressively longer. And all the time he was encouraging us with that soft voice. Encouragement from such a source was almost as good as the training. You see, he was building up our confidence, something that a lot of previous Waterford teams lacked. Eventually we believed that we were as good as any team in the country – and we were!

Pat Fanning's prediction that there was an All-Ireland in the team nearly came to pass in 1957 but everyone knew that Waterford had a team that, at last, could challenge any other in the country. The following year turned out to be a disaster, however and the senior hurling team were crushed by Tipperary in the Munster final at Thurles. This was a huge setback and a great deal of self-doubt was engendered amongst the supporters. A series of crazy rumours circulated concerning the team's preparations, the wildest being that a certain official had given the team some unspecified 'pills' before the game. A friend of mine suggested that if this were true then it must have been sleeping pills that they were given. A county board meeting towards the end of 1958 proposed that the system of selecting the senior hurling team be changed and after a vote it was decided that the county champions should have only one representative (instead of two) with four others being elected by the county board members. This was strenuously opposed by Mount Sion, who had just won the county title for the sixth year in succession. At a Mount Sion club meeting the committee unanimously instructed its selectors to withdraw completely from the county senior hurling selection committee. The committee discussed John's role as trainer of the county team and it was agreed to let matters stand pending further developments at the county board.[200] John was unhappy with the set-up and he resigned as the county trainer but as 1958 gave way to 1959 the clamour grew to have him back and this culminated in a strongly

---

200   Mount Sion club minutes, 8 October 1958

worded plea in the *Munster Express* of 16 January 1959. I give the article in full.

> With the present Waterford hurling team nearing the pinnacle of success, the call for a team trainer becomes very much apparent. The county's destinies must be placed in the hands of one fully qualified for the job. From him must be won respect, discipline and a willingness to respond to every task. The man must know his hurling, and his hurlers. He must be capable of exerting from his charges that vital ounce so necessary for success. Experience too, must play a leading hand, with inspiration a major trump card.
>
> To fill this role, Waterford possesses no more qualified exponent than John Keane. Without question, he was probably the greatest hurler ever to wear the county jersey. For over twenty years John was in the top flight of hurling greatness and won fame not alone for his playing ability but for the excellent mode of sportsmanship which endeared him to friend and foe alike. During his playing career John was known to have filled every team position with distinction, and gained inter-provincial honours in numerous defensive and attacking roles. Under his guidance Waterford won renown in the gallant bid for 1957 All-Ireland honours when the minimum margin deprived the Decies of ultimate victory.
>
> I know that the wish of all Waterford Gaels is expressed when I say 'the county again needs John Keane.' His services would be invaluable throughout the coming season and may mean all the difference between victory and defeat. The players for their part had come to rely on the wisdom and advice of the popular cityman. In this vital field of endeavour the county board are demonstrating a complete lack of duty. I trust that this matter, overlooked during recent months, will be soon

remedied and that John Keane can be again persuaded to serve the county he himself served so nobly in the past.[201]

John responded positively and was re-appointed as team trainer – to wonderful effect. The dream was finally realised in 1959 after those two epic All-Ireland final matches against Kilkenny. If ever a team deserved to win the title it was that 1959 Waterford team. In that campaign they beat Limerick, Tipperary (All-Ireland champions), Cork, Galway and then Kilkenny after a replay. Austin Flynn told me an interesting story about John in the lead-up to that replayed final.

> The field in Waterford was having some work done on it and we were training in Dunhill. One night I was really enjoying the training and felt on top of the world when John abruptly stopped the session and said 'All right, lads, you've all done enough. Go in and have a rub-down.' Some of us were a bit annoyed but we did what we were told. It was only after we had won the All-Ireland that it struck us that John knew we

Pat Fanning (County chairman), John Keane (Trainer) and Jim Ware (Selector) in 1959.
(Photo courtesy of Eoin Fanning)

---

201 *Munster Express*, 16 January 1959

had done enough training and that he didn't want us to leave all our hurling on the training pitch. We were super-fit and he knew that any more training would have made us stale.

Waterford players with Jack Dempsey, former world heavyweight boxing champion in New York 1960. (L-R); Joe Harney, Paudie Casey, Jack Dempsey, Tom Cheasty, John Keane with Jackie Condon at front (Photo courtesy of Paudie Casey)

John continued his work with Mount Sion as committee member and senior hurling selector. The Waterford team continued to prosper under his guidance reaching the National League final of 1961 and winning the Munster, National League and Oireachtas finals in 1963. That was the year that saw Waterford achieve the highest score by a beaten finalist in a sixty-minute All-Ireland final (6-8), when the county lost out to an Eddie Keher-inspired Kilkenny team. Pat Fanning once said that he wasn't sure if John Keane, the player, did more for Waterford than did John Keane the manager, leader, trainer, psychologist, coach, advisor and father-figure to the county senior hurling team.

Chapter twenty one
Endgame

John had a keen business brain and he was involved successfully in various business enterprises as the 1960s ran its course, primarily with building firms but also in buying and running his own public house. His family was now complete and his young family became increasingly involved with the Mount Sion club. His eldest son, Tom, once remarked that while his children had inherited John's mathematical brain they had, apparently, missed out on the hurling gene. Despite that comment it is worth noting that Tom had played hurling and football at the highest club level and had won Waterford titles with Mount Sion in various grades in both hurling and football; under-16 football in 1962 and minor hurling in 1964. He had also been a substitute on the Mount Sion team that won the 1972 county senior hurling title and in the same year had captained the club junior hurling team that lost the county final. As a student in University College Cork (UCC) he played for the college in the Kelleher shield (senior football league) in 1963. He also played in the senior hurling league and was on the UCC team beaten by a Glen Rovers team featuring Christy Ring in the league final in 1966. In the same year (when he was secretary of the college hurling club) he was a substitute on the UCC team beaten by Avondhu in the Cork senior hurling final. In his own words he was enthusiastic and fast, but not very good. John's two daughters, Margaret and Catherine, were excellent badminton players and both subsequently married Mount Sion players, Michael Foley and Eamonn Ryan respectively, who won numerous county titles and also represented Waterford in senior hurling.

The last photo of John with his family, taken three months before his death. L-R: Catherine Keane, Eamonn Ryan, Margaret Foley, Michael Foley, May Keane, Gerard Keane, Agnes Keane, John Keane, Rosemary Keane, John Keane, Tom Keane Photo courtesy of Gerard Keane and with the permission of Moriarty Photographers, Killarney

As the 1960s gave way to the 1970s John had recurring bouts of illness. In his last two years he suffered greatly from leg pains associated with his heart condition and spent some time in various hospitals. His nephew, Tomás Ó Cinnéide tells of an illuminating incident that demonstrated John's heroic nature during that time of great pain.

> I knew that John was suffering great pain in his leg, but I didn't realise the toll it was taking on him until the day when Pat Fanning drove him to the Mater Hospital for an operation. Pat and I, with two other members of the family, were carrying John downstairs when his leg was accidentally knocked against the banisters. He gave a terrible cry of pain and grasped the banister in a vice-like grip. The combined strength of the four of us couldn't budge him until at last the pain diminished slightly and John slowly released his grip. When we had at last placed him reasonably comfortably in

the car, his leg pillowed and cushioned, I looked at him and saw, in his ashen face, all the pain he had endured and all the ravages wrought by the endless, sleepless, nights. As you know he did get some relief from the operation but was never quite the same afterwards and was almost always in some pain. In all that time I never once heard him complain.[202]

John subsequently returned to work but he knew that he was seriously ill. He seemed determined to make the most of the time he had left and began to visit the Mount Sion club centre on a regular basis where he enjoyed the company of the hurlers, old and young. He seemed to draw energy and strength from being with them. That fact that he had been seriously ill for a number of years was unknown to most people and that was typical of the man. He didn't complain. He bore his pain with great courage and it was that courage that sustained him during his terrible pain. The pain was almost constant and might have caused a lesser man to break. Pat Fanning recalled his last few days, thus:

> He had a heart condition which probably was the cause of the bad circulation. John had discussed the matter with me and told me that he would not consent to an amputation though he knew the consequences of that decision. He said 'Pat, I would rather go whole!'

Then, in the midst of his pain John decided, almost unbelievably, that he would go on a journey and pay a visit to the friends and former rivals, all hurling men, who he still met on occasions during his line of work. You know, John loved hurling and he was at his happiest amongst hurling men. It turned out to be an epic journey that had a touch of the heroic about it. It was also his last journey. Did he suspect that before he set out? Perhaps! You know, thinking back on it, John's last journey was a sort of pilgrimage; of a man who knew his days

---

202   Interview with Tomás Ó Cinneide

were numbered and who wished to meet again some of the comrades with whom he had shared so much.[203]

He travelled first to Kilkenny where he spent the night with his old friend Jimmy Langton, talking and reminiscing about the great games between John's Mount Sion and Langton's Éire Óg. He came back to Waterford where he spent a sleepless night, tossing and turning with the pain. Then he went on to Kinsale where he met Cork's Jack Barrett. He was a great friend from their days on Munster Railway cup teams. Next stop was Tralee where he was greeted by Jackie Power, the man who was, perhaps, his closest friend from the old Limerick team that John regarded as the greatest of all time. The following morning he set out on the road to Limerick where he planned to meet with Mick Mackey and all the others from that great team, but he never completed his journey. He became unwell on the road between Tarbert and Limerick, knocked on a door and asked the woman who answered it to call an ambulance – but he died before it reached the hospital.

The date was Wednesday 1 October 1975 and he was a mere fifty eight years of age.

When the news of his death reached us, it was sudden and shocking. Séamus Ó Braonáin wrote:

> We heard [it] ... rough and ready, when we went to buy the morning paper ... The newsagent gave it out straight from the shoulder: 'Did you hear that John Keane is dead?' He had taken ill the previous evening ... at Tarbert ... [was] then rushed to Limerick Hospital but he died on the way. John's sentiment which we had several times heard him express, 'If I couldn't live in Waterford, then Limerick is where I would chose,' had proven true in death rather than in life. We, too, died a little that grey October morning. For John Keane was not only a valued and a dear friend for a number of years: not only one of the most marvellously exciting men to spend

---

203 Interview with Pat Fanning

hours in conversation with, listening to his analysis, thesis and synthesis on hurling and hurlers; not only one of the greatest (many say the greatest!) hurlers of all time who could play anywhere with equal magnificence; not only a great trainer, teacher, motivator of younger hurlers; not only a kindly and sensitive gentleman; he was also our original boyhood hero; the sandy-blond, clean-cut, classicist for whom we would have fought with tooth and nail anyone who dared cast the slightest aspersion on his perfection. And heroes ought not [to] grow old. And heroes simply should not die. So we died a little as the lost youth, still hidden out of sight within us, died at last.[204]

Throughout Waterford city people gathered in groups, at work and in the streets, and spoke about the man they had idolised throughout his hurling career. His passing cast a shadow not only over Waterford city and county but throughout the land, for John Keane was known and loved wherever hurling men gathered. But how could John Keane be dead and at the ridiculously early age of fifty eight? The man we thought of as being indestructible should have been in the prime of life.

John's match was over, the final whistle had blown but now only he heard its call. The throngs who had cheered him throughout his glorious career were absent and there were no crowds to surge in and carry him shoulder high in triumph. John Keane was conquered at last.

---

204 Ó Braonáin, *Gaelic Sport*, November 1975

Chapter twenty two

Epilogue

Although John was alone when he died, the thousands gathered on the following day in Limerick when, in Pat Fanning's memorable phrase, 'all Munster honoured him.' This time, however, the multitudes were silent and sombre; there were no exultant cries and no banners waved. It was to Limerick that we travelled on that awful day for the removal of the remains and I will never forget the enormous crowd that greeted us when we arrived at the hospital. On seeing that huge crowd we realized with a great sense of humility that John belonged not just to Waterford but to the nation. That was also seen as the hearse left the mortuary when former All-Ireland hurlers Mick Mackey, Jack Barrett, Jackie Power, John Mackey, Dave Clohessy and Mick Herbert acted as pall bearers, and present and past players lined the route from the hospital for fully two hundred yards down the street. We took him home to Waterford and Mount Sion and to the thousands who had waited silently in the wind and the rain to say a last farewell to the man who had made us all feel so proud. Former Taoiseach, Jack Lynch, and Seán Ó Síocháin, GAA general secretary, read the lessons at the funeral mass on the following day and, as the coffin was borne to the hearse by club and county teammates of different eras, former colleagues of John from the 1938 and 1948 All-Ireland teams formed a guard of honour from the church to the Cork Road.[205] We buried John in the cemetery

---

205 The pall-bearers were representative of the Mount Sion club from its very beginning; Mick Healy, Larry Fanning, Andy Fleming, Larry Guinan, Mick Flannelly, Pat O'Grady, John Flynn, Philly Grimes, Séamus Power, Pat McGrath, Jim Greene, Dicky Roche, Davy Power, Martin Óg Morrissey, Frankie Walsh and Paddy Greene.

overlooking the broad sands of Tramore in the presence of a host of hurlers and GAA men who had known him during his stellar career. Pat Fanning, his voice breaking with emotion, gave the funeral oration over the grave of his friend. It was, possibly, the hardest duty that he ever had to perform.

A meal had been arranged at a Waterford city hotel for the visiting players and officials and as the crowds left the cemetery Pat Fanning noticed a lone figure still standing at the graveside. He was a giant of a man but his head was bowed and his great frame was racked with tears as he struggled to control his emotions. Pat recognised the great Nicky Rackard and, approaching him, told him of the reception and that he was welcome to join the other hurlers. Rackard, his face streaked with tears, declined the invitation and said, 'Pat, I came to bury John Keane and all I want to do now is go home.' The former Limerick star, Jackie Power, accompanied some of the Mount Sion players to the club headquarters and when Power was asked to say a few words he said, memorably 'Today we buried a man who showed us all how to hurl.'

The tributes paid to John during the following weeks were many and fulsome. All referred to his hurling skill, of course, but running through them all were the constant references to his qualities as a man and as a friend. Tom Browne of the *Irish Press* encapsulated those sentiments when he wrote in October 1975:

> A great hurler. No more needs to be said, for it hardly matters now whether you rank him No. 1 or 2 or 3 in the list of all-time greats. Those who saw him play cherish the experience as one that will never be repeated or copied. Centre-back, fullback, centre-forward: it wouldn't matter to Keane for he could be and was among the greats in all those positions. He is irreplaceable, for he was unique. That uniqueness was not only because of his hurling – though that was unparalleled – but also because of his special human qualities. Since his death several hundred people have told me that either they themselves, or their fathers, uncles or other relatives were

great personal friends of John. They were. He made them feel so. No sportsman I have known gave so much of himself to his fans. Somehow he had an innate understanding of what it meant to ordinary people to be able to say they had a chat with John Keane the other day.

'What John Keane?'

'There is only one John Keane. John Keane, the great hurler, of course.'

But let the final words be with Mick Mackey, John's relentless opponent - and great friend. When Mackey heard of John's death he delivered a tribute fit for the ages; one that was all the more potent and eloquent because of its clarity, brevity and frankness. He said simply:

There never was, nor never will be, a greater hurler than John Keane of Waterford.[206]

---

206 From the article *The mighty John Keane of Waterford*, by Seamus O'Brien, in the programme for the Munster senior hurling semi-final, Waterford v Limerick, 14 June 2009

Appendices

Appendix One

JOHN KEANE'S PLAYING RECORD 1931-55

The following statistical record of John's career has been compiled from different sources, but mainly the local and national newspapers. Unfortunately not every match was reported in full (and some were not reported at all) leaving some unavoidable gaps in the record. To supplement the newspaper records I also examined the minutes of the Mount Sion H&F club where I found valuable information. I gleaned more from notes written on match programmes and from scribbles on old photographs.

Please note that the winning team is shown in bold print and both teams are bolded where a match ended in a draw. An asterisk (*) after a team, indicates that the team won the match on an objection.

Abbreviations
POS = John's position on the team;
NK = Not Known;
MH = Minor Hurling;
MF = Minor Football;
JH = Junior Hurling;
JF = Junior Football;
SH = Senior Hurling;
SF = Senior Football;
S/F = Semi-Final;
Tour = Tournament;
Ref = Referee

DATE	COMPETITION	AGE	TEAM	OPPOSITION	POS.
11-Jan-31	1930 East Minor H S/F	13	**Mount Sion/Eire Óg**	De La Salle	NK
30-Jan-31	1930 East Minor H Final	13	**Mount Sion/Eire Óg 9-4**	Portlaw 1-1	LHB
02-Apr-31	1930 Co Minor H Final	14	**Mount Sion/Eire Óg 8-2**	Dungarvan 0-0	NK
06-Nov-31	1931 East Minor H Final	14	**Mount Sion/Eire Óg 7-1**	Portlaw 2-7	NK
1932					
28-Feb-32	Minor F Challenge	15	Mount Sion	Ballytruckle	NK
15-May-32	1932 Munster MH 1st Rd	15	**Waterford 4-1**	Cork 3-2	CF
17-Jul-32	1932 Munster MH S/F	15	Waterford 3-1	**Tipperary 4-7**	LHF
31-Jul-32	U/16 Hurling Challenge	15	**Mount Sion CBS**	Ferrybank	NK
XX-XX-32	SH Schools Challenge	15	**Mount Sion CBS (Won)**	Carrick-on-Suir CBS	FB
XX-XX-32	SH Schools Challenge	15	**Mount Sion CBS (Won)**	Carrick-on-Suir CBS	FB
XX-XX-32	SH Schools Challenge	15	**Mount Sion CBS (Won)**	St Stephen's CBS	FB
XX-XX-32	SH Schools Challenge	15	**Mount Sion CBS (Won)**	Kilkenny CBS	FB
13-Nov-32	SH Schools Challenge	15	**Mount Sion CBS (Won)**	Callan CBS	FB
01-Nov-32	SH Schools Challenge	15	**Mount Sion CBS (Won)**	Callan CBS	FB
1933					
08-Jan-33	1932 County MH S/F	15	**Mount Sion 6-4**	St Stephen's 3-0	FB
12-Mar-33	School Friendly SH	16	**Mount Sion CBS 5-1**	St Stephen's 4-3	FB
19-Mar-33	1933 County JH 1st Rd	16	**Mount Sion 3-4**	St Stephen's 3-2	FB
25-Mar-33	1933 Harty Cup, 1st Rd	16	**Mount Sion CBS 1-7**	Limerick CBS 2-1	FB
12-Apr-33	1933 Dr Hackett Cup	16	**Mount Sion CBS 5-1**	Dungarvan CBS 1-1	FB
17-Apr-33	1933 Harty Cup S/F	16	Mount Sion CBS 2-6	**Thurles CBS 6-4**	FB
30-Apr-33	Inter-Pro Final	16	**Munster Colleges 4-4**	Leinster Colleges 3-1	RFB
21-May-33	Munster MH 1st Rd	16	**Waterford 3-4**	Tipperary 4-1	RFB
25-Jun-33	Munster MH Replay	16	Waterford 2-1	**Tipperary 4-1**	NK
20-Aug-33	Mount Sion JH Tour	16	**Mount Sion 7-4**	Erin's Own 1-2	FB
17-Sep-33	County JH S/F	16	**Mount Sion (Won)**	Croughaun Rangers	FB
01-Oct-33	Eastern MH Final	16	**Mount Sion 4-4**	Passage 2-1	FB
22-Oct-33	1933 County JH Final	16	**Mount Sion 6-3**	Dungarvan 2-5	FB
19-Nov-33	Challenge MH	16	**Mount Sion (Won)**	Carrick-on-Suir	FB
10-Dec-33	Schools Friendly SH	16	**Mount Sion 6-3**	Callan CBS 4-6	FB
1934					
21-Jan-34	1933 County MH Final	16	**Mount Sion 9-3**	Dungarvan 1-0	NK
04-Feb-34	SH Challenge	16	**Mount Sion 3-6**	De La Salle 2-3	FB
25-Feb-34	SH Challenge	17	Mount Sion 3-1	**Mooncoin 4-2**	FB
04-Mar-34	SH Challenge	17	Mount Sion 3-1	**Mooncoin 5-4**	FB
09-Mar-34	County JH 1st Rd	17	Mount Sion 4-6	**De La Salle 5-6**	FB
08-Apr-34	County SH 1st Rd	17	**Mount Sion 3-3**	Dunhill 0-2	FB
22-Apr-34	Trial JH game	17	Waterford 7-2	**Sth Kilkenny 11-10**	FB
29-Apr-34	Inter-Pro Final	17	Munster Colleges 3-1	**Leinster Colleges 5-6**	NK
13-May-34	Munster JH 1st Rd	17	**Waterford 8-3**	Kerry 1-3	FB
17-Jun-34	Munster MH 1st Rd	17	**Waterford 10-9**	Kerry 2-3	FB
24-Jun-34	Munster MF 1st Rd	17	**Waterford 3-4**	Limerick 0-1	RFB
08-Jul-34	Eastern MF S/F	17	**Mount Sion (Won)**	Gaultier	NK
15-Jul-34	Eastern MH S/F	17	**Mount Sion (Won)**	Cathal Brugha	NK
22-Jul-34	Munster MH Final	17	Waterford 0-6	**Tipperary 3-6**	FB
05-Aug-34	County SH League	17	Mount Sion	**Tallow (by 2 pts)**	FB
12-Aug-34	Munster JH Final	17	**Waterford 5-7**	Cork 1-4	FB
26-Aug-34	All Ireland JH S/F	17	**Waterford 4-5**	Galway 3-4	FB
09-Sep-34	Eastern MF Final	17	Mount Sion (Lost)	**Cathal Brugha**	NK
16-Sep-34	Clonea Tour SH Final	17	Mount Sion 2-4	**Carrick Davins 4-5**	FB
23-Sep-34	County SH East Final	17	Mount Sion 1-6	**Erin's Own 4-8**	FB
14-Oct-34	All Ireland JH Home Final	17	**Waterford 5-8**	Kildare 1-3	FB
04-Nov-34	All Ireland JH Final	17	**Waterford 3-5**	London 3-3	FB
11-Nov-34	County MH Final	17	**Mount Sion (Won)**	Fourmilewater	FB

1935

Date	Competition	Age	Team/Score	Opponent/Score	Position
15-Feb-35	National League SH	17	Waterford 2-1	**Cork 5-4**	RHF
03-Mar-35	SH Challenge	18	Mount Sion 3-2	**Carrick Swan 4-4**	FB
09-Mar-35	Dr Harty Cup SH	18	Mount Sion 0-0	**North Monastery 9-3**	FB
24-Mar-35	National League SH	18	Waterford 3-3	Kilkenny 4-6	LHB
31-Mar-35	Inter-Pro Final	18	**Munster Colleges 5-7**	Leinster Colleges 4-4	RFB
XX-Aug-35	County SH 1st Rd	18	**Mount Sion (Won)**	City Divisional Team	NK
15-Sep-35	County SH 2nd Rd	18	**Mount Sion 4-0**	Dunhill 3-2	FB
22-Sep-35	County SH East Final	18	Mount Sion 1-3	**Erin's Own 3-5**	FB
06-Oct-35	National League SH	18	Waterford 5-3	Clare 6-2	NK
17-Nov-35	National League SH	18	**Waterford 4-4**	Tipperary 3-3	FB
01-Dec-35	National League SH	18	Waterford 1-0	**Galway 2-3**	FB

1936

Date	Competition	Age	Team/Score	Opponent/Score	Position
10-May-36	Munster JH 1st Rd	19	**Waterford 8-3**	Limerick 0-4	LFB
15-May-36	Benefit Game	19	**Mount Sion 9-2**	Carrick Swan 8-2	FB
07-Jun-36	Munster SH 1st Rd	19	Waterford 4-4	**Clare 5-7**	CHB
19-Jul-36	County SH 1st Rd	19	**Mount Sion 4-3**	Erin's Own 2-5	CHB
07-Aug-36	SH Friendly	19	Mount Sion (Lost)	**Mooncoin**	NK
23-Aug-36	County SH East Final	19	**Mount Sion 3-4**	Dunhill 2-6	CHB
27-Sep-36	County SH Final	19	**Mount Sion 2-6**	Tallow 1-5	FB
04-Oct-36	National League SH	19	**Waterford 4-5**	Dublin 4-4	CHB
18-Oct-36	National League SH	19	**Waterford 5-4**	Cork 3-1	CF
01-Nov-36	National League SH	19	Waterford 2-3	**Limerick 4-3**	CF
22-Nov-36	B'bricken Church Tour	19	Mount Sion 2-2	**Erin's Own 3-1**	CF
06-Dec-36	SH Friendly	19	Mount Sion 4-2	**Mooncoin 5-1**	NK

1937

Date	Competition	Age	Team/Score	Opponent/Score	Position
07-Feb-37	National League SH	19	Waterford 5-0	**Tipperary 7-2**	CHB
14-Feb-37	Railway Cup SH S/F	19	**Munster 4-6**	Connacht 3-1	RHB
17-Mar-37	Railway Cup SH Final	20	**Munster 1-9**	Leinster 3-1	RHB
21-Mar-37	National League SH	20	**Waterford 2-5**	Galway 1-2	CHB
04-Apr-37	National League SH	20	Waterford 2-1	Kilkenny 5-3	CHB/CHF
11-Apr-37	Sisters of Charity Tour	20	**Mount Sion 8-6**	Thurles Sarsfield 3-4	CHB
18-Apr-37	National League SH	20	**Waterford 3-8**	Clare 3-4	CHB
13-Jun-37	County SH 1st Rd	20	**Mount Sion 8-6**	Dunhill 1-3	CHB
04-Jul-37	Munster SH 1st Rd	20	Waterford 3-2	**Limerick 3-4**	CHB
18-Jul-37	Eastern SH Final	20	Mount Sion 1-6	**Portlaw 3-4**	CHB
24-Oct-37	National League SH	20	Waterford 4-1	**Limerick 5-5**	CHB
31-Oct-37	SH Challenge	20	Waterford 3-7	**Tipperary 5-4**	CHB
07-Nov-37	National League SH	20	**Waterford 3-7**	Clare 3-1	CHB
14-Nov-37	Gaelic League Tour.	20	**Mount Sion 3-2**	Erin's Own 2-4	CHB

1938

Date	Competition	Age	Team/Score	Opponent/Score	Position
20-Feb-38	Cork Grounds SH Tour	21	Waterford 2-3	**Tipperary 2-5**	CHB
17-Mar-38	Railway Cup SH Final	21	**Munster 6-2**	Leinster 4-3	RHB
20-Mar-38	SH Challenge	21	Mount Sion	Carrick Swan	CHB
27-Mar-38	East JF Championship	21	**Mount Sion 0-2**	P.H.Pearse 0-0	NK
24-Apr-38	B'bricken Church SH Tour	21	**Mount Sion 6-7**	Carrigtohill (Cork) 4-1	CHB
08-May-38	Friary SH Tour	21	**Mount Sion 3-8**	Erin's Own 1-5	CHB
26-Jun-38	County SH Championship	21	**Mount Sion 3-5**	Tallow 4-4	CHB
10-Jul-38	Munster SH 1st Rd	21	**Waterford 5-2**	Cork 1-3	CHB
31-Jul-38	Munster SH Final	21	**Waterford 3-5**	Clare 2-5	CHB
07-Aug-38	All-Ireland SH S/F	21	**Waterford 4-8**	Galway 3-1	CHB
04-Sep-38	All-Ireland SH final	21	Waterford 1-6	**Dublin 2-5**	CHB
11-Sep-38	SH Challenge	21	**Mount Sion 6-6**	Carrickshock 6-5	CHB
18-Sep-38	Cork Churches SH	21	**Waterford 5-10**	Cork 4-3	CHB
02-Oct-38	County SH 2nd Rd	21	**Mount Sion**	P.H.Pearse	CHB
09-Oct-38	National League SH	21	**Waterford 4-3**	Limerick 2-5	CHB/CHF

Date	Event	#	Result 1	Result 2	Role
06-Nov-38	Prisoner's Aid SH	21	Waterford 3-7	**Kilkenny 7-6**	CHB
13-Nov-38	National League SF	21	Waterford 2-2	**Wicklow 1-6**	CHF
20-Nov-38	National League SH	21	**Waterford 5-4**	Kilkenny 4-3	CHB

1939

Date	Event	#	Result 1	Result 2	Role
08-Jan-39	County SH Final (1938)	21	**Mount Sion 4-3**	Erin's Own 3-4	CHB
22-Jan-39	B'bricken SH Tour	21	**Mount Sion**	Erin's Own	CHB
05-Feb-39	National League SH	21	**Waterford 5-6**	Clare 2-3	CHB
26-Feb-39	Railway Cup SH	22	**Munster 8-5**	Connacht 0-2	RHB
05-Mar-39	National League SH	22	**Waterford 2-5**	**Cork 3-2**	CHB
12-Mar-39	Senior Football	22	Waterford 0-5	**Wexford 2-6**	
17-Mar-39	Railway Cup SH	22	**Munster 4-4**	Leinster 1-6	RHB
02-Apr-39	National League SH	22	**Waterford 5-7**	Wexford 3-4	CHB
16-Apr-39	Edmund Rice Memorial		Erin's Own 4-3	Eire Óg (KK) 5-5	**Ref**
23-Apr-39	County JF Trial	22	East Division	West Division	NK
30-Apr-39	National League SH Final	22	Waterford 1-4	**Dublin 1-8**	CHB
07-May-39	County JH		Passage	Gaultier	**Ref**
14-May-39	Munster SF	22	Waterford 0-6	**Cork 0-7**	CHF
26-May-39	County JF 1st Rd	22	**Mount Sion**	Gaultier	NK
28-May-39	Feis Loc Garman	22	**Waterford 3-6**	Wexford 2-6	FB
07-Jun-39	County JH		Erin's Own	St Stephen's	**Ref**
09-Jun-39	Mt Melleray S.H.	22	Waterford 1-6	Clare 3-4	FB
25-Jun-39	Munster SH 1st Rd	22	Waterford 4-3	**Cork 7-4**	CHB/CHF
16-Jul-39	County SH 2nd Rd	22	**Mount Sion 6-7**	P.H.Pearse 1-1	CHB
23-Jul-39	County JF 1st Rd Replay	22	**Mount Sion**	Gaultier	NK
30-Jul-39	County JH replay		Clonea 7-4	Carrickbeg/Windgap 1-2	**Ref**
06-Aug-39	County SH S/F	22	**Mount Sion 9-5**	Dungarvan 1-2	FB
27-Aug-39	County SH S/F		St Stephen's	Erin's Own	**Ref**
03-Sep-39	County JF championship	22	**Mount Sion**	St Stephen's	NK
10-Sep-39	Cork Tour		Waterford 3-5	**Cork 6-8**	FB
17-Sep-39	County SH Final	22	**Mount Sion 2-4**	Erin's Own 2-2	FB
24-Sep-39	Knocktopher Tour		Mount Sion 1-2	**Carrickshock 4-4**	FB
08-Oct-39	National League SH	22	Waterford 2-1	**Limerick 3-4**	FB
22-Oct-39	East JF S/F	22	**Mount Sion**	P.H.Pearse	NK
29-Oct-39	East JF Final		**Mount Sion 1-2**	Dunhill 0-2	NK
05-Nov-39	County JF Final	22	**Mount Sion 3-3**	Lismore 0-0	CF
12-Nov-39	B'bricken SH Final	22	**Mount Sion 3-2**	Erin's Own 0-3	CHB
19-Nov-39	National League SH	22	**Waterford 4-4**	Clare 1-4	NK

1940

Date	Event	#	Result 1	Result 2	Role
04-Feb-40	National League SF	22	Waterford 0-0	**Tipperary 8-4**	NK
10-Mar-40	Cork Churches SH	23	Waterford 2-7	**Cork 5-4**	CHB
17-Mar-40	Railway Cup SH Final	23	**Munster 4-9**	Leinster 5-4	CHB
05-May-40	County JF 1st Rd		Newtown 1-4	Dunhill 0-2	**Ref**
12-May-40	County SF 1st rd		Mount Sion 0-5	**Kilrossanty 4-9**	CHF
16-Jun-40	Munster SH 1st Rd	23	**Waterford 3-5**	**Limerick 4-2**	CHB
30-Jun-40	SH Challenge		**Mount Sion 2-7**	**Mullinavat 3-4**	CHB/CF
14-Jul-40	Munster SH Replay		Waterford 3-3	**Limerick 3-5**	CHB
18-Jul-40	SH Challenge	23	**Mount Sion 4-4**	Wexford Juniors 3-1	CHF
11-Aug-40	SH Challenge	23	Waterford 2-5	**Kilkenny 6-3**	CHB
15-Sep-40	County SH 1st Rd		**Mount Sion 11-5**	Clonea 5-3	CHB
29-Sep-40	SH Challenge	23	Mount Sion 4-5	**Mullinavat 6-7**	CHB
06-Oct-40	National League SH	23	Waterford 3-2	**Limerick 3-3**	CHB
13-Oct-40	County SH S/F	23	**Mount Sion 2-7**	Erin's Own 2-2	CHB
20-Oct-40	National League SH	23	Waterford 5-3	**Clare 5-5**	CHB
27-Oct-40	County SH Final	23	**Mount Sion 2-5**	**Dungarvan 1-8**	CHB/CHF
03-Nov-40	National League SH	23	Waterford 3-4	**Kilkenny 2-9**	CHB
10-Nov-40	SH Challenge	23	**Mount Sion 6-3**	St Stephen's 4-2	CHB
24-Nov-40	Tournament Final	23	**Mount Sion 8-8**	Portlaw 3-5	CHB
01-Dec-40	National League SH	23	Waterford 2-4	**Cork 4-2**	CHB
08-Dec-40	County SH Final Replay	23	**Mount Sion 6-5**	Dungarvan 3-2	CHB

1941

Date	Event	Age	Team	Opponent	Ref
16-Feb-41	Railway Cup SH	23	**Munster 7-4**	Connacht 0-5	CHB
17-Mar-41	Railway Cup SH	24	Munster 2-4	**Leinster 2-5**	CHB
23-Mar-41	SH Challenge	24	Mount Sion 4-4	**Mullinavat 4-5**	CHB
20-Apr-41	Green Cross Fund	24	**Waterford 6-2**	Kilkenny 6-1	CHB
27-Apr-41	County SF 1st Rd	24	**Mount Sion**	Erin's Own	NK
22-Jun-41	East SH Final	24	**Mount Sion 2-10**	Erin's Own 1-1	CHB
20-Jul-41	Munster JF	24	Waterford 1-4	**Tipperary 2-2**	CHF
03-Aug-41	SH Challenge	24	**Mount Sion**	St Stephen's	CHB
17-Aug-41	County SH Final	24	Mount Sion 1-5	**Dungarvan 2-6**	CHB
05-Oct-41	SH Challenge	24	**Mount Sion 5-6**	Mullinavat 0-1	CHB

1942

Date	Event	Age	Team	Opponent	Ref
17-Mar-42	Railway Cup SH	25	**Munster 4-9**	Leinster 4-5	CHB
03-May-42	County SH League	25	Mount Sion 1-2	**Portlaw 4-4**	FB
31-May-42	Munster SH 1st Rd	25	Waterford 2-5	**Limerick 4-4**	CHB
07-Jun-42	County SF	25	Mount Sion	Stradbally	NK
21-Jun-42	County SH League	25	Mount Sion 2-3	**Erin's Own 4-4**	NK
06-Sep-42	County SH League	25	**Mount Sion 6-3**	St Stephen's 1-5	NK
25-Oct-42	Tournament final	25	**Mount Sion (Draw)**	P.H.Pearse	NK
08-Nov-42	Defence Forces Tour	25	**46th Batt. LDF. 5-6**	Curragh Comm. 3-6	CHB
22-Nov-42	County JF League	25	**Newtown 1-3**	Fenor 0-2	**Ref**
06-Dec-42	Def. Forces Tournament	25	**46th Batt., LDF 5-2**	Th'town Comm. 4-5	CHB

1943

Date	Event	Age	Team	Opponent	Ref
03-Jan-43	SH Challenge	25	Mount Sion	Mooncoin	CHB
14-Feb-43	Railway Cup SH	25	**Munster 3-5**	Connacht 3-2	CHB
07-Mar-43	SH Tournament	25	St Stephen's 4-4	Mooncoin 3-4	**Ref**
17-Mar-43	Railway Cup SH	26	**Munster 4-3**	Leinster 3-5	CHB
21-Mar-43	SH Challenge	26	**46th Batt. LDF**	**Erin's Own Selection**	CHB
28-Mar-43	Kilkenny SH League	26	Mooncoin 2-6	The Rower 3-6	**Ref**
02-Apr-43	SH Challenge	26	Mount Sion	Portlaw	CHB
02-May-43	SH Challenge	26	**46th Batt. LDF 4-7**	South Comm. 1-3	CHB
13-Jun-43	Munster SH 1st Rd	26	**Waterford 4-5**	Tipperary 1-2	CHB
20-Jun-43	County SH 1st Rd	26	**Mount Sion 3-1**	Erin's Own 2-1	CHB/CHF
04-Jul-43	Munster SF	26	**Waterford 3-7**	Limerick 4-3	CHB
18-Jul-43	County SH 2nd Rd	26	**Mount Sion (Won)**	De La Salle	CHB
01-Aug-43	Munster SH Final	26	Waterford 2-3	**Cork 2-13**	CHB
08-Aug-43	County SH S/F	26	**Mount Sion 6-7**	Portlaw 3-2	CHB
22-Aug-43	Def. Forces SH Tour	26	**46th Batt. LDF 12-3**	Th'town Comm. 3-4	CHB
17-Sep-43	County SH Final	26	**Mount Sion 3-8**	Tallow 1-5	CHB
26-Sep-43	SH Challenge	26	Waterford 4-4	**Cork 4-9**	CHB
17-Oct-43	SH Tournament	26	**Mount Sion 11-5**	P.H.Pearse 3-0	CHB
29-Oct-43	East JF	26	**Mount Sion 1-3**	Butlerstown 0-0	NK
21-Nov-43	4 County SH League	26	Waterford	**Tipperary (Won)**	NK
26-Nov-43	Def. Forces SH	26	**46th Batt. LDF 6-8**	7th Brigade 5-5	CHB

1944

Date	Event	Age	Team	Opponent	Ref
25-Feb-44	SH Challenge	27	Mount Sion	Portlaw	NK
26-Mar-44	Gaelic Field SH Tour	27	**Mount Sion 7-1**	De La Salle 4-3	NK
04-Apr-44	Ballybricken SH	27	**Mount Sion**	**Army 3rd Batt.**	NK
16-Apr-44	4 County SH League	27	**Waterford 3-3**	Kilkenny 2-6	NK
27-Apr-44	B'bricken SH Replay	27	Mount Sion	**Army 3rd Battalion**	CHB
29-Oct-44	Br Rice SH	27	**Waterford 7-8**	Cork 5-6	CHB
12-Nov-44	Gaelic Field SH Tour	27	Mount Sion 2-4	**Erin's Own 4-4**	CHB
03-Dec-44	4 County SH League	27	Waterford 3-2	**Tipperary 5-3**	CHB
10-Dec-44	Ballybricken SH	27	Mount Sion 3-1	**Army 3rd Batt. 4-10**	CHB

1945

Date	Competition	Age	Result	Opponent	Pos
18-Feb-45	4 County SH League	28	Waterford 3-1	**Wexford 3-6**	CHB
25-Feb-45	Augustinian Church SH	28	Rest Of Munster 2-3	**Munster 6-2**	CHB
04-Mar-45	SH Tournament	28	Waterford 2-0	**Kilkenny 3-11**	NK
25-Mar-45	SH Tournament	28	Waterford 3-2	**Cork 5-2**	CHB
XX-May-45	County SH 1st Rd	28	**Mount Sion**	P.H.Pearse	NK
10-Jun-45	Munster SH 1st Rd	28	Waterford 0-3	**Tipperary 3-6**	CHB
26-Aug-45	County SH 3rd Rd	28	**Mount Sion 1-5***	Erin's Own 2-5	CHF
14-Oct-45	SH Tournament	28	Waterford 2-4	**Limerick 5-5**	CHB
21-Oct-45	County SH Final	28	**Mount Sion 3-8**	Dungarvan 2-5	CHF/CF
28-Oct-45	National League SH	28	Waterford 2-3	**Kilkenny 2-6**	CHB/CF
04-Nov-45	SH Tournament	28	**Mount Sion 4-2**	Mullinavat 2-2	NK
11-Nov-45	National League SH	28	Waterford 2-8	**Cork 5-11**	CHB
02-Dec-45	Army Ben. Fund SH	28	Mount Sion 1-6	**Eire Óg (KK) 3-6**	NK

1946

Date	Competition	Age	Result	Opponent	Pos
10-Feb-46	National League SH	28	**Waterford 4-3**	Wexford 1-3	CHB
03-Mar-46	SH Challenge	29	**Waterford 3-5**	Tipperary 4-0	CHB
10-Mar-46	Dr Kinane Cup SH	29	Mount Sion 1-4	**Eire Óg (KK) 3-11**	CHF
07-Apr-46	Benefit Game SH	29	Mount Sion	**Mullinavat (by 2pts)**	NK
12-May-46	SH Challenge	29	Waterford 3-7	**Cork 5-8**	CHF
16-May-46	SH Challenge	29	Mount Sion	Mullinavat	NK
19-May-46	SH Challenge	29	**Mount Sion 3-5**	Glen Rovers (Cork) 2-3	CHF
26-May-46	County SH Championship	29	Mount Sion	P.H.Pearse	NK
09-Jun-46	Fr Dollard Cup SH	29	Mount Sion 2-2	**Carrick Swan 4-10**	NK
30-Jun-46	Munster SH S/F	29	Waterford 1-6	**Cork 3-9**	CHB
28-Jul-46	County SH League	29	Mount Sion 1-2	**Erin's Own 3-3**	CHB/CHF
04-Aug-46	Dunmore East SH	29	Mount Sion	**Mooncoin**	CHF
18-Aug-46	County SH League	29	Mount Sion	De La Salle	NK
03-Nov-46	National League SH	29	Waterford 2-3	**Kilkenny 3-5**	FB
01-Dec-46	National League SH	29	**Waterford 5-1**	Cork 3-2	FB

1947

Date	Competition	Age	Result	Opponent	Pos
02-Feb-47	National League SH	29	**Waterford 5-4**	Wexford 1-1	FB
16-Mar-47	Railway Cup SH	30	**Munster 9-7**	Ulster 0-0	FB
06-Apr-47	Railway Cup SH	30	Munster 1-1	**Connacht 2-5**	FB
13-Apr-47	SH Challenge	30	**Mount Sion 3-7**	Blackrock (Cork) 2-8	NK
04-May-47	SH Challenge	30	**Mount Sion 5-4**	Carrick Swan 0-4	NK
11-May-47	County SH 1st Rd	30	**Mount Sion 3-10**	Butlerstown 0-3	CHF
30-May-47	SH Challenge	30	**Mount Sion 6-3**	Carrickshock 3-6	CHF
06-Jun-47	SH Challenge	30	**Mount Sion 6-7**	Carrickshock 5-9	CHF
29-Jun-47	Munster SH S/F	30	Waterford 1-5	**Cork 3-10**	FB
04-Jul-47	SH Challenge	30	**Mount Sion 4-5**	**Carrickshock 4-5**	CHF
13-Jul-47	County SH 2nd Rd	30	**Mount Sion 7-5**	Meagher's 7-3	CHF
24-Aug-47	County SH 3rd Rd	30	Mount Sion 3-7	**Erin's Own 4-6**	CHF
05-Oct-47	National League SH	30	Waterford 2-6	**Kilkenny 4-10**	FB
26-Oct-47	National League SH	30	**Waterford 4-4**	**Laoighis 3-7**	CHB/FB
16-Nov-47	National League SH	30	**Waterford 5-4**	Wexford 2-3	CHB
30-Nov-47	National League SH	30	Waterford 1-2	**Kilkenny 1-3**	CHB

1948

Date	Competition		Opponent		Result
21-Mar-48	SH Challenge	31	**Mount Sion 3-8**	Thomastown 3-1	CHF
28-Mar-48	National League SH	31	Waterford 2-3	**Dublin 2-7**	FB
02-May-48	County SH 1st Rd	31	**Mount Sion 7-7**	Erin's Own 1-2	CHF
23-May-48	Munster SH S/F	31	**Waterford 4-8**	Clare 5-3	CHF
27-May-48	SH Challenge	31	**Mount Sion (by 4pts)**	Thomastown	CHF
13-Jun-48	County SF S/F	31	St Otteran's (Div. Team)	**Dungarvan**	NK
XX-XX-48	County JF	31	**Mount Sion**	De La Salle	NK
01-Aug-48	Munster SH Final	31	**Waterford 4-7**	Cork 3-9	CHF
08-Aug-48	Munster JF Final	31	**Waterford 2-8**	Limerick 1-7	RCF
15-Aug-48	All Ireland SH S/F	31	**Waterford 3-7**	Galway 1-6	CHF
05-Sep-48	All Ireland SH Final	31	**Waterford 6-7**	Dublin 4-2	CHF
08-Oct-48	Oireachteas SH S/F	31	**Waterford 2-6**	Kilkenny 0-9	CHF
10-Oct-48	National League SH	31	**Waterford 7-8**	Wexford 3-4	CHF
17-Oct-48	Oireachteas SH Final	31	Waterford 2-6	**Dublin 3-6**	CHF
24-Oct-48	National League SH	31	Waterford 3-6	**Kilkenny 3-8**	CHF
31-Oct-48	County SH 2nd Rd	31	**Mount Sion**	Butlerstown	CHF
14-Nov-48	Eastern JF S/F	31	**Mount Sion 1-3**	Dunhill 1-0	NK
21-Nov-48	Eastern JF Final	31	**Mount Sion 2-6**	Windgap 2-0	FF
28-Nov-48	National League SH	31	Waterford 0-7	**Cork 1-11**	CHF
12-Dec-48	County SH Final	31	**Mount Sion 9-8**	Avonmore 0-5	CHF

1949

Date	Competition		Opponent		Result
06-Feb-49	National League SH	31	Waterford 3-5	**Dublin 6-2**	CHF
13-Feb-49	Railway Cup SH	31	**Munster 2-8**	Leinster 1-8	CHF
17-Mar-49	Railway Cup SH	32	**Munster 6-2**	Connacht 2-9	CHF/LFF
20-Apr-49	Gaelic Field SH S/F	32	**Mount Sion 6-11**	Erin's Own 1-0	CHF
10-Apr-49	Gaelic Field SH Final	32	**Mount Sion**	Carrickshock	CHF
24-Apr-49	1948 County JF Final	32	**Mount Sion 1-7**	Cappoquin 0-7	FF
01-May-49	SH Challenge	32	Mount Sion 4-8	**Holycross 6-5**	CHF
08-May-49	County SH championship	32	**Mount Sion 6-5**	St Molleran's 1-1	CHF
15-May-49	SH Tournament	32	**Waterford 4-7**	Cork 2-5	CHF
29-May-49	Belfast Feis SH	32	**Waterford 9-3**	Antrim 3-7	CHB
12-Jun-49	Munster SH	32	Waterford 3-3	**Limerick 3-8**	CHF
24-Jul-49	County SH championship	32	**Mount Sion**	T.F.Meagher's	CHF
14-Aug-49	Munster JF Final	32	Waterford 0-6	**Kerry 2-5**	RFF
21-Aug-49	County SH S/F	32	**Mount Sion 22-12**	Erin's Own 0-0	CHF
18-Sep-49	Kinane Cup SH S/F	32	**Mount Sion 4-11**	Tullaroan 2-8	CHF
16-Oct-49	County SH Final	32	**Mount Sion 4-6**	Clonea 0-6	CHF

1950

Date	Competition		Opponent		Result
19-Mar-50	O'Shee Cup SH	33	**Mount Sion 3-5**	Graigue (KK) 2-3	CHF
02-Apr-50	Kinane Cup SH Final	33	**Mount Sion 7-3**	Holycross (Tipp) 4-4	CHF
16-Apr-50	SH Challenge	33	**Mount Sion 10-6**	Borrisoleigh 5-2	CHF
23-Apr-50	Aug. Church SH	33	**Mount Sion 9-6**	Dungarvan Utd. 7-7	CHF
07-May-50	O'Shee Cup SH Final	33	**Mount Sion 6-10**	Glen Rovers (Cork) 3-1	CHF
14-May-50	County SH championship	33	**Mount Sion 4-12**	Avonmore 2-4	CHF
21-May-50	Kinane Cup SH	33	**Mount Sion 6-4**	Graigue (KK) 2-3	CHF
25-May-50	SH Challenge	33	Mount Sion	Eire Óg (KK)	CHF
04-Jun-50	KK Gaelic Week SH	33	**Waterford 1-10**	Kilkenny 2-3	CHF
25-Jun-50	Munster SH	33	Waterford 0-5	**Cork 1-4**	CHF
16-Jul-50	County SH S/F	33	**Mount Sion 4-7**	Meagher's 1-5	CHF
30-Jul-50	SH Challenge	33	**Mount Sion**	Butlerstown	CHF
10-Sep-50	County SH Final	33	Mount Sion 2-5	**Tourin 3-7**	CHF
15-Oct-50	SH Challenge	33	Mount Sion	Tourin	CHF
22-Oct-50	National League SH	33	**Waterford 4-4**	Dublin 4-4	FF
29-Oct-50	SH Tour S/F	33	**Mount Sion 5-3**	Imokilly (Cork) 3-4	CHF
12-Nov-50	SH Tour Final	33	Mount Sion	**St Finbarr's (Cork)**	CHF

1951

Date	Competition		Result	Opponent	
13-May-51	SH Challenge	34	**Mount Sion 4-6**	Mooncoin 3-4	CHF
27-May-51	National Graves SH	34	Mount Sion 0-8	**Eire Óg (KK) 0-13**	CHF
24-Jun-51	County SH championship	34	**Mount Sion 4-12**	Tourin 1-6	CHF
16-Sep-51	County SH S/F	34	**Mount Sion 8-2**	Cappoquin 1-5	CHF
07-Oct-51	County SH Final	34	**Mount Sion 7-8**	Dungarvan 0-9	CHF

1955

Date	Competition		Result	Opponent	
24-Jun-55	County SF	38	**Mount Sion 1-7**	St Otteran's 1-4	FF
07-Aug-55	County SF East S/F	38	**Mount Sion 1-6**	Kill 1-5	FF
28-Aug-55	County SF East replay	38	**Mount Sion 0-6**	Dunhill 0-3	FF
18-Sep-55	County SF Final	38	**Mount Sion 1-2**	**Brickey Rangers 0-5**	CHF
25-Sep-55	County SF Final Replay	38	**Mount Sion 1-6**	Brickey Rangers 0-6	FF

Appendix Two

Graveside oration by Pat Fanning, former President GAA, 4 October 1975

John Keane was a great hurler, a loyal friend, a committed member of the GAA. All his life he gave of himself to hurling and to the GAA but to the end he insisted that in the GAA he had found happiness and fulfillment and that he owed to the Association a debt he could never repay. That was the man we buried today. I believe something of his story should be re-told. It may inspire some of our young people as he inspired so many of us over so many years.

The name of John Keane is forever enshrined in the hearts of all who love hurling. His story is indeed the story of his club and county. In his bearing, in all that he attempted and achieved, he reflected the very spirit of a hurling county. His courage, his daring, his indomitable spirit and, above all, his unshakeable loyalty remain for many of us a great source of pride and consolation. Let these poor words attempt to capture, for the comrades who served with him and the youth who would emulate him, something of the spirit and character of a truly fine human being.

John Keane came from a family rich in the Gaelic tradition. Reared in a GAA neighbourhood and schooled in that cradle of Waterford hurling in Mount Sion, John took up hurling early. A magnificently proportioned youngster, his natural flair for the game was quickly recognized by the Brothers in the Barrack Street monastery and John Keane's feet were set firmly on the road to hurling fame. His progress was rapid. He figured on teams with boys who were by years his senior. He won county minor honours with Cnoc Síon in '33 and '34. In 1934 the young minor was a star in Waterford's All-Ireland junior hurling triumph. In that Golden Jubilee year of the Association he helped Mount Sion to victory in the county junior championship and this ushered in a new name and a new era in county senior hurling. John Keane, still a minor, had made his mark and for twenty and more years to come, his was to be the outstanding name in our county's hurling story.

1935 saw him a member of the county senior fifteen – as a corner-back. And he was a minor yet. Then in 1937 we saw the blossoming of a great centre half-back whose skill and daring and shining sportsmanship were to fire the blood and grip the imagination not only of Waterford but of all Ireland. Few who saw Waterford's battle with unconquerable Limerick in 1937 will ever forget John Keane's inspired display on the greatest of all hurlers of that era, Mick Mackey of Ahane.

The twenty year old Waterford man that day in Clonmel achieved immortality in one of the greatest man-to-man confrontations ever seen on a hurling field. That day was born a lasting friendship between Keane and Mackey, and Mackey was one of the hurler's who shouldered Keane's coffin in Limerick last week. Talk to Mick Mackey and the name of John Keane inevitably crops up. Hurling men can judge their own kind.

In the aftermath of his death hurling men from the hurling counties have come to echo and confirm Mick Mackey's assessment of John Keane – the hurler and the man. 1937, too, saw John make his first Croke Park appearance on a Munster fifteen. In this inter-provincial sphere he was to achieve further distinction and national recognition. In 1938 he won the Munster title with Waterford and made his All-Ireland appearance against Dublin. But for John, perhaps, the sweetest success of all in that memorable year was Mount Sion's first ever county senior hurling victory. He was now the idol of hurling fans everywhere and one of the most colourful figures in Munster hurling, ranking as a great hurler in one of the greatest of hurling eras. But he and Waterford had yet to win that senior All-Ireland. Towards that end the great defender was committed to attack and, on the forty yards, his keen hurling brain brought a new dimension to forward play. His contribution to the All-Ireland triumph of

1948 is immeasurable. The spirit of Keane as much as his hurling skill was decisive.

He retired from hurling in 1951 but he did not retire from the GAA. He served as Club chairman and county treasurer and it is possible that his greatest contribution to his county and to hurling was made as trainer and advisor to the men of '57 to '63. Now he has departed the scene but the glory of his achievements in victory or defeat lives on and will be forever an inspiration.

John Keane was a simple man who was happiest when in the company of hurling men and he delighted in visiting old rivals throughout the Province and recounting the deeds of other days. During the last two years of his life he had been plagued with ill-health and was in almost constant pain which he bore with patience and fortitude as befitted a man of his stature. Yet his hurling desire to the end was to see hurling and all hurling men prosper in the Decies. He took a particular interest in the young fellows of the present time who always received encouragement and inspiration from him.

Looking back briefly in one final glance at the saga of one man's effort in the cause of hurling, the memories come crowding in. I recall again that day in 1937 at Clonmel, the strapping figure of the youthful Keane, the blond curly head bobbing as he threw back attack after attack, outwitting the legendary Mackey in what is still regarded as one of the finest displays of centre-back play ever witnessed. I recall his greatest display of courage and endurance – perhaps his greatest personal triumph – when at Dungarvan in 1943 he fielded with a badly injured ankle and almost alone broke the back of Tipperary and carried Waterford to a Munster final. Well do I remember cutting the boot from his swollen leg at the end of that excruciatingly painful hour. And I recall, too, an old man of Tipperary who pushed his way to where Keane lay, to shake, as he said, 'the hand of John Keane, the greatest man in Ireland.' And, I see again, Croke Park in 1948 with the figure of John Keane, not quite so full now and the head no longer blonde, still weaving and cutting his way goal-wards for the scores that brought his beloved county to the end of a long, long trail.

That is the John Keane I remember – a great hurler but, above all, a good man. He has gone from us but lives on in our hearts, and his family can be assured that while hurling is played his name will be remembered and the young hurlers of tomorrow will seek to recapture the spirit and emulate the deeds of a man who for so long bestrode the hurling scene like a colossus – John Keane of Mount Sion. God rest you John Keane. You were a good one.

Ar dheis Dé go raibh a anam.

Appendix Three

Tributes

[He was] not only one of the greatest (many say the greatest!) hurlers of all time who could play anywhere with equal magnificence: not only a great trainer, teacher, motivator of younger hurlers: not only a kindly and sensitive gentleman, he was also our original boyhood hero: the sandy-blond, clean-cut, classicist for whom we would have fought with tooth and nail anyone who dared cast the slightest aspersion on his perfection.

Séamus Ó Braonáin, 1975

Whenever hurling connoisseurs meet, his name is mentioned in the same breath as men such as Mick Mackey, Lory Meagher or Christy Ring, for John Keane was of that great mould of powerful athlete. He was a big handsome man, enormously skilful, fearless, fast and scrupulously fair. He seemed indestructible in his strength and his great heart.

Dónal Foley, Irish Times, 1975

A great hurler. No more needs to be said, for it hardly matters now whether you rank him No. 1 or 2 or 3 in the list of all-time greats. Those who saw him play cherish the experience as one that will never be repeated or copied. Centre-back, fullback, centre-forward: it wouldn't matter to Keane for he could be and was among the greats in all those positions

Tom Browne, Evening Press, 1975

John ranks with the all-time greats of hurling. He is to Mount Sion and Waterford what Mick Mackey is to Ahane and Limerick, Christy Ring to Glen Rovers and Cork, Lory Meagher to Tullaroan and Kilkenny. He remains for many of us a man apart, a man who in his physique, his character, his personality, his sportsmanship, his sheer artistry as a hurler and his enduring loyalty to the game he graced for so long, was the very epitome of Mount Sion's and Waterford's hurling spirit.

Cnoc Síon Souvenir Record, 1974

He was worth four or five points to Mount Sion (as a minor hurler) before the match even started and he was usually at full-back in those days.

Billy Howlett (former Portlaw hurler)

John Keane was the greatest all round hurler ever to come out of Waterford and would certainly be numbered among the first six places in any assessment of the most accomplished players in the history of the game.

Paddy Downey, Irish Times, 1975

Who should be centre-half? Jim Regan of Kinsale, Podge Byrne of Dicksboro', Paddy Clohessey of Fedamore, Bobby Rackard of Rathnure? And who on the displays of the past few years could pass by Pat Stakelum of Holy Cross? Yet I will give the palm to none of them, but award it instead to John Keane of Waterford's Mount Sion who was, in his hey-day possibly the best man I have ever seen play in this dominant position.

Pádraig Puirséal, Kilkenny People, 1959

He was to me the absolute perfection when it came to hurling; a master tactician, a skilful ball player, a leader of men, and above everything else a sportsman to his very fingertips.

James Grant, former Secretary Waterford Co. Board, 1984

You see, it doesn't matter at all whether they put Keane up at No. 1 or 2 or 3 on the All-Time-Greats, or whether he is put, undeservedly, lower down. Hurling alone did not make the man. As the modern phrase goes, he was a great human being, apart from the hurling.

Séamus Ó Braonáin, 1975

For nearly 20 years, Keane's was a name to conjure with on the hurling fields of Waterford, of Munster and of Ireland. Keane at centre half-back was the complete hurler. On the ground or in the air, whether the game was hard and close or fast and open, on a soft sod or an iron-hard pitch, he was equally skilled, equally masterful.

Pádraig Puirséal, Evening Press, 1975

He was without a flaw. He was equally brilliant with left or right, overhead or on the ground. He was extremely skilful and with enormous strength.

Pádraig Ó Fainín, ex GAA President, 2008

He's a legend.

Eddie Keher, former Kilkenny hurler, 2001

[He] is mourned by every hurling fan who ever had the privilege and pleasure of seeing him in action. A really great hurler … his passing will leave a gap in the ranks of Ireland's all-time greats of hurling.

The Connaught Tribune, 1975

Today we buried a man who showed us all how to hurl.

Jackie Power, former Limerick hurler, 1975

There'll never be another John Keane

*Christy Ring, as quoted in
Tim Horgan's biography of Ring, p.91*

In November 2009 the Waterford Civic Trust erected a blue heritage plaque on the house where John was born at Barrack Street, Waterford.

Appendix Four

Greatest-ever hurling teams

I have mentioned the 'greatest-ever' hurling teams and this immediately brings to mind the Centenary Hurling Team and the Millennium Hurling team. However, down through the years, there have been many more such selections and the following is a list of such teams that I have researched.

1955: This was the selection of the great Tipperary player Tommy Doyle, taken from his biography *A Lifetime in Hurling* (1955), published in the *Sunday Independent*, 15 May 1955. Doyle's selection was:

> Tony Reddin (Tipp); Johnny Leahy (Tipp); Sean Óg Murphy (Cork); John Joe Doyle (Clare); John Keane (Wat); Paddy Clohessy (Lim); Paddy Phelan (KK); Jim Hurley (Cork); Lowry Meagher (KK); Christy Ring (Cork); Mick Mackey (Lim); Phil Cahill (Tipp); Eudie Coughlan (Cork); Martin Kennedy (Tipp); Mattie Power (KK).

Doyle selected John at right half-back but wrote 'I find it very hard to pass over John Keane and Paddy Phelan both of whom always impressed me as great stylists. John Keane might also be chosen at right-full or centre-back'.

1959: The best ever hurling team since 1922, published in the *Kilkenny People* quoting Moondharrig (Pádraig Puirséal) in the *Irish Catholic*. Puirséal's team was:

Dr Tommy Daly (Clare); Johnny Leahy (Tipp); Sean Óg Murphy (Cork); Eddie Doyle (KK); Garret Howard (Lim); John Keane (Wat); Builder Walsh (Dub); Lowry Meagher (KK); Mick Mackey (Lim); Mick Cahill (Tipp); Terry Leahy (KK); Christy Ring (Cork); Mick King (Gal); Martin Kennedy (Tipp); Mattie Power (KK)

He wrote thus about his selection for centre-back; 'Who should be centre-half? Jim Regan of Kinsale, Podge Byrne of Dicksboro, Paddy Clohossey of Fedamore, Bobby Rackard of Rathnure? And who on the displays of the past few years could pass by Pat Stakelum of Holy Cross? Yet I will give the palm to none of them, but award it instead to John Keane of Waterford's Mount Sion who was, in his hey-day possibly the best man I have ever seen play in this dominant position'.

1961: The best-ever hurling team as chosen in a popular poll conducted by *Gael-Linn* and published in the *Irish Independent*, 17 June 1961. The *Gael-Linn* team was:

Tommy Daly (Clare); Jimmy Brohan (Cork); Nick O'Donnell (Wex); John Doyle (Tipp); Jim English (Wex); John Keane (Wat); Paddy Phelan (KK); Lowry Meagher (KK); Mick Gill (Gal); Jimmy Langton (KK); Mick Mackey (Lim); Eudie Coughlan (Cork); Paddy Barry (Cork); Nicky Rackard (Wex); Christy Ring (Cork).

1965: Greatest-ever team from 1935-65 as chosen by Gaelic Games journalist Raymond Smith.

Tony Reddin (Tipp); Bobby Rackard (Wex); Nick O'Donnell (Wex); John Doyle (Tipp); Jimmy Finn (Tipp); John Keane (Wat); Tommy Doyle (Tipp); Jack Lynch (Cork); Timmy Ryan (Lim); Christy Ring (Cork); Mick Mackey (Lim); Jimmy Doyle (Tipp); Jackie Power (Lim); Nicky Rackard (Wex); Tim Flood (Wex).

1976: John D. Hickey, Gaelic Games columnist of the *Irish Independent* chose the greatest-ever team from his lifetime for the 1976 *Our Games Annual*.

> Tommy Daly (Clare); Bob Rackard (Wex); Nick O'Donnell (Wex); Jim Treacy (KK); Jimmy Finn (Tipp); John Keane (Wat); Paddy Phelan (KK); Mick Gill (Gal); Lowry Meagher (KK); Eudie Coughlan (Cork); Mick Mackey (Lim); Eddie Keher (KK); Paddy Kenny (Tipp); Martin Kennedy (Tipp); Christy Ring (Cork).

1977: Mitchel Cogley, Sports columnist with the *Sunday Independent* selected his greatest-ever team which was published in that paper on 7 Aug 1977.

> Paddy Scanlon (Lim); Willie Murphy (Cork); Nick O'Donnell (Wex); John Doyle (Tipp); Jimmy Finn (Tipp); Willie Rackard (Wex); Paddy Phelan (KK); Bob Mockler (Tipp); Timmy Ryan (Lim); John Keane (Wat); Mick Mackey (Lim); Christy Ring (Cork); Eddie Keher (KK); Nicky Rackard (Wex); Jimmy Kennedy (Tipp).

1981: Seamus O Ceallaigh, a Kilkenny native but Limerick based GAA writer and historian had seen every All-Ireland hurling final between 1922 and 1981 when he published his greatest-ever team in the *Sunday Independent* on 30 Aug 1981

> Tommy Daly (Clare); Willie Murphy (Cork); Sean Og Murphy (Cork); Mick Fitzgibbon (Lim); Des Ferguson (Dub); John Keane (Wat); Tommy Doyle (Tipp); Lowry Meagher (KK); Jim Hurley (Cork); Jimmy Langton (KK); Mick Mackey (Lim); Christy Ring (Cork); Eddie Keher (KK); Nicky Rackard (Wex); Matty Power (KK)

1984: The *Sunday Independent/Irish Nationwide* GAA Centenary Team

Tony Reddin (Tipp); Bobby Rackard (Wex); Nick O'Donnell (Wex); John Doyle (Tipp); Jimmy Finn (Tipp); John Keane (Wat); Paddy Phelan (KK); Lowry Meagher (KK); Jack Lynch (Cork); Christy Ring (Cork); Mick Mackey (Lim); Jimmy Langton (KK); Jimmy Doyle (Tipp); Nicky Rackard (Wex); Eddie Keher (KK)

1984: Waterford Centenary Team

Jim Ware (Erin's Own); Andy Fleming (Mount Sion); Charlie Ware (Erin's Own); Jackie Goode (Dungarvan); Johnny O'Connor (Abbeyside); John Keane (Mount Sion); Mick Hayes (Butlerstown); Séamus Power (Mount Sion); Philly Grimes (Mount Sion); Christy Moylan (Dungarvan); Tom Cheasty (Ballyduff); Frankie Walsh (Mount Sion); Larry Guinan (Mount Sion); John Kiely (Dungarvan); Sonny Wyse (Erin's Own).

2000: An Post/GAA Millennium team

Tony Reddin (Tipp); Bobby Rackard (Wex); Nick O'Donnell (Wex); John Doyle (Tipp); Brian Whelehan (Off); John Keane (Wat); Paddy Phelan (KK); Lowry Meagher (KK); Jack Lynch (Cork); Christy Ring (Cork); Mick Mackey (Lim); Jimmy Langton (KK); Jimmy Doyle (Tipp); Ray Cummins (Cork); Eddie Keher (KK)

2000: Munster Millennium Team

Tony Reddin (Tipp); John Doyle (Tipp); Brian Lohan (Clare); Denis Murphy (Cork); Jimmy Finn (Tipp); John Keane (Wat); Jackie Power (Lim); Jack Lynch (Cork); Philly Grimes (Wat); Jimmy Doyle (Tipp); Mick Mackey (Lim); Christy Ring (Cork); Jimmy Smyth (Clare); Ray Cummins (Cork); Paddy Barry (Cork)

2000: Waterford Millennium team

Jim Ware (Erin's Own); Andy Fleming (Mount Sion); Austin Flynn (Abbeyside); Jackie Goode (Dungarvan); Tony Browne (Mount Sion); John Keane (Mount Sion); Vin Baston (Army & Mount Sion); Séamus Power (Mount Sion); Philly Grimes (Mount Sion); Christy Moylan (Dungarvan); Tom Cheasty (Ballyduff); Frankie Walsh (Mount Sion); Larry Guinan (Mount Sion); John Kiely (Dungarvan); Paul Flynn (Ballygunner)

2009: GAA 125th Anniversary team

In a souvenir magazine for the GAA's 125th anniversary, Sean Moran, the Gaelic Games correspondent of the *Irish Times* selected his team of the past 125 years. It was published on 29 January 2009.

Tony Reddin (Tipp); Bobby Rackard (Wex); Brian Lohan (Clare); John Doyle (Tipp); Brian Whelehan (Off); John Keane (Wat); Paddy Phelan (KK); Lowry Meagher (KK); Jack Lynch (Cork); Christy Ring (Cork); Mick Mackey (Lim); Henry Shefflin (KK); Jimmy Doyle (Tipp); Nicky Rackard (Wex); Eddie Keher (KK)

In discussing replacements for the 1984 team Moran looked at Brian Corcoran (Cork) for centre-back but concluded that 'John Keane was felt to be one of the strongest of the Centenary selections'.

2009: Etihad 125th Anniversary team
Former Tipperary hurler Nicky English was adjudicator in an Etihad Airways promotion to find the 'All Time Hurling Dream Team' where the public were asked to submit their selections. The Etihad 125 'Dream Team' was:

Tony Reddin (Tipp); John Doyle (Tipp); Nick O'Donnell (Wex); Bobby Rackard (Wex); Brian Whelehan (Off); John Keane (Wat); Paddy Phelan (KK); Jack Lynch (Cork); Lory Meagher (KK); Christy Ring (Cork); Mick Mackey (Lim); Henry Shefflin (KK); Eddie Keher (KK); Ray Cummins (Cork); Jimmy Doyle (Tipp).

Brendan Fullam asked several hurlers to select their All-Star team for his book *Giants of the Ash* (1991) and, of those who did so, the following hurlers selected John. John's position on those teams is given in brackets.

Kevin Armstrong, Antrim (LHB); Jim Ware, Waterford (CHB); Mick Daniels, Dublin (CHB); Philly Grimes, Waterford (CHF); Jimmy Heffernan, Kilkenny (CHB); Seán Herbert, Limerick, (CHB); Garrett Howard, Limerick (RHB); Jack Lynch, Cork (CHB); John Mackey, Limerick (CHB); Christy Moylan, Waterford (CHB)

Bibliography

Books

Burke, Frank, *All Ireland Glory: a pictorial history of the Senior Hurling Championship 1887-2004*, (Frank Burke, NULL, 2004)

Carey, Tim, *Croke Park: Cathedral of Sport*, (Cork: Collins Press, 2007)

Comerford, R.V., *Charles J. Kickham: A study in Irish nationalism and literature*, (Dublin, Wolfhound Press, 1979)

Corry, Eoghan, *God and the Referee*, (Dublin: Hodder Headline Ireland, 2005)

Cronin, Jim, *Making Connections; A Cork G.A.A. Miscellany*, (Cork: Cork County Board GAA, 2005)

Cronin, Jim, (ed.), *Munster G.A.A. Story*, (The Munster History Committee, 1986)

deBhraldraithe, Tomás, (Transl. and Ed.), *Diary of an Irish Countryman*, A Translation of Humphrey O'Sullivan's *Cín Lae Amhlaoibh*, (Mercier Press: Cork, 1979)

de Bhulbh, Seán, *Sloinnte Uile Éireann*, (Luimneach: Comhar-Chumann Íde Naofa Teo., 2002)

de Búrca, Marcus, *The GAA: A History*, 2nd Ed, (Dublin: Gill & Macmillan, 1999)

Doheny, Michael, *The Felon's Track*, (Dublin; M.H.Gill & Son, Ltd. 1920)

Dorgan, Val, *Christy Ring: A Personal Portrait*, (Dublin: Ward River Press, 1980)

Dowling, Daniel, *Waterford Streets Past and Present*, (Waterford: Waterford Corporation, 1998)

Fogarty, Weeshie, *Dr Eamonn O'Sullivan: A Man before His Time*, (Dublin: Wolfhound Press, 2007)

Foley, Dónal, *Three Villages*, (Dublin: The Egotist Press, 1977)
Fullam, Brendan, *Giants of the Ash*, (Dublin: Wolfhound Press, 1991)
GAA Book of Lists, (Dublin: Hodder Headline Ireland, 2005
Horgan, Tim, *Christy Ring: Hurling's Greatest*, (Cork: Collins Press, 2007)
Houlihan, Elaine Burke, (comp.), *Tipperary: A Treasure Chest*, (Nenagh: Relay Books, 1995)
Hunt, Tom, *Sport and Society in Victorian Ireland: the Case of Westmeath*, (Cork: Cork University Press, 2007)
Keane, Colm, *Hurling's Top 20*, (Dublin: Mainstream Publishing Company Ltd., 2002)
Keith, Tom, *The Colours Blue & White*, (Midleton: Tom Keith, 1998)
Keith, Tom, (Comp., & Ed.), *A Century of Camogie in the Déise*, (Midleton: Waterford Camogie Archive Group, 2004)
Kelly, Seán, *Rule 42 and All That*, (Dublin, Gill & Macmillan, 2008)
Keogh, Dermot, *Jack Lynch: A Biography*, (Dublin: Gill & Macmillan Ltd., 2008)
King, Séamus, *Classic Munster Hurling Finals*, (Dublin: Gill & Macmillan, 2007)
King, Séamus, *History of Hurling*, (Dublin: Gill & Macmillan, 1996)
Lalor, Brian, (Ed), *The Encyclopaedia of Ireland*, (Dublin: Gill & Macmillan, 2003)
McCann, Owen, *The Greats of Gaelic Games*, (Dublin: Gaelic Publications, 1977)
McCarthy, Justin with Shannon, Kieran, *Hooked: A Hurling Life*, (Dublin: Gill & Macmillan Ltd., 2002)
McCarthy, Kevin, *Gold, Silver and Green: The Irish Olympic Journey 1896-1924*, (Cork: Cork University Press, 2010)
MacLysaght, Edward, *The Surnames of Ireland*, (Blackrock; Irish Academic Press, 6th edition, 1985)
Mehigan, P.D., Kilfeather, Seán (Ed.), *Vintage Carbery*, (Dublin: Beaver Row Press, 1984)

Murray, Robert J., *A Church Grows On a Tree Claim: A History of Sacred Heart Parish*, (Aberdeen S.D: North Plains Press, 1981)
O'Flynn, Diarmuid, *Hurling: The Warrior Game,* (Cork: The Collins Press, 2008)
Ó hEithir, Breandain, *Over the Bar,* (Dublin: Ward River Press Ltd., 1984)
Ó Murchú, Liam, *A Time to Love?* (Dublin: Gill and Macmillan Ltd., 1986)
O'Neill, Michelle, *Reminiscences of Waterford*, (Waterford: 1997)
O'Neill, Phil, *History of the G.A.A. 1910-1930,* (Kilkenny: Kilkenny Journal Ltd., 1931)
Ó Riain, Séamus, *Maurice Davin (1842-1927): First President of the GAA,* (Dublin: Geography Publications)
Ó Tuama, Liam, *The Spirit of the Glen*, (Cork: Fánaithe na Gleanna, 1974)
Ó Tuama, Liam, *Where He Sported and Played: JACK LYNCH, A Sporting Celebration*, (Dublin: Blackwater Press, 2000)
Power, Rev. P., *The Place-Names of Decies*: (London: David Nutt, 1907)
Rackard, Billy, *No Hurling at the Dairy Door*, (Dublin: Blackwater Press, 1996)
Riegel, Ralph, *Three kings: Cork, Kilkenny, Tipperary: the battle for hurling supremacy*, (Dublin: The O'Brien Press Ltd., 2008)
Roche, Dickie, (comp. & written), *The Mount Sion Story: from the beginning in 1932,* (Waterford: 2000)
Roche, Dickie, (comp. & written), *A Story of Hurling in Waterford*, (Waterford: 2005)
Sweeney, Eamonn, *Munster Hurling Legends*, (Dublin: O'Brien Press Ltd., 2002)
Walsh, Denis, *Hurling: The Revolution Years*, (Dublin: Penguin Ireland, 2005)
Walsh, Jim, (comp.), *Sliabh Rua: A History of Its People and Places*, (2001)

Newspapers

Cork Examiner

Connaught Tribune

Dungarvan Leader

Dungarvan Observer

Evening Press

Freeman's Journal

Kilkenny Journal

Kilkenny Leader

Irish Independent

Irish Press

Irish Times

Limerick Leader

Munster Express

Southern Star

Sunday Independent

Sunday Press

The Nation

Waterford Evening News

Waterford News

Waterford News and Star

Waterford Standard

Waterford Star

Weekly Irish Times

Magazines

An Cúl, Vol. 4, No. 2, (Dublin: Gaelic Press Ltd., 1973)
Cnoc Síon 1802-1972, (Waterford: 1972)
Cnoc Síon 1932-1974, Souvenir Record, (Waterford: 1974)
Cuchulainn Annual 1969, (Dublin: Press Cuchulainn Ltd., 1969)
Gaelsport 1987, (Dublin:1987)
Gaelic Yearbook 98, (Dublin: Chieftain Publications, 1998)
Kelloggs Book of G.A.A. Facts, (Dublin: G.A.A. Coisde na nÓg, 1985)
Mount Sion GAA Club 75th Anniversary, (Waterford: Waterford News & Star, 2007)
Our Games Annual, (Dublin: Gaelic Athletic Association, 1962)
Our Games Annual, (Dublin: Gaelic Athletic Association, 1963)
Our Games Annual, (Dublin: Gaelic Athletic Association, 1973)
P.D.Mehigan, *Carbery's Annual 1942-43*, (Dublin: Carbery Publications, 1943)
P.D.Mehigan, *Carbery's Annual 1943-44*, (Dublin: Carbery Publications, 1944)
P.D.Mehigan, *Carbery's Annual 1945-46*, (Dublin: Carbery Publications, 1945)
P.D.Mehigan, *Carbery's Annual 1946-47*, (Dublin: Carbery Publications, 1946)

P.D.Mehigan, *Carbery's Annual 1947-48*, (Dublin: Carbery Publications, 1947)
P.D.Mehigan, *Carbery's Annual 1949-50*, (Dublin: Carbery Publications, 1949)
P.D.Mehigan, *Carbery's Annual 1953-54*, (Dublin: Carbery Publications, 1953)
P.D.Mehigan, *Carbery's Annual 1954-55*, (Dublin: Carbery Publications, 1954)
P.D.Mehigan, *Carbery's Annual 1955-56*, (Dublin: Carbery Publications, 1955)
P.D.Mehigan, *Carbery's Annual 1956-57*, (Dublin: Carbery Publications, 1956)
P.D.Mehigan, *Carbery's Annual 1957-58*, (Dublin: Carbery Publications, 1957)
P.D.Mehigan, *Carbery's Annual 1960-61*, (Dublin: Carbery Publications, 1960)
P.D.Mehigan, *Carbery's Annual 1961-62*, (Dublin: Carbery Publications, 1961)
P.D.Mehigan, *Carbery's Annual 1962-63*, (Dublin: Carbery Publications, 1962)
P.D.Mehigan, *Carbery's Annual 1963-64*, (Dublin: Carbery Publications, 1963)
Portláirge '84
Solo Annual '75, (Dublin: Gaelic Press Ltd., 1975)
Waterford G.A.A. Yearbook 1997: An Déiseach, (Waterford: Waterford Publications Committee, 1997)

Programmes

Munster Hurling Championship 1933
Craobh na Mumhan san Iomáint 1934
Craobh Iomána na hÉireann 1938
Craobh Iomána na hÉireann 1948
Cluichí Ceannais Iomána na hÉireann 1984
Cluichí Leath-Cheannais Iomána na Mumhan 2009

Interviews

Andy Fleming, Austin Flynn, Jack O'Neill, Jim O'Meara, Larry Fanning, Pat Fanning

I have had long conversations, some extending over a number of years, with Pat and Larry Fanning, Paddy Greene and the following members of John's family: Tom Keane, Peggy Keane, Tommy Keane, Mary Doyle, Pat Kelly and Tomás P ÓCinnéide.

I have also spoken with James Grant, former Secretary, Waterford Co. Board, GAA and Tom 'Gum' Kennedy, historian of the Erin's Own GAA club who played alongside John as a young member of the Mount Sion club.

Index

Page numbers with a 'p' refer to a picture on that page

Aintree Grand National, 12
All Ireland
  1934 Junior Hurling, 30, 30p, 31, 32
  1938 Senior Hurling, 52–54, 54p, 55, 55p, 56, 57, 57p, 62
  1948 Minor Hurling, 121
  1948 Senior Hurling, 105, 114, 120–122, 122p, 123, 124, 125p
  1957 Senior Hurling, 220
  1959 Senior Hurling, 222
An Cúl, 94
An Fear Rua, 78

Bachelor's Walk, 12
Ballybricken, 1, 3, 12, 15, 178
Ballyduff, 1, 172
Ballytruckle, 1, 129
Barrack Street, 13–16, 27, 61, 79, 117, 160, 168, 189, 242, 249
Barrett, Jack, 61, 227, 229
Barron, John, v, 219
Barron, Willie, 57p, 91, 98
Barry, Jim, 116, 130
Barry, Mick, 177
Baston, John, 174p
Baston, Vincent, 62, 86, 87, 91–93, 97, 99, 100, 103–107, 110, 114, 116, 118, 129, 132, 186, 195, 198p, 202
Bolger, Martin, 139p, 140
Breen, Dick, 153, 154p
Brennan, Tony, 26
British Army Incident, 14, 15
Browne, Fad, 35, 36, 102, 158, 171
Browne, Tom, 230, 246

Browne, Tony, 102, 158
Buggy, J., 140
Bunmahon, 11
Butler, J., 123
Butler, Jackie, 50p
Butlerstown, 1, 91
Byrne, 'Dashy', 155, 162
Byrne, Locky, 20, 32, 35–37, 50p, 54, 56, 57p, 60, 60p, 138, 141, 147, 150, 152, 153, 154p, 155, 156, 161, 162, 189
Byrne, Podge, 247

Callan, 2
Campbell, Willy, 170
Canon Power, 11
Carew, Eddie, 106, 116, 118, 119, 129, 200
Carrick-on-Suir, 33, 120, 193, 199
Casey, Paudie, 223p
Casey, Wal, 205, 211p
Cashman, Denis, 4
Cheasty, Tom, 223p
Christian Brothers
  Kenneally, Br., 154p
  Malone, Br., 19, 19p, 20, 137, 138
  O'Connor, Br., 97, 138, 145p, 146, 182, 183
  O'Toole, Br., 138
  Rice, Br., 17, 18, 96, 177
  Walker, Br., 138
Clohessy, Dave, 47, 74, 229
Clohessy, Paddy, 247
Clubs
  Abbeyside, 217
  Ahane, 243, 247
  Army 3*rd* Battalion, 177, 182
  Army 7*th* Battalion, 175
  Avondhu (Cork), 224
  Avonmore, 188, 199, 200
  Blackrock (Cork), 187
  Borrisoleigh, 198, 199
  Brickey Rangers, 214, 215
  Butlerstown, 103, 187

263

Cappoquin, 183, 209, 210
Carrick Davin's, 141
Carrick Swan, 141, 150, 187, 205, 206
Carrickshock, 141, 156, 163, 187, 193, 205, 206
Carrigtwohill, 150
Castleconnell, 43
Clonea, 5, 107, 195–197, 212
De la Salle, 6, 140, 141, 179, 214
Dicksboro, 194, 205, 206, 247
Dungarvan, x, 20, 32, 35, 99, 107, 139, 151, 155, 160, 164, 165, 182, 184, 210, 211
Dungarvan United, 199
Dunhill, 35, 141–144, 146, 214
Durrow, 5, 6
Éire Óg (Kilkenny), 163, 186, 199, 200, 205, 207, 208, 227
Éire Óg (Mount Sion), 20, 137, 138
Erin's Own, x, 20, 32–37, 59, 70, 98, 102, 104, 105, 107, 109, 112, 137, 138, 141–144, 146–153, 155–160, 163, 164, 170, 171, 177, 179–182, 186–188, 192–195, 200, 210
Faughs, 153
Fedamore, 247
Ferrybank, 35–37, 159
Ferrybank (P.H. Pearse), 151, 155, 179
Glen Rovers, 96, 169, 186, 198–200, 247
Gracedieu, 6
Graigue, 198–200, 205
Holycross, 193, 199, 200, 247
Kill, 158, 213, 214
Kinsale, 247
Knockboy, 6
LDF 46*th* Battalion, 175
Lismore, 22, 32, 99
Mooncoin, 35, 37, 38, 63, 141, 147, 150, 162, 206, 214
Mount Sion, *see* Separate entry

Mullinavat, 141, 163, 186
O'Rourke's, 83
Portlaw, x, 20, 21, 64, 98, 99, 146, 147, 165, 170, 172, 247
Rapparee, 145
Rathnure, 205, 247
Sarsfields (Cork), 119, 205, 214
St Colmcille's, 140
St Molleran's, 193
St Otteran's, 108
St Stephen's, 59, 155, 163, 170
Stradbally, 95
Tallow, x, 32, 34, 35, 144–146, 150, 151, 172
Thomas Francis Meagher's, 193
Thurles Blues (Sarsfield), 38
Tourin, 202, 204–206, 208, 209
Tullaroan, 38, 195, 198, 205, 206, 247
University College Cork, 224
Colleges
Callan CBS, 22
Dr. Harty Cup, 22, 25, 159
Kilkenny CBS, 22
Munster team, 25–28, 32, 104
St Kieran's, 25
Comerford, R. V., 2
Condon, Jackie, 223p
Connolly, Tom, 211p
Connors, Billy, 174p
Cooke, Noel, 154p
Cooney, Jimmy, 48, 50
Cooper, Richard, 174p
Coughlan, Seán, 95
Creed, Matty, 70
Croke, Andy, 93
Cronin, Jim, 4, 69
Cullen, Martin, 88p, 107, 112
Culleton, Dick, 205
Cummins, Ray, 195
Curley, Mick, 57p, 60, 60p
Curran, Paddy, 206p, 211p
Curran, Tom, 118, 125
Cusack, John, 106, 125
Cusack, Michael, 4

Daly, Ned, 106, 110, 126, 129, 130
Daly, Willy John, 58, 116
Daniels, Mick, 56
Darmody, James (great Uncle), 17
Darmody, John (great Grandparent), 12
Darmody, Katie (Mother), 13, 18, 18p
Darmody, Michael (great Uncle), 17, 18
Darmody, Tom (Grandparent), 13
de Búrca, Marcus, 4
de Bhulbh, Seán, 11
De la Salle, Brothers, 17
De la Salle, School, 18
de Valera, Eamonn, 28, 66
Doheny, Michael, 3
Doherty, Gabriel, vi
Donnelly, John, 154p
Doocey, Dick, 204
Dorgan, Val, 100, 101
Dowling, Michael, 138, 154p, 162
Dowling, Paddy, 62, 73, 74, 83, 97, 98, 154p, 163, 174p, 176, 179, 180p
Dowling, Ramie, 126, 200
Downey, Paddy, 247
Downey, Shem, 126
Doyle, Brian 'Bunny', 35, 139p, 140, 153, 154p, 156, 162, 170, 174p, 176, 206p
Doyle, D., 34, 35
Doyle, Jimmy, 114
Doyle, Mary, v, 262
Doyle, Michael, 25, 138, 139p, 140, 154p, 203, 206p
Doyle, Tommy, 58
Duffy, Charles Gavan, 3
Duggan, Jos., 138
Duggan, Larry, 153, 154p, 156
Duggan, Paddy, 35, 139p, 140, 145, 153, 154p, 155, 161, 162, 166
Duggan, Seanie, 118
Dungarvan, 33, 53, 91
Dunmore East, 91
Dunne, 'Lovely' Johnny, 32
Dunne, May (Wife), 117, 124, 128p, 175, 179, 180p, 225p

Edwards, Frank (IRA), 28
Equipment
  Boots, 56, 69, 90
  Hurley, 16, 69–71, 78, 120, 147, 156, 177, 183, 208, 209, 219
  Jersey, 49, 68, 69, 72, 190, 218, 221
  Sliotar, 68–70, 78, 152
  Togs, 69, 77, 117, 173

Factory League, 212
Fanning, Eoin, v
Fanning, Johnny, 35, 54, 57p, 64, 148, 152
Fanning, Larry, v, 70, 74, 112, 121, 151, 152, 169, 174, 174p, 195, 198p, 202, 207, 211p, 229, 262
Fanning, Paddy, 139p, 140
Fanning, Pat, v, 22, 23, 45, 79, 89, 90, 111, 112, 121, 132, 138, 148, 150–153, 154p, 156, 173, 174p, 202, 204, 205, 206p, 212, 217, 218, 220, 222p, 223, 225–227, 229, 230, 242, 248, 262
Fardy, Nicky, 153
Feeney, Seán, 57p
Ferrybank, 35, 159, 160, 162
  Back in Waterford, 35
Finn, Jimmy, 132
Fives, Jim, 202
Flannelly, Mick, 184, 188, 199, 206p, 211p, 229
Flavin, Jack, 138, 152, 154p, 166, 172, 174p, 206p
Fleming, Andy, v, 19, 20, 29, 62, 73, 74, 83, 87, 97, 98, 102–104, 106, 120, 123, 129, 159, 161, 163, 170, 172, 173, 174p, 176, 179, 186, 188, 189p, 198p, 203p, 206p, 207, 229, 262
Flynn, Austin, v, 217, 222, 262
Flynn, John, 154p, 229

Foley, Dónal, 37, 160, 246
Foley, Michael, 224, 225p
Fullam, Brendan, 58, 120, 190

Gaffney, Billy, 206p, 211p
Gallagher, Jack, 174p, 206p
Gallagher, Mick, 99, 108, 153, 154p, 157, 162, 163, 166, 174p, 176, 189p, 192, 206p
Gallagher, Tom, 188, 199, 206p, 211p
Gallagher, Willie, 206p
Gallow's Hill, 1
Galvin, Willie, 106
Gargan, Joe, 200
Goode, Declan, 35, 50p, 56, 70, 80, 81, 110, 153
Goode, Jackie, 104, 106, 129
Grace, Fr. John, 216
Grace, Paddy, 126
Gracedieu, 1, 4, 13
Grant, James, v, 108, 109, 158, 248, 262
Grant, Mickey, 140
Grant, Ritchie, 194
Grattan Square, 33, 174
Graves & Co., 24, 167, 212
Greaney, Tom, 35, 50p, 57p
Greene, Jim, 229
Greene, Paddy, v, 22, 29, 37, 40, 112, 113, 140, 146, 147, 153, 154p, 156, 163, 174p, 175, 229, 262
Griffith Place, 152
Grimes, Philly, 102, 109, 182, 183, 189, 190, 204, 205, 207, 211p, 215, 217, 229
Grounds
  Ballyduff, 172
  Clonmel, 40, 42, 46, 75–77, 100, 105, 243, 244
  Cork, 29, 32
  Croke Park, 37, 39, 103, 124, 243, 244
  Davin Park, 32, 198
  Dungarvan, 41, 49, 59, 62, 92, 108, 131, 150, 151, 172, 183, 186, 209, 210, 244
  Ennis, 51
  Enniscorthy, 64, 104
  Fermoy, 36, 64, 217
  Fitzgerald Stadium, 75
  Gaelic Field(Waterford), xi, 16, 77, 80, 125, 140, 150, 151, 158, 160, 161, 163, 192, 194, 207
  Lismore, 38, 144, 187
  Mardyke, 32, 98
  Nenagh, 87
  New Ross, 22, 62
  Nowlan Park, 25, 28, 41
  Thurles, 23, 63, 113–115, 117, 131, 220
  Wexford Park, 30
Guinan, Larry, 229

Halpin, Tom, 57p
Hanlon, Johnny, 154p
Harney, Joe, 223p
Harte, Denis, 139p, 154p
Hartery, Johnny, 28
Hartery, Nicholas, v
Hayden, Diamond, 126, 200
Hayden, Séan, 206p, 211p
Hayes, Martin, 88p
Hayes, Matthew, 15
Hayes, Mick, 100, 103, 104, 106, 109, 129, 187
Hayes, Séamus, 138
Healy, Mick, 109, 179, 183, 206p, 211p, 229
Heffernan, Mick, 188p, 206p, 211p
Herbert, Mick, 229
Hickey, John D., 44, 93, 105
Hickey, Martin, 120
Hickey, Mick, 49, 51, 52, 57p, 91–93, 120, 121, 125
Hodgers, Paddy, 27
Hogan, 'Dottie', 35, 140–142
Hogan, Séan, 138
Horgan, Tim, 249
Howard, Garrett, 44
Howlett, Billy, 21, 137, 247

Humphries, Tom, 152
Hurley, Jim, 211p

IRA, 15, 28
Islandikeane, 11

Jackman, Noel, 211p
Jones, Dick, 28

Keane, Agnes, 225p
Keane, Babby (Sister), 24, 25p
Keane, Biddy (Sister), 14
Keane, Catherine (Daughter), 128, 128p, 224, 225p
Keane, Gerard (Son), v, 128, 128p, 225p
Keane, John
  Administration
    Club Chairman, 108, 192, 244
    Club Committee, 137
    County Selector, 99, 107–110, 192, 212
    County Treasurer, 129, 192, 197, 244
  Family
    As child, 15, 16
    Family name, 11
    Grand Parents et al, 12, 13, 17
    Own family, 24, 124, 128, 175, 179, 224
    Parents, Siblings, 12–14, 18, 24, 28, 39, 83, 140, 168, 169
  Health
    Ill-health/Death, 164, 225–231, 242, 243
    Injuries, 22, 88–90, 95, 96, 171–173, 176, 177, 181, 185, 244
    Physique, 12, 21, 27
  Hurling
    Approach from Cork, 168, 169
    First Hurley, 16, 140
    On Hurling, 53, 70, 71, 79, 80, 118, 180, 181, 219, 220, 222
    On other players, 45, 101, 102, 179
    Referee/Umpire, 59, 169, 192, 212
    School/Minor, 18–25, 27, 137, 140
    Sent Off, 210
    Trainer, ix, 27, 108, 192, 212, 217, 219, 220, 222, 223, 244
  Personality
    Character, ix, xi, 26, 76–80, 97, 124, 164, 166–168, 190, 208, 218–222, 224, 225, 227
    Politics, 28
    Resigns from Club, 166, 167
    Team Leader, 21, 22, 37, 40, 96, 132, 154, 155
  Photograph, 11p, 30p, 41p, 50p, 54p, 57p, 60–62p, 73p, 88p, 122p, 128p, 139p, 143p, 154p, 174p, 180p, 184p, 189p, 191p, 198p, 203p, 206p, 211p, 222p, 223p, 225p
  Sporting
    Football, 29, 59, 63, 108, 117–119, 213, 214, 216
    Other Sports, 27, 28
Keane, John (Son), v, 128, 128p, 225p
Keane, Josie (Brother), 14, 24, 25p
Keane, Katie (Mother), see Darmody, Katie
Keane, Kitty (Sister), 24, 25p
Keane, Margaret (Daughter), 128, 128p, 224, 225p
Keane, May (Wife), see Dunne, May
Keane, Molly (Sister), 13, 24, 25p
Keane, Peggy (Sister), v, 24, 25p, 140, 168, 262
Keane, Queenie (Sister), 24, 25p
Keane, Rosemary, 225p
Keane, Séamus, 205
Keane, Thomas (Brother), 14, 15, 24, 24p
Keane, Thomas (Father), 12, 12p
Keane, Thomas (Grandparent), 12
Keane, Tom (Son), v, 128, 128p, 224, 225p, 262
Keane, Tommy, v, 15, 182, 183, 189,

205, 206p, 210, 211p, 262
Keher, Eddie, ix, 223, 248
Kehoe, George, 35, 140
Keith, Tom, 115
Kelly, Pat, 26
Kelly, Pat (brother-in-law), v, 138, 139p, 150, 166, 262
Kenneally, Billy, 28, 129
Kennedy, Catherine (great Grandparent), 13
Kennedy, Martin, 33, 34, 158
Kennedy, Patrick, 83
Kennedy, Tom 'Gum', v, 206p, 211p, 262
Keogh (Kehoe), Michael, 145
Kickham, Charles J., 2, 3
Kiely, Johnny, 217
Kilmacow, 91
Kilmacthomas, 11, 91
Kinane, Dr Kinane Cup, 195, 199
Knockboy, 5
Knockhouse, 4
Kyne, Tom, 99

Langton, Jimmy, x, 40, 102, 126, 130, 200, 207, 208, 227
Lannen, Tom, 107
LDF (Local Defence Force), ix, 66, 91, 167, 168, 175
Leahy, Terry, 126
Lemass, Seán, 83
Lismore, 91
Lucas, Maurice, 16
Lynch, Bill, 35, 36, 153, 154p, 176
Lynch, Jack, x, 23, 26, 26p, 28, 48, 72, 73, 81, 82, 93, 101, 102, 105, 115, 169, 175, 186, 229

macConmara, Donncha Ruadh, 1
MacNamara, Aidan, 95, 154p, 206p
McGabhann, Seán, 154p
McGrath, Jack, 35
McGrath, Ken, 102
McGrath, Pat, 102, 229
McGrath, Tom, 158
McHugh, Maurice 'Budgie', 110
McLysaght, Edward, 11
Mackey, Anthony, 43
Mackey, John, 43, 82, 229
Mackey, John 'Tyler', 43
Mackey, Mick, x, 23, 40–47, 52, 56–58, 60p, 73, 74, 76, 81, 82, 84, 86, 94, 102, 105, 175, 227, 229, 231, 243, 244, 246, 247
Madden, Morgan, 30
Malone, Br., see Christian Bro.
Marnell, Mark, 126
Mater Hospital, 26, 225
Mayor's Walk, 12
Meagher, Lory, 246, 247
Meagher, Thomas Francis, 1, 3
Mehigan, P. D. (Pat'O), 34, 72, 92, 98
Minogue, Frank, 153, 154p, 166, 174p, 176
Mooncoin, 5, 120
Moonvoy, 11
Morrison's Road, 13, 16
Morrissey, Máirtín, 188, 206p, 211p
Morrissey, Martin Óg, 70, 229
Morrissey, Tommy, 154p
Morrissey, Wattie, 153, 154p, 163, 206p
Mount Congreve, 5
Mount Sion
  County Selection, 40, 41, 107, 220
  Eligibility of Players, 143–145, 147, 197
  First County Title
    1930 Minor H. (Mount Sion/ Éire Óg), 20
    1933 Minor H. (exclusive M.S.), 139
    1934 Junior H., 31, 139
    1936 Senior H.(Lost Objection), 144–146
    1938 Senior H., 152, 153
    1945 Senior/Minor H., 183–185
    1953 Senior Football, 213
  Foundation, 138–139

Match Trouble
 Éire Óg (Kilkenny), 207–208
 Brickey Rangers, 215
 Dunhill, 146
 Erin's Own, 148, 181–182
 Photograph, 139p, 143p, 154p, 174p, 184p, 188p, 189p, 191p, 198p, 201p, 203p, 206p, 211p
 Trouble within, 165–167, 170
Mount Sion Avenue, 16, 189
Mountain, Jimmy, 57p
Moylan, Christy, 32, 35, 39, 42, 43, 48, 57p, 60, 60p, 63, 74, 98, 102, 119, 120, 125
Mulcahy, Billy, 184, 211p
Mulcahy, Jack, 126, 200
Mulcahy, Tom, 129
Mullinavat, 12
Munster Football Championship
 1934 Minor, 29
 1948 Junior, 117–119
Munster Hurling Championship
 1932 Minor, 23
 1933 Minor, 24
 1934 Minor, 29
 1934 Junior, 29
 1935 Senior, 32, 33
 1936 Junior, 236
 1936 Senior, 35
 1937 Senior, 41, 46, 47
 1938 Senior, 49, 50, 50p, 51, 52
 1939 Senior, 63, 64
 1940 Senior, 73–76, 91, 92
 1941 Senior, 83
 1942 Senior, 84
 1943 Senior, 88–90, 92, 93
 1944 Senior, 96
 1945 Senior, 99
 1946 Senior, 100
 1947 Senior, 105
 1948 Senior, 108–110, 113, 115, 116
 1949 Senior, 131
 1950 Senior, 131
 1951 Senior, 132
Murphy, Bernie, 93, 116

Murphy, Séamus, 154p

National Football League, 59
National Hurling League, 33–35, 37–42, 44, 48, 57–60, 62, 65, 80, 81, 98, 99, 103, 104, 106, 108, 131, 196, 197
 Debut, 32
 Finals, 62, 63, 223
 Referee, 212
Nestor, Mick, 118, 119
Newgate Street, 14
Norris, Mikie, 39

Ó Braonáin, Séamus, 42, 45, 76–78, 227, 228, 246, 248
O'Brien, Freddie, 217
O'Brien, Mick, 174p
O'Brien, Séamus, 102, 231
Ó Ceallaigh, Séamus, 46
Ó Cinnéide, Tomás, v, 75, 117, 225, 226, 262
O'Connor, Br., *see* Christian Bro.
O'Connor, Johnny, 104, 106, 116, 118
O'Connor, Paddy, x, 141, 143–146, 150, 153, 154p, 155, 162, 166, 174p, 205, 206p
O'Connor, Peter (IRA), 28
O'Donnell, Nick, 200
O'Donoghue, Vincent, 36, 111
O'Donovan, Paddy, 25
O'Donovan, Paddy (Cork), 114, 169
Ó Fainín, Pádraig, *see* Fanning, Pat
O'Grady, George, 74
O'Grady, John, 114
O'Grady, Pat, 229
O'Hanlon, Johnny, 140
O'Hehir, Mícheál, 68
O'Meara, Jim, v, 151, 154p, 159, 162, 171–173, 174p, 179, 187, 188p, 262
O'Neill, Delia, 180p
O'Neill, Jack, v, ix, 262

O'Regan, Johnny, 206p, 211p
O'Regan, Mick, 64
O'Riordan, D., 105
Ó Síocháin, Seán, 229
Ó Súilleabháin, Amhlaoibh, 2
O'Shea, Joe, 174p
O'Sullivan, Terry, 54
Oireachtas Tournament, 124, 223

Pall bearers
   Limerick, 229
   Waterford, 229
Parle, Mick, 140
Passage East, 86, 91
Penkert, Frank, 142
Phelan, Ned 'Gaelic', 5
Phelan, Paddy, 48, 102
Poleberry, 27
Portlaw, 88, 147, 155, 164, 166, 214
Power, Davy, 206p, 211p, 229
Power, Jackie, x, 102, 227, 229, 230, 249
Power, Séamus, 102, 183, 215, 229
Prior's Knock, 15
Puirséal, Pádraig, 247, 248

Rackard, Bobby, 247
Rackard, Nicky, 230
Railway Cup, 39, 40, 48, 60, 60p, 61, 63, 72, 74, 82, 87, 95, 98, 99, 103, 129, 130, 190, 227
   Captain, 59, 60, 130
   Debut, 39
   Dropped, 94
Regan, Jim, 247
Regan, Mick, 22
Reidy, Liam, 200
Rice, Br., *see* Christian Bro.
Ring, Christy, x, 40, 42, 43, 58, 81, 82, 87, 92–94, 100–102, 105, 116, 130, 131, 169, 186, 199, 224, 246, 247, 249
Roche, Dicky, 229

Roche, F., 99
Russell, Paul, 52, 53
Ryan, Bon, 35, 139p, 141
Ryan, Con, 37
Ryan, Eamonn, 224, 225p
Ryan, Lukie, 35
Ryan, Timmy, x, 48, 72, 73, 76

Sallypark, 35
Scanlon, Paddy, 74, 82, 102
Sexton, Thomas, 4
Shanahan, Dave, 107
Sheehan, Pa, 35, 50p, 57p
Simpson, Mick, 154p
Skehan, Mick, 35
Slievekeale, 4, 15, 16, 160
Slieverue, 91
Smith, Anne, vi
St. Ignatius Street, 16
Stakelum, Pat, 247
Stradbally, 19

Tarbert, 227
Time-keeping, 47, 165
Tramore, ix, 11, 12, 28, 91, 230
Transport
   Bicycle, 67, 84, 88, 91, 125, 171
   Bus, 67, 84, 121, 125, 164, 208
   Car, 27, 83, 88, 125, 183, 190, 226
   Lorry, 121
   Plane, 121
   Train, 19, 20, 26, 32, 64, 67, 84, 91, 113, 125, 131, 193, 198
   Walk, 67, 117, 125, 171

Veale, Seán, 95
Vereker, Tom, 211p

Wade, Eddie, 39
Walsh, Charlie, 5
Walsh, Davy, 202, 206p

Walsh, Frankie, 78, 215, 229
Walsh, Jimmy, x, 126, 156, 174p
Walsh, John 'Hopper', 32, 138, 140, 153, 154p, 155
Walsh, Mary (Grandparent), 12
Walsh, Willie, 5, 35, 37, 47, 53
Walsh, Willie 'Doyle', 57p, 174p
Walsh, Willie (Kilkenny), 126
Ware, Charlie, 20, 33, 35, 36, 50p, 52, 56, 57p, 59, 63, 64, 107, 137, 143, 147, 152, 153
Ware, Jim, 74, 90, 93, 98, 99, 105, 106, 114, 116, 129, 130, 156, 171, 222p
Widger, 12
Wild Man from Borneo (horse), 12
Wyse, Mick, 36
Wyse, Sonny, 35, 36, 139p, 158

Yellow Road, 1

English Revision for
Leaving Certificate
Higher Level

English Revision for Leaving Certificate Higher Level

FOURTH EDITION
FOR EXAMINATIONS IN 2005, 2006 AND 2007

Anne Gormley

GILL & MACMILLAN

Gill & Macmillan Ltd
Hume Avenue
Park West
Dublin 12
with associated companies throughout the world

© Anne Gormley 2001, 2002 and 2004
0 7171 3713 9

Print origination in Ireland by
O'K Graphic Design, Dublin

Note: The texts, films and poems in this book are prescribed for the Higher Level Leaving Certificate examinations in June 2005, June 2006 and June 2007.

The paper used in this book is made from the wood pulp of managed forests. For every tree felled, at least one tree is planted, thereby renewing natural resources.

All rights reserved.
No part of this publication may be reproduced, copied or transmitted in any form or by any means without written permission of the publishers or else under the terms of any licence permitting limited copying issued by the Irish Copyright Licensing Agency, Irish Writers' Centre, Parnell Square, Dublin 1.

Contents

Acknowledgments	viii
Preface	x
1. Revision Techniques	1

Paper I

2. Examination Techniques in Paper I	2
3. Comprehension	3
Characteristics of comprehension passages	3
Types of prose writing	3
Structure and form of comprehension passages	7
The language of comprehension	13
Characteristics of well-written answers in comprehension	14
Comprehension vocabulary	17
Exercises on style	22
4. Composition	24
General notes on writing	24
Problems and pitfalls	25
Preparation	27
Planning	29
The paragraph	31
Checklist for writing compositions	40
5. The Language Genres	41
The language of narration	41
The language of argument	49
The language of information	60
The language of persuasion	74
The aesthetic use of language	86
6. Samples of Paper I with Model Answers	95
Structure of Paper I	95
First sample paper: culture and trends	96
Second sample paper: violence and destruction	101
Third sample paper: communication	109
Fourth sample paper: lifestyles	114
Fifth sample paper: home and identity	121
Model answers to comprehension questions	127

Paper II

7. Examination Technique in Paper II	150
Prescribed texts for examination in 2005	150
Prescribed texts for examination in 2006	152
Prescribed texts for examination in 2007	154
Examination technique in Paper II	155
Answering literature questions	156
8. The Study of a Single Text	158
How to answer a question on the study of a single text	158
Sample draft answers	159
Amongst Women (2005 exam)	159
As You Like It (2005 and 2006 exams)	160
Wuthering Heights (2005 and 2007 exams)	161
Death and Nightingales (2006 exam)	162
The Poisonwood Bible (2006 and 2007 exams)	163
Sample complete answers	164
Hamlet (2005 exam)	164
Silas Marner (2005 exam)	166
King Lear (2006 exam)	168
Pride and Prejudice (2006 and 2007 exams)	170
Macbeth (2007 exam)	172
Possible types of questions for the study of a single text	175
9. The Comparative Study of Texts	178
What is a comparative study?	178
Answering a question on the comparative study of texts	179
Draft questions and sample answers	180
Possible types of questions on the comparative study of texts	191
10. Notes on Some Prescribed Texts	193
Amongst Women (2005 exam)	193
Silas Marner (2005 exam)	195
A Doll's House (2005 and 2006 exams: comparative studies only)	197
Jane Eyre (2005 and 2006 exams: comparative studies only)	199
Wuthering Heights (2005 and 2007 exams)	202
Antigone (2006 exam: comparative studies only)	205
Death and Nightingales (2006 exam)	208
Great Expectations (2006 exam: comparative studies only)	209
The Poisonwood Bible (2006 and 2007 exams)	212
Pride and Prejudice (2006 and 2007 exams)	214
Death of a Salesman (2007 exam)	215
11. Notes on Shakespeare Drama	218
Tragedy in Shakespeare	218
Hamlet (2005 exam)	220
As You Like It (2005 and 2006 exams)	229
King Lear (2006 exam)	231
Macbeth (2007 exam)	243

12. Notes on Films	247
Characteristics of films	247
Much Ado about Nothing (2005 exam)	248
The Dead (2005 exam)	250
Strictly Ballroom (2005 exam)	253
Dances with Wolves (2005 and 2006 exams)	255
Il Postino (2005, 2006 and 2007 exams)	257
Witness (2005, 2006 and 2007 exams)	261
On the Waterfront (2006 exam)	264
A Room with a View (2006 and 2007 exams)	267
Henry V (2006 and 2007 exams)	271
My Left Foot (2007 exam)	274
Twelve Angry Men (2007 exam)	277
13. Unseen Poetry	280
Approaching the unseen poem	280
Method of answering questions on an unseen poem	287
Questions and sample answers	287
14. Prescribed Poetry	296
Approaching the question	296
Questions and sample answers	297
Séamus Heaney (2005 exam)	297
Elizabeth Bishop (2006 and 2007 exams)	298
Eavan Boland (2005 exam)	300
Possible types of questions on prescribed poetry	302
15. Answers	304
16. Past Examination Papers	306

Acknowledgments

For permission to reproduce copyright material in this book, grateful acknowledgment is made to the following:

HarperCollins for extracts from *Wild Swans* by Jung Chang;

John Murray (Publishers) Ltd for an extract from *Wheels Within Wheels* by Dervla Murphy;

Peters Fraser Dunlop for an extract from 'The Reaping Race' by Liam O'Flaherty (© Liam O'Flaherty);

Random House Group Ltd for an extract from *An Evil Cradling* by Brian Keenan, published by Hutchinson (© Brian Keenan 1992), an extract from *In Patagonia* by Bruce Chatwin, published by Jonathan Cape (© Bruce Chatwin 1977); and for an extract from *A Far-Off Place* by Laurens van der Post (© Hogarth Press);

Faber and Faber Ltd for an extract from *Lord of the Flies* by William Golding, an extract from *Murder in the Cathedral*, 'The Hippopotamus' and an extract from 'The Waste Land' from *Collected Poems, 1909–1962* by T. S. Eliot, 'Epitaph on a Tyrant' from *Collected Shorter Poems* by W. H. Auden and 'You're' from *Collected Poems* by Sylvia Plath;

Curtis Brown Group Ltd, London on behalf of The Estate of Elizabeth Bowen for extracts from 'Summer Night' from *Look at All Those Roses* (© Elizabeth Bowen 1946) and 'The Demon Lover' from *Ivy Gripped the Steps* (© Elizabeth Bowen 1941) by Elizabeth Bowen;

Extract from *How to Write a Novel* by John Braine (Methuen). Used by permission of David Higham Associates;

Penguin Books Ltd. for an extract from *How Many Miles to Babylon?* by Jennifer Johnston (Hamish Hamilton 1974, Penguin Books 1988). Copyright © Jennifer Johnston 1974;

Excerpts from *The Complete Poems: 1927–1979* by Elizabeth Bishop. Copyright © 1979, 1983 by Alice Helen Methfessel. Reprinted by permission of Farrar, Straus and Giroux, LLC.

Extracts from newspaper articles are from the *Irish Times, Irish Independent, Sunday Business Post, Daily Telegraph,* and *Guardian.*

Photos: The Kobal Collection: 250 © Sam Goldwyn/Renaissance Films/BBC; 252 © Vestron-Zenith; 254 © M & A Film Corporation; 256 © Orion; 259 © Cecchi Gori/Tiger/Canal; 262 © Paramount; 266 © Columbia; 268 © Merchant Ivory/Goldcrest; 273 © Renaissance Films/BBC/Curzon Films; 276 © Granada/Miramax; 279 © United Artists.

The publishers have made every effort to trace copyright holders, but if they have inadvertently overlooked any they will be pleased to make the necessary arrangements at the first opportunity.

Preface

In this revision book, guidelines are clearly set out that will enable you to revise for the Leaving Certificate course at Higher Level. The book gives a series of practical guidelines on how to tackle both Paper I and Paper II. There are notes on the different language genres, together with sample material and commentary, which will help you in dealing with questions on Paper I. There are also a number of samples of Paper I that follow the same form – that is, comprehension and composition – as the examination on Paper I.

The book also deals with Paper II. There are guidelines on how to prepare for the question on both the single study of a text and the comparative study of texts. The notes on all texts are specifically designed for Higher Level. There are also notes on Shakespeare plays, a compulsory question at Higher Level.

Guidelines are also given on answering questions on both prescribed and unseen poetry. The method of answering poetry questions in both the prescribed and the unseen section is clearly outlined. In addition, there are sample answers on both unseen poetry and some of the prescribed poetry on the course.

I hope the practical approach adopted throughout this book will enable you to prepare in an efficient and focused manner for all aspects of this course.

Revision Techniques

1. Make sure you are completely familiar with the syllabus and the requirements for Higher Level. Know exactly how many questions you have to answer on each paper and how much time you have for answering each one. Know what sections or questions are compulsory.
2. Prepare yourself for Paper I, which covers *comprehension* and *composition,* by reading material on topics you are interested in. Gather ideas on these topics and perhaps write them up in a notebook.
3. Study unseen passages for the comprehension section and practise writing answers to these. It can help to compare your own answers with some of the sample answers already done in this book.
4. Practise writing answers on the writing assignments in the different language genres. Make sure your expression is original and striking.
5. Identify clearly what text, whether a play or a novel, you will choose for the detailed question in Paper II, as you will need to know this more thoroughly. Practise writing essays on both the detailed study of a text and the comparative section. Give yourself the same amount of time that you will have in the examination.
6. Clearly establish which three texts you are studying for the comparative question on Paper II. Remember that you can study a film for this question. If you do choose a film, watch it several times and try to familiarise yourself with the central issues and the techniques.
7. Know your texts, whether a book or play, very well. You cannot read your texts often enough. There is no substitute for your own intimate interaction with the text. Understand what you are reading; follow what is happening. If you miss a connection in the story, you will find yourself increasingly puzzled as you read on. Ask yourself the following questions: Why are the characters behaving in this way? How is the plot constructed? Study key passages and sections in great detail. Take note of important quotations and familiarise yourself with the plot and the main features of the characters.
8. In the Shakespeare play, take note of key scenes and soliloquies. Study these in relation to the development of character and the plot.
9. You have two questions to answer on the poetry, so remember to prepare a question on one of the prescribed poets and one on how to answer an unseen poem.

Paper I

2 Examination Techniques in Paper I

1. The total number of marks for this paper is 200, or half the total for the examination. There are 100 marks for the comprehension and 100 marks for the composition assignment.
2. Four comprehension texts are given, each followed by two questions (question A and question B). You must answer *two* questions: question A on *any text* and question B on *any other text*. You cannot answer two questions on the same text.
3. In addition, you must answer one question on a composition or writing assignment.
4. The time limit for this paper is 2½ hours.
5. Spend 75 minutes on the comprehension and 75 minutes on the writing assignment.
6. Give yourself approximately 35 minutes on each comprehension question.
7. Answer the comprehension questions first, since they demand less effort at creative thinking. Both the passage and the questions are clearly laid out.

Comprehension 3

CHARACTERISTICS OF COMPREHENSION PASSAGES

In the comprehension passage, always look for the following:
- *theme* – this is the subject matter of the writing;
- *tone* – this is the relationship between the writer and the reader, *how* the writer is saying what is in the passage;
- *intention or purpose* – this is the reason why the writer wrote the passage.

All three features are related. If a writer's intention is to condemn violence, the theme will reflect that intention. A writer may wish to tell a story, so the subject matter will be presented in the form of a narrative. Another writer may wish to persuade the reader about something and will therefore use a persuasive style of writing.

TYPES OF PROSE WRITING

- Autobiographical
- Argument
- Informative
- Narrative
- Persuasive
- Descriptive

Autobiographical writing

In this kind of writing we get an insight into the mind of the writer. The use of the subjective 'I' is a feature of autobiographical writing.

Example

In May 1953 my mother went into hospital to have her third child, who was born on 23 May – a boy called Jinming. It was the missionary hospital where she had stayed when she was pregnant with me, but the missionaries had now been expelled, as had happened all over China. My mother had just been given a promotion to head of the Public Affairs Department for the city of Yibin, still working under Mrs Ting, who had risen to be party secretary for the city. At the time my grandmother was also in the hospital with severe asthma. And so was I, with a navel infection; my wet-nurse was staying with me in the hospital. We were being given good treatment, which was free, as we belonged to a family 'in the revolution'.

(Jung Chang, *Wild Swans*)

Comment
This is an example of autobiographical writing, in which the writer recounts some details about her life and events in her family during the Cultural Revolution in China.

Argument writing
In writing that is based on argument, the information is presented in a logical and organised manner. The method of the writer here is detached and factual.

Example
>Humankind is under an obligation to preserve its physical health and well-being and to avoid anything that might endanger it. It is wrong to take alcohol in volumes that affect the rightful use of reason and one's consciousness.
>
>Drug addiction, apart from being an offence against the individual human person, is also a destabilising factor in society as a whole. The relationship between rising crime and drug abuse is evident. For that reason, the state has a duty, in the interests of the common good, to make all forms of drug-taking illegal, not to speak of trafficking in them. It would abdicate responsibility if it permissively tolerated any form of so-called 'soft' drugs.

Comment
The style of writing here is based on argument. The tone is clear and factual. The argument is based on the dangers of drug abuse. The writer establishes his argument here on a fact – the need to preserve one's physical well-being. The effects of drug addiction are clearly stated in the parallel between rising crime and drug abuse.

Informative writing
The purpose of this type of writing is to inform or to convey certain facts in a clear and terse manner.

Example
>Pope John Paul has signed a decree recognising a miracle by Pope John XXIII, which will allow for his beatification. He also recognised a miracle attributed to the Dublin-born Benedictine priest Dom Columba Marmion, who died in 1923. Elected to the papacy on the death of Pope Pius XII in 1958, Pope John was already elderly. He was to become the most radical and best-loved pope of the century. The miracle is based on a vision of Pope John by Sister Caterina Capitani at Naples in 1966. Then twenty-two, she was dying of acute peritonitis. She had received the last rites when, on 25 May 1966, she said Pope John appeared and told her he had answered her prayers. Her recovery was immediate. Still alive, she is now nursing in Sicily.

Comment
This extract is taken from a newspaper report. It is a clear example of informative writing, as it gives the reader information and facts about the beginnings of the process of beatification of Pope John XXIII.

Narrative writing

In narrative writing the writer is telling a story. There is a definite arrangement of ideas or sequence of events. Narrative prose puts an emphasis on description – describing people, actions and events in detail.

Example
> One sunny frosty December morning I set out to cycle to the foot of the Knockmealdown Mountains, some eight miles north of Lismore. I took a picnic and ate it by a lively brown stream, and then thought it would be fun to climb to the top of Knockmealdown – an easy little mountain of just under 3,000 feet.
>
> I had been up several times before, with my father and Pappa and sundry guests, and was familiar with the easiest route. But somehow the climb took longer than expected, and as I approached the top the weather began to change. The air lost its crispness and the Galtees to the north-west disappeared as clouds came rolling south over the plain of Tipperary. Before I was half way down both the clouds and the dusk had overtaken me. But I was too inexperienced to be immediately afraid. For ten or fifteen minutes it all seemed a glorious adventure and I never doubted that I would soon hear the stream and feel the road beneath my feet. Not until darkness came, and the mist turned to rain, and a wind began to moan, did panic threaten. Then I stumbled into an old turf-cutting that should not have been on my route, and burst into tears.
>
> (Dervla Murphy, *Wheels Within Wheels*)

Comment
This is an example of narrative writing, which has a strong personal flavour and pays lively attention to small details. The writer recounts in a vivid and intimate manner an incident that affected her deeply. She uses an **anecdote** here, which is a feature of narrative writing – a single incident is told in the form of a story. This incident almost always contains a definite point. Through the incident where the writer got lost in the mountains we learn how unpredictable and dangerous the weather can be.

Persuasive writing

The purpose of persuasive writing is to sway the reader towards a certain viewpoint on the strength of feeling and emotion.

Example
> In the current debate on street violence, I have to say I'm amazed at the cursory mention of alcohol. The truth is that alcohol is responsible for a substantial number of violent attacks.
>
> I don't drink, and sometimes when I walk home at night through Temple Bar I wonder

whether I've stepped into some bizarre alternative Dublin. Between the fresh vomit, the streams of urine, the shouting yobs, the general air of disorder and the occasional acts of violence, the easy availability of alcohol has to be blamed.

All my friends drink, and I don't object to people drinking. But I do object to the acceptance of an atmosphere in which drink-related civil disorder is accepted as unavoidable and the Gardaí just have to contain it as best they can.

Secondly, I don't accept the age-old belief that someone who misbehaves under the influence is socially cleared of responsibility. No one is forced to drink.

So what to do? Prohibition isn't an option, politically or practically. But a tough line on public drunkenness, under-age drinking and drinking in public streets should be enforced. Heavy fines should be imposed and in particular bars that serve under-age drinkers or people obviously drunk should have their night's takings confiscated.

I'm twenty-seven years old, I'm not a reactionary, but I'm appalled at seeing the city I was born and live in deteriorate into a yobbos' paradise. Am I on my own in feeling this?

Comment

This is taken from a letter written to a daily newspaper and is an example of persuasive writing. The writer makes use of colourful analogies, such as 'some bizarre alternative Dublin' and 'a yobbos' paradise', to illustrate his points about drinking. He concludes on a rhetorical question, which is a feature of persuasive writing.

Descriptive writing

Where narrative writing tells us what people and things *do,* descriptive writing tells us what people or things *are like.* Joseph Conrad said that descriptive writing, 'by the power of the written word, makes you hear, makes you feel; before all makes you see.'

This type of writing illustrates the power of the imagination to create unusual images or to juxtapose exciting and dynamic ideas. It differs from factual or argument writing in that it links ideas through word repetition and image association rather than through logic. There is a strong emphasis on drawing descriptions of things or people.

Descriptive writing:
- gives a clear picture
- selects details with great care
- uses precise vocabulary and avoids exaggeration.

Example

As soon as the sun was down, the air was full of bats, cruising as noiselessly as cars upon asphalt; the nighthawk swept past too – the bird that sits on the road and in the eyes of which the lights of your car gleam red a moment before he flutters up vertically in front of your wheels. The little spring hares were out on the roads, moving in their own way, sitting down suddenly and jumping along to a rhythm, like miniature kangaroos. The cicadas sing an endless song in the long grass, smells run along the earth, and falling stars run over the sky, like tears over a cheek.

A few miles out, in the Maasai reserve, the zebra are now changing their pasture, the flocks wander over the grey plain like lighter stripes upon it, the buffalo are out grazing on the long slopes of the hills. My young men of the farm would come by, two or three together, walking one after the other like narrow dark shadows on the lawn.

(Karen Blixen, *Out of Africa*)

Comment
This is a splendid example of the use of detailed and vivid description. In this passage the writer sharply focuses on small details, which is a striking feature of good descriptive writing. For example, note the comparison between the cars and asphalt. The use of similes in writing can lend a richness and immediacy to description.

Note
Some comprehension passages will contain a mixture of styles. The intention of the writer will largely dictate what style they will use. A writer may decide to attack corruption in the political sphere, so, for example, they could use argument and an ironic tone. Another writer may wish to tell a story, so they could make use of anecdote to illustrate a point more effectively.

STRUCTURE AND FORM OF COMPREHENSION PASSAGES

A comprehension passage is made up of:
- paragraphs
- sentences
- words.

The **structure** is the layout of the writing, whether it is written as one continuous piece of prose, structured in paragraphs or is simply a series of sentences.

Paragraphs
A paragraph consists of one main sentence, usually called the **topic sentence**. The rest of the paragraph consists of support for that topic sentence. In a comprehension passage, the paragraphs may be clearly outlined or the passage may simply be one independent piece of writing. When you are studying paragraphs for comprehension, examine:

- the topic sentence – try to find where exactly in the paragraph it comes. Usually topic sentences come at the beginning or end of a paragraph
- the linking devices used by the writer to tie up the different ideas in each paragraph.

Sentences
A sentence may be defined as a group of words that makes complete sense. Sentences may be classified according to:

- their purpose
- their syntax
- their form.

Purpose
According to its mood or purpose, a sentence may be:
declarative – a statement or an assertion:

> John's wife died of cancer.
> Mary broke the vase.
> It's a lovely sunny day.

interrogative – asking a question:

> Have you seen him?
> Where's the cat?

imperative – giving a command:

> Please stop talking.
> Don't burn the toast.
> Close your books.

exclamatory – expressing surprise or shock:

> 'Oh, what a rogue and peasant slave am I!'
> My mother won the lottery!
> Imagine that!

Syntax
According to its syntax, a sentence may be:
simple – made up of one subject and one object:

> The typist made an error.

compound – just two simple sentences connected by a conjunction:

> The typist made an error and then she spilled the coffee.

complex – a simple statement followed by one or two qualifying clauses:

> Computers require a particular set of aptitudes, and if these aptitudes are missing, little can be done and misery is guaranteed to millions of people.

Form
According to form, a sentence may be:
periodic – with the main idea coming at the end:

> Spectacular though the parade was, it passed by largely unnoticed.
> Surprised and excited, the scientists who witnessed the event found themselves wondering, is this how life got started?

loose – the main point coming at the beginning:

> The parade was spectacular, but it passed by largely unnoticed.
> We can make impersonal places, like offices and factories, bear the imprint of our personality: pin-ups on the wall behind the workbench, trendy executive toys, gold pens, silver-mounted portraits on the executive's desk (or, equally revealing, nothing at all).

balanced – having a similarity of thought and a similarity of structure. The purpose can be to create dramatic effect. Balanced sentences can also show that a writer is drawing on different aspects of the subject matter to drive home the point:

> To be a woman writer long meant, may still mean, belonging to a literary movement apart from, but hardly subordinate to, the mainstream: an undercurrent, rapid and powerful.
>
> The true gentleman is too clear-headed to be unjust; he is as simple as he is forceful, and as brief as he is decisive.

inverted – with the subject of the sentence coming in the middle or at the end:

> Seeing a bullfight in Valencia, I understood why people can find it such a fascinating thing. Now in this dawn, how or why he did not know, his brain, without help or knowledge, had made that leap and combined with impeccable logic those two simple but momentous propositions.

antithetical – creating an **antithesis**, which could be described as similar to a balanced sentence but with the balance created by opposing ideas:

> The husband is a ruthless businessman, while his wife is a docile and humble woman.
> The farmer is a just and loyal employer, while his employees are dishonest and unfaithful.
> That girl is strong and powerful in her manner, while her brother is weak and cowardly.

The way writers construct sentences can reveal certain attitudes they may have towards the subject. A series of terse sentences can contribute to the flow of thought in a passage:

> The performance came to an end with two choruses, the second more subtle in its harmonies. The choir stood still and let their voices resonate around the small German church. There was no applause. No-one moved. The conductor did not move. There was a sort of stunned silence, but it was deliberate. It lasted one minute, perhaps more. And then there was a shuffling of papers, but no coughs or whispers. The performers remained still. No-one spoke. People began to move quietly from their seats.

Simple sentences anchor a writer's thoughts securely. However, a series of too many simple sentences can cause the writing to be jerky and monotonous. Examine the following opening on the subject of success, which is made up of a series of simple sentences:

> Swallowing, then inhaling deeply, I plunged forward. 'How could you, after all I have told you? What are you trying to do? What right have you to disfigure such a beautiful area?'
>
> Beneath my steadfast gaze he slowly transformed into a tall, cruel, bellowing devil. 'Vanessa, my dear, I've won. It's all over. Construction is going ahead. All your exaggerated stabbings and jibes didn't work. Who cares about wildlife? Today the only thing that counts is money, and, along with genius, I've a lot of that.'

The sentences' structure here makes the piece of writing incoherent and jerky. The following sentence structure would be more effective:

> As I plunged forward, I inhaled deeply. I began to cry out as I directed my gaze in his direction. 'How could you do this, after all I told you? What are you trying to do? Who gave you the right to devastate and disfigure the whole area, which is so beautiful?'
>
> As I looked at him he slowly changed and began to look like a tall and cruel devil-like

figure. With a slow, measured voice he bellowed: 'Vanessa, my dear, it's all over. I've won. The construction is going ahead, in spite of all your jibes and criticism. In this world, the only thing that counts is money, and, as well as genius, I've got lots of that. So who cares about wildlife?'

Words

It is important to clearly understand how words are used in writing. The same word can be used to persuade, to argue or to describe something. A writer can also use words to draw pictures or images of certain things.

There are different kinds of words. *Pictorial* words draw an image or picture of something. *Concrete* words give a specific idea about something, for example, a heavy man, a round table, a tall girl, a circular motion, an oval face, a hollow cheek, a gaunt child, a green, ripe apple. *Abstract* is the opposite of concrete. It means something that is not specific or tangible, for example, goodness, loyalty, whiteness, truth.

The context of words

Examine the context of certain words. Both the *context* and the *connotations* of words can affect the writer's message or purpose. The same word or set of words can be used to provoke a totally different type of reaction in the reader, depending on its context.

(1) Bombshell from Brazil explodes onto catwalk.

(2) He dropped a bombshell in the department when he announced that he was resigning.

The first sentence is a headline taken from a magazine. The second is an informal and casual use of language, taken from a personal letter.

(1) Torrid time for retailers.

(2) Retailers will have to audit their accounts before the next budget.

(3) He works as a retailer.

The first sentence is a headline from a newspaper, written in a sensational way in order to attract attention. It is an example of an emotive statement. The second is simply a factual account of how retailers will have to organise their accounts before the next budget and it could feature in a newspaper article. The third is a simple assertion or statement that can also be spoken.

(1) Pets find their patch in star-studded glory.

(2) Pets are usually familiar with their own patch in the garden.

(3) She was mending the patch when the pets wandered over to her.

The first sentence is a headline from a newspaper. The second is taken from a book on gardening and deals with the peculiar habits of pets. The third is a statement taken from a story. Thus, we can see that the context of words can affect their meaning in a sentence.

Comprehension

The connotation of words

The connotation of a word is the emotive impact it may have on a reader – the associations, whether positive or negative, it conjures up in the mind. Word connotations all suggest certain attitudes to an idea. Examine the following words and consider the various connotations that spring to mind when you read them:
- cool
- upbeat
- traditional
- soap opera
- obese
- foolish
- raw.

Word connotations can be achieved in different ways: through
- syntax
- alliteration
- assonance
- cacophony
- sibilance
- repetition.

SYNTAX
Syntax can be defined as the order of words a writer uses when constructing sentences. The syntax can play a large part in the communication of certain ideas to the reader and in controlling or manipulating the reader's responses.

ALLITERATION
This is the repetition of consonant sounds, especially the initial consonants of words. Through the alliteration of certain consonants, different moods or emotions can be conveyed:

> He feared he would go mad or fall ill, yet if he once let go, the elaborate scaffolding he had so painfully erected would fall asunder.

The repetition of the *f* sound here is an example of alliteration and serves the function of underlining the emotion of fear within this man:

> I realised I had looked my last on youth and little more,
> For they are not made whole that reach the age of Christ.

The *l* sound here emphasises the sense of loss experienced by the writer.

ASSONANCE
This is the repetition of vowel sounds, which conveys a musical or sensuous impact or a sense of harmony. Look at the following lines of poetry, all of which are examples of the use of assonance, each with a different effect or a different connotation:

> only a man harrowing clods ...
> with an old horse that stumbles and nods ...

The repetition of the *o* sound here emphasises the sense of isolation in the lines.

> Fall, gall themselves, and gash gold-vermilion.

Repetition of the *a* and *o* sounds here depicts a sense of richness.

> ... Nor does long our small
> Durance deal with that steep or deep. Here creep ...

There is assonance in the repetition of the *e* sound, which emphasises a profound sense of disorientation and confusion in the writer.

Cacophony

Cacophony, or *dissonance*, is the opposite of assonance – it consists of the repetition of 'hard' sounds, such as *k*, to suggest a harsh or grating mood:

> Blight and famine, plague and earthquake, roaring deeps and fiery sands
> Clanging fights and flaming towns and sinking ships
> and preying hands.

The connotations underlying the use of cacophony in these lines suggest destruction and devastation.

Sibilance

This is the repetition of *s* and *z* sounds and its use in writing serves the function of appealing to the senses. The following lines, from two different poems, contain some striking examples of the use of sibilance:

> starlight lit my lonesomeness
> when I set out for Lyonesse ...

> turning the silver out of dark grasses
> where the skylark had lain ...

Repetition

A writer can repeat the same word or set of words for purposes of emphasis. This type of emphatic repetition underlines different points more effectively for a writer:

> the beating down of the wise,
> and great Art beaten down.

> he knew he was on the point of breaking through – he knew it ...

> no development has provoked more religious awe, more contentious debate, more lyrical speculation ...

Word connotations can also be achieved by means of:
- irony
- simile
- metaphor.

The combined use of these different techniques can add up to what is termed the *figurative use* of language.

THE LANGUAGE OF COMPREHENSION

Style

'Style' is the ability to present a subject in a way that is best suited to achieving the writer's aim. It is important when understanding a passage to know how to 'read between the lines', to understand how language and imagery both work to create a certain tone or mood and how they all add up to a coherent style.

Note the difference between 'tone' and 'mood'. **Tone** is the relationship a writer establishes with the reader – how the writer is saying what is in the passage. **Mood** is the atmosphere of the piece of writing.

Imagery

Words can also be combined to form images or 'word pictures'. (The use of imagery will form an essential part of the 'Aesthetic Use of Language' section in Chapter 5)

When you see imagery in comprehension pieces or writing, ask yourself the following questions:
- What does it say?
- Why is it used?
- How well does it work in the passage?
- Has it 'sound effects' or certain connotations?

There are different kinds of imagery:

simple:
Easter Island is the loneliest inhabited place in the world. The nearest solid land the inhabitants can see is in the firmament, the moon and the planets.

original:
His instincts threw up their defences against the scandalous notion of being creative.

In some cathedrals you can see demonic winged creatures referring diplomatically to the majesties of political power. The cathedral can therefore be seen as an awesome engine of communication.

Copies of the molecule began to evolve and it began to perform new and unexpected chemical tricks.

vivid or clear:
The matador, gorgeous in green and gold, skipped with unbelievable nimbleness and daring in front of the bull, varying his blows with caresses on the soft nose and deft little side-kicks on the jaws.

exotic:
A hedge of hibiscus bordered the airport buildings. Sunbirds glittering with green and blue iridescence played around it, darting from one scarlet blossom to another, hanging on beating wings as they probed for nectar. I noticed a chameleon motionless except for its goggling eyes, which swivelled to follow every passing insect.

startling:
> The calves sang to my horn, the foxes on the hill barked clear and cold …

> Fury had shrieked 'No lingering! Let me be fell: force I must be brief.'

> O the mind, mind has mountains cliffs of fall
> Frightful, sheer no-man fathomed.

Images can be used for different reasons in writing:

to illustrate a point:
> He is nearly as tall as a Dublin policeman, and preaching literature, he stood on the hearthrug, his feet set close together. Lifting his arms above his head (the very movement that Raphael gives to Paul when preaching at Athens)…

to provoke atmosphere:
> The edge of a colossal jungle, so dark-green as to be almost black, fringed with white surf, ran straight, like a ruled line, far, far away along a blue sea whose glitter was blurred by a creeping mist.

to provoke an emotional impact (the following lines are from an advertisement for perfume):
> Each woman should have her own subtle fragrance – one that will suit her style and that is a true expression of her personality. Each must use it as much to denote what kind of woman she is, her emotions and her aspirations, as to enhance her outward appearance.

Remember, imagery is effective when it conveys what a writer intends in a vivid and economical way. The use of imagery can also help a writer to achieve originality of expression in writing.

CHARACTERISTICS OF WELL-WRITTEN ANSWERS IN COMPREHENSION

1. Your answers must reflect a clear understanding of the content of the passage.
2. Organise your thoughts clearly. Focus on exactly what you are asked. Avoid padding or introducing irrelevant points.
3. Have a thorough grasp of the writer's intention in writing. Be able to understand whether the writing is persuasion, argument or narration.
4. Develop the ability to follow a line of argument and to evaluate the points objectively.
5. Your answers must show a basic knowledge of the constituent elements of writing – how to structure sentences and paragraphs, how to use and understand tone and imagery.
6. Use clear, correct English and lucid argument to support your statements.
7. Answers must be:
   - clear
   - logical
   - factual
   - precise
   - simple, not ambiguous or awkward.

Common errors in comprehension answers
1. Misunderstanding the content of the passage.
2. Using incorrect facts or information in answers.
3. Misunderstanding the questions. Distinguish between such terms as:
   'How does the writer reach the conclusion …?'
   'Why does the writer claim that this is the case …?'
   'Demonstrate from your own experience …'
4. Not giving reasons for answers when asked to do so.
5. Badly structured answers, where the main point is ignored and irrelevancies are introduced and developed.
6. Badly written answers, with faulty grammar, weak expression and poor punctuation.
7. Not answering the question asked, but rambling and going off the point.

Method of tackling comprehension questions
1. Remember, you have *two* questions to answer on comprehension. These must be taken *from two different texts.*
2. Spend approximately 35 minutes on each question.
3. Read the passage through several times in order to grasp the gist or general idea of what it is about. Try to examine what the primary purpose of the passage is – is it informative, narrative or persuasive?
4. Quickly scan the layout of the passage. If the text is divided by sub-headings, many times these headings can provide you with an idea of what the passage is about and how the points are developed.
5. Sometimes it can help to write out one sentence or phrase on the main idea of the passage. This can help to focus your mind and keep to the point.
6. If the passage uses *imagery,* examine why it is used and what point is being made by it.
7. Does the writer intrude in the text and can you see why?
8. In a passage that is factual or based on argument, know how to distinguish facts from opinions. See whether there is evidence to support the points made.
9. Before beginning to write your answers, work on a rough draft – getting your points down in note form – for each question.
10. Tackle every aspect of your question. Keep control of time. Stop when your allotted time is up.
11. Use your own words as much as possible.
12. When reading back, read your answers with a purpose. Check the question and then your answer. Have you answered the question asked? Have you used examples that are relevant and useful? Is your answer clear and logical or is it repetitive and long winded?

The summary
A summary tests your ability to:
- condense material, choose the main points from a piece of writing and express them in appropriate and clear language

- organise material in a coherent and logical manner.

Method of writing a summary
1. Grasp the general gist or message of the writing.
2. Write down the main points in the form of a rough draft.
3. Rewrite the summary in the form of one main paragraph.
4. Include all dates, numbers or statistics.
5. Write your summary in the past tense.

Read the following article (from a 'healthy living' newspaper), then study the sample summary that follows.

Threat to natural health supplements

Today you can walk into any health shop and buy safe health-supporting supplements of your choice at reasonable prices – just as you have been able to do for the last twenty years or so. You can select your vitamins, your garlic or evening primrose oil or other natural remedies from the vast array that is available. You can also discuss your purchase with the sales assistant to make sure it is the right one for you.

But all this could change. In May this year the Irish Medicines Board issued a document entitled *Guide to the Definition of a Medicinal Product*. Without question, this document threatens the rights of health-conscious consumers to buy effective and safe supplements of their choice. If the proposals in this document become law, many safe and popular products could disappear from the shelves, simply because the IMB has decided to reclassify them as medicines and not food supplements. Enforcement of the proposals would require most products to have a medicinal licence, which, even if it were possible to obtain one, would cost thousands of euro and take several years of clinical trials and scientific work for each product. Of necessity, these costs would be passed on to the consumer.

The IMB claims this is an issue of safety; but reclassifying supplements would not make them safer. Products at present produced under food law have to be 100 per cent safe; medicines do not.

As you would expect, consumers are extremely unhappy with this situation and are asking why the IMB has decided to pre-empt legislation, which is expected towards the end of this year, by bringing out their own guidelines.

Sample summary

Safe health supplements of your choice can be obtained at reasonable prices from any health shop. You can select vitamins, garlic, evening primrose oil or other natural remedies that are available. This could change. In May this year the Irish Medicines Board issued a document entitled *Guide to the Definition of a Medicinal Product*. If its proposals become law, many products could be reclassified as medicines rather than food supplements. The enforcement of these proposals would require that these products have a medicinal licence. This would cost thousands of euro, which would have to be paid for by the consumer.

The IMB claims this is an issue of safety. Products now covered by food law have to be 100 per cent safe; medicines do not. Consumers are unhappy with this situation and are questioning the IMB's decision to pre-empt legislation by issuing their own guidelines.

Remember, in comprehension a good Honours pupil must be able to ask and answer the following questions:
1. What was the writer's intention in writing this passage?
2. Who is the intended audience for this passage? Are the techniques used suitable for this audience? Explain why or why not.
3. Is the writing structured clearly in paragraphs, and if so, does each paragraph fit into the scheme of the writing as a whole?
4. Is the writer appealing to our emotions or to our intellect? Why is this so?
5. Does the nature of the subject justify the use of the emotions employed? Remember that emotion must be restrained in writing if it is to achieve the desired effect.
6. If the writing is based on argument, do you find the arguments convincing? If so, why?
7. Is the style uniform or does it vary? If so, why is this? Does the style suit the subject or is it too dull or too ornate?
8. What do the style and the subject matter tell us about the writer?
9. Look at the writer's choice of words to see whether they are relevant, excessive, appropriate, precise, etc.

COMPREHENSION VOCABULARY

You should know the difference between the following words:

analyse: 'take apart' an idea or a statement in order to consider all its aspects
compare: show the similarities or the differences between things ('compare with': make a comparison; 'compare to': suggest a similarity)
contrast: show the differences between things
criticise: point out mistakes and weaknesses in a balanced way
define: give the precise meaning of a concept
discuss: explain a passage and give details, with examples
disprove: produce arguments that show something to be false
evaluate: discuss, but go on to judge for and against
explain: offer a detailed and exact explanation of an idea or principle
illustrate: give examples that demonstrate and prove a point
justify: give the reasons for a position
prove: give answers that demonstrate the logical position
state: express the points briefly and clearly
summarise/outline: give only the main points – not details
trace: give a description in logical or chronological order of the stages of a process

Study the meaning of the following literary terms
alliteration: repetition of the same initial consonant:
   the beating of the baton
   leafy with love

allusion: a reference; allusions can be:
—scientific:
  Newton's laws in physics
—literary:
  Heaney's poetry is rich in symbolism
—historical:
  the Wild Geese fled

ambiguity: the use of an expression or word that has a number of possible meanings in such a way that it is difficult to tell which meaning is intended:

  love is blind

analogy: a comparison that points out a relationship or similarity between two things
aphorism: a short, powerful maxim: a concise statement of truth:

  brevity is the soul of wit
  borrowing dulls the edge of husbandry

archaism: a term that is obsolete or no longer in use:

  perchance
  methinks
  thou

assonance: the rhyming of vowel sounds within words:

  thought her too proud
  watery hazes of the hazel

atmosphere: the feelings or emotions evoked by nature or a piece of music, art, etc.
balance: placing two parts of a sentence or words within a sentence in such a way as to be in opposition to one another:

  People who are powerful renounce coercive power but not the power that rests on persuasion.
  Fools step in where angels fear to tread.

bias: a prejudice: favouring one side in an argument
cadence: the rhythmical rising and falling of language in writing or speech
caricature: the portrayal of a person in which certain characteristics are exaggerated so that the person appears ridiculous
cliché: a hackneyed expression so overused as to have lost its impact:

  slowly but surely
  up for grabs

climax: the culminating moment in a play, poem or piece of prose
colloquial: belonging to common or ordinary speech: informal language
connotations: reverberations or what is implied by a word
diction: the writer's choice of words
digression: turning aside from the main subject
ellipsis: the omission of words, usually indicated by *omission points* (…)
emotive: tending to arouse emotion or feelings
empathy: the complete association of the self with another being
epigram: a short sentence expressing a witty thought or shrewd comment

euphemism: a mild expression in place of a harsh one
figurative language: language that contains many figures of speech, such as metaphors or similes
hyperbole: exaggeration to achieve a certain effect
idiom: an expression peculiar to a certain language
image: a word picture
implication: something that is hinted at or suggested rather than stated explicitly
inference: a judgment or conclusion derived from a statement
invective: wordy abuse or denunciation
irony: an incongruous contrast between the words used and their implication
lucid: vivid or clear
lyrical: literally, like a song; figuratively, full of praise:

   he waxed lyrical about her talents

maxim: an adage: an established principle or truth expressed in a concise form:

   present fears are less than horrible imaginings
   brevity is the soul of wit

metaphor: a comparison between two things without using 'like' or 'as'
mood: the feeling or atmosphere created by a piece of writing
moral: concerned with the good or bad of human behaviour
oratorical: eloquent
paradox: a statement that is apparently contradictory but might be true in a way
parenthesis: an aside
pathos: pity, sadness or tenderness created by a writer
personification: investing inanimate things with human qualities
platitude: a trite or commonplace remark
polemics: the art of controversial discussion
precis: a summary
pun: a play on words that are similar in sound but different in meaning
quip: a sharp retort
rhetoric: persuasive and impressive speech or writing
sarcasm: bitter or wounding remarks made at the expense of another person
satire: exposing folly by means of ridicule
simile: the comparison of two things, using the words 'like' or 'as':

   as plain and as unadorned as the unclouded sky – and about as beautiful

slang: extremely informal expressions that are fashionable for a time but usually go stale very quickly
syntax: the grammatical arrangement of words in the form of sentences
tone: the voice of the writer or speaker
verbosity: wordiness: using more words than necessary, especially pompous ones:

   we would labour with all the wit of us, all the strength of us, to reach our goal [we would try with all our strength and intelligence to reach our goal]
   on a six-monthly basis [every six months]

Common vocabulary errors
Be aware of the difference in meaning between the following sets of words.

advance: progress, going forward:
> the advance of medicine, the advance of old age, the advance of time

advancement: promotion or helping forward:
> The Government is working for the advancement of education

affect (a verb): This word has different meanings:
(*a*) to produce an effect on:
> The climate affected his health

(*b*) to move or influence:
> The news affected relations with Japan
> The film affected me deeply

(*c*) to pretend something, to pretend to feel:
> He affected shock at the news

effect (a noun): the result or consequence of an action:
> The effects of the nuclear fall-out were disastrous

When used as a verb it means to cause or bring about:
> The prisoners tried to effect an escape

agree with: to regard something with approval:
> I agree with the minister's new proposal

agree to: to give consent:
> They were forced to agree to the plans for the new building, though they did not like them

allusion: an indirect reference:
> She drew on several literary allusions in her lecture

illusion: a false image:
> He has illusions of greatness

delusion: a false belief with no basis in fact:
> He suffers from delusions ever since the accident
> She is under the delusion that she can write well

anecdote: a short story
antidote: a medicine used to counteract the effects of a poison or disease

approve: to give consent to:
> The committee has approved the budget

approve of: to think well of, to regard with favour:
> He did not approve of the plan to build an extension to the house

artful: cunning or deceitful:
> He is an artful planner when it comes to getting more money

artless: natural, innocent:
> She is a simple, artless girl

assent/consent: both words mean 'agree to' and both take the preposition 'to'. Assent is immediate agreement; consent is agreement after some consideration.

cancel: to put off altogether
postpone: to put off until later

censor: to examine books, films or plays with the intention of suppressing anything offensive.
censure: to criticise strongly:
> The teacher censured the pupil for cheating in the examination

compare to: to state a resemblance between two things:
> Shakespeare compared the world to a stage and men and women to players

compare with: to place side by side and note the resemblances, but mainly the differences:
> Most working people are better off compared with how they were in the fifties

credible: believable:
> a credible story

creditable: deserving of merit:
> a creditable achievement

credulous: ready to believe anything

defective: faulty:
> The computer is defective

deficient: lacking in something:
> You're deficient in vitamin C

definite: certain:
> a definite offer

definitive: final, complete:
> a definitive explanation

disinterested: detached, not emotionally involved, objective
uninterested: not interested, not paying attention:
> A judge should be disinterested in a case, but not uninterested

instantaneous: immediate, over in an instant:
>an instantaneous reaction
>death was instantaneous

simultaneous: happening at the same time:
>simultaneous translation

its (a possessive adjective):
>The cat is licking its paw
>The world is using up its resources

it's: a contraction of 'it is' (a pronoun and a verb):
>It's a fine day

lose (a verb):
>I lose my keys frequently
>I've lost my confidence in the Government

loose (an adjective):
>The door handle is loose

stationery (a noun):
>The stationery shop is on the corner

stationary (an adjective): at a standstill:
>The car is stationary

Exercises on Style

Examine the following sentences, then rewrite them correctly. (You can compare your answers with those on pages 304–305.)

1. Shorten and increase the vigour of the following sentences:
   (a) Looking at the house from the outside I would imagine there to be about twenty rooms in the house.
   (b) The writer uses short to the point sentences with humour and sarcasm to keep the reader interested in the passage.
   (c) Boyle full of self delusion sees himself as the man of the house.
   (d) Many of these sort of teenagers result from homes where parents are unable to control them properly or the mother is at work and has no time for her children.
   (e) I would be delighted if you could please write back to me and tell me if and when you are available to do it for me.
   (f) What he means by this is that wherever there is a place it is made a place by people being there.
2. Criticise the following sentences under the headings repetition, punctuation and use of clichés:

(a) When he states his points of arguments he doesn't condemn himself to one side he tries to incorporate the other side too.
(b) You could find it in a magazine which rich people buy, you wouldn't find it in a newspaper because there are too many pictures.
(c) The house is enormous and is not the usual type of house, it appears to be an old house that has been restored.
(d) The environment where a person lives can tell you a lot about that person, if for instance you were in an untidy house you would presume that the owner was a laid back easy going character.
(e) The image I get from Oprah on her programme tells me what type of person she is and her way of life, and I think her home would be the best way to tell me about her.
(f) This would indicate to me that this is a family which leads a classy lifestyle by the mirror and the picture of the woman with the pearls.

3. Rewrite the following sentences by eliminating the repetition and improving the grammar:
   (a) The play is filled with jealousy and betrayal one sign of this is Iago.
   (b) In university students consistently analyse their actions with great scrutiny feverishly fearing that they may unwaveringly upset a fellow peer or teacher.
   (c) I am writing this letter to you to let you know what type of images and photographs I want included in my photo gallery.
   (d) The surplus between cost and selling price arose.
   (e) Trade fairs are a commercial feature today many being in new exporting markets.
   (f) I believe the writer puts across his argument very well and he also perceives human tendencies and exposes them in his argument very well.

4. Rewrite the following sentences and eliminate ambiguity:
   (a) I find myself grappling to maintain my popular personage.
   (b) The application of time and motion study to this section will of course result in appreciable improvement from the production standpoint.
   (c) Regrettably I'm stuck steadfast in this tedious unwelcoming claustrophobic condition where no one knows the despair filled plight I must participate in every day and the lonesome state I am in.
   (d) Re your order for Boxhead golf clubs of 15 ult., we beg to advise that these are out of stock.
   (e) During the winter the 15:20 train (which during the summer runs on weekdays but not on Sundays) will not run on Sundays.
   (f) To these people they soldier on, perhaps living on very little for many years struggling in their quest for success.

4 Composition

GENERAL NOTES ON WRITING

How to write effectively

Good, effective writing is a craft that can be acquired with hard work and a knowledge of the basics. Successful writing involves taking into account a number of different things. It means:
- knowing how to construct sentences so that they form effective and clear paragraphs
- constructing paragraphs and linking them together to achieve a coherent unity and structure
- selecting the appropriate style for your reader
- mastering the conventions of spelling and punctuation
- polishing and revising what you have written.

Every form of written communication must take into account the following elements:
- a writer
- an audience or 'receiver'
- the purpose of the communication.

Before you start writing, clearly establish:
- what the purpose of your communication is
- what your subject matter is
- the type of reader and what expectations they have.

Effective writing means that what you have written is both relevant and appropriate to the situation. For effective writing, therefore, bear in mind the following elements:
- purpose
- topic or subject

- context
- audience
- language or techniques.

Genres of writing

The prose composition should be an attempt to present a reasonable and logical interpretation of the topic you choose. The Leaving Certificate course offers you the opportunity to write in a variety of genres, including:
- the language of narration
- the language of argument
- the language of information
- the language of persuasion
- the aesthetic use of language.

As we have already seen in the section on comprehension, none of these methods are completely clear cut. In other words, a piece of informative writing will involve some amount of persuasive techniques, while writing an argument means that you must communicate information in a certain way.

The art of writing a composition can be mastered with time and effort. It is essential in writing a composition that you take into account certain things, such as pre-composition writing and the different features of the language genres, together with some basic knowledge of how sentences work to form paragraphs and how paragraphs are constructed to form a full composition.

Your composition must be your own individual response to the subject. It is important, therefore, not to regurgitate material or to learn compositions off by heart. Nor is it advisable to write a composition simply 'off the top of your head', without any preparation. It can be useful to use fifth year and perhaps some holiday time to read and prepare material on different styles of compositions. Remember, the best compositions are written on topics that you enjoy, therefore, learn to identify your own style and work at cultivating various interests.

PROBLEMS AND PITFALLS

Content

One of the main problems is in knowing what exactly to write. The fact of having to write on an unseen topic at Higher Level can be confusing and unsettling for many people. The content in compositions must reflect a certain maturity of approach and a balance of judgment, particularly when writing on factual topics. Avoid digression or introducing irrelevant information. Avoid repetition of ideas.

The language genres

The different language genres or styles for the English course have certain distinctive features. It is important to be aware of these aspects and to know how to use them.

Writer's block and exam paralysis
Overcoming exam paralysis and starting to put pen to paper is another problem.

Lack of unity and structure
There is also the difficulty of organising ideas, of knowing exactly how to construct a paragraph and how to select relevant information and discard useless ideas. Sometimes pupils have problems in writing a suitable opening paragraph.

Poor timing
Time and time management can be a further problem.

Faulty style
Faulty style can be shown in many different ways, such as excessive repetition, poor spelling and bad grammar.

Misinterpreting the question or the title
This can occur from a careless reading of the titles.

Solving these problems
1. Gather ideas from newspapers or magazines that deal with current affairs and keep a notebook in which you can jot down ideas. Identify your style of writing and what genres appeal to you. The advice from your teacher can be invaluable here. For the most part you write best on subjects that you enjoy or feel strongly about.
2. Study the guidelines in this section on how to write in the different language genres (Chapter 5). Know exactly what is required for each genre. Also, study the sample material provided for each genre, particularly the commentary after each one.
3. The main thing in overcoming exam paralysis is to put pen to paper and simply write until your thoughts become coherent.
4. Some of the pre-writing strategies, such as 'brainstorming' and writing a rough outline, can help you to structure your ideas and organise your thoughts more clearly. The section on paragraphing, especially on introductory paragraphs, offers some guidelines and sample material to help you construct opening paragraphs (see pages 31–39).
5. Set deadlines for yourself when writing throughout the year. Remember, you have approximately 75 minutes in the exam to write the composition.
6. Pay attention to such details as spelling, handwriting and grammar. Correct all spelling errors and check that every word you use is the right one. Read your work aloud if possible – this can alert you to all repetition, not only of words but also of ideas. Study the section on style (page 13) and learn how to eliminate common errors in both grammar and spelling.
7. Read the questions and titles slowly and take account of every word and the possibilities or connotations of each word.

PREPARATION

Pre-writing activities

The success of a finished product depends to a great extent on the preparation that has gone into making it what it is. This also applies to a piece of writing. Some of the more important pre-writing activities include:
- brainstorming
- clustering
- outlines
- free writing.

Brainstorming

This is the process of throwing your imagination into high gear and trying to trigger as many ideas as possible on the topic. It can be useful to use such techniques as 'trigger questions' (why? how? where? what? when?) to generate ideas on the topic.

Look at the following samples of how you can brainstorm a topic.

Topic 1: The modern magazine
What exactly is a magazine?
What qualifies it as modern?
What is the difference between a modern magazine and an old-fashioned one?
Who decides that a particular magazine is modern or not?

Topic 2: The place of colour in life
What exactly is colour?
Why are there different kinds of colours?
What place has colour in life?
How does colour affect us?

Clustering

Draw together all the points you have generated from your brainstorming. Begin by 'clustering' your ideas or assembling them into groups. For example, look at the brainstorming above on the topic 'the modern magazine'. Answer some of the questions, then cluster these answers.

For example, you can discuss the different types of magazines today. You may go on to discuss whatever is modern or popular – clothes, beauty tips, love, favourite types of food or holidays. You could also contrast today's publications and trends with those of the past. When you group these ideas together you will have the basis for an outline.

Outlines

Outlines form another part of pre-writing activities. The use of outlines can be very helpful when you are planning a writing activity, particularly a composition. Outlines are the result of brainstorming and drawing up clusters of ideas before you set about the process of writing. Outlines have the following advantages:

- They organise your thoughts.
- They clarify exactly where you are going in the composition.
- They help to provide a direction for a flow of ideas in the composition.
- They help to overcome exam paralysis. Staring at a blank page can be a daunting experience and the rough outline can be a life-saver here.
- They help you to organise and structure paragraphs.

Rough outlines help you to organise your thoughts; they show what needs to be emphasised and what needs to be eliminated, where repetition occurs, etc. Many common errors can be eliminated through the outline, such as:
- gaps in the logical development of ideas
- excessive repetition
- omission of central ideas and information on the subject
- going off the point
- insufficient evidence and examples.

The following is an example of brainstorming a topic, then clustering the ideas together and finally drawing up an outline. Examine the method closely and try to follow it in your writing assignments.

Topic
Compose a persuasive composition that seeks to establish the need for a greater awareness of sex stereotyping.

Sample brainstorm
Use trigger questions on the topic:
- What is sex stereotyping?
- How is this created?
- Where is this situation most in evidence?
- What can be done to remedy it?

Sample clustering
Answer the questions from your brainstorming session, then cluster or gather together these answers; for example:

> *The problem consists of stereotyping people because of their sex.*
> *Sex stereotyping can be seen in certain types of advertisements – the helpless woman, the resourceful man.*
> *Some television serials stereotype male and female characters – the slim, tall women, the strong men in fast cars.*
> *There needs to be a more balanced presentation of male and female roles in the media.*

Sample outline
Establish greater awareness of stereotyping in society.

Opening paragraph
The images of Mother cooking a meal, Father watching television on Saturday evening. Father objecting to slogan in advertisement on television – 'So simple even he can do it'.

Paragraph 2
Images of chaos when Father runs the house. Order and harmony with the presence of Mother. The recognition of this type of stereotyping in advertising.

Paragraph 3
Discuss how some areas of professional life limit and isolate people. 'Female jobs': secretaries, cleaners, nurses. 'Male jobs': technicians, drivers.

Paragraph 4
The media constantly consolidate these images. For example, in *The Simpsons*, the intelligent and resourceful mother and daughter nevertheless do the housework.

Paragraph 5
The effects of this on society. Friction between men and women as pressures to conform intensify. The typical image that women mechanics or bus drivers have to be resilient and tough to survive.

Concluding paragraph
The need to tackle this issue: men and women to deal with their limitations and transcend the pressures coming from the media. Television programmes need to broaden people's outlook on this issue.

Study this composition (which is given in full on pages 84–5) and read the commentary.

Free writing
Free writing is a helpful method of warming up before you begin the process of writing in a formal and coherent manner. The main idea underlying this activity is to put pen to paper and to get going on the writing process immediately. Simply write about anything you choose and in whatever way you like, not caring about punctuation, spelling or structure. Write without stopping. Don't stop to plan, organise or edit. It can help to concentrate on a topic and to set yourself a time limit. The main idea is to generate as many words as possible on paper.

PLANNING

1. Be decisive with regard to selecting what topic or question you are going to write about.

2. Rephrase the title as a question (if it is not already in the form of a question); this will help to generate ideas on the subject.
3. Brainstorm the topic by using trigger questions such as who? why? how?
4. Cluster ideas that are related. Be clear about what direction your essay is taking. Don't introduce irrelevant material or go off the point.
5. Select material for paragraphs. Fully write out the topic sentence of each paragraph.
6. Your composition must have a general unity of impression. This will be shown in a clear, conclusive and satisfactory ending and in a logical development of thought between the paragraphs.

Ten basic hints on writing a composition

1. Write every day. Write a paragraph on any topic in order to improve your expression and your flow of thought.
2. Cultivate your own ideas on current events. You can do this by having a notebook in which to collect ideas throughout the year.
3. Understand the topic fully, otherwise don't write on it.
4. Always engage in some of the pre-writing activities – brainstorming, clustering, free writing and drawing up outlines – before writing seriously on the topic.
5. Avoid errors made in previous writing work by learning spellings and correcting mistakes in grammar.
6. Identify your strengths and weaknesses in writing. Work at eliminating the weaknesses and improving the strong points.
7. Write simply. Choose a simple word instead of a more obscure expression. Avoid using clichés: 'few and far between', 'in the heel of the hunt', 'to tell you the truth'.
8. Work at writing interesting and arresting openings.
9. Draw up your own list of quotations and clever phrases and use them in written work.
10. Don't make general or global statements without supporting them with clear, specific examples and evidence.

Ten do's

1. Write a paragraph every day on any topic. Leave it to 'cool', then come back later and correct it.
2. Always brainstorm your title and always write rough drafts.
3. Organise your paragraphs, putting the most important ideas first.
4. Write interesting and exciting opening paragraphs.
5. Make your composition a reasonable length – three to four pages of standard paper is usually sufficient.
6. Make sure the ideas you use are relevant. Use your own ideas.
7. Make your conclusion clear, fairly substantial and non-repetitive.
8. Vary the length and structure of your sentences.
9. Link your literature course to your composition; weave in quotations or ideas naturally and fluidly.
10. Read your composition aloud in order to hear your mistakes.

Ten don'ts
1. Don't go off the point – stick to the topic.
2. Don't use direct speech unless it is necessary.
3. Don't use two different ideas in one paragraph.
4. Avoid self-conscious expressions: 'I hope to prove …' or 'I feel that I have shown …'.
5. Avoid the use of clichés and repetitive phrases.
6. Don't use quotation marks unless you are quoting.
7. Avoid the use of a definition in your opening paragraph.
8. Don't conclude your composition in mid-air.
9. Don't conclude on one sentence.
10. Don't reproduce compositions that have been learned off by heart.

THE PARAGRAPH

Every piece of prose composition is based on knowing how to build sentences to form an effective paragraph. A paragraph is like a miniature composition – it should have a clear beginning, a middle and a conclusion.

Each paragraph deals with one section of your subject. Each paragraph has one main idea or topic sentence, together with support or examples. The paragraph must have unity – all ideas, examples, statistics or illustrations must be related to the main idea.

Paragraphs can be connected by linking or transitional devices, such as 'nevertheless', 'furthermore', 'however', 'if', 'or', 'so'. Paragraphs can be of any length; however, avoid extremes, that is, writing a paragraph that is either very long or very short. Generally speaking, there should be a variety in the construction of paragraphs within the composition.

Features of paragraphs
- clarity
- unity
- emphasis
- coherence
- transitional or linking devices between paragraphs.

Clarity
Good writing aims at communicating effectively to your readers, not merely impressing them. The main idea must be clear to your reader. Generally speaking, the topic sentence usually comes either at the beginning or end of a paragraph.

The following paragraph is an example of clear writing.

> When the Black and Tan lorry left the strand road to swing instead towards the centre of the town, the Dummy was lounging at the corner house. All evening he had stood there in the mild warmth of the October sunlight, and though he was startled he did not move.

But when the lorry passed close to him, his eyes narrowed and his head inclined slightly towards the wide strand on his left. He counted the turns. The engine slowed, revved, dropped again. It was going towards Freddie's house. By the time it stopped completely he was hammering loudly at one of the small cottages which faced the strand.

(James Plunkett, *The Web*)

COMMENT
The main or topic sentence is clearly set out in the opening sentence of this dramatic piece of writing. The remaining sentences demonstrate the reaction of the character to the arrival of the Black and Tan lorry in the town.

Unity
Unity occurs in a paragraph when the main idea is clearly stated and all examples or supporting material are related to that main idea.

So great and deep a cave, of course, had to be dark. But it was even darker than François had expected when he crawled through the narrow entrance. Then he could tell from the feel of the sand underneath his hands that he was inside it in depth. He looked carefully all round him but could see nothing to indicate the presence of Xhabbo, Nuin-Tara, and Nonnie. Were it not for Hintza, who, as always, unless ordered away, was close to him, he could easily have thought himself to be alone. The darkness indeed was so dense that it was almost tangible, and as he stood up, silently and slowly, his left hand brushed the air in front of his face as if to clear the black matter from his eyes. It was a most unpleasant feeling, as if this profound darkness around him had found an ally within, inflicted on them all by the tragic events of the day. The whole was not just a sensation conveyed by the senses but a powerful emotion arguing with the voice of despair that the last light was about to be extracted from life on earth.

(Laurens van der Post, *A Far-Off Place*)

COMMENT
The theme or main point of this paragraph is the extreme state of darkness within the cave. Every sentence relates to the opening sentence here. The writer draws some vivid images of the effects internally and externally on the characters.

Emphasis
Emphasis comes from the position of the key sentence within the paragraph. This sentence can occur anywhere in the paragraph.

The following two paragraphs show the effect of placing the topic sentence in a distinctive position within the paragraph.

Colour tends to be a subconscious element in films. The use of colour in films is strongly emotional in its appeal, expressive and atmospheric rather than conspicuous or intellectual. Psychologists have discovered that most people actively attempt to interpret the lines of a composition, but they tend to accept colour passively, permitting it to suggest moods rather than objects. Lines are associated with nouns, colour with adjectives. Line is sometimes thought to be masculine; colour feminine. Both lines and colour suggest meanings, then, but in somewhat different ways.

COMMENT

The opening sentence here is the topic or main sentence. Every other sentence is developed from this main sentence and illustrates an example of how colour is accepted as a subconscious element of films.

Coherence

Coherence means the logical flow of thought between ideas. All the sentences in a paragraph must relate to the topic sentence and to one another. There must be a link between one sentence and another in such a way that the reader will clearly see a logical progress and development in thought within the paragraph.

There are different ways of achieving coherence within a paragraph. A writer can use linking or transitional words, such as 'moreover', 'but', 'furthermore'. The writer may also use the repetition of the same word, phrase or sentence to link the ideas within the paragraph. The following paragraph is an example of the smooth and logical flow of thought from one idea to another.

> Michael Gill and his wife came last. Gill had begun to reap with the slow methodic movements of a machine driven at low pressure. He continued at exactly the same pace, never changing, never looking up to see where his opponents were. His long lean hands moved noiselessly, and only the sharp crunching rush of the teeth of his reaping-hook through the yellow stalks of the rye could be heard. His long drooping eyelashes were always directed towards the point where his hook was cutting. He never looked behind to see had he enough for a sheaf before beginning another. All his movements were calculated beforehand, calm, monotonous, deadly accurate. Even his breathing was light, and came through his nose like one who sleeps healthily. His wife moved behind him in the same manner, tying each sheaf daintily, without exertion.
>
> (Liam O'Flaherty, *The Reaping Race*)

COMMENT

This is an example of a coherent and fluid stream of thought between one idea and another. The writer cleverly registers each of Gill's movements as he carries out the task of reaping the sheaves of rye. Each sentence is linked to the preceding one, and each flows effortlessly and fluidly along to give a striking image of two people caught up in a reaping competition.

Remember, in order to achieve coherence within a paragraph:
1. Clearly establish your topic sentence.
2. Do not introduce two topic sentences or two different ideas in one paragraph.
3. Make sure that every point made in the paragraph has some relation to this topic idea.

4. Every sentence must develop or advance the preceding ideas or build up to a climax if the topic sentence comes at the conclusion of the paragraph.
5. Do not digress or introduce irrelevant statements into the paragraph.
6. Use linking devices to help provide a smooth and logical continuity within the paragraph.

Linking devices

The use of transitional words or phrases not only serves the function of linking ideas within the same paragraph, but can also serve as a link between the different paragraphs. Linking devices can elaborate and develop a writer's argument.

Look at the following examples of how linking devices can be used in different ways.

To show contrast between ideas:
- But,
- Nevertheless,
- Still,
- Although,
- Conversely,
- Yet,
- On the contrary,

To emphasise a point:
- For example,
- For instance,
- In fact,
- Indeed,

To show cause and effect or the consequences of something:
- Therefore,
- Thus,
- As a result,
- Accordingly,

To show relations of time and sequence:
- Then,
- Later,
- Afterwards,
- Next,
- Meanwhile,
- Soon,

To sum up or conclude:
- In conclusion,
- Finally,
- To sum up,

Examine the following two extracts, which are on different subjects and have clear linking or transitional devices, both within and between them. Then carefully study the commentary.

Passage 1

Dare to be dangerous by embracing the hottest colour of the season – red – in shades veering from poppy to plum. On the catwalk, red mixed boldly with tamer neutral tones to create a sophisticated look. Even Prada, the most minimalist of designers, included a bold red knee-length coat in the autumn-winter collection. For those without dominatrix tendencies there was a more subtle offering from Valentino, who showed a beautifully delicate yet stunning bodice-style dress that fell just above the ankle.

If you're wary of red, then embrace it with caution. This season leather is one of fashion's most basic allies because it never goes out of vogue. If leather does not appeal to you because you think it requires too much attitude to wear it, then think again.

The main thing to keep in mind is contrast. Match it with cool jerseys or delicately soft wools for maximum appeal. For most of us, the only thing standing in our way of going hell for leather is cost. If you want to get a leather effect without getting into ferocious debt, then the only way to do it is with PVC.

COMMENT

This extract is from a newspaper account of the latest colours and style in clothes. It is written for a general audience and, obviously, for women. Note how the linking word 'if' is used to offer an alternative to the colours and styles that are mentioned. Also, such terms as 'for those' and 'for most of us' are clearly persuasive and designed to win the reader around to accepting the idea that is being expressed.

Passage 2

Watching Irish politics over the last fifteen years has been like practising deep-space astronomy. It used to be that astronomers watched the skies and noted what they could see. Now, trying to work out what is going on in the wider universe, they pay as much attention to what they cannot see. By observing the motions of heavenly bodies they guess at the forces that must be operating on them. From the way known objects behave, they can be pretty sure that bodies they cannot yet see are affecting them. Eventually, as they look harder, they get clear images of where those bodies are buried.

So it has been with political life. It's been obvious to anybody looking at it with half an eye that invisible forces have influenced its movements. Decisions have been made, actions taken that are simply inexplicable unless we assume the presence of some unseen force, some hidden pull.

We have to conjecture that this force is corruption. But, until the McCracken Tribunal, we couldn't see it with the naked eye, name or place it.

Even now we haven't got the clear, sharp images of our political universe that would allow us to understand exactly how it has worked. However, we still have to work on the assumption that there are many black holes, uncharted but discernible by their effects.

COMMENT
In this article several clear transitional devices are used to signal a relation between the different ideas. The writer proceeds to develop the argument by using certain linking terms, such as 'it used to be', 'by observing' and 'now it is'. The use of certain words and phrases, such as 'eventually' and 'so it has', shows the reader what the results of such findings have been. The writer draws a contrast between the ideas by using the linking words 'but' and 'however' and the phrase 'even now we haven't got'.

The introductory paragraph

The introductory and the concluding paragraphs are the two most important paragraphs in your composition. The introductory paragraph has two main functions:
- to capture your reader's attention
- to introduce your material and demonstrate your stance or approach to the subject.

The opening paragraph of your composition must be interesting and arresting for your reader. Avoid openings that are predictable and dull, for example, definition-style openings:

Fashion may be defined as …
This technological age may be seen as …
'This great stage of fools' is a saying that is true because it is all round us …

Make sure your opening paragraph is original or takes an original slant on the topic. It can help to use an anecdote, a quotation or a surprising statistic. Look at the following paragraph:

The new youth
If the whole point of each fresh generation is to moult, revolt and supplant its parents, to crash through the creaky barriers of the establishment – quite simply, to inherit the earth – then it must be disconcerting to be young right now. The old battles are over. And the new ones, whatever they might be, have not yet taken shape – aside from the sense of helplessness that the very earth the young are inheriting is increasingly damaged. There is no world war; there is no cold one either. For many people in their twenties that good fortune is offset by a yawning lack of common purpose: even the horrors of the Balkan wars did not generate the solidarity of common conflicts. And so the battle cry of the young, 'Do it yourself, for yourself', sounds suspiciously like a Nike ad.

COMMENT
This paragraph takes an interesting and original angle on the subject. A variety of sentence structures and vocabulary is used and the images used are relevant and punchy.

Now study the following paragraphs (taken from pupils' actual work) and examine the commentary following each one.

Hairstyles

I glance at the mirror illuminated by tiny white lights which make you look frighteningly pale and pudgy and just as quickly averted my eyes. This mirror does absolutely nothing for one's appearance, I thought grimly. My hair dripping wet was stuck to my face and there was a big white patch on my forehead where my make-up used to be until some over-eager employer decided to herself that I didn't need make-up on that part of my anatomy. This is too humiliating. I decide that I'll do it myself in future. The future always turns into the next time, though. Vanity and pressure from my friends prevail. It's unfashionably long, look at your split ends, and don't you know that rubber bands break your hair? were constantly being hurled at me, so after one particularly spirit-crushing evening of abuse I made an appointment at the hairdresser's. The 'Guillotine'. How appropriate, I think, as I make the phone call with a certain amount of dread.

COMMENT

This is an example of a weak opening. No real statement is made and no topic sentence is established. The sentence structure is too long and confusing. The writer here seems to be unpacking the contents of her mind onto paper in a disorderly and confusing manner. There is no clear topic sentence and there is poor organisation of thought within the paragraph.

REWRITTEN VERSION

I glanced at the mirror, illuminated by tiny white lights, which make one look frightfully pale and pudgy. I quickly averted my eyes. I began to think grimly: This mirror does absolutely nothing for one's appearance. I stood before the mirror. My hair, which was dripping wet, stuck to my face. There was a big patch on my forehead where my make-up had smudged. I felt humiliated and decided to do it myself next time. But personal vanity, combined with pressure from my friends, prevailed over everything. Comments such as 'It's unfashionably long,' 'Look at your split ends' and 'Don't you know that rubber bands break your hair?' had been hurled at me repeatedly. So, after one of these sessions of abuse from my friends, I made an appointment with a hairdresser called the 'Guillotine'. How appropriate, I thought as I made the phone call, not without a certain amount of dread.

The advertising jungle

The world in which we live today seems intent on bombarding us with images of ultra-shining cars that are so clean you can see yourself in them.

Image after image jumps off our television screens out of our radios in through our car windscreen, off roadside hoardings, in a desperate attempt to force us into buying products we don't need and if we really thought about it don't even want. Tempting us to part with our hard earned money so that we can build up more and more material goods which will in turn make us all much better people, because don't forget the more we have and the more we own the better we are, forget about the man down the road who has no money for food.

COMMENT
There is no clear direction in this paragraph. The punctuation is weak and the paragraph has no clear topic sentence. The writer uses excessive repetition. The words 'advertising' and 'jungle' are not even mentioned.

REWRITTEN VERSION

> Today's world of advertising seems to bombard us from all angles with numerous images, from those of ultra-shiny cars to the latest trends in clothes or that super-modern gadget for your kitchen. Images assault us from everywhere, be it the television screen, the radio or on hoardings. All are united in the fact that they represent an attempt to manipulate us into buying products we do not need or even want. These images are designed to tempt us to part with our hard-earned money in order to accumulate more material goods. Furthermore, we are enticed into buying more, under the illusion that the more we have the happier and more fulfilled we will be. Of course these advertisements do little for the man down the road who has not even got the money for food.

The concluding paragraph

Your concluding paragraph is your final statement on the topic of your composition. It is the last impression left on your reader and therefore it is vitally important.

A good conclusion has two purposes:
- to round off the main points or ideas in your composition satisfactorily
- to provide a general unity of impression.

Avoid conclusions that repeat the main ideas of your composition in the same words. On the other hand, you should avoid going to the other extreme by introducing a different approach or new ideas in your conclusion, which will only serve to frustrate your reader. One happy medium between the two extremes is referring back to the introductory paragraph and developing the anecdote or statistic or simply the point that was made there. This method can ensure that there is a unity in your composition. If, for example, a composition on 'European Union: where to go to from here?' begins like this:

> Ever since the term 'European' was first used, in the time of Charlemagne, its interpretation has been disputed. What does it mean to be European today? For those in other continents it simply means the people who live in this one. And there are an awful lot of people living here, from Austrian farmers to Norwegian taxi drivers, who don't identify themselves as European ...

the conclusion could consist of the following:

> A European Union in the future would be a world mode of what I call 'liberal order'. By this I mean an order without a single dominant power, flexibly open to different alliances of states on different issues and ultimately committed to the peaceful resolution of all

conflicts between its members. It is only in this way, I believe, that the hopes and fears of the three different kinds of Europeans will possibly be reconciled in a way that has never been achieved since the days of Charlemagne. This is the Europe we need and this is the Europe I urge on my fellow Europeans.

Examine the concluding paragraph of the following composition on 'Isn't it time to limit the use of private cars?'.

Until the time when responsibility is taken for this problem, the situation will only continue to worsen. Those who sit alone each morning in their cars and complain about the traffic must realise that they play a role in creating the problem itself. The public transport services too, while complaining about the difficulties they face, must realise that the inadequacy of their systems also contributes to this problem. If the problem is left unaddressed we may reach the time when limiting the use of private cars will be necessary. To avoid this situation, we must take co-operative action now and eliminate 'urban gridlock'.

COMMENT
This is an example of a concluding paragraph that makes a clear statement on the issues raised in the title. The writer here ties up certain ideas and presents some solutions in a clear and vigorous manner.
  Remember that your conclusion must show that you have complete control over your subject.

Rules for a good style
1. Write to communicate, not to impress. Know exactly what you want to say, then go ahead and say it.
2. Put your statements in a positive form. Make your statements or ideas clear and definite.
3. Choose a specific and concrete word. Avoid the use of vague or abstract expressions.
4. Use an active verb rather than a passive one. Your writing is more effective and forceful when you use active verbs.
5. Avoid repeating yourself in the same words. Repetition has to be used correctly, otherwise it can weaken the writing.
6. Vary the length and structure of your sentences.
7. Every sentence must have a subject, a verb and an object.
8. Always consult a dictionary when you are not sure how to spell a word or to check the meaning of a word.
9. Get used to writing and rewriting.
10. Learn the basic rules of correct punctuation thoroughly.
11. Know how to link your paragraphs correctly. The section on paragraphs (pages 31–8) gives examples of transitional or linking devices and how to use them correctly.

Checklist for writing compositions

Before you begin writing compositions, consider the following questions.

Content
- Are you presenting original and interesting ideas?
- If you are writing in the 'language of argument', have you presented the arguments in a balanced way and supported all statements made with sufficient evidence?
- Have you commented on the significance of quotations or examples in the development of your argument?
- Have you arrived at your own conclusions or relied too heavily on the interpretations of other people?

Organisation
- Does your introduction give a clear idea of what your composition is about?
- Does each paragraph fit into the pattern of your composition and advance the main point, or are there gaps in the development of ideas or digressions that sidetrack your points?
- Are the transitions between the paragraphs effective? Do they unify a paragraph and provide a logical development of thought between each paragraph?
- Does your conclusion link to your opening and tie in all the ideas in an interesting way? Is the conclusion positive? Is there a strong unity of impression from your conclusion?

Language
- Is the language used appropriate to the subject?
- Have you used the exact word to convey the precise meaning?
- Have you used language that is clear and comprehensible and avoided ambiguous expressions?
- Have you avoided slang and jargon?
- Are your sentences varied in length?
- Are the tenses of verbs consistent throughout?

Mechanics
- Have you avoided grammatical errors?
- Is your composition properly punctuated?
- Are all words correctly spelled?
- Are quotations or dialogue introduced correctly?
- Is there any unnecessary repetition of ideas, words or phrases?

5 The Language Genres

Study the notes below on the different language genres. In each section there are notes and guidelines on how to understand and write in the different genres; use these to guide you through the exercises.

THE LANGUAGE OF NARRATION

In the language of narration, or *narrative writing,* the writer is telling a story. Narrative writing is to be found in novels and short stories, plays, poems, histories, letters, some expository essays and reviews. Non-fictional narrative includes biography, autobiography and travel literature.

In an autobiography the writer narrates an account of his or her own life and experiences. Generally these events are narrated in chronological sequence. A biography is the study of one person's life and achievements written by another person. Travel literature records details of journeys and the writer's impressions of places visited in a way that lends a distinctive shape to the narrative.

Features of the language of narration
1. The ability to tell a story that has an effective narrative shape, with a beginning, a middle and a conclusion that are all clearly defined. There must be a distinct arrangement in the sequence of events presented.
2. The story must have a fairly definite location and context.
3. The story should be interesting and original. Clichés and stereotyping are avoided.
4. In a good narrative the writer introduces some personal commitment or experience.
5. All description must be both vivid and realistic.
6. Sometimes an anecdote can be used as part of a narrative. Here a single incident is told in the form of a short story. The incident almost always contains a definite point.
7. The characters presented must be realistic.
8. The story must have atmosphere. There has to be a certain setting; this can be a country, a certain type of house or a distinct period in history.

Sample passages

I lived in Portstewart, one of the small villages on the coast. I rented a small room at the top of an old dank two-storey Victorian terrace house. The house was the last one in the terrace, and from its window I could look out on the grey, ever-restless ocean. I can still remember the view from the window and the constant changes in the sea. The weather in that part of the north of Ireland was never the kindest, though when the summer came, the landscape round us, the easy access to Donegal and to the remoter parts of the North gave the area its own particular delight.

An old retired couple who owned the house lived in two rooms on the ground floor. Mr Paul was in his eighties, and I remember him going for his nightly walk accompanied by his walking-stick and his small mongrel dog. His bent figure would brave even Portstewart's weather as he walked along the sea front. I never saw the old man at any other time apart from these walks. I heard him occasionally in his own room. His wife, his second, would sit quietly in the kitchen beside the old range, constantly knitting and offering us cups of tea as we came in from the pub or back from studying. She never bothered us much, was always friendly, and enjoyed a cup of tea with those of us who would sit and chat with her.

Mr Paul became ill very suddenly. We were not surprised, aware even then that age can be cruel. But what moved me most was his rapid decline, the fact that I never saw him walking bent double against the wind, and the sight of his walking-stick always lying in the hall. It became a strange kind of symbol. Late into the night I could hear him coughing and throwing up. The fact that we were only aware of this man's illness through his rasping cough and his wife's ministrations lent the house a kind of ominous gloom.

One evening I came in from the cold and straight to the kitchen to heat myself at the range. Mrs Paul sat alone. There was a silence I couldn't understand. I recall now that her knitting-needles were for once not in evidence. There was no steam coming out of the old kettle normally kept simmering on the hot plate. Her face was very still. It took her some time to look up, to acknowledge me coming into the room. 'Would you like a cup of tea?' I asked. She looked up slowly, and I remember her old, lined but still quite beautiful face as she said calmly and without emotion: 'My husband is dead.'

(Brian Keenan, *An Evil Cradling*)

COMMENT

An Evil Cradling describes Brian Keenan's experience as a hostage in Lebanon. This extract recounts an incident in his life and is written in an autobiographical and narrative style. The passage is built around a series of small, effective devices, all of which are a hallmark of good narrative writing. The use of the autobiographical 'I' adds an air of realism to the writing. The imagery and language are precise and homely, and this quality of simplicity lends an arresting impact to the writing.

Question A
1. Show how the writer builds up atmosphere in the passage.
2. Identify several details that contribute to drawing vivid descriptions in the passage.

Question B
Write a short narrative description of some experience that affected you greatly. In your description concentrate on drawing some realistic details of character.

> When the news of my birth reached Dr Xia he said: 'Ah, another wild swan is born.' I was given the name Erhong, which means 'second wild swan'.
>
> Giving me my name was almost the last act in Dr Xia's long life. Four days after I was born he died, at the age of eighty-two. He was leaning back in bed drinking a glass of milk. My grandmother went out of the room for a minute, and when she came back to get the glass she saw that the milk had spilled and the glass had fallen to the floor. He had died instantly and painlessly.
>
> Funerals were very important events in China. Ordinary people would often bankrupt themselves to lay on a grand ceremony – and my grandmother loved Dr Xia and wanted to do him proud. There were three things she absolutely insisted on: first, a good coffin; second, that the coffin must be carried by pallbearers and not pulled on a cart; and third, to have Buddhist monks to chant the *sutras* for the dead and musicians to play the *suona*, a piercing woodwind instrument traditionally used at funerals. My father agreed to the first and second requests but vetoed the third. The communists regarded any extravagant ceremony as wasteful and 'feudal'.
>
> Traditionally only very lowly people were buried quietly. Noise-making was considered important at a funeral, to make it a public affair: this brought 'face' and also showed respect for the dead. My father insisted that there could be no *suona* or monks. My grandmother had a blazing row with him. For her, these were essentials, which she just had to have. In the middle of the altercation she fainted from anger and grief. She was also wrought up because she was all alone at the saddest moment of her life. She had not told my mother what had happened, for fear of upsetting her; and the fact that my mother was in the hospital meant that my grandmother had to deal directly with my father. After the funeral she had a nervous breakdown and had to be hospitalised for almost two months.
>
> (Jung Chang, *The Wild Swans*)

COMMENT
One of the features of good narrative is describing a specific time and location. Here the writer concentrates on certain significant events that occurred when she was born, how her grandfather died and the small details about the funeral ceremony. We also learn about her Communist background and about certain customs in China.

Question A
1. Sum up in your own words the main points you have gathered about the tradition of funeral ceremonies in China.
2. What is the tone of the extract? Support your answer by reference to the passage.

Question B
Rewrite the passage in the form of a dialogue. In writing your dialogue concentrate on registering some striking features of the characters represented.

Writing in the language of narration

The skills of good narrative composition come from practice. Writing a narrative composition essentially requires the ability to write a short story. The story should have one point of view and there should be a definite arrangement of ideas. A story must be original and interesting for your reader. A good story springs from your own experience.

How to write a narrative composition
1. Tell the story in one tense; the past tense is generally best.
2. It can help to put your own experience into the narrative – personal experience authenticates the flavour of a narrative.
3. The structure of your story can be straightforward and in chronological sequence or it can be told in flashback. Remember, your story must have a shape – a clear beginning, middle and conclusion.
4. Use the third-person narrator to tell your story. Avoid the use of too much dialogue, as it can break up the flow of thought. Remember, dialogue needs to be written well in order to read well.
5. Understand the terms 'plot', 'character' and 'dialogue' when writing a narrative composition and know how to use them correctly.

Plot
A plot can be defined as the series of events that make up a story.
- The plot must move forward towards a definite conclusion.
- The plot must include some element of change. The situation depicted at the beginning of the story must change as the story unfolds.
- All events of the plot must carry the narrative forward.
- There has to be a pace in the plot. Balance your beginning, middle and conclusion carefully to give your story a shape.

   Remember when planning your plot to have:

- change in the story
- pace and movement in the narrative
- general shape at the conclusion.

Characters
Because stories are about people, your characters must be real, recognisable figures. Your readers must be able to recognise the characters in your story; if not, they will not arouse any interest. You can reveal the true nature of your characters through dialogue and description. Concentrate on one or two significant features of a character when describing them, rather than on several points.

When you are describing a character, don't tell everything at once – use implication or suggestion instead. For example, look at the following descriptions:

> The sister, Catherine, was a slender worldly girl of about thirty, with a solid, sticky bob of red hair, and a complexion powdered milky white. Her eyebrows had been plucked and then drawn on again at a more rakish angle, but the efforts of nature towards the restoration of the old alignment gave a blurred air to her face. When she moved about there was an incessant clicking as innumerable pottery bracelets jingled up and down upon her arms. She came in with such a proprietary haste, and looked around so possessively at the furniture that I wondered if she lived there.
> (F. Scott Fitzgerald, *The Great Gatsby*)

COMMENT

Here the writer concentrates on registering some small details in the picture given to us of this character. Note how the writer describes the woman's hair as a 'sticky bob of red hair'. The image of the bracelets jangling up and down her arms is striking and clear.

Look at the effect achieved in the following description of a character:

> Mrs Reed was a woman of robust frame, square-shouldered and strong limbed, not tall, and though stout, not obese: she had a somewhat large face, the under-jaw being much developed and very solid; her brow was low, her chin large and prominent, mouth and nose sufficiently regular; her skin was dark and opaque, her hair nearly flaxen; her constitution was sound as a bell, illness never came near her; she was an exact clever manager, her household and tenantry were thoroughly under her control.
> (Charlotte Brontë, *Jane Eyre*)

COMMENT

The writer concentrates on drawing a clear and animated image of a certain type of person. The physical appearance of the woman is registered vividly through a series of small and precise points, such as her robust frame and the fact that she is strong-limbed but not obese. Remember, good description concentrates on making the reader clearly see what is being drawn.

Dialogue

Learn to master the art of writing effective dialogue before beginning a narrative composition. The function of dialogue is to reproduce live speech. Never allow dialogue simply to slip into a conversation – it must have a purpose. Remember that one of the main features of effective dialogue is the ability to convey conflict in a realistic manner. Conversation or good dialogue can add pace and variety to an otherwise dull story.

Learn how to punctuate dialogue correctly. Use quotation marks at the beginning and end of each section of direct speech. Separate the dialogue from the narrative by means of commas. The first word in every piece of direct speech begins with a capital letter. Use a new paragraph each time there is a change of speaker.

Study the following examples of the use of dialogue in composition, then read the commentary:

> 'How would you like to go to school then, child Alexander, hey?'
>
> The question took me completely by surprise, but anyway my mother answered for me. 'Frederick.' Her voice had a warning in it.
>
> He smiled briefly in her direction. 'Hey then, my boy?'
>
> 'I hadn't really thought about it, Father.'
>
> 'Well, think about it. Now's the time. Meet a few chaps of your own age. Broaden. Polish you up a bit. Games,' he said, without any enormous conviction. 'Pass the celery, please. And things.'
>
> I passed him the celery.
>
> 'Mr Bingham is more than adequate.' Her voice was north-north-east cold.
>
> 'Perhaps a widening of outlook would do no harm. There are other subjects which Mr Bingham ...'
>
> 'He is delicate, Frederick. You must not put his health at risk.'
>
> 'In your eyes he is delicate, my dear. I see few signs of it. He has just eaten a most remarkable lunch.'
>
> 'Dr Desmond ...'
>
> 'Dr Desmond is an ass.'
>
> 'Frederick, *pas devant* ...'
>
> 'My dear good woman, you know perfectly well that Dr Desmond will say anything you want him to say.'
>
> (Jennifer Johnston, *How Many Miles to Babylon*)

COMMENT

This extract depicts the strain in the relationship between husband and wife. The dialogue conveys in a terse manner the primary features of these two characters.

Mood and atmosphere

Note the difference between the terms 'mood' and 'atmosphere'. Mood is the way the writer feels; atmosphere is how the place and setting are described.

Every story needs an atmosphere. Atmosphere is created in a narrative by a careful blending of people, events and setting. Your atmosphere must help to draw your reader into your story. While the use of imagination can help to build up an atmosphere, remember that the imagination must be controlled in writing. This is necessary in order to make your writing more realistic and authentic.

Sample composition

The following composition is written in the language of narration. It is taken from actual pupils' work and is graded according to the standards required at Higher Level. Study it carefully and pay particular attention to the commentary that follows.

The exercise was: 'Write on some experience that left a deep impression on you. Use a narrative or imaginative style in your composition.'

Awakenings
Even now, thirty years after experiencing the bullfight at San María, my pulse still races when it calls to mind
The rippling lengths of bleached canvas overhead
The golden glimmering bullring far below.
I presumed that by sitting half way up the crowded amphitheatre we would be safe,
To a certain extent removed from it all,
Protected from the ferocious intensity below.
We were not.

That summer Pat, Kilty, John Drennan and myself were enjoying a cycling tour of the Iberian Peninsula. Three young students; none older than twenty. We had been in the country for three weeks and had not yet succeeded in understanding the Spanish mind-set. All we had ascertained was that they were tanned, aloof, beautiful and gibbering.

The breakthrough came on a bright Sunday afternoon in late July. It so happened that my bicycle became punctured a few miles outside a modest uphill village called San María. Because of the severity of the puncture we had to venture into the town for an unscheduled stop.

The wife of the local garage owner – an olive, leathery-skinned woman – explained to us that he was at the bullfight, of course. Glad of a temporary respite, we all wheeled our bicycles to the stadium. We were all country boys and therefore had gone hare-coursing and hunting at home. Our voices grew to an animated pitch of feverish excitement as we neared the giant theatre.

Nearly all the seats had been taken half an hour before the event began. Luckily we managed to find three seats half way up the bustling amphitheatre.

Our hungry eyes and ears scanned the onlookers. There were people of all ages and both sexes, delight and excitement clearly visible on their faces. The hushed, reverential noise of the crowd was unlike anything I had previously experienced at hurling matches at home. It was strange and unsettling.

Only when the bull entered did I understand the reason: the close, undeniable presence of death among us. I was in no way prepared for my utter dread of the bull – a gruesome, malevolent presence. He lashed out at the crowd in general, thundering left and right. His red nostrils flared, and the muscles of his silky sweat-covered trunk contracted uncontrollably into spasms.

To my left a samba band announced the arrival of *el matador*. He was a man of twenty-two years – only slightly older than us, a local from a neighbouring upland village. As usual, his father was also a matador before him. It was said that he was a fine fighter, already in a few short years having exceeded the skill, grace and creativity of his father.

To my unaccustomed eye he was short and of slight build. Yet his puny presence had already managed to dissipate some of the bull's choking and stifling sense of menace.

The matador walked towards the bull, the crowd fell quiet, he stopped. Beast and matador silently studied each other. The bull seemed to recognise who exactly he encountered, both the purpose and significance of the encounter. This mutual appraisal lasted no more than fifteen seconds. The bull charged.

Closer and closer the ton and a half of agitating muscle charged. The matador remained motionless. His guttural growl grew to fever pitch. The matador clicked the heels of the delicate dust-covered shoes, recognising a distant face in the crowd.

Then at the last possible instant the matador stepped sideways, totally unconcerned. The crowd erupted.

Amidst the dizzying heat and deafening roars of 'Toro, toro,' a strange thing happened. Choked with fear, I experienced the most potent sense of humanity that to this day I have ever felt. Every sinew in my body pulsed with an immense feeling of pride of race. Every deft little side kick and neat little blow increased my pride in belonging to the human race.

The matador's complete superiority over the bull held me spellbound. Like everybody else, I was far too caught up in the celebration of the matador's prowess even to notice the brutish suffering of this animal. That was it. The breakthrough.

It all now made sense to me. The scenario before me had framed the idea: who exactly these people were. At first I had been horrified by the Spaniards and how lightly they weighed the life of an animal, too cosmopolitan and blasé to care for the suffering of a simple beast. I had missed the point entirely. They understood death more than I. They recognised their own place within nature as humans. They moved within nature, a powerful force with a profound understanding and respect for her.

When the time came to leave and seek out the mechanic, my whole body shook with a vibrancy and energy. It lasted for days, but the lesson learned returned with me to Ireland, the brutal lesson that I had learned amid the heat and bleached canvas, a lesson that eroded my prejudices and gave me a deeper insight into my humanity and even my own soul.

Comment

Grade B1

This composition has an effective narrative shape. It has a clear beginning, middle and conclusion. Furthermore, the narrative is given a distinct location and time. Both the language and description used are original and clear. The story has a dramatic immediacy. There is a wide variety of sentence structure. The terse sentence structure conveys an energy and pace to the narrative. The loose and informal paragraph structure contributes to the flow of the narrative. There is a strong sense of unity in the viewpoint.

The writer is perhaps trying to do too much in too short a space. He wishes to convey the powerful impact on him of having experienced a bullfight and to draw the conclusion that it has left a mark on him for ever. However, this is not achieved in enough detail or depth. The conclusion is somewhat abrupt. The characters in the narrative need to be developed in greater detail.

The first page is too formal. Perhaps the writer is trying too hard to impress. Phrases such as 'because of the severity of the puncture', 'I presumed' and 'having ascertained' are awkward and stiff. The use of the term 'gibbering' to describe a language the writer does not understand is offensive. However, the style of the narrative begins to flow steadily as the story develops.

Exercises on writing in the language of narration
1. Write a suitable conclusion to the following paragraph, which is written in a narrative style: 'The village to which our family had come was a scattering of some twenty or thirty houses down the south-east slope of a valley. The valley was narrow, steep and almost entirely cut off; it was also a funnel for winds, a channel for the floods and a bird-crammed, insect-hopping sun-trap whenever there happened to be any sun. The sides of the valley were rich in pasture and the crests heavily covered in beechwoods.'
2. Write a narrative composition on the experience of being a refugee.
3. Write on one of the following topics, using a narrative style:
   'A new millennium'
   'My first job'
   'Fragile Earth'
   'My experience of visiting the home of a pop star'.
4. Take each of these opening sentences and write a narrative-style composition:
   'They began to move up just at dusk, and by the time night fell and the first flares became visible …'
   'His hat had rolled a few yards away, and his clothes were smeared with the filth and ooze of the floor on which he had lain …'

THE LANGUAGE OF ARGUMENT

Argument is a form of rational persuasion. The 'language of argument' attempts to prove a particular point by using logic or evidence.

It is important to understand the difference between argument and persuasion. Argument assumes that a reader is objective, is able to follow a logical train of thought, to weigh up evidence and will not be prevented by emotion from accepting the conclusions to which the logic or the evidence points. Argument differs from persuasion in that it appeals to reason and logic rather than to emotion or feelings.

Writing that uses the language of argument includes legal documents, scientific and medical journals and newspaper reports.

Features of the language of argument
1. In a well-constructed argument, claims must always be supported. A claim is a statement that is arguable. Claims can be supported by:
   - providing data or evidence
   - facts
   - examples
   - statistics, where information is presented in the form of numbers.
2. Good argument must be supported by evidence that is valid. An argument is valid when the conclusion follows logically from the premise or the preceding statements. To test the validity of an argument:

- assess the truth of the premise
- assess the truth of each argument
- assess the truth of each sub-argument.
3. Argument is effective when evidence and reasoning are both presented in a persuasive manner so as to convince the reader that certain opinions are preferable to others.
4. In understanding the language of argument it is important to distinguish between a fact and an opinion. A fact is something that really exists or occurs – it can be verified or proved by an objective or detached observer. The process of confirming that a statement is true is known as verification.

A fact differs from an opinion because facts can be *verified,* whereas opinions must be *supported.* An opinion is a judgment or a belief regarding something that is held by a person. It can be based on a logical inference from the facts. The following statements are examples of facts:

> The weather has got warmer over the last few years.
> The Leaving Certificate examination brings with it a great deal of pressure on pupils.

We can add some opinions to these facts; for example:

> The weather has got warmer over the last few years, therefore we need to do something about global warming.
> The Leaving Certificate examination brings with it a great deal of pressure on pupils, so perhaps it should be abolished.

To test factual statements we must examine the evidence. To test statements of opinion we must:
- examine the evidence of fact
- examine the inferences drawn from it.

An *inference* is an interpretation of a fact – it is the product of a subjective reasoning process. We make inferences about things many times without realising it. For example, we meet someone we know very well but they don't greet us, so we may infer that we have done something wrong or that they are in bad humour. The reality may be quite different – they may simply be distracted or tired.

The following example will illustrate more clearly the difference between a fact (or argument), an opinion and an inference:

Fact
All the planets in the solar system are spheres.

Inference
As the planets in the solar system are spheres, the Earth must be a sphere.

Opinion
All the planets in the solar system are wonderful.

COMMENT
The first statement is a fact. The second statement is an inference that proceeds from the first one, and in this case it is true. The third statement is merely an opinion – not all people will agree with it.

The processes or stages of argument
There are different processes or stages of reasoning in argument:
- deductive reasoning
- inductive reasoning
- *a priori* reasoning
- *a posteriori* reasoning.

Deductive reasoning
Deductive reasoning begins with a general law and moves to a particular case.

> All the planets in the solar system are spheres.
> The Earth is a planet in the solar system.
> Therefore the Earth is a sphere.

The first two statements are called *premises*. They lead to the conclusion in the third statement. These three statements add up to a logical structure, which is called a *syllogism*. However, not all deductive arguments are true.

> All tigers are cats.
> Our pet is a cat.
> Therefore our pet is a tiger.

Though the first two premises are true, the concluding premise is false and therefore the argument is false. For an argument to be valid, all premises or statements must be true.

Inductive reasoning
Inductive reasoning begins with observing individual phenomena and from them arriving at a general law.

> John is a man.
> John is mortal.
> Therefore all men are mortal.

The structure of inductive reasoning is based on establishing certain evidence about something and then drawing a conclusion. Inductive argument can be false; for example:

> Joan is a woman.
> Joan is a teacher.
> Therefore all women are teachers.

A priori reasoning
A priori ('from the former') reasoning goes from known causes to imaginary effects; it is a form of deductive reasoning.

> They have been working all day, so they must be tired.
> He crashed his car, so therefore he will buy a new one.

A posteriori reasoning
A posteriori ('from the latter') reasoning moves from known facts to probable causes.

> She suffers from migraine, so she must be stressed.
> The meat is not cooked, so the oven must be broken.

Fallacies in argument
A fallacy is faulty reasoning or a false or misleading argument. It is important to recognise unsound ways of reasoning or fallacies in argument, such as the following:
- faulty generalisation
- glittering generalities
- begging the question
- ignoring the question
- *non sequitur*
- false dilemma
- emotional appeals.

Faulty generalisations
These occur through drawing the wrong conclusions from certain information. Such generalisations can be unqualified. In most cases the statement 'killing is wrong' can be considered true; however, killing in self-defence may be justifiable, so this statement could be considered an example of an unqualified generalisation.

Hasty generalisations or jumping to conclusions is another example of a faulty generalisation. For example, an article that claims that most rock stars commit suicide would be an example of a hasty generalisation.

Generalisations about things involve reaching a conclusion on the grounds of certain facts or evidence. For example, if pollution causes certain animal and plant life to die, then scientists could draw up a valid or true generalisation about the evil effects of pollution.

Glittering generalities
This is a method of obscuring an argument by deliberately keeping it vague. Glittering generalities usually involve making sweeping statements or extravagant claims about something. Some examples can be the use of certain phrases or expressions:

> The best you can get
> Tremendous value
> For tens of thousands of pupils, exams are approached with total apprehension.

Statements of this type are vague and abstract. Examine what the facts are here – what is the writer saying?

Begging the question
Begging the question means taking the point that is being disputed for granted – using the claim to support itself. In this type of argument a statement or idea is presented in such a way that presumes to be true what still has to be proved.

> We must believe that God exists because it says so in the Bible, which is the word of God.

Here proof for the existence of God is based on an assumption of His existence and so amounts to no proof at all.

> We have to accept change because without change there is no progress.

This statement presupposes that change and progress are synonymous, something that is not necessarily true.

Ignoring the question
In this type of argument the question or issue being discussed is ignored altogether.

Non sequitur
A *non sequitur* ('it does not follow') is a conclusion that cannot validly be inferred from the premise or assertion.

> All rats eat rice.
> All rice is good.
> Therefore all rats are good.

> John is an Irishman.
> All Irish people are rich.
> Therefore John is rich.

The conclusions here are examples of generalisations that do not follow from the preceding statements.

False dilemma
This offers a choice between only two answers or two courses of action, ignoring alternative possibilities.

> The Taoiseach should abandon the budget or else resign.
> Either you welcome all immigrants to Ireland or you're a racist.

Emotional appeals
Emotional appeals include name-calling, labelling and using loaded terms.

> They're very traditional in their beliefs.
> She's fanatical about politics.
> He's a red.

Emotional appeals invariably lead to *non sequiturs*.

Sample passages

Study the following article, which makes use of the language of argument.

'It was like something straight out of *The Godfather*,' said the taxi driver, appalled at the circumstances in which Sergeant Andy Callanan died in Tallaght this week. And so it was, horrible almost beyond belief, the kind of thing we thought could happen only in a film.

Now we know different. And the taxi driver's comment is sickeningly relevant, given the belief, firmly held in some quarters, that our cinema and television screens are awash with mindless violence and that this has dreadful social implications.

And the awful manner in which the garda lost his life again raises questions about our culture, how and why it is being influenced by fictional images of violence and the links between screen violence and violence in real life. This is made all the more real by suggestions that the perpetrator of the appalling incident in Tallaght may have been influenced by a recent episode of the television series *The Bill*, featuring a scene in which a policeman was doused with petrol by someone who had a grudge against the force.

The questions and the debate about them are not new. In the United States – the home of Hollywood – the director Oliver Stone is still embroiled in controversy over his film *Natural Born Killers*. The best-selling novelist John Grisham (author of *The Firm* and *The Pelican Brief*), one of whose friends was shot by a couple claiming they had been inspired to carry out the shooting by *Natural Born Killers,* insists that Stone should bear some of the responsibility.

Are films, television plays and videos capable of influencing people to carry out acts of violence? The debate has been joined on this side of the Atlantic by Audrey Conlon, the deputy film censor, who outlined her thinking in a television interview yesterday. 'People tend to have very strong views on censorship and classification. And very often you find yourself in a corner – perhaps not trying to defend your situation but certainly trying to explain what your job is about.'

So what is the most criticism a film censor gets? Do people think the censors today are too lenient or too tough? 'Both. In one corner you can have someone saying, "You can see anything now in the cinema; you can watch anything on video." And then the next day you'll meet someone who'll ask, "Why do we need censorship? Given that the whole media environment has changed so much, are you relevant?" The fact is that it is an area that a lot of people are interested in, particularly parents, who are concerned about what children are viewing.'

When the Video Recordings Act (1989) was introduced it meant that extra staff had to be appointed to the Film Censor's office to deal with video classification, and Ms Conlon was appointed by the Minister for Justice, Máire Geoghegan Quinn. Ms Conlon says she didn't have particularly strong views about films before becoming a censor. 'But I was always very interested in media. I'm a bit of a media junkie. When I go to a hotel somewhere the first thing I do is click on the television to see what's on CNN, and I've always been a reader of newspapers.'

In an age in which technological developments in broadcasting will very soon give us access to two or three hundred television channels, is there still a role for the censor and a place for censorship? 'Yes. But I would prefer not to use the word censorship. People's ideas and perceptions of censorship were probably formed by what they heard about what happened here in the nineteen-forties and fifties. That's not the way the system operates at the moment. Censorship now works with a fairly light hand. Very few mainstream films are banned; but there very definitely is a need for censorship, and it's a need supported by over forty years of research.'

In other words, even in the nineteen-nineties there's a need, in Ms Conlon's opinion, to regulate in some way the material that we as a society view, especially the material that our children view. 'What the censor's office now is essentially doing is classifying material.' Which of course means that a lot of the control and responsibility is being handed back to the home. 'Certainly in the home the responsibility is being handed to the parents; but what we are giving them through the classification system is good guidelines – good consumer advice. And we're saying to them that in our opinion, based on our experience, if we classify this as 12 we are encouraging you not to let your six-year-old see it.'

Apart from the awful business in Dublin, that concern was reinforced by reports this week that two boys were motivated to try to murder a friend as a result of watching the horror film *Scream*. Little wonder that Ms Conlon would say that violence is now the main concern of the censorship office, with particular concern for its potential effects on younger people. 'This concern is not just something that we concocted ourselves. It is supported by about forty years of research, and it's research that has been done all over the world. And the conclusion is – and there will always be dissenting voices – that the mass media do bear some responsibility for contributing to violence. That's it in a nutshell.'

Does this exclude real events, like war coverage? 'No. What we see on our screens – all mediated images of violence – all contribute.'

So are we becoming desensitised to violence? The research would certainly suggest that we are and this conclusion appears to have the support of serious researchers, meaning in the end that we are all in danger of being desensitised. 'It drips into our culture. And it appears to have done so this week with horrific consequences.'

Question A
1. What devices has the writer used to support his arguments? Refer to anecdotal evidence, factual information, classification and possible use of statistics in your answer.
2. Are the points made in this article convincing? Has the writer made use of personal opinion or invalid or unsubstantiated claims? If so, give examples.

Question B
Write an article for a local newspaper commenting on some violent videos that you believe have a harmful effect on young people. In your article make some suggestions about how to remedy this situation.

Writing in the language of argument
When you are writing in the language of argument, the emphasis is on being able to write in a discursive manner – presenting facts and argument on a certain topic and arriving at a conclusion. In this type of writing you are trying to convince your reader that your argument is valid.
- Take a definite stance on the topic. For example, in a composition on 'Spare the rod and spoil the child', you may decide to agree or disagree. The important thing is to clearly establish, both to yourself and to your reader, what your own stance on this issue is.
- Identify your audience, whether you are writing for a group of young people, educated professionals or a class of schoolchildren.
- Establish what tone or point of view you will use.
- Draft an outline of the main ideas for each paragraph and put the most important ideas first.
- Write in a balanced way. Avoid giving a one-sided presentation.
- Support every fact you present with evidence.

Remember, good argument writing is clear and concise. It is structured on original ideas, organised thought and a balanced and logical presentation of facts. For that reason:

- use language that is formal and precise
- express ideas in a logical manner
- use transitional words to link your ideas
- anticipate the reader's opposing views
- defend your own ideas in a forceful and clear way
- avoid the use of clichés, repetition, emotional or offensive language, euphemisms and double-speak.

Sample composition

The following composition is written in the language of argument. It is taken from actual pupils' work and is graded according to the standards required at Higher Level. Study it carefully and pay special attention to the commentary that follows. The task was to write an article for a serious journal in which you challenge or support the statement 'There are actually people who take pride in their race. This is stupid.'

> As we celebrate the beginning of a new century, the desire to reflect on our history and actions is at a peak. This is a unique time to learn from our mistakes and take pride in our achievements. In the twentieth century the human race advanced in some areas more than it has in the entire course of its history. However, for all our vast and wonderful achievements, the dark and destructive stain of racism remains as a reminder that in some ways we still remain almost at the same level of civilisation as the animals. This inhumanity and injustice to our fellow humans overshadows our greatest achievements and reminds us too clearly of the savage and primitive state that remains latent within.
>
> The idea that a particular race of people could be superior to others is an absurd belief. In the words of Kofi Annan, Secretary-General of the United Nations, 'We may have different religions, different languages, different-coloured skin, but we all belong to the one human race. We all share the same basic human values.' Undoubtedly there are many things that we can take pride in: the first landing on the moon or the first transatlantic voyage. Yet is it possible that such events can compensate for the brutal reality of two world wars and the mindless violence perpetrated in places such as Africa and Europe, and all carried out in the name of racism? Indeed, the few moments of glory in humankind's achievements are nothing compared with some of the grave atrocities that have been committed on our fellow humans.
>
> Undoubtedly racism today takes on many different aspects, from antagonising a group of Travellers at their halting site to barring someone from entry to a club because of their social status or depriving people of educational or welfare benefits due to them.
>
> We may ask the question, what is it that makes a person believe they are superior to another race? We are all cast from the same mould, though decorated differently. Perhaps this mistaken belief in one's superiority could stem from our past, when competition was fierce and indeed competition was the name of the game. The survival of the fittest may still survive in our subconscious thoughts today. If this is the case, then we differ little from our savage ancestors in lacking the spirit of open-mindedness to see the human race in its entirety.

While racism has been a blot on the pages of history for decades, it was only during the colonial years, when thousands of African slaves were traded like cattle between the white settlers of America, that the topic came to the forefront. To this day a rift divides the two cultures and it has seen the growth of terror groups such as the Ku Klux Klan. Up to the sixties African-Americans had little or no rights and were still slaves to society. However, through the painstaking efforts of such people as Martin Luther King, enormous developments and inroads have been made. All this bitter hatred and animosity could have been avoided, however. It is totally unjustifiable and incomprehensible to believe that a person should consider themselves to be superior because of the colour of their skin. In fact, it defies logic.

Extremist views pose the greatest problem in this particular area. Pride in one's achievements becomes converted into a brutal and radical form of racism, and in turn this is translated into profound hatred for different ways, whether the difference is manifested in religion, culture, background or beliefs. Underlying this intransigent attitude is fear – fear of whatever is different. This fear becomes channelled into hatred and can be seen most strikingly in groups such as Combat 18 and neo-Nazism.

In these cases, violence and intimidation become the only method of communication. Diplomacy is non-existent. The results generated by such regimes are devastating. Humankind must learn that violence and injustice produce only suffering and sterility.

Adolf Hitler is an example of one such extremist. The name itself is enough to send a shiver along the spine of any humane individual. Yet he is worshipped as a god for many others. Hitler managed to find a scapegoat for the problems he confronted, both personal and political, in just about anybody, from Jews to Communists. Under his brutal 'final solution', six million Jews and up to twenty million Russians became victims of Nazi concentration camps and were butchered and slaughtered by the malignant SS. His vision of an all-dominant 'Aryan' race that would triumph over humankind and last for centuries ultimately failed. Hitler has earned the unique title of having carried out more murders than any other being in history, all in the name of pride and a wilful blindness to the supposed superiority of one's race.

Racism today is deeply entrenched in the heart of our society. It is evident in all walks of life, from international politics to the area of the media. The recent move to elect Jörg Haider – a well-known master wordsmith for racism and xenophobia – in Austria sent a chill reminder across the world. It may be an interesting irony that Hitler himself was born in the same place. Many people began to fear that history would repeat itself, having borne witness to Haider's strong adherence to Hitler's views. Some people began to fear the consequences of Hitler's legacy in the wake of such political manoeuvring. In the light of this fact, Austria was politically isolated around the world. Public opinion made the statement that his beliefs are not acceptable at the start of a new century, since we know exactly what they led to in the thirties and forties. It is vitally important that a marker be put down, that when extremism is mainstreamed, something profound is happening in Europe today.

As we look back on our past we begin to realise how racism and the belief in one's superiority over another person have proved to be a disastrous combination. We are all members of the same human race. We are all entitled to the same rights and treatment because of our status as human beings. Basic unwillingness and an inability to accept this point inevitably causes conflict and war. The bloodstained history books are a colourful enough reminder of the utter pointlessness of racist beliefs. It is only when we undertake to unite and combat the various limitations within our own nature and within life in general that we can truly begin to become masters first of all of ourselves, and then perhaps we will attain some form of control over this world of ours.

COMMENT
Grade A2
This composition on the topic of racism is written in the form of an argument. It is clearly structured into a series of paragraphs, all of which deal with the subject in a factual and logical manner. The material used in the article has been well researched, and the examples and supporting evidence are both relevant and topical. The points that are made are clearly supported with evidence. Remember, good argument requires evidence and support to sustain it. The conclusion is effective and there is a distinct unity of thought throughout the composition.

POINTS FOR DEVELOPMENT
The topic of racism has been broadened to include many other types of discrimination. The tendency to blur the meaning of 'racism' by using it as an all-purpose term for prejudice is reflected in its use here to describe discrimination against Travelling people and even discrimination on grounds of social class, while the references to the slave trade and the causes of two world wars reflect an unawareness of colonialism as distinct from racism. The scope chosen by the writer is very wide and it may not be possible to treat all of it in sufficient depth.

Perhaps the language and style could have more energy, contrast and colour. Some of the sentences are a little too weighty and the argument lacks clarity at times. Always remember that good writing is clear writing.

Writing exercises
1. Write a speech for a group of businesspeople on how you consider they could help eradicate some of the injustices in 'Third World' countries.
2. Write the speech you would give at a seminar entitled 'The power of the media'. Clearly describe your views on how the media have been either a positive or a negative influence on society.
3. Write an article for a magazine using the language of argument on the topic 'The greatest of evils and the worst of crimes is ignorance'.
4. Write a letter to a local newspaper using the language of argument on both the positive and the negative changes you have seen in Ireland over the last few years.

THE LANGUAGE OF INFORMATION

The objectives of this type of language can be to:
- convey information in a succinct or terse manner
- give instructions or make requests
- persuade or influence the reader to adopt an attitude or act on a certain issue or matter.

The language of information is to be found in reports, journalism (newspaper, television and radio), instructions, memos and letters, summaries, bulletins, forms and questionnaires. Each of these forms has different objectives. Reports give a factual account of a situation or set of circumstances. Media accounts usually give a report of events in a clear and factual manner. Instructions offer a clear, concise explanation of how to do something. Memos are short messages written in an informal style. Summaries give a condensed account of information. Forms and questionnaires request information in a plain, compact manner.

Features of the language of information

1. There is clear organisation of information. All arguments and information must be presented in a logical and coherent manner.
2. The content is relevant. Do not digress from the main point in what you are writing; avoid introducing useless or irrelevant information.
3. Use an appropriate style and expression. In general, the style required for functional writing is clear and factual. Avoid the use of colourful language and images, such as:

   Performance has plummeted unexpectedly and with increasing force because of a catastrophic lack of in-service training of staff in this area.

   Use simple, factual language instead, for example:

   The lack of in-service training for staff has caused performance to fall greatly.

4. Use short sentences. Convey the information as briefly as possible.
5. Use the precise number of words. Avoid verbose or long-winded statements.
6. Use concrete words rather than abstract ones.
7. Use each word in a way that clearly illustrates its meaning. For example, look at the following sentences.

   Check L's report.

   Does this mean check the report that L has completed or check the report on L? What does 'check' mean anyway?

   Record sales figures for last year.

   Does it mean write down the sales figures for last year or that the sales figures for last year exceeded those of other years?

8. Avoid the use of slang, jargon, buzzwords and commercialese. *Slang* is very informal language. *Jargon* is the inappropriate use of the terminology of a

specialised profession. *Buzzwords* are fashionable terms often used in advertising or informal conversation. *Commercialese* consists of dated or stereotyped formulas of a kind once popular in business correspondence:

Enclosed herewith [I enclose]
Your letter is to hand [I have received your letter]
With reference to same [With regard to …]
I trust this will meet your expectations [I hope this is agreeable]

In addition, good informative writing has the following features.
- It must be simple, clear and concise.
- The information presented must be comprehensive – it must deal with all aspects of the subject.
- It must be appropriate for the intended audience.
- The tone of the language must be objective.

In this section we will examine the different features of reports, instructions, letters and memos, etc. and study how to write them for examination purposes.

Reports

As we have seen, reports give a factual account of a situation. The main function of a report is to study or analyse material or information and to present this in a clear and standard form. Report writing can have different objectives, for example:
- to inform the reader about something or to research information
- to evaluate or explain a situation or a set of circumstances
- to provoke debate on an issue.

THE LAYOUT OF A REPORT

Some of the following headings may be used in a report. Not all reports demand such detailed layout; however, it is good to be familiar with these terms in order to know how to use them.

terms of reference: the instructions that are given to those writing the report about what they have to investigate. For example, a report could have the following terms of reference: 'To report on the number of school-leavers who emigrate and work abroad.'
introduction: this fully sets out:
- the main details of the report
- the questions under investigation
- the time limits
- the material or methods used.

work carried out: this section will contain detailed information on what has been done to find out information, for example, any statistics that have been gathered.
findings: under this heading comes the main body of information gathered. The material in this section must be organised carefully and any irrelevant points must be discarded – only information bearing on the issue must be included in this section.

conclusions: these are based on the terms of reference and the findings. They should flow naturally from all the evidence and findings and should be clear, simple and objective.

recommendations: these will include your own interpretations of any improvements or points that can be taken into account as a result of your findings. Present these simply and if possible in the form of a list.

summary: a condensed version of the report. Summaries provide a short, succinct account of both findings and conclusions. A good summary should concentrate on giving an outline of the main points, in particular the conclusions and recommendations.

acknowledgments: a list of those people and organisations that helped in any way during the research of the report.

references: any publications or other publicly available material that was used; these also should be acknowledged.

appendixes: subsidiary material gathered together at the end of the report, usually numbered. Make use of headings and sub-headings.

SAMPLE REPORT

This is an example of a report using some of the headings described above.

Report on television viewing by pupils aged between 15 and 18

Introduction
At the request of the Minister for Education and Science, a report on television viewing by young people has been authorised. The number of hours and the types of programmes watched will be studied. A list of recommendations will be drawn up.

Procedures
A detailed questionnaire on the amount of time spent watching television and on the types of programmes watched was issued to all secondary schools in the country. This questionnaire was aimed at the 15–18 age group.

Findings
Pupils generally watched between ten and twenty hours of television a week. Among the more popular types of programmes were serials, such as *Friends*, *Neighbours* and *Home and Away*. Boys generally watched more sports programmes than girls. Boys also spent more time on the internet than watching television.

Conclusions
Very few pupils engaged in selective viewing of television programmes. More than 80 per cent of viewing has little educational content. Many of the programmes watched were sentimental serials with little or no substance. The literary ability of pupils in this group has declined, perhaps in part because of the smaller amount of time spent reading and writing.

Recommendations
1. More programmes with an educational or informed content should be broadcast in the evenings.
2. Parents should take a more decisive part in monitoring television viewing.
3. Local libraries should provide more video and internet facilities to stimulate young people to carry out research, read and study.

Commentary
A good title helps to provide a clear focus on what the report is about. The introduction sums up all aspects of the report – the reasons why the report is being undertaken, time limits, details of those carrying out the report and who authorised it.

Remember that the style of report writing must be factual and objective. Avoid the use of emotive and ambiguous language.

Remember to sign and date a report.

How to write a report
Before you begin, ask yourself the following questions:
- What is the purpose and the theme of this report?
- What objectives am I hoping to achieve?

Remember, a report is effective when:
- it is understood without too much effort
- the findings are acknowledged to be valid and are acted on.

Preliminary work
Because reports have very different objectives, it is necessary to put in a great deal of work in preparing the material before beginning the process of writing it. This preliminary work will determine the quality of the result and will enable you to structure and organise your material more effectively.
1. Establish the purpose or objective of the report. Is it to describe or evaluate a situation or set of circumstances? Is the report explaining a procedure or situation?
2. Once you have established the purpose of the report, decide on a title; this will help you to concentrate more clearly on what exactly the report is all about. You may be asked to write a report on how secondary school girls use their free time at weekends. You could use a title such as 'The use of free time at weekends by schoolgirls aged 14–17'. Establishing a title will help you to limit the topic and to concentrate more clearly on what exactly you must write.
3. Find out who will read the report. This will affect the style of your report. Writing a report for the school committee will demand a different style from one for the managing director of a company.
4. Establish whether the report has a time limit, and if so, what this is.
5. Look at the resources at your disposal. What budget have you been allocated? What equipment have you got? What materials will you need?
6. Study how to structure your report. Will your report be structured in sections with sub-headings? Will the report be a summary?

CHECKLIST FOR REPORTS
1. Does the title clearly indicate the nature of the report?
2. Are the objectives of the report clearly stated?
3. Are all the terms used in the report clearly defined?
4. Is the report written in the correct tense? (Generally reports are written in the past tense.)
5. Is the language of the report clear? Are there obscure phrases, evidence of bias, emotive terms or intemperate language in the report?
6. Are all the claims made substantiated clearly by facts?
7. Are the conclusions based on evidence?
8. Are the recommendations feasible?
9. Is the report signed and dated?

Media accounts
Media accounts of some event or happening generally give a factual and objective description of what they are reporting. However, such accounts are often influenced by a number of things – the type of publication, the readership aimed at or the writer's own viewpoint on the event.

Instructions
Instructions can be written on technical or human subjects. Technical subjects involve giving detailed guidelines on certain procedures, such as changing a fuse, fixing the plug of a hairdryer or changing the bag on a vacuum cleaner. These types of instructions will use specialised vocabulary and perhaps a series of numbered stages or steps.

On the other hand, instructions can be written on human subjects, such as 'How to increase your self-confidence', 'How to benefit from the points scheme' or 'How to cope with exam stress'. In these type of instructions the use of generalised vocabulary and illustrations will help a great deal. The style will be more relaxed and informal.

In writing instructions, as in all writing situations, take into account:
- your subject matter
- your audience
- the best techniques that can be used to communicate that subject matter to the audience.

Examine the following set of instructions on 'taking your children out of the rat race', then study the commentary that follows it.

Taking your children out of the rat race
Quality bus corridors, rising house prices, corrupt politicians, lack of child care facilities, the cost of the latest football strip – has your blood pressure shot up yet? If not, you're in a minority. It seems that stress levels for most of us have increased at a similar pace to economic growth. Have you noticed how aggressive other drivers have become? Or how casual and dismissive shop assistants are? Perhaps it is all symptomatic of the negative aspects of prosperity. The outcome of our new-found status is a population that appears

less caring and more interested in promoting self-interest. In the middle of all this material mayhem, it is important for parents not to lose sight of the core values. How many of the following do you do regularly?

- Talk to your children. Do you know what your children did at school today? If not, why not?
- Play with your children. There can surely be no more rewarding experience for a parent than getting lost in the child's world. Your child likes nothing more than spending time with parents – no toy or bag of sweets is more cherished.
- Tell your child about your own experiences. Younger children love to hear about what life was like when Mammy and Daddy were the same age. This is also a useful strategy if you suspect that your child is experiencing some difficulties. For example, if you suspect that your child is being bullied, talking about when you were young can be a useful way of getting your child to open up.
- Listen. It's not an easy skill. Go for a walk and let the child do the talking. Sit and simply shoot the breeze. Try to say nothing. Let your child lead the conversation.
- Be yourself. There is no such thing as a perfect parent or a perfect child. Being trendy or over-generous will not enhance the relationship with your child; being yourself will. That means getting into the habit of leaving work outside the front door and tuning into the home environment as you find it.
- Inform your child about what is happening in the world.
- Watch your child. Children like nothing better than having their parents watching their activities. Whether this involves cringing as your child rides a bicycle with no supports for the first time or freezing on the sideline of a football pitch for an hour, your child will appreciate it.
- Be present. Stress makes us spend all our time reflecting on the past and planning for the future. It means we miss the most important time of all. Try to come into the present and enjoy the magic and beauty of your children as they are today.
- Say 'no' sometimes. There is a temptation to make up for lost time with material goods. This can lead to frustrations on both sides when it becomes impossible to supply all your child's desires.

COMMENT

This passage is written in an information format. Note the informal, almost chatty style of introduction. The layout is clear and unambiguous; all points are signalled and no excessive information is used.

WRITING INSTRUCTIONS

1. Work out exactly what you want to achieve. What is the purpose of the instructions? Are you trying to teach children how to cook, to outline the stages of a game or to instruct people how to operate a machine?
2. Instructions must be clear. Make your statements specific.
3. Make sure there is a logical sequence in the stages of your instructions. Each stage should follow logically from the preceding one.
4. Say one thing in each sentence and make sure your different stages are manageable.

5. Put the most important item in each sentence at the beginning.
6. Use the imperative form of the verb.
7. Use short sentences and short paragraphs.
8. Avoid jargon.

SAMPLE INSTRUCTIONS
Study the layout of the following set of instructions.

Tableware care

Detergents
Many different automatic dishwashing detergents are available. Choosing the correct one is vitally important because some detergents with a high alkaline concentration can cause permanent damage to your tableware. Whenever possible, choose a detergent that can provide a good hygienic result without damaging your tableware and never use more than the recommended quantity.

Temperatures
A washing temperature of 60°C (140°F) is accepted as the most suitable for the effective removal of food particles while minimising the risk of damaging the glaze or decoration. Excessively high temperatures will reduce washing efficiency and may damage your tableware.

Scraping
Use a plastic or rubber scraper to remove food residues. Do not use metal utensils, which can cause marking. Ideally, also spray with water before washing.

Racking
Make sure that racks and baskets are plastic or plastic coated. Replace damaged baskets immediately, as exposed metal will cause marking. Avoid the use of metal scourers. Rack your tableware correctly to ensure that items do not vibrate against each other during the wash cycle. Avoid placing cups of differing heights in the same basket.

Cutlery
Always wash cutlery separately in specially designed cutlery baskets to prevent marking of the tableware.

Microwave ovens
Tableware with metallised decorations, for example gold, is not suitable for use in microwave ovens.

Thermal shock
Ceramic tableware is not designed to withstand thermal shock, so avoid moving your tableware from a freezer to a hot oven or hob, or from a hot oven to a cold surface. Do not place tableware on or near a naked flame.

Staining
If glaze staining is a problem, use a recognised destainer or soak the tableware in a weak solution of bleach or washing soda crystals. Avoid using abrasives to remove staining.

Memos

A memo can be defined as a brief and informal letter. The main differences between a letter and a memo are:
- a memo is informal
- the message is immediate
- memos are written in offices or other workplaces.

In general, both letters and memos involve:
- getting the reader's attention
- making a claim
- supporting the claim by justification or explanation
- calling for action; this may include what you want the reader to do, what you will do or both.

Memos generally explain or outline all details in a short, compact form. Avoid long sentences and pompous words. Use information that is relevant; avoid digressing. Maintain a polite and courteous tone.

MEMO
Use of folders
It appears that manila folders are being used for internal data and for communication with the regional sales offices, when it would be more satisfactory to use paper clips or simply staples on these documents. In the interests of economy it is suggested that for all internal and external mail, wherever practicable, either of the above two methods should be adopted.

COMMENT
This memo is long-winded and redundant. The sentence structure is too long and confusing. Avoid the use of such phrases as 'wherever practicable'.
An alternative version could be written as follows:

The use of folders is costing our company extra money. As an alternative, please staple documents or use paper clips.

Letters

There are different kinds of letters. *Formal letters* include business letters, letters of complaint, job applications, sales letters and letters to the newspaper. *Personal letters* include letters of condolence and letters to a friend or pen-pal.

When writing any kind of letter:
- know what you want to say

- set out your information logically and in paragraph form
- use the correct layout and the correct tone.

Examinations on the writing of letters and memos are testing:
- the coherent organisation of information
- the use of appropriate expression
- accepted standards of layout.

Features of a letter
1. Use the correct layout and make it pleasing to the eye.
2. The sender's address is usually written in the top right-hand corner. (A letter on behalf of an organisation or a company will be on a printed letterheading that includes the name and address.)
3. Write out the date fully, for example, 23 January 2005. All letters must be dated, as they constitute a written record of a transaction.
4. Reference numbers are usually written either above or below the recipient's address.
5. Begin the letter by addressing the person by name or alternatively 'Dear sir/madam'.
6. The first sentence contains the main point of your letter.
7. Conclude your letter with either 'Yours sincerely' or 'Yours truly'. Remember, 'Yours' begins with a capital letter; 'sincerely' has an *e*; 'truly' has no *e*.
8. Use the correct tone for the context. Use a formal, tactful and courteous style, especially if you are conveying unwelcome information.
9. Choose appropriate language. Avoid clichés, wordy statements and jargon. The language should be clear and simple.

How to write a letter
1. Decide what you want to say.
2. Set out your information logically and organise it into paragraphs. In a letter, paragraphs are signposts for the reader that enable him or her to follow your message more clearly.
3. Choose a suitable tone when writing letters. Remember to be factual and not emotional in letters.
4. Use correct spelling and punctuation.
5. Choose the correct vocabulary for the person who is being addressed.
6. Avoid verbose language and clichés. Choose fresh, concise language that is free from jargon.
7. Write the main point of your letter in the first sentence.

Sample letters
Read the following letters, then study the commentary carefully.

LETTER OF APPLICATION FOR A SUMMER JOB

> 14 Moygrave Park
> Cork
>
> 13 May 2006

Mr John Naughton, Personnel Manager
Bel Computers Ltd
Cloneen Industrial Estate
Cork

Dear Mr Naughton,

    I wish to apply for the position of computer operator advertised in the *Cork Examiner* on Thursday last. I am a fifth-year pupil at Crescent Comprehensive College, Cork, where I have just completed a special course in computers. I also spent some time during my transition year working in a computer firm as part of my work experience.

    I feel that I would be capable and proficient in carrying out this job. I would be available to start work from 1 June until September.

    I enclose a copy of my CV and I will supply you with two recent references should you require them. You can contact me by telephone at (021) 6372334.

Yours sincerely,

Neil Dolan

COMMENT

This letter clearly sets out the important details concerning this applicant. The writer makes use of short sentences and short paragraphs, which contributes to making the points striking and clear.

LETTER TO A NEWSPAPER

> 4 Carew Park
> Blakestown
> Killarney
>
> 6 January 2006

Letters to the Editor
Irish Times
11 D'Olier Street
Dublin 2

Dear sir,

    In recent weeks your paper has carried negative articles about Travelling people. As a

Traveller and a member of the Irish Association of Travelling Women, I would like to invite the writers of these articles to live for a week in a Travellers' site so that they can experience for themselves what it means to live without running water, toilets or refuse collection.

Your articles imply that Travellers cause dirt and litter, which they leave to the local authority to clean up. I would challenge the writers to keep a site clean with no bin collections, no running water and no toilets, not to mention settled people dumping their own rubbish in skips on Travellers' sites. Many of these sites are indeed a disgrace, but whose fault is it?

Mr Davis states that Travellers refuse to work, even when there is a labour shortage. I would like them to tell me who will give Travellers a job, when they are followed by security people even as they go innocently into shops.

Finally, Traveller parents have been criticised for making their children beg, subjecting them to 'emotional and physical slavery'. Yes, there is a minority of Traveller children who beg – usually because of severe hardship at home – but anyone passing along any city street knows that the majority of people begging nowadays are settled people and are mostly adults.

It does not befit your paper to allow space for articles and letters such as those of Mr Graham and Ms Moore, which contribute to anti-Traveller prejudice and make the work of Travellers' organisations much harder.

Yours sincerely,

Margaret Rushe

Comment

This letter is a complaint against unjust claims and statements made about Travelling people. The style is clear and to the point. The sentence structure is short and the vocabulary used is precise.

Remember, when writing a letter of complaint you must:
- concentrate clearly on the results you want, rather than on the incompetence of the people involved
- describe your problem clearly without giving way to anger; control of emotion is essential to get the desired result
- keep a record of all contacts and transactions made
- make sure you are complaining to the right person
- keep letters of complaint short.

Notices and bulletins

Notices place the emphasis on layout and attracting the reader's attention through short, catchy phrases and words. Their main aim is to attract the attention of different people. For that reason, their position on a noticeboard must be:
- well positioned for all to see
- big and attractively laid out
- up to date.

Notices are effective only if they produce the results that were intended. For that reason, the language should be vigorous and direct. The presentation should be simple and bold and the message comprehensible to everyone. Keep messages brief. The opening or heading should be an eye-catcher.

> **Learn German – free!**
> If you would like to start learning German, hand in your name to the Personnel Office before Friday, 10 October.
>
> Classes will be held at 6 p.m. in Block D on Tuesdays and Fridays. Classes will last one hour and are free.
>
> **Remember –**
> - you have nothing to pay
> - you can drop out whenever you like if you don't enjoy learning German.
>
> Places are limited! Hand in your name to Mary Dawson *now*.

COMMENT
The information in this notice is reduced to a minimum. The vocabulary is simple and sentence structure and paragraphs are short. The layout makes it eye-catching. Note how two devices from advertising are used:
- the headline, which aims at catching attention
- the appeal to action at the conclusion.

Forms and questionnaires
In filling out forms:
1. Read the instructions carefully and follow them.
2. Leave no part of the form unanswered.
3. Supply all details fully, such as first name and surname, dates of attendance at courses, etc.
4. Where sections do not apply to you, draw a line through them or write *not applicable*.

A *questionnaire* is a document that is circulated in order to obtain information by means of a series of carefully designed questions. This information is then collated and deductions are made about the issues involved.

Sample composition
The following composition is written in the language of information. It is taken from actual pupils' work and is graded according to the standards required at Higher Level. Study it carefully and pay particular attention to the commentary that follows it. The task was: 'Write an informative newspaper article about your home town or parish, concentrating especially on the qualities that make it unique or memorable.'

> Lying south of Limerick rests the parish of Donaghmore. With a present population of approximately 2,600 and an area of 8,500 acres, this parish has evolved over the centuries as one of the most distinctive and distinguished areas of County Limerick.

Since its beginnings as a parish in the thirteenth century, the area has undergone considerable change and its inhabitants have witnessed and participated in some of the important events in local history. From the arrival of St Patrick to this land in the fifth century to the War of Independence in 1921, this parish has contributed greatly to the rich heritage of the south of Ireland.

What makes the chronology of this parish so monumental and atypical has been the consistent involvement in both cultural and sporting activities. Rich architectural features are a striking hallmark of this parish. These bear witness to some of the more impressive changes that have been a constant feature of this region. As you saunter along the road or drive through the narrow laneways, you will see the ancient ruins of castles and churches nestling snugly alongside more modern structures.

This particular parish has played a large part in our history. The Great Famine of 1845 brought about considerable change for the Irish people at that time. Community spirit was at a low ebb, with the brutal reality of emigration rampant everywhere. It is ironic that precisely at a time of profound neediness and suffering the parish managed to construct one of the richest churches in the region, magnificently decorated with some outstanding stained-glass windows and fronting a large and elegant roof – an undoubted architectural achievement!

A singular feature of Famine times was the famous Mass paths, and of course my parish boasts several – those secret paths where many local people stole silently along in early morning time, in spite of the danger involved, and attended their Mass gathered around a rock in a large bare field. Such are the strong remnants of a deep Christian community, which still remain in evidence today.

One of the clearest documented facts is that some people from my parish participated in the Boer War of 1899.

Clearly, some of the most memorable achievements of the people from this region will be in the area of sports. One of the greatest moments in history is recorded on the first Sunday of September 1973, when Éamon Grimes of Rootiagh captained Limerick to win the All-Ireland senior hurling title, a feat that has yet to be repeated by any Limerick man. Undoubtedly this was one of the proudest and most extraordinary events in the lives of many parishioners. Some other strong links in the sporting scene include Dromore Celtic and Glenview FC, which figure predominantly in the Limerick soccer scene. Indeed, my parish is home to one of County Limerick's oldest and most well-established GAA clubs, South Liberties, which has attained numerous trophies over the years.

One of the striking features of some of the buildings bears witness to the existence of that strong feature of Irish educational life, the hedge school. In a corner of a large field lie the ruins of one of the most famous hedge schools in the country, a place that testifies to the eager attempts of the Irish to overcome oppression and struggle to retain some vestige of their identity by keeping the Irish language alive.

No parish would be complete without a focal point for its young people and my parish stands foremost in providing a large hall, which is well endowed with stage and dance floor. Our local group may not be the outstanding rock metallers but they do supply our lively youth with some good entertainment every weekend.

One of the most striking achievements of my community has been the establishment of a strong community centre, situated in the heart of the parish. It is here that the various social and educational activities take place and it is here that many young people find an outlet for their various talents, from tap-dancing to disco dancing, and from community work to teaching arts and crafts.

Spearheaded by some students and a keen drama teacher, Youthbrief, a popular drama group, has set the parish on the map. Not only has this drama group been at the centre of a national festival, but they have managed to entertain the local community on many long winter nights with various performances of *Riders to the Sea* and *The Playboy of the Western World*. This universally popular entertainment has become one of the most organic and dynamic initiatives undertaken in recent years.

In addition, there are voluntary projects that are organised and run by some young people of my parish. These embrace different activities, from visiting the old people, helping with odd jobs and shopping to teaching literacy skills to the local Travelling community.

The community centre provides a rich forum for organising and sustaining these varied activities. Every Saturday the organisers of this community, who work voluntarily, run a disco for young and old alike to finance the different projects. Classes are held every Tuesday and Wednesday morning for all mothers. Here they have an opportunity to develop and improve various skills, from cookery to guitar, to acquiring another language or brushing up an already rusty one. To facilitate their lives, an extension has been added on to the centre where crèche facilities make it easy to relax and enjoy the morning in peace and perhaps engage in gossip and chat about the local news.

There are a host of various activities and areas of interest in this exciting community. This is an area that is characterised by a striking sense of good will, an area that is unique in the support and consolidation offered by its members to the old and disadvantaged. Truly my community is both unique and noteworthy.

COMMENT
Grade: A2
In this piece the writer has structured the information clearly into separate paragraphs, all of which deal with a distinct aspect of the subject. Each of these paragraphs gives a graphic and detailed insight into some particular feature of this parish that makes it noteworthy.

Remember, good informative writing has to be both clear and concise. This composition has hints of a personal touch, which prevent the subject from becoming boring. The whole article is comprehensive – it gives a thorough insight into the more striking features of this community and covers the central aspects of its life. The writer uses a variety of sentence structure and vocabulary to communicate the points effectively. The subject is handled confidently; this is evident in the style, which is smooth flowing and lucid.

Exercises on writing in the language of information

1. You are the secretary of a city youth club. Write a report that you will submit to the Department of Education and Science with an application for a grant. Include details of all the activities of your club and the numbers who attend.
2. You are the manager of a small restaurant. Write a list of instructions for your employees on the procedures to be followed in the event of a fire.
3. You wish to object to an advertisement that you consider to be unsuitable for viewing on television. Write a letter to the Advertising Standards Body clearly setting out your objections.
4. As a journalist for a local newspaper, write a factual report on an All-Ireland rugby match.

THE LANGUAGE OF PERSUASION

The 'language of persuasion' is used by writers to try to influence the way in which a person may think or act. Its primary purpose is to influence how a reader thinks. This is the type of writing that forms the framework of political speeches, advertising writing and marketing.

Persuasion can be achieved in different ways:
- by manipulation
- by appealing to emotions
- by argument.

The language of argument and that of persuasion are quite similar; however, the techniques used in both are distinctive. Because the aim of the persuasive writer is to manipulate feeling and emotion, there is a heavy reliance on emotive vocabulary and on using feeling and emotion to elicit agreement or acquiescence. Persuasive writing can be found in letters, political speeches and addresses, film reviews, some newspaper reports and advertising.

Features of persuasive writing

Because persuasive writing has as its aim convincing you about something, most of the techniques used are directed at the emotions or the senses rather than the intellect. The language of persuasion relies on emotive argument to communicate its message more forcefully to the reader.

All types of persuasive writing use the same tactics. It is worth examining the following features of persuasive writing, in particular in the area of advertising, to persuade or convince:
- slogans
- repetition
- statistics
- imperatives and commands
- rhyming
- rhetorical questions

- buzzwords
- tones.

Slogans

A slogan can be described as a point made without any support, often in the form of a short, punchy phrase. Advertisements usually contain slogans.

> If you ache when you wake ...
> When it pours, we reign.
> You can with a Nissan.
> Every Rolex takes twelve months to make; no wonder time is so valuable.
> When you're healthy on the inside, it shows on the outside.

The purpose of a slogan is to fix an image in your mind, so the writer will use graphic images and perhaps a play on words wherever possible.

Repetition

Repetition is a hallmark of persuasive writing, in particular of advertising.

> Introducing PURE COLOUR nail lacquer with a treat at the House of Fraser.
> Pure impact. Pure luxury. Pure colour. Pure treat.

The following extract from an article on drugs is a clear example of how repetition can be used effectively in persuasive writing:

> We know that good education and good training policies work. We know that strict regulation is much more effective in keeping drugs such as alcohol and tobacco away from children than the anarchic market in illegal drugs has ever been. We know, above all, that what we're doing now is, by any objective standards, a failure so disastrous that no change could ever make things worse.

The repetition of the phrase 'we know' gives a strong and emphatic punch to the ideas here.

Statistics

Statistics are also used by persuasive writers. The use of statistics may lend an air of authority to an otherwise dubious claim.

> A nationwide study by a team of doctors has demonstrated that in 97 per cent of headaches, X works to give relief.
> Up to 80 per cent sleep better on the Tempur mattress.
> Syndol gives relief in half an hour.
> Now 82 per cent of people in the country have opted for the Maxi central heating system.

Imperatives and commands

These are also a feature of persuasive writing. Imperatives demand immediate action:

> Buy now ...

> Use this coupon to send for our free brochure ...
> Send in this form and you will receive ...
> Order today ...
> Pay in the next ten days and you will receive ...
> All you have to do is ...

Rhyming
Very often persuasive writing uses words that rhyme, which can give a sense of movement to the piece of writing.

> A flawless look ... imperceptible, undetectable.
> Firm up your flab in five weeks.

Rhetorical questions
A rhetorical question is one to which an answer is not really expected – the question usually implies the answer and is used merely as a persuasive device.

> Have you problems getting your wash white?
> Would you believe there are bikes that cost more than this car?
> What really kills weeds?
> What gas heating is more simple than ...?
> Why not enjoy life with a Sunrise Scoota?
> What other cereal will provide a better balance of the things your body needs?

Buzzwords
Buzzwords are fashionable, often pseudo-technical terms that are usually meaningless – 'empowerment', 'cyberspace', 'out there', 'in terms of', 'the bottom line'. They are widely used in persuasive writing to impress the reader.

Tones
Tone is the relationship a writer establishes with the reader. It is an important ingredient of effective persuasive writing. A writer wishing to persuade can adopt any number of tones, including:
- humorous
- ironic or satirical
- didactic or instructive
- oratorical.

HUMOROUS TONE
A writer can use humour to illustrate a point, as in the following paragraph about computers:

> Bugs are the usual excuse for computer breakdown, but a London company had a particular problem with rats that liked to eat the insulation around the cables. Rodent exterminators were brought in and laid tubs of poison underneath the floorboards. The

rats just dragged the dishes out of the way to get at the insulation. The ratters then spread special spy-dust, which, instead of laying a trail to the rats' nest, got swept into the air-conditioning system and made the staff sneeze.

The humour here mocks the attempts of humans to deal with computer breakdown.

Ironic tone

Both irony and satire can be used for purposes of ridicule or mockery. Irony can also be used to hammer home a point effectively. In the following paragraph the writer makes clever use of irony to condemn the growth of 'warlords' in eastern European countries:

> Much of the former Yugoslavia is now ruled by warlords. Their vehicle of choice is a four-wheel-drive Cherokee Chief with a policeman's blue light to flash when speeding through a check-point. They pack a pistol but they don't wave it about. They leave vulgar intimidation to the bodyguards in the back, the ones with shades, designer jeans and Zastava machine-pistols. They themselves dress in the leather jackets, floral ties and pressed corduroy trousers favoured by German television producers. They bear no resemblance whatsoever to Rambo. The ones I met at the check-points on the roads of Croatia and Serbia were short, stubby men who in a former life were small-time hoods, small-town cops or both. Spend a day with them touring their world and you'd hardly know that most of them are serial killers.

Satirical tone

In satirical writing the folly of human nature is exposed to ridicule. Dickens possesses the remarkable gift of drawing an exquisitely satirical portrait in some of his characters. The following passage is an example of humorous satire that describes Pip eating his Christmas dinner as a child:

> Among this good company I should have felt myself, even if I hadn't robbed the pantry, in a false position. Not because I was squeezed in at an acute angle of the table-cloth, with the table in my chest and the Pumblechookian elbow in my eye, nor because I was not allowed to speak (I didn't want to speak), nor because I was regaled with the scaly tips of the drumsticks of the fowls and with those obscure corners of pork of which the pig, when living, had had the least reason to be vain. No; I should not have minded that if they would only have left me alone. But they wouldn't leave me alone. They seemed to think the opportunity lost if they failed to point the conversation at me, every now and then, and stick the point into me. I might have been an unfortunate little bull in a Spanish arena, I got so smartly touched up by these moral goads.

(Charles Dickens, *Great Expectations*)

The following description is an example of how character portrayal can be used effectively to gain maximum satirical effect:

> The worst of it was that that bullying old Pumblechook, preyed upon by a devouring

curiosity to be informed of all I had seen and heard, came gaping over in his chaise-cart at tea time, to have the details divulged to him. And the mere sight of the torment, with his fishy eyes and mouth open, his sandy hair inquisitively on end, and his waistcoat heaving with windy arithmetic, made me vicious in my reticence.

The description of Pumblechook's physical appearance is based on a series of small graphic details – 'gaping over in his chaise-cart at tea time', 'fishy eyes', 'mouth open', 'sandy hair inquisitively on end'. The combination of these striking and effective details with a distinct tone of satire makes this piece a splendid example of ironic satire.

Didactic tone
Didactic writing sets out to instruct or teach the reader about something. The writer uses the imperative 'must' or 'have to' and a dogmatic tone in this type of writing.

> I have learned that many people who take astrology seriously were first attracted to the field by reading horoscopes in the newspapers. It is deplorable that so many newspapers now print this daily nonsense. At the start the regular reading is a sort of fun game, but it often ends up as a mighty serious business. The steady and ready availability of astrological 'predictions' can, over many years, have insidious influences on a person's judgment. Faith in astrology and other occult practice is harmful in so far as it encourages an unwholesome flight from the persistent problems of real life. Other solutions must be found by people who suffer from the frustrations of poverty, from grief at the death of a loved one or from fear of economic or personal insecurity.

The purpose of this passage is to persuade the reader against falling victim to astrology. The tone is an explicit condemnation of reliance on astrological predictions. The writer uses a dogmatic tone to point out the fact that faith in such practices results in an unwholesome escape from the problems that are a part of daily life.

Oratorical writing
Oratorical writing is also used by the persuasive writer, though it is more suited to the spoken than to the written word. Some features of this type of writing are:
- a magnificent flow of thought
- the use of rhetorical questions
- a fine command of expressions and language.

Examine the following speech of St John Rivers to Jane Eyre, all in an oratorical tone:

> I am the servant of an infallible master. I am not going out under human guidance, subject to the defective laws and erring control of my feeble fellow-worms: my king, my lawgiver, my captain, is the All-perfect. It seems strange to me that all round me do not burn to enlist under the same banner – to join in the same enterprise.
>
> Humility, Jane, is the groundwork of Christian virtues: you say right that you are not fit for the work. Who is fit for it? Or who that ever was truly called, believed himself worthy of the summons? I for instance am but dust and ashes. With St Paul I acknowledge

myself the chiefest of sinners: but I do not suffer this sense of my personal vileness to daunt me. I know my Leader: that he is just as well as mighty; and while he has chosen a feeble instrument to perform a great task, he will, from the boundless stores of his providence, supply the inadequacy of the means to the end. Think like me, Jane – trust like me. It is the Rock of Ages I ask you to lean on: do not doubt but it will bear the weight of your human weakness.

(Charlotte Brontë, *Jane Eyre*)

In this extract, St John Rivers is urging Jane to leave everything and become his wife out on the missions. The tone is emotive. Examine the use of repetition and rhetorical questions: these are effective rhetorical devices in moving an audience over to your side and are hallmarks of oratorical writing.

The following is an example of a political speech written in an oratorical tone:

Ladies and gentlemen, I would like to talk to you for a moment about the present situation. Never before has this country faced such a crisis and what is now needed is a great deal of courage and honesty. Should we fail to deal with the economic crisis at once, the situation could be disastrous. It is at moments such as this that the true character of a nation shines through. I believe that the right action taken now will resolve the problems that have faced us so menacingly. What we must all realise is that the way ahead is hard and sacrifices must be made, but on no account and in no circumstances must our resolve be shaken. It is obvious that those who do not firmly believe as I do that this is so are mistaken. Were we to act as they suggest we would face a situation from which we might never recover and this must not be allowed to happen. I sincerely hope that you will join with me in saying 'Yes' to what I am proposing, because saying 'No' would mean not only that I was defeated but that I was wrong.

This is an example of a speech that relies for its effect on arousing the emotions of the audience. Note the reliance on emotive vocabulary in the sentence beginning 'Should we fail to deal …'. In oratorical writing there is a certain degree of exaggeration, which is also a hallmark of persuasive writing. Phrases such as 'never before has this country faced such a crisis' and 'were we to act as they suggest' rely for their effect on exaggeration and drama.

Writing in the language of persuasion
A good persuasive writer must be able to:
- express their views clearly and logically
- foresee all possible angles of opposition and be able to tackle them effectively.

Before you begin any type of persuasive composition, be aware of the following points:
- know your audience
- know your subject
- establish the correct tone with your audience
- state your purpose clearly and confidently
- use persuasive techniques.

Know your audience
Have a good knowledge of who your reader or audience is. A rousing talk on drug dependence is hardly likely to stimulate a group of pensioners. Similarly, an excellent article describing the advantages of pension schemes will not attract the attention of a group of teenagers. Identify as clearly as possible who your readers are, what level of knowledge they have about the subject and their motivations and interest in reading the composition. Know what type of persuasion will affect your reader.

The following headlines are taken from different magazines and are written in a persuasive style. Identify the intended audience in each case.

> When pop stars have to talk love, they only talk to their fave mag, *TV Hits*
> They're the cutest twosome in pop – but what makes Marvin and Tamara tick?
> Why we adore Dior

These headlines are obviously taken from magazines that are aimed at young people. Naturally this type of approach could not be adopted in an educational publication or a medical journal.

Know your subject
It makes no sense to start writing about something you know nothing about, particularly when you are trying to persuade somebody to adopt your viewpoint. Consider the following two paragraphs on how fashion in clothes is the deliberate creation of waste:

> Fashion today is nothing more than creating a lot of waste. People buy clothes they do not need and so waste them. This is particularly the case with women, because they are in a sense more slaves of fashion than men. Thus clothes designers produce new designs each year and they in turn contribute to this development of waste.

There is very little in this argument that will make you adopt any serious viewpoint. On the other hand, look at the following passage on the same theme:

> Over the years, the great majority of men have successfully resisted all attempts to make them change their style of dress. The same cannot be said for women. Each year a few so-called top designers in Paris or London lay down the law and women the whole world over rush to obey. The decrees of the designers are unpredictable and dictatorial. This year they decide, in their arbitrary fashion, that skirts will be short and waists will be high; zips are in and buttons are out. Next year the law is reversed, and far from taking exception, no one is even mildly surprised.
>
> If women are mercilessly exploited year after year, they have only themselves to blame. Because they shudder at the thought of being seen in clothes that are out of fashion, they are annually blackmailed by the designers and the big stores. Clothes that have been worn only a few times have to be discarded because of the dictates of fashion. When you come to think of it, only a woman is capable of standing in front of a wardrobe packed full of clothes and announcing sadly that she has nothing to wear. Changing fashions are nothing more than the deliberate creation of waste. Many women squander

vast sums of money each year to replace clothes that have hardly been worn. Women who cannot afford to discard clothing in this way waste hours of their time altering the dresses they have. Hemlines are taken up or let down; waislines are taken in or let out; necklines are lowered or raised and so on.

The writer here gives examples to support the argument and the examples chosen are graphic and relevant. Remember to research your subject before beginning the process of writing.

Establish the correct tone with your audience
Once you have identified your audience, adapt your message and tone accordingly. You cannot use a lofty or philosophical tone with a group of schoolchildren; neither can you use a colloquial tone in a speech to the board of management of your school. Similarly, do not use formal language if you are writing on pop music for a teenage magazine.

It can help sometimes to introduce a note of humour or irony into your writing in order to gain the attention of your reader more readily.

State your purpose clearly and confidently
Outline clearly in your opening paragraph what your intention is.

Use persuasive techniques
Some examples can be the use of effective images or anecdotes to support your viewpoint. These can also serve the function of arousing certain emotions about your topic in readers and getting them on your side.

The following paragraphs are an excellent example of how humour and the anecdote work together to communicate a point effectively:

> As everyone knows, 'getting away from it all' involves a lot more than just physical distance. For me, though, it has to be shoes: one hint of even the shortest weekend break and I feel I should get into shoes so comfortable I could conceivably sleep in them. I have a particular antipathy to flat shoes because the stupid things make me feel short, fat and flat footed.
>
> This antipathy to flatties took on a more sinister note on a recent trip to Galway, when, as usual, I took the first, quavering step to really relaxing by donning my old school trainers. They're made of canvas with three bright blue stripes and they're flatter than a glass of Seven-Up left in the sun. They go down very well in trendy night clubs and at casual brunches in friends' back gardens when everyone usually has a good chat about how they don't make trainers like that any more. This is all very well, but after two days of short wanders to the beach and back to the pub I was practically bed-ridden, with legs bent like nutcrackers. It didn't take an Einstein or even a Dr Scholl to work out that this complete seizure in the leg department was the result of wearing flat shoes for the first time in – oh, dear – seven years. The tendons in my calves were used to being made tight by two inches of heel and were complaining loudly about being stretched to their natural length.

The writer of this passage uses a familiar and homely vocabulary that is accessible to the ordinary reader. The humorous tone makes it a lively piece of writing. The writer also varies the structure of the sentences.

Remember
Bear in mind the following guidelines when writing a persuasive composition or article.
1. Avoid making sweeping statements or vague and broad generalisations, such as:

   All pupils suffer from extreme examination pressure.
   All governments are corrupt.
   All teenagers take drugs.
   All women are victims.

2. Don't make unsupported statements. Support each point you make with sufficient evidence or effective illustrations.
3. Avoid using an aggressive or bitter tone, as it will only alienate your reader.
4. Don't distort the truth. While a certain amount of hyperbole or exaggeration is permissible in persuasive writing, it is never acceptable to distort or pervert the truth or to tell a lie in your writing.

Sample composition

The following passages are written in the language of persuasion. They are taken from actual pupils' work and are graded according to the standards required at Higher Level. Study them carefully and pay particular attention to the commentary that follows.

The task here was: 'Write a persuasive article for a teenage magazine on the subject of dieting and weight.'

> **Lighten up – you'll never get stuck in the aisle**
> You're walking down the aisle of a crowded bus and straight ahead you see the last vacant seat. Approaching it in slow motion, you realise that there are steel bars on each side of the seat. Everyone is watching as you sit down. Squeezing against the bars of the seat are your bulges of fat and they're multiplying by the second. Wide-eyed passengers point and stare as you struggle to get out of your seat and walk back down the aisle in sheer terror. Oh, the relief when the alarm wakes you up to the Divine Comedy's 'National Express'.
>
> A few weeks ago our transition-year class in St Jude's was busily discussing ideas for our magazine, *Voice from the Well*. We all got distracted and started to talk about weight. Within minutes we were heatedly deploring the emaciated appearance of Monica in *Friends*.
>
> Women through the ages have wasted their time worrying about their weight and their appearance and I think it's about time we confronted our fears. We might feel tempted to blame anorexic actors, gaunt girl-groups or the supercilious models of today for making size six a figure. We could say that women's magazines are the cause of such mass misery, bombarding us as they do with revolutionary diets that just don't work. But the simple truth is that women were concerned about their weight and appearance long before such things even existed.

According to a tour guide in Bath, a lift built to honour Queen Victoria in one of the finest hotels in the city made no difference to her lifestyle. She overheard a peasant saying something like 'Oh, my goodness, would you look at the Queen's flat ankles', and she fled the city in a huff, never to return. I can't help but feel a little sympathy for the petulant queen because, in the words of Julian Browne, obesity is a condition that proves that the Lord does not help those who help themselves.

Imagine having to ask your sister to help you crush your lower chest cavity with a corset every morning and you would wonder how any woman could ever have inflicted those elephant-tusks of discomfort on herself. Yet women once chanced breaking the odd rib to gain some control of their figure.

Today dieting seems to have replaced the corset. After all, it takes a lot of self-discipline to stick to a diet consisting of a rice cake for breakfast, a cup of tea for lunch and no dinner at all. Lots of women would be quite happy to be a little less pear shaped, but successful control freaks, like Courtney Cox and Calista Flockhart, go much further and, not surprisingly, have been accused of being anorexic.

Scientists have proved that a woman with Barbie Doll proportions could not survive, yet many women strive for what they see as perfection.

'All the other reindeer used to laugh and call him names …' If you ever really thought about that jolly Christmas song, you'd realise that it isn't so jolly after all. You might even say that Rudolph epitomises our cultural over-emphasis on physical appearance. Poor old Rudolph was stigmatised for having a red nose and was accepted only when it dawned on the other reindeer that he might come in handy because of it. Being fat is also highly stigmatised and women tend to use their weighing scales to evaluate their physical attractiveness. The average female was dismayed when *Titanic* star Kate Winslet was described as 'too fat to be attractive'.

On groggy-eyed days, when you sit sluggishly at the back of the classroom and feel your hair, you suddenly realise that the strange shampoo you used that morning must have been conditioner. Then you feel as if you had poured petrol over yourself before coming to school. And just as you were forgetting about your facial volcanoes you're asked to analyse the Prince of Morocco's line in *The Merchant of Venice* – 'Mislike me not for my complexion.' By the time you get home and collapse in front of the telly nauseated with self-pity you're simply in no form for irritating Special K advertisements.

If you compare yourself with others you may become vain and bitter, for, as the 'Desiderata' says, 'there will always be greater and lesser persons than yourself.' You might never be a Naomi Campbell or a Kate Moss, but the chances are too that you'll never realise your recurring nightmare and make headlines for getting stuck in the aisle of a bus. I suggest that we all lighten up and become more like Rudolph. Do something useful, like buying a nice cream bun. Perhaps some shops and bakeries might even think of putting up a little sign saying 'Thank you for not dieting.'

COMMENT

Grade A2

This is a witty and light-hearted piece of writing on the topic of weight and dieting. The opening anecdote is entertaining and catches the reader's attention immediately.

The language and style are both vibrant and humorous. There are some light-hearted yet clever hints of satire and sarcasm. The examples that are used are familiar and topical. There is clear identification of the audience – the article is written for a teenage magazine and the examples and illustrations used are interesting and relevant. There is an energy and vibrancy in the ideas presented; it is clear that the writer is enthusiastic about the topic. The writer here seems to be very much in control of her subject at every stage. The writing is immediate and accessible, as the writer constantly addresses the reader.

Perhaps some of the references could be developed in more detail and depth to gain that higher mark. Also, the narrative moves on a bit too abruptly at times.

For the next composition, the task was: 'Compose a persuasive composition that seeks to establish the need for greater awareness of sex stereotyping today.'

> Mam is cooking the evening meal. She glances at the saucepans every now and then as she runs the cloth over the kitchen work-top. This completed, she picks up the sweeping-brush. All this time, Father sits in his armchair, gazing with glassy eyes at the television screen. He hasn't moved from his cosy sanctuary for hours. He and the armchair have become one, as if he had been melted into it in a liquid state and now they are inseparable. As my mother runs the brush over the floor, she protests feebly about the noises coming from the television. A typical scene on a Saturday in my house!
>
> Suddenly, in a feat of incredible athletic ability, my father springs from his chair and dives for the television. (The remote control is broken and he hasn't got around to fixing it.) He reaches the mute button in less than one second and before my eyes have become adjusted to the sight of him actually out of his chair he is seated comfortably again. 'I hate that advertisement,' he declares in disgust. 'I'm sick of this incessant campaign against men. We're just as capable as women and I'm tired of being told otherwise.'
>
> It could be one of a range of advertisements running at the moment that irritate my father – the advertisements that suggest that men can do housework only with this wonderful product and should do so to seek approval from women; an advertisement that features a woman spelling out the slogan 'So simple even he can do it'; an advertisement that depicts utter chaos when Father is looking after the house and only with the return of the female is order restored.
>
> These advertisements are nothing less than harmful. Women have been so oppressed and victimised in the past that now it seems we have veered too much to the other extreme. Now, marketing strategies base their tactics on portraying an image of a highly effective, highly capable woman, not realising that this excessive portrayal of supposed outstanding female talent runs the risk of undermining the male counterpart. Sex stereotyping still exists, in however subtle a form, and it is imperative that this issue is recognised and addressed as such.
>
> Sex stereotyping affects us all, whether we realise it or not. As may be deduced from my earlier anecdotal reference, my parents fit neatly into this category of male and female stereotypes as depicted by the media. My mother does most of the cleaning and housework, while my father carries out the 'male' jobs, such as washing the car and fixing

whatever is broken. Although, genetically speaking, my father would be as capable of vacuuming and cleaning sinks as my mother, it is not difficult to see how this situation has evolved.

From birth they have been assaulted with images that subtly engrave on their consciousness certain ideas about the different roles of males and females in society. Who can blame them for their actions when they have experienced such brainwashing? My parents are certainly not alone in this. Can you think of a single household in which there are no preconceived notions about male and female roles? I certainly cannot. While many people may recognise the inanity and prejudice underlying such advertisements, there are other, more subtle methods that consolidate this attitude. Take, for example, the famous *Simpsons,* a programme that is watched by multitudes, both old and young, every night of the week. This programme is a key example of sex stereotyping in its depiction of an intelligent and hard-working daughter and a lazy, troublesome and intellectually challenged son. The long-suffering mother is more intelligent than her husband and looks after all the housework and child care. This type of presentation is more insidious, as it adopts a simple and fairly unassuming story line and cleverly uses the medium of comedy to communicate its content.

It is my firm belief that sex stereotyping is one of the greatest sources of friction between males and females in our society. Every person, whether male or female, holds some preconceived ideas about the opposite sex, whether they realise it or not. These prejudices on both sides sometimes lead to conflict and an unspoken agreement that it is the duty of all women to join together in hostility against men. Men feel compelled to defend their position and 'band together' against women. American chat shows illustrate how prominent this male-female conflict has become in American society. It is hardly surprising that the divorce rate in America is the highest in the world and this is enough to provide ample evidence for the link between sex stereotyping in society and the damage done to male-female relations.

In the world of sport the damage done by sex stereotyping is once again in evidence. Society puts such pressure on both men and women to conform that people may become afraid to seek the job they truly want. Male nurses and female mechanics need to be strong individuals to deal with the inevitable mockery and harassment they will receive as a result of their career choice.

Sex stereotyping is a problem that must be addressed fully. In an age such as ours it is disturbing to think that we cannot behave as we please or choose whatever career we wish because of the reproductive organs we were born with. Both males and females must face their different strengths and limitations squarely and sincerely and try to transcend all the pressures to behave in a particular way. Since the mass media seem to be one of the main methods through which this attitude towards males and females springs, the problem needs to be remedied within this context. Media programmes and presentations of these issues must broaden the scope of their research and work at depicting a wider vision of the different roles of both males and females.

COMMENT
Grade B1
This composition is an example of an organised piece of writing that is clearly constructed into different paragraphs, all of which keep to the topic throughout. The writer's enthusiasm for the subject is evident from the lively and rather witty style. The writer also makes use of some current examples and illustrations from the media to support the statements made. However, as is typical of a lot of young people's writing, many very generalised statements are made, for example, 'Women have become so oppressed and victimised in the past that now it seems we have veered too much to the other extreme.' Remember that facts must be supported at all times by clear examples or statistics.

Exercises on writing in the language of persuasion
1. Write a short, persuasive article for a local newspaper on the value of having sport as a compulsory part of the curriculum. Aim your article at a general readership.
2. Compose a persuasive article for a popular magazine on the topic 'Is it now time for men's liberation?'
3. Compose a persuasive composition for a teenage magazine that seeks to establish the need for a greater degree of selectivity in the viewing of television programmes.
4. Write out an advertisement for your favourite make-up, aiming it at members of your own class. In the advertisement include price, special offers and the imperative use of language.
5. Write a persuasive letter to a local newspaper about ways in which the environment could be kept cleaner.

THE AESTHETIC USE OF LANGUAGE

This section deals with the way in which language can be used to create an aesthetic effect in writing to create concepts of beauty and harmony through the use of words that add up to striking images of things. The emphasis here is on the use of language as an artistic or creative medium.

Writing in which language can be used aesthetically includes fiction, drama, films, and poetry.

Features of the aesthetic use of language
1. The use of imagery: the capacity of words to create pictures. Imagery can also be defined as word pictures; it is the way a writer uses words to conjure up a picture or image of something. Imagery is the basis of all writing, but in particular in the writing of poetry, drama, certain types of fiction and, in a different manner, in films.
2. A stress on how language can be used in an artistic way.
3. The different ways in which words can be used to create concepts of beauty and harmony.

Read the following descriptive passage, then study the commentary that follows.

> Smoke was rising here and there among the creepers that festooned the dead or dying trees. As they watched, a flash of fire appeared at the root of one wisp, and then the smoke thickened. Small flames stirred at the bole of a tree and crawled away through leaves and brushwood, dividing and increasing. One patch touched a tree trunk and scrambled up like a bright squirrel. The smoke increased, sifted, rolled outwards. The squirrel leapt on the wings of the wind and clung to another standing tree eating downwards. Beneath the dark canopy of leaves and smoke the fire laid hold on the forest and began to gnaw. Acres of black and yellow smoke rolled steadily towards the sea. At the sight of the flames and the irresistible course of the fire, the boys broke into shrill, excited cheering. The flames, as though they were a kind of wild life, crept as a jaguar creeps on its belly towards a line of birch-like saplings that fledged an outcrop of the pine rock. They flapped at the first of the trees, and the branches grew a brief foliage of fire. The heart of flame leapt nimbly across the gap between the trees and then went swinging and flaring along the whole row of them. Beneath the capering boys a quarter of a mile square of forest was savage with smoke and flame. The separate noises of the fire merged into a drum-roll that seemed to shake the mountain.
>
> (William Golding, *Lord of the Flies*)

COMMENT

This passage is highly dramatic and vivid. The effect here is achieved through a series of energetic verbs and vocabulary: 'a flash of fire appeared', 'the smoke increased, sifted, rolled outwards'. The writer is intent on conveying movement and energy. Through the expert combination of certain techniques, such as the use of intense imagery, splendid descriptions and energetic language, he paints a highly effective image of the whole scene.

Now look at the following extract, which has many examples of the figurative use of language:

> As the sun set, its light slowly melted the landscape, till everything was made of fire and glass. Released from the glare of noon, the haycocks seemed to float on the aftergrass: their freshness penetrated the air. In the far distance, hills with woods up their flanks lay in light like hills in another world – it would be a pleasure of heaven to stand up there, where no foot ever seemed to have trodden, on the spaces between the woods soft as powder dusted over with gold. Against those hills, the burning red rambler roses in cottage gardens along the roadside looked earthy – they were too near the eye.
>
> The road was in Ireland. The light, the air from the distance, the air of evening rushed transversely through the open sides of the car. The rims of the hood flapped, the hood's metal frame rattled as the tourer, in great bounds of speed, held the road's darkening magnetic centre streak. The big shabby family car was empty but for its small driver – its emptiness seemed to levitate it – on its back seat a coat slithered about, and a dressing case bumped against the seat. The driver did not relax her excited touch on the wheel: now and then while she drove she turned one wrist over, to bring the watch worn on it into view, and she gave the mileage marked on the yellow signposts a flying, jealous, half-

inadvertent look. She was driving parallel with the sunset: the sun slowly went down on her right hand.

(Elizabeth Bowen, 'Summer Night')

COMMENT

This is a splendid example of how language can be used in a highly creative and aesthetic fashion. In the extract, the writer gives us some beautiful images of nature. Note, for example, her reference to colour: 'everything was made of fire and glass', 'the woods soft as powder dusted over with gold', the 'burning red rambler roses'. All the images used are rich and sensuous and serve the function of painting a powerfully clear picture of an Irish landscape in summer.

The following extract, from the verse play *Murder in the Cathedral,* is a good example of how language can be used aesthetically:

Chorus:
Numb the hand and dry the eyelid,
Still the horror, but more horror
Than when tearing in the belly.
Still the horror, but more horror
Than when twisting in the fingers,
Than when splitting in the skull.
More than footfall in the passage,
More than shadow in the doorway,
More than fury in the hall.
The agents of hell disappear, the human, they shrink and dissolve
Into dust on the wind, forgotten, unmemorable; only is here
The white flat face of Death, God's silent servant,
And behind the face of Death the Judgment,
And behind the Judgment the Void,
more horrid than active shapes of Hell;
Emptiness, absence, separation from God;
The horror of the effortless journey, to the empty land
Which is no land, only emptiness, absence, the Void,
Where those who were men can no longer turn the mind
To distraction, delusion, escape into dream, pretence;
Where the soul is no longer deceived, for there are no objects, no tones,
No colours, no forms to distract, to divert the soul
From seeing itself, foully united for ever, nothing with nothing,
Not what we call death but what beyond death is not death
We fear, we fear. Who shall then plead for me,
Who intercede for me, in my most need?

(T. S. Eliot, *Murder in the Cathedral*)

COMMENT
This passage is written in a highly poetic style, which is also a feature of the language of aesthetics. The vocabulary is rich and poetic; images are lyrical and emphatic. The writer uses splendid and fluid rhythms, together with effective repetition, to conjure up some frightening images of Hell and loss.

Writing in the language of aesthetics
The ability to write in order to demonstrate the aesthetic quality of language involves a capacity to use images. Language that is aesthetic is rich in beautiful imagery and description. Learn the art of writing description well. Good descriptive writing concentrates on giving a clear, vibrant picture. Good description concentrates on involving all the senses.

Method of writing descriptive composition
1. Select details of what you are describing with great care and concentrate on registering a few small points.
2. Be selective in what you write about when describing. Do not include every feature, but concentrate on one or two.
3. Refer to location in some way. This can be the geographical context, the country or region, the landscape or the time, season or historical period.
4. Remember, effective imagery is created through the association of words. This can be achieved by:
   - similes, metaphors or rhythm
   - direct description.
5. Use images and language that appeal to the different senses. Visual images can include features of colour or shape and size. The use of images that appeal to the ear create a deep and lasting impression on your reader.

> The scullery was water, where the old pump stood. And it had everything else that was related to water: thick steam of Mondays edgy with starch; soapsuds boiling, bellying and popping, creaking and whispering, rainbowed with light and winking with a million windows. Bubble bubble toil and grumble, rinsing and slapping of sheets and shirts, and panting Mother rowing her red arms like oars in the steaming waves. Then the linen came up out of the pot like pastry or woven suds or sheets of moulded snow.

The effect of this description is to conjure up a vivid picture of the scullery and how the washing was done. The writer draws on all the senses – the sense of smell by the starch and the soapsuds and the sense of touch in the references to slapping the sheets and 'rowing her red arms like oars in the steaming waves.'

Describing people
The ability to draw effective description of character requires:
- drawing an image of their inner character, motivations, moods or situation
- painting a picture of the background, age, professional situation or emotional state.

Sometimes a writer will use the actions of a character or their particular environment to depict internal dispositions.

> Towards the end of her day in London Mrs Drover went round to her shut-up house to look for several things she wanted to take away. Some belonged to herself, some belonged to her family, who were by now used to their country life. It was late August; it had been a steamy showery day: at the moment the trees down the pavement glittered in an escape of humid yellow afternoon sun. Against the next batch of clouds, already piling up ink-dark, broken chimneys and parapets stood out. In her once familiar street, as in any unused channel, an unfamiliar queerness had silted up; a cat wove itself in and out of railings, but no human eye watched Mrs Drover's return. Shifting some parcels under her arm, she slowly forced round her latchkey in an unwilling lock, then gave the door, which was warped, a push with her knee. Dead air came out to meet her as she went in.
> (Elizabeth Bowen, 'The Demon Lover')

The following passages show how language can be used in an aesthetic way. They are taken from actual pupils' work and are graded according to the standards required at Higher Level. Study them carefully and pay particular attention to the commentary that follows.

The first assignment was: 'Compose an imaginative series of reflections on the topic "autumn".'

> September and October can be the very worst months of the year. Look at the weather: rain, wind, mist and damp; wind blowing in relentlessly from the Atlantic, heralding the first onslaughts of winter. Fog and mist roll in and sometimes for days on end the countryside is enveloped in a thick blanket of grey. It clings to river banks, shrouds mountain tops, nestles in valleys and between the folds of hills. It deadens sound, obscures sight and creates an eerie, ghostly atmosphere.
>
> There is dampness everywhere. On walls! On windows! On floors! Housewives become irritated and drivers frustrated as the damp of their windscreens lessens visibility. There is mud and mire on city paths and country lanes and as you walk you hear the squelch as the water and mud ooze up around your shoes. Old people tread warily as all around 'moist green leaves rest in rotting rust.' Everywhere shoes make a lovely crunching, crackling, rustling, popping sound as you walk on the carpet of leaves underfoot.
>
> Then again you may awake some October morning and the world appears transformed. You swish back your curtains and lo! you look out into a dazzling world, your eye marvels at the dizzy blue sky overhead and here and there scattered in the high dome of the heavens, clouds like puffballs and torn tufts of cotton-wool glide lazily in the vast expanse of blue. You open your front door and your eye is assaulted and bombarded with glowing, jewel-bright colours. What colour! Hedgerows, wood ditches, forests and fields are clothed in a glorious array of colour: vivid orange, fiery reds, bright yellows, garish mustards, dull browns and sombre black.
>
> Trees, shrubs, flowers are now beginning to wear a tattered, forlorn look. They are no longer clothed in the glossy, green, luxuriant foliage of high summer. Trees are taking a

gaunt, skeletal look as they raise brittle, bare branches to the sky. Ominous-looking brown and black spots are appearing like some malignant disease on the ripe blooms of roses and flowers. Leaves look as if they are sickening for some fatal disease: they shrivel up, become crisper and crisper and then in the first gales of autumn flutter gently to the ground, yielding up their fragile, tenuous hold on life and lie decaying on the ground.

   Meanwhile, frenzied and feverish preparations go on in both the animal and the human world. Take a walk in your local woods – but tread carefully. Move stealthily through the undergrowth and you may see a sudden flash and a brown bushy tail belonging to a busy squirrel who is hurriedly scuttling out of your way as he clutches a pawful of nuts. You may hear a rustling sound and lo! you may see a mole or badger digging out their winter home in preparation for hibernation. Look overhead and your eye will marvel at the sight of birds congregating on wires, twittering excitedly in anticipation of their annual winter holiday when they migrate to sunny southern climates.

   In cosy country kitchens filled with a smell of turf, plump, bustling housewives are sweating as they bend over hot stoves making delicious jams, pickles, mouth-watering pies and potent wines and ales and reminding us only too well of those vivid words of Shakespeare, 'and greasy Joan doth keel the pot.' Out in the straw-strewn farmyard the red-faced farmer is busy bringing in the last of the crops. In both town and country, young folk with long, doleful faces are making last-minute and begrudging preparations for returning to school.

COMMENT
Grade: B1
This article is written in an imaginative and highly descriptive style. There is a strong emphasis on describing colour, movement and shape, which is a hallmark of good, effective description. Some of the images used are rich and sensuous.

AREAS FOR DEVELOPMENT
The opening of this composition is a bit too obvious. Openings have to be dynamic and arresting for the reader. There is an atmosphere of 'purple prose' throughout, a conscious striving for effect, giving the whole piece an unnatural air.

   Perhaps the writer could concentrate on developing the description in more detail. Concentrating on the lives of people would perhaps broaden the scope and develop the theme in greater detail. The conclusion needs to be developed in more detail and depth, as it is a bit too abrupt and flat and a little disappointing.

The next passage is from an aesthetic composition on the topic 'Memories'.

'Children of the sun'
The black nannies congregated on the corner of Gillian Road, shouting out greetings of 'Sanibonai' and 'Ngikhona' in their loud, cheerful voices. The coarse sound of their voices was softened by the beautiful musical lilt of their language. Their vibrant exclamations hovered on the still hot air and their infectious laughter lingered over the neighbourhood.

   Faint echoes of the carefree chatter floated out over the vast, dry, empty land in front and were carried downwards over the gently sloping field of burnt dry tufts of grass, which crackled underfoot, and sand of almost the same yellowish-brown shade, until they reached the river. The gurgle of the deep brown water mimicked the buoyant giggles and the hadida bird's call from above echoed across the vlei. Children's playful shouting and a dog's excited barking reverberated among the cloud-like rocks bordering the river. Two bluish-white trees, though quite bare, provided the only source of shade from the blazing sun. But the refreshing sound of flowing water made the sun's crude heat more bearable.

The only refuge from a scorching midday sun was beneath the cool, clear blue waters of a swimming pool. Happy and carefree children screamed in delight while splashing around in the water, duck-diving and dodging the bees and wasps that hovered on the surface. Around the edge of the pool, steam rose from the slabs of slate, roasting any feet that ventured out of the pool.

Towards early afternoon little brown bodies lay glistening in the sun, stretched out on towels, shivering with warmth and with the ticklish feeling as each tiny droplet evaporated.

But peace and serenity did not last long. Sharp ears perked up as the familiar tinkling tune of the ice cream man drifted through the air. And the legs that had been stretched out in the sun sprang to life in anticipation. Money in shrivelled hands and children in swimming costumes with stringy wet hair ran barefoot down the driveway in glee. And it didn't matter that the ice creams melted before they reached their mouths or that the raspberry sauce dropped down onto bronzed feet and made their toes stick together. The children walked slowly back up the driveway, heads bent forward in an attempt to catch as much of the liquid as possible. They sat on the patio's stone steps licking the ice creams, with dots of white on their noses and red sauce smeared around their mouths, happy and content.

Even when empty, the patio held all the voices and memories of the neighbourhood. It was a place where many stories had been told, jokes shared and tears shed. Overlooking the swimming pool and surrounded by luscious green tropical plants, its cold stone floor and cool shade were both refreshing and relaxing. Out in front, the garden sloped down towards the road, bordered on one side by a tall white wall and on the other by the long driveway running adjacent to a boundary of trees, plants and hedges.

Once darkness fell, the lush flowerbeds, trees and shrubs provided an ideal place for 'tip the lantern' and, starting from the bottom of the garden, the children tried to sneak their way up to the top beside the patio without being seen. Scrapes and bruises on bare legs and arms were ignored as little bodies wormed their way through soil and plants like camouflaged snakes.

The rustle of shrubs was covered up by the shrill of the crickets, whose sound was so constant that it was forgotten but would be missed if absent.

Gay chatter drifted across from the adults around the candle-lit patio table, where they still sat hours after the braai was over. Floating candles on the pool created a magical glow and the warm night was softly scented with the mingled fragrances of sweet pea and honeysuckle.

Life revolved around nature and the outdoors. Trees, plants, bushes and shrubbery provided innumerable playgrounds. A forest of tall bamboo supplied rich, cool shade and a soft leafy floor for exhausted children and an ideal storage place for caterpillars in shoe boxes, waiting for them to spin cocoons.

Long scrape marks on the syringa barks all over the neighbourhood marked the struggles of scratched legs' attempts to overcome the initial challenge of the bare tree trunk, before climbing through green leaves and rough branches. The tall sky-rockets were much easier to climb, for the thick coniferous foliage started at ground level. But a challenge was always welcomed and syringas, with their beautiful, sweet-smelling pink flowers, had better-shaped branches for tree-houses.

Grubby children solemnly collected wood, planks and ropes from old compost heaps and fields full of shoulder-height yellow grass. They emerged laden with precious materials and covered in blackjacks. Planks of wood were wedged between branches and tied meticulously, and gradually the tree-houses were erected. These were the sites of many tree parties and secret nocturnal meetings when even the crickets were asleep.

The silent whispers in this magical land of the large trees at night was a stark contrast to the shouting of children at play on the road during the day. BMX bikes skidded in the earth, sending up clouds of dust behind them. The bikes, which were once brightly coloured and shiny, were now almost indistinguishable from one another, for each was coated in the same layer of dry brown dust.

A stranger could not tell which children belonged where, for wooded stiles, built by the gardeners, provided easy access for barefoot children from garden to garden. Sandy children with messy hair, skimpy clothing and dirty bottoms scrambled in all directions.

But every Monday afternoon they all headed in the same direction, muttering Bible verses under their breath that should have been learned over the past week. Children from even further afield than Gillian Road came to Good News Club, and the competition for a perfect memory verse record and the ultimate prize was tough.

But behind all the competitiveness, the love shown and taught among friends and neighbours shone back through the glowing eyes of their happy children.

COMMENT
Grade: A1

This is a highly original piece of writing and approach to the topic. The images and language are vivid and poetic, all of which are strong features of the aesthetic use of language. The whole composition is clearly punctuated with its striking emphasis on colour, sounds and smells. There are some splendid touches of poetry, for example, the sibilance in the lines 'around the edge of the pool, steam rose from the slabs of slate, roasting any feet.' The imagery used is varied, rich and sensuous: 'little brown bodies lay glistening in the sun, shivering with warmth.'

This passage is written to emphasise how language can be used in an aesthetic manner. For that reason the subject matter does not have to be developed or analysed in a deep or weighty manner; instead there is a heavy reliance on the aesthetic use of language, harmony, the use of images, sound patterns and poetic touches.

Exercises on writing in the language of aesthetics

1. Write a descriptive article for a holiday magazine on a city scene preparing for a new millennium.
2. Compose a sketch or dramatic scene for a play on any topic you are interested in. Concentrate on drawing out specific features of the characters you are presenting.
3. Write a poem or a short story, paying particular attention to the use of imagery or description, on any scene from country life or nature that has impressed you.
4. Write a series of diary entries on your experiences in settling in another country.

6
Samples of Paper I with Model Answers

STRUCTURE OF PAPER I

Study the following samples of Paper I. They follow the same layout as the examination at Higher Level. In each paper there are four different comprehension texts. Some of these texts may include a photograph or an advertisement. Each text is followed by a number of questions, which correspond to the type of questions that will be asked in the examination.

Suggested answers are provided for the comprehension questions on each text (see pages 127–50). The purpose of these answers is to suggest a method of approaching a particular question. None of these answers are definitive – a variety of approaches may be adopted.

To improve your technique in answering comprehension questions, try answering the questions yourself first, then compare your own answers with the suggested answers provided.

PAPER I
Time allowed: 2½ hours.
- This paper is divided into two sections: Section I COMPREHENDING and Section II COMPOSING.
- This paper contains *four* texts on a general theme.
- Both sections of this paper (COMPREHENDING and COMPOSING) must be attempted.
- Each section carries 100 marks.

Section I: Comprehending
(100 marks)
- Read each of the texts carefully a number of times.

- Two questions, A and B, follow each text.
- You must answer a Question A on one text and a Question B on a different text. You must answer only one Question A and only one Question B. These questions carry equal marks.
- N.B. You may NOT answer a Question A and a Question B on the same text.

Section II: Composing
(100 marks)
Write a composition on *any one* of the topics provided.

The composition assignments are intended to reflect language study in the areas of information, argument, narration and the aesthetic use of language.

FIRST SAMPLE PAPER: CULTURE AND TRENDS

This paper contains *four* texts on the general theme of culture and trends.

Section I: Comprehending
(100 marks)

Text 1

Vitamin pills increase the risk of lung cancer and heart disease among smokers, according to a report to be published by the World Health Organization (WHO). The claim – which concerns tablets that contain beta-carotene, a form of vitamin A – will shock millions of smokers who believe that popping the pills can prevent cancer and limit the damaging effects of their habit.

The warning follows an international meeting in Lyon at which scientists agreed that non-smokers who take beta-carotene pills and related carotenoid supplements in the hope of preventing cancer are probably wasting their money.

Dr Harri Vainio of the International Agency for Research on Cancer, a WHO body comprising twenty-three experts from ten countries, said: 'Our group came to the conclusion that, until further information becomes available on how beta-carotene and other carotenoids influence the processes leading to cancer, none of these substances should be promoted to the general population as a tumour-preventive treatment.'

Beta-carotene, the best known of the six hundred identified carotenoids, is a pigment that gives colour to many foods, including carrots, apricots and oranges. It is also present in dark-green leafy vegetables.

QUESTION A
1. Identify the writer's purpose in this passage. Does the writer succeed in achieving this purpose? Make reference to the passage to support your answer.
2. What type of readership is targeted in this piece of writing? Support your answer by reference to the passage itself.

Question B

Write an original and witty article for a popular teenage magazine on the subject 'We are what we wear.'

Text 2

Hellfire and hyperdrive: the Gospel according to *Star Wars*

'I am trying to bring up my children with Jedi values' – so wrote an earnest Christian recently in a discussion on an internet site devoted to modern culture. The combination of Christianity and *Star Wars* may seem one of the more bizarre bits of merchandising in the hype around *The Phantom Menace*, but now a Methodist university chaplain in Liverpool has written an entire book on the subject. 'I'm not into buying light-sabres, running around pretending to be Princess Leia or anything like that,' said the Rev. David Wilkinson, who worked for six years as an astrophysicist before his ordination. He claims to be only a moderate fan, though he has already seen *The Phantom Menace* twice in the line of duty. But, he says, this is the way that schoolchildren and students get their moral discussions nowadays. 'I went to a school the other day and spoke to a group of around a hundred people. Half of them had already seen it on pirate video, even before the official release.'

Though *The Phantom Menace* has been generally panned, Wilkinson sees it as in some respects the most theologically interesting of the films, because it centres on a character changing sides. 'How does the boy Anakin Skywalker turn into the evil Darth Vader? What is it that conspires within us to produce evil?' That the answers to this question are not necessarily Christian ones does not bother him, though conservative Christians around the world have complained that *Star Wars* spreads New Age heresies.

In the climactic scene of *Return of the Jedi*, where Darth Vader returns to his original team and chucks the evil Emperor into the glowing maw of the hyperdrive, Wilkinson sees an echo of the Christian theme of redemption through self-sacrifice. He sees the Force as a sign of hope: 'It's not a picture of God, but it's raising the question of God. There is a tension in the films between the scientific-materialistic world view and the transcendence – the good guys rely on the Force and the bad guys rely on the Death Star. They even use a robot army in *The Phantom Menace*, which is an illustration of a Western technological society trying to stamp out any sense of the transcendent.'

On the other hand, to most people the Force is nothing like the idea of a Christian

God. The interesting bits of Christianity, from the Book of Job onwards, are adaptations to the fact that the spaceship does not rise miraculously from the swamp, even when the good guys want it to, really badly. This does not worry Mr Wilkinson. It seems to him that *Star Wars*, though it is one of the greatest consumerist phenomena of the age, opens up a vision of a world beyond technological consumerism. It is designed to appeal to the kind of characters – 'a small boy and a whiny teenager' – who would never have anything to do with normal church life.

It's all an imposing theory and will make an interesting companion to an earlier book he published on *The Spirituality of The X Files*. Both phenomena, he says, show evidence of a tremendous need to believe in the reality of stuff outside our narrow imaginations and to anchor myth with detailed reality. There is a key difference, he insists. Christianity's gospel stories weren't made up in the way that those about Skywalker and Darth Vader were. *Star Wars* fans, of course, might not agree.

QUESTION A
1. Briefly explain the arguments the writer uses to draw a parallel between Christian ideas and those underlying the presentation of *Star Wars*.
2. What techniques does the writer use to back up or substantiate the claims made in the above passage?

QUESTION B
Write a short review of a film you enjoyed watching.

Text 3

Eating at Mama's

For the first time since the decline of Dadaism we are witnessing a revival in the fine art of meaningless naming. This thought is prompted by the film *Trainspotting* and by the opening of a new play on Broadway called *Virgil Is Still the Frogboy*. The play is not about Virgil: no frogs feature therein. The title is apparently taken from a Long Island graffiti, to whose meaning the play offers no clues. This omission has not diminished the show's success.

As Luis Buñuel knew, obscurity is a characteristic of objects of desire. Accordingly, there is no train-spotting in *Trainspotting*, just a predictable, even sentimental movie that thinks it's hip. (Compared with the work of, say, William Burroughs, it's positively cutesy.) The film has many admirers, perhaps because they are unable to understand even its title, let alone the fashionably indecipherable slang of the dialogue. The fact remains that *Trainspotting* contains no mention of persons keeping obsessive notes on the arrival and departure of trains. The only railway engines are to be found on the wallpaper of the central character's bedroom. Whence, therefore, the choo-choo moniker? Some sort of pun on the word 'tracks' may be intended.

Nowadays, dreary old comprehensibility is still very much around. A new film about a boy-man called Jack is called *Jack*. A film about crazed basketball fans is called *The Fan*. The new version of Jane Austen's *Emma* is called *Emma*.

However, titular mystification continues to intensify. When Oasis sing 'You're my wonderwall', what do they mean? I intend to ride over you on my motorbike, round and round at very high speed? Surely not.

And *Blade Runner*? Yes, I know that hunters of android replicants are called 'blade runners'. But why? And yes, William Burroughs (again) used the phrase in a 1979 novel and, to get really arcane, there's a 1974 medical thriller called *The Bladerunner* by the late Dr Alan Nourse. But what does any of this have to do with Ridley Scott's film? Harrison Ford runs not, neither does he blade. Shouldn't a work of art give us the keys with which to unlock its meanings? Perhaps there aren't any; perhaps it's just that the phrase sounds cool, thanks to those echoes of Burroughs, 'Daddy Cool' himself.

In 1928 Luis Buñuel and Salvador Dali co-directed the surrealist classic *Un Chien Andalou*, a film about many things but not about Andalusian dogs. So it is with Tarantino's *Reservoir Dogs*. No reservoir, no dogs, no use of the words 'reservoir', 'dogs' or 'reservoir dogs' at any point in the film. No imagery derived from dogs or reservoirs, or dogs in reservoirs, or reservoirs of dogs. Nothing; or as Mr Pink and co. would say, '. . . nothing'.

The story goes that when the young Tarantino was working in a video shop his distaste for fancy European writer-directors such as Louis Malle manifested itself in an inability to pronounce the titles of their films. Malle's *Au Revoir, les Enfants* defeated him completely ('Oh reservoir les . . .'), until he began to refer to it contemptuously as – you guessed it – 'those, oh reservoir dogs'. Subsequently he made this the title of his own film, no doubt as a further gesture of anti-European defiance. Alas, the obliqueness of the gibe meant that the Europeans simply did not comprehend. 'What we have here,' as the guy in *Cool Hand Luke* defiantly remarked, 'is a failure to communicate.'

But these days the thing about incomprehensibility is that people aren't supposed to understand. In accordance with the new *zeitgeist**, therefore, the title of this piece has in part been selected – 'sampled' – from Lou Reed's advice – 'Don't eat at places called Mama's' – in the diary of his recent tour. To forestall any attempts at esotericism, I confess that as a title it means nothing at all, but then the very concept of meaning is now outdated.

Welcome to the new incomprehensibility: gibberish with attitude.

* *Zeitgeist*: spirit of the times.

QUESTION A
1. What is the main thrust of the writer's arguments in this passage?
2. Comment on:
    i) the writer's use of reference in the above passage
    ii) the style of the passage.

QUESTION B
'Welcome to the new incomprehensibility: gibberish with attitude.' How apt a conclusion to the passage is this statement? Give reasons for your answer.

Text 4

QUESTION A

1. What type of lifestyle is suggested by this picture? Support your answer by reference to details in the photograph.
2. What kind of statement is this photograph making?

QUESTION B
Compose a short introductory paragraph that might accompany this photograph.

(For suggested answers on first sample paper see pages 127–31.)

Section II: Composing
(100 marks)

Write a composition on *any one* of the following.
1. Write a narrative composition on your experience of making a film or of an interview that you carried out with a film star.
2. Write a letter to your local newspaper on what you consider to be the advantages of health food shops.
3. Choose an exotic region that you would like to visit. Write a descriptive account of your trip and the particular cultural experiences that impressed you.
4. Write a persuasive speech for a debate entitled 'Discrimination is still rampant today.'
5. '*Star Wars*, though it is one of the greatest consumerist phenomena of the age, opens up a vision of a world beyond technological consumerism. It is designed to appeal to the kind of characters – "a small boy and a whiny teenager" – who would never have anything to do with normal church life.' Compose a series of arguments on what you consider the relationship between religion and ordinary life should be.
6. Imagine that you are working on the set of a film being made about your locality. Compose an imaginative account of your experiences of working with the film crew.
7. 'Vitamin pills increase the risk of lung cancer and heart disease among smokers, according to a report to be published by the World Health Organization (WHO).' Write an informative article for a teenage magazine on the importance of healthy eating.
8. Write the speech you will deliver for a debate on the topic 'Young people today are slaves of fads and fashions.'

SECOND SAMPLE PAPER: VIOLENCE AND DESTRUCTION

This paper contains *four* different texts on the general theme of violence and destruction.

Section I: Comprehending
(100 marks)

Text 1

Animal cruelty and mass murder

Shortly before the killings at the US Capitol building in Washington, the chief suspect in the case shot sixteen cats with his father's revolver. This vitally important incident was barely mentioned in reports of 'the assault on the front door of democracy'. It should have received banner headlines.

In England a few years ago the 'Butcher of Hungerford', Michael Ryan, tested his vast array of weapons on cats and wildlife before blowing away his neighbours. At the age of fourteen he had set animals alight just to watch them burn. Yet the police never considered him a threat to society – not until Michael declared open season on humans.

Recently two schoolchildren in Arkansas made world headlines when they shot their teacher and several pupils. As it happened, the children had been taught from an early age to hunt and kill animals – and to enjoy doing it. Video footage showed them pumping bullets into deer at point-blank range, with smirking adults standing over them.

After the murders a local policeman was quoted as saying, 'We just don't understand how something like this could happen in our small, peaceful, deer-hunting community.'

In Britain, neighbours had seen two children who abducted and killed a younger child cutting the heads off live pigeons. Gangsters Bonny and Clyde tortured livestock on a farm before embarking on their killing spree. In one of Ireland's most gruesome murder cases, the killer admitted in court that exposure to cruelty in a meat plant where he worked had brutalised him. After watching pigs die without being stunned, which his co-workers found amusing, he 'hadn't the slightest remorse' about using a butcher's knife on his victims.

The people involved in these and similar crimes had different motives, backgrounds and psychological profiles. But they all had one thing in common – ill treatment of animals had made them insensitive to human suffering.

For example, one study found that sport hunters in the US were seven times more likely to beat their wives than non-hunters. This disturbing tendency was attributed to an 'excessive need among hunters to control and dominate their environment'.

In Ireland firearms abound. Our gun culture is getting out of hand. Parts of the countryside have become a virtual battlefield, with bird and animal corpses littering the woods and fields. We should tackle this issue before 'harmless' taking of life spawns a major tragedy. One effective measure would be to have all weapons electronically tagged. Police could then monitor their use and whereabouts. Sadistic or over-zealous gunmen could be given the same treatment, depending on how the situation developed.

It is, after all, a matter of life and death.

QUESTION A
1. Do you consider this passage to be an example of effective writing? Give reasons for your answer.
2. Distinguish the facts from the opinions in this passage.

QUESTION B
Write two paragraphs, using a descriptive style, on a street scene at night.

Text 2

A light flapped over the scene, as if reflected from phosphorescent wings crossing the sky, and a rumble filled the air. It was the first move of the approaching storm.

The second peal was noisy, with comparatively little visible lightening . . .

Then there came a third flash. Manoeuvres of a most extraordinary kind were going on in the vast firmamental hollows overhead. The lightning now was the colour of silver, and gleamed in the heavens like a mailed army. Rumbles became rattles. Gabriel from his elevated position could see over the landscape at least half-a-dozen miles in front. Every hedge, bush, and tree was distinct as in a line engraving. In a paddock in the same direction was a herd of heifers, and the forms of these were visible at this moment in the act of galloping about in the wildest and maddest confusion, flinging their heels and tails high into the air, their heads to earth. A poplar in the immediate foreground was like an ink stroke on burnished tin. Then the picture vanished, leaving the darkness so intense that Gabriel worked entirely by feeling with his hands.

He had stuck his ricking-rod, or poniard, as it was indifferently called – a long iron lance, polished by handling – into the stack, used to support the sheaves instead of the support called a groom used on houses. A blue light appeared in the zenith, and in some indescribable manner flickered down near the top of the rod. It was the fourth of the larger flashes. A moment later and there was a smack – smart, clear, and short . . .

Heaven opened then, indeed. The flash was almost too novel for its inexpressibly dangerous nature to be at once realised . . . It sprang from east, west, north, south, and was a perfect dance of death. The forms of skeletons appeared in the air, shaped with blue fire for bones – dancing, leaping, striding, racing around, and mingling altogether in unparalleled confusion. With these were intertwined undulating snakes of green, and behind these was a broad mass of lesser light . . .

Oak had hardly time to gather up these impressions into a thought . . . when the tall tree on the hill before mentioned seemed on fire to a white heat . . . It was a stupefying blast, harsh and pitiless, and it fell upon their ears in a dead, flat blow, without that reverberation which lends the tones of a drum to more distant thunder. By the lustre reflected from every part of the earth and from the wide domical scoop above it, he saw that the tree was sliced down the whole length of its tall, straight stem, a huge riband of bark being apparently flung off. The other portion remained erect, and revealed the bared surface as a strip of white down the front. The lightning had struck the tree. A sulphurous smell filled the air; then all was silent, and black as a cave in Hinnom.

(Thomas Hardy, *Far from the Madding Crowd*)

QUESTION A
1. Show how the writer succeeds in building up atmosphere in this extract.
2. Comment on how the writer makes use of small details to draw a realistic picture of the storm in this extract.

QUESTION B
Write a conclusion of about 150 words to this extract. In particular, concentrate on the effects of the storm.

Text 3

What is it possible to say about the loss of lives resulting from the Northern troubles? This. That so far it has all been in vain, quite purposeless. No cause was advanced in any way which would have not been better served by peaceful means. Who can say what this island would have been like if the depraved culture of violence had not once again taken root? Aside from the 3,600 lives lost, how much else has been lost? What opportunities to learn, to be civilised, to create art and order were squandered in the cretinous squalor of war?

If we had listed the dead of 1916–22, described who they were and how they died, if we had studied the barbarous injustice of their fate, if we had dwelt on the sufferings of their families, if we had made the immorality of political violence a keystone of our political culture we would not have tolerated the violation of law and life of the last thirty years.

Catalogue
There might be an excuse for being ignorant of the events of 1916–22. There is no excuse now for ignorance over the events of 1966–99. The definitive catalogue of those who died in our troubles, how, where and when they died, who their families were and how else their families might have suffered, has been produced by David McKittrick and published by Mainstream Publishing. It is the saddest, most sobering, most heartbreaking book I have ever read. Not a page of it is without an almost unbearable tragedy; each tragedy is real, each one was lived by actual people, each one spread vast repercussions through family, friends and the broader community to which they belonged.

Numbers numb. Very soon after one starts counting deaths they lose meaning. Three hundred, four hundred, five hundred; people become ciphers, their identity, their purpose in life, the people they loved and the people who loved them in return vanish behind the metronome ticking of digits passing through our minds. That is how we have been able to bear the unbearable during these troubles. We let the shutters of statistics conceal the mountain range of human suffering behind them.

In the greatest single piece of historical scholarship in either journalism or historical studies that has ever been conducted in this country, David McKittrick has liberated the dead from the limbo of statistics. The unliving live again. He has followed up each death, back to the first killings in 1966, and up to the most recent, that of Charles Bennett last year – the numbered corpses and their poor bereaved families come back to life on the page. And in their merely literary resurrection they serve as a terrible indictment of the culture of political violence that finds so many apologists throughout Irish life.

Utter futility
A page of David's masterpiece should convince any civilised person that a resort to violence to solve the communal problems of Ireland is no more than a celebration of idiot-barbarism. And it is not enough to say this is the case today. The resort to violence in the name of the Republic has been marked by two enduring features. The first is the enormous suffering it has caused, the second is its utter futility. The war for a united Irish republic has been going on intermittently now for nearly eighty-five years. It is no closer to achievement today than it was when the violent accounts were opened in Dublin in 1916 and two unarmed police officers – Constables Lahiffe and O'Brien – were murdered in the centre of Dublin.

How are these murders commemorated today? They are not. Children are not taught about these poor men butchered while doing their duty. They are not taught about

Countess Markievicz capering around the body of the policeman she had just shot in St Stephen's Green joyfully shrieking, 'I shot him, I shot him.' There is a statue to her not far from where she gunned down this blameless man; he has vanished from history, as have the hundreds of others who died that Eastertide.

Those who are ignorant of the realities of the Easter Rising and of the violence of 1919–22 could be forgiven their ignorance. The issue is not individual atrocities. The issue is violence itself. That is the atrocity. It is the atrocity which we have had to live with for the greater part of this century, an atrocity which in each generation has re-emerged. But until the publication of *Lost Lives*, it has always been possible to hide the true evil of violence. Not any more. There can be no more searing indictment, not merely of the individual deeds of violence but of the political culture which justifies it, than this book.

Monstrosity
I defy anyone to browse through the pages of *Lost Lives* without being stunned by the sheer monstrosity of all that we have done, or allowed to be done, over the last thirty years. Evil, unspeakable evil, rose in our midst and we as a people were too weak, too indecisive, too pusillanimous to deal with it. And here now is a record of the consequences; in its encyclopaedic detail, in its towering integrity and in its moral compassion it could be the most influential study of Irish history that has ever been presented.

I know of no work which can alter behaviour as this one can, should, must. The argument it presents against the use of violence, for all that it is implicit, is compelling and complete.

Nothing more needs to be said. Buy *Lost Lives*. Nobody on this island can have an excuse for not knowing about the evils of violence. Nobody who can work through the 1,600 pages of murder it covers will ever find an excuse or a pretext for political violence again.

QUESTION A
1. Consider this passage as an example of effective persuasive writing.
2. In what type of publication would you read this type of article?

QUESTION B
Write a speech for your class, of about 200 words, outlining the reasons why you think they should read this book.

Text 4

Photograph A

Photograph B

Photograph C

Photograph D

Photograph E

QUESTION A
1. Study photographs A–E and briefly describe what comment is being made in each case.
2. Pick one photograph and identify three different techniques that are used to communicate its particular message.

QUESTION B
Write a headline that could accompany each photograph.

(For suggested answers on second sample paper see pages 131–6.)

Section II: Composing
(100 marks)

Write a composition on *any one* of the following.
1. 'There might be an excuse for being ignorant of the events of 1916–22. There is no excuse now for ignorance over the events of 1966–99.' Write out a speech for a debate in which you would either challenge or support this statement.
2. Write a narrative composition on your experience of seeing a street fight.
3. 'In Ireland firearms abound. Our gun culture is getting out of hand. Parts of the countryside have become a virtual battlefield, with bird and animal corpses littering the woods and fields.' Write a letter to the newspaper on your own views of the hunting and shooting of wild animals.
4. 'The lightning now was the colour of silver, and gleamed in the heavens like a mailed army.' Use this statement as the starting point for a short story. Concentrate on using vivid, descriptive language.
5. Compose a series of arguments on the subject 'Violence has become a hallmark of our society.'
6. Write the dialogue for a screenplay on the subject 'Peaceful solutions'.
7. In an article intended for a serious magazine, write a persuasive account of your own experience of the horrors of war.

THIRD SAMPLE PAPER: COMMUNICATION

This paper contains *four* texts on the general theme of communication.

Section I: Comprehending
(100 marks)

Text 1

A: Pope redefines the nature of Paradise

Just days after a leading Jesuit magazine redefined concepts of Hell, the Pope turned his attention yesterday to Paradise, declaring that it was not a place above the clouds where angels played harps, but a 'state of being' after death.

The Heaven in which we will find ourselves is neither an abstraction nor a physical place among the clouds, he told seventy pilgrims in St Peter's Square.

Looking invigorated and tanned after his summer break in the Italian Alps, the Pope, who has suffered from a series of debilitating illnesses, said he wanted to make it clear that Paradise was 'a living and personal relationship with the Holy Trinity'. Just as Hell was separation from God, so Paradise was 'close communion and full intimacy with God. Heaven is a blessed community of those who remained faithful to Jesus Christ in their lifetime and are now at one with his glory.'

At the end of last week, *Civiltà Cattolica*, the magazine of the Society of Jesus, said Hell was not a place where the souls of the damned were tortured eternally by fire and demons, as represented by Dante and others, but a state of being in which those who had consistently rejected God and 'consciously chosen not to do good' were condemned to permanent banishment from God's presence.

Earlier this year the Pope, rejecting artistic images from Michaelangelo to Blake, told pilgrims they should not see God as an old man with a white beard but rather as a supreme being with both masculine and feminine aspects.

Although many writers, such as Milton, have propagated a literal idea of Paradise, others have taken a sceptical view, with Proust observing in *Remembrance of Things Past* that 'the true paradises are the paradises we have lost on earth.'

The Pope told his listeners that they could gain some 'intimation' of what Paradise would be like by following the 'sacramental life, of which the Eucharist is the centre', and by devoting themselves to 'fraternal love for their fellow beings'.

B: Paradise redefined

Heaven must be one hell of a place.

Paradise is no longer the place it used to be. Like one of those seaside resorts most frequently compared to it, its delights are looking tackier with time. So the Pope, the principal salesman of this time-share retreat, has suggested that the prospectus be sent for a reprint. Apparently, the traditional selling points – the angels and ambrosia and eternal sunshine – now seem a little outmoded. Heaven, the Pope told pilgrims yesterday, is not a physical place above the clouds but a state of being after death, and Paradise a living personal relationship with the Holy Trinity.

Of course, the Pope is quite sensible in making such suggestions. The human condition is thrown out of kilter by the prospect of perpetual bliss. Man's earthly delights are held in delicate balance by desires that admit of only passing satisfaction if they are not to destroy themselves. Unlimited pleasure, much like retirement to the Costa, can seem rather less than perfect when offered in perpetuity. And surely, deep down, Disraeli knew that even a glutton would soon sicken of ortolans eaten to the sound of soft music.

Anyway, eternity must keep pace with the times. Our less sophisticated forebears may have been beguiled by the prospect of a simple blow-out banquet, but life on earth in their day must have been pretty tough to endure. How easy it must have been to imagine Elysian satisfactions when an ingrowing toenail could make existence a living hell.

It was only when Plato came up with his ideas about archetypes, of ideal worlds that were so much more real than his own, that Paradise had to start measuring up to increased expectations. From then on, unthinkable bliss had to adapt itself to the ideals of different religions, each trimming and tweaking it according to their various systems of value. The Pope now adds his own interpretation to this visionary pageant, but he finds himself facing the same problem that has perplexed all those who have grappled with portrayals of perfect happiness. Like the great spiritual poets Dante and Milton before him, the pontiff is finding out how notoriously hard it is to make Heaven sound even half as good as Hell. Certainly, to the average Christian teenager, his papal ideal of chilling out with the Paraclete will not sound like too much fun. Perhaps everyone should be left to conjure up his own personal vision of the expected afterlife, for in the end all anyone can really guess is that Heaven is bound to be one hell of a place.

QUESTION A
1. Study the two articles above and identify the purpose of each. Comment on which you consider to be more effective in achieving that purpose. Give your reasons why.
2. In what type of publication would you expect to find each article? In your answer take into account the type of language and arguments that are used.

QUESTION B
Write a short review, of about 150 words, for a popular magazine on what you consider the main priority of a journalist should be.

Text 2

Brutal but moving

A few poignant moments – a whisper, a glance, a touch – are the only glimpses of true humanity in this film, in which the outlook for the future is portrayed as very bleak indeed. Set on the streets of Belfast, the story of the 'Boxer' unfolds in a chaotic world where violence is a part of everyday life and where to fall in love may be not just dangerous but deadly.

Danny Flynn, played magnificently by Daniel Day-Lewis, is a former IRA man trying to build a life on the outside after spending fourteen years in prison. His long years inside have convinced him that it's time to do things differently, but in a world where order is imposed by the authority of the IRA, that means breaking social mores.

As is his custom, Daniel Day-Lewis immersed himself completely in the role, and once again his strict method has paid dividends. His emotional portrayal of Danny is complex, subtle and utterly convincing. His training with Barry McGuigan turned him into a muscular fighting machine, and the scenes in the ring are every bit as compelling as those in *Raging Bull* and that other great, under-rated boxing film, *The Big Man*.

QUESTION A
1. Identify the writer's main purpose in this article.
2. Comment on two different techniques used by the writer to achieve this purpose. Make reference to the passage to support your answer.

QUESTION B
Write two paragraphs for a serious journal on the topic 'Family life is in conflict with television.' In the first paragraph outline the problems you see in this area. In the second paragraph propose some solution to these problems.

Text 3

A virtual nation

The pioneers of telecommunications have always looked further than others, seeking new ways to bring people together over seemingly impossible distances. Now, with the birth of Turly, worldwide portable telecommunications has been achieved. In the space of seven short years since the company was spun off from its founder, Motorola, Iridium has turned a vision into a reality.

Like many great inventions, Iridium has grown out of a simple challenge. On holiday in the Caribbean in 1985, Karen Bertinger found she could not call the United States on her mobile phone. 'Why can't you make my phone work out here?' she asked her husband, Bary Bertinger, an executive with Motorola. She convinced him that there was a real need for a system that would provide wireless communication between any two points on the planet and that's where the Iridium story really begins.

But to quote Thomas Edison, arguably the greatest telecommunications pioneer, 'Genius is one per cent inspiration, ninety-nine per cent perspiration.' In this respect, Iridium is no different from any other major technological leap forward – from the original idea flowed thirteen years of tireless hard work as the talents of more than 10,000 people were harnessed with the single goal of making the vision a reality.

Now satellites are in place, circling the globe in their orbits 780 kilometres above Earth. Agreements have been signed with more than 300 telecommunications providers.

The palm-sized Iridium handsets are in production and will soon be available to the first customers, bringing them the power to make and take calls anywhere in the world, using one telephone, with one number and receiving only one bill. What was once a visionary project is now a technological and commercial triumph.

QUESTION A
1. Clearly describe how the writer illustrates the opening statement: 'The pioneers of telecommunications have always looked further than others, seeking new ways to bring people together over seemingly impossible distances.'
2. Do you think the writer effectively develops the argument here? Support your points by detailed reference to the text.

QUESTION B
Write an original and interesting opening paragraph on the topic 'Isn't it time to limit the use of private cars?'

Text 4
QUESTION A
1. Write a description of the photograph that accompanies the advertisement on page 113. What do you consider to be the relation between the photograph and the advertisement?
2. Identify three different techniques used by the writer. In your answer take into account the layout of the advertisement together with the writer's use of words.

QUESTION B
Write a speech for your class on what you consider to be the benefits of having a mobile phone.

(For answers on third sample paper see pages 136–40.)

Section II: Composing
(100 marks)

Write a composition on *any one* of the following.
1. Write a prose composition, using the language of argument, on the topic 'The media's role is to uncover and expose the truth.'
2. Imagine you are a journalist who has been asked to report on a famine or war in a country in southern Africa. Compose an imaginative article on that topic.
3. 'To quote Thomas Edison, arguably the greatest telecommunications pioneer, "Genius is one per cent inspiration, ninety-nine per cent perspiration."' In light of this statement, write an informative article for a serious journal on your views of recent technological developments.
4. 'The Pope turned his attention yesterday to Paradise, declaring that it was not a place above the clouds where angels played harps but a "state of being" after death.' Write a narrative account of your vision of Paradise.
5. Compose a persuasive speech either for or against the argument that the media must respect people's privacy.
6. 'Looking invigorated and tanned after his summer break in the Italian Alps, the Pope, who has suffered from a series of debilitating illnesses, said he wanted to make it clear that Paradise was a "living and personal relationship with the Holy Trinity".' Imagine you are asked to represent the young people of Ireland at an international conference in Rome. Compose an autobiographical sketch on your impressions of attending the conference and your experience of having a private audience with the Pope.
7. Write a persuasive letter for a serious journal on your ideas about the topic 'Freedom of information is a necessary right in a democracy.'

FOURTH SAMPLE PAPER: LIFESTYLES

This paper contains *four* texts on the general theme of lifestyles.

Section I: Comprehending
(100 marks)

Text 1

Reach for the stars

Seriously rich women are different from you and me – they have time to think ahead. Do you know what you are going to wear on New Year's Eve? Neither do I. But there they were this week, lining the front rows at the final Paris *haute couture* showings, picking their frocks for the party to end all parties.

Ivana Trump thought she might go for Thierry Mugler; Muna al-Ayub seemed certain to choose Dior; Catherine Deneuve was considering Yves Saint-Laurent; while Joan Collins was enraptured by Valentino. The Bride of Wildenstein hadn't made up her mind. Nan Kempner, the American socialite, chuckled throatily. 'When you get to my age

darling, every day seems like New Year. So I shall be at home in bed, in New York, wearing nothing at all.'

The New Year's soirées were a fabulous brief for the couturiers. Even Paco Rabanne, who seems convinced that Paris will be wiped out during the eclipse on the eleventh of August (he thinks that the Mir space station will crash to Earth) had spared a thought for the socialising that will doubtless continue elsewhere. Rabanne, who retired from the couture circus after his show on Sunday, produced his own made-to-measure version of Mir. There was no sense of millennium minimalism – this was a season for vamps and voluptuaries and for the visionary designers to create their ultimate fantasies. It was a season of sybaritic fashion moments and a time to wallow.

Exotic skins (crocodile, python) and furs (fox, rabbit, mink, marmot) fashioned skirts and dresses, trimmed the inside of coats and caressed the cleavage. Fabulous plumage (guineafowl, ostrich, bearded vulture) soared from heads, was woven into knits and trailed from hems of taffeta opera coats.

Brocade glistened with jewels, crystals winked from silk tulle and knickers sparkled with gold studs. There were miracles of invention, such as velvet appliquéd with mink, rabbit painted to look like panther and tweed interlaced with feathers. Not everything was what it seemed. John Galliano's Brer Fox and rabbit toppers were real; his boar's head hat was papier mâché.

Flight was a key inspiration, whether expressed in billowing parachute gowns, paratrooper gear, woman-as-bird or woman-as-satellite. Fashion was reaching for the stars – enough to make the imagination soar.

QUESTION A
1. Who are the intended target audience of this article? Support your answer by reference to the passage.
2. In what type of publication would you read this type of review? Give reasons for your answer.

QUESTION B
Write an imaginative and witty opening paragraph for a teenage fashion magazine on the topic of hairstyles.

Text 2

Does anywhere on Earth sound more exotic? Or does the name Bali evoke an image long since past of a Mecca for artists in the nineteen-thirties and hippies in the nineteen-sixties? Does it offer adventure, romance, peace and quiet, spiritual rejuvenation? Well, yes. Bali has volcanoes, jungles, elephants, wild monkeys, amazing birds, vistas of rice paddies, azure seas, gleaming sands, colourful culture and captivating music and dancing. It also has bungee jumping, go-karting, paragliding, white-water rafting, paint balling and an internet café – this last lot are present because Bali is to Australians what Torremolinos is to British and Irish people.

The views of the jungle and rice paddies opposite are luscious. At night the sound of the stream at the bottom of the gorge and the clatter of insects provide an auditory environment just as compelling.

Plenty of tours will take you on a boat to a desert island or bird park. In any of these places you will come across the monkeys. As well as being charming, they are adept pickpockets, but can usually be bribed with food to return whatever they have purloined. Who is to say whether or not the nearby vendors who sell you the titbits of food are in league with the monkeys?

QUESTION A
1. Do you consider this to be an effective piece of persuasive writing? Give reasons for your answer.
2. Identify the facts in this passage.

QUESTION B
Write out an advertisement that would accompany this article. Include a slogan and an arresting caption and concentrate on using some persuasive techniques in the language you use.

Text 3

The wind blew the smell of rain down the valley ahead of the rain itself, the smell of wet earth and aromatic plants. The old woman pulled in her washing and fetched the cane chairs off the terrace. The old man, Anton Hahn, put on boots and a waterproof and went into the garden to check that all the catchments were clear. The peon came over from the barn with an empty bottle and the woman filled it with apple *chicha*. He was drunk already. Two red oxen stood yoked to a cart, bracing themselves for the storm.

The old man walked round his vegetable garden and his flower garden bright with annuals. Having seen that they would get the full benefit of the rain, he came inside the house. Apart from its metal roof nothing distinguished it from the houses of a southern German village, the half-timbering infilled with white plaster, the grey shutters, the wicket fence, scrubbed floors, painted panelling, the chandelier of antler tines and lithographs of the Rhineland.

Anton Hahn took off his tweed cap and hung it on an antler. He took off his boots and canvas gaiters and put on rope-soled slippers. His head was flat on top and his face creased and red. A little girl with a pigtail came into the kitchen.

'Do your wish your pipe, *Onkel?*'

'*Bitte.*' And she brought a big *meerschaum* and filled it with tobacco from a blue-and-white jar.

The old man poured himself a tankard of *chicha*. As the rain slammed on the roof, he talked about the Colonia Nueva Alemania. His uncles settled here in 1905 and he had followed after the Great War.

'What could I do? The Fatherland was in a bad condition. Before the war, no family could have enough sons. One was a soldier. One was a carpenter, and two stayed on the farm. But after 1918 Germany was full of refugees from the Bolsheviks. Even the villages were full.'

His brother lived on the family farm on the borders of Bavaria and Württemberg. They wrote letters once a month but had not met since 1923.

'The war was the biggest mistake in history,' Anton Hahn said. He was obsessed by the war. 'Two peoples of the Superior Race ruining each other. Together England and Germany could have ruled the world. Now even Patagonia is returning to the *indigenas*. This is a pity.'

He went on lamenting the decline of the West and, at one point, dropped the name Ludwig.

'Mad Ludwig?'

'The King? Mad? You call the King mad? In my house? No!'

I had to think fast.

'Some people call him mad,' I said, 'but, of course, he was a great genius.'

Anton Hahn was hard to pacify. He stood up and lifted his tankard.

'You will join me,' he said.

I stood.

'To the King! To the last genius of Europe! With him died the greatness of my race!'

The old man offered me dinner, but I refused, having eaten with the soprano two hours before.

'You will not leave my house until you have eaten with us. After that you may go where you will.'

So I ate his ham and pickles and sun-coloured eggs and drank his apple *chicha*, which went to my head. Then I asked him about Wilson and Evans.

'They were gentlemen,' he said. 'They were friends of my family and my uncles buried them. My cousin knows the story.'

The old woman was tall and thin and her yellowing skin fell from her face in folds. Her hair was white and cut in a fringe across her eyebrows.

'Yes, I remember Wilson and Evans. I had four years at the time.'

It was a hot, windless day in early summer. The Frontier Police, eighty of them, had been hunting the outlaws up and down the Cordillera. The Police were criminals themselves, mostly Paraguayos; you had to be white or Christian to join. Everyone in Río Pico liked the North Americans. Her mother, Doña Guillermina, dressed Wilson's hand, right here in the kitchen. They could easily have gone over into Chile. How could they know the Indian would betray them?

'I remember them bringing in the bodies,' she said. 'The *Fronterizas* brought them down on an ox-cart. They were here, outside the gate. They had swelled up in the heat and the smell was terrible. My mother sent me to my room so I shouldn't see. Then the officer cut their heads off and came up the steps, here, carrying them by the hair. And he asked my mother for preserving alcohol. You see, this *Agencia* in New York was paying five thousand dollars a head. They wanted to send the heads up there and get the money. This made my father very angry. He shouted them to give over the heads and the bodies and he buried them.'

The storm was passing. Columns of grey water fell on the far side of the valley. Along the length of the apple orchard was a line of blue lupins. Wherever there were Germans there were blue lupins.

By the corral a rough wood cross stuck out of a small mound. The arching stems of a pampas rose sprang up as if fertilised by the bodies. I watched a grey harrier soaring and diving, and the sweep of grass and the thunderheads turning crimson.

The old man had come out and was standing behind me.

'No one would want to drop an atom bomb on Patagonia,' he said.

(Bruce Chatwin, *In Patagonia*)

QUESTION A
1. Good narrative writing depends for its effect on vividly recording small details. In the extract above, identify how the writer has drawn some vibrant description by means of small details.
2. From your reading of this extract, comment on the type of person you think the narrator is. Give reasons for your answer.

QUESTION B
1. Sum up in your own words the anecdote given above and say how much it contributes to the power of the passage.
2. Point out some features of narrative writing from the passage.

Text 4
QUESTION A
1. Identify the target audience of the advertisement on page 120.
2. Do you consider this to be an effective advertisement? Give three reasons for your answer.

QUESTION B
Write a paragraph of about 100 words on your reaction to this advertisement.

(For answers on fourth sample paper see pages 140–4.)

Section II: Composing
(100 marks)
Write a composition on *any one* of the following.
1. 'By the corral a rough wood cross stuck out of a small mound. The arching stems of a pampas rose sprung up as if fertilised by the bodies. I watched a grey harrier soaring and diving, and the sweep of grass and the thunderheads turning crimson.' Compose a descriptive account of some particular scene in nature that impressed you. Concentrate on using some original images and small details in your descriptions.
2. 'But there they were this week, lining the front rows at the final Paris *haute couture* showings, picking their frocks for the party to end all parties.' Write a review for a magazine on a fashion show you attended.
3. 'Or does the name Bali evoke an image long since past of a Mecca for artists in the nineteen-thirties and hippies in the nineteen-sixties?' Compose an article, using a persuasive style, on what you consider to be the advantages of taking holidays abroad.
4. 'Apart from its metal roof nothing distinguished it from the houses of a southern German village, the half-timbering infilled with white plaster, the grey shutters, the wicket fence, scrubbed floors, painted panelling, the chandelier of antler tines and lithographs of the Rhineland.' Write a narrative account of your experiences abroad. Include some details of your impressions of the people, food and culture.
5. 'Travelling broadens horizons.' Taking this topic as the subject for a debate, write out the arguments you would use in your speech.
6. Compose a series of diary entries by a person who is engaged in working on a Third World project. Include details of the people, their lifestyle, food and culture.
7. Write a letter to a local newspaper on your opinion of modern culture.

Fifth sample paper: home and identity

This paper contains *four* texts on the general theme of home and identity.

Section I: Comprehending
(100 marks)

Text I

The Westernisation of the world

A traditional scene

In Singapore, Peking opera still lives, in the back streets. On Boat Quay, where great barges moor to unload rice from Thailand, raw rubber from Malaysia or timber from Sumatra, I watched a troupe of travelling actors throw up a canvas-and-wood booth stage, paint on their white faces and lozenge eyes and don their resplendent vermilion, ultramarine and gold robes. Then, to raptured audiences of bent old women and little children with perfect circle faces, they enacted tales of feudal princes and magic birds and tragic love affairs, sweeping their sleeves and singing in strange metallic voices.

The performance had been paid for by a local cultural society as part of a religious festival. A purple cloth temple had been erected on the quayside, painted papier mâché sculptures were burning down like giant joss-sticks and middle-aged men were sharing out gifts to be distributed among members' families – red buckets, roast ducks, candies and moon-cakes. The son of the organiser, a fashionable young man in an Italian shirt and gold-rimmed glasses, was looking on with amused benevolence. I asked him why only old people and children were watching the show. 'Young people don't like these operas,' he said. 'They are too old-fashioned. We would prefer to see a high-quality Western variety show – something like that.'

He spoke for a whole generation. Go to almost any village in the Third World and you will find youths who scorn traditional dress and sport denims and T-shirts. Go into any bank and the tellers will be dressed as would their European counterparts; at night the manager will climb into his car and go home to watch television in a home that would not stick out on a European or North American estate. Every capital city in the world is getting to look like every other, and not just in consumer fashions – the mimicry extends to architecture, industrial technology, health care, education and housing.

Perverting development
The Third World's obsession with the Western way of life has perverted development and is rapidly destroying both good and bad in traditional cultures, flinging the baby out with the bath water. It is the most totally pervasive example of what historians call cultural diffusion in the history of mankind. Its origins lie in the colonial experience, in which a variety of European conquerors suffered from the same colonial arrogance. Never a doubt entered their minds that native cultures could be in any way – materially, morally or spiritually – superior to their own and they firmly believed that the benighted inhabitants of the darker continents needed enlightening. And so there grew up, alongside political and economic imperialism, that more insidious form of control – cultural imperialism. It conquered not just their bodies but the souls of its victims, turning them into willing accomplices.

Reference-group behaviour
The most insidious form of cultural imperialism works by what sociologists call reference-group behaviour, found when someone copies the habits and lifestyle of a social group they wish to belong to or to be classed with and abandons those of their own group. This desire to prove equality surely helps to explain why Kwame Nkrumah of Ghana built the huge stadium and triumphal arch of Black Star Square in its capital, Accra. Why the tiny village of President Houphouet-Boigny in Côte d'Ivoire has been graced with a four-lane motorway, starting and ending nowhere, a five-star hotel and an ultra-modern conference centre. The aim was not to show the old imperialists but to impress other Third World leaders in the only way everyone would recognise: the Western way. Fashions and dress codes have also fallen victim to this compulsion to Westernise. In post-war Turkey a ruthless policy was pursued which saw the replacement of the Arabic script with the roman alphabet, while the wearing of the traditional hat, the fez, became a criminal offence. Launching this campaign the president declared: 'The people of the Turkish Republic must prove that they are civilised and advanced persons in their outward respect also. A civilised international dress is worthy and appropriate for our nation and we will wear it. Boots or shoes on our feet, trousers on our legs, shirt and tie, jacket and waistcoat – and of course, to complete these, a cover with a brim on our heads. I want to make this clear. The head covering is called a hat.'

QUESTION A
1. Briefly describe the writer's views on the impact the 'obsession with the Western way of life' has made upon the people of the Third World.
2. Do you consider this passage to be an example of effective writing? Give reasons for your answer.

QUESTION B
Write a descriptive passage of between 150 and 200 words for a holiday brochure, describing what you consider to be the ideal holiday. In preparing your writing, pay careful attention to the way the author of the above passage uses detail in the opening two paragraphs.

Text 2

Pioneers: A view of home

I'm just a little picky about what I take pride in. There are actually people who take pride in their race. This is stupid. Not that anyone should be ashamed of his or her race, it's just that when you think about it you had nothing to do with it. Not your race, not your age, not your nationality. Not even your name.

Family feud

Recently I was watching a repeat of a television show called *Family Feud*, in which two families compete in guessing the answers to the silliest questions. The 'right answer' was the one that had been given earlier by a fabled 'one hundred people'. (We asked a hundred people to name a friendly neighbourhood bird and the families had to guess what this one hundred had said – 'buzzard'.) Whichever family reached 350 points first was the winner. A black family consisting of father, mother, two daughters and a son-in-law were playing a white family of father, mother and three sons in uniforms. As luck would have it the black family won. The show's presenter went over and shook the hands of the white family and thanked them for coming. Then one of the sons piped up with: 'Well, we can still fly.' I guess they were Air Force, but mostly that was a racist remark: you blacks may know what one hundred people think, but hey – we whites can fly. Totally unnecessary. And tacky. I don't object to the boys being proud of flying – if I could fly I'd be proud of myself when I board a flight! No. It was the context in which the remark was made. As if 'Well, after all, we're still white' could make up for the fact that they lost.

We are not so important after all

It's so clear, now that we have photographs from the moon and man-made satellites even farther away, that Earth resembles nothing so much as a single cell in the human body. What a concept – that the planet on which we live is no more than a specimen on a slide. We, who think humans are nature's invention, may well turn out to be no more than the life we see swimming in an ordinary drop of water. What is really important then? What does that do to our notions of race, fatherland and home?

Where is home?

They say home is where when you go, they have to take you in. I rather prefer the idea that home, when you could go anywhere, is where you would prefer to be. The true joy of being a black American is that we really have no home. Europeans bought us, but the Africans sold. We might not have come to America of our own volition, but that is true of so many of the people who have come here from the overcrowded, disease-ridden cities of Europe. And what of those who had to flee religious persecution, or the unspeakable Catholic Inquisition, starvation in Italy or the black rotten potatoes lying in the fields of Ireland? No one came to the New World in a cruise ship; they all came because they had to. They were poor, hungry, criminal, persecuted individuals who would rather chance dropping off the end of the earth than stay inert, knowing that both their body and spirit were slowly having the life squeezed from them. A pioneer has only two things – a deep desire to survive and an equally strong will to live. Home is not the place where our possessions and accomplishments are deposited and displayed – it is this earth that we have explored, the heavens we view with awe, these humans who, despite the flaws, we try to love and those who try to love us. It is the willingness to pioneer the one trek we all can make, no matter what our station or location in life – the existential reality that wherever there is life, we are at home.

QUESTION A
1. In your own words, characterise the attitudes of the writer of this passage to questions of identity and belonging.
2. Consider this passage as an example of predominantly persuasive writing.

QUESTION B
Write a short letter (100–150 words) to the television company which produces the show *Family Feud*, commenting on the behaviour of the families as described in this passage.

Text 3
In this passage taken from *How to Write a Novel*, the English novelist, John Braine, establishes a link between the appearance and atmosphere of places and the people who live in them.

> **Writing about home**
> People are places, and places are people. This isn't to dazzle you with its originality; it's simply another working rule. Whenever you write about places you also write about people. It isn't always that you mention the people when you write about the place. Sometimes it's necessary, sometimes it isn't. On the whole the best way is to concentrate on making the reader see the place.
>
> The most revealing place of all is the home. Imagine yourself suddenly in the home of a complete stranger. Within five minutes you'll have an accurate general picture of what sort of person he is. There are obvious guides, like the kind of books or, for that matter, the absence of books, and the pictures and ornaments, and the quality of the furniture. There are different kinds of tidiness, from the house-proud to the clinically obsessive; different kinds of untidiness, from profusion to squalor. There is, over and above all, the atmosphere of a home. Some people have the gift of creating comfort, some have not. But be careful about this. If you describe a home properly, if you see it accurately, there's no need to say anything about the atmosphere. Or, to be more precise, your reader instantly makes the inference of falling between a shot of a man swaying on a windowsill ten storeys up and the same man sitting on the ground.
>
> This isn't to say that we are exclusively the creatures of our economic environment. We aren't, for instance, made what we are by our homes (using the word in its narrowest sense). We make our homes. We were there first, so to speak. We even make impersonal places, like offices and factories, bear the imprint of our personalities: pin-ups on the walls behind the workbench, trendy executive toys, gold pens, silver mounted portraits on the executive's desk (or, equally revealing, nothing at all).

QUESTION A
1. Describe accurately and concisely the author's illustration of his opening statement: 'People are places, and places are people.'
2. Do you think he states his argument well? Support your points by detailed reference to the text.

QUESTION B
Imagine yourself in the home of some well-known figure from the world of entertainment or political life. Write a short account (150–200 words) for a popular magazine of what you imagine this home to look like and give some indication of what you have chosen to include as significant detail.

Text 4
QUESTION A
1. What lifestyle is suggested to you by the collection of images on page 127?
2. How is this lifestyle suggested?
3. In what type of publication would you expect to find images such as this? Refer to the images in support of your point of view.
4. Compose an introductory paragraph of about 200 words that might accompany this image in the publication you have chosen in response to question 3.

QUESTION B
Imagine you are employing a graphic designer to compile such a photo gallery of your own life. Write a brief letter to him or her in which you outline the kind of images or objects you would include, giving the reasons for their inclusion.

Section II: Composing
(100 marks)
Write a composition on *any one* of the following.
1. 'Home, when you could go anywhere, is where you would prefer to be.' 'Home is not the place where our possessions and accomplishments are deposited and displayed.' In an article intended for a serious journal, present a case for or against one of these views of home.
2. 'There are actually people who take pride in their race. This is stupid.' Write an article in which you challenge or support these views.
3. 'Tales of feudal princes and magic birds and wars and tragic love affairs.' Compose a fable or fairytale suggested by one or more of the details in this quotation. You may, if you wish, give your composition a modern setting.
4. 'If you describe a home properly, if you see it accurately, there's no need to say anything about its atmosphere.' Write an informative newspaper article about your home town, parish or locality, concentrating especially on the qualities that make it unique or memorable.
5. 'Fashions and dress codes.' Compose a persuasive article or a speech for a debate that discusses the issue 'We are what we wear.'

6. 'The most revealing place of all is the home.' Compose a series of thoughtful diary entries of a person returning to their native country after an absence of some years.
7. 'Days in my life.' Imagine you are working in the household of the person in the images under Text 4. Compose an autobiographical sketch or dramatic scene in which you characterise your experience in the house and comment on your relationship with the householder.

(For answers on fifth sample paper see pages 144–49.)

Model answers to comprehension questions
First sample paper (pages 96–101)

Culture and trends: Text 1
ANSWERS TO QUESTION A

1. The purpose of this passage is to warn the reader about the dangers of taking certain vitamin pills. The writer succeeds in conveying this point clearly. The passage begins by pointing out the fact that certain types of vitamin pills may increase the risk of lung cancer and heart disease among smokers. To substantiate or back up this statement the writer makes reference to a number of different sources, in particular a report by the World Health Organization. The article develops its points by showing the conclusions that have been drawn from an international meeting in Lyon. References are also made to some words of Dr Harri Vainio, which are used to support the main statement of the article – that beta-carotene should not be promoted to the general population as a tumour-preventive treatment.

2. This article is aimed at the ordinary reader who is concerned about their health. In particular it addresses itself to those people who might be inclined to take vitamins as a food supplement. The article opens with a straightforward assertion: 'Vitamin pills increase the risk of lung cancer and heart disease among smokers.' It then develops its points by using several short, terse statements about the dangers of certain types of pills. This approach is ideal for the ordinary reader who simply wants clear information on the topic.

ANSWER TO QUESTION B

We are what we wear

'You!' the choreographer pinched my arm to guide me. 'You'd be better off dancing in the back row. And for God's sake, why don't you smile?'

I glanced round the stage. *Joseph and His Amazing Technicolour Dreamcoat* is set not long after biblical times, so we would all probably have been stoned for wearing these pastel pink and blue-and-white halter-neck tops and short skirts. In the other corner the producer was vainly trying to teach the fellas how to dance in their gold slave-skirts. Perhaps the previous six hours of standing inconspicuously in the background trying to remember the words to 'Ba, ba, ba, ba, ba, ba, ba' had caused something in my head to snap. But as I looked at the pompous producer gesticulating wildly I saw a curly-haired Adolph Hitler in black leggings. I turned my attention back to the choreographer and bared my teeth.

'That's better.'

'Good humour is one of the best articles one can wear in society.' William Makepeace Thackeray, a contemporary of Dickens and author of *Vanity Fair*, knew the importance of a smile. A smile is not only a sign of humour or pleasure, because the face we present to the outer world is rarely our real face. We rarely show what we really feel in our facial expressions or in our actions. In the words of Billy Joel, 'We all have a face that we hide away forever, and we take them out and show ourselves when everyone has gone.'

So we smile our way through the day, though in fact we may feel angry and annoyed beneath the smile. We smile at customers, the boss or the fact that we have just lost our job. Very few smiles have any real significance; they are simply a part of the suit of armour we don in order to face the world, like the masks we wear on a stage.

Society expects us to conform to a certain standard or idea in what we wear. Jung believed that the psychological struggle throughout life is to become more and more yourself, to continually discover and sculpt your own sense of uniqueness. However, my grandad laughs when I suggest he wear jeans. Him? Wear jeans? It is as if I had suggested he wear a frilly pink leotard to his next Legion of Mary meeting.

Both the clothes we wear and the hairstyles we fashion give scope for expression, though only within the glass confines of our particular culture, age, sex and social status. This kind of predictability led Bill Vaughan to observe that 'before you know it, the little girl in the frilly feminine dress is a woman in blue jeans.'

The old adage of first impressions being lasting only exacerbated my self-consciousness in my first week in first year. The existence of certain norms leaves the way open to all types of stereotyping. So within seconds of setting our eyes on new people, we make general and rigid judgments about them, right down to the very soles of their shoes.

We all know that being a teenager is often like being the reluctant star of a slapstick comedy, so I wasn't too surprised when the usually austere face of my home economics teacher contorted into a devilish grin. As she tore a hole in the top of the L&N shopping bag for my head, she was a fifteen-stone child delighting in having found a 'look what happens when you forget your apron' example.

The closest I can get to an analogy of rattling back to my table to cook those scones amid the stifling laughter is the way an early Christian would have worn a punishment sack. While the comfort of wearing horsehair was a noble and self-sacrificing deed, I on the contrary felt both victimised and absurd. Just as wearing a clown suit rids you of inhibitions about acting the clown, so too does sporting a plastic bag give you the freedom to act as scatter-brained as someone who . . . well . . . wears a plastic bag.

Take for example the distressing case of King Louis XIV of France. The narcissism of men as portrayed on those shampoo ads that we see today is a faint echo of the male pursuit of beauty under his reign. In the country where the Eiffel Tower was initially considered an eyesore, the Sun King introduced the wig and the rouged men of his day would compete for the longest, curliest locks. As if that wasn't feminine enough, Louis also encouraged the late sixteenth-century innovation of high heels, which he wore to increase his own modest height.

'It will make or break him, so he's got to buy the best, 'cause he's a dedicated follower of fashion.' The Kinks could just as well be talking about Julius Caesar. Caesar kept for his own exclusive use the very thread of history: silk. Because it was sleek and synonymous with splendour and lustre, the Chinese guarded the secret of silk for more than two thousand years and decreed death by torture to those who disclosed it. It makes you wonder whether Cleopatra was interested in Julius the man or simply his silken image.

We are all guilty of judging by appearance. No one would give Superman a reporting job because he just does not fit the image. But we must try to remember that what we wear is just a fraction of who we really are. After all, the only difference between Superman and Clark Kent lies in a pair of glasses and a different outfit. It takes a lot longer than a few seconds to catch a glimpse of the other side of a person's mask. Stevie Wonder never wanted pity for his blindness because he has the precious gift of never judging a book by the cover. 'The people I feel sorry for,' he said, 'are those with sight but who still cannot see.'

Culture and trends: Text 2
ANSWERS TO QUESTION A
1. The writer begins by referring to a Methodist university chaplain in Liverpool who has written a book on the subject of linking the film *Star Wars* with Christianity. This man – Rev. David Wilkinson – states that the film *Star Wars* is one of the most interesting films theologically because it centres on a character changing sides. He goes on to pose the question: what is it in us that produces evil? He draws a parallel between the situation in the film where the evil Emperor is thrown into the glowing maw of the hyperdrive and the theme of redemption through self-sacrifice. He goes on to claim that the Force is a sign of hope. While it is not a picture of God, it is raising the question of God. The tension in the film is based on a scientific-materialistic world view and the idea of transcendence. In the film, we are told, the good guys rely on the Force and the bad guys rely on the Death Star. Rev. Wilkinson maintains that *Star Wars* is one of the greatest consumerist phenomena of the age, as it opens up a vision of a world beyond technological consumerism.

2. The writer uses the following techniques in order to develop the arguments in the passage. The passage opens with reference to words expressed by 'an earnest Christian' on how they are trying to bring up their children with Jedi values. The writer moves on to outline how there exists a direct correlation between some of the values of Christianity and those underlying the film *Star Wars*. He uses some words expressed by Rev. David Wilkinson in order to substantiate this claim.

The article develops by illustrating the clear correlation between certain Christian ideas, such as the theme of redemption and self-sacrifice, and those that are shown in the film.

ANSWER TO QUESTION B

One of the films which I have truly enjoyed watching is *Life is Beautiful*. The film consists of two parts, which are closely related. In the first part, Guido (played by Roberto Benigni) falls in love with a school teacher in the town of Arezzo. The second part of the film takes place five years later and deals with the Nazi occupation. Guido, his wife and son are taken to a concentration camp because Guido is part-Jewish. Here, Guido uses all his wit and ingenuity to keep his son alive. For me the striking effect of this film is its ability to show the triumph of the human imagination over adversity. Guido pretends to his son that the death camp is a resort and that all the inhabitants are engaged in a game and the best players will win an enormous prize.

Some people have objected to the fact that this film trivialises the Holocaust. However, I disagree with this view. For me, the film portrays death and suffering in a highly realistic manner. The effect of this serves the purpose of identifying more clearly the enormous horror of the Holocaust. This becomes very obvious for me when Guido himself is compelled to face the ultimate horror in the picture of the piled-up bodies.

I enjoyed this film very much, as it gives a very realistic and human portrayal of characters who suffered from the horrific effects of war and genocide.

Culture and trends: Text 3
ANSWERS TO QUESTION A

1. The writer begins his argument by stating that we are witnessing a revival in the art of giving names which are totally meaningless to things. To support this statement he uses several examples from films, for example *Trainspotting*, *Blade Runner* and *Reservoir Dogs*. The stories of these films have nothing whatsoever to do with their titles.

To illustrate his argument more clearly, the writer uses a humorous and almost ironic anecdote. In this anecdote we learn how Tarantino supposedly got the title *Reservoir Dogs* for his film because of his inability to pronounce the title of the film *Au Revoir, les Enfants*.

The writer concludes his argument by claiming that nowadays things are not meant to be understood; the more incomprehensible they are, the better. The concept of meaning has become outdated.

2. i) The writer's references mainly deal with cinematic allusions. He supports his main argument about the revival of the 'fine art of meaningless naming' by referring to a play, *Virgil Is Still the Frogboy*, and the films *Trainspotting* and *Blade Runner*. He also refers to several film directors, among them Luis Buñuel and Louis Malle, and to William Burroughs. He mentions the actor Harrison Ford in order to comment humorously that in the film *Blade Runner* he neither runs nor blades and to emphasise the fact that the title has nothing whatsoever to do with the film's content.

Then, to demonstrate the fact that dreary comprehensibility does still exist, the writer makes reference to the films *Emma* and *The Fan*.

ii) A number of very effective features of style are used in this passage to support the writer's main points. The tone of the entire passage is ironic and humorous. The writer uses colloquial expressions that would be familiar to the American reader, such as 'positively cutesy', 'hip' and 'Daddy Cool', all examples of the writer's use of colloquial language and his mocking use of buzzwords.

The writer makes effective use of illustrations to support his argument. For example, the reference to the title of the film *Trainspotting* illustrates his main point that incomprehensibility is popular nowadays. In addition, there are copious references to various film directors and their films. The use of the colourful anecdote also illustrates very effectively how the young Tarantino got the name for his film *Reservoir Dogs*.

The sentence structure is varied; most of the sentences are brief, snappy statements that are in keeping with the colloquial or informal tone that is used. The writer also uses a series of short paragraphs that are clearly linked.

ANSWER TO QUESTION B
The conclusion of this passage is very suitable for the preceding argument and the tone used in it. The whole thrust of this article, conveyed by a series of striking examples, is how we are now confronted with a culture of incomprehensibility. The examples the writer uses throughout are taken from popular films and the work of modern artists. The writer also shows how directors give their films names that have nothing to do with their content. The examples he gives include films such as *Reservoir Dogs* and *Trainspotting*.

The conclusion is very effective. It succinctly sums up the writer's central arguments in a neat, effective and compact manner.

Culture and trends: Text 4
ANSWERS TO QUESTION A
1. The lifestyle suggested to me by this photograph is one of poverty and need. The clothes of the two boys are old and torn. The bigger boy has no shoes and the ground is rough and seems to be filled with rubble. In addition, the cart is roughly made: it seems to be made of a cardboard box and wiring and the wheels are broken. The metal bar propelling this old car is also rough-and-ready. The boys, however, seem to be happy. We can tell this from the smile on the face of the older boy and the fact that they are united in the picture.
2. The statement that seems to be made in this photograph is of a sense of initiative on the part of the boys. Even in conditions of poverty these two boys can find something to smile about – the older boy is happy as he pushes the younger boy along in this home-made cart. There is a strong sense of unity between the two, shown in the small detail of both boys holding the one pole and driving forward.

ANSWER TO QUESTION B

> Even in the midst of extreme hardship and poverty, Kiko and Yami can still find something to smile about. Born and bred in the Kikuyo tribe in the North Kenyan mountains, both boys were left destitute at an early age. Their father abandoned their mother and ran to the mountains and later on their mother died from disease and starvation. These two boys survived and now live with their uncle, spending their time entertaining each other and the kids from the nearby village by giving each other joyrides in the local BMW.

Second sample paper (pages 101–9)
Violence and destruction: Text I
ANSWERS TO QUESTION A
1. This passage is a dramatic example of persuasive writing. The writer's contention is that cruelty to animals is closely allied to cruelty and violence against people. The passage opens with a series of short anecdotes that illustrate the main point – how certain people who inflict cruelty on animals become dominated by a thirst for

violence, which is then used on humans. Each point made by the writer is clearly laid out in a series of neat, concise paragraphs, which make it easy to follow the writer's train of thought.

The writer uses language that is accessible and effective. Phrases such as 'pumping bullets', 'gruesome murder cases' and 'the countryside has become a virtual battlefield' serve the function of hammering home more forcefully the writer's message about the profound impact of violence on human consciousness.

The writer concludes by using an authoritarian tone in order to motivate the reader to do something about the problem: 'We should tackle this issue', 'It is, after all, a matter of life and death.' This tone is a hallmark of effective persuasive writing.

2. The following are examples of facts used in the article. (i) The chief suspect in the killings at the Capitol in Washington shot sixteen cats with his father's revolver. (ii) Michael Ryan, also called the 'Butcher of Hungerford', tested his weapons on cats and wildlife before shooting his neighbours. At the age of fourteen he had set animals alight. (iii) In Arkansas two schoolchildren, who had been taught by adults to hunt and kill animals, shot their teacher and several pupils. (iv) Neighbours in Britain had seen two children who abducted and killed a younger child cut off the heads of live pigeons. (v) Bonny and Clyde tortured livestock before they embarked on a killing spree. (vi) In Ireland a murderer claimed that exposure to cruelty in a meat plant had brutalised him. (vii) Research shows that sport hunters are seven times more likely to beat their wives than non-hunters.

The following are examples of opinions expressed in the article. (i) The killings at the Capitol in Washington should have received banner headlines. (ii) The violence in sport hunters is attributed to an excessive need among hunters to control and dominate their environment. (iii) Our gun culture is getting out of hand. Parts of the country have become a virtual battlefield. (iv) We should tackle this issue before the killing of animals spawns a major tragedy. (v) One effective measure would be to have all weapons electronically tagged so that police could monitor their use. Sadistic or over-zealous gunmen could be given the same treatment.

Answer to question B

A street scene at night

It is almost three hours since the black veil of darkness covered the city. Now and then a sliver of moonlight penetrates through the smog and illuminates the streets below. The screeching of tyres – scarcely audible above the booming noise of nightclubs – fills the air as two stolen cars race each other down the main street, driven by teenage joyriders. A lone drunk stumbles along the footpath, using parked cars for handrails.

Across the street in a dark and gloomy alleyway two wretched tramps huddle in a doorway begging for money. One of them covers the scars of a lifetime of pain and suffering beneath a coarse, wrinkled face and dull beard. Drops of rain slowly trickle down an old rusty drainpipe. At the side of the disco a young man deals drugs to his clients before they enter the club. Other people pass by in fancy clothes eager for a night of enjoyment.

Violence and destruction: Text 2
ANSWERS TO QUESTION A

1. The writer builds up atmosphere in the passage by drawing a dramatic description of nature as the storm begins to break. The atmosphere is a distinct one of threat and violence. The world of nature almost begins to take on a life of its own as the storm gathers momentum.

The passage opens with a reference to the light 'flapping' and the rumbles from the thunder filling the sky. As the lightning begins to flash, we witness how the whole atmosphere becomes transformed; every hedge, bush and tree becomes distinct in the landscape. The animals begin to react in wild confusion. This atmosphere of violence and tension intensifies as the passage develops. Just as the storm unleashes itself onto the world of nature, we become exposed to the profound destruction in its wake. The tall tree on the top of the hill is struck by lightning. As Gabriel struggles with the haystacks, his ricking-rod is also struck by a flash of lightning.

2. The writer concentrates on a series of sharp details to paint a striking, realistic image of the development of this storm. He uses a number of similes to describe the destruction in the world of nature. As the storm begins to break we are told how 'A light flapped . . . as if reflected from phosphorescent wings . . .'. Then the lightning is compared to the colour of silver and we are told how it gleams 'like a mailed army'. With the outbreak of the storm, Hardy describes how every hedge, bush and tree 'was distinct as in a line engraving'. Through the use of a colourful simile the writer shows us the image of a poplar tree, which is 'like an ink stroke on burnished tin'. When the lightning strikes the landscape and trees, we are told how 'all was silent, and black as a cave in Hinnom'. Through the use of such vivid and precise similes the writer succeeds in painting an authentic picture of the whole landscape.

Hardy also makes use of personification to depict how nature assumes a lifelike quality. As the storm batters its way across the landscape, the lightning flashes are like 'forms of skeletons' appearing in the air, 'dancing, leaping, striding, racing around, and mingling altogether in unparalleled confusion'. These images are given added intensity through the writer's emphasis on colour: 'undulating snakes of green', 'black as a cave', 'the colour of silver'.

The writer makes use of a number of small but effective details, as well as personification, similes and active verbs, to paint a truly realistic and authentic picture of the whole scene.

ANSWER TO QUESTION B

> All night the storm raged on. At last the heavens opened and began to rain down huge undulating sheets of water. At six o'clock the dawn began to break in a sombre ash colour. The air began to stir and the temperature changed. Some of the trees began to rock to the base of their trunks and the twigs clashed in strife as the wind gathered in intensity. For miles around one could see nothing but havoc: trees lay sprawled on the ground uprooted from their bases and lying in twisted and gnarled positions. Gates and fences were smashed and broken. The barrier around the paddock was battered and completely

destroyed. The storm had wreaked its full havoc. All that remained was the general devastation, which fronted the whole landscape. Morning came on, heavy, dull and leaden in intensity.

Violence and destruction: Text 3
ANSWERS TO QUESTION A
1. This is a very good example of writing as propaganda. The writer opens the article with a number of rhetorical questions: 'What is it possible to say about the loss of lives?', 'Who can say what this island would have been like?', 'How much else has been lost?'. Rhetorical questions are a hallmark of such writing and are a powerful device for gaining the reader's attention.

The writer makes use of emotive vocabulary in order to present his controversial views and images, such as 'the most sobering, most heartbreaking book . . . not a page of it is without an almost unbearable tragedy'. This type of language is very effective, as it serves the function of involving the reader on an emotional level.

Another feature of persuasive writing is the use of repetition. This device illustrates a writer's points or arguments in an emphatic way. The following examples of emphatic repetition illustrate the writer's arguments very well: 'each tragedy is real, each one was lived by actual people, each one spread vast repercussions through family, friends . . .'.

Another feature of persuasive writing is the use of metaphor and images. The writer of this article makes abundant use of images, particularly metaphors, to express an idea more forcefully through such images as 'we let the shutters of statistics conceal the mountain range of human suffering behind them', 'liberated the dead from the limbo of statistics'.

One effective device in persuasive writing is the technique of reinforcing a positive or affirmative statement by means of a negative. The writer of this article succeeds in doing this in a highly effectual and striking way in statements such as 'The issue is not individual atrocities. The issue is violence itself' and 'Not a page on it is without an almost unbearable tragedy; each tragedy is real, each one was lived by actual people'.

The most arresting feature of this passage is the one-sided view it presents of complex and controversial events, which are reduced here to a simple emotional level, the purpose of which is to undermine the legitimacy of any alternative point of view.

The writer concludes the article by making use of the imperative: 'Nothing more needs to be said. Buy *Lost Lives*. Nobody on this island can have an excuse . . .'.
2. This article would probably appear in a newspaper aimed at a readership already inclined to agree with such opinions. The views put forward are expressed in such a provocative manner that there is little likelihood that they would convince an objective reader at the level of rational argument. The article uses highly selective facts and dubious analogies, such as equating the Northern violence with the War of Independence, all aimed at rousing the reader to an emotional involvement that will make them more ready to accept the writer's extreme views.

Answer to question B

I would like to inform you about a book called *Lost Lives*. My purpose in addressing you today is to put forward a number of reasons why you should buy this book. *Lost Lives* addresses itself directly to our own history. It deals with all the deaths arising from political conflict in this century, from 1916 up to the events of the last thirty years. There can be no excuse for not knowing about the history of these events. This book describes the enormous suffering experienced by a huge number of families because of these deaths. Many negative as well as positive acts characterised the struggle for national independence and the negative ones must be confronted honestly. Some people use these facts to put forward a one-sided view that gives the impression that the recent campaign of violence was not only wrong but happened for no reason. They try to ignore the years of sectarian discrimination and repression that led large numbers of people – wrongly, in my opinion – to resort to violence. We must study the causes as well as the effects of political violence if we are serious about making certain that it never happens again.

Violence and destruction: Text 4
Answers to question A

1. Photograph A shows someone who is engaged in a parachute jump. He is being helped by two other people who are sitting in a plane. The main comment that is made in this photograph seems to be that this man is trusting absolutely in his two friends. It shows his dependence on other people and what can be achieved by people working together in harmony. In addition, the photograph seems to be suggesting the enormity of the world of nature and how small we humans seem to be within it.

Photograph B shows the football champion Jack Charlton playing with a schoolgirl and attempting to paint her face. It is a situation of fun, as can be seen from the stance of the girl, who is turning away and laughing. The expression of the other girl in the picture is also one of amusement. In some ways this photograph could represent the need for heroes and a type of hero worship.

Photograph C shows two elderly women studying an old cannon. The comment that seems to be made by this picture is how fascinating antique things can be. The fact that they are looking at a cannon, which has a pile of cannonballs beneath it, could also make a statement about the grim reality of war.

Photograph D shows a family at the seaside with their young son. He has made friends with a dog and is obviously fascinated by it. The photograph shows the power and meaning of friendship and communication.

Photograph E shows a man standing on a rough, rocky surface with his face hidden. In the distance stand two donkeys. The man appears to have climbed, as he is leaning on the stick and wears what appear to be walking boots. The significance of this photograph could be that the man is reflecting deeply on something, perhaps in a spirit of prayer or repentance.

2. Photograph A: This is a very effective image in depicting how humans engage in the art of flying. Two men seated in an aeroplane are holding a rope that is attached to another man, who is in mid-air. This serves the function of emphasising the unity of

the action and how they can achieve so much when working together in unison. In addition, a contrast is drawn between the man and the enormity of the landscape behind him. The face of the man who is in mid-air shows a sense of satisfaction at a feat that has been accomplished.

ANSWER TO QUESTION B
Photograph A : 'A leap of faith'
Photograph B : 'Picasso Jack'
Photograph C : 'The way we were'
Photograph D : 'Man's best friend or kid's worst enemy?'
Photograph E : 'The pilgrim'

Third sample paper (pages 109–14)
Communication: Text 1
ANSWERS TO QUESTION A

1. The primary purpose of the first article is to give a detached and objective account of certain words expressed by the Pope on the subject of Heaven. The writer uses an informative style in order to achieve this purpose. For example, the writer tells us how the Pope turned his attention to Paradise after the publication of a magazine that redefined concepts of Hell. The writer repeatedly refers to the actual words used by the Pope on the subject of Paradise. These statements are objective and clear: Paradise is 'a state of being' after death, a 'living and personal relationship with the Holy Trinity', 'close communion and full intimacy with God'.

The writer develops the points made by using a number of short paragraphs, each of which contains a different point made by the Pope on the subject of Heaven and Hell.

The second article is on the same subject, but the purpose of the writer here is distinctly different. This writer uses a subjective approach in commenting on the Pope's words. Much of the article is based on using certain kinds of tone, in particular sarcasm and irony. There are many ironic references throughout the passage, which serve the function of mocking or undermining the validity of the Pope's address. The writer's use of phrases such as 'even a glutton would soon sicken of ortolans eaten to the sound of soft music', the delights of paradise 'looking tackier with time', 'the Pope, the principal salesman of this time-share retreat' are all sarcastic.

The opening of the passage is both dramatic and sensational: 'Paradise is no longer the place it used to be.' The function of this approach is to shock the reader. The language is colloquial and casual; phrases such as 'chilling out with the Paraclete', 'a simple blow-out banquet', 'unlimited pleasure much like retirement to the Costa', are designed to entertain rather than inform the reader.

The first article has the function of informing the reader about the actual address of the Pope in a much more factual manner. The writer here is more objective and detached. The second article serves the function of shocking and startling the reader. The whole approach is informal and even sensational.

2. The first article would most likely be found in a serious newspaper or journal. The writer appeals to reason and logic in developing the points in the article. Each point is supported by a clear example, which is obviously well researched and rational. There is direct reference to the actual words spoken by the Pope and both evidence and facts are used throughout the article to illustrate each point made.

On the other hand, the second article would most likely appear in a tabloid newspaper. The language and approach are clearly designed to shock. There are few facts mentioned and no reference to any ideas mentioned by the Pope.

ANSWER TO QUESTION B

> In my opinion the main responsibility of a journalist is to serve the prevailing ethos of society. People have a right to the truth; they need to be informed correctly about the truth surrounding public events in order that they can play their part in society. However, commercial success and profitability are often in conflict with truth and with the needs of society.
>
> A journalist has the responsibility to ferret out the truth and to publish it. An effective journalist, in my opinion, should have the aim of informing and educating the public, not merely reflecting surface symptoms. The journalist is an advocate of truth and the primary consideration should be both the truth and the welfare of the reader.

Communication: Text 2

ANSWERS TO QUESTION A

1. The primary purpose of the writer here is to give a review of the film *The Boxer*. The writer sets out the main details of the plot and the chief features of the central character.

2. The writer opens the review on an emotive tone: 'a few poignant moments – a whisper, a glance, a touch . . .'. This approach serves the function of attracting the reader's attention. The writer then moves on to give the main outline of the plot. He uses facts and names to give us certain information. We know, for example, that the story is set in Belfast and that the main character is Danny Flynn, a former IRA man. The writer also uses certain images, such as how the film unfolds in a chaotic world and how falling in love is both dangerous and deadly. This type of imagery clearly shows the nature and style of this film. The writer concludes by commenting on how the central actor performs in this film. The evaluation is subjective; for example, the writer comments how Daniel Day-Lewis's portrayal of the central actor is 'complex, subtle and utterly convincing'.

The whole review is structured into a series of short, compact paragraphs. This particular structure makes it easy to follow the writer's development of ideas and the flow of thought. As a result of this approach, the review flows swiftly along. Note how the writer uses a minimum of words. Look at the second sentence, for example: 'Set on the streets of Belfast, the story of the "Boxer" unfolds in a chaotic world where violence is a part of everyday life and where to fall in love may be not just dangerous but deadly.'

Answer to question B

The main question which must be asked is 'Will family life be able to resist the massive competition of television in our civilised society today?' The content of many television programmes presents a great number of unsolved problems and anxieties for a child. Often questions and themes continue to worry children subconsciously and this can cause the appearance of mental or bodily disorders that are inexplicable to parents. In addition, sustained television viewing can reduce a child's creative imagination and impulses and can cause a deficiency in their literacy and cultural development. Some of the consequences of excessive television viewing are laziness, indifference, lack of concentration and increased aggressiveness.

I feel that parents must play a part in preventing television from dominating and dictating life in their homes. Parents can stimulate children's creative capacities by playing with them from an early age. In this way children develop their talents, learn how to give and take and how to narrate imaginary stories and so stimulate their imagination. This in turn will enable them to communicate better on every level.

It can be helpful for the whole family to watch a particular programme together. This can create an opportunity to react and perhaps discuss the subject matter of that programme. Also, family life needs to be safeguarded by ensuring that television does not dominate the household at meal times. Meal times are a great opportunity to consider the others in the house and give ourselves to them and find out how their day was. Television is only an instrument that we must dominate and that must not be allowed to dominate us.

Communication: Text 3
Answers to question A

1. The writer develops this statement by claiming that with the birth of Turly, worldwide portable telecommunications has been achieved. Then the writer moves on to show how this company, founded by Motorola, has changed a vision into reality through Iridium.

To illustrate this point, the writer uses a short anecdote about Karen Bertinger, who was on holiday in the Caribbean in 1985 and was unable to phone the United States on her mobile phone. She convinced the company's chief executive of the need for a system that would provide wireless communication between any two points on the planet.

The writer goes on to declare that the work of bringing this into operation was based on a great deal of effort. Many people's talents were harnessed in order to bring this idea about.

The writer declares that there are now satellites circling 500 miles above the earth.

The Iridium handsets are palm sized and are now in production. The writer shows how these handsets are now in operation and will give people the power to make and take calls anywhere in the world. They will use only one telephone and one number and will receive only one bill. The writer concludes that what was once a visionary project is now a commercial success.

2. The writer uses effective argument to develop the points made in this passage. The article opens with a deductive argument, that is, the writer makes a general statement about how pioneers of telecommunications have always looked further than others in order to expand their possibilities. The article goes on to illustrate this point by citing a particular example – that the birth of Turly has managed to bring about worldwide telecommunications.

This argument is given effective clarity by means of the short but effective anecdote about Karen Bertinger, who managed to convince the company of the need for a wireless system of communication between any two points on the globe.

To illustrate the point that this project necessitated a lot of hard work, the writer refers to Thomas Edison's remark that 'genius is one per cent inspiration, ninety-nine per cent perspiration.' The writer develops this point in more detail by means of statistics. 'From the original idea flowed thirteen years of tireless hard work as the talents of more than 10,000 people were harnessed.' There is also a reference to the presence of satellites 500 miles above the earth and how agreements have been signed with more than 300 telecommunications companies.

The writer concludes by describing the nature of Iridium handsets – how they are palm sized, can make calls anywhere and involve only one number and one bill.

ANSWER TO QUESTION B

> Particularly in the past five years, the economic boom has brought prosperity for many people. There are disadvantages to all this growth and acceleration, however. With the development of Dublin as the centralised economic and social nucleus of the country, there has been a huge increase in the number of cars in the city. In the past seven years alone, car ownership in the greater Dublin area has increased by forty-two per cent. This has given rise to a situation where Dublin's most commonly used words are now 'gridlock', 'chock-a-block' and 'bumper-to-bumper'. The unprecedented growth in the number of cars on the road is a rapidly worsening problem that Ireland, and in particular Dublin, now faces.

Communication: Text 4
ANSWERS TO QUESTION A
1. The photograph shows us a picture of a man who is standing with one leg on the ground while the other is stretching in the air. At the same time the man is reading a book. This stance suggests that he is completely set for action. Everything in his life is under control.

The relationship between the advertisement and the photograph is intended to show that with a mobile phone you are ready to take on anything. In other words, a mobile phone enables you to take control of your life.

2. The writer uses an effective caption underneath the photograph – 'Total control' – to advertise the mobile phone called 'Ready to Go'.

The advertisement also uses a direct address to the reader: 'Whatever way you look at it, a Ready to Go mobile phone gives you more than freedom, it gives you control over the way you live your life.' The advantages of this type of phone are spelled out in short, punchy statements, all of which are negative but serve the function of hammering home the writer's message: 'No bills, no rental, no connection fee, no hassle!'

Answer to question B

I would like to outline some of the benefits of using a mobile phone. For me, there are numerous benefits, and indeed I feel that a mobile phone is now almost an indispensable means of communication.

One of the chief advantages of having a mobile phone can be seen in the case of accidents and other emergencies. A mobile phone can enable you to make almost immediate contact with a doctor or ambulance. Likewise, a mobile phone can be a lifesaver if you happen to be attacked or trapped in an awkward situation. In the event of a robbery, contact can be made with the local Garda station and the culprit may be apprehended more quickly.

In the world of work, the mobile phone fulfils a number of functions. Mobile phones can be the means of securing an effective business deal. They can help in making contact with someone if you happen to be late for a meeting or if you have to cancel an appointment. Doctors on call must now consider the mobile phone one of their most indispensable instruments.

On a more day-to-day level, the mobile phone enables you to communicate with home if you know you are going to be late and let your family know where you are and how you can be contacted. As we can see, there are considerably more advantages than disadvantages in using a mobile phone.

Fourth sample paper (pages 114–20)
Lifestyles: Text 1
Answers to question A
1. The audience for this type of article is probably women who have a moderate income. The writer begins by attracting the attention of the ordinary reader with the phrase 'Seriously rich women are different from you and me.' Before moving on to capture the exciting and exotic features of this fashion show, the writer asks the question 'Do you know what you are going to wear on New Year's Eve?' The sharp reply in the next sentence – 'Neither do I' – demonstrates clearly that the writer identifies with the ordinary reader, who will not be planning so far ahead. Many of the references are to television and film stars, to 'socialites' and to trendy dress designers.
2. This type of review would probably be published in the features section of a daily newspaper or in a popular magazine. The style is informal and lively. Many of the references to celebrities like Joan Collins and Ivana Trump and fashion designers such as Paco Rabanne, Dior and Yves Saint-Laurent would be familiar to many readers. The language used is simple and accessible to a wide readership, for example: 'there they were . . . lining the front rows . . . picking their frocks for the party to end all parties.'

The writer also makes use of a series of short and clear paragraphs to develop the points made. The images used are graphic: 'Nan Kempner, the American socialite, chuckled throatily', 'the couture circus', 'a season of sybaritic fashion moments and a time to wallow'. In addition, there are lots of examples of the style of clothes displayed at this show. The writer draws on fashion trends to illustrate the styles that dominated: the exotic skins and furs, the brocade glistening with jewels, the crystals winking from silk tulle, the velvet appliquéd with mink and the fabulous plumage soaring from heads, woven from knits and trailing from the hems of taffeta opera coats. These all serve to show how the exotic and novel are a hallmark of the present time.

The writer also uses humour to conclude the article. 'Flight was a key inspiration, whether expressed in billowing parachute gowns, paratrooper gear, woman-as-bird or woman-as-satellite. Fashion was reaching for the stars – enough to make the imagination soar.'

ANSWER TO QUESTION B

Hairstyles

Hairstyles have become the new medium of expression. Hair is clearly not 'hip' these days if it is not bleached, crimped, permed, thickened or fried to within an inch of its life.

One of the most distinguishable species of teenager today is the 'metaller' or, affectionately, the 'headbanger'. These rock-music-loving Neanderthals can be clearly distinguished from the rest of the teenage type by their flowing manes of unkempt hair. This windswept style is all-important to the headbangers. It allows them, literally, to let their hair down at social gatherings such as rock concerts. On the other hand, the skinhead brings a new meaning to the old reliable short back and sides. They prefer the hygienic and practical method of simply shaving all the hair from the head. However practical and hygienic it may be, it must be admitted this looks pretty scary as it glints in the darkness under the multicoloured disco lights.

Certainly hairstyles have become a rather complex issue. Formerly flags and signs distinguished different ethnic groups; nowadays it is hairstyles which distinguish the various groups of people that comprise society today.

Lifestyles: Text 2
ANSWERS TO QUESTION A

1. This is a very effective example of persuasive writing. The article opens with several rhetorical questions, a hallmark of persuasive writing: 'Does anywhere on earth sound more exotic? Or does the name Bali evoke an image long since past of a Mecca for artists . . . Does it offer adventure, romance, peace and quiet . . .?'

The article develops by answering the question using a colloquial tone: 'Well, yes.' The writer gives a list of attractions offered by this exciting place, among them 'volcanoes, jungles, elephants, wild monkeys, amazing birds'. The writer gives a list of the activities that can be engaged in, such as go-karting, paragliding, white-water rafting, paint balling and an internet café. To illustrate Bali's popularity the writer makes use of a simile: 'Bali is to Australians what Torremolinos is to British and Irish people.'

The writer makes use of richly sensuous images, for example: 'The views of the jungle and rice paddies opposite are luscious. At night the sound of the stream at the bottom of the gorge and the clatter of insects provide an auditory environment just as compelling.' The function of such imagery is to attract the reader on an emotive level.

The article concludes by drawing a humorous illustration about the monkeys and the food vendors. This technique adds a sense of colour and interest to the writing.

2. (i) Bali was a Mecca for artists in the thirties and sixties. (ii) There are volcanoes, jungles, elephants, wild monkeys, birds, rice paddies, seas, music and dancing in Bali. (iii) In Bali there is bungee jumping, go-karting, paragliding, white-water rafting, paint balling and an internet café. (iv) Tours will take you by boat to a desert island or a bird park where there are monkeys.

ANSWER TO QUESTION B

Want that perfect paradise?
You have it now in BEAUTIFUL BALI.
Escape to the blissful beaches of Bali, where you can have the time of your life
- wallowing on the golden sandy beaches
- soaking up the glorious sunshine
- lying by cool mountain streams.

Bali has an amazing mixture of adventure sports, magnificent views of the jungle, exotic boat tours and delicious and exciting food.
All you have to do is *book now* for that perfect holiday.
No better value than Bali –
Book your holiday today!

Lifestyles: Text 3
ANSWERS TO QUESTION A

1. The writer opens this section by appealing to the different senses: we can almost smell the rain as it blows down the valley, with 'the smell of wet earth and aromatic plants'. We gain an insight into the habits of this community as they prepare for the oncoming storm. We can visualise the old woman gathering up her washing and the old man putting on his boots and waterproofs before he goes out to the garden. The writer also registers colours vividly with a series of adjectives: 'two red oxen', 'the half-timbering infilled with white plaster, the grey shutters', 'the painted panelling', the 'tobacco from a blue-and-white jar'. As he leaves the house at the conclusion he notes that there is a line of blue lupins, a favourite of German people. There is an emphasis on delineating small details in a vivid and economical way, for example, Anton Hahn takes off a tweed cap and hangs it up on an antler. Features of the characters are shown very vibrantly: 'a little girl with a pigtail', 'his head was flat on top and his face creased and red', the old woman's 'yellowing skin fell from her face in folds', her hair was 'white and cut in a fringe across her eyebrows'.

From the use of small detail we gain an insight into the type of characters represented. We learn that Anton likes his tobacco and *chicha*. We also learn from his conversation that he is bitter about the war and that he is loyal to the former king, Ludwig. In a headstrong gesture he compels the writer to drink to the health of Ludwig and he forces him to stay to dinner in spite of his protestations. It is also clear that these people were humane from their reaction to the death of the two Englishmen. Anton's father had insisted on giving them a proper burial, and before leaving, the writer notes this in the small detail of the rough wooden cross that lay beside the corral.

2. The narrator is observant. This can be seen from his expert and skilful registering of small details in both character and the environment. The old woman is described as 'tall and thin', her skin is 'yellowing' and 'falling from her face in folds'. Anton wears a tweed cap which has its own place: it hangs on an antler. The writer also carefully notes certain customs and habits, such as Anton putting on his rope-soled slippers before he settles down with his pipe and tankard of *chicha*. As the narrator leaves the house he notes the beauty of nature: the arching stems of a pampas rose, the grey harrier soaring and diving. He also observes the small cross over the graves of the two Englishmen who were killed.

The narrator is also fast and resourceful. He makes the mistake of calling the former king 'Mad Ludwig', but is quick to qualify this by claiming 'he was a great genius'.

The narrator is sensitive. He registers the details of the anecdote about the two people who were victims of the frontier police with a great deal of insight and sensitivity. He is also courteous. At the insistence of Anton, he eats what is put before him even though he maintains that he just had a meal with the soprano. He also joins Anton in a toast to King Ludwig out of respect for Anton's view.

ANSWERS TO QUESTION B

1. Wilson and Evans were friends of the Hahns. They were betrayed to the frontier police, who claimed their heads in order to get money. However, the father became angry and insisted on burying them. The anecdote contributes to the power of the passage by showing more clearly the type of people the Hahns were. Though they were Germans and had apparently suffered because of the war, they retained a great deal of humanity and sensitivity, as is evidenced by their reaction to the murder of the two men.

2. The story begins with the narrator coming down into the valley as the rain is starting. It recounts how he meets Anton Hahn and his wife and how he is invited to dinner. He then develops the narrative by giving us an insight into the character of Anton. Through the conversation we learn that Anton is bitter about the Great War – he believes that the war was the biggest mistake in history. We also see Anton's loyalty to the former German king, Ludwig. The reference to the Englishmen shows us another side to Anton's family – the humanity and generous spirit of his father, who insisted on giving the two men a proper burial. The passage concludes with the writer noting the passing of the storm and the blue lupins, which are a favourite of German settlers. Hahn's philosophical comment that no one would want to drop an atom bomb on Patagonia concludes this passage. The narrative has a distinct shape – a definite beginning, middle and conclusion.

There is also a realistic insight into the characters present in this narrative – a hallmark of good narrative writing. The dialogue is immediate and clearly shows the more striking features of these characters, in particular Anton, who is more dominant and headstrong. The style and manner of the narrative shows us different features of the narrator – his capacity for observation, his love of nature, his sensitivity and ability to record small events in a dramatic manner.

Another feature of effective narrative is the ability to draw realistic description. Here, by focusing on a series of details – on colour, movement and shape – we can almost visualise the whole scene before us. Images such as 'So I ate his ham and pickles and sun-coloured eggs and drank his apple *chicha*, which went to my head' and 'The *Fronterizas* brought them down on an ox-cart . . . They had swelled up in the heat, and the smell was terrible' bring the whole situation alive.

Lifestyles: Text 4
ANSWERS TO QUESTION A

1. The intended audience for this advertisement is the ordinary reader. The advertisement addresses itself to the reader who is in a position to help an underprivileged person in another country more effectively.

2. The advertisement is very effective, in the following ways: (i) The photograph of a young boy is highly effective in attracting the attention and sympathy of the reader. The boy's eyes and facial expression suggest someone who is desperately in need and who would greatly appreciate some small help. (ii) The heading at the top of the photograph is arresting and vivid. The underlying idea is one of helplessness in the young boy and his need for effective help, with a clever play on the term 'guardian angel'. (iii) The use of a coupon is a good way for people to find out how to help. In addition, the logo of the organisation Actionaid is clearly positioned and makes it obvious that help is being sought.

ANSWER TO QUESTION B

> My reaction to this photograph is an immediate impression that the boy is in urgent need of help. His eyes and the position of his hand convey a strong impression of a cry for help. The whole image is one of vulnerability and helplessness. This image is reinforced by the words at the top of the photograph: 'An angel in search of a guardian'.

Fifth sample paper (pages 121–6)
Home and identity: Text 1
ANSWERS TO QUESTION A

1. The writer of this article makes several powerful points about the consequences of the Third World's obsession with the Western way of life. He believes it has stunted development and destroyed both the good and the bad in traditional cultures. He contends that this obsession is a striking example of 'cultural diffusion', the roots of

which lie in colonialism. He maintains that colonialism, blinded by its own sense of superiority, imposes its culture while ignoring that of the country it has conquered. The writer concludes that cultural imperialism has become a hallmark of such societies and that it controls both the body and the soul of its victims.

The writer identifies the most insidious form of this type of dominance as 'reference-group behaviour', with the imitation of the habits and lifestyle of another culture and the simultaneous abandonment of one's own. He illustrates this by referring to Ghana and Turkey. In both instances the Western lifestyle was adopted to impress other Third World leaders and to show them that this was superior to their own culture.

2. The passage is a clear example of effective argument for the following reasons.

The writer begins the article with a colourful anecdote to illustrate his argument that adherence to traditional culture in Third World countries is maintained mostly by older people, while younger people prefer to see a performance from the Western world.

The topic sentence in each paragraph stands out clearly and is supported by graphic examples. The writer defines the term 'reference-group behaviour' and then cites examples to support this definition. This method of supporting his points with evidence makes the argument coherent and effective.

The passage concludes very effectively. The writer uses direct reference to an imposition made by the Turkish authorities, which made it compulsory to wear Western dress. The language and tone of the quotation communicate the point with added effectiveness.

ANSWER TO QUESTION B

> We are living in a material world, but you are not a material thing. Even if you were that bony bathing goddess lying on a Mediterranean beach, you know you wouldn't be happy. Sometimes the brochures with the blue skies and the even bluer seas serve only to give you the blues. It's a change of mind that you really want, not a change of scenery. But how do you get what you want, what you really want?
>
> Sri Nisargadatta Maharaj, a guru in India, tells you what you already know: 'You are living in a dream world – seek the truth!'
>
> Enlightenment awaits when you conquer the body and mind. This all-inclusive holiday to India offers you not just a superficial tan, but enables the sun to shine from your very soul as you wallow in a form of eternal bliss. You've heard the message, but the empirical knowledge is the only one of value. Seek!
>
> This magazine also offers you tape-recorded conversations with Sri Nisargadatta Maharaj in the best-selling book *I Am That* for the special price of €10.99.

Home and identity: Text 2
ANSWERS TO QUESTION A

1. The writer speaks about the subject of identity and belonging in the following points: he draws attention to the moral obtuseness underlying racist behaviour in the

anecdote about the television programme *Family Feud*. He goes on to question the importance of our identity by commenting on the size of the planet Earth, which 'resembles nothing so much as a single cell in the human body'. Having stated that the planet on which we live may be little more 'than a specimen on a slide', the writer proceeds to ask the question: How does this affect our notions of home and race?

The writer goes on to contend that home is where you would prefer to be when you are in a position to go anywhere in the world. He concludes by stating that home is the place we belong and where we find our identity. Home is the earth we explore, the people we live with and try to love in spite of their faults, the ability to pioneer the road we have undertaken no matter what situation we are in and the realisation that 'wherever there is life, we are at home'.

2. The passage is an effective example of persuasive writing. The tone of the passage is subjective. The writer uses personal references together with the subjective 'I' to show his objection to people who espouse racist views. The use of the personal pronoun 'we' is a subtle persuasive device which presupposes the reader's acquiescence in what the writer is contending. For example, phrases such as 'Home is not the place where our possessions and accomplishments are deposited and displayed: it is this earth that we have explored, the heavens we view with awe . . .' take for granted that the reader is agreeing with the arguments or points being made.

The writer uses a colloquial tone in order to address the reader more directly. The passage is structured clearly into a series of sub-sections, which make it easy to follow the writer's train of thought. The use of the anecdote about the television programme is a vivid method of illustrating his point about the destructive impact of racism. The writer also uses several rhetorical questions, another useful device to persuade the reader.

The conclusion of this passage is very effective. The writer first of all presents a negative statement, then reinforces this with a series of affirmations in order to hammer home his point more effectively: 'Home is not the place where our possessions and accomplishments are deposited and displayed – it is this earth . . . it is the willingness to pioneer . . .'. This is a very valuable technique for use in persuasive writing.

ANSWER TO QUESTION B

Mallow Road
Cork
13 July 2005

Dear sir,

I would like to draw your attention to the recent edition of *Family Feud* that was broadcast at 8 p.m. on Tuesday, 9 July.

I consider the incident involving the two families to be in very poor taste. It was shocking to see that there are people who can behave with such blindness and arrogance towards another group of people. Programmes and references like this serve to do nothing other than undermine the dignity and integrity of the person. In this particular case the people who came out badly were the white family. A programme of this type only highlights the innate ignorance and insensitivity of some people with regard to the real truth about the human person.

Perhaps, in the event of being unable to show such issues in a balanced and mature manner, you would refrain from dealing with them in any future programmes.

Yours sincerely,
Mary McMahon

Home and identity: Text 3
ANSWERS TO QUESTION A
1. The writer illustrates his argument that 'People are places, and places are people' by maintaining that whenever you write about people you also write about a place. He maintains that the best way to describe a place is to make the reader see it.

He goes on to make the statement that the most revealing place of all is the home. He uses the idea of imagining yourself in the home of a complete stranger. He declares that within five minutes you will know what type of person lives there. This will be revealed clearly through the way objects are positioned: the books (or absence of books), furniture and ornaments. The different kinds of tidiness or untidiness will tell you a lot about the person. The writer claims that if you can describe a home correctly you will not need to talk about the type of atmosphere in it because the description will have done this for you. To illustrate the power of accurate description he uses a graphic image, showing how your reader will be able to make an inference between the image of a man swaying on a windowsill ten storeys up and the same man sitting on the ground.

The writer concludes by stating that we are not 'exclusively the creatures of our economic environment'. It is people who make a home and not the opposite. He cites some familiar examples to support this statement. We make impersonal places, such as offices and factories, bear the imprint of our personality by putting pictures on the wall or by displaying gold pens or 'executive toys'.

2. Yes, I believe that the writer argues his position clearly. He begins with a short, terse sentence that introduces his main argument: 'People are places, and places are people.' A variety of sentence structures is used to develop the argument that we can determine the atmosphere of a place from its description.

Each paragraph is clearly laid out and easy to follow. The writer sets out the topic or main sentence at the beginning of each paragraph. The first paragraph develops the argument by addressing the reader directly in a colloquial tone: 'This isn't meant to dazzle you with its originality: it's simply another working rule.' In the following paragraphs the topic sentences are developed and expanded by means of effective and apt analogies. The second paragraph opens with the statement that 'The most revealing place of all is the home.' To develop this statement the writer uses the argument about being in the home of a complete stranger and how we can make a judgment on what type of person he or she is. The examples used are simple and accessible – the novel description of different types of tidiness and untidiness, the positioning of material things. The concluding paragraph also makes use of familiar and relevant examples, such as the type of accessories one can accumulate in a place of work, whether pictures on the wall, gold pens or 'trendy executive toys'.

ANSWER TO QUESTION B

Hello, and welcome to this special edition of *Empire*. Today we are going to take a peep into the private life and home of none other than Jack Nicholson. The world-famous actor now lives in Los Angeles, where his new three-storey villa is some sight!

Let's start with the outside. The front gates form part of an enormous electric fence, with two security cameras and a tough-looking bodyguard. The long drive up to the house is interesting, filled with exotic plants and luxurious smells. The garden looks like something from ancient Rome, with its two Jacuzzis and its enormous pool surrounded by magnificent marble statues.

Inside this large and lavish house we gain another insight into the type of man Jack Nicholson is through the existence of a small but significant detail: a striking oak cabinet in the front hall. Here we are confronted with not one but two Academy Awards and numerous Golden Globes for Nicholson's many starring roles.

The hall and dining room are filled with prestigious masterpieces, such as works by Van Gogh and Picasso.

The large drawing room contains an amazing view over the lake and in the centre of the parquet floor lies a large leopard-skin rug. The seats are made of black Italian leather and make it enormously difficult to emerge from them once you sink into their luxurious folds. Certainly this home is worth a visit to see how the other half lives!

Home and identity: Text 4
ANSWERS TO QUESTION A

1. The lifestyle suggested to me by this collection of images is one of wealth. The image of the old mansion, together with the pictures of antiques and a horse, suggest a country estate of grandeur and elegance.

2. This lifestyle is suggested by the various pictures, such as the horse, the binoculars which are obviously old and precious and the two dogs that lie indolently on each side of the picture. The picture of the woman with pearls suggests a person of wealth.

3. The type of publication that would show such images is a 'country life' magazine such as *Town and Country* or *Horse and Hound*. Such publications are aimed at a very selective readership, including rich landowners, aristocratic families and other wealthy people.

4. Introductory paragraph for the magazine *Horse and Hound*:

Set in the heart of Connemara, the ancient castle of Ballyglunin Park lies secluded on its own grounds of several thousand acres. The River Cloon flows through the grounds. Stretching out beyond the huge grounds at the back are the splendid stables, which shelter many of the finest thoroughbreds this area has ever seen. The castle itself is famous for its distinctively wide hallway, containing a splendid stained-glass window. This carries the date 1415, the year in which it was taken over by its previous owners, the Butlers. The present owners, the O'Brien family, are renowned for their great love of animals. Once a year Ballyglunin Park opens its doors to host the annual Antique Fair, an event that draws people from all over the country. This castle and its heritage are something we can all take pride in.

ANSWER TO QUESTION B

9 Laurence Terrace
Huntstown
Co. Limerick
14 December 2006

Ms Marie Heraughty
Graphic Design Centre
Arch Row
Belfast

Dear Ms Heraughty,

    I am planning to compile a photo gallery of things that are important to me and that I have accumulated throughout my life.

    I have been given your name by a friend of mine who has praised your expertise in this area. I wish to include some pictures that would show an image of happiness and success. For that reason, perhaps you could include some large maps of the world to show that I have travelled a great deal. I would also like you to include pictures of my home and family, in particular a picture of my youngest daughter.

    Could you contact me at the above address or by phone (061) 2276893 to let me know whether this is possible?

Yours sincerely,
Joan Dunne

Paper II

Paper II, the literature paper, is divided into three sections: fiction, drama and poetry. Each of these sections is dealt with separately below.

7 Examination Technique in Paper II

PRESCRIBED TEXTS FOR EXAMINATION IN 2005

Students are required to study:
1. *One text* on its own from the following texts:
BRONTË, Emily	*Wuthering Heights*
ELIOT, George	*Silas Marner*
McGAHERN, John	*Amongst Women*
SHAKESPEARE, William	*Hamlet*
	As You Like It

2. *Three other texts* from the list below, in a comparative manner, according to the comparative modes prescribed for this course.

   Any texts from the list below, other than the one already chosen for study on its own, may be selected for the comparative study.

   A film may be studied as one of the three texts in a comparative study.

   The comparative modes for examination in 2005 at Higher Level are:
   (i) the general vision and viewpoint
   (ii) theme or issue
   (iii) literary genre.

Texts prescribed for comparative study for examination in 2005
(texts marked with an asterisk are discussed in this book)

ACHEBE, Chinua	*Things Fall Apart*
ANGELOU, Maya	*I Know Why the Caged Bird Sings*
BALLARD, J. G.	*Empire of the Sun*

BARKER, Pat	*Regeneration*
BIELENBERG, Christabel	*The Past is Myself*
BINCHY, Maeve	*Circle of Friends*
BRANAGH, Kenneth (Dir.)	*Much Ado About Nothing* (film)*
BRONTË, Charlotte	*Jane Eyre*
BRONTË, Emily	*Wuthering Heights**
CHANG, Jung	*Wild Swans*
COSTNER, Kevin (Dir.)	*Dances with Wolves* (film)*
ELIOT, George	*Silas Marner**
FRIEL, Brian	*Dancing at Lughnasa*
GORDIMER, Nadine	*The House Gun*
HUSTON, John (Dir.)	*The Dead* (film)*
IBSEN, Henrik	*A Doll's House**
KINGSOLVER, Barbara	*The Poisonwood Bible**
LEONARD, Hugh	*Home Before Night*
LUHRMANN, Baz (Dir.)	*Strictly Ballroom* (film)*
MADDEN, Deirdre	*One by One in the Darkness*
MALOUF, David	*Fly Away Peter*
McGAHERN, John	*Amongst Women**
MEHTA, Gita	*A River Sutra*
MILLER, Arthur	*A View from the Bridge*
MOORE, Brian	*The Statement*
O'CASEY, Seán	*Juno and the Paycock*
O'HANLON, Redmond	*Into The Heart Of Borneo*
OZ, Amos	*Panther in the Basement*
PROULX, E. Annie	*Heart Songs*
RADFORD, Michael (Dir.)	*Il Postino* (film)*
SHAKESPEARE, William	*As You Like It**
	*Hamlet**
SOPHOCLES	*Oedipus the King*
SPARK, Muriel	*The Prime of Miss Jean Brodie*
STEINBECK, John	*Of Mice and Men**
SYNGE, J. M.	*The Playboy of the Western World*
TYLER, Anne	*A Slipping-Down Life*
TWAIN, Mark	*The Adventures of Huckleberry Finn*
WEIR, Peter (Dir.)	*Witness* (film)*

3. **Shakespearean drama**

   At Higher Level a play by Shakespeare must be one of the texts chosen. This can be studied on its own or as an element in a comparative study.

4. **Poetry**

   A selection from the poetry of the following eight poets is prescribed for the Higher Level examination in 2005:

BOLAND
DICKINSON
ELIOT
HEANEY
KAVANAGH
LONGLEY
WORDSWORTH
YEATS

Students will be expected to have studied at least six of the prescribed poems by each poet.

Prescribed texts for examination in 2006

Students are required to study:
1. *One text* on its own from the following texts:
AUSTEN, Jane	*Pride and Prejudice*
KINGSOLVER, Barbara	*The Poisonwood Bible*
McCABE, Eugene	*Death and Nightingales*
SHAKESPEARE, William	*As You Like It*
	King Lear

2. *Three other texts* from the list below, in a comparative manner, according to the comparative modes prescribed for this course.

   Any texts from the list below, other than the one already chosen for study on its own, may be selected for the comparative study.

   A film may be studied as one of the three texts in a comparative study. The comparative modes for examination in 2006 at Higher Level are:
   (i) theme or issue
   (ii) cultural context
   (iii) literary genre.

Texts prescribed for comparative study for examination in 2006
(texts marked with an asterisk are discussed in this book)

ATWOOD, Margaret	*Cat's Eye*
AUSTEN, Jane	*Pride and Prejudice**
BELL, Sam Hanna	*December Bride*
BIELENBERG, Christabel	*The Past is Myself*
BINCHY, Maeve	*Circle of Friends*
BRANAGH, Kenneth (Dir.)	*Henry V* (film)*
BRONTË, Charlotte	*Jane Eyre**
CAREY, Peter	*True History of the Kelly Gang*
CHEVALIER, Tracy	*Girl with a Pearl Earring*
COSTNER, Kevin (Dir.)	*Dances with Wolves* (film)*
CRUISE O'BRIEN, Kate	*The Homesick Garden*
DICKENS, Charles	*Great Expectations**

ELIOT, George	*Silas Marner**
IBSEN, Henrik	*A Doll's House**
IVORY, James (Dir.)	*A Room with a View* (film)*
JOHNSTON, Jennifer	*How Many Miles to Babylon?*
JOYCE, James	*Dubliners*
KAZAN, Elia (Dir.)	*On the Waterfront* (film)*
KEANE, John B.	*Sive*
KINGSOLVER, Barbara	*The Poisonwood Bible**
LEE, Laurie	*A Moment of War*
LIVELY, Penelope	*Moon Tiger*
MADDEN, Deirdre	*One by One in the Darkness*
McCABE, Eugene	*Death and Nightingales**
MILLER, Arthur	*A View from the Bridge*
MOORE, Brian	*The Statement*
NAIPAUL, V. S.	*An Area of Darkness*
O'CASEY, Seán	*Juno and the Paycock*
O'HANLON, Redmond	*Into The Heart Of Borneo*
PROULX, E. Annie	*Heart Songs*
RADFORD, Michael (Dir.)	*Il Postino* (film)*
SHAKESPEARE, William	*As You Like It**
	*King Lear**
	Twelfth Night
SOPHOCLES	*Antigone**
STEINBECK, John	*Of Mice and Men*
TYLER, Anne	*A Slipping-Down Life*
WEIR, Peter (Dir.)	*Witness* (film)*
YOSHIMURA, Akira	*Shipwrecks*

3. *Shakespearean drama*
   At Higher Level a play by Shakespeare must be one of the texts chosen. This can be studied on its own or as an element in a comparative study.

4. *Poetry*
   A selection from the poetry of the following eight poets is prescribed for the Higher Level examination in 2006:
   BISHOP
   DONNE
   ELIOT
   HARDY
   HOPKINS
   LONGLEY
   PLATH
   YEATS
   Students will be expected to have studied at least six of the prescribed poems by each poet.

Prescribed texts for examination in 2007

Students are required to study:
1. *One text* on its own from the following texts:
   AUSTEN, Jane   Pride and Prejudice
   BRONTË, Emily   Wuthering Heights
   KINGSOLVER, Barbara   The Poisonwood Bible
   MILLER, Arthur   Death of a Salesman
   SHAKESPEARE, William   Macbeth
2. *Three other texts* from the list below, in a comparative manner, according to the comparative modes prescribed for this course.
   Any texts from the list below, other than the one already chosen for study on its own, may be selected for the comparative study.
   A film may be studied as one of the three texts in a comparative study. The comparative modes for examination in 2007 at Higher Level are:
   (i)   general vision or viewpoint
   (ii) theme or issue
   (iii) cultural context.

Texts prescribed for comparative study for examination in 2007
(texts marked with an asterisk are discussed in this book)
   ATWOOD, Margaret   Cat's Eye
   AUSTEN, Jane   Pride and Prejudice*
   BRANAGH, Kenneth (Dir.) Henry V (film)*
   BRONTË, Emily   Wuthering Heights*
   CAREY, Peter   True History of the Kelly Gang
   CHEVALIER, Tracy   Girl with a Pearl Earring
   COETZEE, J. M.   Boyhood: Scenes from Provincial Life
   DEANE, Seamus   Reading in the Dark
   DESAI, Anita   Fasting, Feasting
   DEVLIN, Anne   After Easter
   ELIOT, George   Silas Marner*
   FRAYN, Michael   Spies
   HADDON, Mark   The Curious Incident of the Dog in the Night-time
   IVORY, James (Dir.)   A Room with a View (film)*
   JOHNSTON, Jennifer   How Many Miles to Babylon?
   JOYCE, James   Dubliners
   KEANE, John B.   Sive
   KINGSOLVER, Barbara   The Poisonwood Bible*
   LEE, Laurie   A Moment of War
   LIVELY, Penelope   Moon Tiger
   LUMET, Sydney (Dir.)   Twelve Angry Men (film)*
   McCABE, Eugene   Death and Nightingales*

MILLER, Arthur	*Death of a Salesman**
MOORE, Brian	*Lies of Silence*
NAIPAUL, V. S.	*An Area of Darkness*
O'BRIEN, Kate Cruise	*The Homesick Garden*
O'CASEY, Seán	*Juno and the Paycock*
PATCHETT, Ann	*Bel Canto*
RADFORD, Michael (Dir.)	*Il Postino* (film)*
SHAKESPEARE, William	*Macbeth**
	Twelfth Night
	*As You Like It**
SHERIDEAN, Jim (Dir.)	*My Left Foot* (film)*
TAYLOR, Mildred	*The Road to Memphis*
TÓIBÍN, Colm	*The Blackwater Lightship*
TYLER, Anne	*A Slipping-Down Life*
WEIR, Peter (Dir.)	*Witness* (film)*
WILDE, Oscar	*The Importance of Being Earnest*
YOSHIMURA, Akira	*Shipwrecks*

3. *Shakespearean drama*
   At Higher Level a play by Shakespeare must be one of the texts chosen. This can be studied on its own or as an element in a comparative study.

4. *Poetry*
   A selection from the poetry of the following eight poets is prescribed for the Higher Level examination in 2007:
   BISHOP
   DONNE
   ELIOT
   FROST
   KAVANAGH
   MONTAGUE
   PLATH
   YEATS
   Students will be expected to have studied at least six of the prescribed poems by each poet.

EXAMINATION TECHNIQUE IN PAPER II

1. The total number of marks required for Paper II is 200, or 50 per cent.
2. The time allowed for Paper II is three hours and twenty minutes.
3. You must answer from four different sections:
   - one question on a single text (total marks: 60)
   - one question on a comparative study of texts (total marks: 70)
   - one question on prescribed poetry (total marks: 50)
   - questions on an unseen poem (total marks: 20).

4. Divide your time in the following way:
   - The single text: 60 minutes
   - The comparative study of texts: 70 minutes
   - The prescribed poetry: 50 minutes
   - The unseen poetry: 15 minutes.
5. Give yourself five minutes to read back over the paper and to check your answers against the questions asked. *Do not exceed this time.* Remember, good time-keeping in an examination is essential in order to gain the necessary marks. *You will not receive extra marks by writing beyond the time.*
6. Attempt all sections of the paper.
7. Remember, you must answer a question on Shakespearean drama, either as a single text or as part of a comparative study.

ANSWERING LITERATURE QUESTIONS

1. Do the question that you find easiest first. This will cause you to peak; it will boost your confidence and help you with the other sections.
2. Do not rush at answering questions. Spend time working out the implications of the question. Make sure you clearly understand what is being asked in the question. To do this, analyse or decode every aspect of the question.
3. Know the difference between such terms as 'justify', 'analyse', 'discuss', 'compare', 'contrast', 'evaluate', 'assess', 'comment', 'paraphrase'.
4. Remember, you don't have to agree with the question that is asked. Clearly show what stance you are taking on the question. Use evidence from your text or texts to support your stance on the question.
5. Rephrase the question in your own words. It can help to formulate it as a direct question: for example, '*Silas Marner* explores the effects of obsession for money and the need for human love' can be rephrased as 'How are the issues of obsession with money and the need for human loved developed in the novel *Silas Marner*?'
6. Draw a circle around the main points of the question and begin to organise a rough draft.
7. Brainstorm the topic. Use trigger questions: How? Why? Where? When?
8. Begin by *answering* the question asked. Your opening paragraph should simply make a *firm* and *clear* statement on the question that is asked.
9. Use the present tense in your answer. Use modern English as much as you can.
10. Give yourself time to look back over the answers. Check your answer for irrelevant statements, incoherent argument and repetition of ideas.
11. Before you construct a paragraph in your answer, consider:
    - What is the topic sentence or main idea of this paragraph?
    - What relationship has this paragraph to the question?
    - Are the ideas in the paragraph given support through evidence or quotation?
    - Does the concluding paragraph tie up all the ideas and refer back to the question?

    Remember in each paragraph to refer to what is being asked in the question and

remember that each paragraph in your answer has to advance your argument to another stage. Each paragraph is a logical stage in a coherent and developing argument. If the paragraph doesn't have a bearing or relationship to the question, then discard it.

Features of a good answer on literature

1. A unity of impression. All paragraphs relate to one another and to the topic in general. The concluding paragraph must synthesise or tie up all the preceding ideas and arguments.
2. Answers that focus on what is asked, that don't beat around the bush, digress or introduce material that is irrelevant.
3. A style that is familiar and clear to your reader. Remember that you are communicating with, not impressing, your reader. Avoid:
   - awkward syntax
   - long-winded sentences
   - repetition
   - the self-conscious 'I think', 'I hope to prove that', 'I feel I have shown that'. These are redundant and weaken your argument. A good literature essay does not need such statements – it should speak for itself.
4. A clear understanding of the question asked. The opening paragraph must focus your position on the question and show the direction your answer will take.
5. An individual or personal response. Don't rehash notes or critiques – make the answer your own. Support what you say by reference to or quotation from the text.
6. A maturity of response. Answers in the literature section must show that you have evaluated all sides and are presenting an objective, balanced and coherent answer.
7. A structured and organised argument, with supporting evidence that leads logically to a conclusion. Good essays make progress – they advance an argument, explore an issue and arrive at a conclusion.

Incorporating quotations in answers

Every question on the literature paper requires reference to or quotation from the text. Quotations must be positioned in such a way that they play a central role in advancing your argument. The length of quotations must be appropriate to the point being made – give as many words from the text as are strictly relevant to your point – no more and no less. You must explain the relevance of a quotation, how this quotation relates to the point or points being made.

Use a colon or comma to introduce a quotation. 'The novel *Dubliners* represents many instances of male violence. For example, in one story, 'Counterparts', we learn that Farrington, a young man: "aches to revel in violence", and that "the indignities of life enrage him".'

The Study of a Single Text 8

The questions on this section will take for granted that you have acquired a thorough knowledge of the novels or plays you have studied. This means you must:
- know the main features or characteristics of the central characters well
- study the plot and how it develops in the text
- know how language and imagery are used to serve the writer's purpose
- study the principal quotations that describe the motivation of the characters, and the attitude of the writer to the characters and to the issues that are treated in the text.

HOW TO ANSWER A QUESTION ON THE STUDY OF A SINGLE TEXT

1. Rephrase the question. Sometimes it can help to formulate the task as a direct question.
2. Take a definite stance on the question. Decide clearly whether you agree, partly agree or disagree with the question. You are free to take whatever stance you like, as long as you support it clearly with evidence and reference to the text.
3. Your opening paragraph should state clearly, in one or two sentences, your position on the question and the direction your essay will take.
4. Begin to organise your ideas before you start to write the essay. Jot down several points – six or seven – in note form. These will deal with different aspects of the question and will be constructed in paragraphs. The graph illustrates these points more clearly.

How to answer the question on the study of a single text

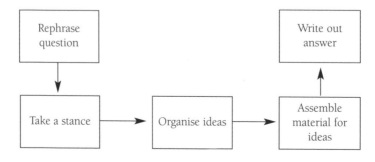

Sample draft answers

Here are sample draft answers to questions on selected texts that illustrate these points. In each case the sample opening paragraph is written out fully; the points for the other paragraphs are written in note form. Closely examine the technique used in answering the questions in this section.

Amongst Women
(2005 exam)
Discuss the position and role of the woman in the novel *Amongst Women*.

Stage 1
Rephrase the question. Examine what part the woman plays in the novel *Amongst Women*.

Sample opening paragraph
There are many different types of female character shown in the novel *Amongst Women*, written by John McGahern and set against an Irish background in the years following the War of Independence in 1921. In spite of the fact that these women have very different types of personality, their role is seen as essentially subservient to that of the male at this particular time in Irish history.

Paragraph 2
Discuss the personality of Rose Brady; that she is an independent girl who had worked in Glasgow and comes home to nurse her sick father. Show how she defies her family and succeeds in marrying Moran.

Paragraph 3
Develop some points that draw out the different characters of the Moran girls: Sheila, Mona and Maggie. Show how they are dependent on Moran's moods, and sensitive to his erratic behaviour.

Paragraph 4
Discuss the changes that take place in the house with the arrival of Rose; how she sets a 'tone that would not be easily wrested from her'. Show the girls' joyful reaction to her personality when she arrives in the house. Show the changes in the lives of the girls with the arrival of Rose; how Maggie manages to go to England and become independent.

Paragraph 5
Develop the relationship between Rose and the Moran family and in particular show how she withstands Moran's erratic and violent behaviour. Show her strength of character in standing up silently for her rights and how she reacts to his verbal violence by announcing that she will leave the house if he thinks she is not wanted. Show how,

through her moral strength, she manages to help the girls attain their independence and find good jobs.

Paragraph 6
Show the girls' progress and how they are very anxious to please Moran by bringing their boyfriends to the house for approval. Draw a contrast between the position and reaction of Luke and Michael to Moran and that of the girls. Develop the point about their unstinting devotion to Moran through all the years in spite of his tempestuous character.

Concluding paragraph
Draw together all the points made. Make reference again to the background of this novel – Ireland in the early twentieth century. Show how the role of the woman was slowly changing from working in the home all day to becoming professionally independent. Sum up the main points on the role of the Moran girls and outline how Rose contributed to helping them, through the particular way she behaved as Moran's wife.

As You Like It
(2005 and 2006 exams)
'The play *As You Like It* is based on a good deal of contrast between different types of worlds and characters.' Test the truth of this statement with reference to the play.

Stage 1
Rephrase the question. The play *As You Like It* projects two different worlds and contrasting characters.

Sample opening paragraph
This is a true statement. *As You Like It* is a happy comedy, which also has its villains and darker sides. Shakespeare has managed to present many contrasting sets of relationships and characters in this lively and fast-paced play.

Paragraph 2
Discuss the two different worlds represented in the play – that of the court and the Forest of Arden. Show how realistic the representation of life is through the picture given of suffering and danger in the forest. The forest is not merely a golden world of youth and romance, but also a place of cold and hunger.

Paragraph 3
Comment on the difference in the relationship between Orlando and his brother Oliver and that between Rosalind and Celia. Outline how one is based on deceit and treachery and the other on love and loyalty. Contrast Oliver's treachery with Celia's loyalty and willingness to suffer for Rosalind.

Paragraph 4
Show the differences between the characters, value systems and lifestyles of Duke senior and his brother, Duke Frederick.

Paragraph 5
Discuss the difference between the values of courtesy and respect in the forest and those of flattery and vanity in the court.

Concluding paragraph
Tie all your ideas together and show how Shakespeare has given a realistic insight into both worlds through his representation of life in the forest and that in the court.

Wuthering Heights
(2005 and 2007 exams)
'Emily Brontë makes use of an original and distinctive method of narration in her novel *Wuthering Heights*.' Assess the truth of this statement in light of your reading of Wuthering Heights. Support your answer by reference to or quotation from the novel.

Stage 1
Rephrase the question. The narrative technique in the novel *Wuthering Heights* is both unique and original. Discuss.

Sample opening paragraph
This statement is true. Brontë makes use of two ordinary narrators to tell this extraordinary story: Lockwood, a young man from London, and Nelly Dean, a housekeeper.

Paragraph 2
Discuss the reason for this extraordinary narrative technique – how it is used as a means of bringing otherwise incredible and supernatural events within the reader's grasp.

Paragraph 3
Discuss Lockwood's narrative in the first four chapters. Develop his character by drawing a contrast with that of Heathcliff and the whole environment of the Heights. Comment on the effect of this. Show how the author is able to introduce the theme of the supernatural (the figure of the ghostly Catherine outside the window) through the medium of Lockwood and so make it credible and acceptable to the reader.

Paragraph 4
Develop the point on how this story is given an anchor in the normal, everyday world by commenting on Lockwood's first reaction to the inhabitants of the Heights. Take particular note of his first reaction to young Cathy.

Paragraph 5
Discuss the character of Nelly Dean. Show how she continually shifts loyalties between Edgar Linton and Heathcliff and comment on how she contributes to bringing about a good deal of the tragedy that happens in the lives of the people in the story.

Paragraph 6
Comment on Nelly's part in facilitating Heathcliff's revenge plans by foolishly allowing young Cathy to be trapped in the Heights and later on to marry young Linton.

Concluding paragraph
Tie up all the points made and restate the particular type of story and genre of this novel. Draw a contrast between the two narrators and their contributions in developing the plot. Show how the novelist skillfully succeeds in revealing an unfamiliar world of heightened passions and violence and yet makes it credible through her extraordinary narrative technique.

Death and Nightingales
(2006 exam)
'Eugene McCabe deals with the issue of politics in Northern Ireland in a realistic and vivid way in the novel *Death and Nightingales*.' Do you agree with this statement?

Stage 1
Rephrase the question. Show how the theme of politics in Northern Ireland is represented in the novel *Death and Nightingales* in a realistic manner.

Sample opening paragraph
McCabe is a writer who deeply explores the beliefs and motives behind extreme political activity and who is sensitive to the complexity of such issues as loyalty and betrayal, specifically in the Northern Irish context. This is clearly evident in the novel *Death and Nightingales,* which is set near the border in the years around 1880. The story deals with the times when Parnell ruled in the nineteenth century and when the agitation underlying the Land League was at its peak. All of these political events are shown in the novel in a vivid and realistic manner.

Paragraph 1
Show how the attitude of Billy Winters mirrors the Protestant landlordism at that time.

Paragraph 2
Draw a contrast between the views of Winters, a Protestant landlord, and that of Liam Ward, a man who espouses the politics of republicanism. Discuss how these characters and their different political beliefs are treated with realism and insight.

Paragraph 3
Discuss the effect of Winters's political ideas in both his family and the community around him.

Paragraph 4
Comment on how the different political viewpoints are represented in the story. In your answer, make reference to or quotation from the novel.

Concluding paragraph
Tie up the different political ideologies represented in the novel and show how all of this mirrors a real Ireland in the 1880s. Comment in particular on the final scene and how it functions to make a distinct statement on the political situation in Ireland.

The Poisonwood Bible
(2006 and 2007 exams)
Discuss the effect of the particular narrative technique in the novel *The Poisonwood Bible*.

Stage 1
Rephrase the question. Show how the narrative is told and demonstrate the particular effects of this method in *The Poisonwood Bible*.

Sample opening paragraph
The novel *The Poisonwood Bible* has a distinct and original narrative method, as it is made up of the voices of five different types of women. These women form part of the Price family, who are Baptists and who spend over twenty years working as white people in the Belgian Congo during the sixties. The particular narrative method mirrors the changes that occurred in the family while also commenting on and highlighting the more dramatic political changes that were wrought in this African country.

Paragraph 1
Speak about the parallel that is drawn between public and private lives, the domestic and political worlds. Show how at times the connection is made explicit – for example, when one of the sisters dies on the same day as Patrice Lumumba.

Paragraph 2
Develop the character of the father Nathan Price and show how the narrative highlights the violence and exploitation within the Price household. Comment on how this mirrors the tyranny and repression of the Belgian Congo and Mobutu's Zaire.

Paragraph 3
Show how at certain stages the narrative is interrupted by the voice of Nathan's wife, Orleanna, who gives her particular version of events that occur in these years.

Paragraph 4
Highlight Adah's narrative and how it deals with the repercussions of Nathan's efforts to convert the natives. She speaks in the voice of the politically and culturally progressive in the story. Her narrative also gives a succinct history of the efforts of colonisation in a period of fifty years in this country.

Paragraph 5
Contrast the narrative of the other sisters – Leah, Rachael and Ruth May – and show how each one develops her own independence and individuality in this particular cultural world.

Conclusion
Tie the various threads of the stories together and show how the narrative technique simultaneously spans twenty-five years of a family with that of a country and its history of political change and violence. Restate the point that each of the different narrative voices shows us the power of freedom and how each member of the Price family reacts in a different manner to the events in Africa in these years.

Sample complete answers

The following are complete sample answers that can be used in the study of a single text. Study the way in which the answers are constructed and in particular the commentary at the conclusion.

Hamlet
(2005 exam)
Deception plays a large part in the play *Hamlet*. Discuss how deception is represented in *Hamlet*. In your answer take into account the language and imagery used by the playwright. Make reference to the text in your answer.

Sample answer
Deception plays a large part in *Hamlet* in the representation of different characters and in the plot. This theme or issue is represented in many different ways and is obviously rooted in the present king of Denmark, Claudius, who has assumed the throne on the basis of murdering his brother, Old Hamlet.

In the court of Elsinore deceit and corruption are rife. The present king, Claudius, appears to be living in incest according to the law at that time. Claudius' first speech in the court of Elsinore shows him to be a king of considerable political skill. He demonstrates extraordinary qualities of decisiveness and self-control as he swiftly combats the threat from Norway. Claudius appears to be a capable politician dedicated to his country's interest, but in reality he is a murderous usurper.

Likewise, Polonius, the chief advisor to the king, appears to be a concerned father and a loyal, faithful, wise man, but the reality is that he is a corrupt plotter who is motivated totally by self-interest. His maxims are superficial and worldly. For example, he tells his son Laertes 'to thine own self be true, | And it must follow, as the night the day, | Thou canst not then be false to any man.' The irony of speeches such as this is that Polonius spends his time in the play deceiving and betraying the people he deals with. He reads his daughter's love letters before the court of Denmark and sends a servant to France to spy on Laertes, with the suggestion that Laertes frequents brothels and has a corrupt lifestyle.

From the very beginning of this play it is clear that Hamlet does not know who to trust. He realises that appearances can be deceptive, 'That one may smile, and smile, and be a villain' (Act I, Scene v). This lack of faith in humankind is rooted in the fact that Claudius has falsely assumed kingship, and furthermore, Old Hamlet has informed Hamlet about the truth of the affair.

Much of the play shows Hamlet having to conceal reality by appearance in order to discover reality, thus the issue of false appearance becomes synonymous with this theme of deception. Hamlet has to test the appearance of things to see if they tally with reality. During this testing period he disguises himself and puts on 'an antic disposition'.

The theme of appearance and reality is reinforced by action and imagery. Polonius tells Reynaldo to cloak his purpose while trying to discover the reality about Laertes. Rosencrantz and Guildenstern try to find out the real cause of Hamlet's madness by masquerading as friends, while in reality they are the king's lackeys. The Ghost himself was deceived by his 'most seeming-virtuous queen'.

The reality of the Ghost's authenticity needs to be tested by Hamlet because 'he may be a goblin damned'. The play within a play is supposed to be entertainment, but the reality is that it is part of the device to test the validity of the Ghost and the true nature of Claudius' character. After the play Hamlet comes upon the praying king, but refrains from killing him as he thinks he is making his peace with God. This is how it appears, but in reality the king is no nearer grace or redemption since he cannot relinquish those things for which he committed the crime, as his own words confirm: 'my crown, mine own ambition and my queen'.

This theme of deception dominates almost every act of the play. In the closet scene Hamlet and his mother seem to be alone yet they are not, as Polonius is hiding behind an arras. Hamlet is enticed into what seems to be a sporting duel in fencing. This is the appearance, but the reality is the intention to cause death by a poisoned sword. In fact, the arras becomes a central symbol to dramatise this theme of deception – Claudius and Polonius spend their time prying into other people's affairs and they use the arras as their prop.

At the end of the play all appearance has broken down and reality and truth are fully exposed. The final scene is the great moment of truth and reality. Shakespeare uses imagery of painting, clothes and acting throughout the play to convey this conflict between appearance and reality and to underscore the deception that governs the atmosphere of this play. Hamlet tells his mother that grief is not to be judged merely by 'his inky cloak' (Act I, Scene ii). He has that 'within which passes show'. Polonius uses the same image to declare: 'the apparel oft proclaims the man'.

Hamlet puts on 'the antic disposition'. The player delivers a powerfully emotional speech while merely acting a part in a drama. Further on we have the 'harlot's plastered face', an image which shows the concealment of reality.

The function of all these types of imagery seems to lie in the idea that in the final analysis ultimate truth will assert itself. All the painting and acting cannot conceal the fact that man is mortal; it cannot hide the reality of man's transience.

Language plays a vital part in communicating the theme of deception in this play.

The play concludes with all painting, acting and cloaking being penetrated and the reality is fully exposed in the figure of Horatio, who deliberately survives to vindicate the truth about the events that have taken place in Denmark.

Comment
The answer begins by taking a clear stance or position on the question and showing how the theme of deception is a central issue in the play *Hamlet*.

The answer then proceeds to develop by giving concrete examples of where and how this is then shown in the play. Certain scenes are selected and shown to be representative of this theme in the play.

The playwright's use of language and imagery are used as an example on how this theme is developed and shown in the play.

A clear conclusion is drawn and the question is restated.

Silas Marner
(2005 exam)
'The novel *Silas Marner* is not just a fairytale but also explores problems that affect real life.' Discuss this statement, supporting your answer by quotation from or reference to the novel.

Sample answer
George Eliot described the novel *Silas Marner* as a 'tale of old-fashioned village life which unfolded itself from the merest millet-seed of thought'. Set in the imaginary village of Raveloe before the onslaught of the Industrial Revolution, the novel celebrates the strong old-fashioned and integrated sense of neighbourliness that prevailed before industrialisation. The central elements of a fairytale – loss of gold, recovery and restoration of happiness – govern the plot, yet the setting, characters, plot, dialect and detailed insight into life at that time prevent the novel from being merely a fairytale.

On one level, the novel *Silas Marner* could indeed be read as a simple fairytale about good and evil, beauty and ugliness, the rich man's folly and the poor man's triumph. Silas, with his bag of linen on his back setting out from Lantern Yard, could seem like a figure from a fairytale as he goes to seek salvation in a distant land. This land is Raveloe, nestled in a snug, well-wooded hollow in the heart of merry England, resembling a hamlet in a fairytale. The stone cottage heightens the air of romance that surrounds this story, resembling as it does a humble woodcutter's home. Even the characters could be figures that have stepped from a fairytale. Eppie, with her golden hair and blue eyes, could be a fairy princess, Dolly a fairy godmother and Dunstan the age-old villain. Godfrey is the wicked brother who suffers for his wickedness and wildness, while Nancy saves him at the end. The evil characters are punished and the good inevitably are rewarded. Like all fairy stories, the novel is made up of inexplicable events, such as the enigmatic disappearance of the gold, Godfrey's hidden past and double life, Dunstan's disappearance and Eppie's mysterious arrival.

The characters also resemble those of a fairytale. Eppie the princess is offered her rightful place in the castle (Red House) at the end, while Silas's capacity to cure with herbs and potents emphasises the elements of mystery and magic that permeate the whole novel.

The language itself has fairytale connotations. The writer tells of the 'sleeping child', the 'shrunken rivulet', the 'song of birds and loving sunshine', 'the guineas rising in the iron pot year after year', with the miser counting his gold.

Despite these fairytale elements, however, the world of the novel is firmly rooted in reality and deals with real issues. Raveloe is set in the 'rich central plain of Merry England, where it was never reached by the vibrations of the coach horn or of public opinion' (Chapter 1). The time is clearly stated before the Industrial Revolution. Raveloe becomes a symbol of a place that enjoys perfect freedom from industrialisation. Places such as the Rainbow are also symbolic of a certain style of life: 'the Rainbow was a luxurious resort for rich and stout husbands, whose wives have superfluous stores of linen' (Chapter 5).

Our first glimpse into the Squirarchy, set against the background of the Napoleonic wars, is given through the Red House, where we see Squire Cass's undisciplined lifestyle. We are told that in a very short space of time he idly feeds his deerhound with enough bits of 'beef to make a poor man's holiday dinner' (Chapter 9). This frequent comment on social waste is another issue that is treated ironically by the author. Early on in the novel we are told that 'there were many chiefs who could farm badly at their ease' (Chapter 1).

The novelist's purpose is not merely to describe character and incident in a vibrant manner, but to sustain, throughout the text, a subtle moral comment on many of the important social issues of the time. Her focus is on how weak will or evil can spread throughout society. For her the greatest sin is voluntary isolation from the community. Both of her leading protagonists, Godfrey and Silas, are reintegrated into Raveloe society. Through solidarity with other people they regain their self-esteem and status.

Eliot frequently interrupts the narrative to moralise or to teach some lesson. She condemns Godfrey's reliance on chance: 'Chance, the god of all men who follow their own devices instead of obeying a law they believe in' (Chapter 9). The writer's view of life is 'as you sow so shall you reap'. Dunstan's soul sows spite and hatred and he meets his death from a broken neck in the stone-pits. Marner's soul is simple and truthful and he is rewarded with the love of Eppie.

Eliot has managed to balance her art in the novel and achieve a perfect blending of fantasy and realism. The fairytale elements are incorporated into a realistic setting where problems that are important to humankind are explored and analysed. She succeeds in creating a novel that not only entertains, but also conveys rich insights into many important social issues of the time.

Comment
This is a question on two aspects of the novel – the fairytale features and the issues which make it a realistic social document.

The answer begins with a quotation from the novelist herself about her purpose in writing the story. It also clearly sets out the background of the story. The answer then develops by showing different aspects of how this novel could be treated on the level of a fairytale.

At each stage this answer makes reference to and quotes from the text to support the points made.

The second part of the answer takes account of the other aspect of the question, showing how the novel deals with real social issues. The answer concludes by referring back to the question and tying up all the points that have been made.

King Lear
(2006 exam)
'The play *King Lear* is a realistic tragedy that depicts the tragic consequences of one man's folly.' Test the truth of this statement with reference to or quotation from the play.

Sample answer
This statement is true. The play dramatises the tragic consequences of one man, in this case a king's folly, and shows the powerful and tragic effects of this action on the people around him. In the figure of Lear we are given a picture of a man who has been dominated by a life of pure power and uncontrolled self-will. A long life of absolute power nourished by flattery and blind obedience to his every whim has made Lear essentially blind to both his own limitations and to the reality of corrupt human nature. Lear has lived the life of an absolute dictator and has therefore generated within himself deeply ingrained faults.

He is choleric and mercurial in temperament and characterised by a presumptuous self-will with absolutely no self-control. He is aptly described as 'full of changes his age is', 'unconstant starts', 'he slenderly knows himself'. All of these defects are cynically assessed by his two daughters, Regan and Goneril, immediately after they have received the power of kingship. They know his nature and flaws very well and are quick to exploit these to serve their own self-interest. Lear arrogantly refuses to listen to anyone who might facilitate this deep-seated blindness and pride. When Kent, his long-standing and loyal servant, tries to intervene and make Lear see the truth, he is immediately banished from the kingdom with a threat of murder over his head. Shortly after this incident, Cordelia, Lear's beloved and faithful daughter, is similarly dispossessed and banished and the kingdom is divided between Lear's two daughters, Regan and Goneril, who later betray him.

Lear is treated with gross injustice by Regan and Goneril. He is thrust out of the palace and forced to survive the storm scenes. Through the picture of Lear, Shakespeare is intent on showing how much of his suffering is self-inflicted. When Lear divides up his kingdom he introduces a principle of calculation or measurement, which both Regan and Goneril adopt and carry to an extreme. Lear also makes a fatal error of understanding. When he introduces this spirit of calculation he is ruthless in his punishment of those who fail to conform to this principle. When his daughters both succeed to power, this spirit of calculation comes to power with them. One by one they dispose of their enemies (or plan to). In the final ironic twist this jealousy consumes them both and they turn on and dispose of each other. Shakespeare's intent is to demonstrate how this becomes a magnificent expression of the self-destructive capacity of this world of evil.

Lear's action affects the characters of the sub-plot, Gloucester and Edgar. At one stage in the play Gloucester, out of loyalty to Lear, decides to go out to Lear in the storm scenes and offer him comfort. By doing this, Gloucester loses his eyesight. Edmund betrays his father, Gloucester, into the hands of the evil Cornwall, who punishes Gloucester with treason and betrayal and plucks out his eyes. Gloucester, however, becomes a better man in this play as a result of suffering. At the beginning of the play he is weak, self-indulgent and over-sensual and the punishment of being blinded begins to generate more self-awareness and insight into humankind. His blindness precedes Lear's madness. When Gloucester realises that it is Edmund who betrayed him he immediately prays to the gods for forgiveness and that Edgar, his other son who he had misjudged, will prosper: 'Kind Gods, forgive me that, and prosper him' (Act III, Scene vii).

Both men suffer because of their weakness and both grow to be better morally through this suffering. It is clear that Lear's fault is one of pride, or an intellectual fault. He fails to judge character and action. He loses his reason and goes mad. At the height of his madness he achieves his deepest insights into human nature and grows both morally and spiritually. The first manifestation of the moral growth is shown in his concern for other people, in this case the Fool:

> poor fool and knave, I have one part in my heart
> That's sorry yet for thee …
> I'll pray and then I'll sleep.
> (Act III, Scene iv).

This manifestation of a concern for other people, this profound growth in humility and attitude of praying is all striking evidence of a deep change in Lear's nature and is shown to be particularly evident at the conclusion, when he is reconciled with Cordelia. He kneels down and begs forgiveness from Cordelia with the words: 'if you have poison for me I will drink it'. He allies himself with Cordelia as 'God's spies', and claims that he will take on 'the mystery of things'. All his earlier pride, arrogance, bad temper and impatience are now supplanted by a deep and sincere repentance. When he meets Cordelia he kneels down and begs her forgiveness. He tells Cordelia:

> Thou art a soul in bliss; but I am bound
> Upon a wheel of fire, that mine own tears
> Do scald like molten lead.
> (Act IV, Scene vii)

So while the play shows us the evil effects of one man's folly and its disastrous effects on the lives of the people around him, it also illustrates the positive aspects of this suffering. Both Lear and Gloucester die better men as a result of their experiences.

Comment
This answer begins by directly addressing the question asked and taking a clear position. In this case it can be seen that the writer agrees with the statement.

The answer then develops by analysing the character of King Lear and showing the implications of his particular faults in the tragedy that ultimately ensues.

A parallel is drawn in the answer between another important character, Gloucester, in order to develop the similarities between both men in the play.

The answer concludes by tying up the main points and drawing certain conclusions or evaluations in light of the analysis made on the question.

Pride and Prejudice
(2006 and 2007 exams)
Would you consider the issues that are represented in the novel *Pride and Prejudice* to be relevant to a modern-day reader?

Sample answer
Austen wrote against the background of mid-nineteenth century England and held a mirror up to life. However, this life has a limited and restricted quality to it because many of her issues and concerns were confined mainly to the middle class. While many of the issues she deals with are still relevant in our modern society, she depicts life and human relationships from the standpoint of a woman in this century. It must also be admitted that her subject matter, which is largely marriage, class distinction, snobbery and human relationships, greatly restricts the scope of her work.

However, while the subject matter of her work may be limited, it is still undoubtedly true that her skills as a novelist surpass any limitations in her work and are certainly relevant to modern-day society. Thus, her psychological perception of character and motivation, her constant humour and her faultless control of tone and narrative method are all exemplary and are still relevant today.

Austen was a critical observer of human nature. Her concerns are morals, human happiness, virtue and self-knowledge and not mere abstract ideas or principles. She exposes the follies and idiosyncrasies of her characters with a profound insight and a subtle and clever irony. Through irony Austen exposes sham values and superficiality and penetrates through falsity in the society around her.

In the novel *Pride and Prejudice*, The Bennets are the main family on which the plot centres. They are a respectable, middle-class family made up of marriageable daughters. It becomes clear from the outset, however, that social interaction between the Bennets and other families, such as the Darceys and the Bingleys, is out of the question. Austen is intent on satirising class consciousness and snobbery. Her vision of life is ironic and irony was part of her method, through which she captured many of the contradictions of life. For Austen, irony is a more truthful mode of communication in a world where she realised that 'seldom does truth belong to any human disclosure'. Irony also served Austen's moral purpose because her vision of life was critical and objective. Therefore, she uses irony as a means of moral and social judgment and through irony she evaluates human behaviour, judges the foibles and follies of her fellow humans and shows the value of virtue. Much of the irony in the novel *Pride and Prejudice* centres on the two main characters, Elizabeth and Darcy, and how they begin to re-evaluate one another as the story develops.

Mr Collins becomes another target of irony from the novelist. He is a clergyman who believes he is doing the Bennet family a great favour by proposing marriage to Elizabeth, the eldest daughter. When Elizabeth declines his proposal he justifies this as something that is not ascribed to the 'usual practice of elegant females'. His high opinion of himself is not daunted and he proceeds to ally himself in marriage to Charlotte. Mr Collins spends a good deal of time in the novel cultivating and flattering his upper-class patron, Lady Catherine de Bourg. It becomes clear that these types of people are still recognisable in our society today.

A good deal of the male characters are governed by this type of empty vanity and petty snobbery. Mr Darcy believes in the dignity of his lineage and he becomes a target of attack many times in the novel. Miss Bingley, who dislikes anyone not as socially accepted as she is, becomes another example of a snob, while Wickham, who will do anything he can to get enough money to raise himself into a higher station, is realistically portrayed throughout. It becomes clear as the story develops that the satire directed at Mr Collins is in reality more subtly directed at the entire social hierarchy, with its shallow values and hollow pretensions.

The plot in *Pride and Prejudice* centres on the relationship between Elizabeth and Darcy and the various prejudices, both within the characters themselves and the society around them. Through the Darcy-Elizabeth and Bingley-Jane marriages, Austen shows the power of love and happiness to overcome class boundaries and prejudices.

Marriage has a central importance in Austen's work and this is apparent in the novel *Pride and Prejudice*. All of her novels end in marriage, which she considers to be 'the origin of change'. The power of marriage to bring fulfilment and happiness is stressed more in Austen's work than in modern society. The relationship between the sexes is more dependent in Austen's world than now, and Austen is intent on showing how the heroine in her story begins to grow morally through marriage. Marriage clearly does not have the same power in our society today, with the liberation of the sexes and feminism.

However, other issues, such as the reality of pride, prejudiced views and class consciousness, are still relevant today. *Pride and Prejudice* certainly provides the reader with a realistic and valid insight into nineteenth-century English life.

Comment

This answer begins by clearly addressing the question, which is the relevance of the novel *Pride and Prejudice* to a modern twenty-first-century reader.

The answer develops by showing what particular issues interest Austen and how some of these are shown to be relevant and how others are not as important today.

Particular examples are taken from the text to support the points made in the answer.

The answer concludes by tying all the ideas together and restating how some issues are still relevant while others are not quite so important.

Macbeth
(2007 exam)

'Would you agree with the statement that the witches in the play *Macbeth* are evil, malevolent creatures who originate deeds of blood and have power over the soul?' Discuss this statement with quotations from or reference to the play.

Sample answer

The witches are indeed creatures of evil who have access to secret knowledge; from the beginning of the play they know Macbeth's name: 'Hail to thee, Thane of Glamis'. However, the witches' power is limited. They can incite, tempt and induce characters to do evil, but they can never cause a character to commit sin or carry out evil deeds except indirectly. We see the limited quality of their powers early on in their own reference to the sailor:

> Though his bark cannot be lost,
> Yet it shall be tempest-tost.
> (Act I, Scene iii)

The witches are agents of evil who seek to reverse the normal order of things and thereby obscure reality. From the outset they make their role clear – to create hurly-burly from what is stable. The essence of their intention can be summed up in the lines

> Fair is foul, and foul is fair
> Hover through the fog and filthy air.
> (Act I, Scene i)

The witches are clearly intended to represent the metaphysical world of evil spirits roaming around Scotland. Their meetings take place in conditions suggestive of cosmic disorder. Their function on a symbolic level is to mirror the spirit of evil roaming around Scotland. They belong to the equivocal world of seeming. Their every action is a perversion of the natural order. They hover in 'the fog and filthy air'. They appear amid thunder and lightning. They are neither wholly male nor female; they look like women yet have beards:

> you should be women,
> And yet your beards forbid me to interpret
> That you are so.
> (Act I, Scene iii)

It is Banquo who recognises this satanic quality inherent in their natures when he asks the question:

> What! Can the devil speak true?
> (Act I, Scene iii)

Banquo also recognises their manner of working:

> And oftentimes, to win us to our harm,
> The instruments of darkness tell us truths,
> Win us with honest trifles, to betray's
> In deepest consequence.
> (Act I, Scene iii)

Evil works through deception in the play. Shakespeare works the theme of appearance versus reality into the texture of his drama in order to clarify the whole theme of evil. The witches as instruments of evil operate in terms of false appearance. Their verse style is an indication of their function; their incantatory utterances communicate only ambiguous and uncertain meanings. In other words, the witches are 'imperfect speakers'.

Macbeth is in some way unconsciously bound up with the evil world of the witches from the very beginning of the play. His first words, 'so foul and fair a day I have not seen', are an unconscious echo of the witches' words in Act I, Scene i. From his first encounter with them, Macbeth falls victim to their fatal temptations. After this first meeting with them (Act I, Scene iii), Macbeth begins to move in a world of darkness, which is the domain of evil. It is no surprise, therefore, to hear him say shortly afterwards, 'Stars, hide your fires!' Macbeth is simultaneously attracted and repelled by the prophecies. He is 'rapt' in a world apart from his fellows. His soliloquy

> Two truths are told,
> As happy prologues to the swelling act
> Of the imperial theme.
> (Act I, Scene iii)

shows us how he is beginning to become involved in the dark world of half truths. This interior battle within Macbeth between good and evil is dramatised as a see-saw rhythm in his musings and in particular his soliloquies:

> This supernatural soliciting
> Cannot be ill, cannot be good;
> (Act I, Scene iii)

It is obvious that Macbeth has begun to vacillate within himself in this juggling with the sense of good and evil. The witches tempt Macbeth with the possibility of kingship. However, he himself is his own destroyer. He is the one who falls victim to their fatal temptations and carries out murder after murder in his quest for 'sovereign sway and masterdom' (Act I, Scene v). So the witches indeed give rise to deeds of blood and violence through their subtle temptations, but they do not have power over the soul. Macbeth and his wife, Lady Macbeth, each end up as their own destroyer. They both go to their own damnation freely.

After carrying out the murder of Duncan, Macbeth is dominated by a sense of guilt and an agony of restlessness. His mind is full of scorpions, he cannot sleep and he stays alone, moody and savage. Everything within him condemns itself for being there. There is a fever in his blood, which urges him on to ceaseless action in his search for oblivion. Ambition, love of power and an instinct for self-preservation are too potent in him to permit him to give up. Motivated by a new will to live and a renewed desire for the crown, he challenges 'Fate' to come 'into the list'. He is 'bent to know, by the worst means the worst'. A frightful result ensues. He speaks no longer of conscience, remorse or pity, but instead becomes active and purposeful in his dedication to evil. By the time he has reached the witches in Act IV, Scene i, his relationship with them has changed. He is determined that

> Things bad begun make strong themselves by ill:
> (Act III, Scene ii)

His decision at this stage is free, fully conscious and deliberately calculated. He wishes to know the future even though there is universal chaos. After this last encounter with the witches, the whole flood of evil in his nature is unleashed. The final stage of their operation against him is shown in Hecate's words:

> raise such artificial sprites
> As by the strength of their illusion
> Shall draw him on to his confusion:
> (Act III, Scene v)

The apparitions that the witches show to Macbeth are mocking illusions. They offer a false confirmation of his own desires while at the same time symbolising through tragedy and violence the final birth of a new order. In this way they turn out to be dramatically ironic. It is Macbeth's tragedy, however, that he accepts the version of the world offered to him by the witches. Yet at no stage do they compel acceptance of what they offer to him. The crime to which they incite him is committed by himself and the responsibility for succumbing to the temptation is Macbeth's alone. He is his own betrayer. Macbeth's security depends on assumptions such as Birnham Wood moving to Dunsinane and the fact that no man born of a woman will harm him. His life depends on appearances like these. His realisation about the falsity of this world of appearance and half-truths comes too late; only at the end of the tragedy does he realise that the witches have been

> juggling fiends...
> That palter with us in a double sense;
> (Act V, Scene vii)

The witches tempt and entice. As evil agents they are catalysts with limited powers, but bring to the surface the latent evil that lies buried in the subconscious mind. Macbeth is his own destroyer and at every stage in the play freely chooses his own course of action and freely commits himself to the world of evil and violence.

Comment
This is a question about the witches and whether or not they are creatures of absolute evil who control the soul of a character. The answer shows how the evil inherent in the

witches is not absolute, but simply sparks evil in others.

The first section of this answer explains the nature of the witches in the play and shows how they operate in deceiving characters.

The answer then develops by showing us the particular manner of the witches' evil operation in the play – their misleading language and statements.

The peculiar relationship between Macbeth and the witches is then outlined and Macbeth's free reactions are clearly drawn.

The answer concludes by demonstrating how the evil that governs the play begins in the witches' initial incitements, but is freely adopted by Macbeth himself and carried to a dreadful extreme.

Possible types of questions for the study of a single text

Amongst Women
(2005 exam)
1. 'The role of the woman is central in McGahern's novel *Amongst Women*.' Discuss this statement with quotation from or reference to the novel itself.
2. 'The novel *Amongst Women* is a realistic insight into Ireland in the early years of the twentieth century.' Would you agree with this statement? Make reference to the novel in your answer.
3. What particular aspect(s) of this novel do you consider to be relevant to life in the twenty-first century? Make reference to the novel in your answer.

As You Like It
(2005 and 2006 exams)
1. The nature and effect of virtue forms an important part of the play *As You Like It*. Discuss the impact of virtue in the lives of two main characters in the play. Support your answer with relevant quotation from or reference to the play.
2. Comment on the role and projection of the women characters in the play *As You Like It*. Support your answer with relevant reference to or quotation from the play.
3. What aspects of this play are relevant for a modern audience? Support your answer with relevant quotation from or reference to the play.

Wuthering Heights
(2005 and 2007 exams)
1. 'The most interesting aspect of *Wuthering Heights* is the pattern of human relationships, especially the relationship between Catherine and Heathcliff.' Discuss this statement with reference to the novel.
2. 'The novelist has succeeded in creating an exciting world of imagination and passion.' Discuss this statement, making reference in your answer to the writer's use of language and imagery.
3. 'Even though Catherine dies halfway through the novel her presence dominates the entire plot.' Would you agree with this statement? Support your answer by reference to the text.

Death and Nightingales
(2006 exam)
1. 'The novel *Death and Nightingales* gives us a realistic insight into Irish rural life in the nineteenth century.' Would you agree with this statement? Support your answer with reference to or quotation from the novel.
2. '*Death and Nightingales* is a novel governed by a great deal of contradictions.' Would you agree with this statement? In your answer refer to one or two characters.
3. 'Politics and violence lie at the heart of the novel *Death and Nightingales*.' Test the truth of this statement with reference to or quotation from the novel.

The Poisonwood Bible
(2006 and 2007 exams)
1. Discuss the position of the white woman in the novel *The Poisonwood Bible*.
2. Analyse the realistic features of African life in the novel *The Poisonwood Bible*.
3. What aspects of this novel would you consider to be relevant to the society we live in today?

Hamlet
(2005 exam)
1. Discuss the death theme in *Hamlet*. In your answer, make reference to or quotation from the play.
2. How does the structure of the play help the playwright's purpose? In your answer, take into account the importance of significant scenes and the playwright's use of language and imagery. Make reference to or quotation from the play.
3. What is the significance of the character of Horatio in this play? Make reference to or quotation from the play.

Silas Marner
(2005 exam)
1. 'The novel *Silas Marner* is a realistic social document.' Would you agree with this statement? Support your answer by reference to the novel.
2. Discuss the power of love to redeem in this novel. Make reference to the main plot and the sub-plot in your answer.
3. What is the role of the villagers in the novel *Silas Marner*? Support your answer by reference to the novel.

King Lear
(2006 exam)
1. Comment on Shakespeare's distinctive use of imagery in *King Lear*. In your answer, take into account the purpose of such imagery and its effect in the play. Make reference to or quotation from the play.
2. What is the significance of the main plot and the sub-plot in *King Lear*? In your answer, make reference to characters, structure and the imagery used.

3. Why is the Fool a central part of the structure of this tragedy? In your answer, take into account his role in the storm scenes. Make reference to or quotation from the play.

Pride and Prejudice
(2006 and 2007 exams)
1. 'A realistic insight into the pettiness and snobbery which governed English life in the nineteenth century.' Would you agree with this statement about the novel *Pride and Prejudice*?
2. How relevant are the issues represented in the novel *Pride and Prejudice* to modern society? In your answer make reference to or quotation from the novel.
3. 'Austen makes subtle use of irony to criticise the social prejudices of her society.' Discuss this statement of the novel *Pride and Prejudice*. Make reference to or quotation from the novel in your answer.

Macbeth
(2007 exam)
1. Discuss the way in which the language and imagery used in the play contribute to creating a world of evil and violence. Make reference to or quotation from the play in your answer.
2. What relevance does this play have for a modern audience? Support your answer by reference to the play.
3. 'Banquo is not an innocent soldier who scorns the prophecies of the witches; he is a man whose upright principles have been deeply compromised.' Would you agree with this assessment of Banquo's character? Support your answer by quotation from or reference to the text.

Death of a Salesman
(2007 exam)
1. 'The play *Death of a Salesman* sets two different worlds side by side: the dreams of the past and the agonies of the present.' Would you agree with this statement? Support your answer by refence to the play.
2. Comment on the relevance of this play for a modern audience. Make reference to the play in your answer.
3. 'Linda is a tragic heroine who deserves the sympathy of the audience more than Willy.' Would you agree with this assessment of the character of Linda? Support your answer by reference to the play.

The Comparative Study of Texts

WHAT IS A COMPARATIVE STUDY?

A comparative study of texts (play, novel or film) means the ability to focus on similarities or differences between texts, under such headings as:
- the genre and techniques used by the writer
- the treatment of different issues or themes
- the social or cultural background or context
- the general vision or outlook of the text.

The genre of a text
(2005 and 2006 exams)
Is the text:
- a tragic play?
- a romantic novel?
- an autobiography?
- a travel book?

Plot and sub-plot
A plot is the sequence of events that happen in a story. A sub-plot is a lesser story within it, which may reflect the central action of the text.

Soliloquy
A soliloquy is a speech made by a character when alone; it is often an insight into the soul of a character.

Narrative technique
This is the way the story is told in the text. A story can be told in the *first person* or *third person*. In first-person narration the story is told from the point of view of the writer or

narrator ('I'). In third-person narration the writer has an overview of the whole story, like an uninvolved outsider who observes events.

Themes or issues
(2005, 2006 and 2007 exams)
This is the central message presented by the writer, for example the themes of evil and the supernatural world in *Macbeth* or the theme of revenge and passion in *Wuthering Heights*. At Higher Level you must examine how a theme is developed in the text and what the writer's approach to it is.

Cultural context or social background
(2006 and 2007 exams)
The setting of a text includes the physical or geographical background, for example, the marshes in *Great Expectations* or the moors in England in the novel *Wuthering Heights*.

Under the heading 'Cultural context or social background', study the text with regard to:
- its cultural situation
- social customs, particular traditions or rituals
- national or class differences
- beliefs and values held by characters
- the role of women and men
- the importance of work in that society
- religious beliefs and practices
- power structures and political issues.

Some examples of cultural context are Nigeria at the beginning of the colonial period in *Things Fall Apart* by Chinua Achebe and England prior to the Industrial Revolution in the novel *Silas Marner*.

The general vision or viewpoint
(2005 and 2007 exams)
You should be able to compare and contrast the different ways of looking at life in the text and see whether there is a coherence or lack of coherence between these viewpoints.

ANSWERING A QUESTION ON THE COMPARATIVE STUDY OF TEXTS

1. Know exactly what your three texts for this section are. Take one of these as your main text.
2. Spend time choosing your question. Clearly identify what exactly you are asked in the question: is it a question on themes or issues, genre or on cultural context and social background?
3. Begin by working on a rough draft. Work with the main text first. Jot down five or six different points related to the question based on that text. In each point make sure to have a quotation or reference related to that point.

4. Write out your answer in draft form, using the main text only.
5. Look at the other two texts and draw in the main points of each text, showing how they compare or contrast. You can do this in two ways: add on some ideas from the two texts to each paragraph or simply write a separate paragraph on each text, outlining how it is related to the question.
6. All the material from your texts must be tied in to your answer in a fluid and natural way. Don't divide your answer into sub-headings with the title of the texts at the top. The main thing is to link or weave in the texts naturally and to show how they relate to the question, jotting down all points of comparison or contrast between the texts.
7. Organise your points into paragraphs and make sure you have used quotation from or reference to the texts as much as possible.
8. Prioritise and order your points and make sure each point refers in some way to the question asked.
9. Start writing the answer and stop at the end of each paragraph to examine what relevance it has to the question.

DRAFT QUESTIONS AND SAMPLE ANSWERS

In the following examples, the method of organising and assembling material for an answer on the comparative question is shown in rough draft form. There are sample questions on *literary genre, theme or issue, cultural context* and *general vision or viewpoint*. Study the method carefully and try to apply it to the possible types of questions on the comparative section, which are shown at the end of this chapter.

Sample answer on literary genre
(2005 and 2006 exams)
Choose **one** of the following aspects of literary genre as your topic and answer questions (a) **and** (b).
  – the use of powerful imagery
  – the creation of memorable characters
(a) Compare the presence of your chosen topic in two of the texts you have studied as part of your comparative course. Illustrate your comparisons by reference to at least one key moment from each text. (40)
(b) Consider some similarities and/or differences in the way in which a third text deals with the same topic. Support your points by brief textual reference. (30)

Stage 1: Identify texts
  The Past is Myself (novel)
  A View from the Bridge (play)
  Il Postino (film)

Stage 2: Analyse the question
This question is divided into two parts and offers a choice between writing on powerful

imagery or on memorable characters in three different texts. Decide clearly which aspect of the question you will answer, either imagery or characters.

Stage 3: Sketch out the main points from the anchor text
Jot down some main points from your anchor text related to the question. Remember, initially in part (a) you are only asked to compare *two* texts.

Stage 4: Sketch the principal points from the other text
Decide on the other text you will use and begin to draw in some comparisons and contrasts between both texts.

Stage 5: Sketch the principal points from the third text
Take your third text and sketch some points of contrast and comparison based on the points you have made from part (a) of your question.

Stage 6: Concluding paragraph
Summarise your main points and include an evaluation or series of judgments on the similarities and/or differences between the three texts.

Stage 7: Write out your answer fully, remembering to quote from or make reference to the text wherever necessary

Sample answer
(a) The three texts I propose to discuss in this answer are the novel *The Past is Myself*, written by Christine Bielenberg, the play *A View from the Bridge*, written by Arthur Miller, and the film *Il Postino*, directed by Michael Radford.

The two texts I propose to discuss in relation to the creation of memorable characters are the novel *The Past is Myself* and the film *Il Postino*. In both texts we are given some extraordinary insights into different types of people from totally contrasting worlds. In the novel we are exposed to the brutal horror of the Second World War, with all its trauma and betrayal. In contrast, the film is set in a remote but beautiful Italian island, with flowers, sunshine and laughter. Mario is a simple-hearted young man who has a wonderfully sensitive character and a great love for the finer things in life, such as poetry and beautiful landscapes. He is gifted with an extraordinary sensitivity to people and to beautiful things. We see a relationship which is vibrant, rich and alive to all that is wondrous.

The contrast between the worlds represented in the two texts is striking and the creation of memorable characters is both strong and real. In the novel *The Past is Myself*, Christine suffers all the trauma of being separated from her husband during the cruel years of the war in 1939, 1940 and up to the end of the war in 1945. Yet she too is a strikingly warm character who struggles to hold her family together and bring up her three children happily and free from prejudice. There are some similarities between both texts when Christine manages to escape for some years to Rohrback in the Black Forest district. We get glimpses of the warmth of community life and the beauty of the countryside, all of which is echoed in the film *Il Postino*. The grim reality of war is never far away, however, and Christine is forced to face the fact that many of her friends are murdered by the Gestapo for speaking out against the war.

The key situation in this novel, which highlights the strength of relationships between the characters, occurs when Christine is confronted with the fact that her husband, Peter, has been put in jail and his life is in extreme danger because he too has spoken openly about Hitler and the prevailing regime. Christine mobilises all the resources at her disposal and manages to arrange a meeting with Peter. Here we see how heroic and courageous she is. She has risked many dangers and humiliations to visit her husband in prison. During the interview with him she manages to transmit a message to him telling him about the death of his two friends, Adam and Carl. As a result Peter is released and they are reunited with their children. Similarly, in the film *Il Postino* Mario falls in love with a beautiful young woman called Beatrice. They have one child called Pablito. Mario still follows all the news of Pablo, who has returned with his wife to Chile.

The key situation in this film, which highlights the power of the relationship between the simple postman Mario and the poet Pablo, occurs when Mario loses his life at a Communist meeting after having been crushed by the crowd. It is evident how much Mario has been greatly influenced by the force and strength of Pablo's personality and charm. Due to Pablo's strong influence on his life, Mario had been writing poetry and joined the Communist party.

Both stories represent truly memorable characters in vivid and also poignant ways.

(b) The third text is a play written by Arthur Miller, called A *View from the Bridge*. This contrasts with the other two texts in its representation of memorable characters. In this text we are given an insight into different types of relationships in the figure of Eddie Carbone and his wife Beatrice. It becomes clear that the relationship between both characters is at an end and Eddie has become tired of Beatrice. Eddie is infatuated with Beatrice's young niece, Catherine, who happens to be staying with them. Eddie refuses to face this fact at any stage, but instead tries to dominate all her movements and maintain a strong control over her life and her relationships. The key moment in this text, which represents how relationships become fraught with tension and distrust, occurs when Catherine becomes engaged to Rodolpho, a young Italian immigrant who has moved to New York in search of work. Eddie then becomes consumed with jealousy and refuses to allow her to marry, in spite of Beatrice's pleadings.

The contrast between the characters represented in this play and the other two texts is dramatic. Relationships in the play are governed by a great deal of strife and violence.

Comment
This question is divided into different parts. The opening paragraph identifies the two texts and the subject matter of the question, i.e. the creation of memorable characters.

The answer proceeds to develop by drawing a contrast between the two texts in terms of their treatment of memorable characters. The answer also identifies two different key sections in each text that focus on the points which are made about the creation of memorable characters.

The answer then draws in the third text and begins to compare and contrast this text with the points made in the first part of the answer on the two texts.

Text	Genre	General vision/viewpoint
The Past is Myself	Novel	The power of human relationships
A View From the Bridge	Play	The destruction caused by jealousy and passion
Il Postino	Film	The power of human relationships

Sample answer on theme or issue
(2005, 2006 and 2007 exams)
Discuss how the theme or issue of 'love' is treated in the texts you have studied as part of your comparative course.

Stage 1: Identify the texts
    Silas Marner (novel) – the main or anchor text
    The Playboy of the Western World (play)
    On the Waterfront (film)

Stage 2: Analyse the question
This is a question on the issue or theme of 'love' as it is shown in the three texts.

Stage 3: Sketch out the main points from the anchor text
Take the main text (*Silas Marner*) and work out a rough draft on the question, using the whole text. Show how the absence of love destroys Marner. Highlight the negative aspects of a lack of love. Contrast Marner's soul when he begins to love Eppie.

Stage 4: Sketch the principal points on this theme from the other two texts
Begin to make judgments at this stage about the comparisons and contrasts between the three texts.

Stage 5: Start writing up your answer
Throughout your answer, refer back to the question and draw in all three texts.

Stage 6: Concluding paragraph
Make sure to tie together all the points you have made. At this stage make some evaluations or judgments about the theme and the comparisons and similarities in the texts.

Stage 7: Write out the answer fully, using all texts and references

Sample answer
Each of the three texts – the novel *Silas Marner*, the film *On the Waterfront* and the play *The Playboy of the Western World* – deals with the theme of love in a different way. Love is shown to be central to these texts and to influence the actions and dispositions of the central characters.

In the novel *Silas Marner*, Marner, an old weaver, has been banished by his community from Lantern Yard, where he grew up and was educated. This community professed strict Calvinistic beliefs and rejected him, having drawn lots to decide his culpability. His supposed best friend, William Dane, betrays him by slandering his reputation and marrying his girl.

Marner loses his faith in God and humankind and proceeds to settle on the outskirts of a small village called Raveloe. Here he becomes a sterile recluse and spends his days weaving for the local villagers and accumulating tons of gold. As he gets richer, his isolation and self-absorption intensify. He is finally rescued from the clutches of this sterile and destructive isolation by love. Love literally crawls up to his door in the form of a small child who is later named Eppie. Marner adopts Eppie and begins to pour out the love that earlier had been poured into his gold. Love redeems him from the stagnant and negative lifestyle that he had slipped into. It opens up new horizons in his soul: 'his large brown eyes seem to have gathered a more answering gaze'.

As the years unfold and Marner is faced with the responsibility for Eppie's education, he is forced to seek help outside himself. A local woman who is kind and generous, called Dolly Winthrop, lends him a hand. She offers him practical advice on how to rear Eppie and advises him to return to the church and have Eppie christened. Through Dolly's intervention and friendly advice, Marner regains his lost faith and begins to practise his religion again. All of this occurs because of his deep, undoubted devotion and love for Eppie.

As the events unfold in the novel and Eppie becomes a young woman, Marner also blossoms and regains his lost youthfulness and faith in humankind. He begins to see that there is another will which he does not understand, but sees that this is a good will: 'Them as was at the making on us, and knows better and has a better will.'

He achieves his crowning fulfilment when he leads Eppie to the altar for her marriage to Aaron Winthrop, Dolly's son. Undoubtedly, all of this has been achieved through the power of love.

Likewise, the theme of love is treated in a dramatically distinct way in the drama entitled *The Playboy of the Western World*. Set in Mayo in the early twentieth century, most of the action takes place within a small pub, or shebeen, owned by Michael James Flaherty.

The plot centres on the arrival of a dirty young fellow who calls himself Christy Mahon. His arrival in the pub provokes a great deal of curiosity and interest from the locals, among whom figures Pegeen Mike, the fiery daughter of the publican. His story of how he killed his father with 'the blow of a loy' enthrals all of these peasants, who are on the way to a funeral. Hungry for romance, excitement and glamour of any kind, these people, and in particular Pegeen, nourish the illusion of greatness and heroism within Christy to such an extent that, before long, he believes that he really has slit his father with one blow to the belt of his breeches.

Pegeen is a sorry figure, starved as she is of any excitement or romance. She is hungry for a hero in this small and remote place in west Mayo and within minutes her imagination is creating a real hero in the figure of Christy. Initially Christy is surprised at all the attention, but his vanity is flattered and within a few hours both Pegeen and Christy are declaring their eternal love for one another in heightened romantic language.

Before Christy's arrival, Pegeen had been engaged to Shawn Keogh, a dull but rich farmer. Within a few hours of Christy's arrival, she is renouncing Shawn and declaring she will marry Christy. Now with her image of the new glorified Christy, her imagination takes flight and they both foresee a future filled with unparalleled joy and happiness.

Their love is short lived, however. It is rudely shattered with the arrival of Christy's father, Old Mahon, who exposes Christy as a liar and 'a dirty stuttering lout'. Within minutes Pegeen's romantic love is no more. The glamorised and heroic image of Christy as a gallant fellow is cruelly shattered. Pegeen banishes him from the house while at the same time lamenting her loss in the words 'I've lost the only playboy of the western world.'

Love in this text has a more tragic conclusion. Built on shaky foundations where the main characters fail to know one another well enough, we bear witness to the grim irony of the conclusion. Pegeen, hungry for love, creates an ideal figure in Christy. In the course of the play he actually does reach this level from his own interaction within this community. She fails to see and understand this growth, however. She only sees the lie at the end and ironically banishes him, to be left alone with the sterile love of Shawn Keogh.

In the film *On the Waterfront* we are given a totally different setting. This time it is the docklands of New Jersey in the fifties. The story centres on Terry, a young boxer who has been bullied by a criminal gang under Johnny Friendly. Terry feels like a failure and an outsider. He is caught in this murky world of corrupt dealings, as his brother Charley is Johnny's right-hand man. Terry meets a girl called Edie and falls in love with her. It so happens that, unknown to him, Terry had a hand in her brother's death. Their love grows against the backdrop of violence, bullying of dockers from Friendly's gang and corruption. Terry is clearly frustrated and decides to take a stance. Under the instigation of the local priest Terry decides to tell Edie about his involvement in her brother's death.

This revelation leads his relationship with her to another level. Initially, she is shattered and rejects Terry. Terry now takes a clear stand against Friendly's gang, who control the workers in this area, and decides to inform the police. His brother Charley is brutally murdered by the gang. Terry, now totally enraged, challenges Johnny to a fight and ends up badly beaten. He triumphs, however, at the conclusion, by leading the men to regain their position as workers in the docks and defying Johnny's gang. Love enables him to assert his rights and triumph over corruption.

In all three texts love is seen in different characters and distinct contexts. True self-sacrificing love overcomes the evil and negativity of lives in the novel *Silas Marner* and in the film *On the Waterfront*. A love that is glamorised and alien from ordinary life is shown to dissipate easily with the exposure of truth in the drama *The Playboy of the Western World*.

Comment
This is a question on one theme or issue in the three texts you have studied for the comparative course.

Identify your texts clearly. The first paragraph answers the question clearly and shows specifically how in each text the theme of love is reflected and which characters are involved.

The answer develops by discussing one character from the text *Silas Marner* and underlining how love redeems him from his self-imposed isolation.

A contrast is drawn with the next text, *The Playboy of the Western World*. Here we see how love is based on a flimsy relationship between the two main characters. This answer draws a contrast in the type of love shown and illustrates how this kind of love evaporates at the conclusion of the play.

Finally, the answer compares love in the third text. In this case the text chosen is a film. Here again both the background and characters are different. The love, however, is true and good and succeeds in triumphing over the evil in the world of this film.

The last paragraph makes a statement on the theme as it is dealt with in the three texts. Here you have an opportunity to weigh up and draw various comparisons and contrasts between the three texts. In this case the power of selfless, true love is shown to conquer evil, in contrast with the negative quality of love, which is based only on glamour, romance and stylised speech.

Text	Theme/issue	Characters
Silas Marner	Silas is redeemed from isolation through love	Silas and Eppie Eppie and Aaron
The Playboy of the Western World	Love is idealised and evaporates	Pegeen and Christy Pegeen and Shawn Keogh
On the Waterfront	Love unites people and overcomes corruption	Terry and Edie

Sample question on cultural context
(2006 and 2007 exams)
With reference to the texts which you have studied for your comparative course, compare the cultural context in the texts. Say which you would prefer and give your reasons why.

Stage 1: Identify texts
  Jane Eyre (novel)
  A View from the Bridge (play)
  Witness (film)

Stage 2: Analyse the question
This is a question based on comparing three different texts in terms of the cultural context represented in each text.

Stage 3: Sketch out the main points from the anchor text
Identify the type of cultural context represented in the main text, *Jane Eyre*. This will include dealing with various points, such as the role of women and men, the type of work engaged in by people and the social classes represented. The answer should also make reference to the type of religion in this society and various customs or traditions practised.

Stage 4: Sketch the principal points from the other two texts
Take the other two texts, *Witness* and *A View from the Bridge*, and begin to jot down points based on the same headings that you have done on *Jane Eyre*. Try to always keep in mind the similarities and differences between the texts.

Stage 5: Start writing up your answer
Start writing up your answer by dealing with the points from the anchor text first and using some quotations to support your answer.

Stage 6: Concluding paragraph
Write a concluding paragraph that ties up your main ideas but also contains certain judgments on the differences and/or similarities between all three texts.

Stage 7: Write out the answer fully, using all texts and references

Sample answer
Each of the three texts – the novel *Jane Eyre*, the play *A View from the Bridge* and the film *Witness* – have a different cultural context. Each of these represents a different type of world and this is shown in various ways.
  In the novel *Jane Eyre* the cultural context is nineteenth-century England. It is set mainly in an upper-class environment, although there are glimpses of profound poverty when Jane goes to Lowood Institution to study. In contrast with this cultural context, the play *A View from the Bridge*, written by Arthur Miller, depicts life in the New York docklands in the early years of the twentieth century, a life of grim hardship and unemployment in a time when people experienced the reality of poverty and hunger. In the representation of life in this play we see how immigrants are treated and how difficult life becomes because of economic depression and lack of financial security.

In the film *Witness*, directed by Peter Weir, we are given an insight into another totally different world. This time it is New York in the late twentieth century. There are some striking scenes of gangland violence and police corruption evident in the cultural background. Life is no longer sacred and killings are rampant. Money can be seen to be the root of much of the corruption, and drug dealing forms another unpleasant reality in this type of cultural context. Within this film there is an effective contrast drawn between two totally different types of cultural context – the Amish community in America and the violence and squalor of New York City life. Within the Amish community emphasis is placed on values such as friendship, loyalty and peace and order within society. In contrast, in New York guns form an indispensable part of the fabric of life. The Amish people do not believe in violence and therefore their code is to never carry weapons.

There are certain similarities between the film *Witness* and the play *A View from the Bridge*. In both texts, relationships are fraught with tension and strife partly because of corruption and poverty, but mainly because of selfishness and greed. In the figure of Eddie Carbone in the play we are given a picture of a man who tries to dominate the lives of other people and force them to do his will. This is particularly the case with Catherine, who is the niece of his wife Beatrice. Greed and the desire for power form the motivating factors here. Similarly, in the film *Witness*, McFee, the corrupt police officer who is involved in illegal narcotics dealings, tries to kill Book, who is the police detective following the case. Both McFee and Schaeffer, who is head of the police, try to bully Carter, another police officer and friend of Book. They eventually murder Carter. The background of both texts shows a world which is riddled with violence and deceit, a world where people do not trust any more and live in fear of their lives.

The novel *Jane Eyre* shows the imprisonment of the woman in the representation of Bertha Mason, Rochester's mad wife who is kept locked up on the third floor of Thornfield. There are also echoes of imprisonment of women in the play *A View from the Bridge*. Catherine, Beatrice's young niece, is controlled by Eddie, who is clearly in love with her and wants to dominate her activity and life. Later on in the novel *Jane Eyre*, St John Rivers tries to dominate the life of Jane and force her to go with him to Africa and work on the missions. Women are tied by their particular cultural environment and in many ways are not allowed to fully express their natures. Similarly, in the film *Witness* we are given an insight into the lifestyle of an Amish woman. Rachel loses her husband early on in the film and it becomes clear that within a suitable time it will be opportune for her to form an alliance with another man from this same community. However, Rachel is headstrong and independent and shortly after she meets the policeman Book she falls in love with him in spite of the strong opposition from the members of the community.

The particular cultural world I would prefer to live in would be that of *Jane Eyre*. Although Jane experiences a good deal of suffering in her various travels between Gateshead House and Lowood, her world is more exciting and dramatic than that represented in either the play or the film. Jane makes some good friends in Helen Burns and her teacher, Miss Temple. Both these people inspire Jane towards goodness and have a strong influence on her life. As the story develops and Jane gains a position as governess in Thornfield, her experiences broaden and she learns what it is to be independent for the first time in her life. She enjoys her job as governess of young Adele, who is the daughter of a French opera dancer and who has been adopted by Rochester. Jane's life in Thornfield changes when she falls in love with Rochester and they decide to get married. She is a courageous character who embarks on a series of adventures upon the discovery that Rochester is secretly married to the mad Bertha Mason. Jane moves into another cultural world when she leaves Thornfield. At Moor House, she discovers the existence of relatives for the first time in her life and experiences some happy days living with her two cousins and their brother, St John Rivers. Jane's varied cultural experiences throughout the story certainly enrich her on many levels and enable her to acquire that resourcefulness which becomes a hallmark of her character. She finds fulfilment in her union with Rochester in a more humble situation at the conclusion.

In all three texts the particular cultural context that is represented is distinct and striking. Contrast forms the basis of the different worlds represented. We gain an insight into middle-class British life in the novel *Jane Eyre*, while the play *A View from the Bridge* represents the docklands of New York in a vivid and realistic manner. The film *Witness* shows two totally contrasting cultural worlds.

Comment
This is a question based on a discussion of the different types of cultural worlds represented in your three texts on the comparative section.

The first paragraph clearly identifies the three texts and their distinctive genres – play, novel, film.

The answer develops by outlining the setting of each text and giving a short sketch of the particular type of background, either rich, poor or middle class.

A contrast is drawn between the cultural contexts in the different texts. Contrast is also drawn between the different types of cultural contexts represented in the film.

Certain similarities between the different social or cultural worlds are also established in this answer.

The answer uses the position of the woman as an example of how cultural context can be represented in the text.

The answer also identifies one particular text that is preferable to the others in terms of cultural context. Various reasons are given for this preference.

The answer concludes by referring back to the question and restating some of the main points.

Remember, in an answer like this on cultural context, which is very broad, you must limit yourself to speaking about only a few points. You cannot deal with all aspects of the cultural context of three texts.

Sample answer on general vision or viewpoint
(2005 and 2007 exams)
With reference to the texts you have studied for your comparative course, compare the general vision or viewpoint.

Stage 1: Identify texts
  Of Mice and Men (novel)
  A Doll's House (play)
  Dances with Wolves (film)

Stage 2: Analyse the question
You are required to compare the general vision or viewpoint in three texts on your course. Follow the same method as you have done for the two preceding sample answers. Make sure that you are drawing in various comparisons/contrasts between your three texts.

  Remember that your conclusion in every answer on the comparative section must contain not only a summary of your main points, but also an evaluation or series of judgments on the similarities and/or differences between the three texts.

Sample answer
Each of the three texts – *Of Mice and Men* by John Steinbeck, *A Doll's House* by Henrik Ibsen and the film *Dances with Wolves*, directed by Kevin Costner – have a different general vision or viewpoint governing its structure.

  The topic of relationships dominates the general vision of all three texts. In the novel *Of Mice and Men*, we witness how George is deeply concerned with looking after Lennie and ensuring that he will not get into trouble. George's whole life is governed by this concern for someone he loves. It becomes evident from the first moment right through to the end of the text when George shoots Lennie to protect him from Curley's vindictiveness and anger. The overall vision in this text is how human beings really care for one another and the lengths they will go to in order to protect one another from harm.

  In the play *A Doll's House*, relationships also govern the story and the overall general vision or viewpoint. In this instance, however, the relationship between Nora and her husband Helmer is tainted with a good deal of tension and strife. Nora is clearly insecure in the presence of her husband, Torvald, while he continuously treats her like a child in a doll's house. It becomes clear that the relationship between husband and wife here is based on a good deal of misunderstanding of one another's characters and nature. There is a striking contrast here between the overall vision of love and protection inherent in the relationship between George and Lennie and on the other hand the distrust and animosity that governs the relationship between Torvald and Nora. This relationship lacks loyalty and trust, unlike that which is evident between George and Lennie. The culmination of events in the play *A Doll's House* is inevitable. Nora leaves her husband, maintaining that she needs to find her true self, her true personality. As she leaves the house she tells Torvald, 'I must think things out for myself, I must decide.'

  On the other hand, the film *Dances with Wolves* is also governed by relationships between people and dominates the structure of the overall vision. Throughout this film the audience is intimately aware of two contrasting sets of people – the white military officers in North America during the civil war and the native Indian Sioux. Dunbar, a white man who absconds from the military army and who goes to live with the native Sioux and imbibes their culture first hand, learns to appreciate and love certain values, such as peace and loyalty among people. His relationship with the Sioux governs the overall general vision and has echoes of friendship and loyalty, which are also evident in the novel. There are contrasting resonances of violence and strife in his relationships with the white people and the brutality of his beating by white men leaves the viewer with a profound distaste for the value system underlying white culture. This conflict governs the structure of the film and Dunbar's loyalty to the Sioux finally forces him to leave the Indian tribe and submit to white justice in order to protect the Sioux from harm.

The final scene of each text is filled with destruction and devastation. In the novel Lennie dies in an act of mercy at the hands of George in order to save him from a more savage death at the hands of Curley. In the play, the marriage between Nora and Torvald disintegrates with Nora's decision to find her true self, while the film concludes with images of the white army wreaking havoc on all the Sioux tribes and the concluding line stating how the whites finally gain control over the Sioux tribes.

Comment

The answer begins by identifying all three texts and explaining their different genres – film, play, novel.

The answer takes the main or anchor text and identifies the overall general vision or viewpoint.

Then the other two texts are used as a mode of comparison, all the time drawing in examples to support the answer.

Text	Genre	General vision/viewpoint
Of Mice and Men	Novel	Poignant and tragic
A Doll's House	Play	Nora's heroic stance in defending her independence
Dances with Wolves	Film	The reality of destruction and violence

POSSIBLE TYPES OF QUESTIONS ON THE COMPARATIVE STUDY OF TEXTS

Literary genre
(2005 and 2006 exams)
1. Take three different texts on your course and show how each writer uses a different method to tell the story.

2. Compare three different texts under one of the following headings:
   - tragedy
   - social realism
   - romance.
3. With regard to three different texts on your course, discuss the various methods used by each writer in the opening of their texts. In your answer, concentrate on the relationship between the opening and conclusion in each one and discuss which you consider to be most effective.

Themes or issues
(2005, 2006 and 2007 exams)
1. Show how your understanding of a particular theme or issue has been deepened or changed from the study of three different texts on your course.
2. Compare and contrast the issue or theme of self-discovery in any three texts on your course.
3. In three different texts on your course, take one central theme or issue treated by the writer. In the case of each text, show how this theme or issue has been developed or treated by the writer.

Cultural context
(2006 and 2007 exams)
1. With regard to three different texts on your course, show the difference between the value system presented by each writer. State which text you consider to be the most effective and why.
2. 'Racism forms part of the cultural background of many of the texts on your course.' In the case of three different texts, discuss how this issue is treated.
3. Take one central character from three different texts on your course. In the case of each one, outline how the cultural context of each text has influenced that character. Which text do you consider to be the most effective? Give your reasons why.

General vision or viewpoint
(2005 and 2007 exams)
1. Show how the general vision or viewpoint in the texts you have studied as part of your comparative course is or is not related to the actual events which occur in the texts.
2. Compare the general vision or viewpoint in the texts you have studied for your comparative course under one of the following headings:
   - optimistic
   - pessimistic
   - unexpected.
3. Identify the general vision in the texts you have studied as part of your comparative course. In your opinion, which of these was the most interesting? Give reasons for your answer.

Notes on Some Prescribed Texts

AMONGST WOMEN

John McGahern
(2005 exam)

Historical and literary background
This novel is set in Ireland in the times following the Irish War of Independence from 1919–22.

The story
The narrative starts at the conclusion of the story. Moran is an old Republican who was a guerilla leader in the War of Independence. His wife is dead and he is left to bring up their five children: three girls and two boys. Luke is the oldest and he has gone to work in London because he will not tolerate his father's violent behaviour. Moran can never forget the authority he wielded during the war and tries to behave in the same way within his household. He continually uses the rosary to regain control and power over his family. Moran marries a girl called Rose Brady when he is beginning to get old. Initially Rose is idealistic about the marriage, but she soon discovers the true nature of Moran and his capacity for violence and dark moods.

Rose is a selfless person who clearly loves Moran in spite of his strong character and difficult temperament. She encourages the girls to become independent and achieve the best they can in life. Maggie settles in London and eventually marries, as does Sheila. Mona gets a good job in the civil service and remains single. Michael, the youngest, leaves and marries. Luke's refusal to return to Great Meadow, the family home, frustrates and angers Moran greatly. All the rest of the family visit him regularly even though he has been domineering and violent. They are all happy together and have learned to accept Moran's peculiar temperament. Moran dies at the conclusion. Everyone except Luke turns up at his funeral and acclaims him as a truly great and heroic man.

Themes
- power and pride
- the power of the family
- war
- stubbornness

Genre
A social document that is set in Ireland in the period following the War of Independence.

Narrative technique
The story is told in flashback. The opening pages of the novel give a picture of Moran towards the end of his life when his family pay regular visits to Great Meadow. Then the novel is narrated in the third person. There are no formal chapters; the narrative is broken into sections separated by a short space. A lot of the story is told through dialogue, which gives a vivid insight into the various characters.

Cultural context
The background is Ireland in a period following war in the early twentieth century. We hear references to reviving Monaghan Day, which is obviously a tradition of the time. The story is set in the country and outlines the position of the family at that time. Family bonds were strong. The Moran family is united, with the exception of Luke, despite their father's erratic temperament.

We also see the faithful practice of the holy rosary, a prayer that is said by the family every night. Moran makes use of this means to acquit himself and refuses to face his own shortcomings. He also uses it as the only way he can exert his power over people, in this case his family.

Women marry securely in this society. Dependable jobs such as the civil service are recommended. Study at the university is not financially viable for Sheila. The profession of doctor is also not acceptable within this family because the doctors had emerged as the bigwigs in the country that Moran had fought for during the war.

One of Moran's key fears is being poor. For that reason he is miserly with money and even though he eventually gets two pensions he still exerts tight control over the finances. He also takes pride in the land he owns. He uses the land as a refuge, many times escaping from the house to work furiously at hay-making or reaping whenever he loses control of himself.

At the conclusion, on his death, Moran is given the typical Republican burial with the tricolor draped over his coffin.

General vision or viewpoint
The implication at the conclusion is that Moran's family is stronger than ever in their love and allegiance to one another. They truly recognise that Moran played a central part in all their lives. Their attendance at his funeral strengthens this bond between them even more. They realise that each one of them, in different ways, has imbibed

Moran's beliefs and values. They remain loyal to his person and beliefs in spite of everything. Only Luke remains obstinate in his decision not to return home – a reminder that he has inherited a great deal of stubbornness and pride from his own father.

SILAS MARNER

George Eliot
(2005 exam)

Historical and literary background
The historical background of this novel is just before the Industrial Revolution in England in the early nineteenth century.

The story
The opening chapter moves from the past to the present by showing us the attitude of the Raveloe people to the profession of the weaver. It also records Marner's treatment by the brethren in Lantern Yard and how he was banished from that community because he was accused of stealing money from an old parishioner. The community in Lantern Yard was a strict Puritan group who judged his guilt on the basis of drawing lots. Marner's best friend, William Dane, a member of this community, betrays him by slandering his reputation and later goes on to marry Marner's girl.

Marner settles on the outskirts of Raveloe, a small village in the heart of England. There he becomes a recluse for fifteen years and spends his time accumulating money by weaving for the local people. In Raveloe there is a rich family by the name of Cass. Squire Cass is an arrogant man who has two weak and dissolute sons, Godfrey and Dunstan. Godfrey is secretly married to a drug addict and they have a child. Dunstan bribes Godfrey and manages to get his horse. He has an accident outside Marner's cottage and steals his gold. Dunstan later dies when he falls into the quarry near the cottage.

Meanwhile, Molly, Godfrey's wife, decides to pay a visit with her child to Raveloe. It is New Year's Eve and Godfrey is having a party to honour Nancy Lammeter, whom he hopes to marry. Molly dies on the way and her child accidentally crawls into Silas's cottage while he is having a cataleptic fit. Silas discovers the child and thinks that it is his gold returned. He decides to adopt the child and bring it up as his own. He christens it Eppie. A local woman, Dolly Winthrop, helps him to manage Eppie.

Godfrey marries Nancy. They are unable to have a child. Eppie grows up and becomes engaged to Dolly's son, Aaron Winthrop.

Dunstan's body is discovered in the quarry with Marner's gold. Godfrey is forced to tell Nancy about his wife and child. They decide to adopt Eppie but she refuses to leave Marner. At the conclusion Eppie marries Aaron.

Themes
- the power of love to redeem
- deception and betrayal
- the strict and rigid nature of Calvinism
- the self-destructive quality of isolation

Genre
The novel *Silas Marner* belongs to the genre of social realism. It gives a realistic insight into rural life in England before the onslaught of the Industrial Revolution. Under this heading also study the following.

The structure of the novel
The first chapter blends past and present and gives us an insight into the reasons why Marner has settled on the outskirts of the village of Raveloe.

The novel is divided into two parts. There is a time lapse of sixteen years between Part I and Part II. This serves the function of showing the development of the plot: Squire Cass is dead, Nancy is married to Godfrey and Eppie is eighteen years old.

There are two plots: a main plot (Marner's story) and a sub-plot (Godfrey's story). These stories parallel one another.

Eliot makes use of the cataleptic fits to develop the plot. It is significant that in Part II, when Marner has attained happiness in loving Eppie, the fits disappear.

Style
The style of the novel is richly symbolic. The names and locations of places are used as symbols. Raveloe, an easy-going place, lies in the rich central plain of Merry England. Lantern Yard is used ironically. It prides itself on being a strong religious community, yet it is a place that offers no light, and significantly at the conclusion when Eppie and Marner return to look for it, it has disappeared.

Eliot makes use of a didactic or moralistic style to teach or instruct on certain issues, such as duty and personal responsibility for one's actions. She also uses this tone to articulate her views on society at that time. For example, when Dunstan goes to tell his father, Squire Cass, about the accident with his horse, we are told how 'Fleet the deerhound consumed enough bits of beef to make a poor man's holiday dinner.'

The writer makes use of gold as a symbol of love. There are repeated references to Eppie's golden hair, which is obviously intended to replace the stolen gold. Many fairytale motifs are used – the accumulation of the gold by the miserly weaver, the loss of the gold, the recovery of the loss in the form of a child, the villain and the fairy godmother (Dolly).

Cultural context
We gain an insight into the old English way of life before the Industrial Revolution. The novel is set in the days when spinning wheels hummed busily in farmhouses. It celebrates the integrated sense of neighbourliness that was a hallmark of life before the onset of the Industrial Revolution. The whole story spans thirty years of an era of rapid

change in England. The conclusion of the story shows the beginnings of industrialisation in England.

The story is set in the period of the Napoleonic wars when the price of agricultural goods was high, so farmers were free to farm badly at their ease. This is particularly the case in the highest social class at that time, the Squirarchy. Eliot attacks this particular class through the figure of Squire Cass and his two dissolute sons, Dunstan and Godfrey.

Class structures are clearly marked out in the novel. Each person has their own place in society and keeps to it. Godfrey, by marrying below his class, has allowed himself to be dragged into mud and slime.

Calvinism is shown in the portrait of Lantern Yard. The insight given in the novel is dark and negative. They profess a belief in revelation and the drawing of lots. This is how justice is exercised within this community. The beliefs and practices of Lantern Yard are shown to be destructive of human fellowship and community.

General vision or viewpoint

The general vision at the conclusion is that the old community life as exemplified in Raveloe is slowly vanishing with the onset of industrialisation. The Industrial Revolution is seen negatively. When Marner and Eppie return to pay a visit to Lantern Yard, they find that everyone is in a hurry. Eppie describes it as 'a dark ugly place. How it hides the sky, it's worse than the Workhouse.' We learn about the cramped conditions of life and the bad smell.

One of Eliot's beliefs was 'as you sow so shall you reap'. Marner sows love and kindness and so he reaps happiness in the figure of Eppie, who in turn is united in marriage to Aaron. Godfrey sows deception and selfishness and so he reaps a marriage that turns out to be childless. The general vision is that one must live with the results of one's deeds and take responsibility for one's actions. The power of love to redeem is also evident at the conclusion.

A DOLL'S HOUSE

Henrik Ibsen
(2005 and 2006 exams: comparative studies only)

Historical and literary background
This play's premiere was shown in Copenhagen in 1879 in the Royal Theatre. Ibsen's plays were written for a predominantly middle-class urban audience.

The story
The story centres on a married couple, Torvald Helmer and his wife Nora. They have three children. Nora's husband has been a barrister who has just been made manager of the bank. He treats Nora as a child. He is a perfectionist and cannot tolerate failure. Christine Linde is an old school friend of Nora's who has been a widow for three years.

Nora is a spendthrift but she is also very self-sacrificing towards her husband and family. She has borrowed money in order that they could go on a holiday to Italy because he was sick. In order to do this she forged her father's signature. Unbeknownst to her husband, Nora borrows the money from a man called Krogstad, a lawyer who happens to work with Torvald at the bank. He is now a widower and had a relationship with Christine in the past.

Krogstad is to be dismissed from the bank by Torvald for having committed a small indiscretion. Krogstad is desperate to retain his position in the bank so he tries to persuade Nora to intercede with her husband on his behalf. She refuses and so Krogstad writes a letter to Torvald revealing everything. However, Krogstad changes his mind due to Christine's influence, who consents to marry him. Torvald, however, discovers the letter before he hears about Krogstad's change of mind and denounces Nora. He decides to cover up the affair and reinstate Krogstad. Just at that moment it is revealed that Krogstad has changed his mind. Torvald decides to forget about everything and go on as usual with life. Nora, however, stands up to him and decides to leave. She does not want to be a wife who is treated like a doll in a doll's house. She leaves her husband and children at the conclusion with the determination to discover who exactly she is and what life is all about. Torvald is the one who has done this for her all her life.

Themes
- self-liberation
- relationships
- deception and dishonesty
- duty and responsibility

Genre
The play belongs to the genre of social realism. The setting is the Helmers' apartment and the time sequence is about sixty hours' duration. There are three acts.

There is a main plot and a sub-plot which parallel one another. The main plot involves Nora, Helmer and Krogstad, while the sub-plot concerns Mrs Linde and Krogstad.

Style
Both the style and setting are naturalistic. There are seven monologues expressed by Nora which serve the function of informing us of her inner torment.

The particular language of each character reflects their individual personality. For example, Helmer makes use of a lot of paternalisms such as 'skylark', 'squirrel' and 'my little squanderbird' to address his wife.

The setting of the drama is a typical bourgeois drawing room.

Cultural context
The cultural background represented in this play is a middle-class family in the nineteenth century.

Marriage between Nora and Helmer is based on a paternal relationship and financial dominance on Helmer's part. He patronises her while she behaves like a child. Nora represents the middle-class nineteenth-century daughter and wife who are protected from the harshness of the outside world.

The nineteenth-century nanny working for a middle-class family is shown in the figure of Anne-Marie, who looks after Nora's children. While Nora plays with her children and buys them presents, it is Anne-Marie who actually brings them up.

General vision or viewpoint

It is interesting that the play begins with the door opening to let Helmer into the house and it concludes with Nora slamming the door in his face. Throughout the play a certain number of decisions have been taken and choices made by the characters. For the first time in her life, Nora forces Helmer to face the truth about their marriage. Roles are reversed. She recognises that 'our home has never been anything but a playroom, where we have never exchanged a serious word on a serious subject.'

She leaves him, claiming that she needs to be freed from the marriage to educate herself and to learn to think about life and its issues. Helmer is a tragic figure. He sincerely loved his wife even though he has failed to express it well. He is left abandoned and alone to look after the family and face the ensuing scandal. There is a sense that both people need to readdress certain basic issues in their lives, such as the reality of what is involved in marriage.

JANE EYRE

Charlotte Brontë
(2005 and 2006 exams: comparative studies only)

The story

Jane Eyre is an orphan who is thrown upon the protection of relations and living in an out-of-the-way corner of England in a large house called Gateshead Hall. These relatives neglect, mistreat, chastise and abuse her. She becomes dogged, revengeful and superstitious. At length, Jane turns on her persecutors in a fit of rebellion and passion. She is sent to a charitable institution called Lowood. Here in Lowood House she has to prove herself. Through her relationship with Helen Burns and helped by the benign influence of Miss Temple, Jane learns that patience is nobler than passion. She grows up into an independent young woman and takes on the job as teacher in Lowood.

Weary of the monotonous life of a teacher, she advertises for a situation as governess. She becomes engaged as governess to a country gentleman by the name of Mr Rochester who entrusts to her the care of a pretty, frivolous French ward by the name of Adele, the child of an opera dancer. Uknown to Jane, Mr Rochester has kept a lunatic wife on the third floor of Thornfield in the charge of a gin-drinking servant called Grace Poole. The house frequently resounds with demoniac laughter and at one stage the mad wife attempts to burn her husband in his bed. Jane falls in love with Rochester and they decide to get married. On the eve of Jane's marriage, the mad Bertha, as she is called, comes into Jane's room and tears her bridal veil in half.

At the altar steps just before the marriage, Jane discovers that Rochester is already married to Bertha Mason, who lives in Thornfield. She refuses to get married and runs away. She travels across miles of countryside until finally, in a state of exhaustion and near starvation, she drops at the front door of a house. It happens to be the house where three of her cousins live. Shortly after her arrival she discovers that she is the heiress of an uncle who has left her £20,000, which she promptly shares between her three cousins.

One of them, Rev. St John Rivers, is a missionary who proposes settling in India. He urges Jane to accompany him as his wife although clearly he is not in love with her. Jane is on the point of yielding when she hears Rochester's voice calling her. She hastens back to Thornfield where she learns that Rochester's wife has burned it down, killing herself and blinding Rochester. Jane finds Rochester and marries him. He partially recovers his sight and they have a child.

Themes
- the woman
- freedom
- love

Genre
The novel belongs to the romance genre. It is written in an autobiographical form and the subjective view of issues presented in the novel firmly sets it within the tradition of romance genre. Brontë constantly parallels inner states and feelings with nature in a highly vivid manner in this novel. Human emotions, moods, internal states and character development are all mirrored in the natural world. She also uses her setting and scenery in a symbolic manner. Jane's character is portrayed from the core of the personality and developed outwards. This development of her inner life and soul is all portrayed against the dynamic backdrop of nature and natural forces.

The novel has elements of the Gothic novel to it, for example, the idea of the mad wife hidden in the attic and the repeated references to supernatural elements, together with the notion of ghosts and goblins, etc.

The structure of the novel
The plot centres on Jane Eyre, the heroine of the book. Strictly speaking the book is divided into five geographical regions:
- Jane's experiences as an orphan at Gateshead Hall.
- Her education at the institution Lowood Hall.
- Her role as governess in Thornfield.
- Her stay at Moor House.
- Her return to Ferndale and her marriage to Rochester.

The plot develops through depicting Jane Eyre's various fluctuations in fortune and how she comes to terms with the difficulties she encounters.

Narrative technique
In the novel Brontë functions as an omniscient consciousness. She controls the entire narrative but does not intrude her own viewpoint. Jane Eyre is the narrator of the story at the same time as being the central consciousness and the heroine. The narrative is told in the first person.

Cultural context
The cultural context of the novel changes because it is set in five different geographical locations. The novel opens in Gateshead Hall, the rich establishment of the Reeds, who have two pampered and spoiled children. There are overtones of a rich indulgence within this house – the rich red draperies, the butler and the footman all depict a pampered and indolent lifestyle. There is a distinct emphasis on social class and it is because of her position as a poor relation that Jane is consigned to the regions of the nursery and made to manage with a candle and the erratic company of Bessie, the nurse.

The cultural context underlying Lowood Institution depicts the enormous harm which was caused by such institutions in Victorian England. We are given some startling insights into the devastation caused by typhus and disease through the number of people who actually died. It is significant that Jane records how things changed in Lowood. The building was reorganised due to the noxious site, corrupt water system, unhealthy food and poor clothing.

We also get an insight into the upper-class system in England through the style of life revealed within Thornfield. The servants' quarters are downstairs while Rochester keeps his mad wife locked away on the third floor of the mansion. There are repeated references to keys and locks, which denote the theme of imprisonment.

When Rochester returns with a company of friends the lifestyle changes. There are dinner parties, riding parties, more fires are lit, new servants are hired and there is a richer abundance of material things in the house. Jane describes some of these guests as similar to 'white plumy birds' because of their attire. These visitors are haughty, elegant, proud, lofty and distinguished, clearly on a different social level from what Jane is used to.

This novel shows us in a realistic way the particular social position of the governess at that time. The governess existed on a mid-point socially between the servants and the middle classes. Thus, Jane is uncomfortable socially during these dinner parties while the Ingrams and such people are presiding. The return to more homely, domestic values is signalled in the portrait given to us of Moor House at the conclusion.

Through vivid depiction of small details we get a look into different cultural levels, from the poor and deprived class to the rich indolence of the upper class, to the sedate and comfortable middle classes. Brontë paints a rich and realistic vision of English life both in the city and country in the early years of the nineteenth century.

General vision or viewpoint
The novel concludes with Jane happily married to Rochester for ten years and the partial recovery of his sight. They also have a child. The general idea here at the

conclusion is that after a loveless and isolated existence Jane has eventually found happiness and fulfilment.

Rochester is more humble and less arrogant. He acknowledges that his physical maiming is a just punishment for his earlier deeds. The general vision of both characters at the conclusion is that they have grown and developed. Jane, less dependent on other people now, is totally fulfilled as she offers moral support to Rochester, who, formerly cynical and suspicious of others, is now child-like and dependent.

There is also a commentary given to us about St John Rivers. He zealously pursues his missionary goals and is assured of his salvation having lived a life of faith and charitable works. The implication here is that St John Rivers has not wavered at any stage from his relentless pursuit of what he considers to be good.

WUTHERING HEIGHTS

Emily Brontë
(2005 and 2007 exams)

Historical and literary background
Wuthering Heights was first published in 1847 in England. The Brontës lived in Haworth, Yorkshire. The novel is set against the background of the wild moors of Yorkshire.

The story
The story is told by two narrators, Nelly Dean, the housekeeper at Wuthering Heights, and Lockwood, who takes over as tenant of the Heights. The story spans three generations and is centred on two main houses, Wuthering Heights and Thrushcross Grange. It begins with Old Earnshaw, who has two children, Cathy and Hindley, who live in the Heights. Old Earnshaw returns from Liverpool with a bundle, which turns out to be a boy that he found wandering along the streets. He is called Heathcliff from then on. Hindley and he become bitter enemies. However, Cathy and Heathcliff develop a deep and passionate relationship, spending their time on the moors. One day they accidentally meet the Lintons, who live at Thrushcross Grange. Isabella and her brother Edgar live at the Grange with their parents. Cathy is attacked by their dog and is forced to stay in the Grange until she recovers. Heathcliff is sent home in disgrace.

Cathy returns after several weeks from the Grange a changed woman. She is flattered by the attention from the Lintons, particularly Edgar. She develops a double side to her character. She acknowledges to Nelly Dean that it would shame her to marry Heathcliff and he accidentally overhears a part of her conversation. He leaves the Heights for three years and returns when Catherine has been married to Edgar for three years. Heathcliff is changed. He is filled with revenge. He moves into the Heights, where Hindley lives alone. He gambles and succeeds in gaining all the property from Hindley and robs Hareton, Hindley's son, of his lawful inheritance.

Meanwhile, Isabella develops an infatuation for Heathcliff and elopes with him. Cathy warns her, but in vain. Isabella escapes from Heathcliff shortly after her marriage when she discovers his true nature and settles in London. There she gives birth to a boy who is named Linton. She dies shortly after this. Heathcliff uses young Linton to avenge himself on Edgar and Cathy. Edgar and Cathy also have a child, whom they call Cathy. Shortly after giving birth the elder Cathy dies. Heathcliff tricks young Cathy into marrying young Linton and so gains possession of the Heights. Heathcliff dies at the end a tortured soul who is clearly haunted by the presence of the ghostly Catherine. Lockwood buys the Heights from Heathcliff at the conclusion.

Themes
- passion and love
- betrayal and loyalty
- revenge
- the supernatural

Genre
This novel belongs to the genre of romance. In the novel Emily Brontë constantly parallels inner states and feelings with nature – human emotions, moods, internal states and character development are all mirrored in the natural world and in particular in the wild moors.

Narrative technique
There are two different narrators: Nelly Dean and Lockwood. Nelly Dean is an ordinary woman who is housekeeper for three generations of the Earnshaws and later on the Linton household. Lockwood is a young man from London with plenty of money and time on his hands who takes over tenancy of the Heights towards the conclusion of the story. Both of these ordinary and readily identifiable narrators tell a story of extraordinary supernatural dimensions. They serve the function of bringing otherwise incredible and unrealistic events within the reader's grasp and understanding. They are used as a means to give this incredible story a foothold in the normal world of everyday affairs.

The narrative technique also makes use of flashback. The first chapter begins at the conclusion and the remainder of the narrative recounts the events of the story through extended flashback. In many respects, the effect of this device in narration is to disorientate the reader and enable them to realise that this story is not dealing with normal life.

Style
The style of *Wuthering Heights* is that of a 'poetic prose'. As Charlotte Brontë, Emily's sister, states in her preface to the novel: 'It is rustic all through. It is Moorish and wild and knotty as the root of heath. Its colouring is of mellow grey and moorland moss clothes; and heath with its blooming bells and balmy fragrance. Her descriptions of natural scenery are what they should be, and all that they should be.'

The novel makes use of many images on a richly symbolic level. Nature is used in a symbolic manner throughout, symbolising strife, discord and moral decay. The storm, thunder and lightning, together with the repeated references to fire, are all used to show the profound depths of violence and heightened passion that dominate the atmosphere.

The actual locations of the two houses mentioned in the novel, Thrushcross Grange and Wuthering Heights, are also used as symbols. The Grange is set in a leafy valley while the Heights is exposed to 'atmospheric tumult' of every kind. The atmosphere within the Heights exudes a profound spiritual degeneration while that in the Grange is civilised and controlled.

Cultural context

The novel is set in nineteenth-century England. We get a vision of two different lifestyles in the Heights and the Grange. The lifestyle in the Heights is wild and uncontrolled. Within the Grange there is rich luxury, 'a splendid place carpeted with crimson, a pure white ceiling bordered by gold, a shower of glass-drops hanging in silver chains from the centre.'

Through the figure of Joseph we gain an insight into the strict harshness of Calvinism. He is a rigid and intransigent figure who spends his time preaching at the children.

Through Nelly Dean we see the role of the housekeeper. In this particular context Nelly is more a mother figure for the children than an actual employee within the house.

General vision or viewpoint

At the conclusion of the novel Heathcliff is ultimately left with power, a power that he finds intolerable and painful. He is consumed with a hell fire, yet refuses to repent. The heaven of others is entirely unvalued and uncoveted by him. His death is explicitly pagan; he wants no minister, no mourners and no prayers to be said for his soul. In Heathcliff's death there is a sense that evil has destroyed itself, that the fire of hatred and destruction that eats its way through his system and through the novel has burned itself out. His power for wickedness has been his punishment, just as his passion for Catherine was a curse, not a blessing. He destroys himself throughout the book, thereby showing how true Isabella's earlier statement is that 'treachery and violence are a double-ended spear, which wound the inflictors more than the sufferers.'

The actual conclusion of the novel gives the reader an image of a happy, harmonious and natural human love. The ending shows the happy marriage of Cathy to Hareton, Heathcliff's revenge plans are frustrated, property is restored to its rightful owners and Nelly Dean takes delight in her 'children's happiness'. All of this is cleverly juxtaposed with an image of pain, rapture and ghostly phenomena. Two types of love are simultaneously affirmed at the conclusion: the ghostly vision of Heathcliff and Catherine as they wander the moors shows us that in some way they too have attained their heaven, while simultaneously we are given the vision of Hareton and young Cathy in a state of blissful union walking in the moors.

ANTIGONE

Sophocles
(2006 exam: comparative studies only)

Historical and literary background
This play was written in Athens about 441 BC. At this time the theatre was a religious festival and also an aspect of the city's political life. The sources for the Greek dramatists were mainly oral – the drama was made up of myths and stories about the past. The actors wore masks and in the drama they presented to the audience historical figures from their past. The actors made repeated reference to the gods, whom they invoke at several stages during the play.

The story
Creon, the king of Thebes, has forbidden the burial of his nephew Polynices. His sister, Antigone, resolves to defy the decree and to perform the funeral rites for him. She is caught and brought before the king. She pleads that her act is in accordance with the overriding laws of the gods. Creon is unrelenting and condemns her to be imprisoned alive in a cave. Her sister, Ismene, who has refused to participate in Antigone's actions, now claims a share in her guilt and begs for punishment, but the king regards her as demented and insane. Creon's son, Haemon, who is betrothed to Antigone, pleads with his father, but in vain. He leaves with a warning that he will die with her.

The seer Tiresias threatens the king with the terrible consequences of defying the divine laws. Creon remains obstinate and banishes Tiresias. However, he relents and goes to the cave to free Antigone. There he finds his son clasping the dead body of Antigone, who has hanged herself. Haemon lunges at Creon with his sword, but he misses and kills himself instead.

Creon returns to the palace to find that his wife, Eurydice, has killed herself in despair. Creon is filled with repentance for his mistakes.

Themes
- pride
- the law
- the gods.

Genre
This play belongs to the genre of tragedy.

Features of tragedy
The tragedy in this play arises from one man's attempts to enforce his will against that of the gods by refusing to allow the sacred rites that are due to the dead. In Creon an error of judgment, which arises out of a defect in his nature, generates much of the tragic action in the play. This error grows and is shown in a general conceit and moral blindness which swell to enormous proportions until in a tyrannical display of anger he commits the fatal mistake of condemning Antigone to death.

This action leads to disastrous consequences, which take the form of death – the death of his son, Haemon, of Antigone and finally the death of his wife, Eurydice. What is implicit in the conclusion is that Creon has erred against the gods and therefore must accept his punishment accordingly.

Function and language of the Chorus
The Chorus has a double function in this play. It adopts the role of actor and commentator on the action and on the characters. In this play the Chorus represents the citizens of Thebes, who defend tradition and legitimate rule.

The language of the Chorus is a mixture of poetic lyrics and moralising; it also makes prophesies about things that will happen. It acts as a bridge or mediator between the spectators and the stage.

Through the Chorus we gain an insight into the characters of Creon and Antigone. Sophocles skillfully uses the Chorus to depict both character and action. This is achieved through a clever and subtle contrast, which is the essence of this play. We as audience are deceived about the characters of both Creon and Antigone. We are offered false clues about her real nature. The Chorus manipulates our vision by condemning her action repeatedly and by seeming to acquiesce in Creon's opinion and judgment.

Thus the Chorus in this play is at times subject to error, to a partial or limited understanding of things. It passes judgment on character and action and it philosophises, but many times its conclusions are not valid.

At the conclusion it is the Chorus that faces the truth and forces the audience to accept it. The play concludes with the last words from the Chorus, which are meant to convey the moral or message of this play. Its language is clear and definite as it speaks in moral tones about the need for reverence to the gods and the fact that suffering finally teaches wisdom.

Dramatic irony
Sophocles makes skilful use of dramatic irony to illustrate his theme. Because the main theme is a form of arrogance or pride that causes moral blindness, irony plays a central part in this play. Much of the irony is dramatic and tragic.

At the beginning of the play this irony takes the form of a contrast that Sophocles builds between Antigone and Creon. We are made to think that Creon is right in many ways. He puts forward many rational arguments that make us condone and justify his behaviour. On the other hand, Antigone's impassioned defence of her brother and his rights seems to show a pride and arrogance that make us qualify our approval of her words and actions. In other words, Sophocles builds his play on a subtle contrast between the real arrogance of Creon and the apparent arrogance of Antigone. At first we are misled in our judgment of both characters and this underlines much of the dramatic irony.

Through his masterly use of irony, Sophocles shows the disastrous results that can follow from a deep-seated and wilful blindness to reality. In the logic of events that occur at the conclusion we are exposed to the tragic consequences of such blindness and lack of judgment.

Cultural context

The cultural background of this play is Athens in the fifth century BC. We learn that the king exercises an authority that is based on tradition and law. Athenian law at that time was based on certain principles and embodied certain beliefs. It denied tyranny in both theory and practice. The city belongs to the whole body of people. The ancient Greeks held that the laws bound a city together and that if these were broken, the individual was ruined no less than the city. That is why Creon's action in breaking the law by refusing to bury Polynices has such grave repercussions.

The religion of this age had no fixed doctrine and no sacred book. Religion embodied certain views about the nature of people and their relations with the gods. The gods were held in very high respect in this culture and people did not transgress the law held by the gods.

The ancient Greeks also held that the bonds of family possessed a special sanctity. Creon breaks this bond by denying the sacred rites to Polynices, his nephew, and furthermore by sentencing Antigone to death. This was a grave action for Creon. To the ordinary Athenian, the unwritten laws – conscience and religious duty – protected the sanctity of family life. The rites of the dead were also held sacred, as can be seen from Antigone's action on behalf of her brother.

We get an insight into the role of women through many references made by the various characters. Ismene reminds Antigone that 'we are women, we're not born to contend with men' (Penguin edition, line 74). Later Creon claims that while he is alive, 'no woman is going to lord it over me' (line 591). However, Antigone's strong defence of her brother's rights shows that when duty towards the dead has to be shown, there is little difference between the sexes.

The theatre in ancient Greece was an open-air arena. There was a place where the Chorus moved and chanted, known as the orchestra or dancing-place. Beside the orchestra was the platform on which the actors stood. The dress was formal and the actors wore a mask that depicted the dominant traits of the character they were playing.

The use of the Chorus, which usually numbered fifteen, was a distinctive feature of Greek drama. They spoke in choral odes, which were recited in unison. The passage of time and the interludes between the Chorus and the dialogue were marked by music.

General vision or viewpoint

The general vision at the conclusion of this play is truly tragic. Enlightenment comes, but only when all the disasters have occurred, when it is too late. This enlightenment is accompanied by a great deal of suffering. Creon suffers because he has done wrong and refuses to undo his wrong in time. The gods wish him to learn. The implication at the conclusion is that the good action that is put off too long ceases to be effective. His repentance comes too late to avert the catastrophe wrought by the gods. Only at the conclusion does he shed his stiff-necked pride and arrogance.

Once Tiresias leaves, disasters come thick and fast. The gods, once they get to work, act swiftly and surely in an undeniably certain manner. This rapidity of events drives the lessons home to Creon. He has had his chance and missed it; his punishment follows quickly. Eurydice dies, blaming him for the deaths of Haemon and Creon. Creon is humiliated and faced with guilt.

Antigone's death is caused by Creon's error and folly. It is a tragic act, but it is one way of requiting the gods. The concluding speech by the Chorus is about the fact that wisdom comes by acknowledging one's humble state before the gods. People must be humble and reverent. Suffering teaches lessons painfully. In the others' deaths Creon finds a sorrow that humbles and enlightens him. These ideas were in accordance with the ancient Greek religion, which gives him a chance to redeem his error by making a merciful offer to him.

DEATH AND NIGHTINGALES

Eugene McCabe
(2006 exam)

The story
The story is set in Fermanagh in the 1880s. It is based on a rich Protestant farmer called Billy Winters. Billy is married to a Catholic woman, but unknown to him their child is illegitimate and not his own. When Billy discovers this fact he abuses his wife and child, Beth. Later on Winters' wife dies. Beth develops into a strong and beautiful woman who becomes attached to a Fenian revolutionary called Liam Ward. She becomes pregnant by him and he persuades her to steal Winters' money and run away with him. Winters discovers her crime and savagely beats her. Beth later on discovers that Liam intends to kill her and steal the money. She prepares to leave with him in a fishing boat. Liam is unable to swim and Beth uses this as a means to revenge herself on him. As they are out in the lake Beth pulls the plug from the bottom of the boat and watches as Liam drowns in front of her eyes. The story concludes with the reconciliation between Beth and Winters. He declares his undying love for her and promises to look after her for the rest of her life.

Themes
- Anglo-Irish relationships
- politics
- revenge

Genre
This is a novel of social realism.

Cultural context
The cultural context of this novel is rural Ireland in the 1880s, the time when Parnell ruled in the Ascendency. The novel traces the inbuilt violence between Catholics and Protestants, which was a striking feature of life in that time. There are references to the political volatility and instability of Ireland in the 1880s.

General vision or viewpoint
The general vision of this novel is sombre and grim. Throughout the story there is a strong stress on the divisions within a local community. It is clear that the relationship between Beth and Winters will never be normal or stable. In many ways, McCabe seems to be using this relationship to show how the various communities in the North will always be divided because of the tragic inheritance from the past.

GREAT EXPECTATIONS
Charles Dickens
(2006 exam: comparative studies only)

Historical and literary background
The background of this novel is nineteenth-century England. *Great Expectations* belongs to the last period in Dickens' writing. A characteristic of all his work is the effort he made to describe and analyse the whole condition of England. Issues such as utilitarianism, political economy, various forms of religious revivalism and agnosticism are part of the historical background of nineteenth-century literature and they feature in the work of Charlotte Brontë, Charles Dickens and Thomas Hardy.

The publication of novels in serial form was a popular practice and is a feature of the literary background of this time. Dickens' *Great Expectations* and Hardy's *Far from the Madding Crowd* were both published in serial form.

The story
Pip tells his own story. He is born in a village in marsh country in Kent and brought up by his sister, Mrs Joe Gargery, who is inflexible and tyrannical. Her husband, Joe, is a blacksmith. One evening Pip meets an escaped convict in the marshes, who forces him to smuggle out some food. Later Pip is taken by Pumblechook, Joe's uncle, to Satis House to visit Miss Havisham, an eccentric woman who had been deserted at the altar on the day of her marriage and now lives among the decayed ruins of her wedding feast. She has a beautiful young protégée, Estella, whom she is bringing up to despise and humiliate men in order to avenge her own suffering.

Pip is apprenticed to Joe at the forge, where he makes an enemy of Joe's journeyman, Orlick. Mrs Joe is assaulted and left for dead by an unknown agent; not long afterwards she dies. Pip receives news from a London solicitor, Jaggers, that he has received money from an unknown benefactor. He goes to London and begins to lead an idle and useless life. Here he meets Matthew Pocket, who is related to Miss Havisham, and becomes friendly with his son, Herbert.

All this time Pip is under the delusion that Miss Havisham is his patron and benefactor and that she wishes him to marry Estella, but later he discovers that Magwitch, the convict he helped years before, is his benefactor. Magwitch has escaped from transportation and returned to England in order to see Pip, but his life is in danger from another former convict, Compeyson. In fact, this is the man who was engaged to Miss Havisham and who let her down.

Pip is forced to hide Magwitch in a house near the Thames. Orlick, in an act of revenge, tries to murder him. Pip tries to smuggle Magwitch out of the country, but there is a fight between Compeyson and the police. Compeyson is drowned and Magwitch is injured and dies later in prison.

Pip becomes ill and is nursed back to health by Joe, who pays all his bills. It is now that Pip realises how the possession of money has corrupted him. He joins Herbert in Cairo in business. Estella marries Bentley Drummle and is miserable. Joe remarries. After eleven years Pip returns and meets Estella, who is chastened and humbled after a life of suffering. Pip foresees that in time he will marry Estella.

Themes
- freedom
- isolation
- money and the corrupting power of wealth

Genre
This novel belongs to the genre of social realism. It is also a tragedy. Some of the features of social realism are:
- the prison system in nineteenth-century England
- the legal profession in nineteenth-century London
- the position of the working class.

Structure of the novel
The novel is divided into three sections:
- Pip's childhood
- his life in London
- his attempts to save Magwitch.

These three stages correspond to three stages of Pip's moral development.

Style of the novel
Great Expectations has certain elements of the thriller or the mystery novel. Because it was published as a serial, Dickens uses this technique to create a strong degree of suspense at the conclusion of each chapter. The capture by Orlick in the derelict shed and the attempts to get Magwitch down the river unseen at night are features of the thriller.

Dickens possessed a genius for writing description. His method of delineating character was generally *caricature*: a single feature is enlarged and repeated in different situations. The portrait of Pumblechook is an example of the striking use of caricature.

Dickens uses *irony* for several reasons. The title of the novel is bitterly ironic in the light of what happens as events unfold. Dickens mocks the moral blindness of certain characters. Pip allows himself to be deceived by appearance and wealth. When it is revealed to him that he is now to become a gentleman, that he has 'great expectations', he takes leave of the marshes, ironically thinking of the convict: 'If I had thought before with something allied to shame of my companionship with the fugitive…my comfort was that it had happened a long time ago, and that he had doubtless been transported a long way off, and that he was dead to me and might be veritably dead into the bargain.'

Dickens makes use of his rich vein of humour throughout the novel. Some of the humour mocks Pip's self-deception and blindness to reality. There is humour in the young Pip describing to Pumblechook, whom he despises, the exaggerated details of his first visit to Miss Havisham:

> 'Now, boy! What was she a-doing of, when you went in today?' asked Mr Pumblechook.
> 'She was sitting', I answered, 'in a black velvet coach.'
> Mr Pumblechook and Mrs Joe stared at one another – as they well might – and both repeated, 'In a black velvet coach?'
> 'Yes,' said I. 'And Miss Estella – that's her niece, I think – handed her in cake and wine at the coach window, on a gold plate'…
> 'Was anybody else there?' asked Mr Pumblechook.
> 'Four dogs,' said I.
> 'Large or small?'
> 'Immense,' said I. 'And they fought for veal cutlets out of a silver basket.'

The function of the humour here is to mock Pumblechook's hypocrisy.

Dickens possessed many gifts as a writer: an ear for comical expressions, a splendid eye for detail and a confident command of all the rhetorical techniques necessary to sustain the reader's interest.

Cultural context

Two different geographical areas are treated in the novel: the Kent marshes and London. Convicts, decayed mansions, dismal brick houses, boats, candles, the forge – all form part of the cultural background of the novel.

Dickens shows us the cultural, social and moral deprivations of village life. The novel also deals with the nineteenth-century prison system; Newgate is shown in vivid detail and in London we gain an insight into the legal profession through the character of Jaggers. His profession is associated with the perversion of justice: he uses bullying and deception to manipulate people and get them to do what he wants.

The culture of the 'gentleman' in London means having ample money to satisfy lavish tastes and whims. There is no need to work, unless one particularly wants to. The attributes of a gentleman are things that only money can buy: expensive clothes, education, a particular accent. The Blue Boar, a symbol of middle-class accommodation, has no time for Pip when he has no money. Money, power and corruption are central in the world of the novel.

General vision or viewpoint

Dickens changed the ending of *Great Expectations*, which was a development of the theme of vanquished expectations. The original ending had Estella, having suffered greatly at the hands of Drummle, marrying again, this time to a doctor: Pip realises that suffering has enabled her to understand better what he suffered through her.

The novel concludes with Pip's realisation that Joe and his new wife were made for one another and will have a happy life. Pip has matured and is a better person, having made mistakes and suffered. When he meets Estella, she too has grown morally as a result of suffering. It is fitting, therefore, that they should develop a relationship, having come through so much and having deepened to understand the real values in life, values that transcend money and revenge.

THE POISONWOOD BIBLE

Barbara Kingsolver
(2006 and 2007 exams)

The story

The story is based on one family who settle in the Congo in 1959. The father is a Baptist preacher and they have four girls called Adah, Leah, Rachael and Ruth May. The story deals with the various characters and the experiences each member of the family has during these years in Africa, a time when the Belgians occupied the Congo and did not allow the native Congolese to receive a proper education.

Nathan Price, the father, is a shrill Baptist preacher who dominates his family, particularly his wife, Orleanna. Orleanna Price suffers a great deal in the story. Her youngest daughter, Ruth May, dies shortly after she is bitten by a snake. Nathan is deeply concerned because she was not baptised. The whole story traces the growth and development of each of the family members as well as the corresponding political situation in the country in the years between 1959 and 1986. After eighty years of colonial rule, the Congo celebrates liberation and the corresponding inauguration of a black leader in 1960. We learn about Independence Day and how the blacks regain control of their own country again. Nathan begins to change after the war and becomes a tyrant and conqueror in his own home. He is determined to do the will of God in a strong and mighty way. Orleanna passively submits to him.

Rachael is the first one to leave and settle with a black man called Axelroot, who is involved in a lot of double-dealings and eventually leaves her for another woman. She marries several times and eventually inherits a large hotel called The Equatorial in a place called Brazzaville in the French Congo. She manages to organise and run this in an efficient way for various businessmen. Rachael never marries again and remains there, happy in her job of hotel owner and manager.

Lumumba assumes control as president in the Congo. There is a coup organised to put Mobutu in charge of the entire army. Lumumba manages to escape but is recaptured and badly beaten. He dies shortly after this and Mobutu assumes control in 1961. Things begin to deteriorate in the country, there is little food and the country suffers severely from bad drought. The people begin to change with independence and decide to vote in church about the question of whether Jesus Christ is a personal god. The Congolese are beginning to become used to the whole idea of the democratic process.

Nathan Price is voted out of the church and the people rebel against him. Orleanna leaves with Adah and the father is left alone. He is later attacked by the natives and burned. Leah is brought to a mission run by French nuns. Adah goes to study in Emory University to become a doctor. She remains in Atlanta and continues to do research into unusual viruses. She never marries. Leah marries a coloured man called Anatole and they have four sons. She remains in Zaire, which now has changed its name from the Congo.

Themes
- the family
- relationships
- religion
- war

Genre
This is a historical novel, which is narrated by five different voices. Each of the daughters tells her version of the story and then Orleanna, the mother, gives her own insight into the events that occur during these years in the Congo.

The structure of the book imitates the names of the bible – Genesis, the Revelation, the Judges and Exodus. This particular structure serves the purpose of showing that the story is not anti-Bible, but is one that contains another history and belongs to another place.

Cultural context
The background of this book is post-colonial Congo during the years after independence. It is a volatile time politically and we are given much insight into the turbulent years following French rule and the transition of the country from that of Congo to Zaire. In the book we witness the years under Lumumba's rule and also Mobutu, another black leader.

We gain a vivid insight into a country governed by Belgian rule, which is struggling to regain its own independence and establish its culture. There is a great deal of poverty and insecurity in the economy of the country. The initial assumption of democracy by the native Congolese gives rise to a good deal of fear and strife for the white people in the newly developed Zaire.

General vision or viewpoint
The general vision of this novel is drawn against the backdrop of two different stories: the personal history of the Price family and the historical development of post-colonial Zaire, or what was formerly the Belgian Congo. Through the rigidity of Nathan Price's style of missionary activity, there is a strong sense of how self-destructive the whole process of white colonisation becomes. The two stories develop and in many ways parallel one another. This type of structure serves the purpose of highlighting the main issues more forcibly. Accordingly, as each member of the Price family assumes independence and adopts a different lifestyle, we are exposed to the varying changes in

the political situation of the Belgian Congo and the difficulties involved in the assumption of independence and freedom. There is a striking sense of the importance of personal freedom in a country and the corresponding need and preparation for that freedom.

Pride and Prejudice

Jane Austen
(2006 and 2007 exams)

The story
The story is set in England and centres around the Bennet family, who live in Longbourn. The Bennets have a moderate income. There are five Bennet girls and Mrs Bennet is anxious to have her daughters married well. Elizabeth and Jane are the two older girls, who are more rational than the others. Mr Bingley, a man with plenty of money, moves into Netherfield, a large estate near the Bennet family. Mr Bingley falls in love with Jane, but under the influence of another rich gentleman by the name of Mr Darcy he abandons his pursuit of Jane because she does not have enough money.

Mr Darcy is regarded by everyone in the area as proud and arrogant. He falls in love with Elizabeth and proposes to her. She refuses him because she believes he is a snob. In addition, she dislikes his treatment of Mr Wickham, an officer in the regiment. It turns out that Wickham is a fortune hunter who used the Darcy family to get money. Wickham elopes with Lydia, Elizabeth Bennet's younger sister, and Darcy is forced to pay him money in order that he will marry Lydia.

Mr Bingley returns from London and proposes to Jane, who accepts him. Elizabeth changes her mind about Darcy and they get married at the end. Jane marries Mr Bingley.

Themes
Pride
The title of the novel is *Pride and Prejudice* and this pride can be seen in the figure of Darcy. Darcy believes he is superior to everyone and in particular despises Mrs Bennet, Elizabeth's mother. When he initially proposes to Elizabeth she notices that his references to her own family and his possible association with them would be a 'degradation'. Darcy changes throughout the novel and becomes more humble and acknowledges that his pride governed his behaviour and that he is prepared to rectify it.

Marriage
Marriage is a central theme in all of Austen's novels. The plot of this novel is constructed around the relationship between Elizabeth and Darcy. Austen is interested in the complexities of human relations. Marriage was the means by which many of the women characters escaped a life of spinsterhood. Look at the case of Charlotte, who marries the dull and stupid Mr Collins. Her reasons are practical, as she tells Elizabeth:

'I am not romantic. I ask only a comfortable home.' Elizabeth's standards for a happy marriage are based on love. The union between Lydia and Wickham is brought about because, as we are told in the novel, 'their passions were stronger than their virtue'. Darcy ends up assisting Wickham in his profession while Elizabeth helps Lydia out with money.

Money
Wealth and affluence are a hallmark of this society. Darcy is a wealthy landowner whose estate, Pemberley, is large and rich. Many of the characters in the novel are introduced in terms of their social position and wealth. The novel deals with certain characters who are rich and filled with pride and snobbery. This is the case in particular with Lady Catherine de Bourg, who is related to Darcy and who refuses to tolerate his marriage to Elizabeth on the grounds that her family is not wealthy or prestigious enough.

Genre
This novel is written in the third-person narrative voice. Austen uses irony in her narrative as a means of showing the truth about situations and people as well as a means of moral and social judgment. She also makes use of humour as a tool to entertain and sometimes to satirise.

Cultural context
The background of this novel is England in the mid-nineteenth century. Austen's social world is restricted to dealing mainly with the middle classes.

The mode of transport is carriage and horses. Many of the activities carried out by the characters consist in sedentary occupations such as quadrille, backgammon and whist parties.

General vision or viewpoint
Throughout this novel relationships between men and women are a central topic. It becomes evident that the right selection of a marriage partner is a critical and a central choice to be made in life. The novel shows us the development of various relationships between different types of people and how they culminate in marriage. Most of these marriages are happy, while some are simply expedient and practical. Marriage, however, seems to be a key factor determining happiness and fulfilment in life.

DEATH OF A SALESMAN

Arthur Miller
(2007 exam)

Historical and literary background
This drama spans a period of forty years from the early twentieth century, a time of dramatic change in lifestyle from an era of abundant job opportunities to one of increasing unemployment because of growing mechanisation. Money and power are primary values in the play.

The story
Willy Loman, the central character of the play, has been a travelling salesman for the Wagner Company for thirty-four years and is now sixty-three years of age. He is married to Linda and they have two sons, Biff and Happy. Biff has been living away from home and is unable to sustain a secure job. The relationship between Biff and Willy has been strained ever since Biff discovered that his father was unfaithful to his mother. Linda and her two sons are worried about Willy's behaviour. Willy decides to approach Howard Wagner, who is the son of the man he worked for thirty-four years ago. Willy wishes to work in New York City, closer to his home. However, Willy learns that he has no job because he has been a failure while working in New England. Willy is devastated at losing his job and goes to Charley, who is an old friend, to borrow more money in order to pay his insurance premium. Charley offers Willy a job but he refuses out of pride.

When Biff tries to communicate with Willy about his failures in finding work and getting a loan, Willy refuses to listen to him. Later on Biff returns home to find Willy planting seeds and talking to his brother Ben, who has been dead for nine months.

At the conclusion, Willy crashes the car and commits suicide. He hopes that he will gain twenty thousand pounds from the insurance. Tragically, nobody turns up for Willy's funeral and he dies a forgotten man.

Themes
- family relationships
- self-deception and self-realisation
- personal failure
- work

Genre
The play is a tragedy. The main character, Willy Loman, refuses to face reality and ends by committing suicide, thus destroying any possibility of happiness for himself or his family.

The structure of the play
Under the title of this play the following words are written: 'Certain private conversations in Two Acts and a Requiem'. This play dramatises a mind in turmoil. The structure of the play fluctuates between the past and the present. The time span of the play is only a twenty-four-hour period. There is no logical time sequence in the play. Willy's mind moves to the past twenty years before and focuses in particular on one year – 1928.

The style of the play
Many of the characters, with the exception of Linda, Willy's wife, use clichés and generalisations.

Certain symbols are used, such as the flute, which is connected with Willy's father. The idea of planting seeds suggests that Willy is anxious to reap some fruit in his life, to see something flourish.

Cultural context
The play shows the culture of America in the early twentieth century, a period of dramatic changes in society. After World War I there followed an increase in industrial production, but this was accompanied by a slump in the late 1920s, which resulted in high unemployment and a shortage of money. The increase in high-rise apartments in the city of New York is so intense that Willy feels the city is stifling him.

General vision or viewpoint
The general vision of life at the conclusion of this tragedy is grim and pessimistic. The disastrous failure to communicate basic emotions and ideas seems to be the tragic culmination of Willy's life and efforts. This failure destroys his family life and relationships. The basic need to be loved and understood is evident from Willy's situation. The conclusion dramatises the tragic lifestyle that results when the individual is unable to feel loved or understood.

11
Notes on Shakespeare Drama

In this chapter we will study the main techniques Shakespeare used in his tragedies. There are also notes on *Macbeth*, *Hamlet* and *King Lear* under the headings 'Themes and issues', 'Genre', 'Cultural context' and 'General vision or viewpoint'.

TRAGEDY IN SHAKESPEARE

Tragedy in Shakespeare involves a central figure who is an exceptional person, a hero of high stature, whose sufferings are extreme. This person is invested with qualities that raise him above his fellows. In Shakespearean tragedy this situation of loss or catastrophe results in recognition by the hero of the consequences of his mistakes or flaws; this is usually accompanied by a state of moral growth and finally death, which must arouse the sympathy and pity of the audience.

Primary features of a Shakespeare tragedy

1. The hero is a person of high status, such as a king, prince or a military leader.
2. This hero is endowed with a fatal flaw, which brings about an exceptional degree of suffering or calamity.
3. The flaw in the character is a form of evil that triggers off the tragic events of the play. These generally lead to the death of the protagonists.
4. Evil in Shakespeare is self-destructive – it annihilates itself.
5. The supernatural forms a part of the structure of his plays, for example, the storm in *King Lear*, the ghost in *Hamlet*.
6. Chance or accident plays a part in developing the plot. In *King Lear*, Edgar meets his father, the Earl of Gloucester, at opportune times, for example, when he is filled with despair and wants to commit suicide. Edgar manages to save his life. In *Hamlet*, there are many instances of the use of chance and coincidence, such as when young Hamlet discovers the letters which contain a plot on his life or when he encounters pirates who manage to escort him safely back to Denmark.

7. The conclusions of Shakespeare's plays are distinctive. They always dramatise a qualified form of redemption with the restoration of good, harmony and justice, but this is always of a mitigated kind. In other words, it is achieved at the expense of death and destruction of the good. The example of Cordelia in *King Lear*, together with the number of deaths in this play alone, qualifies the complete triumph of good over evil.

To sum up, a Shakespeare tragedy is a story of exceptional suffering experienced by a person of high status and culminating in death.

When you are studying the Shakespeare play:
- examine the central scenes that contribute to the development of the action and plot in the play
- examine the main features of the central characters or protagonists and in particular take note of their flaws or shortcomings
- examine how these flaws or defects contribute to the tragic events that occur in the play
- study the main characters' recognition of their flaws and how they grow in self-awareness towards the conclusion of the play
- examine the soliloquies; remember that soliloquies are an insight into a character's soul and give us a deep knowledge of what they are thinking and the reasons for their actions.

Examine soliloquies under the following headings:
- Where do they occur?
- What gives rise to them?
- What do they tell us about the character?
- What do we learn about the plot?
- What images are used and why?

Study the summaries of all the soliloquies at the end of the notes on *Macbeth*.

Historical and literary background

The literary and historical background of Shakespeare's plays is late sixteenth-century and early seventeenth-century England. The tragedies *Hamlet*, *Macbeth* and *King Lear* were written in the same period, 1600–8.
- This was a time of conflict between a traditional way of life and the new.
- The political framework of sixteenth-century England was hierarchical.
- Rulers at that time, whether king, prince or general, were regarded as divinely appointed. Usurpation of kingship was considered to be an act of sacrilege.
- The audience came from all strata of society.

Hamlet

(2005 exam)

The story

Claudius is king of Denmark when the play opens and he has recently married Gertrude, his late brother's wife. Gertrude has one son, Hamlet. He is a student in the University of Wittenberg and his closest friend is Horatio. Denmark has been at war with Norway over land lost by Fortinbras, king of Norway. His son, young Fortinbras, is raising an army against Denmark in order to reclaim these lands.

A ghost appears to two soldiers, Marcellus and Bernardo, while they are on guard duty outside the palace of Elsinore (Helsingør); it is dressed like Old Hamlet, the late king. The two guards tell Horatio, who decides to inform Hamlet. The following night Hamlet meets the Ghost, who informs him that he is his father and that he was murdered by his brother, Claudius. He orders Hamlet to avenge this deed.

Hamlet tells no one but instead adopts an 'antic disposition' – pretending to be mad – to deal with this predicament. Meanwhile, Claudius has successfully averted a war with Norway and has drawn up a peace treaty.

Polonius is the principal advisor to Claudius. He has a son, Laertes, who goes to France, and a daughter, Ophelia, who is in love with Hamlet. Polonius warns Ophelia to stay away from Hamlet, because they are not socially compatible.

Some players arrive at the palace and Hamlet takes this opportunity to organise a play, called *The Mousetrap*, wherein he hopes to 'catch the conscience' of Claudius – he wants to test his reaction as he watches the play in order to confirm his guilt.

Rosencrantz and Guildenstern, two old school friends of Hamlet, have been hired by Claudius to spy on Hamlet. He realises this and constantly makes fools of them.

When the play is put on before the court, the king reacts by calling for lights and disappears to his chapel to try to repent. Hamlet decides not to kill him then – he would rather catch him in the commission of a sinful act so that his soul would be lost for ever. Hamlet confronts his mother; here he accidentally kills Polonius, who is spying behind the arras (a hanging screen or tapestry), thinking it is Claudius.

Hamlet is dispatched to England in the care of Rosencrantz and Guildenstern, who are supposedly responsible for his safety but in fact have orders to kill him. Hamlet reads the letter containing their orders, substitutes another one arranging that Rosencrantz and Guildenstern be killed instead and returns to Denmark to confront Claudius.

Ophelia goes mad from unrequited love and the death of her father and she commits suicide.

Laertes has returned from France because of his father's sudden and strange death. Claudius manipulates him and organises a duel in which Laertes will kill Hamlet with a poisoned sword. He also arranges that a chalice of wine will be poisoned in case his plot should miscarry. By accident, Laertes is pierced with the poisoned sword at the same time that he wounds Hamlet with it. Before he dies he repents and tells Hamlet that Claudius is the villain. Hamlet kills Claudius with his sword and forces him to drink from the poisoned chalice. Gertrude has also drunk some wine from this chalice and she dies.

When Hamlet dies, young Fortinbras becomes king of Denmark and Horatio survives to expose the truth.

Themes
- revenge
- deception or false appearance
- woman and frail womanhood

Genre
Tragedy
Hamlet belongs to the category of revenge tragedy. This revenge is initiated by the injunction from the Ghost to revenge the 'foul and unnatural' deed of Claudius. A young, sensitive prince receives a commission from a ghost to carry out the deed of revenge. Adopting 'an antic disposition' as a weapon to deal with the corruption around him, he delays the deed of revenge for different reasons. Finally, he obtains an opportunity in the concluding scene, having banished Ophelia and driven her into a state of madness and attacked his mother for her sinful deed.

The tragedy concludes with the death of the main protagonist and many of the leading characters.

The structure of the play
The main plot centres on Hamlet and the task he is compelled to carry out as a result of the Ghost's revelations and specific injunction to revenge Claudius's 'foul and unnatural' deed. The sub-plot is structured around the family of Polonius and his two children, Laertes and Ophelia.

The whole play *Hamlet* centres on revenge. Hamlet is faced with a wicked but superficially attractive uncle whose evil is poisoning the state (the body politic). Hamlet cannot appeal to law, as Claudius is the law.

Act I is made up of five scenes. By the conclusion of Act I the details of the plot have been set in motion. Hamlet has met the Ghost and has been informed of his need to avenge. All the main characters have been introduced and we have been given an insight into their main characteristics. The conclusion of Act I reveals Hamlet in a state of profound perplexity and confusion with the deed he is compelled to execute. Both his words and actions from now on show a profound disintegration. This could stem from the fact that his conscience is in revolt against the task and thus his mind is divided:

> The time is out of joint. O cursed spite,
> That ever I was born to set it right!
> (Act I, Scene v)

Act II deals with the interaction of the main plot and the sub-plot. We see Polonius's hypocrisy as he sends a servant to spy on his own son, Laertes. The king employs two old school friends, Rosencrantz and Guildenstern, to spy on his nephew, Hamlet. The Players arrive and they provide Hamlet with an idea for his revenge plan.

The two central events in Act III consist of the play within a play scene and the closet scene. Hamlet has verified the authenticity of the Ghost and forced his mother to acknowledge that she is guilty.

In Act IV, Laertes returns from France and Hamlet is shipped to England. Both Laertes and Hamlet grapple with each other in the graveyard scene. Ophelia goes mad and commits suicide.

In Act V, the final scene concludes with the resolution of the conflict in the deaths of the leading protagonists.

Some of the scenes have titles and these have a particular bearing on the structure of this tragedy. Shakespeare cleverly introduces a play within a play, as it were. This is the scene (Act III, Scene ii) where Hamlet verifies the words of the Ghost, thereby catching the conscience of Claudius.

This scene is significant for the following reasons: Claudius sees his own act of poisoning. Gertrude sees a mirror of her own distasteful behaviour. Hamlet sees a nephew killing an uncle, i.e. himself and the deed he is called upon to do. Thus, Hamlet obtains the evidence he needs in Claudius's reaction after this play.

Both the nunnery scene and the closet scene (Act III, Scene i) deal with the theme or issue of woman. Both scenes are similar in so far as they both show Hamlet overwhelmed with a profound and powerful sense of emotion.

Another scene which has structural significance in the development of the plot is the scene called the graveyard scene (Act V, Scene i). This is a richly ironic scene. It is also structurally important, as it comes before the death of the leading protagonists and it speaks in ironic terms about life after death. While the two gravediggers are clowns who are meant to provide a type of comic relief, there are unmistakable notes of grim irony permeating this scene. One of the first statements made is that the gravemakers' houses last till doomsday. This powerfully reinforces the permanence and power of the grave.

Another aspect of the structure of these tragedies is Shakespeare's use of the soliloquy, which forms an integral part of a Shakespearean tragedy. Most of the soliloquies show the characters analysing and speculating on the consequences of their own or other people's actions. Claudius's first two soliloquies show his complete acknowledgement of guilt and disgust with his life of insincerity and hypocrisy:

> How smart a lash that speech doth give my conscience!
> The harlot's cheek, beautied with plastering art,
> Is not more ugly to the thing that helps it
> Than is my deed to my most painted word:
> O heavy burden.
> (Act III, Scene i)

After he has seen his own deed of murder enacted in the play within a play scene, Claudius rushes in guilt to his private chapel and begins his prayer with the words:

> O, my offense is rank, it smells to heaven;
> It hath the primal eldest curse upon't,
> A brother's murder!
> (Act III, Scene iii)

However, Claudius may possess the capacity to feel guilty and in need of repentance, but his ambition for power is far greater. His final soliloquy in Act IV, Scene iii reveals an attitude where he has coarsened his conscience and ruthlessly suppressed any openness to repentance or amendment of his behaviour:

> And England ...
>   thou may'st not coldly set
> Our sovereign process, which imports at full,
> By letters congruing to that effect,
> The present death of Hamlet.
> (Act IV, Scene iii)

The queen's aside, which is the only one in the play, also reveals a sensitivity of conscience:

> To my sick soul, as sin's true nature is,
> Each toy seems prologue to some great amiss,
> So full of artless jealousy is guilt.
> (Act IV, Scene v)

Most of Hamlet's soliloquies reveal a character who is deeply sensitive and is possessed with a refined moral conscience. The Hecuba soliloquy and his speech in Act III, Scene ii after the performance of *The Mousetrap* play are the only soliloquies which specifically show his plan of attack and the development of the plot:

> the play's the thing
> Wherein I'll catch the conscience of the king.
> (Act II, Scene ii)

After he has proved the Ghost's authenticity, Hamlet announces his intention with respect to his mother, which he will execute in the closet scene: 'I will speak daggers to her, but use none'.

Many of the soliloquies reveal a dilemma within the character and with their conscience in particular. Overall, Hamlet's soliloquies reveal a deeply reflective and philosophical nature that is endowed with an acutely sensitive moral conscience.

Imagery and language in the play

Early on in the play, Polonius tells Claudius that he would 'find truth even if it is within the centre' (Act II, Scene ii). In many ways this statement could sum up the essence of Hamlet's motto underlying his use of language and imagery in the play. Hamlet needs imagery for his 'antic disposition'. His language and imagery are all designed to unmask people, to strip them of their false appearance and to expose them in their true nature. It also reflects his real ability to penetrate to the real essence of things, to break down the barriers erected by hypocrisy.

Through the simile of the pipe he shows Rosencrantz and Guildenstern that he has seen through their intent:

> You would play upon me you would seem to
> know my stops, you would pluck out the heart of my
> mystery ...
> (Act III, Scene ii)

The protective mask of his assumed 'antic disposition' enables him to communicate basic truths in some strikingly colourful ways. For example, he tells Rosencrantz and Guilenstern that they are 'sponges' that 'soak up the king's countenance, his | rewards, his authorities' (Act IV, Scene ii). He wishes to ridicule their hypocrisy and corrupt ambition. The sponge metaphor unmasks their deception and reveals how they have become willing dupes in Claudius's hands.

Hamlet seeks to lead his mother to the truth by means of images, 'a mildewed ear blasting his wholesome brother ...', 'a cutpurse', 'a king of shreds and patches'.

The poison symbol becomes the leitmotif of the imagery in the play, where imagery and action reflect one another. The corruption of Denmark and its people is seen as an insidious poison. The graphic details of Claudius's murder are not enacted on the stage, but instead are depicted in terms of vivid images of corruption, such as 'the leprous distilment', 'vile and loathsome crust'.

Poisoning becomes the means whereby all the main characters die. This powerful imaginative pattern built up of poison, decay, corruption and sickness depicts the unwholesome moral condition of Denmark. The image of an ulcer infecting and eating away the body becomes the central image in the play.

The unnecessary fighting between Norway and Poland is a kind of tumour which grows from too much prosperity:

> This is the imposthume of much wealth and peace,
> That inward breaks ...
> (Act IV, Scene iv)

Hamlet's mother and her association with Claudius takes off the 'rose from an innocent love and sets a blister there.'

Claudius's use of disease images has different implications. The health of Denmark and its security is related to Claudius's security. All is governed by self-interest. Hamlet's free reign in the kingdom is seen as a distinct threat to Claudius's security and life; it is like

> diseases desperate grown
> By desperate appliances are relieved ...
> ... like the hectic in my blood he rages.
> (Act IV, Scene iii)

Images operate on different levels in the play. On the one hand they can depict truth for Hamlet and help him to expose and strip away false appearance. On the other hand, imagery gives him the freedom he needs to cloak his real purpose behind ambiguity, puns, word play, quibbles and ambiguities. To those people he distrusts and dislikes he deliberately misconstrues them and attaches irrelevant and dubious meaning to what they say. He particularly treats Polonius in this manner because he sees through the fact that Polonius is a meddlesome and prying old fool. At one stage Hamlet tells Polonius that he is a fishmonger and when he denies it Hamlet cynically claims:

> Then I would you were so honest a man.
> (Act II, Scene ii)

Thus, Hamlet's hostility for a character is revealed through his use of ambiguous language, for example, his repeated use of misleading comments to Claudius. Our first insight into the relationship between both Claudius and Hamlet reveals these undercurrents of bitterness, when Claudius asks Hamlet:

> How is it that the clouds still hang on you?

to which Hamlet bitterly replies:

> Not so, my lord. I am too much in the sun.
> (Act I, Scene ii)

Later on Claudius greets Hamlet with the words:

> How fares our cousin Hamlet?

to which Hamlet replies:

> Excellent i'faith of the chameleon's dish: I eat
> the air promise-crammed, you cannot feed capons so.
> (Act III, Scene ii)

Hamlet finds such evasion essential as a weapon of self-defence because he finds himself in a world where he does not know who to trust, surrounded by people who use deceit and lies to probe and uncover the truth about other people.

Much of the language and imagery used in the play is richly symbolic and serves the primary function of depicting the central issues and themes.

Cultural context

The particular cultural context of the play *Hamlet* must take into account certain attitudes towards the following:
- kingship/aristocracy and the political landscape
- marriage
- the role of women
- the particular system of values at that time.

The type of kingship that forms the background of the tragedies is monarchy. The king was God's representative on Earth; no person had a right to kill him. Claudius himself echoes this idea when he hypocritically tells Gertrude:

> There's such divinity doth hedge a King,
> That treason can but peep to what it would,
> Acts little of his will.
> (Act IV, Scene v)

Therefore, to murder a lawfully elected king amounted to sacrilege. Furthermore, to marry a brother- or sister-in-law was tantamount to incest in this society. Thus, at the opening of the play the reigning king, Claudius, is guilty of both regicide (the murder of a lawful king) and incest because of his marriage to Gertrude, his brother's wife. When the Ghost appears, he brings with him an injunction to Hamlet, the young prince of Denmark and the next in line to the throne, to exercise the code of morality and revenge this foul deed.

The political panorama is one of peace except for Fortinbras's attempts to mount an army against Poland. We learn from Hamlet that this action is the result of excess wealth and corruption which has been experienced by Norway and Poland. Claudius is an effective and adept politician who knows how to manage any threat on peace to his kingdom swiftly and adroitly.

We get a distinct impression that marriage is not held in very high esteem by either Gertrude or Claudius. From the Ghost's words, we learn that Claudius is guilty of adultery as well:

> Ay, that incestuous, that adulterate beast ...
> (Act I, Scene v)

The Court of Elsinore is therefore corrupt. This corruption is rooted in both Claudius and Gertrude, king and queen of Denmark, and seeps out like a poison corrupting the culture, the value system and the people involved in this society.

The role of women in this society is largely seen in a negative manner. Both of the women in the play, Ophelia and Gertrude, are seen as weak and frail. They allow themselves to be used by men and in general they are treated with contempt and cynicism by the men in the play. Both Polonius and Laertes treat Ophelia as a child – described as a 'green girl', they patronise her and intrude into her private life and relationships.

The value system which is shown to be upheld by the characters seems to be contradictory at times. Shakespeare presents some distinctly Christian values, particularly within Hamlet's mode of behaviour. However, this value system seems to conflict and clash with a more barbaric and primitive mode of reasoning in Hamlet. Early on in the play, Hamlet will not commit suicide because it is a mortal sin:

> Or that the Everlasting had not fixed
> His canon 'gainst self-slaughter!
> (Act I, Scene ii)

Yet later on in the play he seems to have no problem with murdering Claudius and wanting to catch him in an act where his heels will kick at heaven and his soul will be as damned and black as hell.

At the conclusion of the play, Hamlet sees himself and his future in the hands of God:

> There's a divinity that shapes our ends,
> Rough-hew them how we will.
> (Act V, Scene ii)

Although Hamlet can speak with great conviction about heaven and God's plans for men – 'there's a special providence in the fall of a sparrow' – he can still organise the murder of Rosencrantz and Guildenstern with 'no shriving time allowed'.

Hamlet is quick to preach about marriage and the sacred character of matrimony to Gertrude. Her marriage to Claudius has made all marriage contracts void, religion is a mockery and a rhapsody of words. Her deed of incest has taken off the rose from an innocent love and set a blister there instead.

Yet in action Hamlet seems to have no qualms at the conclusion in stabbing the king and forcing him to drink from the poisoned chalice with the words 'thou incestuous, murderous, damned Dane'.

Murder, revenge and punishing evil with evil are fundamentally opposed to the Christian ethic, these are contradictions that are not resolved at the conclusion of the play. They could stem from the fact that for a great deal of the play Hamlet was governed by conflicting emotions and this could have clouded his rational faculty and prevented him from acting in a consistently sound fashion.

General vision or viewpoint

This play begins with darkness, uncertainty, questioning, falsehood and selfishness and ends with certainty restored, self-sacrifice vindicated and justice restored through the medium of Horatio, who has never concurred with evil and is compelled by Hamlet to remain alive in order to bear witness to the truth. Treachery is seen to breed treachery, murder to breed murder. Evil is seen to destroy itself. The conclusion is the redemption of society from corruption and deceit and the peaceful death of the tragic hero:

> Good night sweet prince:
> And flights of angels sing thee to thy rest!
> (Act V, Scene ii)

In all Shakespeare's tragedies, evil is shown to be self-destructive. Through the logic of events, Shakespeare shows that there is a universal moral law that one transgresses at one's peril.

Summary of the soliloquies

Hamlet's soliloquies

In many of Hamlet's soliloquies we gain an insight into a character whose mind seems to be divided. This may stem from the enormous task of revenge imposed on him by the Ghost. In his soliloquies Hamlet also shows a profound philosophical capacity.

1. Act I, Scene ii. This is Hamlet's first appearance in the play. He professes a belief in God and an avoidance of suicide because of that belief. He shows disgust at his

mother's hasty remarriage and expresses a desire for revenge. *Imagery*: Classical images show his scholarship and learning: his father is a Hyperion, Claudius is represented as a satyr and his mother is like Niobe. Disease images, such as 'unweeded garden' and things 'rank and gross in nature', reflect this theme of moral corruption.

2. Act I, Scene v. This soliloquy occurs after the Ghost's disclosures as an expression of Hamlet's moral shock at the Ghost's revelations. He has to lock this horror inside: 'thy commandment all alone shall live ... volume of my brain, | Unmixed with baser matter'. *Imagery*: the 'smiling damned villain' reflects the theme of insincerity and false appearance.
3. Act II, Scene ii. This is the Hecuba soliloquy. The tears of the Players as they enact the drama of Hecuba lead to this soliloquy and make Hamlet realise his inaction. He condemns himself for his tardiness in acting against his uncle. For the first time in the play he articulates the fact that the Ghost may not be authentic: 'the spirit that I have seen may be a devil' (line 587). He announces his plot: to 'catch the conscience' of Claudius by staging a play.
4. Act III, Scene I. This soliloquy occurs just before the nunnery scene and is the one that has earned Hamlet the title of 'prince of philosophical speculators'. He engages in some profound reflections on life, death and the meaning of suffering. He claims that his indecisiveness and lack of resolution stem from too much thinking.
5. Act III, Scene ii. This soliloquy occurs after the play within a play scene, when Claudius's guilt has been exposed. Hamlet ironically announces that 'I could drink hot blood' (line 372–3) and 'do such bitter business as the day would quake to look on.' He announces his intentions regarding his mother: 'I will speak daggers to her, but use none' (line 377).
6. Act III, Scene iii. This soliloquy occurs in the prayer scene, when Hamlet fails to kill Claudius in the chapel. He offers reasons why he will not kill him: he wants to catch him in an act that will damn his soul. These reasonings contradict his earlier beliefs as a Christian.
7. Act IV, Scene iv. Fortinbras is passing through Denmark on his way to capture a small tract of land in Poland. This is similar to the Hecuba soliloquy, as Hamlet compares himself to Fortinbras and again reproaches himself on his delay in setting about his revenge. Spurred on by Fortinbras' spirited activity, he steels himself to perform bloody deeds.

Claudius's soliloquies
Claudius's first two soliloquies show that he has a moral conscience. The third shows how he has become more deeply immersed in guilt and evil-doing.
1. Act III, Scene I. This is Claudius's first acknowledgment of his guilt. It reflects the fact that he has a conscience and shows the burden of his life of deceit and hypocrisy. *Imagery*: The 'harlot's cheek, beautied with plastering art' conceals her ugliness, reflecting the theme of duplicity and insincerity.
2. Act III, Scene iii. This soliloquy occurs in the prayer scene, where Claudius is struggling with himself to repent. He acknowledges his crime: 'My offence is rank'.

He enumerates the reasons why he committed the murder: 'My crown, mine own ambition, and my queen.' The priorities here are interesting: 'his queen' figures last on his list.
3. Act IV, Scene iii. Claudius, now fully immersed in evil-doing, has organised the murder of Hamlet. *Imagery*: 'like the hectic in my blood he rages'. The disease imagery reflects the threat on Claudius's peace and security while Hamlet lives.

Ophelia's soliloquy
Act III, Scene i. This soliloquy occurs at the conclusion of the nunnery scene and is an ironic soliloquy. Ophelia laments the destruction of Hamlet's splendid qualities and blames it on madness. In her next appearance in the play she will be the one to be stricken with madness because of her treatment at the hands of Hamlet.

Gertrude's aside
Act IV, Scene v. Here Gertrude has just learned of Ophelia's madness. Like Claudius, she acknowledges that she is guilty of sin: 'to my sick soul as sin's true nature is …'

AS YOU LIKE IT

(2005 and 2006 exams)

The story
The story opens with the fact that Duke Frederick has taken over the dukedom from his brother, Duke senior, and banished him to the Forest of Arden. There Duke senior lives like Robin Hood with some noblemen. Rosalind, Duke senior's daughter, has stayed with her cousin Celia, Duke Frederick's daughter. They are both good friends and do not want to be separated from one another.

Orlando is the youngest son of Sir Rowland de Boys, who was a good friend of Duke senior. Oliver is Orlando's brother. He is jealous of Orlando and wishes evil against him. He even states himself that he is 'full of ambition … a secret and villainous contriver' (Act I, Scene i). Oliver castigates Orlando to Charles, who is a good wrestler, and arranges a wrestling match between both in the hope that his brother will be defeated.

However, Orlando defeats Charles and is immediately banished from the kingdom by Duke Frederick. At this stage Orlando has met Rosalind and they have fallen in love. Duke Frederick banishes Rosalind from the court with the penalty of death if she disobeys. Celia decides to join her in her banishment. They adopt disguises and false names. Rosalind disguises herself as a young boy and assumes the false name of Ganymede, while Celia takes the name of Aliena.

Touchstone is a clown who meets Audrey, a peasant goatherd, and they decide to get married.

In the meantime, Adam, who is Oliver's servant, warns Orlando about his brother and warns him to leave. Adam offers to protect Orlando and offers him gold. Orlando flees to the Forest of Arden, where he meets the exiled Duke senior. Orlando appeals to the Duke to give them food and bases his appeal on the customs and courtesies of a civilised society, even though he is now living in the middle of the forest. Rosalind and Celia meet Orlando in the forest and the disguised Rosalind begins a conversation with Orlando about the authenticity of his love. There is a great deal of comic and ironic humour governing this part of the play.

Oliver has been commanded by Duke Frederick to find Orlando and capture him. Oliver meets with Rosalind and Celia and tells them that he has repented of his evil intentions against his brother and is sorry. Oliver and Celia fall in love with one another. Jaques de Boys enters to tell them all how Duke Frederick has repented and become converted, and in addition he has returned all the lands stolen to his exiled brother.

The play concludes happily with the marriage of four couples – Orlando and Rosalind, Oliver and Celia, Touchstone and Audrey and Phebe, a shepherd, and Silvius, a shepherdess.

Themes
- romantic love and loyalty
- deception
- relationships
- women
- contrast between the court and the country

Genre
A comedy in five acts. A good deal of the dialogue in this play is based on ironic humour.

Cultural context
There are two different cultural contexts in this play. We get an insight into the values of court life in Act I. The remainder of the play is based in and around the Forest of Arden. The values that are represented in the forest have a dual nature – we are exposed to an ideal pastoral world on the one hand and an actual forest where people are afflicted with fatigue and hunger on the other. There are continuous contrasts drawn in the cultural world of the play between the realities of forest life and the flatteries that dominate the court.

In the Forest of Arden there is also a good deal of respect for the values of the civilised court, such as respect, gentleness, courtesy in speech and action, respect for status and rank, etc. The play manages to highlight how a creative compromise can exist between the two different worlds.

General vision or viewpoint
The general vision or viewpoint inherent in this play is based on the idea of celebrating certain values in life, such as love and friendship. Romance and intrigue govern the plot of this play and it becomes apparent that friendship and loyalty between various characters are important values. The conclusion gives us a happy vision of the unity of

four couples in marriage. What appears to be dominant throughout this play is that certain ideals, such as courtesy and love, that have permeated the play's structure are neither sentimentalised nor destroyed at the end.

KING LEAR

(2006 exam)

The story

Lear is an old man when the play opens. He decides to divide his kingdom among his three daughters by means of a childish love test based on words. When Cordelia refuses to co-operate she is stripped of her dowry and banished to France. Lear's other two daughters, Goneril and Regan, take over the kingship. They are shrewd operators who have fully assessed Lear's flaws. They plot together so that they will not suffer from his unpredictability.

Shortly after Lear abdicates he moves to Goneril's house with a hundred knights; this was one of the conditions of his agreement. Here he has a violent confrontation with Goneril about the number of knights he needs. Regan arrives and the love scene is ironically parodied, with the two daughters haggling over the number of his knights in a grotesque mimicry of the love test. Lear is thrust out into the storm with his Fool and the Earl of Kent.

The Earl of Gloucester has two sons. One of them, Edmund, is 'illegitimate'. Edmund deceives Gloucester about Edgar, his 'legitimate' son, and convinces him he is a villain who is ready to murder him. Edgar is forced to go on the run and to play the role of a mad beggar. He meets Lear on the heath in the storm, and together they reach some profound insights into human nature. Later the Earl of Gloucester is blinded by the Duke of Cornwall (Regan's husband) for helping Lear. Gloucester becomes filled with despair and wanders to Dover to commit suicide. He is saved by Edgar, who discloses his identity to him shortly before Gloucester dies, presumably from a heart attack.

Lear becomes reconciled with Cordelia, who returns to England with an army to save him. Both Lear and Cordelia are imprisoned by Edmund, who leads the English army against the king of France. Cordelia is hanged, and Lear dies of a broken heart.

Goneril and Regan become consumed by lust for Edmund and they kill one another. Edmund is slain by Edgar. Only the Duke of Albany (Goneril's husband), the Earl of Kent and Edgar survive to sustain the gory state of England at the conclusion.

Themes
- blindness to human nature
- the value of suffering and the corresponding growth in insight and moral awareness
- justice
- the child-parent relationship
- good and evil.

Blindness to human nature

The play *King Lear* is a drama of pride. A long life of absolute power, nourished by flattery and blind obedience to his every whim, has made Lear essentially blind to both his own limitations and to the reality of corrupt human nature. Lear has lived the life of an absolute dictator and has therefore generated within himself deeply ingrained faults 'of long engraffed condition'.

Choleric and mercurial in temperament, he is characterised by a presumptuous self-will with absolutely no self-control: 'full of changes his age is', 'unconstant starts', 'he slenderly knows himself'. All of these defects are cynically assessed by his two daughters, Regan and Goneril, immediately after they have received the power of kingship. Lear arrogantly refuses to listen to Kent when he tries to get him to see the true natures of Goneril, Regan and Cordelia. Instead he banishes both Kent and Cordelia and hands over the kingdom to Goneril and Regan, who later betray him.

Similarly, in the sub-plot Gloucester, who is gullible and also blind to the reality of human nature, is deceived by Edmund into believing his legitimate son, Edgar, is a villain.

It is only at the conclusion of the tragedy that both characters grow in insight and moral awareness and learn their children's true natures.

Suffering and growth in moral awareness

The world of the play *King Lear* is a world of suffering. This is brought home to us many times in the play, for instance, Lear's rage and loss of sanity in the storm scenes, together with the violence inherent in the blinding of Gloucester. There are numerous images of suffering and cruelty.

Yet this suffering is shown to have a positive purpose. It is through suffering that both Lear and Gloucester attain insight. Many times their insights echo one another, which reinforces the deliberate parallel that Shakespeare draws between the main plot and the sub-plot.

Both of them recognise their own responsibility for their predicament – Lear's words that his suffering is a 'judicious punishment' are a direct echo of Gloucester's words, 'O my follies'. They come to understand the true natures of their children. Lear describes Goneril and Regan as 'two pernicious daughters' and speaking about Cordelia he acknowledges that 'I did her wrong'.

When Gloucester is blinded by Cornwall and Regan flaunts the truth about Edmund and Edgar before him, Gloucester cries out 'then Edgar was abused'. They both grow in self-knowledge. Lear realises in the storm scenes that he is 'an infirm, weak and despised old man', while Gloucester declares that 'I stumbled when I saw'.

Their high status had allowed them to become blind to the reality of the world around them; stripped of their status they are stripped of their delusions: 'Yet you see how this world goes' Lear states, and Gloucester replies, 'I see it feelingly'.

Both men achieve moral growth and develop new qualities within themselves. Shortly after he is blinded, Gloucester wanders across the heath in despair and meets with Edgar, who brings him to Dover. At this stage his horizons have been broadened through extreme suffering and, for the first time in his life, he becomes aware of the plight of other people. He speaks about justice and the unequal distribution of wealth in the lines

> So distribution should undo excess,
> And each man have enough.
> (Act IV, Scene i)

Earlier Lear had come to a similar conclusion and had realised he had paid too little attention to the poverty around him:

> O, I have ta'en
> Too little care of this,...
> That thou mayst shake the superflux to them,
> And show the heavens more just.
> (Act III, Scene iv)

Lear's central experience is his growth in moral awareness under the impact of suffering; profound agony on the heath, together with the loss of everything, both physical and spiritual, free his heart from the bondage of selfish self-absorption. He loses everything in the world, but gains an appreciation of his own soul and of human nature. He learns the real nature of humility, endurance, love and understanding. His path is not straightforward; he moves from an overweening pride and arrogance through rebellious anger bordering on despair to an eventual patience and humility of soul.

Lear's arrival at truth is through a paradox, by means of 'reason in madness'. In other words, he has to lose his sanity to gain insight and self-awareness, and moreover many of the most profound lessons that he learns in the play are through the medium of the professionally mad Fool.

Shakespeare clearly means to show us through this tragedy that 'he was a man more sinned against than sinning'. His sufferings are out of proportion to his original fault.

Likewise, Gloucester grows to be a better man towards the conclusion of this tragedy by means of suffering. Gloucester's nature at the beginning of the play is self-indulgent and over-sensual and so he suffers the punishment of being blinded. His blindness precedes Lear's madness. We see the first stage of his moral growth when he undertakes to stand by Lear and give him support even at the risk of his own life. This act of going to 'relieve' Lear out on the heath and offer him consolation and comfort costs him his eyes. Afterwards, when Gloucester realises that it is Edmund who betrays him, he immediately prays to the gods for forgiveness and that Edgar will prosper: 'Kind Gods, forgive me that, and prosper him!' (Act III, Scene vii).

Both men suffer because of their weakness and both grow to be morally better men through this suffering. Lear's fault is one of pride, or an intellectual fault. He fails to judge character and action. He loses his reason and goes mad. At the height of his madness he achieves his deepest insights into human nature and grows both morally and spiritually. The first manifestation of the moral growth is his plea to the Fool to go into the hovel before him:

In, boy; go first. You houselesss poverty, –
Nay, get thee in. I'll pray and then I'll sleep.
(Act III, Scene iv)

This manifestation of a concern for other people, this profound growth in humility and attitude of praying is all striking evidence of a deep change in Lear's nature and is shown to be particularly evident at the conclusion when he becomes reconciled with Cordelia. He kneels down and begs forgiveness from Cordelia with the words 'if you have poison for me I will drink it'. He allies himself with Cordelia as 'God's spies', and claims that he will take on the 'mystery of things'.

All his earlier pride, arrogance, bad temper and impatience are now supplanted by a sincere repentance. When he meets Cordelia he kneels down and begs her forgiveness. He tells Cordelia:

Thou art a soul in bliss; but I am bound
Upon a wheel of fire, that mine own tears
Do scald like molten lead.
(Act IV, Scene vii)

So while the play shows us a cruel world of suffering, it also illustrates the positive aspects of this suffering. Lear and Gloucester both die better men as a result of their experiences.

Justice
When the play opens, Lear, as king of England, is justice. The play is structured upon the consequences of a grave error and abuse of justice by a king within whose powers justice lies. When Lear relinquishes his crown to Goneril and Regan and abdicates his right to dispense justice, for the first time in his life he becomes subject to justice. In this position, Lear is better able to assess human systems of justice, the full reality of his kingdom and of power as he himself wielded it for so many years.

The entire play shows the corruption and hypocrisy inherent in human systems of justice in the England of Lear's reign. The mock trial scene in Act III, Scene vi analyses and exposes the system of justice and kingship in the kingdom.

The mock trial is conducted by Lear, who is completely mad, the Fool, whose job it is to act like a madman, and the simulated or pretended madness of Edgar. The whole scene is an ironic comment on how depraved and perverted the existing systems of human justice are.

The scene also confronts the problem of evil. Lear asks the fundamental question, 'Is there any cause in nature that make these hard hearts?' (Act III, Scene vi). The scene is positioned and structured in a striking manner to reinforce the two themes of evil and injustice.

Immediately after this scene, Gloucester is put on trial in a grossly unjust manner. Immediately before he punishes Gloucester Cornwall acknowledges that:

… we may not pass upon his life
Without the form of justice, …
(Act III, Scene vii)

Yet he maintains that: 'our power | Shall do a courtesy to our wrath, which men | May blame, but not control'. In other words, Cornwall is perfectly capable of manipulating and perverting justice in order to satisfy his own revenge. Ironically, in this act of injustice he meets with his own death at the hands of a servant.

There is another trenchant image of justice given to us in Act IV, Scene vi. Here we are exposed to the great image of authority in the farmer's dog, who barks at a beggar. Even 'a dog's obeyed in office' is the implication of such ideas; in other words, those who wield authority are corrupt. Here, justice is useless and ineffective.

The storm symbolises divine justice. However, there is no consistent statement made on the theme or issue of divine justice. In the death of the bad characters, Albany sees the judgment of the heavens at work. When he hears that Cornwall dies in the act of plucking Gloucester's eyes out, Albany cries out:

> This shows you are above,
> You justicers, that these our nether crimes
> So speedily can venge!
> (Act IV, Scene ii)

Edgar repeats this type of sentiment when he tells Edmund in the final scene:

> The gods are just, and of our pleasant vices
> Make instruments to plague us.
> (Act V, Scene iii)

The play does not reflect justice in every character's fate. Cordelia is hanged and Lear dies afterwards of a broken heart. There is no coherent or unifying conclusion drawn in the play about the impact of divine justice.

The overall impression left to us about the human system of justice is that of the power and strength of corruption, unbridled evil and general abuse within the system.

The child-parent relationship
One of the central issues dealt with in this play is that of the relationship between parents and their children. This issue or theme is reflected both in the main plot and the sub-plot.

Out of a foolish mixture of both tenderness and blindness, Lear gives everything away to two daughters and banishes the third. He does this through a fatal error involving love and language. He believes that true love is expressed in words and hyperboles and so he is deceived by Regan and Goneril's meaningless and empty platitudes. Likewise, he interprets Cordelia's silence as a lack of love.

At the same time as Lear is suffering from the cold ingratitude of his two daughters, Edgar falls from the rank to which his birth entitled him. This happens because of his father Gloucester's blindness and his brother Edmund's devious plots. Edgar is forced to assume the shape of a beggar tormented by evil spirits in order to survive detection. Both characters are driven out onto the heath where they endure a profound degree of suffering and degradation.

In some ways Lear and Edgar have a share of the blame in the tragedy which befalls them. Lear confuses his royal function with his parental role. Expecting his daughters to flatter him like his courtiers, he will reward them with land in return. It is the king of France who has to remind him that this is wrong with the words 'Love's not love | When it is mingled with regards that stand | Aloof from th'entire point' (Act 1, Scene 1).

Edgar is naive and gullible and allows himself to be deceived by his own brother, Edmund. He accepts Edmund's story about Gloucester's anger without a moment's questioning and for the rest of the play adopts the role of a disguised runaway.

The evil which happens to both Lear and Edgar may be a mixture of their own flawed natures plus their treatment by their families. Lear is treated with gross injustice by Regan and Goneril. He is thrust out of the palace and forced to survive the storms. The two sisters are then left to deal with their unadulterated lust for Edmund. This eventually consumes them both and they end up destroying one another. In fact, Albany, Goneril's husband, predicts this fact when he condemns his wife for her treatment of her father:

> Tigers, not daughters, what have you perform'd?
> A father, and a gracious aged man ...
> Most barbarous, most degenerate! have you madded ...
> If that the heavens do not their visible spirits
> Send quickly down to these vile offences,
> It will come,
> Humanity must perforce prey on itself,
> Like monsters of the deep.
> (Act IV, Scene ii)

This is what actually occurs in the story of both sisters; destroyed by their jealous passion for Edmund, they end up killing one another.

In contrast, Cordelia continues to love her father in exile. Together with her husband, the king of France, she organises an army to save her father. At the play's conclusion, her love remains steadfast and Lear is able to anticipate a life in prison with pleasure now that he has her with him:

> ... Come, let's away to prison;
> We two alone will sing like birds i' the cage.
> (Act V, Scene iii)

Likewise, Edgar performs a similar function in the sub-plot. He prevents his father from committing suicide and it is through him that Gloucester learns the value of endurance:

> ... Men must endure
> Their going hence, even as their coming hither.
> (Act V, Scene ii)

Throughout the story of Regan and Goneril there is the recurrent idea that the breaking of human ties, especially those of blood and loyalty, are both abnormal and unnatural. On the other hand, the qualities of love and endurance, which are each manifested in different ways by Edgar and Cordelia, are shown to be binding and positive forces in this play.

Good and evil

One of the central questions asked in this play is what the cause of evil is: 'let them anatomise Regan; see what breeds | about her heart. Is there any cause in nature that | makes these hard hearts?'

The play shows the release of evil and its subsequent course. It dramatises the conflict between good and evil, which may be summed up as follows: evil may triumph for a short time but ultimately good asserts itself and emerges victorious at the conclusion. However, the cost of this victory results in the destruction of much that is good and the evil in the play turns out to be self-destructive.

This can be illustrated in the following way. In the stories of Edmund, Goneril and Regan we see the evil that was rooted in both Lear and Gloucester set free in the world. When Lear divides up his kingdom he introduces a principle of calculation or measurement which both Regan and Goneril adopt and carry to an extreme. He also makes a fatal error of understanding. When he introduces this spirit of calculation he is ruthless in his punishment of those who fail to conform to this principle. His daughters both succeed to power and this spirit of calculation comes to power with them. One by one they dispose of their enemies (or plan to). In the final ironic twist this jealousy consumes them both, and they turn on and dispose of each other. This is a magnificent expression of the self-destructive capacity of this world of evil.

Similarly, Edmund's wicked nature stems from Gloucester's weaknesses. Gloucester wants to do as the world does, to forget morality, to be comfortable. Likewise, Edmund wants to have what the world has: 'lands by wit', to 'grow' and 'prosper'. Edmund's worldliness stems from Gloucester's attitudes.

On the other hand, Edgar and Cordelia, who both symbolise goodness, endure and continue to love their fathers while they are exiled and give themselves selflessly in order to redeem them.

The final act exposes the ultimate showdown between both sets of characters and the good emerges victorious.

However, there is a certain qualification to this good when we bear witness to the deaths of the leading protagonists, Lear, Cordelia and Gloucester. In other words, good triumphs, but at a price.

Genre

King Lear is a tragedy. The general sequence of a tragic work follows the story of a hero or a central protagonist who is endowed with a fatal flaw that causes suffering, the loss of everything and finally death.

In the context of this play, Lear's main flaw consists of an overweening pride and blindness to human nature. Shortly after he has abdicated his kingship he suffers a violent confrontation with Goneril and Regan and is forced to accept their terms or face humiliation and poverty out on the heath.

In an extreme state of degradation and suffering throughout the storm scenes he learns the meaning of life and grows in humility and self-knowledge. All of this occurs with the help of his Fool, who plays a key role here.

Likewise, Gloucester is blind to the reality of human nature and fails to see through the wickedness of his son, Edmund. Ironically, it is only when he is physically blinded that he attains a real insight into the truth.

Both characters acknowledge their earlier flaws and both develop and grow to see the real truth about people and about themselves.

Plots and parallel meanings

This play is made up of two plots that echo one another in theme. The deliberate parallels that are set up between the two plots serve the function of realism – to give credibility to a play where the characters and events would otherwise be incredible.

Another effect of this deliberate repetition is to universalise and broaden the themes, such as filial ingratitude and evil.

The story and theme of the sub-plot are repeated in the main plot. Two credulous fathers are betrayed by selfish and unscrupulous children. Both are victims of false appearances. Both are weak, gullible and poor judges of character. Both lack sound judgment and are old men. The Fool teaches Lear while Edgar teaches Gloucester.

The Fool plays a central role in the structure of the play. This role is primarily paradoxical: the supposedly wise king is being taught lessons in wisdom and folly by a fool. We see this mainly in the storm scenes. The Fool is a foil for Lear and also a form of relief, countering Lear's madness. He is used almost like a Chorus, as he harps all the time on Lear's transgressions. His role forms a curious mixture of faithful service and severe condemnation. He offers relief to the gloom of the tragedy.

The Fool represents the voice of reality for Lear. He appears in Act I, Scene iv, when Kent has just manifested his loyalty for Lear by attacking Oswald, Goneril's cunning servant. Lear is about to pay Kent for his action when the Fool enters and mockingly offers Kent his coxcomb. The implication here is that Lear is a fool if he thinks he can repay people with money now that he has handed over everything to his wicked children. The play is full of comments like this, where the Fool mocks Lear's self-deceit and essential blindness to human nature. The Fool is not only Lear's teacher but also echoes Lear's conscience. It is significant that Lear is given few soliloquies in the play. The implication could be that the Fool articulates all his insights and that it is against the backdrop of the storm scenes and the Fool's whirling and sometimes ambiguous statements, which are reflected in the sequence of events, that Lear achieves his moral growth.

The relationship between Lear and his Fool is part of the tragic movement of the play – the downward movement towards the ultimate exposure and defeat, when the king is degraded to the status of the meanest of his servants. We watch the royal sufferer being progressively stripped, first of extraordinary power, then of ordinary human dignity, then of the very necessities of life when he is more helpless and abject than any animal. However, there is a more dreadful consummation than this reduction to physical nakedness. Lear hardly feels the storm because he is struggling to retain his mental integrity, his knowledge and his reason, which for him are the essential marks of humanity itself. From the time when his agony begins and he feels his sanity threatened, he gradually becomes aware of the sufferings of others: 'Poor fool ... I have one part in my heart | That's sorry yet for thee'. His sympathies are aroused and broadened; he realises that all men are one in pain: 'take physic, pomp; | Expose thyself to feel ...'

In the role of the Fool we are confronted with the paradoxical reversal of wisdom and folly. At the beginning of the play Lear and Gloucester are both blind fools. When Lear loses his sanity his vision is enlarged, as his wits begin to leave him he begins to see the truth about himself and when they are wholly gone he begins to have spasmodic flashes of insight in which he sees the truth about the world. The Fool prophetically exclaims that Lear would make a good fool. When he loses everything – his kingdom, his sanity and his honour – becoming an outcast from society, he attains truth. What is this truth which he attains?

This truth is linked to the idea of suffering and attaining a strong and firm endurance through suffering: 'give me patience', he prays, and later on he tells Gloucester to be patient: 'thou must be patient; we came crying hither'.

In the hour of Lear's helplessness during the storm on the heath, king and fool, master and slave as they have been so far, become something different – the bond between them grows closer. In the process of madness we become aware of a deep relation of contraries (opposites) – that of wise man and fool. The essence of this relationship consists in a reversal of accepted values: the supposedly wise man of the opening scenes, the Lear who was in a position to have his slave whipped and to exercise his own will without contradiction, has become the fool, as his own acts have shown. Through his behaviour and language, the Fool offers advice, all of which is based on practical wisdom.

The Fool is an all-powerful auxiliary for both the main plot and the sub-plot. When the Fool leaves the play in the last storm scene (Act IV, Scene vi), we can assume that Lear has grown in moral awareness and it remains for him to be reconciled with Cordelia.

Soliloquy
The soliloquy is a fundamental part of the structure of a Shakespearean tragedy. Shakespeare uses both the public and the private soliloquy in his plays, as each type has a different function. Many of Lear's soliloquies are public, where he articulates his condemnation of humankind. In the storm scene (Act III, Scene iv), he becomes aware for the first time in his life of the full reality of poverty within his kingdom and acknowledges that he has done nothing to remedy the situation. Likewise, Edgar, Edmund and Kent use the public soliloquy to give reasons for the way they are acting. Edmund is the character who has the most soliloquies, which show how he will manipulate events and use opportunities to his own advantage. All of his soliloquies show him to be exceptionally intelligent, cynical and unprincipled.

Edgar's three soliloquies serve different functions. He gives us an insight into the quality of life in the kingdom as it existed under Lear as the Bedlam beggar who was pelted in the villages and looked upon as mad. He also plays the role of moraliser, or preacher of good and evil, in his soliloquies, such as in the speech where he compares his role to Lear's:

> When that which makes me bend makes the king bow;
> He childed as I fathered!
>
> (Act III, Scene vi)

Style and language

Shakespeare's style is richly poetic. In his plays the important characters speak in verse while the minor characters use prose. Language and imagery become an avenue of understanding in Shakespeare's plays and there is a wide variety of images and language patterns used in *King Lear*, much of which communicates the playwright's central message and themes.

Nature and the storm scenes

The five storm scenes are symbolic of moral discord. The storm dovetails personal conflict and external convulsion well, as the storm that has broken out in Lear's mind is admirably fused with the description of the warring elements. The external storm is itself a projection of his inner state, which is expressed in the form of a single poetic reality. Thus related to the action of the elements, Lear assumes a stature which is more than merely personal. Throughout the storm scenes Lear bears the main weight of suffering. He is surrounded by human beings, each of whom is used in a different way to illuminate some aspect of his predicament. The Fool, Kent and Edgar bear some of his tragic burden and provide an insight into some of his tragic situation. Gloucester, who joins him, parallels his suffering and fall in fortunes.

Lear's first appearance in the storm shows him in a state of hostile condemnation and rebellion. He calls upon the storm to destroy the entire universe and the whole world of nature:

> And thou, all-shaking thunder,
> Strike flat the thick rotundity o' the world!
> Crack nature's moulds, an germens spill at once,
> That make ingrateful man!
>
> (Act III, Scene ii)

The cause of his anger is still self-love and self-pity, a sense of outrage that he, Lear, king of England, could suffer such a degree of humiliation.

The Fool is the character who points out to him the deeper causes of his tragedy. He does this mainly through his language, much of which is made up of puns, riddles, word play and ironic speeches where he teaches Lear to adopt a self-interested and calculating attitude. The irony of speeches like this is that he repeatedly fails to follow his own advice – he insists on following Lear, who has nothing.

In the following lines the Fool reminds Lear that they both have a small amount of wit:

He that has a little tiny wit,
With heigh-ho, the wind and the rain,
Must make content with his fortunes fit,
Though the rain it raineth every day.
      (Act III, Scene ii)

There is a profound sense of man's infirmity together with a strong feeling of power and greatness during the storm.

It is within the storm scenes in the company of three different types of mad people that Lear penetrates through to the essential truth of human nature, stripped of the false trappings of sophistication, and he finds in the half-naked Edgar the image of 'unaccommodated man'.

It can certainly be stated that the storm scenes are the most dramatic in the play, where the Fool leaves the play and Lear goes mad. The paradox of the play, 'reason in madness', is also enacted in the storm scenes.

Gloucester's first stage in moral growth occurs when he goes out into the storm to offer comfort and consolation to Lear, the action which costs him his eyes.

Animal or bestial imagery

There is a recurrent idea in the play of animals preying upon one another like monsters in the deep. The animal or bestial imagery suggests one human exploiting and destroying another for his own wicked ends.

Men and women are continually referred to as beasts or monsters. Goneril is referred to as a 'sea monster', a 'serpent', a 'wolf', a 'vulture' and a 'kite'. In Act III, Scene iv, Lear refers to the sisters as 'pelican daughters' feeding on their father's blood. Edgar calls his brother a 'toad spotted villain'. All of this imagery serves the function of depicting the bestial level reached by man when evil possesses him.

Images of sight and blindness

Much of the symbolism or imagery reflects two of the central ideas in the play: sight and blindness. Since both protagonists begin in a state of moral blindness to the full reality of their children and human nature, this imagery plays an important symbolic role.

Because the play concerns itself with two old men who are blind to the reality of their own lives and to the nature of other people, Shakespeare makes use of irony to dramatise these ideas.

Irony serves several functions in the play. It illustrates the profound discrepancy between the real nature of things and their mere appearance. Shakespeare uses irony as a technique to show blindness in characters. Certain characters, such as Gloucester, Lear and Edgar, are essentially blind to the truth about themselves and others, thus as Lear banishes Kent, his loyal servant and the only one who will tell him the truth, he ironically prays to Apollo, the god of light.

Edmund uses a false letter to frame his brother, then adopts the role of confidante to Edgar by advising him to stay out of Gloucester's way. Edgar is blind to evil and corruption in nature, particularly in his brother Edmund's nature, and we hear him ironically telling Edmund how 'some villain has done me wrong' (Act I, Scene ii).

The play is full of ironic reversals. Gloucester gains full insight only after he has been physically blinded. Lear, king of England, learns his wisest lessons on human nature and on life in the context of extreme degradation and in the company of the Fool.

Irony functions as a moral commentary on the wicked characters and is another means of graphically illustrating the profoundly self-destructive quality of evil.

Cultural context

England and the medieval court form the primary cultural background of *King Lear*. The play deals with the culture of kingship and monarchy at that time. The characters are drawn from the aristocracy or nobility. They are public figures whose actions and subsequent sufferings become universalised.

The plot of the play deals with inter-family relationships and the ensuing intrigue, rivalry and conflict. Lear makes a fatal error regarding the nature of kingship – at the beginning of the play he believes he can abdicate the duties of king and retain merely 'the name and all th'addition to a King' (Act I, Scene i).

Lear has been king of England for many years; he has no male heir and so roles change and he hands over his authority to Goneril, Regan and their husbands. In this act of abdication Lear disrupts the social order and causes general anarchy in his kingdom.

The blinding of Gloucester is a barbaric act that co-exists with Christian insights expressed by Lear in some of the storm scenes and at the conclusion of the play. In prison with Cordelia he sees them both as 'God's spies', taking upon themselves 'the mystery of things'.

The play deals with particular matters, such as clothes and courtly deference, that are an inherent part of this cultural environment. Lear sheds the symbols of wealth – rich clothes and fine speech – in his movement towards truth. The play shows the human being reaching truth when stripped of these false cultural adornments. Lear finally sheds his sanity and descends to a state of physical and emotional nakedness.

General vision or viewpoint

At the conclusion of this play there is a certain sense of reconciliation, harmony and justice. Love is not a victory in the play; the victory at the conclusion brings with it much tragedy.

The play presents a world of extreme suffering and many characters express negative philosophies. This suffering, however, brings the benefit of knowledge and awareness. There is an element of justice in the world, but it is not absolute; evil is punished, but good is not always rewarded. The play illustrates the value of endurance and love in the face of cruelty and evil.

The conclusion, therefore, is neither completely pessimistic nor optimistic; people are not shown as mere playthings of a blind or capricious power, nor is the world given over wholly to darkness. There is a blending of loss and sorrow, but also a certain peace at the exposure of evil as well as awe and apprehension in the face of the unfathomable mystery of evil.

In the figures of Albany and Edgar there is a sense of stability and a realistic note in the words:

> All friends shall taste
> The wages of their virtue, and all foes
> The cup of their deservings.
> (Act V, Scene iii)

The general vision or viewpoint offered to us at the conclusion of this tragedy is that life is grim and tough, but people can survive it.

MACBETH

(2007 exam)

The story

The play is set in Scotland where, at the beginning of the play, Duncan is king. Scotland is at war with Norway. Macbeth is captain of the Scottish forces and possesses the title 'Thane of Glamis'. Lady Macbeth is his wife. Both characters are exceedingly ambitious. Macbeth is rewarded with the title 'Thane of Glamis' because of his valour and personal courage in the battle against Norway. Before he hears of this reward, on his return from the battlefield he meets three witches. They prophesy to him that he will be king hereafter. They tell Banquo, another general, that he will be father to kings. Macbeth is clearly influenced by these prophecies and it is obvious that he has secretly nourished ambitions for kingship.

Lady Macbeth persuades her husband to murder Duncan, who comes to spend the night in their castle at Inverness. After the murder, Duncan's two sons, Malcolm and Donalbain, escape to England and Ireland, respectively. Banquo begins to suspect that Macbeth is the murderer, but he himself is killed shortly before the banquet, which officially inaugurates Macbeth as king. At the banquet, Banquo's ghost appears to Macbeth to mock him. Lady Macbeth defends Macbeth loyally. Macbeth slaughters Macduff's wife and children because Macduff goes to England for help. In England the king is called Edward. He is a good and saintly man who offers to help them regain the throne of Scotland and get rid of Macbeth. In England an army of 10,000 men is mobilised and Siward, a general, together with Macduff and Malcolm, resolves to kill Macbeth and restore Malcolm as lawful king of Scotland.

Meanwhile, Lady Macbeth, who has committed herself fully to evil-doing, now begins to go mad and finally commits suicide. Macbeth pays one last visit to the witches, who show him three false visions. He is misled into thinking he will never be killed by any man born of a woman. However, Macduff kills him in the end, telling him that he was ripped untimely from his mother's womb. In the end, Malcolm is invested with kingship and order is restored to Scotland.

Themes
- evil and deception, false appearance and equivocation
- ambition
- kingship
- loyalty and betrayal
- the supernatural.

Genre
The play is from the genre of tragedy and explores the world of supernatural evil.

The witches represent the metaphysical world of evil spirits. They can be seen as archetypal tempters recreating the original temptation that led to the fall of man.

Structure of the play
The play is divided into five main acts. The final destruction of evil and the triumph of good are shown in the concluding scene. The banquet scene is used ironically. It is supposed to confirm Macbeth's power as king, yet as the events proceed in this scene, Macbeth steadily loses control and the scene concludes in chaos. Furthermore, the conclusion of this scene demonstrates the beginnings of the rift between Lady Macbeth and her husband. She becomes haunted by guilt-ridden fantasies, while he develops into a ruthless, hardened murderer.

The plot revolves around the witches' wicked instigations to tempt Macbeth with thoughts of kingship and the evil consequences that ensue.

Style of the play
There is an abundance of blood-dominated imagery, which shows the power of evil and violence in the play.

Irony
Both Macbeth and his wife become victims of irony in this play because their hunger for kingship overrides all moral considerations and turns out to be a disastrous state of being for them. The many references to washing, cleansing and sleeping are all used in a deeply ironic way throughout the play. Both become obsessed with guilt and sleeplessness as a result of their crimes.

Soliloquies
Shakespeare's soliloquies serve many functions. The three characters that use soliloquies in this play are Macbeth, Lady Macbeth and Banquo. In general, the soliloquy furnishes us with a deeper insight into the mentality of that particular character and we can also gain information about the plot. The images used in a soliloquy usually highlight themes or main features of the character.

Cultural context
Under this heading are the following:
- kingship
- the witches
- the political situation.

The monarch at this time was a sacred figure with divine sanction. No earthly individual had a right to put an end to the rule of a king – this was God's right only. Therefore, regicide, or the killing of a king, was no ordinary crime.

The witches represent the supernatural world of evil that was prevalent in Scotland in the early seventeenth century.

The political situation is unstable. The values of order, harmony and stability are shown to be insecure. Under Duncan's rule Scotland has been subjected to rebellion from within (the betrayal of Cawdor) and invasion from without (the war with Norway).

General vision or viewpoint
Malcolm's victory restores order and harmony to Scotland. The leafy branches disguising the advance of the troops are symbolic of new life and hope for Scotland. Malcolm is the 'medicine of the sickly weal', who must 'purge' Scotland of the evil which Macbeth has reduced it to.

Both Macbeth and Lady Macbeth have betrayed themselves by falling for what is equivocal and illusory and now find that their actions and lives are meaningless. Time, life and death have lost all meaning for both. Macbeth's surrender of himself to evil has brought about nothing but a deep sense of emptiness and the futility of life:

> Tomorrow, and tomorrow, and tomorrow,
> Creeps in this petty pace from day to day,
> To the last syllable of recorded time;
> And all our yesterdays have lighted fools
> The way to dusty death.
> (Act V, Scene v)

Evil is shown to be self-destructive in all of Shakespeare's tragedies. Through the logic of events, Shakespeare shows that there is a universal moral law that one transgresses at one's peril.

Summary of the soliloquies
Macbeth's soliloquies
1. Act I, Scene iii. Macbeth's latent ambition is evident. He shows his vacillating moral outlook: 'cannot be ill, cannot be good'. His references to imaginary fears are ironic in light of the banquet scene and Lady Macbeth's breakdown.
2. Act I, Scene iv. Duncan's action in nominating his son Malcolm as successor to the throne is ironic and leads to this soliloquy. Macbeth uses the images of 'black' and 'deep' to show the evil nature of his desires.

3. Act I, Scene vii. This reveals the depths of Macbeth's conscience. It deals with the theme of justice and is a splendid assessment of Duncan's virtuous nature. There is an acknowledgment by Macbeth of his fatal flaw: 'I have no spur …'.
4. Act II, Scene i (the dagger soliloquy). This reveals the fact that Macbeth's moral sense has become corrupted. *Images of evil*: 'pale Hecate', 'bloody business', 'on the blade and dudgeon gouts of blood'.
5. Act III, Scene i. Macbeth's assessment of Banquo's qualities shows the threat to Macbeth while Banquo lives. The images show Macbeth's acknowledgment of the immorality of his deed: 'filed my mind', 'mine eternal jewel given to the common enemy of man'.
6. Act IV, Scene i. Macbeth announces his intention of destroying the Macduff family. He seeks to erase his bitter sense of how meaningless his life has become through this act of gratuitous violence: 'The very firstlings of my heart shall be | The firstlings of my hand'.
7. Act V, Scene iii. Macbeth gives us a glimpse of how hollow his life has become. He enumerates all the values he has lost because of his reign as a tyrant.

Lady Macbeth's soliloquies
1. Act I, Scene v. This is Lady Macbeth's assessment of her husband's character. She commits herself to evil to remove the obstacles that stand between him and the kingship. Images used here include 'the golden round', referring to kingship.
2. Act I, Scene v. She calls on evil to denature her (unsex her) in order to be filled with the necessary amount of murderous cruelty. In these soliloquies she suppresses not only her femininity but also her humanity.
3. Act III, Scene ii. This reflects dissatisfaction with kingship. Images here show us the quality of her life, a state of 'doubtful joy'.

Banquo's soliloquy
Act III, Scene i. Banquo's only soliloquy occurs when Macbeth has taken over kingship. It reveals that the virtuous Banquo may have been seduced by temptation and become morally tainted. Images that reflect a latent ambition that the witches' prophecies may come true include 'their speeches shine', 'May they not be my oracles as well, | And set me up in hope'.

12
Notes on Films

CHARACTERISTICS OF FILMS

This chapter contains some guidelines that can be used in answering questions in the 'comparative study' section. There are also notes on all the films on the prescribed syllabus for Higher Level.

Much Ado About Nothing (2005 exam)
The Dead (2005 exam)
Strictly Ballroom (2005 exam)
Dances with Wolves (2005 and 2006 exams)
Il Postino (2005 and 2006 exams)
Witness (2005 and 2006 exams)
On the Waterfront (2006 exam)
A Room with a View (2006 exam)
Henry V (2006 and 2007 exams)
My Left Foot (2007 exam)
Twelve Angry Men (2007 exam)

A film is about people, places and situations. The way they are shown and the reason they are shown in a particular way varies greatly. A film is a narrative – it tells a story. Being able to say what a film is about, or the meaning of the story, is another way of identifying the themes or issues treated.

It is important to understand what particular values or views of life are represented in a film. A film can promote or criticise certain issues, depending on the stance taken by the director on the themes or issues being presented.

Examine what values or understanding of life the film emphasises or criticises. Ask yourself the following questions:
- Is there a coherent message or moral in the film? If not, why not?
- How does the film leave you at the end? Depressed? Sad? Happy? Why?

Film genres
A film-maker structures the story or narrative in a particular way. In other words, the viewpoint adopted by the film-maker in relation to the subject is what constitutes the film's genre. Film genres include detective story or thriller, western, romance, biography and social realism.

Features of the film genre
Films are made up of images that are photographed within a particular frame – the rectangle that contains the image. The camera frame controls what the audience sees and how they see it. According to what the film-maker is trying to say, this frame can control certain actions and eliminate others or it can direct attention in a particular direction, either towards an object or person or away from them.

Understanding the genre of a film means being able to ask and answer certain questions:
- Is there a pattern of striking camera movements, long shots or abrupt transitions?
- Why does the film end on this image?
- Why does the film start in the way it does?
- When was the film made?
- What does the title mean in relation to the story?
- Why are the credits presented in this particular way? Why are they presented against a particular background?

Every film uses patterns of repetition that are contrasted with certain important moments. One of the first steps in analysing the meaning of a film is recognising these patterns and understanding why they are important.

MUCH ADO ABOUT NOTHING

By William Shakespeare; directed by Kenneth Branagh
(2005 exam)

Historical and literary background
Mediaeval Italy as seen through the eyes of William Shakespeare (sixteenth-century England) forms the historical background of this film.

The story
The story concerns two sets of lovers: Claudio and Hero and Beatrice and Benedick. Don Pedro, Prince of Aragón, returns victorious from battle with his 'illegitimate' brother Don John. Claudio is a follower of Don Pedro and he falls in love with Hero. Don John is jealous of his half-brother and he sullies Hero's reputation by implying that she is a wanton and unfaithful woman. Claudio believes him and breaks off their proposed marriage. Meanwhile, Beatrice and Benedick spend their time sparring and insulting one another. Eventually they fall in love and decide to get married. Hero's reputation is salvaged and the film concludes with the two couples marrying. Don John is punished for his lies.

The plot develops by means of parties, picnics, courtships, witty scenes, parodies and many comic interludes.

Themes
- relationships
- love
- deception/misunderstanding
- marriage
- happiness

Love and courtship
The various entanglements that the different couples engage in throughout this humorous and light-hearted film dominate much of the content.

Deception and intrigue
This issue forms the framework for much of Shakespeare's work. Here Don John's jealousy of his brother gives rise to his efforts to defame Hero's reputation. Happily, things turn out well at the conclusion.

Structure and style
Visual images and photography
There are many images of large, bright gardens, with typical Sicilian architecture. There is a lot of sunshine and open spaces.

Music
The music is rich and joyous.

Genre
Romantic comedy.

Cultural context
The film is set in Messina, in Sicily, in the mid-seventeenth century. At the beginning we are given a picture of men returning from battle. They are seen as heroic and chivalric figures who have sacrificed their lives for other people. The women in the film are beautiful, gentle creatures who live in luxury, read poetry, eat rich food and drink wine. The lifestyle is rich and luxurious, filled with dance, song, wine and joy. They recite poetry, sing songs and talk about heroic deeds of romance and courage. Marriage is important in this society and virtues such as chastity and purity are held in high regard. The conclusion shows us an image of perfect happiness in the marriage of the two couples.

General vision or viewpoint
The overall general vision or viewpoint of this film is one of reconciliation and peace in the wake of misunderstanding and deception. In the unity of both couples in marriage we are given an image of perfect happiness and concord. The villain is destroyed and good triumphs at the conclusion.

THE DEAD

Directed by John Huston
(2005 exam)

Historical and literary background
The film is an adaptation of James Joyce's short story 'The Dead' in *Dubliners*. The film is set in Dublin in 1904.

The story
Two elderly sisters, Miss Kate and Miss Julia Morkan, hold their annual dinner party for their friends and relatives. They invite various people, including their nephew Gabriel and his wife Gretta. Mary Jane is the niece of the two Miss Morkans and plays the organ. They invite many young couples and spend the evening dancing and engaging in friendly conversation. Aunt Julia sings an old song called 'Arrayed for the Bridal'.

Freddy Malins turns up drunk and his mother is disgusted. Mr Browne is an older man and a friend of the two aunts who belongs to 'the other persuasion' and enjoys his drink. The party is formal and polite except for the frequent interruptions from Freddy, who continues to make irrelevant remarks. Most of the conversation revolves around music and the past. Aunt Kate talks in animated tones about how the top gallery of the Old Theatre Royal used to be packed in their day. Mrs Malins mentions that Freddy is off to Mount Melleray at the weekend. This gives rise to a conversation about the religious practices of the monks. Mr Browne thinks that repentance and indulgences are great things: a type of 'free insurance'. They make allusions to how the monks sleep in their coffins to remind them of their last end.

Gabriel gives a speech after they have had dinner. It is filled with references to the people who have gone before and to everyone's responsibility to enjoy the present times. He reminds them of their duties and loving affections for those who are alive. He makes a toast to his two aunts, who are sincerely moved.

As Gabriel and his wife take their leave and cross the Liffey on O'Connell Street Bridge, Gabriel notices that his wife is deeply moved by the song 'The Lass of Aughrim'. On their way home in the carriage Gabriel makes some attempts to engage his wife in conversation, but it is clear that she is distracted and removed from him. He feels a deep disquiet.

Back in the bedroom of the guesthouse where they are staying for the night, Gabriel tries to find out from Gretta what's wrong. He then discovers that she is lamenting the death of a young man called Michael Furey, who died of a broken heart because of her.

Gabriel questions her a few times about whether or not she loved him. It is clear she has never forgotten Michael in all her years married to Gabriel. As she falls asleep on the bed, crying profusely, Gabriel moves to the window and, looking out through the net curtains at the countryside, sees snow falling.

The film concludes with Gabriel's voice speaking about how small a part he has played in his wife's life and how he has never known what it is to really love. In prophetic vision, Aunt Julia is shown laid out on her bed while Gabriel struggles to express his sympathy to Aunt Kate. Gabriel's voice continues to speak about the fact that soon everyone will be only shades and will die. He notes that the snow is falling and that he too will be like everyone else from the past: he will dwindle and dissolve just like the snow.

Themes
- relationships
- memories
- mortality
- love

Genre
The genre of this film is social realism. It is set in a specific time in Dublin in the early twentieth century and gives us a deep insight into the different types of relationships between people.

The film is told mainly through dialogue and there is a long monologue at the conclusion spoken by Gabriel, the central character.

Camera angles
There are many shots of dark buildings from the outside and shadowy halls and rooms.

The camera focuses equally on every character during dinner and enables the viewer to gain an insight into the personality of each one. There are several shots of Gabriel alone, obviously fretting over his feelings of inadequacy.

Prophetic vision
The director makes use of prophetic vision only once in the film. This occurs at the conclusion, when Gabriel is reflecting from the window about the imminent death of Aunt Julia and he looks into the future and sees her laid out on the bed with the rosary beads twined between her fingers. The use of prophetic vision here highlights the theme of death, which is particularly evident in the concluding sequence.

Cultural context
The culture is that of Dublin in the early twentieth century. Behaviour is formal and polite. There are frequent scenes of the cab, which is an old black carriage drawn by a horse and driver. The large lamps on the streets and the candles and paraffin lamps seen from within the house clearly establish the time period.

Clothes are distinctive of this time – the men wear large black bowler hats while the women have long gowns to the ground. The style of clothes is rich and elegant. There are many images of photographs and mementos on the table, which suggests that the past is important in the lives of these people.

General vision or viewpoint

Gretta's disclosures about her love for Michael Furey in the past leads to the long monologue from Gabriel as he contemplates the snow falling outside his bedroom window. It is clear that although these two people have been married for some time, they still do not know each other very well. Gabriel has never fully experienced what it is to really love someone, while his wife has lived in the past and has sustained a schoolgirl love for someone who died when he was seventeen years old. The disclosure from his wife leads to Gabriel's contemplations about the future and the fact that all people will die; they will be merely shades.

The general vision at the conclusion is negative and depressing. There are many scenes of bleak, empty graveyards and snowy countryside. It is as if the world of nature will obliterate humankind's efforts and everything will be reduced to nothingness.

STRICTLY BALLROOM

Directed by Baz Luhrman
(2005 exam)

Historical and literary background

This film is set in Australia during the 1970s.

The story

The story centres on the main character, Scott Hastings, and his attempts to win the Australian Pan-Pacific Dancing Competition. The film opens with Scott taking part in the Waratah Dance Championships. Barry Fife controls these competitions and will not allow dancers to change their style or steps. However, Scott wants to dance his own steps and this brings him into conflict with Barry Fife and his own mother, Shirley, who is determined that he shall win. Initially, Liz is Scott's dancing partner, but she refuses to dance with him because of his efforts to be innovative in his dancing style.

Scott's mother spends a great deal of

time convincing him to conform to the rules of the Dancing Federation. Scott refuses and meets Fran, whose family is Spanish in origin. Fran lives with her grandmother and father at the back of a small bar. Fran and Scott spend a lot of time practising how to dance and secretly improve their steps, unknown to anyone.

Meanwhile, we learn more about Scott's father, Doug. We see him surreptitiously putting on records and dancing on his own a lot. It is clear that his wife outwardly despises him, as he is not a very assertive character. As the story develops, we also learn how Doug had the potential to be a prestigious dancer, but had tried to dance his own steps and was banned by the Federation.

Finally, Scott and Fran enter the Pan-Pacific Competition even though they are opposed by all the members of Scott's family and receive threats from Fife. The final sequence plays the song 'Love is in the Air', and everyone in the hall moves onto the dance floor in spite of Barry Fife's protestations and dances their own individual style. Fife's corrupt manoeuverings are defeated at the conclusion.

Themes
- power and corruption
- deception
- self-expression and individuality
- love and romance

Genre
This film belongs to the genre of romance with touches of absurd humour throughout. The director makes use of caricature to mock, as is seen in Barry Fife's capacity to bully people.

There are also comic touches in the documentary-style interventions from Shirley, who is intent on trying to explain to the viewer how her son must become a champion.

Camera angles
A variety of camera angles are used, mainly of different styles of dancing and of the various events.

Flashback
The film opens with a flashback to the Waratah Championships, which establishes the competitive atmosphere of the film. It also introduces the leading characters who will govern the story's plot.

Cultural context
There are different social classes represented in the film. The culture is that of Australia, but it is restricted to dancing events and competitors.

We gain an insight into a contrasting cultural world through Fran's story. Her background represents a more traditional way of life than the flashy ballroom scenes. The Spanish culture is represented through the figure of her father and his friends and the flamboyant style of dancing which we see in their house.

General vision or viewpoint

The defeat of Barry Fife's wicked manoeuvrings and the success attained by Scott and Fran in dancing in an individual style represent a change in the traditional system, which has obviously operated in this federation for years. The fact that Doug, Scott's father, was considered a failure when in reality he was trying to perfect his art made him appear weak in his own family. With the introduction of a new style of dancing, expressed by Scott and Fran, not only is Fife's corrupt system exposed and destroyed, but Doug's status as a dancer is restored and he is vindicated before his family.

The values of love and selflessness are made apparent in the sincere union of Scott and Fran.

DANCES WITH WOLVES

Based on the book by Michael Blake; directed by Kevin Costner
(2005 and 2006 exams)

Historical background
The background of this film is America during the Civil War (1861–5).

The story

The story is that of a white man, John Dunbar, who goes to live with Native Americans and learns about their civilisation first hand. He is an officer in the Union army who runs away from a field hospital as his foot is about to be amputated. He rides his horse in a suicidal charge at the Confederate lines; when he survives he is given his choice of any posting. He chooses the frontier, because 'I want to see it before it's gone.' He is sent to an isolated outpost in the Dakota region, where he is the only white man for miles around. He starts to keep a journal. When he comes into contact with the Sioux he begins to document the way in which they slowly get to know one another.

Racism is deeply entrenched in the white American culture. Dunbar, however, is able to squarely face attitudes and acknowledge the reality of prejudices against races and peoples. As he begins to discover the culture of the Sioux, so do we. He first meets them on an open prairie. Later he meets Stands-with-a-Fist, a white woman who came to live with the Sioux as a girl. When Dunbar goes to live with the Sioux he is given the name Dances-with-Wolves.

Dunbar marries Stands-with-a-Fist. He warns the Sioux that the white men are coming, so they decide to leave the camp. He returns to look for his diary but is arrested by the soldiers and badly beaten. They take him across country to put him on trial for deserting, but they are attacked by a Sioux band and Duncan escapes while the soldiers are slain. When he returns to the camp he is uneasy, as he knows that this incident will endanger them. Both he and Stands-with-a-Fist decide to leave. The film concludes with an image of soldiers in pursuit of the tribe, with a caption that states: 'Thirteen years later, their homes destroyed, their buffalo gone, the last band of free Sioux submitted to white authority at Fort Robinson, Nebraska.'

The plot is based on Dunbar's integration with the Sioux culture and his rupture from the colonial culture of the white man. It is developed by means of a series of social relationships and confrontations. Dunbar decides to face 'justice' at the conclusion.

Themes
Loyalty and betrayal
Early in the film, Dunbar is honoured and given a commission to take up a post wherever he likes because of his loyalty to the Union army. We bear witness to the profound loyalty within the Sioux nation. At the conclusion of the film, Dunbar decides to leave the camp because of his allegiance to the Sioux and give himself up to the white authorities.

Racism
This theme is expressed in the white men's hatred and their greed for power, which gives rise to a great deal of brutality and needless suffering. The comment at the conclusion is grim, as it demonstrates the extinction of a once-powerful race of people.

Love and friendship
These values are manifest in the Sioux and contribute to building powerful bonds of harmony and order. We see the strong unity within the tribe and the ways in which they obey the elders. Each member is treated with a profound sense of dignity and their individuality is respected. Because of this atmosphere of trust, fellowship and love, the culture flourishes.

Structure and style
Visual images and photography
There is a striking variety of camera angles in the film. The settings include huge, broad landscapes, an American army post and a Native American village. Many of the long shots depict the harmony that exists between the Native Americans and the world of nature, such as in the amazing buffalo chase. In one exemplaary sequence Dunbar is pictured riding on horseback surrounded by a group of Sioux. The mixture of close-up and medium shots serves the purpose of emphasising his unity with this cultural system.

Music
The music is dramatic and intense. Much of the music is triumphant and exultant as it depicts the great joy within the Sioux tribe when they slay the buffalo and when they fight their enemy.

Genre
Epic western.

Cultural context
The cultural context of this film is the American frontier during the Civil War (1861–5). We are given an insight into two different cultural systems – the American military and the Sioux (Dakota) nation. There is a striking contrast between the two cultures. In the Sioux culture there is an emphasis on such values as order, harmony, unity, fellowship and a respect for the individuality and dignity of people. We see how meetings are conducted, with the chief, who embodies the traditional wisdom of their world, having the last word. He is treated with profound respect by all.

On the other hand, the culture of the white man is based on greed and war. Most of the images underlying this cultural system are negative and destructive. When Dunbar is assigned to a post in Fort Hayes we see an officer commit suicide shortly afterwards in a violent manner. All the officers are brutal and violent. The needless slaughter of the buffalo is only one of many examples that bear witness to the violence that seems to dominate the white culture.

General vision or viewpoint
The viewpoint offered at the conclusion of this film is sobering, as we are shown the brutalising effects of colonialism and war. On the other hand, the powerful value and consolidating strength of love and fellowship is evident from the Sioux culture. The vision of the destruction of the Sioux nation and its value system by the white man is both brutal and realistic.

IL POSTINO

Directed by Michael Radford
(2005, 2006 and 2007 exams)

The story
Mario is a young man who lives on an island off the coast of Italy. His father tells him to find a job so he applies for a job as a postman. He discovers that he has to bring the mail every day to a Chilean poet called Pablo Neruda, who has been exiled to Italy because he is a Communist. Giorgio is Mario's boss and he has great veneration and respect for Pablo. Pablo writes love poems and as a result he receives a lot of mail from women. Pablo lives with his wife in a beautiful part of the island called Cala di Sotto. Mario gets one of Pablo's books and asks him to sign it for him but is upset that Pablo has not signed his full name, Mario Ruoppolo. Mario begins to read the book and

becomes fascinated with it. Friendship blossoms between Mario and Pablo. Mario begins to speak to Pablo about poetry and metaphors and becomes a Communist as well. Mr Di Cosmino is a local politician who spends his time looking for votes from the locals on the island.

After a while Mario falls in love with a beautiful girl called Beatrice. Mario asks Pablo to write him a poem for Beatrice. Beatrice lives with an aunt who opposes her relationship with Mario. Some time later the couple marry and Mario asks Pablo to be his best man. At the wedding Pablo receives a letter allowing him the freedom to return to Chile. Beatrice becomes pregnant and Mario decides to call the child Pablito. Mario follows all Pablo's movements by reading the newspapers and hears that he has been to Russia to receive an award. Mario receives a letter one day from Pablo's secretary asking him to send on some of the objects he left behind in the house. Mario returns to the house and begins to reminisce about all the good times he enjoyed while Pablo was there. Mario decides to tape the different sounds of the sea and the wind on the cliffs for Pablo. However, he never sends him the tape.

Shortly after this, Pablo returns to the island with his wife for a visit. Pablo meets Pablito, Mario's child, and Beatrice tells him that Mario is dead. He died as he was reading a poem he had written, dedicated to Pablo. The crowd at a Communist meeting crushed him. The story concludes with the image of Pablo walking along the beach and listening to Mario's words on the tape.

Aspects of the story
Tension
The tension in the film occurs when Mario begins to fall in love with Beatrice and her aunt intervenes. Beatrice's aunt goes to Pablo to complain that Mario is corrupting her niece with lines of poetry.

Climax
At one stage Beatrice secretly slips away from the house at night to meet Mario and her aunt follows her, armed with a shotgun.

Resolution
Mario and Beatrice finally marry. The priest opposes Pablo for best man because he is a Communist. In the end, however, Mario succeeds in having Pablo as best man.

Themes
- friendship
- politics
- relationship
- love
- loyalty

Friendship
One of the main themes in the film is the strong relationship between Pablo, the Chilean poet, and Mario, the Italian postman. Their relationship begins through Mario's fascination with Pablo's lifestyle and his poems. This friendship grows throughout the film and Mario becomes a Communist, following in Pablo's footsteps.

Love
Pablo Neruda, the Chilean poet in the film, is known as the poet of love. This theme is shown in a very tender and sympathetic way. The love between Mario and his wife Beatrice is deep and strong. This love is not destined to last long, however, as Mario dies when his son is very young.

Relationships
Mario and Pablo
This relationship governs much of the action in the film. It is a strong bond, showing us how deeply each of these two characters feels about life and relationships. Pablo is very upset when he discovers that Mario has died at a Communist rally. He is also greatly moved when he begins to listen to Mario's poem, which he had written for Pablo.

Mario and Giorgio
The relationship between Mario and Giorgio, his employer in the post office, is amusing and endearing. Giorgio is a typical Italian who also admires the poet Pablo.

He continually reminds Mario how to behave with respect when he is delivering the post to this great poet.

Genre (2005, 2006)
The genre of this film is social realism with a touch of romance. It is set in Italy and gives us a vivid picture of a small but united community.

Camera angles
There are many contrasting scenes used in this film to highlight the beauty of the Italian landscape and also many shots of the distinct type of buildings in this small village.

Social setting
The film is set on a small Italian island, where the people live by fishing. It is a simple community, with simple values and a traditional way of life. The people are humble and pleasant and even though they do not have much money they seem to be content. We also see some glimpses of the political life of the island. The local politician, who is called Di Cosmino, fails to honour his promises when he becomes elected and the people find they have been betrayed and left without money. On the other hand, the voice of Communism is heard through the figure of Pablo, who is a kind person and who shows a deep concern for the ordinary person.

Cultural context
The particular cultural context is based on the values of a simple Italian village that survives mainly on fishing. There are realistic insights into certain types of characters such as the man who runs the post office and who employs Mario. We also see glimpses of the political life in this community through the figure of Di Cosmino. Certain values of honesty and simplicity are set against those of self-interest and corruption. The women who are represented in the film work hard and seem to suffer a great deal in their lives, mainly from the poverty that surrounds them.

General vision or viewpoint
The treatment of human life and relationships in this film is tender and poignant. The general vision in this film is based on the inevitable suffering and joy inherent in life. Relationships are central in life and can contribute to changing the quality of a person's life and outlook. This is evident from the fact that Mario was greatly influenced by Pablo, the Chilean poet, and became a Communist as a result. Pablo too was changed in his relationship with Mario and learned to appreciate certain values, such as loyalty and goodness. The overall general vision is positive.

WITNESS

Directed by Peter Weir
(2005, 2006 and 2007 exams)

The story

The story begins in 1984 in a community of Amish people in Pennsylvania. The opening sequence shows the funeral of Jacob, the husband of a young Amish woman called Rachel. She has a son called Samuel. Everyone in the community is dressed in black.

Rachel decides to pay a visit to her sister in Baltimore, taking Samuel. They arrive at the central train station and have to wait three hours there. The child wanders into the men's toilet and witnesses a man being killed with a knife by two other men. Samuel manages to escape. A police officer called John Book takes on the case. The man who was killed was a policeman. Rachel and Samuel are forced to stay and identify the man who carried out the crime. While Samuel is in the police station he sees a photograph of a coloured policeman and recognises him as the man who carried out the murder. The policeman is a narcotics officer, called McFee. Book goes to Paul Schaeffer, who is head of the police. Book realises that after a narcotics raid four years before, McFee has become involved in illegal dealings in narcotics worth over $22 million.

Paul tells Book that the FBI will take care of things. Book is shot at by McFee shortly after this in a car park. He then realises that the police are involved in the murder. Book decides to flee back to the Amish community with Rachel and Samuel. He rings his friend Carter in the police force and tells him to destroy all documentation on the affair.

Book sustains gunshot wounds and is forced to take refuge in the Amish community. His wounds are severe, but eventually he is restored to health. He begins to learn all the Amish customs and imbibes their culture, which is free from violence and governed by peace. He falls in love with Rachel.

Schaeffer and McFee carry out investigations to find Book. Carter is interrogated by Schaeffer and eventually killed. At one stage, some of the community go into town with Book and are antagonised by some local boys. The Amish do not fight, but Book is angered and fights the boys. The local police inform Schaeffer and his gang and they come to the Amish village to kill him. Book is in the barn and one of the men comes in with a gun. Book manages to kill him by making him fall into a huge container of grain. He picks up the man's gun and shoots McFee. Schaeffer comes into the barn with a gun held to Rachel's head. He warns Book that he will shoot her if he does not surrender. Book throws down his gun. In the meantime Samuel has rung the bell and all the Amish community come running from the fields to help. Schaeffer holds a gun to Book and leads him out of the barn. Book then stands with the community and attacks Schaeffer verbally. Schaeffer surrenders and is led away by the police. Book leaves Rachel and the community and returns to his job in Philadelphia at the end of the film.

Aspects of the story
Tension
The story is based on corruption in a police force and its attempts to capture the young Amish boy and kill him. Tension is built up through the film by means of dramatic music and certain camera angles, such as the three figures of the policemen walking slowly into the Amish village armed with guns.

Climax
The climax of the film occurs after Book has fought with the gang of young boys who insulted the Amish people in the town. Shortly after this, Schaeffer, McFee and another police officer decide to enter the village by force.

Resolution
The resolution occurs in a violent way. Book kills two of the police officers while the third, Schaeffer, is arrested. The resolution of the film shows us the strength and unity of the Amish people. Samuel, the young boy, rings the bell and this brings the whole community running from the fields to help whoever is in distress. The resolution reinforces our understanding of how strong the bonds of friendship and loyalty are here.

Themes
- violence and corruption
- loyalty and friendship
- trust
- peace and good will
- justice

Loyalty and friendship
These virtues are strongly evident within the Amish community, in striking contrast to the grim, corrupt reality of deception and lies in New York. Book is concerned not to expose Samuel to further danger and for that reason he discontinues the investigation into the crime. Book's friend Carter is also a police officer, who loses his life because of his loyalty to Book.

Peace and the power it brings
It is within the Amish community that, for the first time in his life, Book experiences the consolations of peace and hard work. In the Amish community violence is seen as destructive and for that reason none of the people carry a weapon of any type. When Book is living there he is forced to hand over his gun and we see him adapting readily to their simple but peaceful lifestyle.

Relationships
Book and Rachel
This relationship governs the story in the film. Their love for one another is strong and sincere. The relationship between them cannot continue, however, because each belongs to a different world.

Book and the Amish community
We see how Book comes to appreciate the values of the Amish community, even though he comes from a radically different background. It is within this community that Book learns certain values, such as brotherhood and loyalty. He is a sensitive character and the community appreciates this. We see him grow as a person during the time he stays there.

Genre
The genre of this film is social realism. It makes use of a variety of camera angles to show the contrast between two different communities.

Social setting
There are two different social or cultural worlds represented in this film – the Amish community in Pennsylvania and the predominantly white police force. The two worlds contrast dramatically – the Amish do not believe in violence, human life is sacred and they carry no weapons. They do not react to intimidation or any kind of threat. They are self-sufficient and live by farming. Values such as family, work, unity within the

community and peace are sacred to the Amish people. Their style of dress is almost puritanical. The women wear stiff, long, pinafore-style dresses and hats on their heads, while the men are dressed in black suits unless they are working on the farm. The culture of the New York police force, however, is dominated by corruption and systematic violence.

Cultural context
The cultural context which is represented in this film is based on two totally contrasting worlds – the New York police force and the Amish community in Pennsylvania. Both worlds are dramatically opposed. The New York police force is riddled with corruption and violence and forms the catalyst of the plot. In contrast, there is a distinctly opposing vision given in the Amish community. Here, values of peace and respect for the sanctity of human life are foremost. Clothes, style of dress and behaviour, speech and food form a distinct contrast in both cultural worlds. Human life is sacrosanct in the world of the Amish, while life seems to be expendable and held in little value in New York.

General vision or viewpoint
The general vision or viewpoint in this film is based on the fact that justice finally wins out in the end. Schaeffer, the corrupt head of the police, is eventually overthrown because of the unity among the Amish people. The loyalty and peace-loving values inherent in this Amish community triumph over the evil forces of corruption and violence at the end and the evil characters receive justice. Good triumphs, but at a price, as two police officers are murdered.

ON THE WATERFRONT

Directed by Elia Kazan
(2006 exam)

Historical and literary background
This film was shot on location in Hoboken, New Jersey in 1954.

The story
Terry is a young worker on the docks. He was a boxer, but has now stopped. Terry looks after a flock of pigeons on the roofs of the houses. A man called Johnny Friendly controls the docklands and the workers there. He is the one that decides who gets work and who does not. He is a bully and a criminal. Terry's brother, Charley, is Johnny's right-hand man. Terry also works for Johnny. Under Johnny's instigation, Terry sets a trap for Joey, a fellow worker on the docks, who is going to testify against Friendly's behaviour in the courts. Terry is not fully aware of the implications of this trap and it turns out that Johnny kills this man. After this Terry meets Edie, the dead man's sister, and they fall in love.

The local Catholic priest, Father Barry, is outraged at the behaviour of Friendly's gang and the fear that he is spreading among the workers and so he begins to mobilise them to fight against injustice and form a union. The priest organises a meeting in the church, but Johnny's men beat up those who attend and smash the church's windows. Johnny's men kill a worker on the docklands, named K. O. Doogan, because he tries to stand up to him and get his rights.

Terry talks to the priest and decides to tell Edie about his involvement in the death of her brother. She is heartbroken. Terry decides to give testimony against Johnny Friendly.

Friendly challenges Charley to straighten Terry out and get him to say nothing. Terry refuses and Johnny's gang kills Charley. Terry testifies in the courtroom against Friendly. Friendly is given a warning and allowed out on parole. Terry's friends kill all the pigeons on the roof as punishment for his action. Terry decides to go down to the waterfront and get his rights. He has a fight with Johnny and is badly beaten by his men. All the workers, including the priest, gather round him and challenge him to walk along the docks in defiance of Friendly's gang. Terry leads the men and they regain their rights over Friendly's gang. Friendly is beaten at the conclusion.

Themes
- oppression and violence
- loyalty and betrayal
- redemption through love
- human rights

Genre
The genre is a mixture of gangster and high drama. The film is set along the docklands of New York. The black and white photography makes the time of the film realistic.

Dialogue
Dialogue between the characters is realistic and highlights the features of New Yorkers at that time.

Music
The soundtrack includes music by Leonard Bernstein.

Symbols
The pigeon becomes a symbol of Terry's plight as he is caught between his love for Edie and Friendly's gang. Terry tells Edie at one stage that 'the city is full of hawks, they spot a pigeon and they are down on top of them'. He goes on to tell her that pigeons are very faithful; they get married and stay that way. He proves this at the end by boldly confronting Friendly and his gang.

Fences, gates and wiring are used to show the imprisonment experienced by these people.

Camera angles
A wide variety of camera angles are used in the film. Many scenes are shot from a point high above, showing how people are merely pawns in this system.

Cultural context
This film deals with the culture of America and the docklands during the fifties. The workers are set in conflict with Friendly's gang, who operate as a type of mafia. The landscape is bleak, dark and clearly depressed. These workers are pawns in Friendly's hands, who know they need the money to buy food.

The church becomes a vehicle for the workers to unite against oppression.

Edie represents the situation of women in these times. She is being educated in a convent by nuns and is clearly an innocent girl who has been protected from the evil and corruption of the world.

General vision or viewpoint
Terry's valiant struggle to overcome his previous failure in boxing is shown in his fight against Friendly and in the courage with which he challenges him to fight.

The final scene is dramatic, showing the injured and almost blind Terry struggling to walk and regain control of his body in a heroic fight against the gang of criminals. He is triumphant against Friendly's evil syndicate and so he is able to enlist the help of the other men along the docks. His heroic fight against oppression enables them to overcome their fear and cowardice and to take a clear stance against the bullying and corruption of Friendly's gang. The workers regain their rights and their control over the workplace at the conclusion. Justice and harmony are re-established. Friendly is defeated and has to answer to the law.

A ROOM WITH A VIEW

Based on the book by E. M. Forster; directed by James Ivory
(2006 and 2007 exams)

Historical and literary background
The film is based on the novel by E. M. Forster, first published in 1908, a time when England was still a colonial power.

The story
Lucy Honeychurch, a young Englishwoman, is on a visit to Florence, chaperoned by her cousin, Charlotte Bartlett. They have been led to believe that they will have a wonderful view at the Pensione Bertolini, but they are disappointed when they arrive.

An English father and son overhear them when they express their dissatisfaction and promptly offer to exchange rooms. Charlotte, for her young cousin's sake, is offended at this presumption, especially since the young man is dangerously attractive. However, the rector of Lucy's parish in England, Mr Beebe, happens to be staying there as well; he offers to act as an intermediary and the rooms are exchanged without further ado.

The next morning Charlotte tours the city with Eleanor Lavish, a novelist she met at dinner the night before. Lucy goes for a walk alone and witnesses a violent street fight, in which a young man is seriously injured. She becomes weak and faints from the shock of what she has seen. Luckily, George Emerson, the young man she had met in the *pensione* (guesthouse), is there to help her back to her lodgings.

The following day all the English visitors arrange to go sightseeing as a group and the Emersons belong to the party. George and Lucy become separated from the others, and in a cornfield he kisses her. Charlotte witnesses what happens and after they return to the city she arranges for them to leave their rooms the next day. The women agree not to tell anyone what has happened to Lucy.

Back in England, Lucy accepts a proposal of marriage from Cecil Vyse, a pompous and arrogant snob. By chance, the Emersons take a house in the village of Summer Street, close to the Honeychurch residence. Mr Beebe and Lucy's brother, Freddy, invite George to go swimming in a nearby pond on his first day in the village. The men are high-spirited and naked and they chase each other around the pond. Unfortunately, this occurs at the same time that the ladies are taking their afternoon walk in the woods and they come upon the men in all their naked glory.

Freddy befriends George and he is regularly invited to the Honeychurch home to play tennis. Lucy is perturbed by George's renewed proximity; the contrast between George and the stuffy Cecil is obvious, which unsettles Lucy.

When Charlotte comes to stay with the family she is concerned for Lucy, fearing that George's presence will do harm to her engagement to Cecil. One day Cecil is reading aloud and criticising what he considers to be a dreadful novel and both Lucy and George are listening. The book happens to be by Eleanor Lavish, the woman who stayed in the same *pensione*, and is set in Florence. Cecil reads a paragraph exactly describing the scene where George kissed Lucy. On the way back into the house, out of sight of the others, George repeats the performance.

Lucy is upset by this and hurt that Charlotte told Eleanor Lavish after they had agreed not to tell anyone about what had happened in Italy. In Charlotte's presence she asks George to leave. George gives a passionate account of his love for her and tries to make her see that Cecil cares for her only as he would a prize possession. Lucy denies the fact that she may love George, but all the same she breaks off her engagement with Cecil soon afterwards.

When George sees that Lucy will not have him he decides to leave Summer Street, as he cannot bear to be near her. Lucy is shocked to see the furniture being removed from the house. Mr Emerson talks to her and makes a heartfelt plea to her to stop denying the truth. Realisation dawns on her that she does love George after all and the film ends with the two lovers on their honeymoon in the same *pensione* in Florence, where they kiss at the window of the 'room with a view'.

Themes

Love
A Room with a View is essentially a love story with a happy ending. Within the first ten minutes Lucy exchanges glances with George Emerson across the dinner table and we know that something is going to happen. Even Charlotte Bartlett can see this. She senses danger immediately and is extremely protective of Lucy.

The relationship develops the next day when George catches Lucy as she faints with horror at the sight of blood after a street fight. Lucy is naturally wary of him and gives the distinct impression that she does not trust her own feelings where he is concerned. On the way back to the *pensione* they pause for a while looking down on the river and George simply says, 'Something tremendous has happened.'

Unlike Lucy, who is unsure of her feelings, George knows that he is attracted to her and he acts on his instincts. He takes the opportunity to kiss her a second time after Cecil has read the paragraph based on their first encounter in Italy. He is more spontaneous when he acts like this, though he is reserved in company.

It is clear to the viewer that Lucy is attracted to George, but class barriers prevent her from admitting her love for him. It is only when her refusal to accept his love drives him away that she is jolted into the realisation that she does love him after all and cannot bear the thought of losing him.

The story draws a contrast between the idea of love and real love as it is evinced in everyday life. Cecil Vyse proposes to Lucy because he desires a wife who is suitable to his needs. Lucy comes from a fitting family, is attractive and she plays the piano very well. Cecil is emotionally shallow, but Lucy refuses to acknowledge that their relationship will be hollow and insincere. It is only when George arrives and passionately declares his love for her that Lucy realises what true love is.

Self-deception and self-realisation
It is obvious from the start that Lucy deceives herself about her feelings for George. On the day they meet, George's father is intrusive, pushy and generous almost to the point of rudeness, which emphasises the fact that they are from different classes. Charlotte is horrified at his manner and Lucy unconsciously knows that a relationship between herself and George would be unacceptable to her family.

On her return to England she is courted by Cecil Vyse, a man from the highest social class. This fact underlines the gap between herself and George. Lucy accepts Cecil's proposal of marriage because it seems the right thing to do. Cecil is neither physically nor emotionally attractive to her and as the story unfolds she finds him more unbearable, particularly when compared with George.

The plot is based on the fact that Lucy is lying not only to everyone else but to herself as well. Finally, realising that she cannot suppress her feelings any longer, she transcends the social barriers that separate her from her lover. Much of the viewer's enjoyment of this film comes from observing Lucy's struggle to admit her true feelings to herself and watching her succumb to them in the end.

Class

To the English upper and middle classes at the turn of the century, social position was crucial. In *A Room with a View*, snobbery, pretentiousness and the accompanying hypocrisy are glaringly exposed. Charlotte's attitude towards Mr Emerson in the *pensione* is a striking example of this. The Miss Alans, an elderly couple, also illustrate this when they sympathise with Charlotte and Lucy for having to endure Mr Emerson's insistence on exchanging rooms.

Cecil Vyse is an insufferable snob who sneers at everything that does not meet his standards. In fact, he shows how social standing and gentility do not necessarily go together: he is quite rude about Lucy's brother, Freddy, because he is not an academic and he makes Lucy's mother feel that she is not good enough for him.

It is Cecil who unwittingly organises the letting of the cottage in Summer Street to the Emersons. This is not done out of good will but to get the better of the owner and to punish him for being (in Cecil's opinion) a snob. It doesn't occur to him that George Emerson will be invited to socialise with people as genteel as the Honeychurch family.

It is because of her position in society that Lucy accepts Cecil's proposal and refuses to consider George's advances. There is too much at stake for her to contemplate disgracing herself and her family; the fact that Cecil continuously reminds her of the difference between his position and George's reinforces the point. It is Cecil who precipitates his own downfall through this approach, as Lucy begins to see that he is more in love with the idea of who he is than with selflessly giving himself to her in a loving relationship.

In the end, Lucy has the courage to overcome the social barriers that divide her and George and to follow her instincts. Much of the film concentrates on Lucy's emancipation from the restrictions imposed on her by her family and the society that surrounds her.

Structure and style

Visual images and photography

The Florentine scene, with the view as the main focus, is a striking feature of the film. Art is an important topic, as the architecture of Florence illustrates. The stone carvings on the streets and the inside of a church are examined, paintings in the art gallery in London also feature and Cecil compares Lucy to a Leonardo da Vinci painting. The lovers kiss in a beautiful cornfield and later on in green countryside. The colour green is evident everywhere – England's lush landscape is seen in the swimming episode and in the tennis parties.

There are no significant changes in the lighting at any point in the film. Italy and England in the summer are both awash with light. England indoors is often in shadow, which sometimes varies according to the scene. When Lucy is refusing George the room is particularly dark. Most of this shadowy lighting reflects their relationship.

Language

The actors' accents are clearly drawn. Cecil Vyse in particular has what he considers to be a superior accent. His speeches are in a haughty tone and this is more exaggerated when he is criticising or demeaning someone. His language makes him sound and look ridiculous. Mr Emerson speaks with a plain and unadorned accent. He comes across as a more honest character who speaks as he feels and he stands out in contrast to Cecil, and in particular to the company he meets in Florence and England.

Symbols
The piano is a symbol in the film. Lucy plays it regularly, expressing her strongest emotions through her playing. It is Mr Beebe who is struck by the fact that her personality does not match the way she plays. He makes the point that if Lucy lived as she played, 'it will be very exciting for us, and for her.' He suspects that she will break out some day and that 'one day music and life will mingle.'

Genre
Romance.

Cultural context
Two contrasting cultural backgrounds are depicted in this film: upper-class England and Florence. Bourgeois England is restrained and rigid, with great importance attached to certain codes of behaviour. Women are not allowed to travel alone but have to be chaperoned. The style of life is stiff and formal, which is shown in dress, speech, movement and social behaviour.

The culture of Florence, on the other hand, is rich and flamboyant. The atmosphere is open and bright; the streets are exciting and fascinating. We see open, airy streets and squares, impressive monuments and striking architecture. The Italians are a colourful and varied people; they have no problem chatting to foreigners or even engaging in a violent street fight. Thus, the social codes are radically different.

General vision or viewpoint
The general vision or viewpoint seems to be ambivalent about the England the film portrays. In one way it could be seen as a lightly critical satire of Edwardian society, while on another level it could be an affectionately observed comedy of manners.

HENRY V

By William Shakespeare; directed by Kenneth Branagh
(2006 and 2007 exams)

The story
Henry V is king of England. As the film opens, we witness Henry planning to wage war on France over some disputed titles. He meets with some members of his advisory committee.

The French ambassador arrives with a packet of tennis balls from the French Dauphin. This gesture is a deliberate insult to Henry, who was formerly characterised as a reckless young man going by the name of Prince Hal.

Henry is determined to wage war on France as a result of this incident. Charles VI is king of France. Charles and his council are convinced of the superiority of the French army over the English. The English army numbers 12,000 men in comparison with the French, who number 60,000. The French troops prepare for battle with the English at Agincourt. Henry is unsure of the loyalty of his army and disguises himself on the eve of battle. In a series of conversations with various English soldiers, Henry becomes convinced of their support and loyalty and realises that their patriotism and determination are true and strong. Henry mobilises his troops continuously, urging them to fight for God and for England. He believes he is doing the right thing by engaging in battle. Just before the battle itself, he again urges his men to fight bravely for England, especially on this feast day of Crispin. The English are victorious and in spite of their relatively small numbers manage to massacre 10,000 French soldiers while sustaining few casualties themselves, as some noblemen are slain (only twenty-five men). Henry maintains that it was God who fought for them on this special feast day.

England is triumphant and Henry secures the hand in marriage of Katharine, the French princess. The film concludes with an image of the French king consenting to all reasonable terms and he signs the document in front of the English king. He gives Katharine to Henry in marriage. They pray for neighbourliness and Christian accord between their two countries. He prays to God to bind their two kingdoms together and that no jealousy will prevail. The French and English will receive each other in peace and harmony.

Aspects of the story
Tension
The tension in this film is evident in the constant exchanges between the ambassador from France and Henry. France is determined to fight the English and decline their request to hand over the throne peaceably.

Climax
The climax of the film is reached when the French and English troops have fought and it is clear that the English have won. The small number of English casualties also indicates that the French have been completely overwhelmed and their throne is now under English control.

Resolution
A peace agreement is drawn up between England and France. In addition, Henry secures Katharine's hand in marriage. This bond will bring about unity between the two countries.

Themes
- war
- violence
- loyalty
- goodness
- friendship/love

War
War in this film is seen as a glorious and brave event. Henry engages in many speeches to his troops, praising their courage and valour and declaring that this war has God's blessing. We see an image of the ideal hero in the figure of Henry V. He is brave in battle and loyal to his troops.

Goodness
There are many examples of this theme in the film. In the figure of Henry V we are shown a man who is kind and generous towards his subjects. We also see much good in Charles VI, king of France, a quiet and dignified man who believes in justice and mercy. The fact that Henry frequently invokes the name of God to help him on the battlefield also indicates that he believes in the justice of his cause.

Relationships
Henry and Charles VI
Henry is insulted by the French king's gesture of sending him tennis balls to remind him of his earlier, frivolous days when he was called Hal. Charles, king of France, is not keen to wage war, but is encouraged to do so by the young Dauphin. The two kings are reconciled at the end and Charles gives his consent for Henry to marry his daughter, Katharine.

Henry and Fluellen
Captain Fluellen maintains strict control over the English army out of loyalty to Henry, his king. At one stage a former friend of Henry, called Vardolf, is captured by Fluellen's troops and brought before Henry, having robbed a church. Henry decides to hang him in front of all the men to show that France must be treated with respect while his troops are marching through it.

Genre
The genre of this film is social realism and is based on the historical play written by William Shakespeare.

Camera angles
The film makes use of a variety of camera angles to highlight the bloody scenes of battle.

Social setting
The film is shot in both England and France. The play on which the film is based covers the period of six years from 1414 to 1420.

Cultural context
There are two contrasting world culturally. The film is shot in England and France. In both worlds there are some excruciating violent scenes. The time period is England and France in the fifteenth century. The particular cultural background is that of a Catholic king on the throne of England. Many of Henry's speeches are filled with references to God and his goodness and justice.

General vision or viewpoint
The general vision or viewpoint throughout this play is positive. Henry is a king who possesses a profound faith in God and his way of working. In the film the overall impression is that good will win and justice will prevail. The British troops fight a bloody battle against the French army, but they are constantly animated by Henry, who possesses a sure faith in divine providence. This faith stands to him at the conclusion. With England's victory over France and the securing of Katherine, the daughter of the French king, in marriage, justice and peace will prevail under Henry as king.

MY LEFT FOOT

Based on the book by Christy Brown; directed by Jim Sheridan
(2007 exam)

Historical and literary background
The background of this film is working-class Dublin in the 1930s, a time of poverty and hardship.

The story

My Left Foot is based on the autobiography of Christy Brown, a writer and painter who was born with cerebral palsy into an impoverished family. The film begins with the mature Christy arriving at the house of Lord Castlewellan to participate in a presentation for charity. It then develops by means of flashback as it recalls Christy's attempts to overcome the limitations imposed by his condition. He is a strong and determined character who comes from a tough social background in which a person is expected to make out for himself.

Poverty is a central feature in the lives of the characters. Christy's father's moods fluctuate, as he finds it hard to accept Christy's limited ability. His mother, on the other hand, is a stalwart figure who quietly perseveres and patiently encourages Christy through all his vicissitudes. All his family unites to encourage him in his attempts at painting. It is significant that the first word he writes is 'Mother'.

His mother is an indispensable agent in his growth, continually sacrificing herself so that he will get all the help and encouragement he needs.

Later, Christy's father dies as he tries to build a room where Christy can carry out his work undisturbed. Christy falls in love with his therapist, who helps him to develop his talents. At the conclusion he marries the nurse, Mary, who is seen with him during the reception in the house of Lord Castlewellan.

Themes
Courage
The principal theme of this film is courage in the face of adversity, seen in the life of

Christy Brown and his family. The superhuman struggle to overcome the personal limitations imposed by cerebral palsy and the corresponding courage that is shown by the characters triumph at the conclusion of the film.

Family
The power of the family is another theme of *My Left Foot*. We see how the support of his family generates a positive attitude in Christy, with the mother as a central figure of power and unity.

Love
The theme of love and the need for emotional security features strongly. It is seen as a powerful emotional force that transcends personal limitations and builds up the person.

Class
We get an insight into the class structure of society in this film. Christy belongs to the working class, while Lord Castlewellan's background is the Anglo-Irish ascendancy class; this is shown through such symbols as the big car, the butler and the long avenue lined with trees.

Structure and style
Visual images and photography
Close-ups are used to focus our attention on Christy's attempts to communicate, to show his frustrations or simply give expression to his feelings. Close-ups of the mother portray her anguish and suffering, while those of the father show his perplexity and confusion with the whole situation.

The streets are long and dark, suggesting the poverty of working-class Dublin. When Christy becomes famous the lighting significantly becomes brighter and there are more open spaces, as money has enlarged his possibilities.

Sound
The music is intense and dramatic, underlining the frustrations and tensions of the story.

Language
The language used is the Dublin working-class dialect of English.

Genre
Biography.

Cultural context
The cultural background of this film is working-class Dublin in the early twentieth century, a time of relative poverty. Families are large but united and traditional hospitality and neighbourliness still exist. We see this in the frequent offers of

neighbourly help, the street games organised by local teenagers and the family meals. The Catholic faith is a strong feature of life in this society, evident in the many religious images. The local pub is an important focal point in the life of the community. Significantly, when Christy writes his first words on the slate, his father carries him down to the pub for his first pint of stout. Christy is being initiated into manhood.

General vision or viewpoint
The general vision of this film is positive. The impression we are left with at the conclusion is the importance of struggle and optimism in the face of difficulties. The power of the mother is a central facet in consolidating unity and strength within Christy in spite of all the odds; she is a continuous source of hope and optimism.

Christy's own tenacity is also evident, not only in the way he develops his talents to an outstanding degree but in the strength with which he deals with people. This is evident at the conclusion when he nags the nurse to such a degree that she agrees to meet him that night. Later on he marries her.

TWELVE ANGRY MEN

Directed by Sidney Lumet
(2007 exam)

The story
The story takes place in one room with twelve men who form part of a jury for a murder trial. The twelve men are assembled together to decide on the guilt of a young boy who has been accused of murdering his father. None of the men are given names. One member of the jury (we learn at the conclusion that he is called Davis) declares that the young boy is not guilty while the other eleven members firmly maintain that he is. The film is made up of dialogue to establish the truth about the circumstances. Each man attempts to offer a rational explanation on what he thinks has happened. They attempt to bring the matter to a quick conclusion while the member of the jury who supports the boy remains firm. The men are anxious to finish quickly and bring the whole matter to a reasonable conclusion, as all of them are strongly convinced of the boy's guilt.

As the film proceeds and the dialogue develops between the men, it becomes clear that many of the men who maintain the fact of this boy's guilt are governed by deep-seated prejudices. Some of these men maintain that the young boy's background of poverty and drugs makes his guilt inevitable. Another member of the jury is clearly prejudiced emotionally. He has a photograph of his own son, who has not spoken to him for over two years. It becomes clear that as a father he has failed to establish good communication with his son and for that reason he is antagonistic towards the young man on trial. Each scene shows us how the different men change their minds on the verdict. The men are restless and impatient and we see much hostility between them. They decide to take a secret vote and one new man from the jury votes that he is not guilty. They continue to argue among themselves, declaring that they cannot send a boy to his death in the electric chair on evidence that is not foolproof.

One by one the members of the jury begin to change their minds, having established that they now do not agree with the witnesses, doubting the truth of their testimony. They bring in the knife and while one is declaring that this is a unique knife, Davis produces a similar knife, which he bought in a local shop. One of the members is a foreigner, who reminds them to forget their personal prejudices and that they are deciding on the life of another human being. They also establish that the woman who testified to seeing the young boy killing his father wore glasses, but did not want to do so in court for reasons of vanity. Through building up a good deal of small details they begin to realise that they could be wrong and that the boy could be innocent. Gradually, as the evidence which had been brought against this boy begins to crumble, each man starts to change his mind and declare the boy not guilty. The film concludes with one man eventually breaking down and crying because his prejudice against the boy was rooted in a bad relationship with his own son. Every one of the twelve men vote not guilty at the conclusion.

Themes
- prejudice
- truth
- integrity
- justice

Genre
This is a classic black and white movie. All of the action takes place in one room. There are a few dramatic camera angles, ranging from close-ups to some well-composed medium shots. The music is plaintive and consists of a solo flute by Kenyon Hopkins.

Cultural context
The film is set in middle-class America. The opening sequence focuses on tall, imposing pillars of justice outside Manhattan's general sessions offices. It is set on a stifling hot summer's day, which mirrors the various passions and prejudices of the different men. The jury is made up of an all-male white group, mainly of middle-class status. The cultural background of the young boy accused of murdering his father is Puerto Rican. Much of the dialogue in the film reveals the different and contrasting cultural prejudices of the characters.

General vision or viewpoint
At one stage, one member of the jury reminds another man in the room that what they are speaking about is 'not an exact science'. The whole film dramatises how uncertain human judgment can be and how it can be subject to error in small details. The importance of human life and its sacred quality is reaffirmed throughout this film. From the beginning, Davis, who refuses to condemn the young boy, is unsure of the facts of the case, but his main contention is that a young boy's life is at stake. Each member of the jury is forced to face their own personal prejudices and emotional states and try to squarely acknowledge the truth about the situation given the limitations of the facts presented. The need for deliberation and exact testimony in the judicial system becomes evident from the very beginning of this film.

13
Unseen Poetry

APPROACHING THE UNSEEN POEM

The first thing you must do when tackling an unseen poem is try to understand its meaning. The tone and the choice of words will help to convey the poem's meaning. You will find that the more times you read the poem, the more the meaning will become clear to you.

Some modern poetry has no clear and unequivocal meaning, and in fact is not meant to have a definite meaning. In many instances the meaning can be quite obscure, so don't worry about understanding the meaning immediately.

Remember, a poem can have many different interpretations. It is important to take risks when reading and to try to understand a poem's meaning.

A poem is based on communicating some emotion(s) to the reader through a particular choice of words and structure. To understand more deeply what the content or meaning of a particular poem is, we need to examine the following:
- ideas: the content or subject matter
- persona
- language.

Ideas
1. State the idea or attitude expressed in each component part or in each verse.
2. Are there key words or word repetitions strategically placed in order to express the main ideas? (Remember, poetry is emotion and may communicate through syntax, repetition or image association rather than logic.)
3. See why the verses are structured in the particular way they are.
4. Try to understand the relationship between the different parts of a poem – this will help to reveal its structure.
5. The theme(s) can be elicited or drawn out from grasping how the particular ideas or responses are developed in the poem.

Persona
1. Who is speaking in the poem? Is it the poet or is the poet pretending to be someone else?
2. To whom is the poet speaking – to a particular person or to a general audience?
3. What do we learn about the poet from the poem?

Language
When you analyse the style of a poem – that is, the language, tone, point of view and techniques used – it will help towards gaining a deeper understanding and interpretation of the poem.

The particular way in which language is used in a poem helps to give a shape and structure to the poem's thought and meaning.

The language of poetry is made up of:
- imagery
- words
- rhyme and rhythm
- alliteration
- onomatopoeia
- ambiguity
- sound
- grammar
- metre.

Imagery
Imagery is any form of descriptive writing. Imagery focuses the meaning of the poem as a whole; it can also function to create atmosphere and establish a certain pattern within a poem. A poet can make use of language in many different ways to create imagery or word pictures. Don't just identify imagery – be able to say what its function in poetry is.

Imagery creates atmosphere and establishes a pattern within a poem. Imagery is effective when it is central to the poem's meaning.

When studying imagery in a poem, know how to identify the following:
- metaphor
- simile
- symbol.

Both metaphor and simile compare one thing with another. In a metaphor this similarity is implied, while a simile shows the comparison through the use of the words 'like' or 'as'. Similes are closer to ordinary speech; metaphors are more condensed and economical.

> Simile: The fog descended like a blanket.
> Metaphor: The blanket of fog descended.

A symbol is a word that stands for or points to a reality beyond itself. For example,

flowers can symbolise the shortness of life. Some other examples include:
- sunrise: a new beginning
- water: purity
- a river: life
- the sea: eternity
- a garden: order
- spring: new life and energy
- autumn: maturity, fulfilment
- winter: old age and death

When you are examining symbols, an act of imagination is required before the meaning becomes fully clear. Aim at capturing the way in which a symbol glows or echoes with meaning. The statement or ideas that are being made do not make sense on the surface level – the sense or meaning of symbols must be inferred from some association, comparison, contrast or inversion of images and ideas used in the poem.

For example, take the following lines from T. S. Eliot's poem 'The Waste Land':

> Unreal City,
> Under the brown fog of a winter dawn,
> A crowd flowed over London Bridge, so many,
> I had not thought death had undone so many.

The fog and the winter dawn have many different meanings; they could refer to the spiritual apathy and stagnation that were a feature of the time when Eliot was writing the poem.

With regard to imagery in poetry, ask yourself the following questions:
- What does it say?
- Why is it used?
- Has it got connotations or sound effects?
- Does it fit into the context?
- How well does it acccomplish its task?

Words

Examine the way words work within a poem.

Appropriateness

Are the words that are used poetic, colloquial or abstract? If so, why?

Associations

Do the words have connotations or associations? Kavanagh here is suggesting religious renewal:

> ... the green waters of the canal
> Pouring redemption for me ...

This line from Eliot suggests fear and violence:

> Fleeing from the foreign faces and the foreign swords.

Allusions
An allusion is a reference to another book, event, person or place. The allusion may be implied or hinted; sometimes the effect of an allusion may be to make something that is being said more significant, more ambiguous or more amusing.

Collocation
This occurs through an explosive, unexpected or sometimes contradictory combination of words, such as 'dense din,' 'tremendous silence'. Consider these lines from Dylan Thomas:

> And as I was green and carefree, famous among the barns
> About the happy yard and singing as the farm was home.

Repetition
Repetition of a key word or phrase at different points can give emphasis to the power of the poem:

> And indeed there will be time ... there will be time, there will be time ... Time for you and time for me ...Time to turn back and descend the stair.

> I am tired with my own life and the lives of those after me,
> I am dying in my own death and the deaths of those after me.

Rhyme and rhythm

Rhythm can be used in poetry to add to the mood or atmosphere and therefore it can contribute to conveying the meaning more clearly. Effective rhythm is one where the stress falls on the crucial or important word. In the best poetry the rhythm and meaning of the words appear as one and not two things. Ask yourself whether it is significant that these thoughts and feelings have been expressed in this particular rhythm.

Internal rhyme occurs when a word in one line rhymes with another word in the same line:

> He found the forest track, he brought back
> This beak ...

The internal rhyme serves to emphasise a sense of movement:

> The grains beyond age, the dark veins of her mother.

The internal rhyme between 'grains' and 'veins' underlines the finality of death. Internal rhyme can serve the function of surprising the reader and quickening the pace of a line.

A line can be *end-stopped* with an *end rhyme* or it can run on into another line in a flow of thought. End rhyme occurs when two consecutive lines rhyme or alternate lines rhyme. Look at the following lines, which are an example of end rhyme:

> If I were a dead leaf thou mightest bear, [a]
> If I were swift cloud to fly with thee; [b]
> A wave to pant beneath thy power, and share [a]
>
> The impulse of thy strength, only less free [b]
> Than thou, O uncontrollable! If even [c]
> I were as in my boyhood, and could be [b]
>
> The comrade of thy wanderings over Heaven, [c]
> As then, when to outstrip thy skiey speed [d]
> Scarce seemed a vision; I would ne'er have striven [c]
>
> As thus with thee in prayer in my sore need. [d]
>
> (Percy Bysshe Shelley, 'Ode to the West Wind')

Rhythm sometimes exists to link words and ideas. It can also be used to suggest speed, calm, anger or monotony. Definite rhythm can make a particular point, for example:

> Only thin smoke without flame
>   From the heaps of couch-grass;
> Yet this will go onward the same
>   Though Dynasties pass.

The absence of rhythm can suggest fear, worry or aimlessness. Uneven rhythm is also used for a particular purpose, for example:

> How the old Mountains drip with Sunset
> How the Hemlocks burn –
> How the Dun Brake is draped in Cinder
> By the Wizard Sun –
>
> How the old Steeples hand the Scarlet
> Till the Ball is full –
> Have I the lip of the Flamingo
> That I dare to tell?

These lines are taken from a poem by Emily Dickinson. The uneven rhythm serves the purpose of building up an atmosphere in nature before the poet herself intrudes into the poem.

Alliteration

This is the repetition of the initial consonant. When you are dealing with an unseen poem, discuss the effect of alliteration – don't just give examples. Ask yourself whether or not it produces a distinctive tone and whether or not it is regularly spaced:

> I caught this morning morning's minion king-
> dom of daylight's dauphin, dapple-dawn-drawn Falcon, in ...

The alliteration of the *m* and *d* sounds here serves the function of conjuring up a sense of richness, majesty and power.

> I should hear him fly with the high fields
> and wake up to the farm forever fled from the childless land.

The idea of time passing is expressed here in the alliteration of the *f* sound.

> O wild west wind, thou breadth of Autumn's being ...

The *w* alliteration here enacts the poet's awe in the presence of such a mighty force.

Assonance
This is the repetition of identical vowel sounds. For example, look at the effect of assonance in the following lines from Tennyson:

> Lo! in the middle of the wood,
> the folded leaf is woo'd from out the bud
> Sun steep'd at noon, and in the moon
> Nightly dew-fed; and turning yellow
> Falls, and floats adown the air.

The combined effect of the assonance of the *a* sound creates an impression of rich abundance in nature.

Onomatopoeia
This is where the word conjures up the sound: 'wheeze', 'buzz', 'splash'.

> watch the crisping ripples on the beach
> Liplapping of Galilee.

Ambiguity
Ambiguity in poetry means the use of words to mean two or more different things. Many times a poet can enrich the meaning of a poem by using words that are ambiguous. Ambiguity can emphasise the many nuances or levels of meaning that can be found in poetic language.
Look at the following line:

> ... dapple-dawn-drawn Falcon ...

Does it mean that the falcon is etched against the landscape of the sky? Or does it mean that the falcon has been drawn out by the dawn into the sky?

> My heart in hiding
> Stirred for a bird ...

Does this mean that his heart is in hiding because he is a priest and therefore detached from the world? Or does it mean that he is literally hiding as he watches the bird in the sky?

> Fathering and all humbling darkness
> Tells with silence the last light breaking …

What exactly is meant by the term 'humbling darkness'? Does it mean that death will humble humankind, including the poet? Does it mean that darkness is death? If so, why 'humbling'?

All these examples illustrate the power of ambiguity in poetry.

Effects of sound

Don't just give examples – show the effect. For example, harshness can be conveyed by the use of the consonants *b, t, k*:

> Blight and famine, plague and earthquake, roaring deeps and fiery sands,
> Clanging fights, and flaming towns, and sinking ships, and praying hands..

A sense of smoothness can be conveyed by the use of certain vowels and also by the *s* sound:

> There is sweet music here that softer falls.

Grammar

Consider some of the grammatical devices used in poetry.
- The omission of 'and', verbs or commas. Ask yourself why.
- Adding 'and', commas, verbs or capital letters when not usual. Ask why.
- Short sentences. What is their purpose?
- Long sentences. Anger? Boredom? Movement?
- Unusual syntax. Look at the purpose.
- Word compounds – 'world sorrow', 'blue-bleak', 'leafy-with-love'. What are they saying? Why are they used?
- Word compression – using the smallest number of words to achieve maximum intensity. This can be used to convey a dense or intense meaning or it can be deliberately ambiguous.
- The unusual use of words – 'Pitched past pitch of grief,' 'More pangs will, schooled at forepangs, wilder wring'.
- Nouns made into verbs. Why?
- Coining of words. Why?

Metre

- A very short line can express emotion: joy, anger, hatred.
- A very long line – what effect has it?
- Run-on lines can express movement, speed, growth or development.

Method of answering questions on an unseen poem

Remember that a poem is made up of content or subject matter. This content is shaped in a particular way and adds up to what is known as the structure or form.
1. Aim first of all to give a general summary of what the poem is about and the different stages in the poem.
2. Read the poem through several times to grasp some idea of the meaning.
3. Examine the title of the poem and see what relation it may have to the content.
4. Assess what type of poem it is. Is it narrative, an argument, a philosophical insight into life, an ode, a lyric, a sonnet?
5. If the poem is a narrative, understand the main events. When you understand why the events follow one another in a particular way you will understand how the poem is designed. There are three elements common to poems that tell stories: expectation, surprise and reversal.
6. If the poem is a meditation on life, get the general meaning of what is being said.
7. If the poem is an argument, follow the main stages. Ask yourself why the argument moves from that stage to this. Look at the conclusion of the argument. Is it logical? Is it effective? Has it achieved what it set out to do? Am I convinced? Identify the main points and the different stages of the argument.
8. Look at the words and see whether they carry symbolic or emotive meaning. Ask yourself why this is so. Look for a particular *tone* – this is the voice, mood or outlook of the poet.
9. Show how figures of speech contribute to the poem. Remember, figures of speech can be metaphors, symbols, personification, similes, etc. Many times poems convey their meaning by implication, suggestion, word connotations or associations and not through explicit statement.
10. Be aware of your reaction to the poem. What thoughts or feelings do the words stir up in you? Remember that a poem does not have to make complete sense. Many times the power of poetry comes from its ability to establish or suggest many different levels of meaning and many possibilities.

Questions and sample answers

Attempt your own answers first, then compare them with the sample answers given.

Epitaph on a Tyrant
W. H. Auden

>Perfection, of a kind, was what he was after,
>And the poetry he invented was easy to understand;
>He knew human folly like the back of his hand,
>And was greatly interested in armies and fleets;
>When he laughed, respectable senators burst with laughter,
>And when he cried the little children died in the street.

1. Write a short note on the structure of this poem.
2. What is the tone of the poem?
3. Comment on the poet's use of language.

Sample answers

1. The structure of this poem consists of one stanza. The poem is called 'Epitaph on a Tyrant' and for that reason the poet neatly and compactly expresses his tribute to this tyrant in six short sentences. There are no run-on lines; instead the poet uses end rhyme, in the words 'fleet' and 'street', 'after' and 'laughter', 'understand' and 'hand'. The function of this rhyming scheme is to convey an ironic vision of a man whose life yielded destruction.

> Perfection, of a kind, was what he was after, [a]
> And the poetry he invented was easy to understand; [b]
> He knew human folly like the back of his hand, [b]
> And was greatly interested in armies and fleets; [c]
> When he laughed, respectable senators burst with laughter, [a]
> And when he cried the little children died in the street. [c]

2. The tone of the poem is satirical: the poet is mocking or satirising the tyrant. In the second line he suggests that this tyrant's poetry was easy to understand. In other words, his deeds and life were motivated by selfish interests, such as trying to dominate people and murdering them. For example, 'when he cried the little children died in the street'. The effect of the whole poem is sobering.

3. The language used is restrained and terse. The poet seems to be wary of expressing himself in too much language. This poem is a portrait of a man who wielded power through bullying and brute force. The poet wishes to paint a graphic picture of this tyrant and for that reason he uses images that are arresting and dramatic. The poem is made up of one stanza, which says it all. The poet does not repeat himself and therefore the effect is much more dramatic and intense.

The Hippopotamus
T. S. Eliot

> The broad-backed hippopotamus
> Rests on his belly in the mud;
> Although he seems so firm to us
> He is merely flesh and blood.
>
> Flesh and blood is weak and frail
> Susceptible to nervous shock;
> While the True Church can never fail
> For it is based upon a rock.

The hippo's feeble steps may err
In compassing material ends,
While the True Church need never stir
To gather in its dividends.

The 'potamus can never reach
The mango on the mango-tree;
But fruits of pomegranate and peach
Refresh the Church from over sea.

At mating time the hippo's voice
Betrays inflections hoarse and odd,
But every week we hear rejoice
The Church, at being one with God.

The hippopotamus's day
Is passed in sleep; at night he hunts;
God works in a mysterious way –
The Church can sleep and feed at once.

I saw the 'potamus take wing
Ascending from the damp savannas,
And quiring angels round him sing
The praise of God, in loud hosannas.

Blood of the Lamb shall wash him clean
And him shall heavenly arms enfold,
Among the saints he shall be seen
Performing on a harp of gold.

He shall be washed as white as snow,
By all the martyr'd virgins kist,
While the True Church remains below
Wrapt in the old miasmal mist.

1. Discuss the use of contrast in this poem.
2. Comment on how the form of the poem develops the theme.
3. Examine the images in the poem and show how they contribute to the particular vision presented in the poem.

Sample answers

1. The poet develops his thoughts by drawing a contrast between the image of the hippopotamus and the Church. There is a striking contrast between the two images –

the broad-backed hippopotamus resting in the mud on his belly and the image presented to us of the Church that can never fail, based, as it is, 'upon a rock'. The poet seems to be illustrating the difference between the impermanence of material things, as shown through his symbol of the hippopotamus, and the permanence and power of the spiritual, as evinced in the images of the Church. Each stanza develops this contrast. As the poem develops we bear witness to the growing power of the Church, while simultaneously witnessing the weakness of material things. Images such as 'the 'potamus can never reach | The mango on the mango-tree' show the failure of material things to achieve permanence.

On the other hand, the poet may be illustrating the continuity and permanence of the Church in such lines as: 'But fruits of pomegranate and peach | Refresh the Church from over sea.'

At the conclusion of the poem, the poet skilfully fuses this contrast. The hippopotamus is surrounded by singing angels; he is seen among the saints and washed clean by the blood of the Lamb. Perhaps the poet is painting an image of the fate of those who are faithful to the Church.

2. The poem is structured in a series of nine stanzas, all of the same length. Each of the stanzas is structured in the same manner – four lines of verse – which makes subtle use of end rhyme. For example, look at the effect of the rhyme between the following words in the last three stanzas:

> I saw the 'potamus take wing [a]
> Ascending from the damp savannas, [b]
> And quiring angels round him sing [a]
> The praise of God, in loud hosannas. [b]
>
> Blood of the Lamb shall wash him clean [a]
> And him shall heavenly arms enfold, [b]
> Among the saints he shall be seen [a]
> Performing on a harp of gold. [b]
>
> He shall be washed as white as snow, [a]
> By all the martyr'd virgins kist, [b]
> While the True Church remains below [a]
> Wrapt in the old miasmal mist. [b]

The poet's use of rhyme between words such as 'wing' and 'sing', 'savannas' and 'hosannas' illustrates the striking contrast between the material and the spiritual worlds. He also makes effective use of repetition, for example, 'enfold' and 'gold' paint an image of triumph and glory at the conclusion.

3. The poet makes use of the unusual image of a hippopotamus to put forward his theme of the power of the Church. The images that describe the hippopotamus are earthy and real – resting in the mud on his belly, the vivid image of his broad back, his

voice betraying 'inflections hoarse and odd' at mating time. These are images that are related to the earth, to earthly things. On the other hand, the images that describe the Church's activity are more positive and unified, such as 'While the True Church need never stir | To gather in its dividends' and 'The Church can sleep and feed at once' and suggest an internal harmony and sense of oneness. The poet's use throughout the poem of emphatic repetition in phrases such as 'the True Church' intensifies this dramatic power of the Church.

Exposure
Wilfred Owen

I

Our brains ache, in the merciless iced east winds that knive us …
Wearied we keep awake because the night is silent …
Low, drooping flares confuse our memory of the salient …
Worried by silence, sentries whisper, curious, nervous,
    But nothing happens.

Watching we hear the mad gusts tugging on the wire,
Like twitching agonies of men among its brambles.
Northward, incessantly, the flickering gunnery rumbles,
Far off, like a dull rumour of some other war.
    What are we doing here?

The poignant misery of dawn begins to grow …
We only know war lasts, rain soaks, and clouds sag stormy,
Dawn massing in the east her melancholy army
Attacks once more in ranks on shivering ranks of grey,
    But nothing happens.

Sudden successive flights of bullets streak the silence.
Less deadly than the air that shudders black with snow,
With sidelong flowing flakes that flock, pause and renew,
We watch them wandering up and down the wind's nonchalance,
    But nothing happens.

II

Pale flakes with fingering stealth come feeling for our faces –
We cringe in holes, back on forgotten dreams, and stare, snow-dazed,
Deep into grassier ditches. So we drowse sun-dozed.
Littered with blossoms trickling where the blackbird fusses.
    Is it that we are dying?

Slowly our ghosts drag home: glimpsing the sunk fires, glozed

With crusted dark-red jewels; crickets jingle there;
For hours the innocent mice rejoice: the house is theirs;
Shutters and doors, all closed: on us the doors are closed –
    We turn back to our dying.

Since we believe not otherwise can kind fires burn;
Nor ever suns smile true on child, or field or fruit.
For God's invincible spring, our love is made afraid;
Therefore, not loath, we lie out here; therefore were born,
    For love of God seems dying.

Tonight, His frosty will fasten on this mud and us,
Shrivelling many hands, puckering foreheads crisp.
The burying-party, picks and shovels in their shaking grasp,
Pause over half-known faces. All their eyes are ice,
    But nothing happens.

1. This poem is a powerful comment on the effects of war. Identify the main feelings expressed in the poem. Show how these feelings are conveyed through the language and imagery.
2. Show how the poet has structured his thought in the poem and what the effect of such a structure is.
3. Identify the particular tone and attitude towards life in the speaker.

Sample answers
1. The poem opens with an image of men worn out and fearful as they struggle to keep awake on a bitterly cold night. There is a feeling of tension in the last line of the first stanza, which is underlined by the poet's use of sibilance: 'Worried by silence, sentries whisper, curious, nervous'. The whole feeling is one of fearful apprehension about what is going to happen. These feelings are given added momentum and intensity by the reiterated use of the short, terse line 'But nothing happens.' The poet paints some powerful images of fear and dread and builds the reader up to an expectation of something momentous and dreadful. Then the line 'But nothing happens' serves the function of emphasising this anxiety even more.

    There is a strong feeling throughout the poem of the futility and waste of war. This is achieved by the use of the rhetorical question in the concluding line of the second stanza: 'What are we doing here?' In a sense the poet answers this question in the next stanza, in the grim line 'We only know war lasts, rain soaks, and clouds sag stormy'. The brutal impact of war is registered vividly in these images.

    As the poem develops, the feelings within the poet change. In the fifth stanza the poet asks, 'Is it that we are dying?' This leads him on to some nostalgic reminiscences about his past life, the reality of life at home and his loved ones. But these images are brutal and grim. The only reality of his former family life is mirrored in images such as 'sunk fires … Shutters and doors, all closed: on us the doors are closed'. The only reality is death.

Towards the end of the poem the poet's feelings become almost hopeless as he continues to depict the devastation caused by war. The sixth stanza is gloomy and shows how the poet's dreams have been killed by war to such an extent that even his love is gone:

> . . . our love is made afraid;
> Therefore, not loath, we lie out here; therefore were born,
> For love of God seems dying.

There are undertones of hopelessness and near-despair in these lines. The conclusion of the poem is filled with some chilling images:

> The burying-party, picks and shovels in their shaking grasp,
> Pause over half-known faces. All their eyes are ice …

With these images of frost and snow, the poet seems to be saying how war robs people of feeling. The men's faces are only 'half-known': war has generated indifference and unfeeling attitudes.

2. The poem is structured in eight stanzas of equal length. Each stanza concludes on a short emphatic statement or question, which underlines the futility of war. In each stanza the poet has drawn a parallel between the world of nature and the plight of these men who are hiding in the trenches. The images from nature are wild and savage: 'the merciless iced east winds that knive us … the mad gusts tugging on the wire, | Like twitching agonies of men among its brambles … The poignant misery of dawn'. The function of such imagery is to emphasise the brutality experienced by these men because of the war.

The structure is coherent and compact. The particular effect of such a structure is to illustrate the real impact caused by war on the lives of people and how it wreaks devastation.

3. The tone of this poem is deeply dispiriting and negative. The speaker seems to lose faith in life as the poem develops and progresses. In the opening stanza he is caught in a situation of extreme suffering, surrounded by icy winds and a fearful apprehension and confusion about what is happening: 'drooping flares confuse our memory of the salient … | Worried by silence …'. This sense of bewilderment and confusion on the part of the speaker is given an added intensity by the concluding line of each stanza, such as, 'But nothing happens', 'What are we doing here?'

The tone of the poem reaches a climax of suffering as the men cringe in holes. The poet tries to escape from this anguish in the trenches by recalling images of home and loved ones. But these efforts only conjure up more images of death and loss and so the tone intensifies in its dark, pessimistic strain. This gives way to some sobering reflections on life, war and love. The poet concludes that he finds it hard to accept that 'kind fires burn; | Nor ever suns smile true on child, or field or fruit.' The alliteration here underlines the dark, negative aspect of the speaker's vision of things. The pointlessness of war and the loss of everything, including one's identity, are given striking expression in the concluding stanza, as the dead bodies are only half-known to the people who come to bury them.

You're
Sylvia Plath

Clownlike, happiest on your hands,
Feet to the stars, and moon-skulled,
Gilled like a fish. A common-sense
Thumbs-down on the dodo's mode.
Wrapped up in yourself like a spool,
Trawling your dark as owls do.
Mute as a turnip from the Fourth
Of July to All Fools' Day,
O high-riser, my little loaf.

Vague as fog and looked for like mail.
Farther off than Australia.
Bent-backed Atlas, our travelled prawn.
Snug as a bug and at home
Like a sprat in a pickle jug.
A creel of eels, all ripples.
Jumpy as a Mexican bean.
Right, like a well-done sum.
A clean slate, with your own face on.

1. What particular vision of things is given in this poem? Take into account the poet's unusual use of words.
2. Comment on the language used in this poem and how it communicates the ideas.
3. Write a short comment on the tone of the poem.

Sample answers

1. The title of the poem is 'You're'. The poem gives us an image of a certain type of character, who is happy as they act like a clown with their feet to the stars. As the poem develops, we get an insight into the type of character represented in the poem's title, 'wrapped in yourself like a spool'. There are implications of an isolated and deep character, 'trawling your dark as owls do'. The poet makes sustained use of simile to paint some interesting images for us of this unusual character: 'gilled like a fish', 'mute as a turnip', 'like a sprat', 'snug as a bug'. The general effect of the lines is of an impenetrable and inaccessible character, 'vague as fog and looked for like mail. | Farther off than Australia.'

This portrait is varied. The character represented is as 'Jumpy as a Mexican bean', yet 'Right, like a well-done sum.' The poet uses a wide variety of imagery to paint this highly original portrait of a most interesting character.

2. The writer uses language in a highly original way. Much of the effect of this poem comes from the writer's striking use of simile. Almost every image is structured on some

clever similes: 'Gilled like a fish', 'Wrapped up in yourself like a spool', 'Right, like a well-done sum.' The use of the image 'feet to the stars' in the opening lines is cleverly juxtaposed with the metaphor 'high-riser' in the concluding line of the first stanza. The poet uses alliteration of the *r* sound to conjure up a sense of comfort and ease – 'like a sprat in a pickle jug, | A creel of eels, all ripples.' The effect is intensified by the use of assonance in 'creel of eels, all ripples.'

3. The tone of this poem is detached and factual. The poet is painting a strong picture of different features of a character and she does this through recording a series of clear, factual images in an objective tone: 'Clownlike, happiest on your hands, | Feet to the stars, and moon-skulled.'

14 Prescribed Poetry

In this chapter there are some sample questions on the prescribed poetry. A method of organising and assembling material for an answer on prescribed poetry is given. Study this method carefully and apply it to the questions on the prescribed poetry at the end of this chapter.

Approaching the question

1. Rephrase or rewrite the question.
2. Take a stance on the question – decide to agree, disagree or partly agree.
3. Begin a draft of your answer, writing down seven or eight points that will form the framework of your answer. These points must be on different aspects of the question and must contain quotations or references. In addition, these points will form the basis of each of the paragraphs of your answer. The graph illustrates these points more clearly.

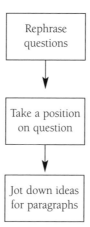

Remember, a good Higher Level answer must be structured in paragraphs and all must develop the question asked. The concluding paragraph must tie up all your ideas and refer back to the question. In addition, a good conclusion makes a definitive statement on the question.

Prescribed Poetry

QUESTIONS AND SAMPLE ANSWERS

Study the following questions and draft answers on the poets Séamus Heaney, Elizabeth Bishop and Eavan Boland. Follow the method given in answering questions like these. It can help to fully rewrite these questions as a first step. In your answers, always use quotations from or references to the poems.

There is a complete answer on Eavan Boland following the two draft answers.

SÉAMUS HEANEY

(2005 exam)

Question 1

'The value of tradition and a keen sense of the past are strong issues dealt with in the poetry of Séamus Heaney.' Discuss this statement with reference to or quotation from the poetry of Heaney on your course.

Stage 1: Rephrase the question
'Séamus Heaney's poetry deals with the past and with tradition or old customs and folklore.' Discuss.

Sample opening paragraph
This statement is true. Séamus Heaney has written a variety of different types of poems. In many of these poems he is concerned with the influence of the past on the present state of the country. In addition, he uses his poetry to show certain traditions, such as the blacksmith's work in an ordinary forge or the simple rural lifestyle in Ireland long ago, and to celebrate the skills that sustained the farming community.

Paragraph 2
Heaney believes that we need to become more aware of our tradition in order to possess a true sense of identity. Show how Heaney celebrates certain traditional practices in skills such as bread-making in the poem 'Sunlight' or making horseshoes in 'The Forge'. Develop points about the real values manifested in the two central characters, the blacksmith and his aunt, in both poems.

Paragraph 3
Develop Heaney's own point about how 'our sense of the past, our sense of the land and perhaps even our sense of identity are inextricably interwoven'. Make reference to poems such as 'The Harvest Bow', 'A Constable Calls' and 'Sunlight' to develop these points and show how these ideas are reflected in the poems.

Paragraph 4
Discuss how Heaney speaks about Irish culture and the rich inheritance of the past in the poem 'Bogland'. Develop your answer by talking about the various aspects of

bogland represented in the poem. Make reference to the rich and original metaphors that are used here.

Concluding paragraph
Sum up Heaney's attitude to tradition and the past in the poems you have discussed. Draw together the main points and reflections on both tradition and the past from the five poems you have discussed. Show how Heaney has illustrated these insights effectively and has given clear, coherent expression to his ideas through a variety of techniques, such as the original use of metaphor, symbolism and contrast. Show how Heaney's voice percolates through many of these poems.

ELIZABETH BISHOP

(2006 and 2007 exams)

Question 2
'Elizabeth Bishop's poems move from description towards moments of discovery, which can be joyful or devastating.' In your reading of Elizabeth Bishop's poetry, did you find this statement to be true? Support your answer by quotation from or reference to the poems on your course.

Stage 1: Rephrase the question
Would you agree with the statement that the poetry of Elizabeth Bishop moves from describing or drawing pictures to revealing moments of insight, which can be either happy or traumatic?

Sample opening paragraph
This statement is true. Bishop's poems move from describing and evoking certain moments of profound illumination and insight towards the revelation of a situation that can be either joyful or devastating. She is a highly subjective poet, as most of her topics spring from her own experience. The poems I propose to discuss are 'The Fish', 'At the Fishhouses' and 'In the Waiting Room'.

Paragraph 1
Discuss her descriptions in 'The Fish' and in particular her meticulous use of sharply observed detail.
   Pay attention to her use of colour and small details in lines such as:

> He was speckled with barnacles,
> fine rosettes of lime,
> and infested
> with tiny white sea-lice …

Show how the fish almost becomes an objective symbol of the poet's own problems in the image of the rainbow (line 75): 'until everything was rainbow, rainbow, rainbow!'

Discuss this central moment of illumination and show how this discovery is positive, a source of joy and added wisdom.

Paragraph 2
Discuss 'At the Fishhouses' and look at how Bishop uses a succession of vivid details in her description:

> an old man sits netting,
> his net, in the gloaming almost invisible,
> a dark purple-brown,
> and his shuttle worn and polished.

Describe and discuss how all these details conjure up a distinct atmosphere of seafaring people.
   Comment on her use of small details in lines such as:

> The five fishhouses have steeply peaked roofs
> and narrow, cleated gangplanks slant up
> to storerooms in the gables
> for the wheelbarrows to be pushed up and down on.

Discuss how the change comes in this poem (line 45 onwards) and how the poet achieves this through her use of images that are now cold and deep. Discuss the reason for the repetition of certain images and how the colours change:

> The water seems suspended
> above the rounded grey and blue-grey stones.

The mode of discovery in the poem is gradual, deep, reflective and sobering. Discuss the fact that while this vision is neither joyful nor devastating, it certainly is a moving and emotional experience for the poet. Perhaps it is a wisdom that comes to her from her background – a neurotic mother and her own abandonment as a child.
   Show how her vision at the conclusion is sobering, that this experience is unalterable:

> It is like what we imagine knowledge to be:
> dark, salt, clear, moving, utterly free,
> drawn from the cold hard mouth
> of the world, derived from the rocky breasts
> forever, flowing and drawn, and since
> our knowledge is historical, flowing and flown.

Paragraph 3
Show how 'In the Waiting Room' takes a simple situation and uses a descriptive and narrative approach to probe the meaning of her own sex on a deeper level.
   Discuss the originality of approach – how on the basis of a simple descriptive narrative the poet merges the vision of herself with that of her aunt.
   Show how she experiences a crisis of identity in the context of ordinary, banal images encountered in a waiting room:

> The waiting room
> was full of grown-up people,
> artics and overcoats,
> lamps and magazines.

Note her emphasis on the colour and movement of the volcano spilling over in rivulets of fire:

> the inside of a volcano,
> black, and full of ashes;
> then it was spilling over
> in rivulets of fire.

Note the description of the black women:

> black, naked women with necks
> wound round and round with wire
> like the necks of light bulbs.

Comment on how she reacts to these images with fear and disgust.

Paragraph 4
Discuss 'Sestina' and how it is structured on some graphic domestic imagery. Comment on how it depicts a child seated at a kitchen table watching her grandmother preparing tea.
   Discuss how the poet juxtaposes the image of the kettle boiling with the recurrent reference to 'drops of tears'. Show how these images change and develop in the poem to reveal a sorrowful moment of insight.
   Develop the idea of how the whole notion of sorrow is firmly implanted in the child's mind by the conclusion of the poem.
   Show how the reference to the child drawing 'another inscrutable house' underlines this unfathomable aspect of life and domestic bliss, which is a strong feature in Bishop's poetry.

Concluding paragraph
Discuss how all four poems operate on the level of simple, vivid and keen descriptive detail.
   Show how this vision differs in each of her poems, revealing either joy or heartache. Conclude by showing how these various illuminations or insights display different aspects of the poet's life.

Eavan Boland

(2005 exam)

Question 3
'Boland's poetry celebrates the domestic and the role of women in a world that is often

violent and threatening.' Discuss this view, supporting your answer by quotation from or reference to the poems by Eavan Boland on your course.

Answer
Eavan Boland is a woman who writes against the background of Ireland and its history. She writes about a rich variety of different themes in her work. It is unquestionably true that Boland does celebrate women and their role in both the domestic situation and society in general. In addition, she communicates her vision of women against the backdrop of a world that is undoubtedly characterised by war and violence.

Many of her poems deal with the position of the woman. In all of them we are exposed to various facets of the woman, from her domestic role as caring mother in poems such as 'The Pomegranate', 'This Moment' and 'Child of Our Time' to the oppressed plight of a sterile woman in Famine times doomed to a life without children. Other poems, such as 'Outside History', discuss the role of the many women who were not recorded in the annals of Irish history in times of oppression for Ireland. 'Child of Our Time' vividly represents the situation of a mother confronting the death of a child because of needless acts of violence.

A simple poem entitled 'The War Horse' draws a dramatic parallel between a tinker's horse that is let loose from a camp on the Enniskerry Road and the influx of terrorist violence in the south of Ireland. Setting the scene in suburbia, Boland dramatically succeeds in fusing together the powerful image of a wild horse as it trots along the road of suburban Dublin one evening. This image becomes a sustained metaphor in the poem, through which she articulates her own insights and views on the reality of war and its impact on the south of Ireland.

In fifteen stanzas, all only two lines in length, Boland conveys the movement of this horse, the destruction left in its wake together with her own personal reactions to the whole situation, which are clear and sincere. She comments on how the horse has destroyed only a rose, which is expendable, a leaf of the laurel tree and a crocus. She uses these images to draw in the political theme and to articulate a strong and serious question about the reality of the commitment on the part of the south to terrorist violence: 'why should we care | If a rose, a hedge, a crocus are uprooted | Like corpses, remote, crushed, mutilated?'

She reiterates the fact that we are safe, however, that our fear of commitment has not been clearly or fully formulated and how, with the disappearance of the horse, this fear has vanished: 'But we, we are safe, our unformed fear | Of fierce commitment gone'. She moves on to show us how the neighbours use the shelter of the curtains to hide: 'Neighbours use the subterfuge | Of curtains.' Boland's reaction is one of gratitude when the horse passes her, 'Thankfully, passing us.' As she pauses she tells us that for a second only her blood is still with atavism. She is motivated by pride in her remote ancestors, but she returns to the present reality of the smashed rose, which reminds her of Ireland's violent history in the past.

In the poem 'The Famine Road' we are confronted with an image of a young woman who is unable to bear any children. She is dehumanised and humiliated, just like the victims of the Famine in the mid-nineteenth century. The world of British imperialism and colonisation are all set against the backdrop of this woman's plight. The poem is recounted from two different standpoints – a clinical, cold doctor and an inhumane, brutal English officer. The world is stark and threatening. The woman's problem is simply dismissed in cold, insensitive tones: 'take it well woman, grow | your garden, keep house, good-bye.'

The poem 'Child of Our Time' is written from the standpoint of a woman and mother in a world of terrorism and violence. The voice of the poem is a mother and woman who witness the needless death of a young child in terrorist violence in a city in the south of Ireland. The whole poem paints a vivid, grim picture of the utter futility of this type of warfare. The speaker addresses the world and pleads with them to learn some type of lesson from the death of this child.

It is certainly clear that Boland is a poet who represents Ireland and in particular the situation of the woman as woman and as mother. Through a rich range of various themes and poetic techniques, Boland succeeds in drawing some vibrant pictures of female sterility against a backdrop of oppression and famine. She uses some of her poems to articulate her public condemnation of violence and its consequences. She writes from the standpoint of a mother who witnesses the senseless waste of young life through the brutality of war. She is a valuable and realistic mouthpiece on behalf of a community suffering from the enormous impact of war and violence.

POSSIBLE TYPES OF QUESTIONS ON PRESCRIBED POETRY

1. How did Boland's poetry affect you as a reader? In shaping your answer you might consider the poet's themes and concerns, the poet's style or your favourite poems.
2. 'A nineteenth-century poet who has both a fascination and relevance for the modern reader.' Would you agree with this estimation of Dickinson? Support your answer by appropriate quotation from or reference to the poems on your course.
3. 'Yeats deals with themes that are not only Irish but have a universal dimension.' Would you agree with this statement? Support your answer with reference to or quotation from the poetry on your course.
4. 'Michael Longley's poetry is a celebration of the personal and the individual in a world of public strife and violence.' Discuss this statement in the light of your study of Longley's poetry.
5. 'Séamus Heaney is essentially a poet of rural Ireland.' Discuss this statement, relating it to the imagery and language he uses in his poetry. Support your answer by reference to or quotation from the poems on your course.
6. 'Robert Frost makes use of nature and natural images to delineate human emotions and to create a particular atmosphere in his poetry.' Test the truth of this statement with reference to the poems you have studied for your course.
7. Examine how relevant the poetry of Sylvia Plath is for a modern reader. In your answer take into account the particular techniques she uses to communicate her themes.
8. 'The insights given to us in Elizabeth Bishop's poetry have a universal aspect and they are given a very particular location and time setting.' Discuss this statement

with regard to any two poems by Bishop on your course. Support your answer by quotation from or reference to the poems you have studied.
9. 'Hopkins is a unique and original poet whose poetry is compelling and timeless.' Would you agree with this estimation of Hopkins's poetry? Support your answer by reference to or quotation from the poems you have studied.
10. 'Yeats explores complex issues that are highly relevant to modern society.' Would you agree with this statement? Make reference to the poems by Yeats on your course in your answer.
11. Write an essay in which you outline your reasons for liking or disliking the poetry of Derek Mahon. Support your points with quotations from or reference to the poetry of Mahon that you have studied.
12. 'John Donne's poetry offers the reader some valuable insights on both the poet himself and his world.' Would you agree with this statement about Donne's poetry? Support your answer by reference to the poems of Donne that you have studied.

More detailed information on prescribed poetry is available in *New Explorations Critical Notes* (edited by John G. Fahy).

Separate revisions of these notes are available for the 2005, 2006 and 2007 exams.

15
Answers

Answers to question 1 (page 22)
(a) When you look at the house from the outside it seems to have about twenty rooms.
(b) The writer makes use of short, terse sentences with both humour and sarcasm in order to maintain the reader's interest in the passage.
(c) Boyle, who is filled with self-delusion, sees himself as the man of the house.
(d) Many teenagers of this type come from homes where the parents are unable to control them properly or where the mother is at work and hasn't enough time for her children.
(e) I would be delighted if you would reply and let me know whether or not you are available and the possible times.
(f) By this statement the writer means that people usually make a place what it is by their presence there.

Answers to question 2 (page 22)
(a) When he states his arguments he gives a balanced account of both sides.
(b) This can be found in a magazine bought by rich people. It would not be likely to feature in a newspaper, as there are too many photographs.
(c) The house is not the usual type, as it is old, enormous and appears to have been restored.
(d) The environment surrounding a person can usually tell you a lot about them. If, for instance, you were in an untidy house you would presume that the owner was an easy-going type of character.
(e) The impression I get of Oprah from her programme gives me some indication of the type of person she is and of her lifestyle. I think her home would also tell me a lot about her.
(f) The picture of the mirror and the woman with the pearls suggests that this family has a luxurious lifestyle.

Answers to question 3 (page 23)
(a) The play is filled with examples of both jealousy and betrayal. For example, this is evident in the figure of Iago.

(b) University students consistently analyse their actions, for they may upset a friend or a teacher.
(c) I wish to inform you of the type of photographs and images that I would like included in my gallery.
(d) The difference between the cost price and the selling price rose.
(e) Trade fairs are a common commercial activity nowadays, many of them held in export markets.
(f) I believe the writer expresses himself and his observations of human motivations very well.

Answers to question 4 (page 23)
(a) I find myself struggling to retain my popularity.
(b) A time-and-motion study in this section would improve output.
(c) I am stuck in this claustrophobic condition, with no one knowing either the despair or the loneliness I am experiencing.
(d) We regret to inform you that the Boxhead golf clubs you ordered on 15 July are not in stock.
(e) The 15:20 train that runs on weekdays in summer will not run on Sundays in either winter or summer.
(f) These people soldier on, living on very little as they struggle for success.

16 Past Examination Papers

LEAVING CERTIFICATE EXAMINATION, 2003

English – Higher Level – Paper 1

Total Marks: 200
9.30 – 12.20

- This paper is divided into two sections, Section I COMPREHENDING and Section II COMPOSING.
- The paper contains **three** texts on the general theme of JOURNEYS.
- Candidates should familiarise themselves with each of the texts before beginning their answers.

- Both sections of this paper (COMPREHENDING and COMPOSING) must be attempted.
- Each section carries 100 marks.

SECTION I – COMPREHENDING

- Two Questions, A and B, follow each text.
- Candidates must answer a Question A on one text and a Question B on a different text. Candidates must answer only one Question A and only one Question B.
- **N.B.** Candidates may NOT answer a Question A and a Question B on the same text.

SECTION II – COMPOSING

- Candidates must write on **one** of the compositions 1–7.

SECTION I
COMPREHENDING (100 marks)
TEXT 1
THE FIRST GREAT JOURNEY

The following is an extract from The Jason Voyage in which the author, Tim Severin, sets out to test whether the legendary journey of Jason's search for the Golden Fleece could have happened in fact. The book was published in 1985.

It was King Pelias who sent them out. He had heard an oracle which warned him of a dreadful tale – death through the machinations of the man whom he should see coming from the town with one foot bare ... The prophecy was soon confirmed. Jason, fording the Anaurus in a winter spate, lost one of his sandals, which stuck in the bed of the flooding river, but saved the other from the mud and shortly appeared before the king. And no sooner did the king see him than he thought of the oracle and decided to send him on a perilous adventure overseas. He hoped that things might so fall out, either at sea or in outlandish parts, that Jason would never see his home again.

1. So begins the first voyage saga in western literature: the tale of Jason and the Argonauts in search of the Golden Fleece. It tells of a great galley manned by heroes from ancient Greece, which sets out to reach a land far in the east. There, in the branches of an oak tree on the banks of a great river, hangs a sacred fleece of gold, guarded by an immense serpent. If the heroes can bring home the fleece, Prince Jason, the one-sandalled man, will win back his rightful throne from his half-uncle, the usurper King Pelias. On their voyage, so the story recounts, the heroes meet all manner of adventures: they land on an island populated only by women who are eager to make husbands of the Argonauts; a barbaric tribal chieftain challenges them to a boxing match, the loser of which will be battered to death; the dreadful Clashing Rocks bar their path and only by a whisker do they save their vessel from being smashed to shards. A blind prophet, who is being tormented by winged female demons, gives them guidance; and when the heroes finally reach the far land, the king's daughter, Princess Medea, falls so madly in love with Jason that she betrays her family, helps Jason steal the fleece, and flees back with him to Greece.

2. Small wonder that such an epic tale has echoed down through the centuries. Homer said that it was already a 'tale on all men's lips' when he came to write the *Odyssey*. And now, twenty-two centuries later, my companions and I also set out to commemorate those heroes of old, but in a different manner. Whereas storytellers and poets had accompanied the Argonauts in verse, we hoped to track them in reality. So we rowed out aboard the replica of a galley of Jason's day, a twenty-oared vessel of 3000-year-old design, in order to seek our own Golden Fleece – the facts behind the story of Jason and the Argonauts. Our travel guide was a copy of the *Argonautica*, a book by the Greek poet Apollonius, wrapped in layers of plastic to guard it from the rain and sea spray aboard an open boat. Pessimists calculated that unless favourable winds helped us on our way, we would have to row more than a million oar strokes per man to reach our goal.

3. Our galley, the new *Argo*, was a delight to the eye. Three years of effort had been devoted to her research, design and construction, and now her elegant lines repaid every minute of that care. Fifty-four feet long, from the tip of her curious snout-like ram to the graceful sweep of her tail, she looked more like a sea animal than a ship. On each side the oars rose and fell like the legs of some great beast creeping forward across the quiet surface of the dark blue Grecian sea. Two painted eyes stared malevolently forward over the distinctive nose of her ram, and at the very tip of that ram a hollow handhold breathed like a nostril, as it burbled and snorted with the water washing through the cavity.

4. To me, the tale of Jason and the quest for the Golden Fleece had long held a special fascination. Like most people I first read about Jason in school, but as a historian of exploration studying the great voyage epics of literature, I began to realise just how important the Jason story is. It holds a unique position in western literature as the earliest epic story of a voyage that has survived. The actual ship that carried the heroes, the immortal *Argo*, is the first vessel in recorded history to bear a name. To a seaman this has powerful appeal: for the first time a boat is something more than an inanimate floating object, an anonymous vehicle. *Argo* is a named, identifiable boat that has a character of her own. In the ancient telling of the story *Argo* could speak with a human voice, and at crucial moments state her own opinions. Even the description of her crew as the 'Argonauts' or 'Sailors of *Argo*', comes from the boat herself. In a modern world accustomed to hearing of astronauts, cosmonauts, and even aquanauts, it was worth remembering that the Argonauts were the first epic adventurers of the distant past.

N.B. Candidates may NOT answer Question A and Question B on the same text. Questions A and B carry 50 marks each.

QUESTION A

(i) 'Small wonder that such an epic tale has echoed down through the centuries.' How, in Paragraph 1 (beginning 'So begins the first voyage saga ...'), does the writer establish the truth of this statement? (15)

(ii) How, in the course of this extract, does the writer establish links between the voyage of Jason's *Argo* and the voyage of his own boat, the new *Argo*? (15)

(iii) Would your reading of the above extract from Tim Severin's book encourage you to read that book in full?
Give reasons for your answer supporting them by reference to the extract. (20)

QUESTION B

A Journey Through Time
Imagine that you have discovered a time capsule containing a number of items from the distant **or** more recent past. Write a letter to a local or national newspaper announcing your find and describing the items contained in the capsule. (50)

TEXT 2
A STRANGE COMPANION

This extract is adapted from The Golden Horde, Travels from the Himalaya to Karpathos, *published in 1997, in which sixty-five year old Sheila Paine describes her travels through some of the turbulent territories of the former Soviet Union. The extract begins at the point when Sheila returns to Saratov station to try once again to buy a ticket for a train journey.*

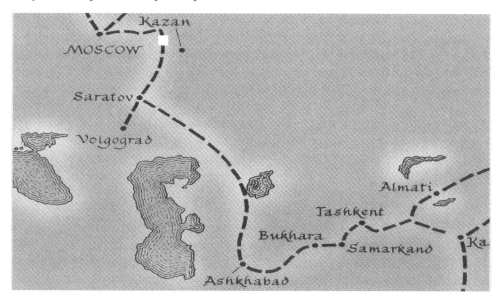

The scene at Saratov station was exactly as I had left it, as if none of the crowds had ever managed to get tickets or to go home or to depart on trains. I joined the battle to buy a ticket once more until, totally exasperated, I was driven to shout out loud, 'God, where do they find these people?' Behind me a voice repeated, 'Yes, God, where are they finding these people?' I turned to see a slim, fine-featured girl with a long blonde ponytail, wearing heavy mountaineering boots, jeans and anorak, and carrying a massive orange rucksack. She held out her hand. 'I'm Alexandra,' she said.

I had a travelling companion.

Alexandra had taken a year off studying to travel. She had huge funds of energy but very little money. 'I need no money,' she said. 'I am of those travellers who live with the inhabitants.'

At the end of three further hours of queuing and pleading, the woman behind the grille was still saying *niet* – no. During my attempts to buy a ticket I tried to look rather lost and forlorn and held up my money deferentially, bleating 'Ashkhabad please'. Alexandra's approach was spectacularly different. She pummelled her rucksack, kicked the wall with her hefty boots, flung her passport to the ground, screamed 'I kill these people', clenched her fists and punched the grille. However, neither of our techniques worked until Alexandra said, 'You have twenty dollars?' 'Yes,' I replied handing her a particularly crisp clean note. Some time later she returned grinning broadly and waving two tickets. 'We just didn't understand the system,' I said.

In all travelling it's usually best to go along with whatever the wind blows you and, as Alexandra had by total chance become part of my journey, I decided to stick with her and just see how things went. I had never met anybody quite so extraordinary and, although she might spell trouble later, she had succeeded in getting us on the train from Moscow to Ashkhabad. As we went to board the train I noticed that right at the end of the platform there was a scene of mayhem. A rusty coach with missing windows and our number on it had been tagged on to the train and was already full. Old women were being pushed through the windows head first, their boots and woolly stockings dangling above the platform. Alexandra went to work with her boots on the dense mass of people at the carriage door and we finally found our places in an open compartment with four bunks. Men lay draped on the luggage racks like leopards lounging on tree branches, some sat on the floor and others were piled on our bed. Now Alexandra used her rucksack to push them along and by the time the train pulled out the passengers had, by some hefty manipulation on her part, been reduced to those with places – the two of us, an old lady nursing toothache in a sparkly scarf, two polite young Turkmen – and an assortment of shifty men with no tickets and dozens of boxes of smuggled cigarettes.

We were to be on the train for three days and three nights.

The train trundled through golden open steppeland. At various stations people sold small silvery salted fish, cucumbers, tomatoes and beer. The old lady with the toothache shared her crushed hard-boiled eggs. Alexandra produced a huge bag of boiled millet, a dry loaf and a big silver knife. The men in the luggage racks leant down and helped themselves to everything. I rubbed vodka on the old lady's tooth and gave her aspirin.

The train chugged on. Men on horseback rode over the steppe herding their horses and sheep. The scene had changed from Russian to Mongol. At night it was bitterly cold as the wind howled through the glassless window. 'You should think to bring your sleeping bag,' said Alexandra.

By the second morning tempers were frayed. The old lady had produced more hard-boiled eggs, Alexandra her millet and bread. Then, suddenly all hell broke loose.

'I kill him. My knife. Where is my knife? I kill who steals it.'

Boots and arms lashed out, eyes stared down. Then, plop, in all the thrashing the knife fell from the grasp of a fat-lipped luggage-rack man on to the bed below.

The old lady got off the train in the night at one of the bleak Soviet towns along the banks of the Amu Darya river. A miserable place, she had said, and so far from her daughter in Saratov. The polite young Turkmen had helped her off while the fat-lipped thief on the rack above had grabbed her bed. He was now fast asleep.

'Some poor girl will be married off to him,' I said.

At the thought of this Alexandra leapt up, threw his baggage off our beds on to the floor and hid his shoes further along the coach.

N.B. Candidates may NOT answer Question A and Question B on the same text. Questions A and B carry 50 marks each.

QUESTION A

(i) What impression do you get of the railway station at Saratov from your reading of the above extract? Support your answer by reference to the text. (15)
(ii) To what extent would you agree with Sheila's description of Alexandra as 'extraordinary'? Support your view by reference to the text. (15)
(iii) Would you like to have shared this train journey with Sheila and Alexandra? Give reasons for your answer. (20)

QUESTION B
You have been asked to give a short talk on radio about an interesting journey you have made. Write out the text of the talk you would give. (50)

TEXT 3
DESTINATIONS

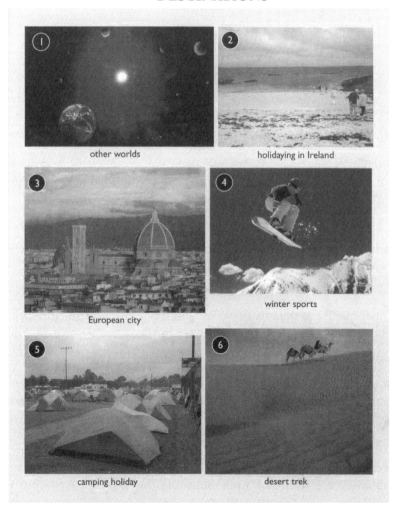

N.B. Candidates may NOT answer Question A and Question B on the same text.
Questions A and B carry 50 marks each.

QUESTION A

(i) Write **one paragraph** that would serve as an introduction to this collection of images entitled **Destinations**. (15)

(ii) Choose **one** of the images and write an account of the kind of journey suggested by it. (15)

(iii) Briefly describe another destination that would fit in well with the collection printed here and give a reason for your choice. (20)

QUESTION B

The Holiday from Hell

Write three or four diary entries that record the details of a disastrous holiday (real or imaginary) that you experienced. (50)

SECTION II
COMPOSING (100 marks)

Write a composition on **any one** of the following.

Each composition carries 100 marks.

The composition assignments below are intended to reflect language study in the areas of information, argument, persuasion, narration and the aesthetic use of language.

1. Imagine you are a member of Tim Severin's crew on board the new *Argo* in TEXT 1.

   Write a letter (or series of letters) to a personal friend or family member in which you describe some of your adventures.

2. 'It tells of a great galley manned by heroes from ancient Greece.' (TEXT 1)

   Write a persuasive article or essay in which you attempt to convince people of the meaning and importance of heroes in life.

3. '… a tale on all men's lips…' (TEXT 1)

   Write a newspaper article in which you outline your views in a serious or light-hearted manner on the part played by story telling or gossip in everyday life.

4. 'We just didn't understand the system.' (TEXT 2)

   You have been asked by the school principal to give a talk to your class group on the importance in life of 'understanding the system'. Write out the talk you would give.

5. '… huge funds of energy but very little money.' (TEXT 2)

   Using this as your title, write a personal essay.

6. 'In all travelling it's usually best to go along with whatever the wind blows you…' (TEXT 2)

   Write an article for a magazine for young adult readers in which you give advice to people intending to travel abroad for work or on holiday.

7. Write a short story suggested by one or more of the images in TEXT 3.

LEAVING CERTIFICATE EXAMINATION, 2003

English – Higher Level – Paper 2

Total Marks: 200
1.30 – 4.50

Candidates must attempt the following:-
- **ONE** question from SECTION I – The Single Text
- **ONE** question from SECTION II – The Comparative Study
- **THE QUESTIONS** on the Unseen Poem from SECTION III – Poetry
- **ONE** question on Prescribed Poetry from SECTION III – Poetry

N.B. Candidates must answer on Shakespearean Drama.
They may do so in SECTION I, The Single Text (*Macbeth*)
Or in SECTION II, The Comparative Study (*Macbeth*, *Othello*, *Twelfth Night*)

SECTION I
THE SINGLE TEXT (60 marks)

Candidates must answer **one** question from this section (A – E).

A **WUTHERING HEIGHTS** – Emily Brontë

  (i) '*Wuthering Heights* is a novel full of passionate extremes.'

   Write a response to the above statement supporting your views by reference to the text.

   OR

  (ii) 'The novel, *Wuthering Heights*, is dominated from start to finish by the character of Heathcliff.'

   To what extent would you agree with the above view of the novel? Support your answer by reference to the text.

B **THE REMAINS OF THE DAY** – Kazuo Ishiguro

(i) 'derbyshire*The Remains of the Day* is a fascinating study of lost potential, of what might have been.'

Discuss this view of the novel, supporting the points you make by reference to the text.

OR

(ii) Write an essay on one or more aspects of *The Remains of the Day* that particularly appealed to you as a reader. Support your answer by reference to the text.

C **DEATH OF A SALESMAN** – Arthur Miller

(i) '*Death of a Salesman* is a tragedy about an ordinary man in an unforgiving world.'

What is your opinion of this assessment of the play? Support your answer by reference to the play.

OR

(ii) 'BIFF: We never told the truth for ten minutes in this house!'

What do you think of this judgement of the Loman family? Support your answer by reference to the play.

D **AMONGST WOMEN** – John McGahern

(i) '*Amongst Women* is a novel in which everything revolves around the concerns of the central character, Michael Moran.'

Write a response to this view of the novel.

OR

(ii) 'Issues of family loyalty are central to *Amongst Women*.'

Discuss this view, supporting your points by reference to the text.

E **MACBETH** – William Shakespeare

(i) 'We feel very little pity for the central characters of Macbeth and Lady Macbeth in Shakespeare's play.'

To what extent would you agree with the above view? Support your answer by reference to the play.

OR

(ii) 'In *Macbeth*, Shakespeare presents us with a powerful vision of evil.'

Write your response to the above statement. Textual support may include reference to a particular performance of the play you have seen.

SECTION II
THE COMPARATIVE STUDY (70 marks)

Candidates must answer **one** question from **either A** – The Cultural Context **or** B – The General Vision and Viewpoint.

In your answer you may not use the text you have answered on in **SECTION I** – The Single Text.

N.B. The questions use the word **text** to refer to all the different kinds of texts available for study on this course, i.e. novel, play, short story, autobiography, biography, travel, and film. The questions use the word **author** to refer to novelists, playwrights, writers in all genre, and film-directors.

A THE CULTURAL CONTEXT

1. Write an essay in which you compare the texts you have studied in your comparative course in the light of your understanding of the term, the cultural context. (70)

   OR

   (a) With reference to **one** of the texts you have studied in your comparative course, write a note on the way/s in which the cultural context is established by the author. (30)

   (b) Compare the ways in which the cultural context is established by the authors of **two other texts** on your comparative course. (40)

B THE GENERAL VISION AND VIEWPOINT

1. 'The general vision and viewpoint of texts can be quite similar or very different.'

   In the light of the above statement, compare the general vision and viewpoint in at least two texts on your comparative course. (70)

   OR

   (a) What did you enjoy about the exploration of the general vision and viewpoint in **any one** of the texts you read as part of your comparative study? Support your answer by reference to the text. (30)

   (b) Write a short comparison between **two other texts** from your course in the light of your answer to part (a) above. Support the comparisons you make by reference to the texts. (40)

SECTION III
POETRY (70 marks)

Candidates must answer **A** – Unseen Poem – **and B** – Prescribed Poetry.

A UNSEEN POEM (20 marks)

Answer **either** Question **1** or Question **2**.

The poet, Rosita Boland, reflects on the tragedy of a war-torn region in our world.

BUTTERFLIES

In Bosnia, there are landmines
Decorated with butterflies
And left on the grassy pathways
Of rural villages.

The children come, quivering down
Familiar lanes and fields.
Hands outstretched, they reach triumphant
For these bright, elusive insects –
Themselves becoming wingéd in the act;
Gaudy and ephemeral.

1. Write a short response to the above poem, highlighting the impact it makes on you.
(20)

OR

2. Comment on the following statements supporting your answers by reference to the poem, *Butterflies*.

   (a) The poem makes very effective use of irony. (10)

   (b) The poem uses beautiful language to capture an ugly reality. (10)

B PRESCRIBED POETRY (50 marks)

Candidates must answer **one** of the following questions (**1–4**).

1. 'Why read the poetry of John Donne?'

   Write out the text of a talk that you would give, or an article that you would submit to a journal, in response to the above title. Support the points you make by reference to the poetry of John Donne on your course.

2. 'We enjoy poetry for its ideas and for its language.'

   Using the above statement as your title, write an essay on the poetry of Robert Frost. Support your points by reference to the poetry by Robert Frost on your course.

3. If you were asked to give a public reading of a small selection of Sylvia Plath's poems, which ones would you choose to read? Give reasons for your choices supporting them by reference to the poems on your course.

4. *Dear Séamus Heaney…*

   Write a letter to Séamus Heaney telling him how you responded to some of his poems on your course. Support the points you make by detailed reference to the poems you choose to write about.

ACKNOWLEDGMENTS (2003 EXAMINATION PAPER)

For permission to reproduce copyright material in this examination paper, the publishers gratefully acknowledge the following:

Sheil Land Associates on behalf of G. T. Severin for an extract from *The Jason Voyage*;

The Penguin Group (UK) for an extract from *The Golden Horde* by Sheila Paine and accompanying map by Martin Collins

The Gallery Press for 'Butterflies' from *Dissecting the Heart* by Rosita Boland.

The publishers have made every effort to trace copyright holders, but if they have inadvertently overlooked any they will be pleased to make the necessary arrangements at the first opportunity.

LEAVING CERTIFICATE EXAMINATION, 2004

English – Higher Level – Paper I

Total Marks: 200
9.30 – 12.20

- This paper is divided into two sections,
  Section I COMPREHENDING and Section II COMPOSING.
- The paper contains **three** texts on the general theme of WORK AND PLAY. Candidates should familiarise themselves with each of the texts before beginning their answers.
- Both sections of this paper (COMPREHENDING and COMPOSING) must be attempted.
- Each section carries 100 marks.

SECTION I – COMPREHENDING

- Two Questions, A and B, follow each text.
- Candidates must answer a Question A on one text and a Question B on a different text. Candidates must answer only one Question A and only one Question B.
- **N.B.** Candidates may NOT answer a Question A and a Question B on the same text.

SECTION II – COMPOSING

- Candidates must write on **one** of the compositions 1 – 7.

SECTION I
COMPREHENDING (100 marks)
TEXT 1
THE IMPORTANCE OF PLAY

The following text is adapted from the writings of Vivian Paley, a teacher who has written over many years about the importance of play in the lives of small children. Paley's books include descriptions of how children play and the stories they tell. The extracts used in this text are taken from her books, The Boy Who Would Be a Helicopter *(1990) and* You Can't Say You Can't Play *(1992).*

1. In my early teaching years I paid scant attention to the children's play and did not hear their stories, though once upon a time I too must have invented such wondrous stories. Indeed, my strongest childhood memories are of the daily chase of good and bad guys on the playground. Nothing else mattered, only the play. We acted out fear and friendship and called into being characters who would speak the lines. Luckily, life

cannot erase this storytelling instinct; it is always there, waiting to be resurrected.

2. Play is the primary reality of the young school child. Imagine two dozen children in self-selected acting companies, each group performing a different drama, moving through one another's settings, proclaiming separate visions of life and death, inventing new purposes and plots, and no one ever inquires, 'What's going on?'

'Y'wanna play tiger? Sabre tooth?'
'Superman! I shotted you.'
'Wah, wah, mommy, mommy!'
'Ghostbusters! Green Slimer!'
'Meow, meow, nice kitty.'
'Are you the dad, Simon? Here's our cave for good bears.'

Not one child asks, 'What is everyone doing? Who are these crawling, crouching, climbing people?' There is no confusion, only the desire to fit into someone's story or convince a classmate to enter yours.

3. The deep importance of shared play is clearly evident in the reaction of a child who is told that he or she 'can't play', can't be a part of someone else's story. Lately I have become more aware of these voices of exclusion in the classroom. 'You can't play' suddenly seems too overbearing and harsh, resounding like a slap from wall to wall. So I propose to my class group that we try out a new rule: You can't say, 'you can't play'. The children who find the idea appealing are the children most often rejected; the loudest in opposition are those who do the most rejecting. 'But then what's the whole point of playing?' Lisa wails.

4. Later, shy Clara speaks for herself. 'Cynthia and Lisa built a house for their puppies and I said can I play and they said no because I don't have a puppy only I have a kitty.' This is the longest sentence she has spoken in school to date. 'They said I'm not their friend.' Clara hugs her tattered kitty and sniffs back her tears.

'We said if she brings in a puppy she can play,' Lisa explains. Even the victim does not know how to react. 'I'll ask my mommy if she could get me that kind of puppy like they have,' Clara offers.

'They has to let her play,' Sheila insists, 'unless they really don't want to.'
'But it was my game!' Lisa cries. 'It's up to me!' She is red-faced and tearful.
'Okay, I won't play then, ever!'

5. Being told you can't play is a serious matter. It hurts more than anything else that happens in school. Everyone knows the sounds of rejection: You can't play; don't sit by me; stop following us; I don't want you for a partner; you're not going to be on our team.

6. The children I teach are just emerging from life's deep wells of babyhood and family. Then along comes school. It is their first real exposure to the public arena in which everything is to be shared and everyone is meant to be equal. And free

acceptance in play, partnerships and teams is what matters most to any child.

N.B. Candidates may NOT answer Question A and Question B on the same text.

Questions A and B carry 50 marks each.

QUESTION A

(i) What impression of the teacher, Vivian Paley, do you get from the above passage? Support your view by reference to the text. (15)

(ii) From your reading of the passage, what did you learn about the two children, Clara and Lisa? (15)

(iii) Would you agree or disagree with the view that the writer has made a convincing case for the 'deep importance of shared play' in the lives of children? Support your point of view by reference to the text. (20)

QUESTION B

'Then along comes school.'

You have been asked to give a short talk to a group of students who are about to start first year in your school. Write out the text of the talk you would give. (50)

TEXT 2
PAUL'S FIRST DAY AT WORK

The following text is adapted from the novel, Sons and Lovers, *by D.H. Lawrence, which tells the story of Paul Morel who, in this extract, begins work at Thomas Jordan & Son – suppliers of elasticated stockings. The novel was first published in 1913.*

On Monday morning, the boy got up at six, to start work. His mother packed his dinner in a small basket, and he set off at a quarter to seven to catch the 7.15 train. Mrs Morel watched him proudly as he trudged over the field. Her elder son, William, was doing well in London and now Paul would be working in Nottingham – her humble contribution to the grandeur of work itself.

At eight o'clock Paul climbed the dismal stairs of Jordan's Factory, and stood helplessly against the first great parcel-rack, waiting for somebody to pick him up. Two clerks had arrived before him and were talking in a corner as they took off their coats and rolled up their shirt sleeves. The younger one spied Paul.

'Hello!' he said. 'You the new lad? All right, you come on round here.'

Paul was led round to a very dark corner.

'You'll be working with Pappleworth,' the young man explained. 'He's your boss, but he's not come in yet. So you can fetch the letters, if you like, from Mr Melling down there.'

The young man pointed to an old clerk in the office.

'All right,' said Paul.

'Here's a peg to hang your cap on – here are your entry ledgers – Pappleworth won't be long.'

Paul sat on a high stool and read some of the letters: 'Will you please send me at once a pair of lady's silk, spiral thigh stockings, without feet, such as I had from you last year...' or 'Major Chamberlain wishes to repeat his previous order for a silk, non-elastic bandage.'

He nervously awaited the arrival of his 'boss' and suffered tortures of shyness when, at half past eight, the factory girls for upstairs trooped past him. Mr Pappleworth arrived at twenty to nine.

'You my new lad?' he said. 'Fetched the letters?'

'Yes.'

'Copied 'em?'

'No.'

Mr Pappleworth sat down beside him, seized the letters, snatched a long entry book out of a rack in front of him, flung it open, seized a pen, and said: 'Now look here – you want to copy these letters in here. Think you can do it all right?'

'Yes.'

'All right then – let's see you.'

Paul rather liked copying the letters, but he wrote slowly, laboriously, and exceedingly badly. He was doing the fourth letter and feeling quite busy and happy, when Mr Pappleworth reappeared.

'Strike my bob, lad, but you're a beautiful writer!' he exclaimed satirically. 'How many h'yer done? Only three! I'd 'a eaten 'em.

'Come on, my lad, oh, com on... Polly will be crying out for them orders. Here – come out. You'd better watch me do it.'

Paul watched the weird little drawings of legs and thighs and ankles which his chief made upon the yellow paper. Mr Pappleworth finished and jumped up.

'Come with me,' he said as he dashed through a door, down some stairs and into the basement where a little group of girls, nicely dressed and in white aprons, stood talking together.

'Have you nothing else to do but talk?' said Mr Pappleworth.

'Only wait for you,' said one handsome girl, laughing.

'Come on then, Paul,' said Mr Pappleworth handing over the orders.

'See you later, Paul,' said one of the girls.

There was a titter of laughter. Paul went out, blushing deeply, not having spoken a word.

Later, at one o'clock, Paul, feeling very lost, took his dinner basket down into the stack room in the basement, which had the long table on trestles, and ate his meal hurriedly, alone in that cellar of gloom and desolation. At five o'clock all the men went down to the same dungeon and there they had tea, eating bread and butter on the bare dirty boards, talking with the same kind of ugly haste and slovenliness with which they ate their meal. After tea, work went more briskly. Paul made out invoices and prepared his stack of parcels for the post. When the postman finally came everything slacked off and Paul took his dinner basket and, wondering if every work day would be like this, ran to catch the 8.20 train. The day in the factory was just twelve hours long.

N.B. Candidates may NOT answer Question A and Question B on the same text.

Questions A and B carry 50 marks each.

QUESTION A

(i) What impression do you get of Paul's workplace from reading the above passage? Support your answer by reference to the text. (15)

(ii) How would you describe the attitudes of the other workers (including Mr Pappleworth) to Paul, the new arrival at Jordan's Factory? Illustrate your answer by reference to the text. (15)

(iii) What advice would you give to the management of Jordan's Factory about how they might improve working conditions for new employees like Paul? (20)

QUESTION B

Employee Assessment

Imagine that Mr Pappleworth is asked, on the basis of Paul's first day at work, to write a report giving his impressions of Paul Morel as an employee. Write the text of his report. (50)

TEXT 3
WORK AND PLAY

The following text consists of a written and a visual element. The visual part of the text is a selection of images of people at work. The written element is an extract from a magazine article on the topic, Work and Play.

WORK AND PLAY

There is a natural rhythm to the lives of most people, what we might call the rhythm of work and play, of effort and relaxation, of chore and recreation. For most of us there is a clear dividing line between the work we have to do and our leisure time, the time that is our own exclusively. The division extends also to the kinds of activities that for us constitute work and play. Certainly, there are those among us who seem always to be working, who are so absorbed in work that play can scarcely be said to exist for them. There are those too whose existence seems a perpetual holiday, who are derisively referred to as having 'never worked a day in their lives'.

And there is another group of people who work in areas normally thought of as play, or whose work *is* the play, the recreation of others. Among these we find the professional sportsman or woman, the actor, the filmmaker, the musician, the writer, the comic, the juggler, the high-wire-walker, the lion tamer. These we think of as the lucky ones, the privileged few who turn play itself into work. We imagine them engaged in a kind of work which must always be enjoyable for them and a kind of play that even puts food on the tables of their families. Not for them, it seems, the daily grind from nine to five; not for them the ache of longing for life's all too brief holiday periods. In the eyes of the majority they indeed lead a charmed life, living as they seem to do for the sheer joy of performance!

It is not, however, a matter of carefree play when the professional footballer is dismissed from the field or when the actress fluffs her lines. And I leave it to your imagination to consider the fate that might befall the lion tamer!

N.B. Candidates may NOT answer Question A and Question B on the same text.

Questions A and B carry 50 marks each.

QUESTION A

(i) What, in your view, is the most important point the writer of the above extract makes about 'the group of people... whose work is the play, the recreation of others'? Support your answer by reference to the text. (15)

(ii) What impact does the visual text make upon you? Support your answer by reference to the images. (15)

(iii) Do you think that the written and the visual elements of the text go well together? Illustrate your answer by reference to the text as a whole. (20)

QUESTION B

My Kind of Work

Write a letter to **one** of the people from the collection of visual images in this text, indicating what appeals **and/or** does not appeal to you about the work which that person does. (50)

SECTION II
COMPOSING (100 marks)

Write a composition on **any one** of the following.

Each composition carries 100 marks.

The composition assignments below are intended to reflect language study in the areas of information, argument, persuasion, narration, and the aesthetic use of language.

1. '…my strongest childhood memories…' (TEXT 1)

   Write a personal essay in which you explore some of your earliest memories of childhood.

2. 'Everyone knows the sounds of rejection…' (TEXT 1)

   Write an article for publication in a serious newspaper or journal in which you draw attention to the plight of a person or group of people whom society has rejected.

3. '… the grandeur of work…' (TEXT 2)

   Write a speech (serious or light-hearted) in which you address your classmates or peer-group on the importance of work in our lives.

4. '"See you later, Paul," said one of the girls. There was a titter of laughter.' (TEXT 2)

   Write a short story suggested by these words.

5. '… the rhythm of work and play…' (TEXT 3)

   Write an article for a magazine for young adult readers in which you give advice to people on the best way to find a healthy balance between work and play in their lives.

6. '… the sheer joy of performance!' (TEXT 3)

   Using the above phrase as your title, write a personal essay.

7. Write a short story suggested by one or more of the images in TEXT 3.

LEAVING CERTIFICATE EXAMINATION, 2004

English – Higher Level – Paper 2

Total Marks: 200
1.30 – 4.50

Candidates must attempt the following:-
- **ONE** question from SECTION I – The Single Text
- **ONE** question from SECTION II – The Comparative Study
- **ONE** question on the Unseen Poem from SECTION III – Poetry
- **ONE** question on Prescribed Poetry from SECTION III – Poetry

N.B. Candidates must answer on Shakespearean Drama.
They may do so in SECTION I, The Single Text (*Macbeth*)
Or in SECTION II, The Comparative Study (*King Lear*, *Macbeth*, *Twelfth Night*)

SECTION I
THE SINGLE TEXT (60 marks)

Candidates must answer **one** question from this section (**A – E**).

A   **WUTHERING HEIGHTS** – Emily Brontë

    (i)   'Emily Brontë's novel, *Wuthering Heights*, causes the reader to wonder which is the more powerful force – love or hate.'

         Write a response to this statement, supporting your views by reference to the text.

OR

    (ii)   Write an essay on the aspects of the novel, *Wuthering Heights*, that you found most interesting or enjoyable to read. Support your points by reference to the text.

B   **SILAS MARNER** – George Eliot

    (i)   'The novel *Silas Marner* has much to teach us about the importance of love for human happiness.'

         Discuss this view of the novel, supporting your answer by reference to the text.

OR

    (ii)   'The life lived by the people of Raveloe is an appealing one.'

         Write a response to this view of the novel, *Silas Marner*, supporting your answer by reference to the text.

C   A DOLL'S HOUSE – Henrik Ibsen

(i) 'Nora retains our sympathy at the end of the play but Torvald does not.'

To what extent would you agree with this view? Support your answer by reference to the play.

OR

(ii) 'The relationship between Nora and Torvald is powerfully conveyed in the title of the play, *A Doll's House*.'

Write a response to this statement, supporting your views by reference to the text.

D   AMONGST WOMEN – John McGahern

(i) '*Amongst Women* is a powerful portrayal of a family whose world has its joys and its sorrows.'

Discuss this view of the novel, supporting your points by reference to the text.

OR

(ii) 'Of all the members of the Moran family, it is Rose, Michael's wife, who most deserves our admiration.'

Write a response to this view of Rose, supporting your points by reference to the text.

E   MACBETH – William Shakespeare

(i) 'Shakespeare's *Macbeth* invites us to look into the world of a man driven on by ruthless ambition and tortured by regret.'

Write a response to this view of the play, *Macbeth*, supporting the points you make by reference to the text.

OR

(ii) 'The play, *Macbeth*, has many scenes of compelling drama.'

Choose one scene that you found compelling and say why you found it to be so. Support your answer by reference to the play.

SECTION II
THE COMPARATIVE STUDY (70 marks)

Candidates must answer one question from **either** A – Theme or Issue **or** B – Literary Genre.

In your answer you may not use the text you have answered on in **SECTION I** - The Single Text.

N.B. The questions use the word **text** to refer to all the different kinds of texts available for study on this course, i.e. novel, play, short story, autobiography, biography, travel writing, and film. The questions use the word **author** to refer to novelists, playwrights, writers in all genres, and film-directors.

A THEME OR ISSUE

1. 'Exploring a theme or issue through different texts allows us to make interesting comparisons.'

    Write an essay comparing the treatment of a single theme that is common to the texts you have studied for your comparative course. (70)

OR

2. 'Any moment in a text can express a major theme or issue.'

    (a) Choose a moment from each of two texts you have studied for your comparative course and compare the way these moments express the same theme or issue. (40)

    (b) Show how a third text you have studied expresses the same theme or issue through a key moment. (30)

B LITERARY GENRE

1. 'Literary Genre is the way in which a story is told.'

    Choose **at least two** of the texts you have studied as part of your comparative course and, in the light of your understanding of the term Literary Genre, write a comparative essay about the ways in which their stories are told. Support the comparisons you make by reference to the texts. (70)

OR

2. 'Texts tell their stories differently.'

    (a) Compare **two** of the texts you have studied in your comparative course in the light of the above statement. (40)

    (b) Write a short comparative commentary on a third text from your comparative study in the light of your answer to question (a) above. (30)

SECTION III
POETRY (70 marks)

Candidates must answer **A** – Unseen Poem – **and B** – Prescribed Poetry.

A   UNSEEN POEM (20 marks)

Answer **either** Question **1 or** Question **2.**

Margaret Walker is an African American poet. In this poem she celebrates the experiences of the African Americans.

I WANT TO WRITE

> I want to write
> I want to write the songs of my people.
> I want to hear them singing melodies in the dark.
> I want to catch the last floating strains from their sob-torn
>
> throats.
>
> I want to frame their dreams into words; their souls into
>
> notes.
>
> I want to catch their sunshine laughter in a bowl;
> fling dark hands to a darker sky
> and fill them full of stars
> then crush and mix such lights till they become
> a mirrored pool of brilliance in the dawn.

1. Write a response to the above poem, highlighting the impact it makes on you.
(20)

OR

(a) Write down one phrase from the poem that shows how the poet feels about her people. Say why you have chosen this phrase. (10)

(b) Does this poem make you feel hopeful or not hopeful? Briefly explain why. (10)

B   PRESCRIBED POETRY (50 marks)

Candidates must answer **one** of the following questions (**1 – 4**).

1. 'There are many reasons why the poetry of Gerard Manley Hopkins appeals to his readers.'

In response to the above statement, write an essay on the poetry of Hopkins. Your essay should focus clearly on the reasons why the poetry is appealing and should refer to the poetry on your course.

2. Imagine you were asked to select one or more of Patrick Kavanagh's poems from your course for inclusion in a short anthology entitled, 'The Essential Kavanagh'.

Give reasons for your choice, quoting from or referring to the poem or poems you have chosen.

3. 'Speaking of Derek Mahon…'

Write out the text of a public talk you might give on the poetry of Derek Mahon. Your talk should make reference to the poetry on your course.

4. 'I like (or do not like) to read the poetry of Sylvia Plath.'

Respond to this statement, referring to the poetry by Sylvia Plath on your course.

ACKNOWLEDGEMENTS 2004 EXAMINATIONS

For permission to reproduce copyright material in these examination papers the publishers gratefully acknowledge Harvard University Press for adapted extracts from *The Boy Who Would Be a Helicopter* and *You Can't Say You Can't Play* by Vivian Paley. These extracts were adapted by the State Examinations Commission exclusively for the purposes of the Leaving Certificate English (Higher Level) examination paper (2004) and do not purport to be the author's original published texts.

The publishers have made every effort to trace all copyright holders, but if they have inadvertently overlooked any they will be pleased to make the necessary arrangements at the first opportunity.